STRUCTURED AND OBJECT-ORIENTED PROBLEM SOLVING USING C++

Third Edition

Andrew C. Staugaard, Jr.

Prentice Hall
Upper Saddle River, New Jersey 07458

Library of Congress Cataloging-in-Publication Data

Staugaard, Andrew C.
    Structured and object-oriented problem solving using C++/ by Andrew C. Staugaard, Jr.—3rd ed.
        p.   cm.
    ISBN 0-13-028451-3
    1. C++ (Computer program language) 2. Structured programming. 3. Object-oriented programming (Computer science) I. Title.

QA76.73.C153 S717 2001
005.13'3—dc21

                                                                    2001021851

Vice President and Editorial Director, ECS: *Marcia J. Horton*
Acquisitions Editor: *Petra J. Recter*
Editorial Assistant: *Karen Schultz*
Vice President and Director of Production and Manufacturing, ESM: *David W. Riccardi*
Executive Managing Editor: *Vince O'Brien*
Managing Editor: *David A. George*
Production Editor: *Patty Donovan*
Director of Creative Services: *Paul Belfanti*
Creative Director: *Carole Anson*
Art Director: *Heather Scott*
Assistant to Art Director: *John Christiana*
Art Editor: *Adam Velthaus*
Cover Designer: *Marjory Dressler*
Manufacturing Manager: *Trudy Pisciotti*
Senior Marketing Manager: *Jennie Burger*

 © 2002 by Prentice-Hall, Inc.
Upper Saddle River, New Jersey 07458

Printed in the United States of America
10   9   8   7 6   5   4   3   2   1

ISBN 0-13-028451-3

Prentice-Hall International (UK) Limited, *London*
Prentice-Hall of Australia Pty. Limited, *Sydney*
Prentice-Hall Canada Inc., *Toronto*
Prentice-Hall Hispanoamericana, S. A., *Mexico City*
Prentice-Hall of India Private Limited, *New Delhi*
Prentice-Hall of Japan, Inc., *Tokyo*
Pearson Education Asia Pte. Ltd., *Singapore*
Editora Prentice-Hall do Brasil, Ltda., *Rio de Janeiro*

To my loving wife, Janet, whose patience endures forever.

CONTENTS

SE102: SOFTWARE PARADIGMS 308

8 FUNCTIONS IN-DEPTH 313

SE103: THE STRUCTURED PARADIGM 377

9 ONE-DIMENSIONAL ARRAYS 385

10   CLASSES AND OBJECTS IN-DEPTH   439

13   POINTERS 551

14   INTRODUCTION TO DATA STRUCTURES AND ADTs 585

MULTIDIMENSIONAL ARRAYS   645

PREFACE

Welcome to the third edition of my C++ text. The highly successful first edition was one of the first textbooks available for teaching C++ in the first programming course. The text was introduced at the 1994 ACM Conference in Phoenix when many were arguing the virtues of teaching C++ and OOP versus Pascal and structured programming in the first programming course. I argued at that time, and still argue, that students need to be taught problem solving early-on using both the structured and object-oriented paradigms and, because of its hybrid nature, C++ is the only language suited to learning both of these paradigms. Since then, many institutions have made the switch from Pascal to C++ for just this reason, as well as the intense industry support for the C++ language. As a result, this third edition continues to provide an introduction to both structured and object-oriented problem solving techniques using the C++ language. Of course, many improvements have been made based on using the text in numerous classrooms all over the world since 1994.

As with earlier editions, the text starts from the beginning, assuming no previous knowledge of C, or any other programming language. The text is appropriate for any introductory programming (CS1) course using the C++ language as well as experienced programmers wanting an introduction to structured and object-oriented problem solving techniques using the C++ language.

New features in this third editions include:

❏ An introductory "getting acquainted" chapter that provides an overview of basic hardware and software concepts and gets students started early with the proverbial "Hello World" program.

❏ A comprehensive Visual C++ tutorial in Appendix C using Microsoft's popular Visual Studio integrated development environment (IDE).

❏ Learning modules strategically placed throughout the text on topics of GUIs, graphics, and software engineering. These modules are optional, but encouraged to provide a rich background for further study of these important topics.

❏ The use of the Unified Modeling Language (UML) class diagrams for object-oriented design.

❐ A series of software engineering modules that follow the Foo.com company programming team from a disastrous build-it, fix-it spaghetti code program, to a structured design, and finally an object-oriented design of their program using the Unified Modeling Language, UML. With these modules, the student gets an understanding of the bigger software engineering picture. In addition, the UML module prepares the student for planning and designing their own classes in Chapter 10.

❐ The use of the ANSI/ISO *string* class throughout. However, C-strings are also covered in the chapter on arrays.

❐ Coverage of the ANSI/ISO Standard Template Library (STL) *vector, stack, queue,* and *list* classes.

❐ A text CD that includes an introductory edition of Microsoft's Visual C++ as well as all example, case study, and Visual C++ tutorial source code.

❐ An instructor's CD that includes PowerPoint presentations organized by chapter, a test bank with answer keys which includes chapter tests as well as comprehensive mid-term and final exams, the solutions to all the chapter questions and programming problems, and all the example, case study and tutorial source code.

❐ A companion Web site at *www.prenhall.com/staugaard* that includes chapter objectives, on-line review tests that are automatically graded, a glossary of terms, downloadable example, case study and tutorial source code, and a syllabus manager.

APPROACH

The text emphasizes problem solving techniques using the C++ language. In fact, problem solving is the essential theme throughout the text. The student begins mastering the art of problem solving in Chapter 2, using problem abstraction and stepwise refinement via the "Programmer's Algorithm." Emphasis is first based on the structured (procedural) paradigm building *gently* into the object-oriented paradigm using seeds planted in the earlier chapters. This approach gradually prepares the student for in-depth coverage of classes and objects later in the text, while building essential structured programming concepts.

This third edition is based on the highly successful earlier editions that have been widely used in CS1 courses since 1994. Previous editions have been adopted at large and small institutions alike. One of the many reasons for the success of these earlier editions is that the text is highly readable and student oriented, with a teachable pedagogy and excellent features. The text provides sufficient material for a fast-paced one semester course or slower paced two semester course sequence.

FEATURES

❐ Highly readable and student oriented.

❐ Thoroughly instructor and student tested via first and second edition adoptions at large and small institutions alike.

❐ Early introduction to problem abstraction and stepwise refinement in Chapter 2 and used as a theme throughout the text using "Problem Solving In Action" case studies.

❐ A *gentle* introduction to classes and objects, beginning in Chapter 2. In-depth coverage of C++ classes and objects in Chapter 10.

❏ The "Programmer's Algorithm": A step-by-step process used to get students started on the right programming tract by considering problem definition, solution planning via algorithms, and good documentation. Problem solving using problem abstraction and stepwise refinement, prior to coding, is stressed throughout the text. All "Problem Solving in Action" case studies follow these proven software engineering techniques.

❏ Tip and note boxes for students throughout.

❏ Section-by-section quick-check exercises for students to check their progress with all answers in an appendix.

❏ Examples that pose problems and then give solutions immediately.

❏ Chapter questions with solutions on an instructor's CD.

❏ Chapter programming problems with solutions on an instructor's CD.

❏ Comprehensive glossary of general computer science as well as object-oriented programming terms.

TO THE INSTRUCTOR

This text has been written to teach structured and object-oriented problem solving techniques using the C++ language at the freshman level in a CS1 type of course. In today's market, it is imperative that students know both paradigms. Students need to understand the roles of and relationship between classes and objects early-on while at the same time learning classic program structuring techniques. I have found that there is no "paradigm shift" when class and object concepts are integrated into the structured paradigm. Structured, or procedural, programming is built around functions, and object-oriented programming is built around classes. Do the two have any relationship whatsoever? Yes! The classes that we build are constructed using elements of structured programming, namely functions. As a result, the structured paradigm is embedded within the object-oriented paradigm. This is why we need to study structured programming first, integrating object-oriented concepts where the opportunity arises, and *gently* move into object-oriented programming.

Some will say that you can't teach programming using C++, because the language is too complicated. I disagree. There is no need to teach every detail of the language in a beginning course. I have used a subset of C++ to teach fundamental structured and object-oriented concepts and have found that beginning students do not have any more difficulty using C++ than Pascal or JAVA with this approach. In addition, learning C++ has the added benefit for the student of learning a very widely used industry standard.

The text can be taught in one or two terms, depending on the ability of the students. In a two term sequence, I would suggest coverage through the topic of functions (Chapters 1–8). Then, begin the second term with arrays and finish out the book (Chapters 9–15). Make sure to cover the strategically placed learning modules on software engineering. These modules provide the student with an understanding of the bigger software engineering picture.

The text begins with a "getting acquainted" chapter that provides an overview of fundamental hardware/software concepts and ends with a section on getting started with C++. If you are using Visual C++, I suggest that you assign the first part of the

Visual C++ tutorial in Appendix C at this time so that students learn how to enter, compile, and execute a C++ program in the Visual C++ environment. Chapter 2 is devoted entirely to problem solving using problem abstraction and stepwise refinement. These concepts are presented in detail here and used as a theme throughout the text. The chapter discusses problem solving using what I call "The Programmer's Algorithm" and should be covered thoroughly. The programmer's algorithm is a step-by-step process that I have used to get students started on the right programming track by considering problem definition, step-by-step solution planning via algorithms, and good documentation. I have employed a pseudocode algorithmic language for problem solution that is generic, simple, and allows for easy translation to the coded C++ program.

Chapter 3 introduces the concepts of data abstraction and ADTs as well as traditional data types, classes, and objects. Here is where we begin planting the seeds of object-orientation to prevent any possible "paradigm shift" for the student when object-oriented programming is covered in-depth in Chapter 10. I suggest that you emphasize the concepts of classes, objects, and ADTs here to get students accustomed to object-oriented concepts. In addition, Chapter 3 introduces students to C++ functions, the common denominator of both paradigms.

In Chapters 4–7, students learn about program I/O, decision making, and iteration. These chapters provide the "nuts and bolts" required to write workable C++ programs. The sequence, decision, and iteration control structures available in C++ are covered thoroughly, emphasizing program logic and the required C++ syntax. The common pitfalls of program logic design are pointed out throughout this material via program debugging tips and programming notes. Again, I have integrated object-oriented concepts within these traditional structured programming topics, especially in Chapter 4 when using the C++ I/O classes and objects. Chapter 4 also introduces files so that students can begin reading and writing their own files early. Again, this opportunity is used to integrate object-oriented concepts into the discussion through the use of C++ file stream classes and objects. Detailed file manipulation is covered later, in Chapter 12.

At this point, your students have a solid knowledge of the important role of functions for both the structured and object-oriented paradigms. Since Chapter 2, they have been designing structured programs using functional decomposition and have observed the role of functions relative to object behavior. In Chapter 8, functions are covered in-depth. This chapter has been greatly improved over time, based on my experience of teaching C++ functions. I have incorporated easy-to-follow guidelines for building function interfaces relative to the topics of return values and parameter passing. It is critical that students understand this material in order to become successful C++ programmers and understand the object-oriented concepts presented in later chapters. The last section of this chapter discusses the important topic of problem solving with recursion. Recursion is introduced via a simple compound interest example, followed by and in-depth discussion of how recursion works and when it should be applied.

Students get their first exposure to data structures in Chapter 9, which discusses one-dimensional arrays. Again, I feel it is important that students have a solid knowledge of arrays and their manipulation. As result, this chapter covers traditional C-type arrays, including C-strings, and not some array class built by the author to hide the details and pitfalls associated with arrays. I have also used this topic to present several classic searching and sorting algorithms that are essential at this level. The ANSI/ISO *vector* class is discussed at the end of the chapter, after the students have mastered C-type arrays.

At this point, the student is prepared to learn about classes and objects in-depth. Again, there will be no paradigm shift here, because we have integrated these topics into the course since Chapter 2. In-depth coverage of classes and objects is provided in Chapter 10 and a solid introduction to class inheritance is provided in Chapter 11. In Chapter 10, students learn how to design their own classes using UML and convert their UML class diagrams into workable object-oriented programs using C++. Chapter 11 expands on the material in Chapter 10 by discussing inheritance. Many texts avoid the topic of inheritance. However, inheritance is one of the cornerstones of OOP and is relatively easy to cover at this point. Chapter 11 provides the student with a solid understanding of inheritance through a comprehensive banking example. The chapter closes with a discussion of polymorphism and dynamic binding.

File manipulation is discussed in-depth in Chapter 12. Here, the student learns how to read, write, append, and change disk files using C++. The topic of files in C++ provides a great opportunity to show how C++ employs inheritance to create reusable code. Here, the student learns how to employ inheritance through the C++ file stream class hierarchy to implement files.

The important topic of pointers is "addressed" in Chapter 13 in preparation for their use to build linked data structures in the next chapter. Pointers are fundamental to programming in C++ and should be covered thoroughly. This material, combined with the material on classes and objects in the previous two chapters, prepares the student to learn about the classic stack, queue, and linked-list ADTs in Chapter 14.

Chapter 14 provides an introduction to ADTs in preparation for an advanced course in data structures. The classic stack, queue, and linked list ADTs are covered thoroughly. In this chapter, ADTs are covered at two levels: The purely abstract level using the black box interface approach, and at the implementation level using C++ classes. Here is where the student really appreciates object-oriented programming, because ADTs are naturally implemented using C++ classes. The chapter closes with a discussion of the ANSI/ISO *stack, queue,* and *list* classes, after the students have mastered the building of their own stack, queue, and list classes using arrays and pointers.

The text closes with a chapter on multidimensional arrays. The chapter focuses primarily on the manipulation of two-dimensional arrays and closes with a comprehensive case study which applies two-dimensional arrays to simultaneous equation solution using Cramer's rule. If you wish, you can cover this chapter immediately after covering one-dimensional arrays in Chapter 9 without any loss in continuity.

The code in the text is portable and meets the new ANSI/ISO C++ standard as close as possible at this time. Finally, the following supplements are available to support this text:

❐ An instructor's CD that includes PowerPoint presentations organized by chapter, a test bank with answer keys that includes chapter tests as well as comprehensive mid-term and final exams, the solutions to all the chapter questions and programming problems, and all the example, case study, and tutorial source code.

❏ A companion Web site at *www.prenhall.com/staugaard* that includes chapter objectives, on-line review tests that are automatically graded, a glossary of terms, downloadable example, case study and tutorial source code and a syllabus manager.

❏ A student laboratory manual and workbook for those using TURBO C++ that provides over 30 laboratory exercises that guide the student through program development with minimal instructor involvement. (ISBN 0-13-63962-5)

TO THE STUDENT

The market demands that computing professionals know the latest problem solving, programming, and software engineering techniques. This book has been written to provide you with an introduction to both structured and object-oriented programming techniques—two of the most important and widely used techniques within the industry. The text emphasizes problem solution through the use of problem abstraction and stepwise refinement throughout. You will learn to attack problems using a "top/down" as well as an "inside-out" strategy. By the end of the text you will have the knowledge required to solve complicated problems using either the top/down structured approach or inside-out object-oriented approach.

Make sure that you go through all the examples and "Problem Solving in Action" case studies as well as the software engineering learning modules. These have been written in short, understandable modules that stress the fundamental concepts being discussed. The case studies and learning modules are integrated into the text at key points in an effort to tie things together and prepare you for future topics.

Finally, above all, get your hands dirty! You cannot become a competent programmer by just reading this book and listening to your instructor's lectures. You must get your hands dirty at the machine by developing *your own* C++ programs. Get started early by sitting down at a computer, getting acquainted with your C++ compiler, and writing *your own* C++ programs. In fact, included on the CD that accompanies this text is Microsoft's introductory version of Visual C++. I suggest that you get your hands dirty right now and install this program on your system. Then, go through the first part of the Visual C++ tutorial in appendix C to learn how to enter, compile, and run a C++ program using Visual C++.

TO THE PROFESSIONAL

The C++ programming language has taken the commercial software development industry by storm. Most of today's window-based software is being developed using C++ because of its object-orientation. Whether you are an experienced programmer or a novice, you will find that this book provides the "nuts and bolts" required to get you writing C++ programs quickly. In fact, this book is all that you will need to begin learning the C++ language. The text provides comprehensive coverage of structured programming using the C++ language and a sound introduction to object-oriented programming, both of which are essential in today's programming market. An introductory version of Microsoft's Visual C++ is provided on the CD that accompanies this book. In addition, a Visual C++ tutorial is provided in appendix C to get you started using Visual C++ quickly.

ACKNOWLEDGMENTS

Contributions to this text have come from many circles. From the academic world I would like to thank David Teague, Western Carolina University; Kathy Liszka, University of Akron; David Hudak, Ohio Northern University; Buster Dunsmore, Purdue University; George Luger, University of New Mexico; Keith Pierce, University of Minnesota; and Bob Holloway, University of Wisconsin, at Madison. All have reviewed the manuscript over the years and have made valuable contributions.

From the industrial world, I would like to thank Bjarne Stroustrup of Bell Labs, now part of Lucent Technologies, who reviewed the first edition manuscript and made many valuable suggestions relative to teaching C++ to beginning students as well as the language philosophy and details.

From the student world, I would like to thank my own students who, over that past ten years, have inspired the creation of this text and have made many valuable suggestions. Special thanks to one of my former students, Riley White, who prepared the Visual C++ tutorial material in Appendix C as well as the Windows template used in the GUI and graphics modules.

From the publishing world of Prentice Hall, I would like to thank my acquisitions editor, Petra Recter, the assistant editor, Sarah Burrows, and the production editor, Patty Donovan of Pine Tree Composition, Inc.

Enjoy!

Andrew C. Staugaard, Jr.

GETTING ACQUAINTED WITH COMPUTERS, PROGRAMS, AND C++

Chapter Contents

Chapter Objectives

When you are finished with this chapter, you should have a good understanding of the following:

- The hardware components of a typical computer system, including CPU, RAM, ROM, secondary storage, and I/O.
- Different levels of programming languages, including machine, assembly, and high-level languages.
- The use of a compiler in translating and running C++ programs.
- Why C++ has become such a popular language.
- A short history of the C++ language.

1

- The difference between structured versus object-oriented programming using C++.
- The general structure of a C++ program.
- How to enter, compile, debug, and execute a C++ program.

INTRODUCTION

In this first chapter, you will begin your learning journey in the important topic of problem solving, using the C++ programming language. This chapter has been written to provide you with an introduction to computers, computer programs, and C++ in general. You will first review the hardware that makes up a typical computer system. Then, you will learn about the relationship between the computer system and the computer programs that operate the system.

The four major steps required to create a working C++ program are ***edit, compile, link,*** and ***run.*** In this chapter, you will get your hands "dirty" early by performing these steps to create your first C++ program.

1.1   THE HARDWARE

You undoubtedly have seen some of the hardware components of a computer. These are the physical devices that you can see and touch, such as those shown in Figure 1.1a. This typical PC system obviously has a keyboard and mouse for user input, a display monitor for output, and magnetic and CD disk drives for program and data storage. Two very important parts of the system that cannot be seen, because they are inside the console, are the ***central processing unit*** and its ***primary memory.***

The block diagram in Figure 1.1b shows all of the major internal hardware sections of the system. From this figure, you see that the system can be divided into five functional parts: the central processing unit (CPU), primary memory, secondary memory, input, and output.

The Central Processing Unit (CPU)

The central processing unit (CPU) is the brain and nerve center of the entire system. This is where all of the calculations and decisions are made. In a PC system, the entire CPU is contained within a single integrated-circuit (IC) chip called a ***microprocessor.***

A ***microprocessor*** is a single integrated-circuit (IC) chip that contains the entire central processing unit (CPU) of a PC.

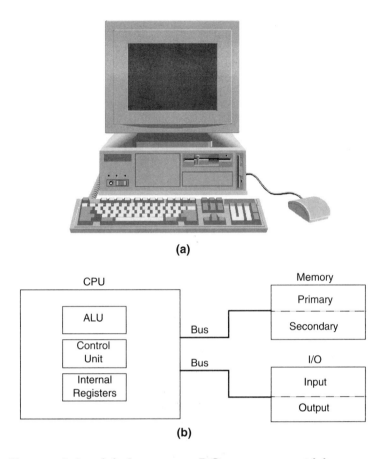

(a)

(b)

**FIGURE 1.1   (A) A TYPICAL PC SYSTEM AND (B) ITS
HARDWARE STRUCTURE, OR ARCHITECTURE.**

In fact, a microprocessor is what distinguishes a PC from a minicomputer or mainframe computer. In minicomputers and mainframe computers, several ICs make up the CPU, not just one as in a PC. A typical microprocessor IC is pictured in Figure 1.2. The CPU contains three functional parts: the *arithmetic and logic unit (ALU)*, the *control unit*, and the *internal registers,* as shown in Figure 1.3.

The Arithmetic and Logic Unit (ALU)

As its name implies, the arithmetic and logic unit performs all of the arithmetic and logic operations within the CPU. The arithmetic operations performed by the ALU include addition, subtraction, multiplication, and division. These four arithmetic operations can be combined to perform just about any mathematical calculation, from simple arithmetic to calculus.

Logic operations performed by the ALU are *comparison* operations that are used to *compare* numbers and characters. The three logic comparison operations are equal, less than, and greater than. These three operations can be combined to

FIGURE 1.2   A MICROPROCESSOR CHIP IS THE CPU OF A PC SYSTEM.

form the three additional logic operations of not equal, less than or equal, and greater than or equal.

Table 1.1 summarizes the arithmetic and logic operations performed by the ALU. The symbols listed in the table are those that you will use later to perform arithmetic and logic operations when writing C++ programs.

The Control Unit

The control unit area of the CPU directs and coordinates the activities of the entire system. This area interprets program instructions and generates electrical signals to the other parts of the system in order to execute those instructions. The control unit communicates with other sections of the CPU via internal signal paths called *buses.* The control unit often is likened to a traffic cop or orchestra leader, because it directs the activity of the entire system.

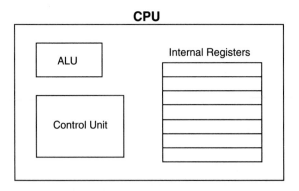

FIGURE 1.3   THE CPU CONSISTS OF AN ALU, CONTROL UNIT, AND INTERNAL REGISTERS.

TABLE 1.1 **A SUMMARY OF ARITHMETIC AND LOGIC OPERATIONS PERFORMED BY THE ALU AREA OF THE CPU**

Arithmetic Operation	C++ Symbol
Addition	+
Subtraction	−
Multiplication	*
Division	/
Modulus (Remainder)	%

Logic Operation	C++ Symbol
Equal to	==
Not equal to	!=
Less than	<
Less than or equal to	<=
Greater than	>
Greater than or equal to	>=

Internal Registers

The internal register area of the CPU contains temporary storage areas for program instructions and data. In other words, these registers temporarily hold information while it is being processed by the CPU.

Primary Memory

Primary memory often is called main working memory. The reason for this is that *primary,* or *main memory* is used to store programs and data while they are being "worked," or executed, by the CPU. Figure 1.4 shows the two types of primary memory: *random-access memory (RAM)* and *read-only memory (ROM)*.

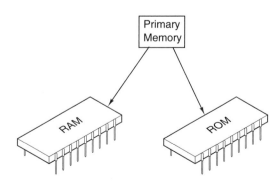

FIGURE 1.4 PRIMARY MEMORY CONSISTS OF RAM AND ROM.

Random-Access Memory (RAM)

Random-access memory is memory for you, the user, along with the programs and data that you are using at any given time. When you enter a program or data into the system, it goes into RAM. This is why the amount of RAM often is quoted when you buy a computer system. You most likely have heard the terms 32 megabyte (32 MB), 64 megabyte (64 MB), and so on, when describing a PC system. This is the amount of RAM, or user memory, that the system contains.

Bits and Bytes. Now, what is this megabyte stuff? Well, all digital computers operate on binary values. A binary value is a collection of bits, where a *bit* is simply a 0 or 1. Thus, we say the binary value 1010 is a 4-bit value. Likewise, the value 10101001 is an 8-bit value. The term *byte* is normally used to describe an 8-bit binary value. Thus, 100 bytes is 100×8, or 800 binary bits (0's and 1's). When describing large binary values we commonly use prefixes such as kilo (K), mega (M), and giga (G). Here, the letter K stands for the value 1024 (approximately one thousand), and M for the value K^2, or 1024×1024 (approximately one million), and the letter G stands for K^3, or $1024 \times 1024 \times 1024$, which is approximately one billion. Table 1.2 summarizes these quantities. Thus, a 64 MB system has $64 \times 1024 \times 1024 = 67,108,864$ bytes of RAM. The more bytes of RAM a system has, the more room there is for your programs and data. As a result, larger and more complex programs require larger amounts of RAM.

By definition, RAM is *read/write memory.* This means that information can be written into, or stored, into RAM and read from, or retrieved, from it. When writing new information into a given area of RAM, any previous information in that area is destroyed. Fortunately, you don't have to worry about this when entering programs, because the system makes sure that the new program information is not written over any important old information.

Once information has been written into RAM, it can be read, or retrieved, by the CPU during program execution. A read operation is nondestructive. Thus, when data are read from RAM, the RAM contents are not destroyed and remain unchanged. Think of a read operation as a "copy" operation.

One final point about RAM: It is *volatile.* This means that any information stored in RAM is erased when power is removed from the system. As a result, any programs that you have entered in main working memory (RAM) will be lost when you turn off the system. You must always remember to save your programs on a secondary memory device, such as a disk, before turning off the system power.

TABLE 1.2 A SUMMARY OF TERMS ASSOCIATED WITH BINARY VALUES

Term	Meaning
bit	0 or 1
byte	8 bits
kilobyte (KB)	1024 bytes
megabyte (MB)	1,048,576 bytes
gigabyte (GB)	1,073,741,824 bytes

64 MB RAM

Memory Addresses	Memory Contents (Data)
67,108,863	10010011
67,108,862	10010110
.	.
.	.
.	.
1	11010111
0	10110111

FIGURE 1.5 **RAM** CONSISTS OF BYTE-SIZED BINARY CHUNKS LOCATED BY ADDRESSES, BEGINNING WITH ADDRESS **0.**

Also, be aware that RAM can be placed in other parts of the system, such as a printer. This allows the CPU to send large amounts of data to be printed to the printer and stored there without clogging up the primary system RAM.

You have probably heard the terms *cache memory,* or simply *cache,* and *virtual memory.* These are different than RAM but serve a similar purpose. Cache is high-speed RAM that is usually contained within the same chip as the CPU. Instructions waiting to be processed are fetched from primary memory and placed in the cache so that they are ready for execution when the CPU needs them. Virtual memory is hard-disk memory that is being used by the CPU as RAM when no more actual RAM is available. The term "virtual" means "illusion." Thus, when the CPU needs more memory space, it borrows hard-disk memory to create the illusion that it is reading/writing RAM. In this case, the apparent size of the system RAM is unbounded. However, system performance is seriously degraded, since it takes much longer to access an electromechanical disk drive than it does actual semiconductor RAM.

Figure 1.5 shows how binary data are stored in RAM. In most of today's systems, memory is byte-oriented. This means that data is stored in RAM in byte-sized chunks as shown in the figure. Each byte is located by a memory address, just like the post office locates you via your postal address. Memory addresses begin with 0 and extend up to the amount of memory for a given system. So, in a 64 MB RAM, the first byte of memory is located at address 0 and the last memory byte is located at address $64 \times 1024 \times 1024 - 1 = 67,108,863$. Why -1 in the calculation? Because the addresses start with 0, right?

Read-Only Memory (ROM)

Read-only memory often is called *system memory* because it stores system-related programs and data. These system programs and data take care of tasks such as reset, cursor control, binary conversions, input/output (I/O), and so on. All of these system programs are part of a larger operating system program that is permanently stored in ROM or on a disk. In IBM PC and compatible systems, the system software stored in ROM is called **BIOS.** The operating system, **DOS** or **Windows,** is stored on disk and works with BIOS to perform **transparent** system operations. The term transparent means that the user is not aware of the underlying system operations being performed.

As its name implies, read-only memory can only be read from and not written into. Consequently, information stored in ROM is permanent and cannot be changed. Because the information is permanent, ROM must be **nonvolatile.** This means that any information stored in ROM is not lost when power is removed from the system. Due to this feature, ROM programs often are called *firmware.*

Secondary Memory

Secondary memory, sometimes called **bulk,** or **mass storage**, is used to hold programs and data on a semipermanent basis. The most common type of secondary memory used in PC systems are magnetic disks, shown in Figure 1.6.

A floppy disk, like that shown in Figure 1.6a, gets its name because the actual disk is flexible, rather than rigid, or hard. The disk is coated with a magnetic material and enclosed within a 3½-inch hard plastic cover. When inserted into a disk drive, the disk is spun on the drive at about 300 rpm. A read/write recording head within the drive reads and writes information on the disk through the access slot, or window, in the disk jacket. Virtually all systems today include a built-in hard disk drive like the one shown in Figure 1.6b. In fact, a hard-drive system is a must when working with professional-level integrated program development software such as you find with most C++ compilers.

When writing programs, you will first enter the program code into the system primary memory, or RAM. When *saving* C++ programs, you must create a work file name for the program. This work file name creates an area, or file, on the disk

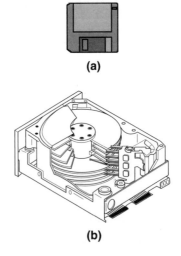

(a)

(b)

FIGURE 1.6 THE COMMON (A) 3½-INCH DISK AND (C) HARD DISK.

where your program will be saved. As you enter and work with your program in RAM, you will periodically save the program on the disk so that it is permanently stored. When you save the program, the system simply copies the program from RAM and saves it on the disk under the work file name that you created. This process is illustrated in Figure 1.7a.

Saving a program on disk allows you to retrieve it later. To read a program from disk, you simply **load** the work file name assigned to the program. This tells the system to read the work file and transfer it into primary memory (RAM), as illustrated in Figure 1.7b. Once it is in working memory, the program can be compiled, executed (run), or changed (edited). Of course, if any changes are made, the program must be saved on disk again so that the changes are also made on the disk. By the way, all C++ program files must have a file extension of *.cpp*.

We should not fail to mention **compact disk,** or **CD,** storage. Today's CDs are optical storage devices and most CD drives are read-only devices. Their high-density and read-only features make them great for storing audio, video, and large application software installation programs such as your C++ compiler. Even though they can be written to with a special CD burner drive, they are not commonly used for file write operations like that required of magnetic hard drives. It is hoped that someday the CD technology and associated price will allow CDs to replace magnetic hard disks.

Input

Input is what goes into the system. Input devices are hardware devices that provide a means of entering programs and data into the system. The major input devices for a PC system such as the one pictured back in Figure 1.1a are the keyboard and

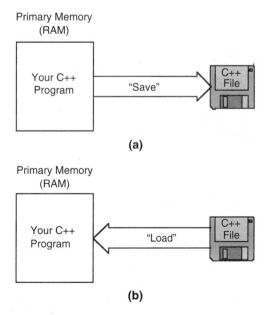

FIGURE 1.7   (A) SAVING A PROGRAM ON DISK, AND (B) LOADING A PROGRAM FROM DISK.

mouse. The computer keyboard contains all of the characters that you will need to write a program. In addition, there are also special control functions and special control keys that provide for system operations such as cursor movement. A mouse provides a means to input commands by pointing and clicking on a *graphical user interface,* or *GUI,* screen. We say that GUI programs are *event-driven*, which means they are controlled by the pointing and clicking events generated by a mouse.

The disk drive is another form of input device, because it also provides a means of loading programs and data into the system. There are many other types of input devices used with computer systems, such as modems, network cards, and so on. However, the keyboard, mouse, and disk drive are the primary input devices that you will be using when learning how to write C++ programs.

Output

Output is what comes out of the system. Output devices are hardware devices that provide a means of getting data out of the system. The four major output devices with which you will be concerned are the display monitor, printer, disk drive, and modem. The display monitor is just the screen in front of you. It allows you to observe programs and data that are stored in primary memory (RAM).

A printer provides you with a hard copy of your programs and data. During a printing operation, the system actually copies information from primary or secondary memory to the printer. Thus, any information to be printed must be stored in primary or secondary memory.

A disk drive is also an output device, because information stored in primary memory can be written to the disk. You could say that a disk drive is an I/O device, because it provides a means of getting information both in and out of the system.

Finally, a modem lets you communicate over the telephone or cable networks with other computers.

The Fetch/Execute Cycle

The fetch/execute cycle is what takes place when you *run* a program. To run a program, you must first enter it into primary memory via the keyboard or load it from disk. Once in primary memory, the program must be *compiled.* The compiling process is performed by a C++ compiler. The compiler converts the C++ instructions into executable binary machine code that can be run by a particular CPU. Your program cannot be run, or executed, until it is free of errors and completely compiled. The compiler checks the program for errors and generates error messages and warnings to you via the display monitor. The compiling process associated with C++ will be discussed in more detail in the next section.

Once a C++ program has been translated into binary machine code, the machine instructions are *fetched* from primary memory or cache and *executed,* or *run,* one at a time as shown in Figure 1.8.

Observe the *fetch/execute* cycle within the CPU. The control unit first fetches a given program instruction from primary memory or cache. The instruction is then decoded, or translated, to determine what is to be done. Next, the control unit

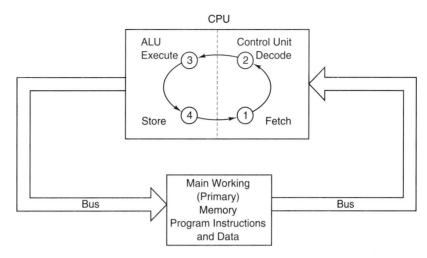

FIGURE 1.8   **THE FETCH/EXECUTE CYCLE BETWEEN THE CPU AND
MAIN WORKING MEMORY.**

makes available any data required for the operation and directs the ALU to perform the operation. The ALU executes the operation, and the control unit stores
the operation results in an internal register or primary memory. The resulting data
are temporarily stored in an internal register or primary memory until they are
used for another operation or sent to an output device such as a disk or printer. In
summary, you can see from Figure 1.8 that the four basic fetch/execute cycle operations are *fetch, decode, execute,* and *store.* That's it in a nutshell!

 Quick Check

1. List the three major areas of a PC's architecture.
2. A CPU contained within a single integrated-circuit is called a(n) _____.
3. List at least three arithmetic and three logic operations performed by the ALU
   area of a CPU.
4. List three things that are found in a CPU.
5. A 128-MB system has _____ bytes of RAM.
6. Programs stored in ROM are often called _____.
7. Explain what takes place between the CPU and memory when you run a program.
8. Instructions waiting to be processed are fetched from primary memory and
   placed _____ memory so that they are ready for execution when the CPU
   needs them.

1.2   PROGRAMMING AND SOFTWARE

If computer hardware can be likened to an automobile, computer software can be likened to the driver of the automobile. Without the driver, nothing happens. In other words, the computer hardware by itself can do nothing. Therefore, computers are dumb. We have to tell them exactly what to do. The hardware system requires software that provides step-by-step instructions to tell the system what to do. A set of software instructions that tells the computer what to do is called a *computer program.* A *programmer* is a person who writes a computer program. One thing that a programmer must always keep in mind, even when programming in a high-level language, is that a computer always blindly follows orders. For example, take the instructions found on most shampoo bottles: *wash, rinse, repeat.* As a human, you know that you only need to wash and rinse a second time if your hair really needs it, but a computer would wash and rinse forever. In programming terminology, this is known as an infinite loop. Programmers have to be careful to tell a computer when to stop in a case where instructions must be repeated.

Unfortunately computers don't speak English, so we have to use their language. That is where programming comes in. At the most basic level, computers communicate using binary codes (1's and 0's). Programmers don't generally use binary, though. Instead we use high-level languages. These high-level languages, such as C++, are translated to a series of 1's and 0's that the computer can understand. To communicate instructions to the computer, computer programs are written in different language levels. In general, computer languages can be categorized into one of three major levels: *machine language, assembly language,* and *high-level language.*

> A *computer program* is a set of software instructions that tells the computer what to do.

Machine Language

All of the hardware components in a computer system, including the CPU, operate on a language made up of binary 1's and 0's. A CPU does not understand any other language. When a computer is designed, the CPU is designed to interpret a given set of binary instructions, called its *instruction set.* Each instruction within the instruction set has a unique binary code that can be translated directly by the CPU. This binary code is called *machine code,* and the set of all machine-coded instructions is called the CPU's *machine language.*

A typical machine-language program is provided in Figure 1.9a. To write such a program, you must determine the operation to be performed, and then translate the operation into the required binary machine code from a list of instruction set machine codes provided by the CPU manufacturer. As you might imagine, this is an extremely inefficient process. It is time-consuming, tedious, and subject to a tremendous amount of error. In addition, simple operations, such as multiplication and division, often require several lines of machine code. For these reasons, machine-language programming is rarely used. However, remember that high-level

01001100	mov bx, offset value	x = 2;
11101001	mov ax, [bx]	if (x<=y)
10101010	add ax, 5	x = x + 1;
10001110	sub ax, 2	else
00001111	inc ax	x = x – 1;
(a)	(b)	(c)

FIGURE 1.9   (A) MACHINE LANGUAGE, (B) ASSEMBLY LANGUAGE, AND (C) HIGH-LEVEL LANGUAGE.

language programs are always translated to machine language to enable the CPU to perform the fetch/execute cycle.

Assembly Language

Assembly language is a step up from machine language. Rather than using 1's and 0's, assembly language employs alphabetic abbreviations called *mnemonics* that are easily remembered by you, the programmer. For instance, the mnemonic for addition is ADD, the mnemonic for move is MOV, and so forth. A typical assembly-language program is listed in Figure 1.9b.

The assembly-language mnemonics provide us with an easier means of writing and interpreting programs. Although assembly-language programs are more easily understood by us humans, they cannot be directly understood by the CPU. As a result, assembly-language programs must be translated into machine code. This is the job of another program, called an *assembler*. The assembler program translates assembly-language programs into binary machine code that can be decoded by the CPU.

Although programming in assembly language is easier than machine-language programming, it is not the most efficient means of programming. Assembly-language programming is also tedious and prone to error, because there is usually a one-to-one relationship between the mnemonics and corresponding machine code. Also, assembly language is specific to a given CPU or family of CPUs. For example, Intel's family of CPUs employ a different assembly language than Motorola's family of CPUs. The solution to these inherent problems of assembly-language programming is found in high-level languages.

This does not mean that assembly language is not useful. Because of their one-to-one relationship with machine language, assembly-language programs are very efficient relative to execution speed and memory utilization. In fact, many high-level-language programs include assembly-language routines, especially for those tasks requiring high-speed software performance.

Operating Systems

An *operating system,* or *OS,* is the "glue" that binds the hardware to the application software. Actually, an operating system is a collection of software programs dedicated to managing the resources of the system. These resources include memory management, file management, I/O management, monitoring system activity, system security, and system performance, just to mention a few.

In the early days, operating systems, such as DOS and Unix, were text-based. Today, however, most operating systems like Windows and the Macintosh operating systems are GUI-based. The acronym "GUI" stands for "graphical user interface," implying a windows-based user interface.

Until not too long ago, assembly language was used to develop operating systems, due to its execution efficiency and its ability to access system components directly. Then, in the 1970s, Bell Telephone Laboratories (now part of Lucent Technologies) developed a high-level language called C to write the Unix operating system. The C language is sometimes referred to as a "mid-level" language since it contains many of the high-level commands of a high-level language, but also many of the "bit-level" commands of an assembly language.

High-Level Language

High-level languages overcome the programming tediousness inherent in assembly languages. Also, high-level languages are not CPU dependent. Therefore, a high-level language program written for a PC that uses an Intel CPU will look the same as that written for a Mac which uses a Motorola CPU. However, the downside to high-level languages is that the programs they produce are not as fast and memory efficient as their assembly language counterparts.

A high-level language consists of instructions, or statements, that are similar to English and common mathematical notation. A typical series of high-level statements is shown in Figure 1.9c. High-level-language statements are very powerful. A typical high-level-language statement is equivalent to many machine-code instructions.

High level programming languages are constructed so that ambiguities are not possible. This means that each program instruction has only one possible meaning. If a sentence can have more than one meaning, we say that it is ambiguous. Look at the following sentence: In the dark night crawlers roam. Does this sentence mean that *night crawlers roam in the dark* (whether the dark is a cellar, a closet or the outdoors), or does it mean that *crawlers roam in the dark night* (which is almost definitely outdoors)? You will not find such ambiguity in high-level programming language instructions, because they are constructed so that different interpretations are not possible.

High-level languages were developed in the early 1950s to take some of the work out of programming. When programming in a high-level language, you do not have to concern yourself with the specific instruction set of the CPU. Rather, you can concentrate on solving the problem at hand. Once you learn a given high-level language, you can program any computer for which a compiler exists to translate your program into the CPUs machine language.

You must be aware that even when programming in a high-level language, the system must still translate your instructions into machine code that can be understood by the CPU. There are two types of system programs that can be employed for this purpose: a **compiler** and an **interpreter.** A compiler is a program that accepts a high-level–language program and translates the entire program into machine code all at one time, before it is executed by the CPU. On the other hand, an interpreter translates and executes one high-level statement at a time. Once a given statement has been executed, the interpreter then translates and executes the next statement, and so on, until the entire program has been executed. Although interpreters do have their advantages, especially during the debugging stage, C++ employs a compiler. For this reason, let's look more closely at the operation of a compiler.

Figure 1.10 illustrates the basic functions of a compiler. The compiler acts as the interface between your program and the machine. Here's how a typical C++ compiler works. Once you have entered a C++ program into the system using your C++ editor, the program must be translated into machine code by the compiler. Your C++ program is referred to as a ***source program,*** and the machine-language program that is generated by the compiler is called an ***object program***. C++ source programs usually have a *.cpp* file-name extension, and the corresponding object program has a *.obj* extension.

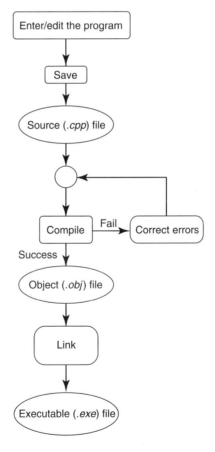

FIGURE 1.10 THE C++ COMPILER AND LINKER TRANSLATE SOURCE CODE INTO MACHINE CODE THAT CAN BE EXECUTED BY THE CPU.

> A *source program* is the one that you write in the C++ language and that normally has a file extension of *.cpp*. An *object program* is the binary machine language program generated by the C++ compiler, which always has a file extension of *.obj*.

As the program is being translated, the compiler checks for errors. After the program is compiled, the compiler displays a list of error messages and warnings. In addition, many C++ compilers will place the cursor on the display monitor at the point in your program where a given error was detected. After you correct all the errors, you must execute the compiler again until you get a successful compilation.

Once compiled, your program must be ***linked.*** The linking step integrates your program with any additional routines that are required for proper program execution. These routines can be other high-level programs, assembly-language programs, or operating-system routines. The linking step produces an executable file with an *.exe* file-name extension. Errors can also occur during the linking step, especially if any required routines are not available or cannot be located. Your C++ software will also report any linking errors.

Finally, when the entire program has been successfully compiled and linked, you can execute, or run, your program. When you run your program, the CPU is actually executing the machine-language program generated by the compiler/linker.

Why C++?

As you are probably aware, there are several popular high-level languages, including COBOL, Pascal, FORTRAN, BASIC, Ada, Java, and C/C++, among others. Each has been developed with a particular application in mind. For instance, COBOL, which stands for *CO*mmon *B*usiness *O*riented *L*anguage, was developed for business programming. FORTRAN, which means *FOR*mula *TRAN*slator, was developed for scientific programming. BASIC, which stands for *B*eginners *A*ll-purpose *S*ymbolic *I*nstruction *C*ode, was developed for simple general purpose programming. Pascal was developed primarily for education to teach the principles of structured programming. Java was developed for use on networks consisting of different CPU platforms, like the Internet.

The C language is a ***structured language*** that allows complex problems to be solved using a modular, ***top/down,*** approach. The C++ language contains the C language for structured programming, but in addition extends the C language to provide for ***object-oriented programming (OOP).*** Object-oriented programming allows complex problems to be solved using a more natural object approach, similar to the way in which we humans tend to look at the real world. It allows complex programs to be developed using ***objects*** that can communicate by exchanging messages. More about this later. Thus, C++ is a hybrid language, allowing for both structured and object-oriented programming.

As stated earlier, the C++ language evolved from the C language and, in fact, contains the C language as a subset. As a result, C++ is a popular choice for software development because of its ability to employ structured programming concepts through its C language subset as well as object-oriented concepts. In fact, most of the commercial software developed today is written using C or C++. The

C++ language is so popular that the American National Standards Institute (ANSI) and the International Standards Organization (ISO) have created a standard specification for the language so that all C++ compilers translate a C++ program in the same way. Industry standards facilitate the *portability* of a language.

The C language is a **structured language** that allows complex problems to be solved using a modular, **top/down,** approach. The C++ language contains the C language for structured programming, but in addition extends the C language to provide for **object-oriented programming (OOP).** Object-oriented programming allows complex problems to be solved using more natural **objects** that model the way we humans think about things.

Portability is that feature of a language that allows programs written for one type of computer to be used on another type of computer with few or no changes to the program source code. Compilers that conform to the ANSI/ISO standard make C++ a portable language. This means that your C++ program can be translated for a Windows machine using a Windows-based C++ compiler and also be translated for a Unix machine using a Unix-based C++ compiler. Both translated programs will execute the same on their respective machines. Of course, both compilers must conform to the standard.

Some C++ History

First, there was the B language, then C, and then C++. All were developed at Bell Telephone Laboratories (now a part of Lucent Technologies) and, like all high-level structured languages, have their roots in ALGOL. The B language was developed by Ken Thompson at Bell Labs, in an effort to develop an operating system using a high-level language. Prior to B, operating systems were developed using the assembly language of the particular CPU on which the operating system was to run. Using the B language as a basis, Dennis Ritchie developed the C language at Bell Labs. The main purpose for the C language was to develop an operating system for the Digital Equipment Corporation (now part of Compaq) PDP-11 minicomputer. The resulting operating system became known as *Unix.* In fact, most versions of Unix today are written almost entirely in C. The C language was originally defined in the classic text *The C Programming Language*, written by Brian Kernighan and Dennis Ritchie (1977). In fact, the C language became such a popular commercial language that an ANSI standard for C was released in 1989.

As you already know, the C++ language is an extension of the C language. Bjarne Stroustrup at Bell Labs enhanced the C language in the early 1980s by adding object-oriented programming (OOP) capability. The obvious goal of Dr. Stroustrup was to maintain the efficiency of C while providing the power of OOP to the language. The resulting language became known as C++. You will realize where the ++ came from when you learn about the C++ *increment* operator later in this text. Because C++ is an enhancement of C, any C program is also a C++ program; however, the opposite is not true.

The Art and Science of Programming

Once you decide that you want to learn how to program, the first step is to learn a programming language. With this book, you are well on your way beginning the first step. In general, programming works like this: You type in the computer program instructions using a programming language, compile the program into machine readable form (called an executable), then you run the executable program. Additionally, most compilers have a built-in debugger that allows you to step through the code (i.e., run each instruction one at a time) to make sure everything is running correctly.

The way a program is designed and run can be loosely described by the way a train travels. The train has a station where it begins, and it has to know where it is going. To get to where it's going, the track layout must be planned. Then the workers must lay out the track, taking care to make the track flow smoothly so that the train will not crash. The final step is to send a test train down the track to make sure the track is safe for general traffic. If the test train encounters any problems, they must be fixed.

The building of the track takes time. It must be planned out well, and any unforeseen problems must be worked around during construction. This is all very important because once the track has been built, every train that travels down the track will follow it blindly—they are not able to swerve around obstacles. They are limited to traveling the path defined by the train track.

Similarly, a programmer must decide what he or she wants the program to accomplish, plan out how the program will accomplish it, then actually sit down and *code* the program, working around any unforeseen problems encountered during the coding process.

A program is built line by line. The program begins at the first statement and flows through each statement, executing the instructions found on each line as it comes to them.

Shortly into the coding process, the programmer must begin **debugging.** This is the process of searching for and fixing any errors in the program. There are two categories of errors in programming: *syntax* and *logical.* A **syntax error** is generally easy to find and correct. It is an error in following the rules of the programming language. A program with a syntax error will not compile. Most compilers will tell you exactly what and where the error is. For example, if you forget to put a semicolon at the end of a line of code in C++, the compiler will tell you and will point you to the line where the error is. It will not, however, put the semi-colon at the end of the line for you.

A **logical error** is harder to find. A program with a logical error will compile and run, but it will not act as expected. To correct a logical error, the programmer generally has to step through the program (run the code one line at a time in a debugger) to find the error, then rework the program design to fix the error.

Once the program is working well (i.e., it compiles, and it runs correctly every time), it is finished except for future enhancements and maintenance. Like the finished train track it is ready to be used. Just like any train can go down the track and end up where it wants to go, any user can run the program and accomplish the task that he or she wants to accomplish.

Quick Check

1. What is the major difference between C and C++?
2. List the steps that must be performed to translate a C++ source code program to an executable program.
3. What is meant by portability?
4. What is the difference between a compiler and an interpreter?
5. What are the three levels of language used by computers?
6. Your C++ program code is referred to in general as _____ code and has a file extension of _____.
7. The code generated by a C++ compiler is referred to as _____ code and has a file extension of _____.
8. The code generated by a C++ linker is referred to as _____ code and has a file extension of _____.
9. What is the purpose of an operating system.

1.3   GETTING STARTED WITH C++: "HELLO WORLD"

It is now time to get your hands dirty by entering, compiling and executing your first C++ program. The program you will execute is the classic "Hello World" program that all computer science students have executed at some time in their early programming learning years. So, find yourself a computer with a C++ compiler and read on. Here is the "Hello World" program that you will execute:

```
1    /*
2    NAME: ANDREW C. STAUGAARD JR.
3    CLASS: CS1
4    PROGRAM TITLE: HELLO WORLD
5    DATE: 5/16/01
6    THIS PROGRAM WILL DISPLAY THE MESSAGE "Hello World"
     TO THE SYSTEM MONITOR
7    */

8    //PREPROCESSOR SECTION
9    #include <iostream.h>                    //FOR cout

10   //MAIN FUNCTION SECTION
```

```
11  int main()
12  { //BEGIN MAIN FUNCTION BLOCK
13          cout << "Hello World";           //DISPLAY MESSAGE TO MONITOR
14          return 0;
15  } //END MAIN FUNCTION BLOCK
```

The program code lines are numbered to facilitate our discussion. First, lines 1 through 7 provide an introductory **block comment** that shows the programmer, class, date, and purpose of the program. You should always include a comment at the top of your program to identify the programmer and explain the program's purpose. A block comment is *two or more* lines that provide the program reader with information. The comment block begins with a forward slash followed by a star (/*). The C++ compiler will ignore any lines that appear after these symbols until it translates a star followed by a forward slash (*/) which ends the comment block. Next, in line 8, you see a **line comment.** Line comments are used for a single comment line and inserted into a program using double *forward* slashes (//). The double forward slashes tell the compiler to ignore the rest of that particular line. The double forward slashes can appear anyplace on a given line, but anything after // on a given line is ignored by the compiler. Notice that line comments also appear in lines 10, 12, 13, and 14 to describe the purpose of a given section or line of code. We will extensively use comments within the programs in this text to *self-document* the C++ code. We suggest that you do the same in your programs. Comments within your programs make them much easier to read and maintain.

> A **block comment** begins with the symbols /* and is terminated with the symbols */. A **line comment** begins with the symbols // and is terminated at the end of the given line.

Aside from the comments, any C++ program consists of two sections: a **preprocessor** section and a **main function** section.

The Preprocessor Section

The **preprocessor section** of a C++ program can be viewed as a smart text editor that consists of **directives** that always begin with a pound (#) symbol as shown in line 9 of the foregoing program. Although there are others, the preprocessor directive that you will use the most is the *#include* directive. The *#include* directive in line 9 tells the C++ compiler to "include" the code in a file called *iostream.h* as part of your program. Notice that the *iostream.h* file name is enclosed within angle brackets like this: *<iostream.h>*. This is the required **syntax** for the directive.

> The **syntax** of a language is the set of grammar rules required to write code for the language. Any violation of a syntax rule will always result in a compiler error.

DEBUGGING TIP

Program comments are an important part of the program documentation and should be used liberally. In this text, program comments will appear in all caps so that they can be readily distinguished from the program code. At a minimum, the program should include the following comments:

- The beginning of the program should be commented with the programmer's name, date the program was written, date the program was last revised, and the name of the person doing the revision. In other words, a brief ongoing maintenance log should be commented at the beginning of the program.

- The beginning of the program should be commented to explain the purpose of the program, which includes the problem definition and program algorithms. This provides an overall perspective by which anyone, including you, the programmer, can begin debugging or maintaining the program.

- Preprocessor directives should be commented as to their purpose.

- Constant and variable definitions should be commented as to their purpose.

- Major sections of the program should be commented to explain the overall purpose of the respective section.

- Individual program lines should be commented when the purpose of the code is not obvious relative to the application.

- All major subprograms (functions in C++) should be commented just like the main program function.

- The end of each program block (right curly brace) should be commented to indicate what the brace is ending.

Remember, someone (including you) might have to debug or maintain the program in the future. A good commenting scheme makes these tasks a much more efficient and pleasant process.

As you will learn later, C++ has several built-in, or *standard*, **header** files. These files contain things that make your programming job easier. The *iostream.h* header file contains an object called *cout* (pronounced "see-out") that displays information to the system monitor. As another example, the standard *math.h* header file contains mathematical operations, such as square root, sine, and cosine so that you do not have to code these operations if you need them in your program. There are literally thousands of header files available for C++. Some are standard header files defined by the language and provided as part of your compiler such as *iostream.h* and *math.h*, while others are created by programmers for specific applications. Header files facilitate the creation of software **libraries** to support a variety of applications. In fact, you will be creating your own header files in just a few short chapters. If a header file contains some operation that you need in your program, all you have to do to use it is to include it in the preprocessor section of your program using the *#include* directive.

COMPILER NOTE

If you have an ANSI/ISO compatible compiler, you can optionally drop the *.h* file extension and simply code the include statement as *#include <iostream>*. However, if you chose to include *iostream* rather than *iostream.h* you must add another statement after the preprocessor section, as follows:

```
using namespace std;
```

In this text, we will normally include the *iostream.h* file which is compatible with both new and older compilers, unless required to do otherwise in order to use a ANSI/ISO standard library file.

The Main Function Section

The main function section of the program is where all the executable C++ code resides or is executed from. As you will see soon, a structured C++ program is simply a collection of *function* blocks.

A *function* in C++ is a subprogram that returns a single value, a set of values, or performs some specific task, such as I/O.

Notice the syntax shown in line 11 of the foregoing program. The main function identifier is *main()*. The main function identifier is preceded by the word **int.** The reason for this will become apparent later. A left curly brace, {, must follow the main function identifier prior to any other statements. This brace designates the beginning of the main function block and normally appears directly below *main()*. At the bottom of the program in line 15, you see a right curly brace, }. This brace is used to designate the end of the main function block. You must always use a set of curly braces, { }, to designate a block of code in C++. Thus, the set of curly braces in the foregoing program defines the main function block. We say that the set of curly braces *frames* the main function block.

The statement section of *main()* is the main executable body of the program. The program instructions, or *statements,* go here. Each statement must be terminated with a semicolon. Because C++ is a modular language, the statement section of the program often consists of calls to additional function blocks, whose combined execution performs the overall program task. However, our "Hello World" program consists of just two executable statements. The first statement uses the *cout* object to display the "Hello World" message on the system monitor. The second statement is a *return* statement that returns control of the computer to the operating system. Don't worry about the syntax details yet, these will be explained in time.

It is now time to code, compile, link and run the "Hello World" program. Using a text editor, enter and save the foregoing program as *hello.cpp*. **Do not** enter the line numbers, because they are only there for discussion purposes and will create syntax errors if compiled as part of the program. Once saved, compile, link, and run your program. If you are using Visual C++, you can refer to Appendix C to get started.

Quick Check

1. Any C++ program consists of two sections, called the _____ and _____ sections.
2. Write a *#include* directive to include a standard header file called *math.h* into a program.
3. A subprogram that returns a single value, a set of values, or performs some specific task in C++ is called a _____.
4. Line comments are inserted into a C++ program using
   a. left and right curly braces like this {COMMENT}.
   b. a semicolon like this ;COMMENT.
   c. stars and slashes like this /*COMMENT*/.
   d. double forward slashes like this //COMMENT.
   e. none of these
5. Block comments are inserted into a C++ program using
   a. left and right curly braces like this {COMMENT}.
   b. a semicolon like this ;COMMENT.
   c. stars and slashes like this /*COMMENT*/.
   d. double forward slashes like this //COMMENT.
   e. none of these.
6. State at least four places where your program should include comments.
7. All the executable statements reside or are called from function _____.

CHAPTER SUMMARY

Any computer system can be divided into two major components: hardware and software. Hardware consists of the physical devices that make up the machine, and software consists of the instructions that tell the hardware what to do.

There are three functional parts that make up the system hardware, or architecture: the CPU, memory, and input/output. The CPU directs and coordinates the activity of the entire system as instructed by the software. Primary memory consists of user memory (RAM) and system memory (ROM). Secondary memory is usually magnetic and is used to store programs and data on a semipermanent basis. Input is what goes into the system via hardware input devices, such as a keyboard and mouse. Output is what comes out of the system via hardware output devices, such as a display monitor or printer.

There are three major levels of software: machine language, assembly language, and high-level language. Machine language is the lowest level, because it consists of binary 1's and 0's that can only be easily understood by the CPU. Assembly language consists of alphabetic instruction abbreviations that are easily understood by the programmer but must be translated into machine code for the CPU by another program called an assembler. High-level languages consist of Englishlike statements that simplify the task of programming. However, to be understood by the CPU, high-level-language programs must still be translated to machine code using a compiler or interpreter. An object program is generated by a C++ compiler. This is a low-level program, similar to machine language. However, the C++ object program must then be linked with any additional routines that are required for proper program execution. The linking step produces a file that will execute on the platform for which it was compiled.

C++ was developed at Bell Labs by Bjarne Stroustrup to add an object-oriented programming capability to the C language. The C++ language has since been standardized by ANSI/ISO to provide for portability across multiple platforms. Standardization makes the C++ language more portable across multiple platforms such as Windows, Unix, and Mac.

Program comments are an important part of the program documentation and should be used liberally. In C++, a block comment begins with the symbols /* and is terminated with the symbols */. A line comment begins with the symbols // and is terminated at the end of the given line. Aside from the comments, any C++ program consists of two sections: a preprocessor section and a main function section. The preprocessor section can be viewed as a smart text editor that consists of directives, like *#include*. The *#include* directive allows you to include header files which contain needed operations into your program. The main function section of the program is where all the executable C++ code resides or is called from. The *main()* function block must be framed with curly braces, { }. All executable C++ program statements must appear between these two curly braces.

QUESTIONS AND PROBLEMS

QUESTIONS

1. Name the three operational regions of a CPU and explain their function.
2. Explain the term *volatile* as it relates to computer memory.
3. Another name for software located in read-only memory (ROM) is _____.
4. A floppy disk is a form of _____ memory.
5. Name the three levels of software and describe the general characteristics of each.
6. List at least four functions of an operating system.
7. Explain the operational difference between a compiler and an interpreter.
8. A C++ compiler translates a source program into a(n) _____ program.

9. True or false: C++ employs both a compiler and an interpreter to produce an executable program.

10. Explain why C++ is source code portable across all computer platforms, but not object code portable.

11. What is structured programming?

12. The C++ language was developed by _____ (Who?) at _____ (Where?).

13. Object-oriented programming allows complex programs to be developed using simpler programming constructs called _____.

14. The C++ language evolved from the _____ language.

15. What is object-oriented programming?

16. List at least three places where comments should occur in your C++ program.

17. Explain the syntax required for a block comment.

18. Explain the syntax required for a line comment.

19. The two general sections that make up a C++ program are the _____ and _____ sections.

20. What is the purpose of the *#include* directive?

21. Write a directive to include the standard *string* header file into your program. Note that, even though *string* is a C++ header file, it does not have a *.h* extension. This is because the C language contains a *string.h* header file which is different from the C++ *string* header file.

22. Where must all executable program statements appear in a C++ program?

23. What is the purpose of framing and what syntax is required to frame a block of code?

PROBLEMS

1. Use your C++ compiler to find and correct the syntax errors in the following program:

```
/*
PROBLEM 1 (P01_01.cpp)
THIS PROGRAM WILL CALCULATE THE WEEKLY GROSS PAY OF
OF AN HOURLY EMPLOYEE

//PREPROCESSOR DIRECTIVES
#include iostream.h        //FOR cout

//MAIN FUNCTION
int main()
{
    //DEFINE AND INITIALIZE VARIABLES
    int hours = 35;         //WEEKLY HOURS WORKED
    float rate = 6.50;      //HOURLY RATE IN $
    float grossPay = 0.0;   //WEEKLY GROSS PAY

    /CALCULATE PAY
    grossPay = hours * rate
```

```
//DISPLAY RESULTS
cout.setf(ios::fixed);
cout.setf(ios::showpoint);
cout.precision(2);
cout << "Given an hourly rate of $" << rate << endl
     << "and weekly hours of " << hours << endl
     << "the resulting weekly gross pay is $" << grossPay;

//RETURN
return 0;
}//END main()
```

2. Run the program in problem 1. Closely compare the program run to the program code and try to answer the following questions:
   a. What is the purpose of the *iostream.h* header file included in the program?
   b. What is the purpose of the *cout* object in the program?
   c. What is the purpose of the *cout.precision(2)* statement in this program?
   d. What is the purpose of the *endl* command in the *cout* statement?

3. Enter, compile, and run the following program. Does the output generated by the program make sense, especially if you were the customer? Of course not! There is a logic error in the program. A ***logic error*** occurs when the compiler does what you tell it to do but is not doing what you meant it to do. It is an error in thinking on the programmer's part. Use your C++ debugger to locate and correct the logic error. Refer to Appendix C on how to use the Visual C++ debugger if you are using this compiler. (*Hint:* Watch the variable *tax* as you step through the program.)

```
//PROBLEM 3 (P01_03.cpp)

//PREPROCESSOR DIRECTIVE
#include <iostream.h>              //FOR cin AND cout

//MAIN FUNCTION
int main()
{
   //DEFINE VARIABLES
   float rate = 7;                //SALES TAX RATE IN PERCENT
   float cost = 0.0;              //COST OF ITEM
   float tax = 0.0;              //SALES TAX
   float totalCost = 0.0;         //TOTAL COST OF ITEM

   //GET COST FROM USER
   cout << "Enter the cost of the sales item: $";
   cin >> cost;

   //CALCULATE TAX
   tax = rate * cost;

   //CALCULATE TOTAL COST
   totalCost = cost + tax;

   //DISPLAY RESULT TABLE
   cout.setf(ios::fixed);
```

```
cout.setf(ios::showpoint);
cout.precision(2);
cout << "The total cost of the sales item is: $" << totalCost
    << endl;

//RETURN
return 0;
}//END main()
```

4. What do you suppose is the purpose of the *cin* statement in the program given in problem 3?

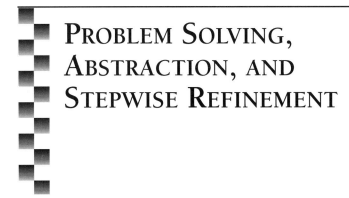

PROBLEM SOLVING, ABSTRACTION, AND STEPWISE REFINEMENT

Chapter Contents

Chapter Objectives

When you are finished with this chapter, you should have a good understanding of the following:

- How to define a problem in terms of input, output, and processing.
- How to plan a problem solution using algorithms.
- The attributes required for a good computer algorithm.
- The role of pseudocode in problem solution planning.
- The use of a problem solving diagram.
- The concept of problem abstraction.
- The concepts of stepwise refinement and modular programming.
- The steps required to test and debug a program.

- Different types of programming errors, including syntax errors, type errors, logic errors, and run-time errors.
- What good program documentation must include.

INTRODUCTION

Programming reduces to the art and science of problem solving. To be a good programmer, you must be a good problem solver. To be a good problem solver, you must attack a problem in a methodical way, from initial problem inspection and definition to final solution, testing, and documentation. In the beginning, when confronted with a programming problem, you will be tempted to get to the computer and start coding as soon as you get an idea of how to solve it. However, you *must* resist this temptation. Such an approach might work for simple problems but will *not* work when you are confronted with the complex problems found in today's real world. A good carpenter might attempt to build a dog house without a plan but would never attempt to build your "dream house" without a good set of blueprints.

In this chapter, you will learn about a systematic method that will make you a good problem solver, and therefore a good programmer—we call it the ***programmer's algorithm.*** In particular, you will study the steps required to solve just about any programming problem. You will be introduced to the concept of ***abstraction,*** which allows problems to be viewed in general terms without agonizing over the implementation details required by a computer language. From an initial abstract solution, you will refine the solution step by step until it reaches a level that can be coded directly into a C++ program. Make sure you understand this material and work the related problems at the end of the chapter. As you become more experienced in programming, you will find that the "secret" to successful programming is good planning through abstract analysis and stepwise refinement, which results in workable software designs. Such designs are supported by languages like C++. In the chapters that follow, you will build on this knowledge to create workable C++ programs.

2.1   THE PROGRAMMER'S ALGORITHM

Before we look at the programmer's algorithm, it might be helpful to define what is meant by an algorithm. In technical terms, it is as follows:

An ***algorithm*** is a series of step-by-step instructions that produces a solution to a problem.

Algorithms are not unique to the computer industry. Any set of instructions, such as those you might find in a recipe or a kit assembly guide, can be considered an algorithm. The programmer's algorithm is a recipe for you, the programmer, to follow when developing programs. The algorithm is as follows:

> **The Programmer's Algorithm**
>
> - Define the problem.
> - Plan the problem solution.
> - Code the program.
> - Test and debug the program.
> - Document the program.

Defining the Problem

You might suggest that defining the problem is an obvious step in solving any problem. However, it often is the most overlooked step, especially in computer programming. The lack of good problem definition often results in "spinning your wheels," especially in more complex computer programming applications.

Think of a typical computer programming problem, such as controlling the inventory of a large department store. What must be considered as part of the problem definition? The first consideration probably is what you want to get out of the system. Will the output information consist of printed inventory reports or, in addition, will the system automatically generate product orders based on sales? Must any information generated by a customer transaction be saved permanently on disk, or can it be discarded? What type of data is the output information to consist of? Is it numerical data, character data, or both? How must the output data be formatted? All of these questions must be answered in order to define the output requirements.

Careful consideration of the output requirements usually leads to deciding what must be put into the system in order to obtain the desired system output. For instance, in our department store inventory example, a desired output would be most likely a summary of customer transactions. How are these transactions to be entered into the system? Are the data to be obtained from a keyboard, or is product information to be entered automatically via an optical character recognition (OCR) system that reads the bar code on the product price tags? Does the input consist of all numerical data, character data, or a combination of both? What is the format of the data?

The next consideration is processing. Will most of the customer processing be done at the cash register terminal, or will it be handled by a central store computer? What about credit card verification and inventory records? Will this processing be done by a local PC, a minicomputer located within the store, or a central mainframe computer located in a different part of the country? What kind of programs will be written to do the processing, and who will write them? What sort of calculations and decisions must be made on the data within individual programs to achieve the desired output?

All of these questions must be answered when defining any computer programming problem. In summary, you could say that problem definition must consider the application requirements of output, input, and processing. The department store inventory problem clearly requires precise definition. However, even with small application programs, you must still consider the type of output, input, and processing that the problem requires.

The reason this inventory problem lends itself to computer solution is that it deals with input, processing, and output, thus lending itself to an algorithmic approach to problem solving. Many real-world problems, such as long-range weather forecasting, do not lend themselves to this approach. So, when trying to define a problem you must first decide if it is a candidate for computer solution. To do this, you must ask yourself whether it lends itself to input and processing that input to producing meaningful output information. Once a problem is identified as a candidate for computer solution, then you need to define the problem in terms of specific input, processing, and output.

When defining a problem, look for the nouns and verbs within a problem statement. The nouns often suggest input and output information, and the verbs suggest processing steps. The application will always dictate the problem definition. We will discuss problem definition further, as we begin to develop computer programs to solve real problems.

PROBLEM SOLVING TIP

Look for the nouns and verbs within a problem statement; they often provide clues to the required input, output, and processing. The nouns suggest input and output, and the verbs suggest processing steps.

Planning the Solution

The planning stage associated with any problem is probably the most important part of the solution, and computer programming is no exception. Imagine trying to build a house without a good set of blueprints. The results could be catastrophic! The same is true of trying to develop computer software without a good plan. When developing computer software, the planning stage is implemented using a collection of algorithms. As you already know, an algorithm is a series of step-by-step instructions that produce results to solve problems. When planning computer programs, algorithms are used to outline the solution steps using Englishlike statements, called *pseudocode,* that require less precision than a formal programming language. A good pseudocode algorithm should be independent of, but easily translated into, *any* formal programming language.

Pseudocode is an informal set of Englishlike statements that are generally accepted within the computer industry to denote common computer programming operations. Pseudocode statements are used to describe the steps in a computer algorithm.

Coding the Program

Coding the program should be one of the simplest tasks in the whole programming process, provided you have done a good job of defining the problem and planning its solution. Coding involves the actual writing of the program in a formal programming language. The computer language you use will be determined by the nature of the problem, the programming languages available to you, and the limits of the computer system. Once a language is chosen, the program is written, or coded, by translating your algorithm steps into the formal language code.

You should be cautioned, however, that coding is really a mechanical process and should be considered secondary to algorithm development. In the future, computers will generate their own program code from well-constructed algorithms. Research in the field of artificial intelligence has resulted in "code-generation" software. The thing to keep in mind is that computers might some-day generate their own programming code from algorithms, but it takes the creativity and common sense of a human being to plan the solution and develop the algorithm.

Debugging the Program

You will soon find out that it is a rare and joyous occasion when a coded program actually "runs" the first time without any errors. Of course, good problem definition and planning will avoid many program mistakes, or "bugs." However, there always are a few bugs that manage to go undetected, regardless of how much planning you do. Getting rid of the program bugs (*debugging*) often is the most time-consuming job in the whole programming process. Industrial statistics show that often over 50 percent of a programmer's time is often spent on program debugging.

There is no absolute correct procedure for debugging a program, but a systematic approach can help make the process easier. The basic steps of debugging are as follows:

❏ Realizing that you have an error.
❏ Locating and determining the cause of the error.
❏ Fixing the error.

First of all, you have to realize that you have an error. Sometimes, this is obvious when your computer freezes up or crashes. At other times, the program might work fine until certain unexpected information is entered by someone using the program. The most subtle errors occur when the program is running fine and the results look correct, but when you examine the results closely, they are not quite right.

The next step in the debugging process is locating and determining the cause of the errors—sometimes the most difficult part of debugging. This is where a good programming tool, called a ***debugger,*** comes into play.

Fixing the error is the final step in debugging. Your knowledge of the C++ language, this book, C++ on-line help, a C++ debugger, and your C++ reference manuals are all valuable tools in fixing the error and removing the "bug" from your program.

When programming in C++, there are four things that you can do to test and debug your program: ***desk-check*** the program, ***compile*** the program, ***run*** the program, and ***debug*** the program.

Desk-Checking the Program.   Desk-checking a program is similar to proofreading a letter or manuscript. The idea is to trace through the program mentally to make sure that the program logic is workable. You must consider various input possibilities and write down any results generated during program execution. In particular, try to determine what the program will do with unusual data by considering input possibilities that "shouldn't" happen. Always keep Murphy's law in mind when desk-checking a program: *If a given condition can't or shouldn't happen, it will!*

For example, suppose a program requires the user to enter a value whose square root must be found. Of course, the user "shouldn't" enter a negative value, because the square root of a negative number is imaginary. However, what will the program do if he or she does? Another input possibility that should always be considered is an input of zero, especially when used as part of an arithmetic operation, such as division.

When you first begin programming, you will be tempted to skip the desk-checking phase, because you can't wait to run the program once it is written. However, as you gain experience, you soon will realize the time-saving value of desk-checking.

Compiling the Program.   At this point, you are ready to enter the program into the computer system. Once entered, the program must be compiled, or translated, into machine code. Fortunately, the compiler is designed to check for certain program errors. These usually are *syntax* errors that you have made when coding the program. A syntax error is any violation of the rules of the programming language, such as using a period instead of a semicolon. There might also be type errors. A *type error* occurs when you attempt to mix different types of data, such as numeric and character data. It is like trying to add apples to oranges.

A *syntax error* is any violation of the rules of the programming language, and a *type error* occurs when you attempt to mix different types of data.

During the compiling process, many C++ compilers generate error and warning messages as well as position the display monitor cursor to the point in the program where the error was detected. Once an error is corrected, you must attempt to compile the program again. If other errors are detected, you must correct them, recompile the program, and so on, until the entire program is successfully compiled.

Running the Program.   Once the program has been compiled, you must execute, or run, it. However, just because the program has been compiled successfully doesn't mean that it will run successfully under all possible conditions. Common bugs that occur at this stage include *logic errors* and *run-time* errors. These are the most difficult kinds of errors to detect. A logic error will occur when a loop tells the computer to repeat an operation but does not tell it when to stop repeating. This is called an ***infinite loop.*** Such a bug will not cause an error message to be generated, because the computer is simply doing what it was told to do. The program execution must be stopped and debugged before it can run successfully.

A ***logic error*** occurs when the computer does what you tell it to do but is not doing what you meant it to do. It is an error in thinking on the part of the programmer. A ***run-time*** error occurs when the program attempts to perform an illegal operation as defined by the laws of mathematics or the particular compiler in use.

A run-time error occurs when the program attempts to perform an illegal operation, as defined by the laws of mathematics or the particular compiler in use. Two common mathematical run-time errors are division by zero and attempting to take the square root of a negative number. A common error imposed by the compiler is a value out of range. For example, C++ limits byte-sized integers to a range of –128 to +127. Unpredictable results can occur if a byte value exceeds this range.

Sometimes, the program is automatically aborted and an error message is displayed when a run-time error occurs. Other times, the program seems to execute properly but generates incorrect results, commonly called *garbage*. Again, you should consult your compiler reference manual to determine the exact nature of the problem. The error must be located and corrected before another attempt is made to run the program.

Using a Debugger.   One of the most important programming tools that you can have is a debugger. A debugger provides a microscopic view of what is going on in your program. Many C++ compilers include a built-in, or *integrated,* debugger that allows you to single-step program statements and view the execution results in the CPU and memory.

DEBUGGING TIP

A word from experience: Always debug your programs in a systematic, common-sense manner. Don't be tempted to change something just because you "hope" it will work and don't know what else to do. Use your resources to isolate and correct the problem. Such resources include your algorithm, a program listing, your integrated C++ debugger, your reference manuals, this textbook, and your instructor, just to mention a few. Logic and run-time errors usually are the result of a serious flaw in your program. They will not go away and cannot be corrected by blindly making changes to your program. One good way to locate errors is to have your program print out preliminary results as well as messages that tell when a particular part of the program is running.

Documentation

This documentation step in the programmer's algorithm often is overlooked, but it probably is one of the more important steps, especially in commercial programming. Documentation is easy if you have done a good job of defining the problem, planning the solution, coding, testing, and debugging the program. The final program documentation is simply the recorded result of these programming steps. At a minimum, good documentation should include the following:

❑ A narrative description of the problem definition, which includes the type of input, output, and processing employed by the program.

❑ A set of algorithms.

❑ A program listing that includes a clear commenting scheme. Commenting within the program is an important part of the overall documentation process. Each program should include comments at the beginning to explain what it does, any special algorithms that are employed, and a summary of the problem definition. In addition, the name of the programmer and the date the program was written and last modified should be included.

❑ Samples of input and output data.

❑ Testing and debugging results.

❑ User instructions.

The documentation must be neat and well-organized. It must be easily understood by you as well as any other person who might have a need to use or modify your program in the future. What good is an ingenious program if no one can determine what it does, how to use it, or how to maintain it?

One final point: Documentation should always be an ongoing process. Whenever you work with the program or modify it, make sure the documentation is updated to reflect your experiences and modifications. Someday you might have to maintain a program written by yourself or somebody else. Without good documentation, program maintenance becomes a nightmare. Just look at what has happened with the Y2K (Year 2000) problem. This is a classic example of a problem caused by large-scale software systems created without good documentation.

 Quick Check

1. English-like statements that require less precision than a formal programming language are called _____ statements.

2. What questions must be answered when defining a computer programming problem?

3. What can be done to test and debug a program?

4. Why is commenting important within a program?

5. What is a syntax error?

6. What is a logic error?

2.2   PROBLEM SOLVING USING ALGORITHMS

In the previous section, you learned that an algorithm is a sequence of step-by-step instructions that solves a problem.

For instance, consider the following series of instructions:

> Apply to wet hair.
>
> Gently massage lather through hair.
>
> Rinse, keeping lather out of eyes.
>
> Repeat.

Look familiar? Of course, this is a series of instructions that might be found on the back of a shampoo bottle. But does it fit the technical definition of an algorithm? In other words, does it produce a result? You might say "yes," but look closer. The algorithm requires that you keep repeating the procedure an infinite number of times, so theoretically you would never stop shampooing your hair! A good computer algorithm must terminate in a finite amount of time. The repeat instruction could be altered easily to make the shampooing algorithm technically correct:

> Repeat until hair is clean.

Now the shampooing process can be terminated. Of course, you must be the one to decide when your hair is clean.

The foregoing shampoo analogy might seem a bit trivial. You probably are thinking that any intelligent person would not keep on repeating the shampooing process an infinite number of times, right? This obviously is the case when we humans execute the algorithm, because we have some commonsense judgment. But what about a computer; does it have commonsense judgement? Most computers do exactly what they are told to do via the computer program. As a result, a computer would repeat the original shampooing algorithm over and over an infinite number of times. This is why the algorithms that you write for computer programs must be precise.

Now, let's develop an algorithm for a process that is common to all of us—mailing a letter. Think of the steps that are involved in this simple process. You must first address an envelope, fold the letter, insert the letter in the envelope, and seal the envelope. Next, you need a stamp. If you don't have a stamp, you have to buy one. Once a stamp is obtained, you must place it on the envelope and mail the letter. The following algorithm summarizes the steps in this process:

> Obtain an envelope.
>
> Address the envelope.
>
> Fold the letter.
>
> Insert the letter in the envelope.
>
> Seal the envelope.
>
> If you don't have a stamp, then buy one.
>
> Place the stamp on the envelope.
>
> Mail the letter.

Does this sequence of instructions fit our definition of a good algorithm? In other words, does the sequence of instructions produce a result in a finite amount of time? Yes, assuming that each operation can be understood and carried out by the person mailing the letter. This brings up two additional characteristics of good algorithms: Each operation within the algorithm must be *well-defined* and *effective.* By well-defined, we mean that each of the steps must be clearly understood by people in the computer industry. By effective, we mean that some method must exist in order to carry out the operation. In other words, the person mailing the letter must be able to perform each of the algorithm steps. In the case of a computer program algorithm, the compiler must have the means of executing each operation in the algorithm.

In summary, a good computer algorithm must possess the following three attributes:

1. Employ well-defined instructions that are generally understood by people in the computer industry.
2. Employ instructions that can be carried out effectively by the compiler executing the algorithm.
3. Produce a solution to the problem in a finite amount of time.

In order to write computer program algorithms, we need to establish a set of well defined, effective operations. The set of pseudocode operations listed in Table 2.1 will make up our algorithmic language, or pseudocode. We will use these operations from now on, whenever we write computer algorithms.

Notice that the operations in Table 2.1 are grouped into three major categories: *sequence, decision,* and *iteration.* These categories are called *control structures.* The sequence control structure includes those operations that produce a single action or result. Only a partial list of sequence operations is provided here. This list will be expanded, as additional operations are needed. As its name implies, the decision control structure includes the operations that allow the computer to make decisions. Finally, the iteration control structure includes those operations that are used for looping, or repeating, operations within the algorithm. Many of the operations listed in Table 2.1 are self-explanatory. Those that are not will be discussed in detail as we begin to develop more complex algorithms.

 Quick Check

1. Why is it important to develop a set of algorithms prior to coding a program?
2. What are the three major control structure categories of pseudocode operations?
3. List three decision operations.
4. List three iteration operations.

TABLE 2.1   PSEUDOCODE OPERATIONS USED IN THIS TEXT

Sequence	Decision	Iteration
Add (+)	If	While
Calculate	If/Else	Do/While
Decrement	Switch/Case	For
Display		
Divide (/)		
Increment		
Multiply (*)		
Print		
Read		
Set or assign (=)		
Square		
Subtract (−)		
Write		

2.3   PROBLEM ABSTRACTION AND STEPWISE REFINEMENT

At this time, we need to introduce a very important concept in programming— *abstraction.* Abstraction allows us to view a problem in general terms, without worrying about the details. As a result, abstraction provides for generalization in problem solving.

> **Abstraction** provides for generalization in problem solving by allowing you to view a problem in general terms, without worrying about the details of the problem solution.

You might have heard the old saying, "You can't see the forest for the trees." This means that it is very easy to get lost within the trees of the forest without seeing the big picture of the entire forest. This saying also applies to problem solving and programming. When starting out to solve a program, you need to get the "big picture" first. Once you have the big picture of the problem solution, the "forest," you can gradually *refine* the solution by providing more detail until you have a solution, the "trees," that is easily coded in a computer language. The process of gradually adding more detail to a general abstract problem solution is called *stepwise refinement.*

> **Stepwise refinement** is the process of gradually adding detail to a general abstract problem solution until it can be easily coded in a computer language.

As an example, consider the problem of designing your own "dream house." Would you begin by drafting the detailed plans of the house? Not likely, because you would most likely get lost in detail. A better approach would be to first make an artist's general-perspective rendition of the house; then make a general floor plan diagram, and finally make detailed drawings of the house construction that could be followed by the builders.

The concepts of problem abstraction and stepwise refinement allow you to *divide and conquer* the problem and solve it from the *top down*. This strategy has been proven to conquer all types of problems, especially programming problems. In programming, we generate a general problem solution, or algorithm, and gradually refine it, producing more detailed algorithms, until we get to a level that can be easily coded using a programming language.

In summary, when attacking a problem, always start with the big picture and begin with a very general, or *abstract,* model of the solution. This allows you to concentrate on the problem at hand without getting lost in the "trees" by worrying about the implementation details of a particular programming language. You then gradually refine the solution until you reach a level that can be easily coded using a programming language, like C++. The *Problem Solving in Action* examples that follow illustrate this process.

Quick Check

1. Explain why abstraction is important when solving problems.
2. Explain the process of stepwise refinement.
3. How do you know when you have reached a codable level of an algorithm when using stepwise refinement?

PROBLEM SOLVING IN ACTION: SALES TAX

PROBLEM

Develop a set of algorithms to calculate the amount of sales tax and the total cost of a sales item, including tax. Assume the sales tax rate is 7 percent and the user will enter the cost of the sales item.

Defining the Problem

When defining the problem, you must consider three things: *output, input,* and *processing* as related to the problem statement. Look for the nouns and verbs within the problem statement, as they often provide clues to the required output, input, and processing. The nouns suggest output and input, and the verbs suggest processing steps. The nouns relating to output and input are *sales tax, total cost,* and *cost.*

The total cost is the required output, and the sales tax and item cost are needed as input to calculate the total cost of the item. However, the sales tax rate is given (7 percent), so the only data required for the algorithm is the item cost.

The verb *calculate* requires us to process two things: the amount of sales tax, and the total cost of the item, including sales tax. Therefore, the processing must calculate the amount of sales tax and add this value to the item cost to obtain the total cost of the item. In summary, the problem definition in terms of output, input, and processing is as follows:

Output: The total cost of the sales item, including sales tax to be displayed on the system monitor.

Input: The cost of the sales item to be entered by the user on the system keyboard.

Processing: $tax = 0.07 \times cost$
                 $totalCost = cost + tax$

Notice that we have indicated *where* the output is going (the system monitor), and *where* the input is coming from (the user keyboard). Where the output is going and the input is coming from should always be indicated for each item in the problem definition. Also, we have addressed output first, because careful consideration of the output requirements often leads you to determining what input data and processing steps are required to produce the desired output information.

Planning the Solution

Now that the problem has been defined in terms of output, input, and processing, it is time to plan the solution by developing the required algorithms. Using the foregoing problem definition, we are now ready to write the initial algorithm. We will call this initial algorithm *main()*. (*Note:* The parentheses after the algorithm name will be used from now on to indicate an algorithm, or function, to perform some given task.) Here is the required initial algorithm, *main()*:

Initial Algorithm

main()
BEGIN
        Read the cost of the sales item from the user.
        Calculate the sales tax and total cost of the sales item.
        Write the total cost of the sales item, including sales tax on the system
        monitor.
END.

Notice that, at this level, you are not concerned with how to perform the foregoing operations in a computer language. You are only concerned about the major program operations, without agonizing over the language implementation details. This is problem abstraction!

We have divided the problem into three major tasks relating to input, processing, and output derived directly from our problem definition. So, the problem definition will always lead you to the *main()* algorithm. The next step is to refine repeatedly the initial algorithm until we obtain one or more algorithms that can be coded directly in a computer language. This is a relatively simple problem, so we can employ the pseudocode operations listed in Table 2.1 at this first level of refinement. Three major operations are identified by the preceding algorithm: *reading* data from the user, *calculating* the tax and total cost, and *writing* (displaying) the results to the user. As a result, we will create three additional algorithms that implement these operations. First, reading the data from the user. We will call this algorithm *readData()* as follows:

First Level of Refinement

readData()
BEGIN
    Write a program description message to the user.
    Write a user prompt to enter the cost of the item (*cost*).
    Read *cost.*
END.

In Table 2.1, you will find two sequence operations called **read** and **write.** The *read* operation is an input operation. We will assume that this operation will obtain data entered via the system keyboard. The *write* operation is an output operation. We will assume that this operation causes information to be displayed on the system monitor. The *readData()* algorithm uses the *write* operation to display a **prompt** to the user and a corresponding *read* operation to obtain the user input and assign it to the respective variable.

STYLE TIP

The *readData()* algorithm illustrates some operations that result in good programming style. Notice that the first *write* operation is to write a program description message to the person running the program—the user. It is good practice always to include such a message so that the user understands what the program will do. In addition, the second *write* operation will display a message to tell the user to "Enter the cost of the item." Without such a prompt, the user will not know what to do. You must write a user prompt message anytime the user must enter data via the keyboard. Such a message should tell the user what is to be entered and in what format the information is to be entered. More about this later.

The next task is to develop an algorithm to calculate the cost of the sales item, including tax. We will call this algorithm *calculateCost()* and employ the required pseudocode operations from Table 2.1, as follows:

calculateCost()
BEGIN
    Set *tax* to $(0.07 \times cost)$.
    Set *totalCost* to $(cost + tax)$.
END.

Finally, we need an algorithm to display the results. We will call this algorithm *displayResults().* All we need here is a *write* operation as follows:

displayResults()
BEGIN
     Write *totalCost.*
END.

That's all there is to it. The illustration in Figure 2.1 is called a **problem solution diagram,** because it shows the overall structure of our problem solution. The problem solution diagram shows how the problem has been divided into a series of subproblems, whose collective solution will solve the initial problem. By using the above algorithms and problem solution diagram, this problem can be coded easily in any language, such as C++.

When you begin coding in C++, you will translate the preceding algorithms directly into C++ code. Each of the algorithms will be coded as a C++ **function.** Functions in C++ are subprograms designed to perform specific tasks, such as those performed by each of our algorithms. Thus, we will code a function called *readData()* to get the data from the user, another function called *calculateCost()* to calculate the total cost of the sales item, and a third function called *displayResults()* to display the final results to the user. In addition, we will code a function called *main()* to sequentially **call** these functions as needed to produce the desired result. Notice that the name of the algorithm, or function, begins with a lower case letter, then each subsequent word in the name begins with an uppercase letter. This naming convention will be used throughout this book for naming both variables and functions.

A *function* in C++ is a subprogram designed to perform specific tasks, such as those performed by an algorithm. In other programming languages, functions might be referred to as *procedures, methods,* or *subroutines.*

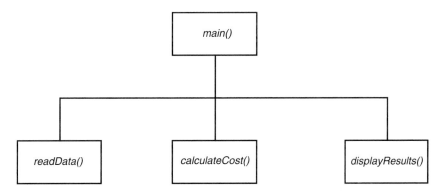

FIGURE 2.1 A PROBLEM SOLUTION DIAGRAM FOR THE SALES TAX PROBLEM SHOWS THE ABSTRACT ANALYSIS AND STEPWISE REFINEMENT REQUIRED FOR SOLVING COMPLEX PROBLEMS.

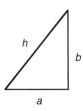

FIGURE 2.2 **SOLVING THE HYPOTENUSE OF A RIGHT TRIANGLE USING THE PYTHAGOREAN THEOREM.**

PROBLEM SOLVING IN ACTION: PYTHAGOREAN THEOREM

PROBLEM

Develop a set of algorithms to find the hypotenuse of a right triangle, given its two right angle sides, using the Pythagorean theorem depicted in Figure 2.2. Construct the final algorithms using the pseudocode instructions listed in Table 2.1.

Defining the Problem

When defining the problem, you must consider three things: *output, input,* and *processing* as related to the problem statement. Let's label the two sides *a* and *b*, and the hypotenuse *h*. The problem requires us to find the hypotenuse (*h*), given the two sides (*a* and *b*). So the output must be the hypotenuse (*h*). We will display the hypotenuse value on the system monitor. In order to obtain this output, the two sides (*a* and *b*) must be received by the program. Let's assume that the user must enter these values via the system keyboard.

The Pythagorean theorem states that the hypotenuse squared is equal to the sum of the squares of the two sides. In symbols,

$$h^2 = a^2 + b^2$$

This equation represents the processing that must be performed by the computer. In summary, the problem definition is as follows:

Output: The hypotenuse (*h*) of a right triangle displayed on the system monitor.
Input: The two sides (*a* and *b*) of a right triangle to be entered by the user via the system keyboard.
Processing: Employ the Pythagorean theorem: $h^2 = a^2 + b^2$.

Now that the problem has been defined in terms of output, input, and processing, it is time to plan the solution by developing the required algorithms.

Planning the Solution

We will begin with an abstract model of the problem. This will be our initial algorithm, which we refer to as *main()*. At this level, we are only concerned about addressing the major operations required to solve the problem. These are derived directly from the problem definition. As a result, our initial algorithm is as follows:

Initial Algorithm

main()
BEGIN
    Read the two sides (*a* and *b*) of a right triangle from the user.
    Calculate the hypotenuse (*h*) of the triangle using the Pythagorean theorem.
    Write the results (*h*) on the system monitor.
END.

The next step is to refine repeatedly the initial algorithm until we obtain one or more algorithms that can be coded directly in a computer language. This is a relatively simple problem, so we can employ the pseudocode operations listed in Table 2.1 at this first level of refinement. Three major operations are identified by the preceding algorithm: reading data from the user, calculating the hypotenuse, and displaying the results to the user. As a result, we will create three additional algorithms that implement these operations. First, reading the data from the user. We will call this algorithm *readData()*.

First Level of Refinement

readData()
BEGIN
    Write a program description message to the user.
    Write a user prompt message to enter the first side of the triangle (*a*).
    Read *a*.
    Write a user prompt message to enter the second side of the triangle (*b*).
    Read *b*.
END.

The next task is to develop an algorithm to calculate the hypotenuse of the triangle. We will call this algorithm *calculateHypot()* and employ the required pseudocode operations from Table 2.1, as follows:

calculateHypot()
BEGIN
    Square(*a*).
    Square(*b*).
    Assign $(a^2 + b^2)$ to h^2.
    Assign square root of h^2 to *h*.
END.

The operations in this algorithm should be self-explanatory. Notice how the *assign* operation works. For example, the statement *Assign square root of h^2 to h* sets the variable *h* to the value obtained from taking the square root of h^2. We could also express this operation as *Set h to square root of h^2*. The *assign* and *set* operations are equivalent; however, the verb objects within the respective phrases are reversed. You should be familiar with either terminology.

The final task is to develop an algorithm to display the results. We will call this algorithm *displayResults()*. All we need here is a *write* operation as follows:

displayResults()
BEGIN
    Write *h*.
END.

PROBLEM SOLVING IN ACTION: CREDIT CARD INTEREST

PROBLEM

The interest charged on a credit card account depends on the remaining balance according to the following criteria: interest charged is 18 percent up to $500 and 15 percent for any amount over $500. Develop the algorithms required to find the total amount of interest due on any given account balance.

Let's begin by defining the problem in terms of output, input, and processing.

Defining the Problem

Output: According to the problem statement, the obvious output must be the total amount of interest due. We will display this information on the system monitor.

Input: We will assume that the user will enter the account balance via the system keyboard.

Processing: Here is an application in which a decision-making operation must be included in the algorithm. There are two possibilities as follows:

1. *If* the balance is less than or equal to $500, *then* the interest is 18 percent of the balance, or

$$interest = 0.18 \times balance$$

2. *If* the balance is over $500, *then* the interest is 18 percent of the first $500 plus 15 percent of any amount over $500. In the form of an equation,

$$interest = (0.18 \times 500) + [0.15 \times (balance - 500)]$$

Notice the use of the two *if/then* statements in these two possibilities.

Planning the Solution

Our problem solution begins with the initial algorithm we have been calling *main()*. Again, this algorithm will simply reflect the problem definition as follows:

Initial Algorithm

main()
BEGIN
    Read the account balance from the user.
    Calculate the interest on the account balance.
    Write the calculated interest on the system monitor.
END.

Because of the simplicity of the problem, only one level of refinement is needed, as follows:

First Level of Refinement

readData()
BEGIN
    Write a program description message to the user.
    Write a user prompt to enter the account balance (*balance*).
    Read *balance*.
END.

calculateInterest()
BEGIN
    If *balance* $<= 500$ Then
        Set *interest* to $(0.18 \times balance)$.
    If *balance* > 500 Then
        Set *interest* to $(0.18 \times 500) + [0.15 \times (balance - 500)]$.
END.

displayResults()
BEGIN
    Write *interest*.
END.

As you can see, the two decision-making operations stated in the problem definition have been incorporated into our *calculateInterest()* algorithm. Notice the use of indentation to show which calculation goes with which *if/then* operation. The use of indentation is an important part of pseudocode, because it shows the algorithm structure at a glance.

How might you replace the two *if/then* operations in this algorithm with a single *if/else* operation? Think about it, as it will be left as a problem at the end of the chapter!

CHAPTER SUMMARY

The five major steps that must be performed when developing software are (1) define the problem, (2) plan the problem solution, (3) code the program, (4) debug the program, and (5) document the program. When defining the problem, you must consider the output, input, and processing requirements of the application. Planning the problem solution requires that you specify the problem solution steps via an algorithm. An algorithm is a series of step-by-step instructions that provide a solution to the problem in a finite amount of time.

Abstraction and stepwise refinement are powerful tools for problem solving. Abstraction allows you to view the problem in general terms, without agonizing over the implementation details of a computer language. Stepwise refinement is applied to an initial abstract problem solution to develop gradually a set of related algorithms that can be directly coded using a computer language, such as C++.

Once a codeable algorithm is developed, it must be coded into some formal language that the computer system can understand. Once coded, the program must be tested and debugged through desk-checking, compiling, and execution. Finally, the entire programming process, from problem definition to testing and debugging, must be documented so that it can be easily understood by you or anyone else working with it.

Your C++ debugger is one of the best tools that you can use to deal with bugs that creep into your programs. It allows you to do source-level debugging and helps with the two hardest parts of debugging: finding the error and finding the cause of the error. It does this by allowing you to trace into your programs and their functions one step at a time. This slows down the program execution so that you can examine the contents of the individual data elements and program output at any given point in the program.

Questions and Problems

Questions

1. Define an algorithm.
2. List the five steps of the programmer's algorithm.
3. What three things must be considered during the problem-definition phase of programming?
4. What tools are employed for planning the solution to a programming problem?
5. Explain how problem abstraction aids in solving problems.
6. Explain the process of stepwise refinement.
7. The writing of a program is called _____.
8. State three things that you can do to test and debug your programs.
9. List the minimum items required for good documentation.
10. What three characteristics must a good computer algorithm possess?
11. The three major control structures of a programming language are _____, _____, and _____.
12. Explain why a single *if/then* operation in the credit card interest problem won't work. If you know the balance is not less than or equal to $500, the balance must be greater than $500, right? So, why can't the second *if/then* operation be deleted?

Problems

Least Difficult

1. Develop a set of algorithms to compute the sum, difference, product, and quotient of any two integers entered by the user.
2. Revise the solution you obtained in problem 1 to protect it from a divide-by-zero run-time error.

More Difficult

3. Develop a set of algorithms to read in an employee's total weekly hours worked and rate of pay. Determine the gross weekly pay using "time-and-a- half" for anything over 40 hours.
4. Revise the solution generated in the credit card problem to employ a single *if/else* operation in place of the two *if/then* operations. As you will see later, an *if/else* operation

does one thing "if" a condition is true, "else" does something different if the same condition is false.

5. A dimension on a part drawing indicates that the length of the part is 3.00 ± 0.25 inches. This means that the minimum acceptable length of the part is 3.0 − 0.25 = 2.75 inches and the maximum acceptable length of the part is 3.00 + 0.25 = 3.25 inches. Develop a set of algorithms that will display "ACCEPTABLE" if the part is within tolerance and "UNACCEPTABLE" if the part is out of tolerance. Also, show your problem definition in terms of output, input, and processing.

6. Develop a problem definition and set of algorithms to process a standard bank account. Assume that the user must enter the beginning bank account balance as well as any deposits or withdrawals on the account. The banking transactions that must be implemented are adding any deposits to the balance and subtracting any withdrawals from the balance. Of course, the program should display the account status, including the old balance, amount of deposits, amount of withdrawals, and the new balance.

7. Develop a problem solution diagram for the banking problem in problem 6.

8. Develop a problem definition and set of algorithms to process a business inventory. Assume that the user must enter five inventory items for a local bait and tackle store. Each entry is to consist of the item name, quantity on hand, and item price. The program should calculate the expected profit on each item and total profit for all items, assuming a profit margin of 20%. The program should then display the expected profit on each item and total expected profit of all items.

9. Develop a problem solution diagram for the inventory problem in problem 8.

10. Develop a set of algorithms that will allow the entry of three integer coefficients of a quadratic equation and generate the roots of the equation. Provide for an error message if complex roots exist.

11. Develop a problem solution diagram for the quadratic equations problem in problem 10.

DATA: TYPES, CLASSES, AND OBJECTS

■ Chapter Contents

Chapter Objectives

When you are finished with this chapter, you should have a good understanding of the following:

- The concepts of data abstraction and abstract data types (ADTs).
- The concept of object behavior.
- The relationship between a class and its objects.
- Functions and their use in C++ programs.
- The primitive data types in C++.
- The Standard C++ Library for the *string* class.
- The C++ Standard Template Library, STL, for data structures and algorithms.
- The C++ *string* class.

- How to define constants and variables in a C++ program.
- How to define string objects in a C++ program.
- Numeric overflow errors.
- Fixed decimal versus exponential format of floating-point numbers.
- How to display information using the C++ *cout* object.
- How to create programmer-defined enumerated data types.
- How to create a C++ program from a set of algorithms.

INTRODUCTION

You are now ready to begin learning the building blocks of the C++ language. The C++ language is what is called an *object-oriented language.* Object-oriented programming, OOP, is built around *classes* and *objects* that model real-world entities in a more natural way than do procedural languages, such as BASIC and C. By natural we mean that object-oriented programming allows you to construct programs the way we humans tend to think about things. For example, we tend to classify real-world entities such as vehicles, airplanes, ATM machines, and so on. We learn about such things by studying their *characteristics* and *behavior.* Take a class of vehicles, for example. All vehicles have certain characteristics, or *attributes,* such as engines, wheels, transmissions, and so on. Furthermore, all vehicles exhibit *behavior,* like acceleration, deceleration (braking), and turning. In other words, we have a general abstract impression of a vehicle through its attributes and behavior. This abstract model of a vehicle hides all the "nuts and bolts" that are contained in the vehicle. As a result, we think of the vehicle in terms of its attributes and behavior rather than its nuts and bolts, although without the nuts and bolts, a real-world vehicle could not exist. How do objects relate to classes? Well, your car is an example, or instance, of the vehicle class. It possesses all the attributes and behavior of any vehicle but is a specific example of a vehicle. Likewise, in object-oriented programming, we create an abstract class that describes the general attributes and behavior of a programming entity, then create objects of the class that will be actually manipulated within the program, just as your car is the thing that you actually drive, not your general abstract notion of a vehicle. You will begin learning about classes and objects in this chapter.

You will get your first exposure to the structure of C++ in this chapter as you learn about the various types of data contained in the C++ language. Data are any information that must be processed by the C++ program. However, before C++ can process any information, it must know what type of data it is dealing with. As a result, any information processed by C++ must be categorized into one of the legal *data types* defined for C++.

The data types that you will learn about in this chapter are the *integer, floating-point, character,* and *Boolean* data types. It is important that you understand this idea of data typing, because it is one of the most important concepts in any language. Once you learn the general characteristics and behavior of each data type, you will learn how to create constants and variables for use in a C++ program.

In addition to the primitive data types employed by C++, this chapter will introduce you to the programmer-defined data type called a ***class.*** Here, the term programmer-defined refers to classes that you, the programmer, will define. The class construct is particularly important for you to learn, because it allows you to create your own classes for developing object-oriented programs.

You will learn that structured, or procedural, programming is built around functions, and object-oriented programming is built around classes. Do the two have any relationship whatsoever? Yes! The classes that we build are constructed using elements of structured programming, namely functions. This is why we need to study structured programming first and gradually move into object-oriented programming. In the next few chapters, you will learn how to build structured programs. In addition, you will start thinking of things in terms of classes and objects. Once you have mastered these fundamental concepts, you will be ready to learn about object-oriented programming in later chapters.

At the end of this chapter, you will be asked to write, enter, and execute your first C++ programs. If you have not already done so, it's probably a good idea for you to familiarize yourself with the operation of your system at this time. You should know how to load the C++ compiler, enter and edit programs, compile programs, debug programs, and run programs. Refer to Appendix C if you are using Visual C++.

3.1 | THE IDEA OF DATA ABSTRACTION AND CLASSES

You might be thinking: "Data are data, what's all this fuss about data?" First, you must think of data as any information that the computer might perform operations on or manipulate. So, let's define a ***data object*** to be any item of information that is manipulated or operated on by the computer. Many different types of data objects exist during the execution of a program. Some of these data objects will be programmer-defined while others will be system-defined.

Now, think about the types of information, or data objects, that a computer manipulates. Of course, a computer manipulates numbers, or ***numeric data.*** One of the primary uses of a computer is to perform calculations on numeric data, right? But what about ***character*** data? Isn't the computer operating with character data when it prints out your name? Thus, numeric data and character data comprise two different ***types*** of data. What makes them different? Well, numeric data consist of numbers, whereas character data consist of alphanumeric symbols. In addition, the operations defined for these two types of data will be different.

> An ***abstract data type,*** or ***ADT,*** describes the data attributes and behavior of its objects.

Now, what's all this ADT stuff? Well, we say that an ADT describes the data characteristics, or ***attributes,*** as well as legal operations, or ***behavior,*** of its objects. Remember the vehicle analogy cited in the chapter introduction. The notion of a vehicle describes things such as engines and transmissions (the attributes), as well as acceleration and deceleration (the behavior), for any actual vehicle objects such as your own car. Well, we can look at data in the same natural way. Take the integers as an example of an ADT. The attributes, or characteristics, of integers is that they include all the whole number data values between minus infinity and plus infinity. Furthermore, there is a set of operations specifically defined for the integers. These operations include addition, subtraction, multiplication, and division, among others, and define the behavior of the integers. Thus, the set of whole numbers from minus infinity to plus infinity, along with their related operations, form an ADT. Any integer value can only be a whole number and only be used in an operation specifically defined for integers just as any actual vehicle looks and behaves like a vehicle. In fact, we say that the set of integers forms an ***abstract data type,*** or ***ADT,*** as shown in Figure 3.1.

You were introduced to the idea of abstraction in the last chapter. You found that abstraction, as applied to problem solving, allowed you to concentrate on the problem solution, without worrying about the implementation details. The same is true with ADTs. Abstract data types allow you to work with data without concern for how the data are stored inside the computer or how the data operations are performed inside the computer. This is referred to as ***data abstraction.*** Let's take the addition operation as an example. Integer addition, by definition, dictates that you must supply two integer arguments to be added, and it will return the integer sum of the two. Do you care about the details of how the computer implements addition or how the computer represents integers in memory? Of course not! All you care about is what information needs to be supplied to the addition operation to perform its job and what information is returned by the operation. In other words, all you care about is *what* must be supplied to the addition operation and *how* the operation will respond. This is called ***behavior***—how the ADT will act and react for a given operation.

FIGURE 3.1   THE INTEGERS CAN BE CONSIDERED AN ABSTRACT DATA TYPE, WHERE THE ARITHMETIC OPERATIONS ON THE INTEGERS DEFINE THE BEHAVIOR OF INTEGER DATA.

> The term **behavior**, as associated with ADTs, has to do with how the ADT will act and react for a given operation.

You will learn more about ADTs and behavior later in the text. For now, it is only important that you understand the concept as applied to C++ ADTs.

The C++ language supports several different ADTs as shown in Figure 3.2.

The primitive data types are those that are simple and are predefined to, or "built into," the C++ language. These consist of integer numbers and floating-point (real, decimal) numbers, as well as character data. In addition, there is an enumerated data type which allows you, the programmer, to define a particular set of data values for a given application. You will learn about these primitive data types shortly.

One of the reasons OOP has been so popular is its support of **code reuse.** Code reuse allows commonly used code to be written just once then, using an OOP property called **inheritance,** the code can be reused and tailored to specific applications as required. In other words, code reuse eliminates the need for "reinventing the wheel" each time a common ADT or operation needs be coded. To facilitate this, the ANSI/ISO standard specifies the **Standard C++ Library.** The Standard C++ Library consists of commonly used ADTs and algorithms. One such ADT is the string ADT that is available in the library via the *string* class. The C++ Standard Library also includes the **Standard Template Library,** or **STL,** which consists of commonly used ADTs called **container classes** that can be used in any C++ program. These are complex data types that include the *vector, list, stack,* and *queue* container classes, among others. These container classes are referred to as complex in the sense that they include primitive data as well as operations needed to manipulate the data that they contain. You will learn about classes contained within these standard libraries as you go through this book.

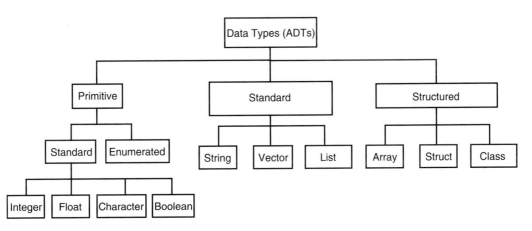

FIGURE 3.2   DATA HIERARCHY IN THE C++ LANGUAGE.

> **Code reuse** is an inherent feature of OOP that eliminates the need for "reinventing the wheel" each time a common ADT or operation needs be coded. Code reuse is supported by the Standard C++ Library.

A **structured data type** is also a complex data type, in the sense that it is made up of other simpler primitive data. As an example, your name, address, and telephone number can be combined to form a **struct,** also referred to as a **record.** This struct obviously consists of integers and characters, both of which are primitive data types. You could store your semester test scores in an **array.** Thus, the array structure would consist of a series of test scores, each of which is a decimal, or floating-point, value. In other words, structured data types are formed using combinations of the simpler primitive data as building blocks. These structured data types differ from the STL container classes in that they are not standardized by any means, but provide you, the programmer, a way to code your own non-standard arrays, structs, and classes.

Of particular interest is the C++ **class** category. The **class** provides the foundation for object-oriented programming (OOP) in C++. You now know that the C++ language includes *standard* classes via its standard class libraries. Well, the C++ class allows you, the programmer, to create your own ADTs. For example, suppose that you have been hired to write an application program to control an ATM machine. The ATM machine is required to handle various types of data with specific operations defined for those data, such as deposit and withdrawal. Doesn't this sound like an ideal application for an ADT, because an ADT is a collection of data along with a set of operations defined for those data? Obviously, there is no standard ATM machine ADT built into the C++ language. However, the C++ class

Quick Check

1. A _____ describes the data attributes and behavior of its objects.
2. Simple data that are predefined within a programming language are called _____ data types.
3. A set of data values created by you, the programmer, to meet a given application is called a(n) _____ data type.
4. Another name for a struct is a _____.
5. What is an ADT?
6. The three major data type categories in the C++ programming language are the _____, _____, and _____ categories.
7. What is meant by the term behavior as applied to classes and ADTs?
8. Why is the C++ class ideal for implementing your own ADTs?
9. The behavior of a class is provided by _____ in C++.

> A *class* in C++ is a programming unit, or construct, that allows you to build your own ADTs. Classes contain data to provide the ADT attributes and functions to provide the ADT behavior.

allows you to build your own ATM ADT, which will define all the data attributes and behavior associated with an ATM machine. A C++ class is composed of primitive data types. In addition, classes include *functions* that operate on the class data. Recall that a function is a subprogram in C++ usually associated with an algorithm of some kind. The data of the class provides the characteristics, or attributes, of the class, while the class functions define the operations, or behavior, of the class. Thus, the C++ class is ideal for implementing ADTs, because it can be used to define the data attributes of the ADT as well as the behavior of the ADT.

3.2   THE PRIMITIVE DATA TYPES IN C++

Recall that primitive data types are built into the C++ language. This built-in feature simply means that the C++ compiler recognizes any legal data values contained in a primitive type. There are four primitive types of data that we need to discuss: *integer, floating-point, character,* and *Boolean.*

The Integer Types

As you know, integers are the whole numbers. They may be positive, negative, or 0. In an algebra course, you most likely learned that there are no theoretical limits to the integers. They can range from minus infinity ($-\infty$) to plus infinity ($+\infty$). However, there are practical limits in the real world of computers. In C++, the largest and smallest possible integer values depend on the particular type of integer and compiler that is being used. In many C++ compilers, standard integers range from -32768 to $+32767$. However, there are different types of integers.

So, you're thinking that integers are integers; how can there be different "types" of integers? Well, the C++ language defines five separate integer types that define five separate ranges for integer data objects. They are **short int, int, unsigned int, long int,** and **unsigned long.** As you can see from Table 3.1, each integer type defines a legal range of integer values for a data object of a given type of integer.

TABLE 3.1   INTEGER TYPES AND CORRESPONDING RANGES IN A TYPICAL C++ COMPILER

Integer Type	Range	Bytes
short int, or **short**	-128 to $+127$	1
int	-32768 to $+32767$	2
unsigned int	0 to $+65535$	2
long int, or **long**	-2147483648 to $+2147483647$	4
unsigned long	0 to 4294967295	4

You might be wondering why there are different types of integers. Why not just define one type that will provide enough range for most applications? For instance, why not use the **long int** type all the time, because it provides the largest range of values? Well, recall that an advantage of C++ is its efficiency relative to execution speed and memory utilization. Each of the preceding integer types employ a predefined number of memory bytes to represent an integer value. For example, if **int** requires 2 bytes of memory to represent a value, and **long int** requires twice as many, or 4 bytes, to represent a value it would take twice as much memory space to represent **long int** integers as it does **int** integers. In addition, it would take twice as long to fetch a **long int** as an **int,** using a 16-bit CPU. So, the idea is to use the type of integer that has enough range to satisfy a given application. For most applications, **int** will do the job and provide for efficient execution and memory utilization.

COMPILER NOTE

Be aware that the ANSI/ISO C++ standard acknowledges that the ranges of the standard data types usually derive from the architecture of the host computer. As a result, the range of the various data types within the C++ language might differ from compiler to compiler. For example, your compiler might specify the range of **int** to be from −32768 to +32767, whereas another compiler might define this range to be from −2147483648 to +2147483647.

EXAMPLE 3.1

Which of the following are *not* legal **int** values according to Table 3.1?

a. +35
b. 35
c. −247
d. 0
e. 3.14
f. 32,767
g. 32768

Solution

The values in a, b, c, and d are all legal **int** values in C++, because they are all whole numbers within the defined range of **int.** Notice that +35 and 35 are both legal representations of the integer value 35.

The values in e, f, and g are not legal **int** values in C++. The value 3.14 is not an integer because it is not a whole number. The value 32,767 is an integer within the predefined range, but is not legal in C++, because it contains a comma. Commas are not allowed as part of numeric values in C++. Finally, the value 32768 is not a legal **int** value in C++, because it is outside of the predefined **int** range.

DEBUGGING TIP

You must be especially aware of the integer range limits imposed by C++ when performing integer calculations within your C++ programs. For example, multiplying two integers could easily produce an integer result beyond this range, resulting in an incorrect result. This is called an **overflow** condition. Depending on where it occurs, an overflow condition might or might not generate an error message during program compiling or execution. Even if no overflow error message is generated, the operation will always produce an incorrect result. These are often the most difficult type of errors to find and fix.

EXAMPLE 3.2

Which of the following **int** operations will generate an overflow condition in C++? (Use Table 3.1 to determine the legal **int** range, and assume that the * symbol means multiplication and the / symbol means division.)

   a. 32 * 1000

   b. 100 * 1000

   c. (100 * 1000)/5

Solution

   a. 32 * 1000 = 32000, which is within the predefined **int** range. No overflow condition exists.

   b. 100 * 1000 = 100000, which is outside of the predefined **int** range. The overflow condition will result in an incorrect integer result.

   c. (100 * 1000)/5 = 100000/5 = 20000. Although the final result is within the predefined **int** range, an overflow condition will occur, thereby generating an incorrect result. Why? Because the multiplication operation in the numerator results in a value outside of the **int** range.

One final point: You probably have noticed that the word **int,** for example, is set in bold type. Such a word in C++ is called a **keyword.** Keywords have a specific meaning to the C++ compiler and are used to perform a specific task. You cannot use a keyword for anything other than the specific operation for which it is intended. C++ contains about seventy keywords, including **int.** You will learn about other keywords in subsequent chapters. In any event, from now on all keywords will be printed in bold type so that you can easily recognize them.

The Floating-Point Types

Floating-point data values include all of the whole number integers as well as any value between two whole numbers that must be represented using a decimal point. Examples include the following:

$$-2.56$$
$$1.414$$
$$-3.0$$

Note in particular that –3.0 is interpreted as a floating-point value because it contains a decimal point. However, the value –3 is interpreted as an integer because it does not have a decimal point. Even though the values –3.0 and 3 are the same, they are stored differently in the computer. All of the foregoing values have been written using *fixed decimal-point* notation. Fixed decimal-point notation requires a sign, followed by an unsigned integer, followed by a decimal point, followed by another unsigned integer. This format is as follows:

FIXED DECIMAL FORMAT FOR A FLOATING-POINT VALUE

(+ or – sign)(integer).(integer)

Another way to represent a very large or a very small floating-point value is with scientific notation, called *exponential format.* With this notation, the floating-point value is written as a decimal-point value multiplied by a power of 10. The general format is as follows:

EXPONENTIAL FORMAT FOR A FLOATING-POINT VALUE

(+ or – sign)(decimal-point value)**e**(integer exponent value)

In both the foregoing formats, the leading + sign is optional if the value is positive. Examples of floating-point values using exponential format include

$$1.32e3$$
$$0.45e-6$$
$$-35.02e-4$$

Here, the letter *e* means "times 10 to the power of." The letter *e* is used because there is no provision on a standard computer keyboard to type above a line to show exponential values. Again, the + sign is optional for both the decimal-point value and the exponential value when they are positive.

EXAMPLE 3.3

Convert the following exponential values to fixed decimal values.

   a. 1.32e3

   b. 0.45e–6

   c. –35.02e–4

   d. –1.333e7

Solution

   a. $1.32e3 = 1.32 \times 10^3 = 1320.0$

   b. $0.45e{-}6 = 0.45 \times 10^{-6} = 0.00000045$

   c. $-35.02e{-}4 = -35.02 \times 10^{-4} = -0.003502$

   d. $-1.333e7 = -1.333 \times 10^7 = -13330000.0$

You might be wondering if there is any practical limit to the range of floating-point values that can be used in C++. As with integers, C++ defines different types of floating-point data that dictate different legal value ranges. Again, the value range is determined by the C++ compiler that you are using. As an example, Table 3.2 summarizes the floating-point types defined for a typical C++ compiler.

The greater the value range, the greater precision you will get when using floating-point values. However, as you can see from Table 3.2, it costs you more memory space to achieve greater precision when using a floating-point type. Again, the application will dictate the required precision, which, in turn, dictates which floating-point type to use. For most applications, the **float** type will assure the proper precision. However, many programmers choose to use **double** all the time to assure precision when memory or execution speed are not considerations.

TABLE 3.2 FLOATING-POINT TYPES AND CORRESPONDING RANGES IN A TYPICAL C++ COMPILER

Float type	Range	Bytes
float	Roughly $\pm 10^{+38}$ to $\pm 10^{-38}$ (7 significant digit precision)	4
double	Roughly $\pm 10^{+308}$ to $\pm 10^{-308}$ (15 significant digit precision)	8
long double	Roughly $\pm 10^{+4932}$ to $\pm 10^{-4932}$ (19 significant digit precision)	10

**TABLE 3.3   COMMON PREFIXES USED IN
DATA COMMUNICATIONS**

Prefix	Symbol	Meaning
pico	p	10^{-12}
nano	n	10^{-9}
micro	μ	10^{-6}
milli	m	10^{-3}
kilo	k	10^{3}
mega	M	10^{6}
giga	G	10^{9}

EXAMPLE 3.4

In data communications, you often see quantities expressed using the prefixes in Table 3.3. Given the following quantities

$$220 \text{ picoseconds (ps)}$$
$$1 \text{ kilohertz (kHz)}$$
$$10 \text{ megahertz (MHz)}$$
$$1.25 \text{ milliseconds (ms)}$$
$$25.3 \text{ microseconds (}\mu\text{s)}$$
$$300 \text{ nanoseconds (ns)}$$

a.   Express each of the listed quantities in exponential form.

b.   Express each of the listed quantities in fixed decimal form.

Solution

a.   To express in exponential form, you simply convert the prefix to its respective power of 10 using Table 3.3. Then, use exponential notation to write the value, like this:

$$220 \text{ ps} = 220\text{e}{-}12 \text{ second}$$
$$1 \text{ kHz} = 1\text{e}3 \text{ hertz}$$
$$10 \text{ MHz} = 10\text{e}6 \text{ hertz}$$
$$1.25 \text{ ms} = 1.25\text{e}{-}3 \text{ second}$$
$$25.3 \text{ }\mu\text{s} = 25.3\text{e}{-}6 \text{ second}$$
$$300 \text{ ns} = 300\text{e}{-}9 \text{ second}$$

b.   To express each in its fixed decimal form, simply move the decimal point according to the exponent value.

$$220 \text{ ps} = 220\text{e}{-}12 \text{ second} = 0.000000000220 \text{ second}$$
$$1 \text{ kHz} = 1\text{e}3 \text{ hertz} = 1000.0 \text{ hertz}$$
$$10 \text{ MHz} = 10\text{e}6 \text{ hertz} = 10000000.0 \text{ hertz}$$
$$1.25 \text{ ms} = 1.25\text{e}{-}3 \text{ second} = 0.00125 \text{ second}$$
$$25.3 \text{ }\mu\text{s} = 25.3\text{e}{-}6 \text{ second} = 0.0000253 \text{ second}$$
$$300 \text{ ns} = 300\text{e}{-}9 \text{ second} = 0.000000300 \text{ second}$$

A *standard function* is a predefined operation that the C++ compiler will recognize and evaluate to return a result or perform some predefined task.

EXAMPLE 3.5

C++ includes several ***standard functions*** that you can call upon to perform specific operations.

One such function is the *sqrt()* function. The *sqrt()* function is used to find the square root of a floating-point number. As an example, execution of *sqrt(2.0)* will return the value 1.414. On the other hand, an operation *not* included as a standard function is the square function. You must write your own *user-defined function* to perform the square operation. More about this later. Now, given the standard *sqrt()* function, determine the result of the following operations:

   a. sqrt(3.5)

   b. sqrt(–25.0)

   c. sqrt(4e–20)

Solution

   a. sqrt(3.5) = 1.87

   b. sqrt(–25) is imaginary and will generate a run-time error when encountered during a program execution.

   c. sqrt(4e–20) = 2e–10

The Character Type

All of the symbols on your computer keyboard are characters. This includes all the upper- and lowercase alphabetic characters as well as the punctuation, numbers, control keys, and special symbols. There are also ***white space*** characters on your keyboard. These are the non-printable characters such as a space, tab, and enter, among others. All C++ compilers employ the American Standard Code for Information Interchange (ASCII) character set shown in Table 3.4.

As you can see from the table, each character has a unique numeric representation code because, in order for the CPU to work with character data, the individual characters must be converted to a numeric (actually, binary) code. When you press a character on the keyboard, the CPU "sees" the numeric representation of that character, not the character itself. Table 3.4 provides decimal equivalents of the ASCII characters.

EXAMPLE 3.6

C++ includes a standard function called *toascii()*. This function is used to generate, or return, the decimal representation for any character. Determine the result of the following operations using Table 3.4.

   a. toascii('A')

   b. toascii('Z')

   c. toascii('a')

    d. toascii('z')

    e. toascii(' ')

Solution

Using Table 3.4, you get the following:

    a. toascii('A') = 65

    b. toascii('Z') = 90

    c. toascii('a') = 97

    d. toascii('z') = 122

    e. toascii(' ') = 32

TABLE 3.4   ASCII CHARACTER CODE TABLE

Dec	Char	Dec	Char	Dec	Char	Dec	Char
0	^@ NUL	32	SPC	64	@	96	`
1	^A SOH	33	!	65	A	97	a
2	^B STX	34	"	66	B	98	b
3	^C ETX	35	#	67	C	99	c
4	^D EOT	36	$	68	D	100	d
5	^E ENQ	37	%	69	E	101	e
6	^F ACK	38	&	70	F	102	f
7	^G BEL	39	'	71	G	103	g
8	^h BS	40	(	72	h	104	h
9	^I HT	41	)	73	I	105	i
10	^J LF	42	*	74	J	106	j
11	^K VT	43	+	75	K	107	k
12	^L FF	44	,	76	L	108	l
13	^M CR	45	-	77	M	109	m
14	^N SO	46	.	78	N	110	n
15	^O SI	47	/	79	O	111	o
16	^p DLE	48	0	80	p	112	p
17	^Q DC1	49	1	81	Q	113	q
18	^r DC2	50	2	82	r	114	r
19	^S DC3	51	3	83	S	115	s
20	^T DC4	52	4	84	T	116	t
21	^U NAK	53	5	85	U	117	u
22	^V SYN	54	6	86	V	118	v
23	^W ETB	55	7	87	W	119	w
24	^X CAN	56	8	88	X	120	x
25	^Y EM	57	9	89	Y	121	y
26	^Z SUB	58	:	90	Z	122	z
27	^[ESC	59	;	91	[	123	{
28	^\ FS	60	<	92	\	124		
29	^] GS	61	=	93	]	125	}
30	^^ RS	62	>	94	^	126	~
31	^— US	63	?	95	—	127	DEL

TABLE 3.5 CHARACTER TYPES AND CORRESPONDING RANGES IN A TYPICAL C++ COMPILER

Character Type	Range	Bytes
char	−128 to +127	1
unsigned char	0 to +255	1

The foregoing example points out several characteristics of character data. First, note that a single character in C++ is enclosed within single quotation marks, even a space. This is a requirement of the language. Second, each character has a unique numeric representation inside the computer. Even a space (SPC in the table) has an ASCII storage value inside the computer. Last, because each character has a unique numeric representation, the characters are ordered. For instance, 'A' < 'Z', because the numeric representation for 'A' (65) is less than the numeric representation for 'Z' (90). Likewise, ' ' < 'a' < 'z', because 32 < 97 < 122.

Recall that there were different types of integer and floating-point values defined by the C++ compiler. These different types define the range of values that are legal for a given type. Well, the same is true of characters. There are two different types of characters defined for C++: **char** and **unsigned char,** both shown in Table 3.5.

The **char** type allows for all the ASCII characters shown in Table 3.4. The **unsigned char** type also allows for all the ASCII characters shown in Table 3.4 but, in addition, allows for an extended character set as defined for the IBM PC. (See your PC documentation for this extended character set.) Again, the application will dictate which character type to use. The **char** type will satisfy most of the applications in this text.

Characters are stored in the machine as integer values, so you can perform arithmetic operations on character data. For instance, you can add 1 to the character 'A' and get the character 'B'. This is an example of the flexibility built into the C++ language; however, with this flexibility comes responsibility. You must be able to predict the results you will get. Other languages, like Pascal, will not allow you to perform arithmetic operations on characters.

CAUTION

C++ will allow you to perform arithmetic operations on character data; however, be careful because the results can be sometimes difficult to predict. What do you get when you add the character 'A' to the character 'B' or when you multiply these two characters?

The Boolean Type

Boolean data, consisting solely of the values **true** and **false,** are the simplest type of data that can be employed in a program. Boolean data play an important role in a program's ability to make decisions, because all program decisions are Boolean decisions, based on whether a given condition is true or false. You will learn this later when we discuss program decision making and iteration.

C++ specifies a Boolean data type called **bool.** This type contains two elements, **true** and **false.** The **bool** type is a scalar type, meaning that the elements within the type are ordered. By definition, **false** is defined to be less than **true.** The words **bool, true,** and **false** are keywords and, therefore, cannot be used for any other purpose in a program.

> **COMPILER NOTE**
>
> Be aware that the ANSI/ISO C++ standard specifies the **bool** type, but compilers sold before release of the standard did not support the **bool** type. If you have an older compiler, it will most likely not support the **bool** type. You can get around this problem by creating your own Boolean data type using enumeration. This will be discussed shortly.

 Quick Check

1. What is the approximate range of values that is provided in a typical C++ compiler via the standard **int** data type?

2. What type of error occurs when, as a result of a calculation, a value exceeds its predefined range?

3. The two ways that floating-point values can be represented in a C++ program are using either _____ or _____ format.

4. Which is larger, the character 'a' or the character 'z'?

5. Which is larger, the character 'a' or the character 'A'?

6. The primitive data type that contains only two elements, **true** and **false,** is the _____ data type.

7. What is white space?

3.3   CONSTANTS AND VARIABLES

From mathematics, you know that a constant is a value that never changes, thereby remaining a fixed value. A common example is the constant *pi* (π). Here, the Greek symbol π is used to represent a floating-point value of approximately 3.14159. This value of π never changes, thus remaining constant regardless of where and how it might be used in a calculation.

On the other hand, a variable is something that can take on different values. In mathematics, the symbols *x* and *y* are often used to denote variables. Using the

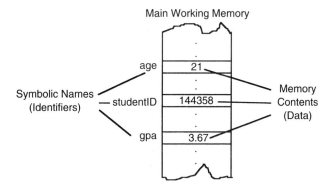

FIGURE 3.3   EACH VARIABLE HAS A SYMBOLIC NAME, OR IDENTIFIER, THAT LOCATES ITS VALUE IN MEMORY.

equation $y = 3x + 2$, you can substitute different values of x to generate different values of y. Thus, the values of x and y in the equation are variable.

The values of variables are stored in main working memory of a computer for later use within a program. Each variable has a symbolic name, called an ***identifier,*** that locates its value in memory. This idea is illustrated in Figure 3.3. The memory contents located by the identifiers *age, studentID,* and *gpa* might change during the execution of the program. As a result, these symbols are called variables.

All constants and variables to be used in a C++ program must be defined prior to their use in the program. The reason that we must define constants and variables in a language is twofold. First, the compiler must know the value of a constant before it is used and must reserve memory locations to store variables. Second, the compiler must know the data type of the constants and variables so that it knows their attributes and behavior. Now, let's see how constants and variables are defined in C++.

Defining Constants

To define a constant, you must use the keyword **const,** like this:

> ### *CONSTANT DEFINITION FORMAT*
>
> **const** *data type   constant identifier* **=** *constant value*;

First, a word about how syntax will be formatted in this text. Words or symbols that must appear as part of the syntax will be shown outright in bold, such as the word **const** and the symbol **=** in the foregoing format box. Those things that you must decide as a programmer will be shown in italic type such as the data type, constant identifier, and constant value in the foregoing format box.

Now, let's look at the syntax required to define a constant. The definition begins with the keyword **const.** The keyword **const** is used to signify that the value of the constant can never change within the course of the program execution. Next, you must specify the primitive data type of the constant, followed by a constant identifier. The identifier is the name of the constant that will be replaced by the constant value during compile time. To identify constants easily within your program, we suggest that your constant identifiers always be in all capital letters. This way, it makes it much more clear that no statement should attempt to alter the constant value. An equals symbol (=) is used to separate the constant identifier from its defined value. Finally, each constant definition must end with a semicolon.

EXAMPLE 3.7

Suppose you wish to use the price of 34 cents for a first-class postage stamp in your C++ program. In addition, your program must calculate the sales tax required for a given sales item based on a sales tax rate of 7 percent. Define appropriate constants to represent the price of a stamp and the sales tax rate.

Solution

By using the format given before, the postage price and sales tax rate are defined as follows:

```
const float POSTAGE = 0.34;
const float TAX_RATE = 0.07;
```

With these definitions, you would simply use the words *POSTAGE* and *TAX_RATE* when performing calculations within the program. For instance, to find the total price of a sales item, you would write the expression

```
totalPrice = price + (price * TAX_RATE);
```

When the program is compiled, the compiler simply substitutes the constant value 0.07 for the *TAX_RATE* identifier. What about the identifiers *price* and *totalPrice* in this expression? Are these constants or variables? You're right—they are both variables, because their values will change, depending on the price of the item. What data type must *price* and *totalPrice* be? In other words, what type of data is required for this application: integer, floating-point, or character? Right again—floating-point, because you must provide for decimal quantities to allow for dollars and cents. Thus, *price* and *totalPrice* must be defined as floating-point variables. You will find out how to do this shortly.

You are probably wondering why we should define constants using identifiers. Why not just insert the constant value into the expression whenever it is needed, like this:

```
totalPrice = price + (price * 0.07);
```

Have you ever known postage or sales tax rates to change? Of course you have! You might say that these types of "constants" are not constant forever. So, when using constants such as these, which might be subject to change in the future, it is

STYLE TIP

Always code your constant identifiers in all caps so that they are easily identified as constants within your program. Always code variable identifiers in lowercase. For a multiword variable identifier, the first letter of the first word should be lowercase, then the first letter of each succeeding word should be uppercase. For example, the two foregoing variable identifiers were *totalPrice* and *price*. This convention will be used throughout this book for variable identifiers.

Notice also in Example 3.7 that the constant identifier *TAX_RATE* is made up of two words, *TAX* and *RATE*. The C++ compiler will not allow you to separate multiword identifiers using spaces. Thus, we have chosen to separate the two words with the underscore symbol (_). You cannot use a dash, -, to separate words within an identifier. This is why we used the underscore symbol in the *TAX_RATE* constant identifier. Also, notice that the variable identifier *totalPrice* is made up of two words. Here, the two words are run together with the first letter of the second word capitalized. To summarize, the following two techniques will be used throughout the text when using multiword identifiers:

1. Uppercase for constant identifiers, separating words within a multiword identifier with the underscore symbol.

2. Lowercase for variable identifiers, capitalizing the first letter of each word in a multiword identifier, except for the first word.

Here are some other rules that govern the use of identifiers in the C++ language:

- An identifier can be any length, but some compilers will ignore any characters after a certain length.

- Identifiers can contain the letters *a* to *z*, *A* to *Z*, the digits *0* to *9*, and the underscore symbol.

- No spaces or punctuation, except the underscore symbol, are allowed.

- Identifiers in C++ are *case-sensitive*. Thus, the identifiers *Tax, tax,* and *TAX* are seen as three different identifiers by the compiler.

much easier to define them in one single place. Then if they need to be changed, you only have to make a single change in your program. Otherwise, a change must be made in each place that you use the constant within the program.

Defining Variables

Before you can use a variable in a C++ program, it must be defined. When you define a variable, the compiler reserves a location inside the computer memory for the variable value. When you define a variable, you are telling C++ what type of data you will be storing for the variable. To define a variable, you must specify its data type, its name, and an optional initializing value. Here's the format:

VARIABLE DEFINITION FORMAT

data type   variable identifier = optional initializing value;

The foregoing format requires that the variable data type be listed first, followed by the variable identifier, or name. We recommend that the first word in a variable name should begin with a lowercase letter, with all subsequent words beginning with an uppercase letter. You can terminate the definition at this point with a semicolon, or you can add an optional equals symbol, =, followed by an initializing value, and then the semicolon to terminate the definition.

PROGRAMMING NOTE

It is always good practice to initialize variables when they are defined. When a variable is not initialized you will not get a compiler error, but some arbitrary value is stored in memory for the variable. If the variable is used later in the program without taking on a value, any operations using the variable will generate "garbage." The term "garbage" is often used in computer circles to describe meaningless data. Generally, numeric variables will be initialized to the value 0 or 1, and character variables will be initialized with a blank.

EXAMPLE 3.8

Suppose you were asked to write a C++ program to calculate the part-time hourly pay for an employee, given his/her rate of hourly pay and hours worked over the given time period. Define the necessary variables that will be used in the program for the calculation.

Solution

To solve this problem, you simply multiply the hourly rate by the number of hours worked like this:

$$p = r \times h$$

where

p is the pay, in dollars and cents.

r is the hourly rate of pay, in dollars and cents.

h is the number of hours worked.

Here, the variable identifiers are given to be p, r, and h. Now, the question is: What data type must these variables belong to? You know that p, r, and h will be used to represent numeric data, so your decision as to their type reduces to integer or floating-point. If you define p, r, and h as integers, you will be limited to using whole number values for these variables within your program; however, this might create a problem because pay, rate of pay, and hourly values often are decimal values. So, let's define them as floating-point variables, like this:

```
float p = 0.0;   // GROSS PAY
float r = 0.0;   // HOURLY RATE OF PAY
float h = 0.0;   // NUMBER OF HOURS WORKED
```

Notice that each variable is defined as a floating-point variable and initialized to the value 0.0. Of course, because these are variables, their values will most likely change during the execution of the program. Notice also that each variable is commented to indicate its purpose within the program.

STYLE TIP

C++ allows identifiers, or names, to be just about any reasonable length. Thus, your programs will become much more readable and self-documenting if you use words, rather than letters and symbols, to represent constants and variables. For instance, the variable definitions in Example 3.8 would be much more readable to a user if you were to define pay, rate of pay, and hours worked like this:

```
float grossPay = 0.0;      // GROSS PAY
float hourlyRate = 0.0;    // HOURLY RATE OF PAY
float hoursWorked = 0.0;   // NUMBER OF HOURS WORKED
```

By using this definition, the actual words (*grossPay, hourlyRate,* and *hoursWorked*) would be used within your program when calculating payroll. So, the statement required to calculate the gross pay would appear in your program as follows:

```
grossPay = hourlyRate * hoursWorked;
```

Notice the use of the equals symbol, =, in this statement. This is the way that you must *set or assign* quantities in C++. Also, notice the use of the star symbol, *, for multiplication.

A word of caution: When using names as variable identifiers, you cannot use any punctuation within the name. For instance, the variable identifier *total(Sales)* or *total-Sales* to represent total sales are illegal identifiers in C++ because of the parentheses in the former case and the dash in the later case. Two legal identifiers would be *totalSales* or *total_Sales.* In the first case, the two words are connected, with the first letter of the second word capitalized. In the second case, the underscore symbol, _, is used to separate the two words instead of a dash. The underscore is okay to use within C++ identifiers. You will see both of these techniques employed for identifiers throughout the remainder of this text.

EXAMPLE 3.9

You must write a program to calculate the sales tax of a sales item using a sales tax rate of 7 percent. Define the appropriate constants and variables.

Solution

First, you must decide what identifiers to use. Always use word identifiers that best describe the related constant or variable. Let's use the word *salesTax* to identify the resulting calculation, the word *price* to identify the cost of the item, and the word *TAX_RATE* to identify the sales tax rate. So, using these identifiers, the sales tax calculation would be

```
salesTax = price * TAX_RATE;
```

Now, the question is: Which of these are variables and which are constants? Obviously, *salesTax* and *price* are variables, because they will change depending on the cost of the item. However, the *TAX_RATE* will be a constant, regardless of the cost of the item. So, we will define *salesTax* and *price* as variables and *TAX_RATE* as a constant, like this:

```
const float TAX_RATE = 0.07;    // CURRENT SALES TAX RATE
float price = 0.0;              // PRICE OF AN ITEM
float salesTax = 0.0;          // SALES TAX OF AN ITEM
```

Notice that both the variables are defined as floating-point, because both will be decimal values. Suppose that you were to define the tax rate as a variable rather than a constant and initialize it to the value 0.07, like this:

```
float taxRate = 0.07;
```

There is no problem with this definition. The compiler will reserve storage for the variable *taxRate* and place the initial value of 0.07 at this storage location. However, the value of *taxRate* could be changed by the program, whereas it could not be changed if defined as a constant. Would this be desirable? Probably not, since the sales tax rate would not likely change during the course of the program execution.

Once a constant or a variable is defined, you can write its value to the monitor like this:

```
cout << salesTax << endl;
```

As you will discover in Chapter 4, *cout* is a standard object used by C++ to display information to the monitor. Each item to be written to the monitor is "sent" to the *cout* object using the **<< insertion operator.** We say that the << insertion operator inserts the item value into the *cout* stream, which "flows" to the monitor. The *endl* defines the "end of line" and is called an ***I/O manipulator.*** More about this stuff later.

The *cout* object is used with the << insertion operator to display information on your system monitor.

EXAMPLE 3.10

Choose an appropriate name and define a variable that could be used to represent any given day of the week. Assume that a day of the week is represented by the first letter of the given day.

Solution

Let's pick a meaningful variable identifier, such as *dayOfWeek*. Now, because the days of the week will be represented by the first letter of each day, the variable must be of the character data type. When defining character variables, you must use the keyword **char** in the variable definition, as follows:

```
char dayOfWeek = ' ';   // SINGLE CHARACTER FOR ANY DAY OF THE WEEK
                        //INITIALIZED WITH A BLANK
```

Notice that the character variable is initialized with a blank character. To code a blank character, simply type a single quote, a space, then another single quote.

Do you see any problems with the definition in Example 3.10? There are no syntax errors, and it is perfectly legal as far as C++ is concerned. But are there any problems associated with using this variable? A character variable is limited to representing a *single* character at a given time. This is why each day of the week must be represented by a single letter. However, using the first letter of each day creates a problem. Does an 'S' represent Saturday or Sunday? Likewise, does a 'T' mean Tuesday or Thursday? The solution to this dilemma is found in the use of strings, the topic of the next section.

Boolean Variables. Variables can be defined for the **bool** type just as you define any other variable—by listing its data type followed by the variable identifier. Here's an example that illustrates this idea.

EXAMPLE 3.11

Define a Boolean variable called *decision* for use in a decision-making operation. Initialize the variable with a value of **false.**

Solution

Boolean variables are often used in a program for decision-making operations. A Boolean variable, called *decision,* can be defined for such a purpose as follows:

```
bool decision = false;
```

With this definition, the variable *decision* can be used in a program, taking on the values of **true** or **false** as required by the program logic.

COMPILER NOTE

Remember that older compilers do not support the **bool** data type. You can get around this problem by creating your own Boolean data type using enumeration. This will be discussed shortly.

Quick Check

1. What are two reasons for defining constants and variables in a C++ program?
2. Define a constant called *PERIOD* that will insert a period wherever it is referenced in a program.
3. Define a variable to store your middle initial.
4. Define a variable to store your grade point average.
5. Define a variable to store your age.
6. Define a variable to store the salary of an employee.
7. What will be returned when the following functions are executed?

```
toascii('B')
toascii('?')
```

8. What characters must employ the **unsigned char** data type?

3.4 STRINGS

A string is simply a collection of characters. Examples of strings include your name, address, and phone number, as well as the sentence you are now reading.

Strings in C++ are always enclosed in double quotes, like this: "C++". Recall that individual characters are enclosed in single quotes. Thus, 'J' denotes an individual character, whereas "J" denotes a string of one character.

A string is not a primitive data type in C++ because, by definition, a string is a complex data type formed by combining simpler primitive data types, namely characters. Also, there are special operations defined for the specific purpose of manipulating strings. Doesn't this sound like a class (data combined with operations defined for that data)? For this reason, C++ provides a *string* class that defines what a string should be (a collection of characters) as well as operations that can be used on a string.

The *string* class is contained in the C++ Standard Library. To use the *string* class, it must be included in your program using a #*include* directive in the preprocessor section of your program like this: #*include <string>*. Notice that there is not an .*h* extension for this header file. This is because there is another header file called *string.h* that is used for C programs. We will be using the C++ *string* header file without the .*h* extension in this book.

Recall that a class describes the attributes (characteristics) and behavior (operations) for its objects. In other words, a class is a blueprint for any objects of the class. You *do not* manipulate a class within your program. Instead, you define an **object** of a given class, then manipulate the object within your program, just as you define a variable of a primitive data type and manipulate the variable within your program.

> **PROGRAMMING TIP**
>
> Double quotes around a number, such as "1234", indicate a string of characters and *not* numeric data. In fact, the string "1234" requires 4 bytes of storage, whereas the **int** 1234 requires only 2 bytes of storage in many compilers. In addition, arithmetic operations cannot be performed on the string "1234". For these reasons, numeric data should be defined using a numeric type and not the string class. In trying to decide what type of data to use, ask yourself: "Will this data ever need to be manipulated arithmetically within my program?" In other words, "Will I ever have to add, subtract, multiply, or divide this data?" If so, it should be defined as numeric data; otherwise, it should be defined as string data. A common example would be your age versus your social security number. Your age might need to be manipulated arithmetically, for example adding years as you get older. However, your social security number will never be manipulated arithmetically. Therefore, your age should be defined as an integer, while your social security number should be defined as a string.

To define an object of a predefined class, you simply list the class name, followed by a space, then the object name like this:

> **OBJECT DEFINITION FORMAT**
>
> *class name   object name = optional initializing value;*

To define a string object, we use the class name *string,* followed by an appropriate string object name, or identifier. For example, suppose you need to create three string objects, one for your name, one for your address, and one for your phone number. Here is how these objects could be created:

```
string myName = "Andrew C. Staugaard, Jr. "       // MY NAME
string myAddress = "999 Code Road, C++ City, USA";   // MY ADDRESS
string myPhoneNumber = "(012)345-6789";              // MY PHONE NUMBER
```

These definitions tell C++ that *myName, myAddress,* and *myPhoneNumber* are objects of the *string* class. In addition, each object is initialized with a string value. The initializing string values are optional. Could the initial string values of these objects be changed? Of course they could, because each object is a variable object. Notice also that the string values are enclosed within double quotation marks and a comment is placed after each object definition. Get used to commenting the purpose of all of your variables and objects, because it's just a good habit to get into.

Once a string object is defined, you can display its value using the *cout* object like this:

```
cout << myName << endl;
cout << myAddress << endl;
cout << myPhoneNumber << endl;
```

This produces a display of:

```
Andrew C. Staugaard, Jr.
999 Code Road, C++ City, USA
(012)345-6789
```

As stated before, the *cout* object along with the << operator are used to display information in C++. The purpose of the *endl* command is to display the strings on separate lines. More about this later. We can even use the *cout* object, along with the << operator to display two strings together like this:

```
cout << "My name is: " << myName << endl;
```

This statement displays the fixed string, "My name is: ", followed by the string stored in the object *myName*. Notice that the fixed string is surrounded with double quotation marks while the string object is not. The << operator tells the *cout* object to display the fixed string, "My name is: ", followed by the variable string, *myName*. Also, notice that there is a space or two after the colon and before the ending quotation marks in "My name is: ". The purpose of the spacing is to separate the colon from the actual name stored in memory. Thus the display will show the following:

```
My name is: Andrew C. Staugaard, Jr.
```

 The << insertion operator is used with the *cout* object to **concatenate** the display items together. The term *concatenate* means to join together.

EXAMPLE 3.12

Using the character variable definition back in Example 3.10 presents a usage problem when representing the days of the week, because a character variable can only represent a single character at a time. Solve this problem by using a string object.

Solution

A string object can be used to represent any number of consecutive characters. So why not define *dayOfWeek* as a string object, like this:

```
string dayOfWeek = " "; //DAYS OF THE WEEK INITIALIZED WITH BLANKS
```

With this definition, the object *dayOfWeek* can be used to represent the entire day of the week word ("Sunday", "Monday", "Tuesday", etc.). Notice that the string object is initialized with an empty string using empty double quotation marks. It is always good practice to initialize variables and objects when they are defined. Of course, during the execution of the program, an actual string value can be stored in *dayOfWeek* using an *assignment* statement, like this:

```
dayOfWeek = "Friday";
```

This assignment stores the string "*Friday*" in memory for the value of the *dayOfWeek* string object. Now, what will the following statement do?

```
cout << "The current day of the week is " << dayOfWeek << endl;
```

You're right, this statement will display the following on the system monitor:

```
The current day of the week is Friday
```

String Operations

Since *string* is a class, it includes operations that are specifically written to manipulate string data. As a result, any object of the *string* class can use these operations to manipulate or provide information about its string. Some of the operations available in the *string* class are summarized in Table 3.6. These will all be discussed in time, as the need arises. But, let's take a special look at the *length()* operation. This operation is a function defined specifically for the *string* class. As a result, you must use a string object to call the *length()* function. The function is called by placing a dot between the string object name and the function. For example, suppose that you wish to display the length of a string in your program. Here is a code segment that will accomplish this task:

```
string employee = "John Doe";
cout << employee.length();
```

Notice that our *employee* string object is calling its *length()* function via the dot operator. This code would simply cause the length of the *employee* string, 8, to be displayed on the system monitor.

PROGRAMMING TIP

You must use the dot, . , operator to call a class function. To call the function, you place a dot between the object name and the function like this: *myObject.classFunction()*.

EXAMPLE 3.13

Write a C++ code segment that will display the length of each of the *myName, myAddress,* and *myPhoneNumber* strings defined earlier.

Solution

To get the length of each string, each string object must call its *length()* function from Table 3.6. This can be done within *cout* statements like this:

```
cout << myName.length() << endl;
cout << myAaddress.length() << endl;
cout << myPhoneNumber.length() << endl;
```

The resulting display is:

```
24
28
13
```

DEBUGGING TIP

Remember that C++ is case-sensitive. Thus, using the string "Hello World" is not equivalent to the string "hello world". And, because of the ASCII ordering of characters, the string "Hello World" is less than the string "hello world". Check this out in the ASCII table and you will see the 'H' is less than 'h'. This first character comparison makes the entire "Hello World" string less than the "hello world" string.

 Quick Check

1. A class called _____ is part of the Standard C++ Library and is used to create string objects.

2. Define a constant string object called *BOOK* that will insert the string "Structured and Object-Oriented Problem Solving" wherever it appears in a program. (*Note:* a constant string object is created by simply preceding the definition with the keyword **const**.)

3. How many bytes of storage are required by the string "The United States of America"?

4. Define a string object called *ssn* that will store the social security number of an employee.

5. Define a string object called *course* that will be initialized to a string value of "Data Structures".

6. Write a statement to display the string stored in the object in question 5.

7. Define two string objects called *firstName* and *lastName* that will store your first and last names, respectively.

8. Define a string object called *myName* and write a statement to concatenate the two strings defined in question 7 into the *myName* string.

9. Write a statement to display the length of the *myName* string in question 8.

TABLE 3.6   SOME STANDARD STRING OPERATIONS

Function	Description	Use of

s.empty()	Returns **true** if the string *s* has no characters.	```string s;```
		```s.empty()```
		returns **true**

s.length()	Returns the length of *s*.	```string s = "Hello World";```
		```s.length()```
		returns 11

s1 == s2	Returns **true** if *s1* equals *s2*, else returns **false.**	```string s1 = "Hello World";```
		```string s2 = "hello world";```
		```s1 == s2```
		returns **false**

s1 != s2	Returns **true** if *s1* does not equal *s2*, else returns **false.**	```string s1 = "Hello World";```
		```string s2 = "hello world";```
		```s1 != s2```
		returns **true**

s1 < s2	Returns **true** if *s1* is less than *s2*, else returns **false.**	```string s1 = "Hello World";```
		```string s2 = "hello world";```
		```s1 < s2```
		returns **true**

s1 > s2	Returns **true** if *s1* is greater than *s2*, else returns **false.**	```string s1 = "Hello World";```
		```string s2 = "hello world";```
		```s1 > s2```
		returns **false**

s1 = s2	Copies, or assigns, *s2* to *s1*.	```string s1 = "Hello World";```
		```string s2 = "hello world";```
		```s1 = s2;```
		s1 now contains "hello world"

s = s1 + s2	Concatenates *s2* to *s1* to form *s*.	```string s;```
		```string s1 = "Hello";```
		```string s2 = "World";```
		```s = s1 + s2;```
		s now contains "HelloWorld"

s1 += s2	Appends *s2* to *s1*.	```string s1 = "Hello";```
		```string s2 = "World";```
		```s1 + = s2;```
		s1 now contains "HelloWorld"

You will have many occasions to manipulate strings within your C++ programs using the string operations shown in Table 3.6. For now, just review each operation in the table so that you get an idea of what can be done with string objects. We will demonstrate the use of many of these operations as the need arises throughout the remainder of the text.

3.5   ENUMERATED DATA

One distinct advantage of using C++ is that it allows you, the programmer, to create your own type of data. Up to this point, you have been using the standard data types of integer, floating-point, character, and Boolean. As you have seen, these types have been adequate for many programming applications. Although these predefined types can be used for just about any programming task, they often are insufficient to describe a problem clearly. You will soon discover that enumerated data types enhance the readability of your program by making it clearer and application-oriented, something we are especially concerned about in problem solving. The more clearly we can express a problem as related to its application, the easier it is for us and others to understand and solve the problem.

Enumerated data types consist of a set of data values that you, the programmer, define for a particular application. The idea of defining your own data types might seem awkward to you at first, but you will soon discover that it provides a convenient means of working with real-world problems. There will be times when none of the standard data types will work conveniently for certain applications. For example, suppose an application problem required the manipulation of the colors red, white, and blue. Because none of the primitive data types include colors as values within their predefined range, you might suggest that each color be set to an integer value using **const** definitions like this:

```
const int RED = 0;
const int WHITE = 1;
const int BLUE = 2;
```

Then, using these definitions, you could actually manipulate these colors within your program. For instance, assuming the variable *color* is defined as an integer, a program might include the following pseudocode operations:

If *color* is RED
     Write "Red is my favorite color"

Because you have set the colors to integer values, the above *If* statement is simply comparing the value of *color* to the integer value assigned to *RED* (0). If *color* equals 0, then the message is generated.

C++ allows a more convenient way to work with nonstandard data through the use of enumerated types. Rather than using numeric assignments as before, you can define the set of colors using the keyword **enum** like this:

```
enum Colors {red, white, blue};
```

Here, the keyword **enum** defines the type *Colors* to include the set of three values, *red, white,* and *blue. Colors* is called a user-defined type because you, the user, have defined it.

Defining Enumerated Types

The general format and syntax for defining enumerated data is as follows:

ENUMERATED DATA DECLARATION FORMAT

enum *type identifier {value #1, value #2, ⋯, value #n};*
type identifier   variable identifier;

As you can see, enumerated data require a two-part definition. First, you must define the data values using the keyword **enum** followed by a type identifier and a list of the values that make up the enumerated type. Notice that the value list is enclosed within curly braces, { }, and a semicolon terminates the definition. Second, one or more variables are defined for the enumerated type. The variable(s) provides access to the enumerated values. The variable identifier, or name, is listed after the same type identifier used in the **enum** definition. For instance, let's go back to our colors example. The desired colors are first defined as an enumerated type, like this:

```
enum Colors {red, white, blue};
```

Then, a variable must be defined for the type, like this:

```
Colors color;
```

Any operations with the enumerated data in your program will then use the variable identifier (*color*), as follows:

If *color* is red
　　Write "Red is my favorite color"

The Ordering of Enumerated Data.   An enumerated type is also a scalar, or ordered, type just like the other types. In fact, the word *enumerated* means "numbered with order." As a result, the C++ compiler assigns an order to the enumerated values such that *value #1 < value #2 < ⋯ < value #n*. This means that in the *Colors* type, *red < white < blue*. As a result, relational operations involving the enumerated type are perfectly legitimate. For instance, consider the following pseudocode:

If (*color* > red) AND (*color* < blue) Then
　　Write "The color is white"

Here, the value of *color* is compared to *red* and *blue*. Using the above enumerated definition for *Colors, color* must be *white* if it's between *red* and *blue*, right? How does it work? The C++ compiler actually assigns integer values to the enumerated data values in the order that they are listed, beginning with the value 0. Thus, in the previous example, *red* is assigned the value 0, *white* the value 1, and *blue* the value 2. Therefore, the previous *If* statement reduces to a comparison of integer values.

EXAMPLE 3.14

Define the following as enumerated types. Define an appropriate variable to go along with the type definition.

   a.   *MonthsOfYear,* consisting of the twelve months of the year.

   b.   *TestGrades,* consisting of the five common letter grades.

   c.   *ArmyRanks,* consisting of the eight common ranks found in the army.

Solution

   a.
```
enum MonthsOfYear {Jan, Feb, Mar, Apr, May, Jun, Jul, Aug,
                   Sep, Oct, Nov, Dec};
MonthsOfYear month;
```

   b.
```
enum TestGrades {F, D, C, B, A};
TestGrades test;
```

   c.
```
enum ArmyRanks {Private, Corporal, Sergeant, Lieutenant,
                Captain, Major, Colonel, General};
ArmyRanks rank;
```

Observe the syntax in the foregoing code. First, the type name must be all one word. No space nor punctuation is allowed. Also, notice that individual words within the type name begin with a capital letter, even the first word. This has been done so as to identify a type name from a variable name in any subsequent code. This is not a requirement of C++, but has been done for clarity. Next, you see that the values are listed inside of curly braces and separated by commas. Finally, a semicolon is required at the end of the value listing to mark the end of a given type definition.

Look at the *TestGrade* type a little closer. Notice that there are no quotes around the character symbols. A common mistake when defining character symbols as enumerated data is to enclose the data symbols in quotes as you would characters. In an enumerated type definition, the character symbols are not treated as characters, but as unique values of the enumerated type.

You should also note the ordering of each definition. The *TestGrade* type is ordered such that an $F < D < C < B < A$. This represents a natural ordering, when you consider the application of grading. If the test grades were defined as characters, the ordering would be the opposite, because of the relative ASCII values of the given characters. In addition, the *ArmyRanks* type is ordered according to the natural order of ranks from the lowest rank

(*Private*) to the highest rank (*General*). Finally, notice that an appropriate variable has been defined for each type using the variable naming convention discussed earlier.

EXAMPLE 3.15

In C++, the Boolean value **true** is represented with the integer 1, and the Boolean value **false** is represented with the integer 0. Define a Boolean type and define a corresponding variable called *flag* that will allow the programmer to use the Boolean values of true and false in a program. Initialize *flag* to **false** as part of the object definition.

Solution

If you are using a compiler that meets the ANSI/ISO C++ standard, you do not need to create your own Boolean type because it is specified as part of the standard and, therefore, is already available as a standard type in your compiler. All you need to do is create a variable object for the **bool** type, like this:

```
bool flag = false;
```

However, if you are using an older compiler that does not meet the ANSI/ISO C++ standard, you must create your own Boolean enumerated type, as follows:

```
enum BOOL {FALSE, TRUE};
BOOL flag = FALSE;
```

Here, the *BOOL* value FALSE is assigned the integer 0, and the *BOOL* value TRUE is assigned the integer 1 by the C++ compiler. As a result, the programmer can employ the identifiers of TRUE and FALSE in a program in lieu of 1 and 0, respectively, when working with Boolean values. This makes the program much more readable. This definition could also be subsequently compiled with a compiler that meets the standard because we have chosen to use the word *BOOL* rather than **bool** and the words FALSE and TRUE rather than **false** and **true.** Why? Well, recall that the words **bool, false,** and **true** are defined as keywords by the ANSI/ISO standard and, therefore, cannot be used in an enumerated type definition.

DEBUGGING TIP

It is important to realize that enumerated type values are *not* variables or strings. Thus, using the data value *white,* for example, as a variable in a program will cause an error. An enumerated data value must never appear on the left side of an assignment, like this:

```
white = red + 1;
```

Another common source of error is to inadvertently define the enumerated data values as strings, like this:

```
enum Colors {"red", "white", "blue"};
```

This will always cause a compile error. Again, the individual data values are *not* strings; they are actually constant value identifiers.

Quick Check

1. Why would you want to create an enumerated data type in your program if a standard data type could be used to do the job?
2. Define an enumerated data type called *Automobiles* which consists of at least ten popular automobile brands.
3. What numeric value does the C++ compiler assign to the first value in an enumerated type?

PROBLEM SOLVING IN ACTION: BANK ACCOUNT PROCESSING

PROBLEM

Your local bank has contracted you to design a C++ application program that will process savings account data for a given month. Assume that the savings account accrues interest at a rate of 12 percent per year and that the user must enter the current account balance, amount of deposits, and amount of withdrawals. Develop a problem definition, set of algorithms, and C++ program to solve this problem.

Defining the Problem

Output: The program must display a report showing the account transactions and balance for a given savings account in a given month.

Input: To process a savings account, you need to know the initial balance, amount of deposits, amount of withdrawals, and interest rate. We will assume that these values will be entered by the program user, with the exception of the interest rate, which will be coded as a constant.

Processing: The program must process deposits and withdrawals and calculate interest to determine the monthly balance.

We will divide the problem into individual subproblems to solve the overall banking problem. Now, try to identify the separate tasks that must be performed to solve the problem. First, the user must enter the required transaction data, which will include the previous month's balance, current month's deposits, and current month's withdrawals. Once the transaction data are entered, the program must add the deposits to the account balance, subtract the withdrawals from the account balance, calculate the interest, and generate the required report. As a result, we can identify five program tasks as follows:

❑ Obtain the transaction data entered by the program user.

❑ Add the deposits to the account balance.

❑ Subtract the withdrawals from the account balance.

❑ Calculate the account interest.

❑ Generate the monthly account report.

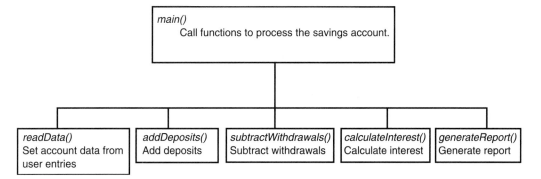

FIGURE 3.4 **A PROBLEM-SOLVING DIAGRAM FOR THE BANK-ING PROBLEM.**

The problem solving diagram in Figure 3.4 shows the structure required for the program.

Planning the Solution

Now we will employ stepwise refinement to develop the required set of algorithms. The initial algorithm level, *main()*, will reflect the problem definition and call the individual subprogram, or function, modules as follows:

Initial Algorithm

main()
BEGIN
    Call function to obtain the transaction data from user.
    Call function to add the account deposits.
    Call function to subtract the account withdrawals.
    Call function to calculate the account interest.
    Call function to generate the account report.
END.

The first level of refinement requires that we show a detailed algorithm for each subprogram module, or function. They are as follows:

First Level of Refinement

readData()
BEGIN
    Write a prompt to enter the current account balance.
    Read *balance*.
    Write a prompt to enter the monthly deposits.
    Read *deposits*.
    Write a prompt to enter the monthly withdrawals.
    Read *withdrawals*.
END.

> *addDeposits()*
> BEGIN
>   Calculate *balance = balance + deposits.*
> END.
>
> *subtractWithdrawals()*
> BEGIN
>   Calculate *balance = balance – withdrawals.*
> END.
>
> *addInterest()*
> BEGIN
>   Calculate *balance = balance + (balance * interest).*
> END.
>
> *generateReport()*
> BEGIN
>   Write *balance.*
>   Write *deposits.*
>   Write *withdrawals.*
> END.

Coding the Program

The foregoing problem solution can be coded easily in any structured programming language. Here is how the foregoing algorithms are translated into C++ code:

```cpp
/****************************************************************
ACTION 3-1 (ACT03_01.CPP)
THIS PROGRAM WILL PROCESS A BANKING ACCOUNT
****************************************************************/

//THIS PROGRAM SHOWS THE BLOCK-STRUCTURED NATURE OF C++
//TAKE A GENERAL LOOK AT ITS OVERALL STRUCTURE

//PREPROCESSOR DIRECTIVE
#include <iostream.h>        //FOR cin AND cout

//DEFINE GLOBAL INTEREST CONSTANT
const float INTEREST = 0.01;      //CURRENT MONTHLY INTEREST RATE

//FUNCTION PROTOTYPES
void readData(double &balance, double &deposits, double &withdrawals);
void addDeposits(double &balance, double deposits);
void subtractWithdrawals (double &balance, double withdrawals);
void addInterest(double &balance);
void generateReport(double balance, double deposits, double withdrawals);

//MAIN FUNCTION
int main()
{
 //DEFINE FUNCTION ARGUMENT VARIABLES
 double balance = 0.0;                         //ACCOUNT BALANCE
 double deposits = 0.0;                        //MONTHLY DEPOSITS
 double withdrawals = 0.0;                     //MONTHLY WITHDRAWALS
```

```cpp
//DISPLAY PROGRAM DESCRIPTION MESSAGE
cout << "This program will generate a banking account report based"
     << "on information entered by the user" << endl << endl;

//CALL FUNCTIONS
readData(balance,deposits,withdrawals);
addDeposits(balance,deposits);
subtractWithdrawals(balance,withdrawals);
addInterest(balance);
generateReport(balance,deposits,withdrawals);

//RETURN
return 0;
} //END main()

//THIS FUNCTION GETS THE MONTHLY ACCOUNT
//INFORMATION FROM THE USER
void readData (double &balance, double &deposits, double &withdrawals)
{
cout << "Enter the account balance: $";
cin >> balance;
cout << "Enter the deposits this month: $";
cin >> deposits;
cout << "Enter the withdrawals this month: $";
cin >> withdrawals;
} //END readData()

//THIS FUNCTION ADDS THE MONTHLY DEPOSITS
//TO THE ACCOUNT BALANCE
void addDeposits(double &balance, double deposits)
{
balance = balance + deposits;
} //END addDeposits()

//THIS FUNCTION SUBTRACTS THE MONTHLY WITHDRAWALS
//FROM THE ACCOUNT BALANCE
void subtractWithdrawals (double &balance, double withdrawals)
{
balance = balance - withdrawals;
} //END subtractWithdrawals()

//THIS FUNCTION ADDS MONTHLY INTEREST
//TO THE ACCOUNT BALANCE
void addInterest(double &balance)
{
balance = balance + (balance * INTEREST);
} //END addInterest()

//THIS FUNCTION DISPLAYS THE MONTHLY ACCOUNT REPORT
void generateReport(double balance, double deposits, double withdrawals)
{
      //FORMAT OUTPUT IN DOLLARS AND CENTS
      cout.setf(ios::fixed);
      cout.setf(ios::showpoint);
      cout.precision(2);
```

```
//DISPLAY ACCOUNT REPORT
cout << "The account balance is currently: $" << balance << endl;
cout << "Deposits were $" << deposits << endl;
cout << "Withdrawals were $" << withdrawals << endl;
} //END generateReport()
```

At this point, the code might look a little overwhelming. However, don't agonize over the coding details; just observe the things that relate to what we discussed in the last few chapters. You will learn all the coding details in time. First, notice the overall structure of the program. A general program comment is at the top of the program, followed by the preprocessor directives, followed by function *main()*, which is followed by the individual function code. Notice that the only purpose of *main()* is to call the individual functions in the order they are needed to solve the problem. The individual functions simply implement their respective algorithms using C++ code.

Second, notice the constant and variable definitions. The constant *INTEREST* is defined prior to *main()* to make it a global constant and accessible to the entire program. This means that it will be accessible to *main()* as well as to all the other functions defined in the program. The variables *balance, deposits,* and *withdrawals* are defined at the beginning of *main()*. These variables are listed as **arguments** in the function calls. A function argument is a data value that the function requires to perform its defined task. More about this later. You should define constants just before *main()*, after your preprocessor directives, and you should define variables before anything else within *main()*. You can define constants within *main()*, and it would make no difference in the simple programs covered in this book, but in more complex programs, it makes a big difference.

A function **argument** is a data value that the function requires to perform its designated task.

Finally, notice the extensive use of comments. The purpose of the program is commented, as well as the purpose of each function. Furthermore, a comment is placed with each constant and variable definition to specify its purpose in the program. The comments are easily identified from the executable code, because they are coded in uppercase characters.

The foregoing C++ code involved the use of functions to implement the various program modules. It won't be long before you are writing structured C++ programs like this. However, we can implement simple problems like this using a *flat* or *inline* approach. The term *flat* comes from the idea that we will flatten the hierarchical structure of the program by coding all the program steps as one long *inline* sequence of statements as part of function *main()*. Here is the *flat* solution:

```
/*******************************************************************

ACTION 3-2 (ACT03_02.CPP)
THIS PROGRAM REPRESENTS THE FLAT SOLUTION TO THE BANKING PROBLEM

*******************************************************************/
```

```
//PREPROCESSOR DIRECTIVE
#include <iostream.h>        //FOR cin AND cout

//DEFINE GLOBAL INTEREST CONSTANT
const double INTEREST = 0.01;     //CURRENT MONTHLY INTEREST RATE
                                  //IN DECIMAL FORM

//MAIN FUNCTION
int main()
{
 double balance = 0.0;            //ACCOUNT BALANCE
 double deposits = 0.0;           //MONTHLY DEPOSITS
 double withdrawals = 0.0;        //MONTHLY WITHDRAWALS

 cout << "This program will generate a banking account report based"
      << "on information entered by the user" << endl << endl;

 //readData(): GET THE MONTHLY ACCOUNT INFORMATION
 //FROM THE USER
 cout << "Enter the account balance: $";
 cin >> balance;
 cout << "Enter the deposits this month: $";
 cin >> deposits;
 cout << "Enter the withdrawals this month: $";
 cin >> withdrawals;

 //addDeposits(): ADD THE MONTHLY DEPOSITS
 //TO THE ACCOUNT BALANCE
 balance = balance + deposits;

 //subtractWithdrawals(): SUBTRACT THE MONTHLY WITHDRAWALS
 balance = balance - withdrawals;

 //addInterest(): ADD MONTHLY INTEREST
 balance = balance + (balance * INTEREST);

 //FORMAT OUTPUT IN DOLLARS AND CENTS
 cout.setf(ios::fixed);
 cout.setf(ios::showpoint);
 cout.precision(2);

 //generateReport(): DISPLAY THE MONTHLY ACCOUNT REPORT
 cout << "The account balance is currently: $" << balance << endl;
 cout << "Deposits were $" << deposits << endl;
 cout << "Withdrawals were $" << withdrawals << endl;

 //RETURN
 return 0;
} //END main()
```

As you can see, each of the former function statements has been coded inline as part of *main()*. This type of implementation is adequate for simple problems such as this. The program code is clear and easy to understand, given the appropriate program comments. For the next few chapters, we will employ flat implementations. Then, as the problems get more complex, we will need to implement the program modules as C++ functions and replace the inline program statements with calls to those functions as we did in the first program. However, before you can do this, you need to learn the basic implementation details of the C++ language. The next four chapters are devoted to this purpose. We will get back to highly structured C++ programs in Chapter 8, where functions are discussed in detail.

CHAPTER SUMMARY

Data abstraction allows us to use data without agonizing over the internal implementation details of the data; this gives rise to the term abstract data type, or ADT. The term behavior has to do with how an ADT will act and react for a given operation. As a result, ADTs exhibit a given behavior, which is determined by the operations defined for the ADT. In C++, the **class** is used to implement ADTs.

C++ is a typed language. This means that all of the data processed by a C++ program must be part of a given data type that is defined within the program. There are three major data type categories: primitive, standard, and structured.

Primitive data types consist of the standard types built into the C++ language. These include the integer, floating-point, character, and Boolean data types. The integer types in C++ include the **short, int, unsigned int, long,** and **unsigned long** types, each of which defines a given range of integers that depend on the particular C++ compiler that you are using.

The floating-point type consists of decimal values that can be represented in either fixed decimal or exponential form. Floating-point constants and variables can be defined as **float, double,** or **long double** types, each of which defines a given precision of floating-point values that depend on the particular C++ compiler that you are using.

Character data include all of the symbols on your computer keyboard which can be white space characters and non-white space characters. Characters are ordered, because they are represented internally using a numeric ASCII code. In C++, there are two character types: **char** and **unsigned char.** The former is used to represent the standard ASCII character set. The latter is used to represent the standard ASCII character set as well as the extended PC character set.

The Boolean type, **bool,** consists of only two data elements, **true** and **false.** C++ compilers developed before the ANSI/ISO standard was released will not support the **bool** type. Boolean values are used in programs to make decisions.

A string is a collection of characters. The Standard C++ Library includes a *string* class from which string objects can be created.

Enumerated types are those that you, the programmer, define when constructing a program. Enumerated types can be employed in your C++ programs to make them more understandable and application-oriented. These data types are defined using the keyword **enum.** Because enumerated types are scalar, the values defined as part of a given type are ordered in ascending order from the first value in the value listing to the last value in the listing.

All constants and variables used in a C++ program must be defined prior to their use in the program. Constants are defined using the keyword **const.** The constant identifier is set to its constant value. Variables are defined by listing the variable data type followed by the variable identifier. An optional initializing value should always be included in the definition. String objects are defined as objects of the *string* class. The class name, *string,* is listed first, followed by an appropriate object identifier. Like primitive variables, string objects should always be initialized when they are defined. Empty strings can be initialized with double quotation marks.

QUESTIONS AND PROBLEMS

QUESTIONS

1. What is an abstract data type, or ADT?
2. Give an example of an ADT.
3. What is meant by the term *behavior,* as related to classes and ADTs?
4. Why is the C++ class ideal for implementing ADTs?
5. Name the four standard primitive types defined in C++.
6. Which of the following are *not* legal integer values in C++? Explain why they are not valid. Assume the **int** data type in this compiler requires 2 bytes of storage.
   a. −32.0
   b. +256
   c. 256
   d. 3,240
   e. 32000
   f. 40000
7. What is an overflow condition, and when will it generate incorrect results in C++?
8. Which of the following are not legal floating-point values in C++? Explain why they are not valid. Assume the **float** data type.
   a. 35.7
   b. −35.7
   c. 0.456
   d. 1.25e−9
   e. −2.5−e3
   f. −0.375e−3
   g. 25
9. Convert the following decimal numbers to exponential notation.
   a. −0.0000123
   b. 57892345.45
   c. 1.00004536
   d. +012.345
10. Convert the following exponential values to fixed decimal notation.
    a. 3.45e−7
    b. −2.25e−5
    c. 2.22e6
    d. −3.45e4
11. Three values in a data communications problem are 15.3 kHz, 2.2 MHz, and 10 ps.
    a. Express each as a floating-point value in fixed decimal form.
    b. Express each as a floating-point value in exponential form.
    c. Express each as an integer value.

12. The following current and voltage values are measured in an electronic circuit: 1 milli-ampere, 32 millivolts, 100 microvolts, and 125 nanoamperes.
    a. Express each current and voltage value in fixed decimal form.
    b. Express each current and voltage value in exponential form.

13. What is the data type or class of each of the following?
    a. 250
    b. −250.0
    c. −16
    d. −3.5e − 4
    e. 'x'
    f. '$'
    g. "2"
    h. "175"
    i. "1.25e − 3"

14. State the difference between a character and a string.

15. Choose appropriate identifiers and define constants to represent each of the following.
    a. A maximum value of 100.
    b. Your name.
    c. Your student number.
    d. Your age.
    e. A period.
    f. Your birth date.
    g. Your school.

16. Define a series of constants that would represent the months of the year.

17. Choose appropriate identifiers and define variables or objects for each of the following.
    a. Grade point average (gpa).
    b. Grade for a course.
    c. Gross pay on a paycheck.
    d. Student name.

18. Suppose that *name* is a string object. Explain what happens as the result of executing the following:

    ```
    cout << name.length();
    ```

PROBLEMS

Least Difficult

1. The = symbol is used in C++ to denote an assignment operation. An assignment operation simply assigns, or copies, the value on the right side of the = symbol to the variable on the left side of the = symbol. For example, the statement

   ```
   value1 = value2;
   ```

   assigns, or copies, *value2* to *value1*. Now, consider the following,

   ```
   //PROBLEM 3-1

   //PREPROCESSOR DIRECTIVE
   #include <math.h>   //FOR sqrt()
   ```

```
//DEFINE CONSTANT
const double VALUE = 2.5;

int main()
{
//DEFINE VARIABLES
  int x = 0;
  int y = 0;
  float a = 0.0;
  float b = 0.0;

//RETURN
return 0;
}//END main()
```

determine the results of each of the following program segments:

a. x = 25;
   b = sqrt(x);
b. y = 5;
   a = sqrt(sqrt(y));
c. x = 1;
   x = x + 1;
   y = sqrt(x);
d. x = 2;
   y = x + x;
   a = (y + 1) * VALUE;
e. x = 2;
   y = x + x;
   a = y + 1 * VALUE;

More Difficult

2. The *cout* object is used in C++ to display a value on the display monitor. The format for this operation is

   ```
   cout << variable or value to displayed << endl;
   ```

   Notice that the << symbols direct the variable or value to the *cout* object. The *endl* command creates a carriage return, line feed (CRLF) and flushes the output stream buffer. Thus, to display the value of the variable *x* in a program, use the following statement:

   ```
   cout << x << endl;
   ```

   Code the program given in problem 1, including the program segments given in part a through part e of the problem. Add a *cout* statement to each of these segments to display the resulting variable value. To use the *cout* object you must include the *iostream.h* header file. Compile, link, and run the program. Verify that the output generated by the program is correct according to the respective program calculations.

3. Design and code a C++ program that will find the sum of three test score values and display the sum on the system monitor. Call the variables *score1, score2,* and *score3,* and assume that they have initial values of 95.3, 78.5, and 85.2, respectively. Use the program structure given in the last chapter. Compile and run your program using your C++ compiler.

4. Expand the program you wrote in problem 3 to calculate and display the average of the three scores. (*Note:* The / symbol is used for division in C++.) Compile and run your program.

5. Design and code a C++ program that will find the total resistance of three series resistors whose values are 3.3k, 2.2k, and 1M. (*Note:* The prefix k stands for the quantity 1000, and the prefix M stands for 1,000,000. The total resistance of resistors in series is the sum of the individual resistances.) Display the total resistance on the display monitor using a *cout* statement. You must include the *iostream.h* file in your program to use the *cout* object. Use the program structure given in the last chapter. Compile, link, and run your program.

6. Design and code a C++ program that will generate a weekly payroll report for Bill Gates. Assume that Bill worked 22.5 hours this week at a rate of $1,000,000 per hour. Also, assume that Bill's payroll deductions were 35 percent of his gross pay. The report should show the number of hours worked, hourly rate, gross pay, payroll deduction amount, and net pay.

7. Use your C++ compiler to find and correct the syntax errors in the following program:

```
//PROBLEM 7 (P03_07.CPP)
//PREPROCESSOR DIRECTIVES
#include <iostream.h>       //FOR cout

//MAIN FUNCTION
int main()
{
 //DEFINE AND INITIALIZE VARIABLES
 double voltage = 0.0;      //VOLTAGE IN VOLTS
 current = 0.001;           //CURRENT IN AMPERES
 double resistance = 4700.0;      //RESISTANCE IN OHMS

 / GENERATE PROGRAM DESCRIPTION MESSAGE
 cout <<"This program will calculate voltage "
      << "given a current value of 0.001 amp \n"
      << "and a resistance value of 4700 ohms. " << endl << endl;
 //CALCULATE VOLTAGE
 Voltage = Current * Resistance

 //DISPLAY RESULTS
 cout.setf(ios::fixed);
 cout.precision(3);
 cout << "Given a current value of " << current << " amperes "
      <<"and a resistance value of " << resistance << " ohms,\n"
      <<"the resulting voltage is " << voltage << " volts." << endl;

 RETURN
 return 0;
} //END main()
```

8. The following is an enhanced version of the program given in problem 7. Enter, compile, link, and run this program using your C++ compiler.

```
//PROBLEM 8 (P03_08.CPP)

//PREPROCESSOR DIRECTIVES
#include <iostream.h>   //FOR cout
#include <iomanip.h>    //FOR setw()
```

```
//MAIN FUNCTION
int main()
{
 //DEFINE AND INITIALIZE VARIABLES
 double voltage = 0.0;         //VOLTAGE IN VOLTS
 double current = 0.001;       //CURRENT IN AMPERES
 double resistance = 4700.0;   //RESISTANCE IN OHMS

 //GENERATE PROGRAM DESCRIPTION MESSAGE
 cout <<"This program will calculate voltage "
      << "given a current value of 0.001 amp \n"
      << "and a resistance value of 4700 ohms. " << endl << endl;

 //CALCULATE VOLTAGE
 voltage = current * resistance;

 //DISPLAY HEADINGS
 cout  << "\n\n\n\n"
       << setw(20) << "RESISTANCE"
       << setw(20) << "CURRENT"
       << setw(20) << "VOLTAGE\n"
       << setw(20) << "----"
       << setw(20) << "----"
       << setw(20) << "----" << endl;

 //DISPLAY VALUES
 cout.setf(ios::fixed);
 cout.precision(3);
 cout  << '\n'
       << setw(20) << resistance
       << setw(20) << current
       << setw(20) << voltage << endl;

} //END main()
```

9. Look closely at the *cout* statements in the program in problem 8. Try to answer the following questions:
   a. What is the purpose of the '\n' character in these statements?
   b. What is the purpose of the *endl* command in these statements?
   c. What is the purpose of the *setw()* function in these statements?
   d. What is the purpose of the *cout.setf(ios::fixed)* statement in this program?
   e. What is the purpose of the *cout.precision(3)* statement in this program?

10. How does the output generated by the program in problem 8 differ from the output generated by the program in problem 7?

INPUT AND OUTPUT OBJECTS

■ Chapter Contents

Chapter Objectives

When you are finished with this chapter, you should have a good understanding of the following:

- The use of the *cout* object to display information.
- How to format a text display.
- How to use the *cin* object for keyboard input.
- How to use the *get()* and *getline()* functions for keyboard input.
- How to read and write disk files.
- How to design and implement user-friendly programs.

INTRODUCTION

In Chapters 1 to 3, you learned the general concepts of problem solving, data abstraction, and C++ program design. In this chapter, you will begin learning the implementation details of the C++ language. In particular, you will learn how to get information into and out of your system via C++ objects. Getting data into the system is called **reading,** and generating data from the system is called **writing.** You will discover how to write information to your display monitor and a disk file. Then, you will learn how to read information from your keyboard and a disk file. Armed with this knowledge, you will be ready to write some *interactive* C++ programs. By interactive, we mean programs that will interact with the user—writing user prompts and reading user input data. Make sure that you do the programming problems at the end of the chapter. You *must* get your hands dirty with some actual programming experience to learn how to program in C++.

Console- vs. Windows-Based Programming

Once upon a time there was DOS (Disk Operating System). DOS used to be the predominant PC operating system, but now that distinction belongs to Microsoft Windows. With Windows, you use a mouse to get around, only resorting to the keyboard when needed. In DOS, the mouse might as well not be there. Almost all commands are given through the keyboard. The screen you see in a DOS environment is called a **console screen.** The typical console screen has a black background and a white (or light gray) prompt with a blinking cursor waiting for you to type in your command.

The drawbacks to consoles are that they are not pretty and not intuitive. A black screen and a blinking cursor are a little daunting to the novice user. However, it is a good environment for learning to program because input and output (the tasks of getting information from the user and writing information to the monitor) are relatively straightforward. All programmers should begin in a console environment such as DOS to get a basic idea of how programming works. Therefore, this chapter focuses on console-based programming. Console-based programs are called **CUI,** or **character user interface,** programs.

Windows-based programs are called **GUI,** or **graphical user interface,** programs. Windows programming doesn't always refer to programs written for Microsoft Windows, even though the windows programs in this book are all for Microsoft Windows. Windows programming is a more generic term referring to programming that involves working with a graphical environment rather than a blank screen and a command prompt.

Windows programs generally look better than console programs, and they are much less daunting for the novice user. Unfortunately, windows programming is very confusing for those not accustomed to it. Even professional windows programmers generally have a *template* to work from to program a windows application, rather than starting each program from scratch. Sample windows programs given in this book cannot simply be typed in, compiled, and run. You must copy the windows program template provided and insert blocks of code into the appropriate places. You will be exposed to windows-based programming through the use of a template in the GUI module that follows this chapter.

A **template** in C++ is a programming unit, or construct, that is comprised of generic container classes, such as Windows and graphics classes, for use by a programmer to develop commonly used application code without starting from scratch each time a different application must be created. The C++ Standard Template Library, STL, uses templates to implement container classes such as *vector, list, stack,* and *queue.* You will use a template in the GUI module that follows this chapter.

4.1   GETTING STUFF OUT

When executing your C++ programs, you usually will want to generate information to one of three hardware devices: a monitor, a printer, or a disk file. In fact, there will be occasions when you will need to generate information to all three of these devices during the execution of a program.

You can write information to a display monitor using a *cout* (pronounced "see-out") statement. The word *cout* is not considered a keyword within C++ and, therefore, is not set in bold type. Rather, *cout* is part of the *iostream.h* header file that invokes predefined routines to accomplish the output task. In fact, *cout* is actually an object defined in the *iostream.h* header file for a standard class called *iostream.* Objects are at the core of object-oriented programming, and you will learn how to define and apply your own objects in C++ programs later in the text. For now, let's learn how to use the predefined *cout* object to write data to the display monitor.

COMPILER NOTE

If you have an ANSI/ISO compatible compiler, you can optionally drop the *.h* file extension and simply code the include statement as *#include <iostream>*. However, if you chose to include *iostream* rather than *iostream.h* you must add another statement after the preprocessor section as follows:

```
using namespace std;
```

This statement avoids extra syntax when using the *cout* and *cin* objects in the standard *iostream* class. In this text, we will normally include the *iostream.h* file unless forced to do otherwise as when using the ANSI/ISO *string* class. The *iostream.h* file will compile with both new and older compilers.

Using the *cout* Object

The general format for a *cout* statement is as follows:

> **COUT FORMAT**
>
> *cout << item #1 << item #2 << item #3 << ⋯ << item #n;*

As you can see, *cout* is followed by a list of the items to be written, which are separated by the << **stream insertion operator.** We refer to *cout* as an **output stream object** that is attached, or connected, to your system monitor. A **stream** is simply a sequence of data flowing from one point in the system to another. Thus, a *cout* statement represents a sequence of data, or stream, flowing from your program to the system monitor. Items are *inserted* into the output stream using the << stream insertion operator. As items are inserted into the stream, they flow to your system monitor, as illustrated in Figure 4.1.

> A **stream** is a sequence of data flowing from one point in the system to another, usually between a logical program object and a physical I/O device.

The best way to understand how *cout* works is to look at the output generated by several different *cout* statements. Probably the simplest use of the *cout* statement is to write fixed, or constant, information. There are two types of fixed information that can be written: numeric and character.

Getting Out Fixed Numeric Information.   When you want to write fixed numeric information, you simply insert the numeric values into the *cout* output stream using the << operator. Thus, the statement

```
cout << 250;
```

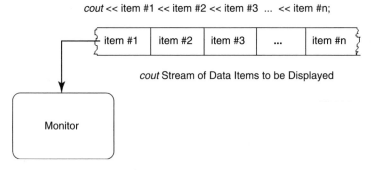

cout Stream of Data Items to be Displayed

FIGURE 4.1   **ITEMS TO BE DISPLAYED ARE INSERTED INTO THE *COUT* OUTPUT STREAM USING THE << STREAM INSERTION OPERATOR.**

generates an output of *250.* The statement

```
cout << -365;
```

generates an output of *-365.*
The statement

```
cout << 1 << 2 << 3 << 4;
```

generates an output of *1234.*
The statement

```
cout << 2.75;
```

generates an output of *2.75.*

When several individual items are inserted into the stream, the output does not generate any spacing between the items. This is why the statement

```
cout << 1 << 2 << 3 << 4;
```

generates an output of *1234.*

Next, notice that when a fixed floating-point value is inserted, you get its fixed decimal equivalent on the output, not the exponential equivalent. Both of these conditions (item spacing and decimal output) can be altered using special formatting options within the *cout* statement. Output formatting will be discussed shortly.

Getting Out Fixed Character and String Information. To write character information, you must enclose the output information in quotes—single quotes for single characters and double quotes for strings. Consequently, the statement

```
cout << 'A';
```

generates an output of the single character *A,* while the statement

```
cout << "This text is great!";
```

produces an output of the string *This text is great!* You can also do the following:

```
cout << "Words" << "More Words";
```

This line will cause *WordsMore Words* to be displayed on the screen. It displays *Words* then it displays *More Words* without putting a space between them. If you want a space, you will have to add it either after *Words* or before *More Words* like this:

```
cout << "Words " << "More Words" ;
```

or

```
cout << "Words" << " More Words";
```

Notice the space after *Words* (but within the quotation marks) in the first example, and before *More Words* in the second example. Both of these statements will output *Words More Words* to the screen. They are different statements, but they do the same thing. This is very common in coding—there are several ways to do most everything, but not all of them make sense to us humans. As an example, look at the following:

```
cout << "Words Mo" << "re Words";
```

This statement will also write *Words More Words* to the screen, even though it may not be easy to see at first.

Finally, to make things easier to read during programming, you can spread a *cout* statement over several lines like this:

```
cout << "Words Words "
     << "Words Words "
     << "Words Words "
     << "Words Words "
     << "Words And More Words";
```

This single statement writes *Words Words Words Words Words Words Words Words Words And More Words* to the screen on one line. Note that *cout* appears only on the first line, beginnning the statement, while a semicolon appears on the last line, ending the statement. Although this statement takes five lines, it is considered to be only one statement. Also, the indentation at the beginning of each line (except the first) is there to make it easier to read the statement. The lines could have begun with no indentation before the << insertion operator and the statement would execute the same. When coding a *cout* statement that is broken up like this, it is very easy to forget to put a space between the output of one string and the output of the next string. Notice the spaces within the quotation marks after the second *Words* in each of the first four lines. These spaces are required to separate the *Words* on the display monitor.

EXAMPLE 4.1

Construct *cout* statements to generate the following outputs:

   a. 3.14

   b. 1 2 3 4

Solution

   a. `cout << 3.14;`

      or

      `cout << '3' << '.' << '1' << '4';`

      or

      `cout << "3.14";`

   b. `cout << 1 << ' ' << 2 << ' ' << 3 << ' ' << 4;`

      or

      `cout << "1 2 3 4";`

Data can be displayed as numeric or character data. This is clearly illustrated in the solution to part a. The value is first displayed as a numeric value, then as a sequence of four characters, then as a string of four characters. The solution to part b illustrates the use of spacing. To get spacing in the output, use blank characters between the output values. Remember that blanks are also characters. As a result, the statements in part b generate blanks, or spaces, where they are inserted using single quotation marks.

Getting Out Variable Information.   The next thing you must learn is how to write variable information. Again, this is a simple chore using the *cout* object: You simply insert the variable identifier(s) into the *cout* stream using the << insertion operator. For instance, if your program has defined *grossPay, rate,* and *hours* as variables, you would write their respective values by inserting them into the *cout* stream, like this:

```
cout << grossPay << rate << hours;
```

The foregoing statement would write the values stored in memory for *grossPay, rate,* and *hours,* in that order. The order of the output will be the same as the listing order within the *cout* statement. However, there would be no spacing between the values. Blank characters must be inserted separately to provide spacing. Let's see how this statement might be used within a complete program.

EXAMPLE 4.2

Suppose your sales of widgets last month amounted to $5,346.00 but your cost for the widgets was $3,045.25. Write a program to calculate and display your profit.

Solution

Of course, you probably would not go to all the trouble of writing a C++ program for such a simple chore. However, let's do it just to get some practice. Suppose we define three variables to represent the sale of widgets last month, the cost of the widgets, and the profit we made on selling the widgets. We will initialize the given sales and cost values and subtract the two to determine the profit we made. The resulting profit will then be displayed using the *cout* object. Here's the program:

```
/*
THIS PROGRAM CALCULATES AND DISPLAYS PROFIT FOR MONTHLY SALES
*/

//PREPROCESSOR DIRECTIVES
#include <iostream.h>              //FOR cout

//MAIN FUNCTION
int main()
{
    //DEFINE AND INITIALIZE VARIABLES
    double sales = 5346.00;     //SALES LAST MONTH
    double cost = 3045.25;      //COST OF SALES LAST MONTH
    double profit = 0.0;        //PROFIT MADE LAST MONTH

    //CALCULATE PROFIT
    profit = sales - cost; //SUBTRACT COST FROM SALES TO GET PROFIT
    //DISPLAY PROFIT
    cout << profit;
```

```
        //RETURN
        return 0;
} //END main()
```

The output produced by the program is

```
2300.75
```

Notice that the output is rather boring. You see that it is simply a number with no apparent meaning. To be meaningful to the user, all output should be appropriately formatted.

Formatting the Output

By formatting an output, we mean structuring it to meet a given application. C++ allows output formatting using special commands within the *cout* statement. For example, the output generated in Example 4.2 is simply the number 2300.75. What a bore! You need to "dress up" your program outputs so that the user of the program understands what's going on. First, you should always use a *cout* statement at the beginning of your program that tells the user what the program is going to do. We will refer to this as a ***program description message.*** A program description message does two things:

1. It tells the user (the person running the program) what the program will do.

2. It provides documentation within the program listing as to what the program will do. As a result, the program listing becomes self-documenting.

A program description message for the program in Example 4.2 might be coded something like this:

```
cout << "\nThis program will calculate monthly profit"
     << "\ngiven sales and cost of sales values." << endl;
```

This one *cout* statement will generate the following output:

```
This program will calculate monthly profit
given sales and cost of sales values.
```

Observe that one *cout* statement is used to write two lines of character information. The trick is to divide the output sentence into two strings on two separate lines. Notice that each string item must be enclosed within double quotes. Also, notice the symbol \n (a *backslash* followed by the character *n*) at the beginning of each string. The \n symbol is treated like a single character and is called an ***escape sequence.*** When inserted into the output stream as a single character or as part of a string, a carriage return/line feed (CRLF) is generated wherever it appears. A CRLF causes the cursor to advance to the beginning of the next line. Thus, in the foregoing *cout* statement, a CRLF is first generated so that the first string item is written on a separate line. Next, at the beginning of the next string, a CRLF is generated to move the cursor to the beginning of the next line before the second string item is written. You may be wondering about the *endl* item at the end of the *cout* statement. The *endl* item does two things: First, like the \n escape sequence, it generates a CRLF, and second, unlike the \n escape sequence, it "flushes" the output stream buffer. This means that everything in the output stream buffer will get written to the screen. The *cout* statement puts everything into a waiting area (called a *buffer*) before it goes to the screen. Placing *endl* at the end of a *cout* statement simply makes sure that everything is cleared out of the buffer and written to the screen. If you do not want a CRLF at the end of your output line, but want to clear the buffer anyway, you can use *flush* instead of *endl.* You probably will never run into a problem with the buffer not being cleared even without using *endl* or *flush,* but it is still a good idea to use them because a potential problem exists without it, especially in networked systems. By the way, *endl* means "end-of-line." Both *endl* and *flush* are referred to as ***I/O manipulators.*** In the code that follows, you will notice the \n escape sequence being used within a *cout* statement for cursor control, whereas the *endl* or *flush* manipulators will be employed at the end of a *cout* statement to flush the stream buffer. Figure 4.2 illustrates how the \n escape sequence and *endl* manipulator control the location of the cursor when used in the *cout* statement.

Now, good style would dictate that output information should be descriptive. In other words, the output information should be self-documenting and easily understood by the user. In Example 4.2, the profit statement could be modified, like this:

```
cout << "\nGiven a monthly sales value of $" << sales
     << "\nand a total cost value of $" << cost
     << "\nthe resulting profit is $" << profit << endl;
```

This one *cout* statement will generate the following output:

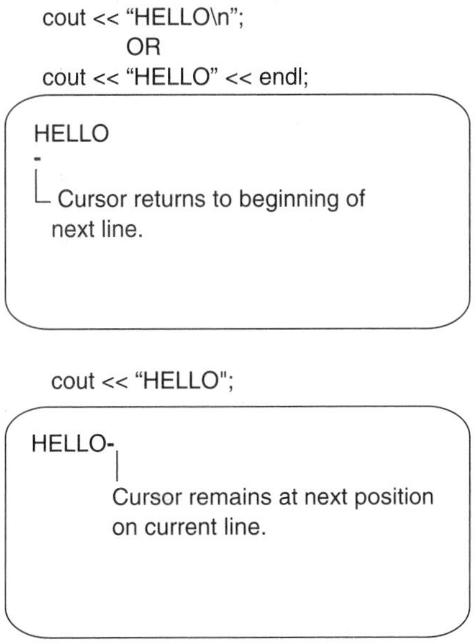

```
cout << "HELLO\n";
        OR
cout << "HELLO" << endl;
```

```
HELLO
-
L Cursor returns to beginning of
  next line.
```

```
cout << "HELLO";
```

```
HELLO-
     |
        Cursor remains at next position
        on current line.
```

FIGURE 4.2   USING THE \n ESCAPE SEQUENCE, OR *endl* MANIPULATOR, FORCES THE CURSOR TO THE NEXT LINE.

```
Given a monthly sales value of $5346
and a total cost of $3045.25
the resulting profit is $2300.75
```

Let's analyze this output. First, observe that a \n escape sequence has been placed at the beginning of each string in the *cout* statement. This generates a CRLF prior to each of the three strings, thereby creating three separate lines on the screen. You treat \n as a single character, just as you would any other character. It can appear as a single character item within single quotes or as part of a string like any other character.

Next, look at the output lines themselves. See how an output sentence is constructed using separate string items. The sentence is formed by separate character strings enclosed within double quotation marks. The monthly sales, cost of sales, and profit values are inserted into the output, between the string items, by inserting the variables (*sales, cost,* and *profit*) when they are needed as part of the output stream. Notice that the character strings and variable items are inserted into the *cout* stream using the << insertion operator. It is important that you see that the quotation marks are around the string information and *not* around the variables.

The same thing could be accomplished with three separate *cout* statements, like this:

```
cout << "\nGiven a monthly sales value of $" << sales;
cout << "\nand a total cost value of $" << cost;
cout << "\nthe resulting profit is $" << profit << endl;
```

EXAMPLE 4.3

Insert the *cout* statements given in the previous discussion into the program developed in Example 4.2 to form a complete program.

Solution

```
/*
THIS PROGRAM CALCULATES AND DISPLAYS PROFIT FOR MONTHLY
SALES
*/

//PREPROCESSOR DIRECTIVES
#include <iostream.h>            //FOR cout

//MAIN FUNCTION
int main()
{
    //DEFINE AND INITIALIZE VARIABLES
    double sales = 5346.00;      //SALES LAST MONTH
    double cost = 3045.25;       //COST OF SALES LAST MONTH
    double profit = 0.0;         //PROFIT MADE LAST MONTH
```

```
//DISPLAY PROGRAM DESCRIPTION MESSAGE
cout << "\nThis program will calculate monthly profit"
     << "\ngiven sales and cost of values." << endl;

//CALCULATE PROFIT
profit = sales - cost; //SUBTRACT COST FROM SALES TO GET PROFIT

//DISPLAY PROFIT
cout << "\nGiven a monthly sales value of $" << sales
     << "\nand a total cost value of $" << cost
     << "\nthe resulting profit is $" << profit << endl;

//RETURN
return 0;
} //END main()
```

As you can see from Example 4.3, the general idea of using the *cout* statement is simple: You place the *cout* statement in your program whenever you want to display information on your system monitor.

Up to this point, you have seen the use of the \n escape sequence (CRLF) to control cursor positioning to format the output. There are other escape sequences that you might need to use from time to time, a few of which are in Table 4.1.

To use any of these escape sequences, simply include them as part of a string or insert them as single characters (using single quotes) into the output stream via the << operator. The purpose of each should be obvious from the action described in the table.

EXAMPLE 4.4

Write a *cout* statement to display the string *Simon says: "Touch your head."*

Solution

```
cout << "Simon says, \"Touch your head.\"" << endl;
```

TABLE 4.1   ESCAPE SEQUENCES DEFINED FOR C++

Sequence	Action
\a	Beep
\b	Backspace
\n	CRLF
\r	CR
\t	Horizontal tab
\v	Vertical tab
\\	Backslash
\'	Single quote
\"	Double quote
\?	Question mark

Here you see the use of the \" escape sequence to insert double quotation marks into the output stream. Why do you have to use the \" escape sequence? Why can't you just insert the quotation marks within the string as needed?

Now, let's learn how the computer "sees" a display screen. Most systems divide a page of text output into twenty five rows and eighty columns as shown by the ***layout chart*** in Figure 4.3. Layout charts are used to lay out, or format, your output. The layout chart allows you to align output information so that the following happens:

❑ Proper margins are provided for header information.

❑ Numeric and character data are properly aligned under column headings and evenly spaced across the page.

❑ The output looks professional.

The first thing to do when using a layout chart is to fill in the chart with the information to be displayed. For instance, suppose you must create three columns of output: the first for a person's name, the second for the person's address, and the third for a person's phone number. Figure 4.4 shows how these three columns might be laid out on a layout chart. Looking at the figure, you can make the following observations:

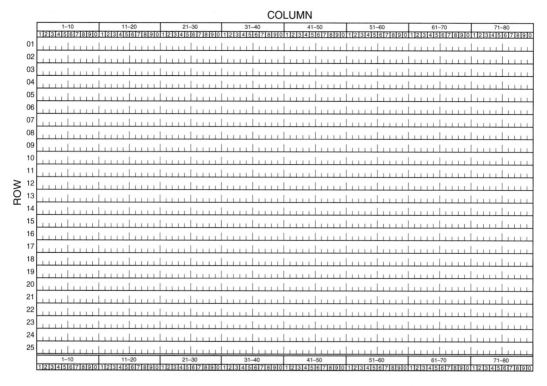

FIGURE 4.3   A TYPICAL LAYOUT CHART.

COLUMN

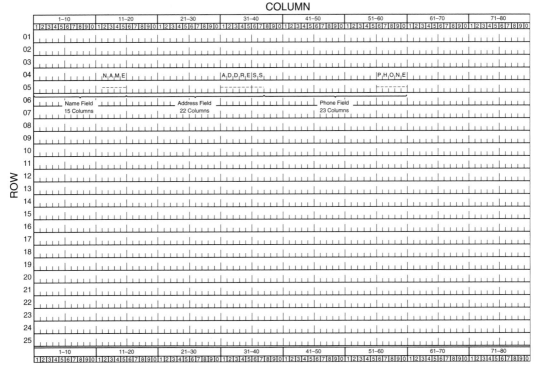

FIGURE 4.4   LAYING OUT AN OUTPUT USING A LAYOUT CHART.

❑ Three headings are located on row 4.

❑ Dashes in row 5 underscore each column heading.

❑ The NAME heading has a field width of 15.

❑ The ADDRESS heading has a field width of 22.

❑ The PHONE heading has a field width of 23.

The ***field width*** of an output item is the number of columns on the monitor that the item will occupy.

Using this information, let's write a program that will display the headings just as they appear on the layout chart. Here it is:

```
/*
        THIS PROGRAM GENERATES THE OUTPUT SHOWN IN FIGURE 4.4
*/

//PREPROCESSOR DIRECTIVES
#include <iostream.h>   //FOR cout
#include <iomanip.h>    //FOR setw()
```

```
//MAIN FUNCTION
int main()
{
 //SKIP THREE LINES AND DISPLAY HEADINGS
 cout <<"\n\n\n"
        << setw(15) << "NAME"
        << setw(22) << "ADDRESS"
        << setw(23) << "PHONE" << endl;

 //DISPLAY HEADING UNDERSCORES
 cout << setw(15) << "----"
        << setw(22) << "-------"
        << setw(23) << "-----"
        << endl;

 //RETURN
 return 0;
}//END main()
```

The first item inserted into *cout* stream is a string of three CRLF escape sequences. Assuming that the cursor is located in the upper left-hand corner of a clear screen, these three escape sequences generate the three blank lines in rows 1, 2, and 3, respectively. Now, looking at the layout chart in Figure 4.4, you see that each heading is designated by a field width that indicates the number of columns that a given output item will occupy. To communicate the field width to the *cout* object, you must use the *setw() **I/O manipulator*** contained in the *iomanip.h* header file. A list of several I/O manipulators is provided in Table 4.2.

Notice that I/O manipulators allow you to manipulate the output stream to obtain some desired effect, in our case using the *setw()* manipulator to set the field width of a given output item. Remember that in order to use some of these manipulators, such as *setw()*, you must include the *iomanip.h* header file in your program.

Any of the manipulators in Table 4.2 can be inserted in the *cout* stream just like any other item using the << insertion operator. The following format shows how the *setw()* manipulator will set the field width for an item to be output.

FIELD WIDTH FORMAT

cout << setw(field width) << output item;

TABLE 4.2 I/O STREAM MANIPULATORS FOR C++

Manipulator	Action
setw(n)	Sets field width to *n*
setprecision(n)	Sets floating-point precision to *n*
setfill(n)	Sets fill character to *n*
ws	Extracts white space characters
endl	Inserts a new line in the output stream, then flushes the output stream
flush	Flushes the output stream

In Figure 4.4, observe that the first output, *NAME,* has a field width of 15 columns. Thus, *setw(15)* tells C++ to assign a field width of 15 columns to the *next* item to be written, which, as you can see from the program, is the string *NAME.* When *NAME* is written, it will be right justified, by default, within this field width. Because it is right justified, *NAME* is positioned at the extreme right-hand side of the field. And, because the word *NAME* requires only 4 columns of output, C++ generates 15 – 4, or 11, spaces prior to *NAME.*

Next, count the number of columns from the *NAME* field in Figure 4.4 to the last *S* in the *ADDRESS* field. You get 22, right? Thus, the *ADDRESS* field width is 22. Therefore, *setw(22)* is inserted into the *cout* stream prior to inserting the item *ADDRESS.*

Finally, counting the number of columns from the *ADDRESS* field to the last letter (*E*) in *PHONE* field, you get 23. Consequently, the *PHONE* field width is set to 23. Notice that the *endl* manipulator is inserted into the stream at the end of the *PHONE* item so that the cursor will be positioned at the beginning of the next output line and the stream buffer is flushed. The same basic idea is then repeated within the next *cout* statement to produce row 5. This statement generates the dashes that provide underscoring for the headings.

EXAMPLE 4.5

Write a program segment that will format a three-column table for *CURRENT, RESISTANCE,* and *VOLTAGE.* Underscore each column heading.

Solution

Using a layout chart, you must first lay out the output headings. Such a layout is shown in Figure 4.5. Here, the table headings are located in row 5, and each heading has a field width of 20. In addition, each heading is underscored by using dashes in row 6. The dashes must also have a field width of 20 to locate them under their respective headings.

The resulting program is as follows:

```
/*
THIS PROGRAM GENERATES THE OUTPUT SHOWN IN FIGURE 4.5
*/

//PREPROCESSOR DIRECTIVES
#include <iostream.h>      //FOR cout
#include <iomanip.h>       //FOR setw()

//MAIN FUNCTION
int main()
{
 //SKIP FOUR LINES AND DISPLAY HEADINGS
 cout    <<"\n\n\n\n"                //SKIP FIRST FOUR LINES
         << setw(20) << "CURRENT"    //DISPLAY HEADINGS
         << setw(20) << "RESISTANCE"
         << setw(20) << "VOLTAGE" << endl;
```

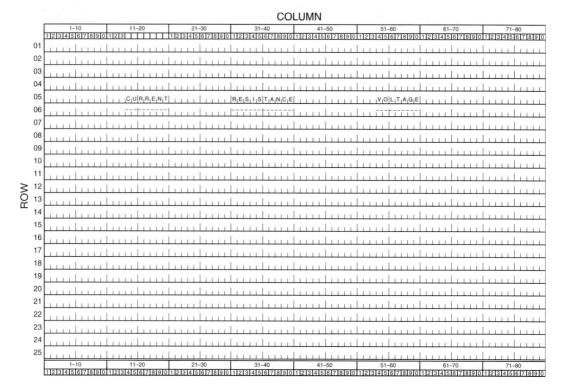

FIGURE 4.5   LAYOUT CHART FOR EXAMPLE 4.5.

```
//UNDERSCORE HEADINGS
cout    << setw(20) << "-------"
        << setw(20) << "----------"
        << setw(20) << "-------"
        << endl;

//RETURN
return 0;
}//END main()
```

EXAMPLE 4.6

Given a current value of 0.001 ampere and a resistance value of 4700 ohms, write a program to calculate voltage using Ohm's law. Ohm's law simply multiplies current by resistance to get voltage. Write the current, resistance, and voltage values using the format developed in Example 4.5.

Solution

The following program will do the job:

```
/*
THIS PROGRAM GENERATES A TABLE OF CURRENT, RESISTANCE AND
VOLTAGE
*/
```

```
//PREPROCESSOR DIRECTIVES
#include <iostream.h> //FOR cout
#include <iomanip.h>  //FOR setw()

//MAIN FUNCTION
int main()
{
 //DEFINE AND INITIALIZE VARIABLES
 double voltage = 0.0;        //VOLTAGE IN VOLTS
 double current = 0.001;      //CURRENT IN AMPERES
 double resistance = 4700.0;  //RESISTANCE IN OHMS

 //CALCULATE VOLTAGE
 voltage = current * resistance;

 //DISPLAY HEADINGS
 cout <<"\n\n\n\n"
      << setw(20) << "CURRENT"
      << setw(20) << "RESISTANCE"
      << setw(20) << "VOLTAGE" << endl;

 //DISPLAY HEADING UNDERSCORES
 cout << setw(20) << "-------"
      << setw(20) << "----------"
      << setw(20) << "-------"
      << endl;

 //DISPLAY VALUES
 cout << setw(20) << current
      << setw(20) << resistance
      << setw(20) << voltage
      << endl;

  //RETURN
  return 0;
}//END main()
```

Here, we have simply combined several things that we have done previously. The headings program segment from Example 4.5 was inserted to generate the required CURRENT, RESISTANCE, and VOLTAGE headings. Notice that the last *cout* statement in the program writes the actual values of current, resistance, and voltage, respectively. Here, the variable identifier is listed after the field-width specifier required to locate the value under the respective heading. You might note that three *cout* statements are used for clarity: one to write the header information, another to underscore the headings, and another to write the variable information.

Formatting Floating-Point Output.   Many application programs require you to display floating-point data. Recall that C++ employs two methods for representing such data: fixed decimal point notation or exponential notation. The way your compiler displays such data depends on several factors, including the size of the data item to be displayed as well as the compiler design itself. In most cases you

COMPILER NOTE

To obtain the output required in these formatting examples, you must start with a clear screen. Many C++ compilers provide a standard function to clear the screen. For example, some DOS and Windows compilers provide the *clrscr()* function as part of the *conio.h* header file. Check your compiler reference manual, or ask your instructor about such a function if you are not using a DOS- or Windows-compatible platform. The ANSI/ISO standard does not identify a standard function to clear the screen, because different platforms use different screen formatting techniques. So, be careful when using such a compiler-specific function because it may not be standard and, therefore, may not be portable across different platforms.

will want to avoid any exponential output and force the compiler to generate a fixed decimal point display. The C++ compiler provides three functions in the *iostream.h* header file to accomplish this task. They are *setf(), unsetf(),* and *precision()*. The *setf()* function is used to set various formatting **flags** for the compiler. C++ provides the *setf()* function to set a flag and the *unsetf()* function to unset a flag.

A **flag** is something that can be turned on or off. You set a flag to turn it on and *unset* the flag to turn it off.

There are three flags that we are concerned about at this time: the *fixed, right,* and *left* flags. Setting the *fixed* flag using the *setf()* function forces the compiler to display a floating-point value *using fixed decimal point* notation as opposed to exponential, or *e,* notation. The number of decimal places provided is specified by the *precision()* function. Both the *setf()* and *precision()* functions must be called by the *cout* object, as follows:

GENERATING DECIMAL POINT VALUES

cout.setf(ios::fixed);
cout.precision(n);

Notice that a dot, **.**, is used by the *cout* object to call the function. This *dot notation* is employed whenever an object calls one of its **member functions.** A member function of an object is simply a function that is part of the object class. More about this later. The statement *cout.setf(ios::fixed)* forces the compiler to generate a fixed decimal output as opposed to an exponential output, and the *cout.precision(n)* statement dictates the number of decimal places to the right of the decimal point to generate. Recall our Ohm's law program from Example 4.6. Suppose that we altered the display part of the program as follows:

```
//DISPLAY VALUES
cout.setf(ios::fixed);
cout.precision(2);
cout  << setw(20) << current
      << setw(20) << resistance
      << setw(20) << voltage << endl;
```

Here, using the *setf()* and *precision()* functions force the following decimal output:

```
CURRENT    RESISTANCE    VOLTAGE
----------  ---------------  -----------
      0.00       4700.00       4.70
```

Notice that the compiler was forced to generate a fixed decimal output with two places to the right of the decimal point. However, do you see a problem here? The problem is that there is not enough precision to display the current value. So, let's change the precision value to 3, like this:

```
//DISPLAY VALUES
cout.setf(ios::fixed);
cout.precision(3);
cout << setw(20) << current
     << setw(20) << resistance
     << setw(20) << voltage << endl;
```

The resulting display is as follows:

```
CURRENT    RESISTANCE    VOLTAGE
----------  ---------------  -----------
      0.001     4700.000      4.700
```

Now we have generated enough precision to display all the values in fixed decimal format.

You can change the precision at any time in the program by calling the *precision()* function as needed, as long as the *setf()* function has been called someplace previously in the program. To place the compiler back in its default display mode, you must use the *unsetf()* function, like this:

```
//DISPLAY VALUES
cout.unsetf(ios::fixed);
cout  << setw(20) << current
      << setw(20) << resistance
      << setw(20) << voltage << endl;
```

Now the output becomes

```
CURRENT    RESISTANCE    VOLTAGE
----------  ---------------  -----------
      0.001     4.7e+03        4.7
```

As you can see, the compiler has chosen to display the resistance in exponential form.

You control the justification of a value within a field by using the *right* and *left* flags. By setting the *left* flag, the output value will be left-justified within its field.

To right justify a value, you set the *right* flag. Recall that output values are right-justified by default. For example, suppose that you want to left justify the table headings and Ohm's law values in the foregoing program. To do this, we will set both the *fixed* and *left* flags using the *setf()* function. Here's the required syntax:

GENERATING LEFT-JUSTIFIED VALUES

cout.setf(ios::fixed);
cout.setf(ios::left);

Notice that *setf()* is called twice and, therefore, is setting two flags: the *fixed* and the *left* flag. Here's the Ohm's law code for left justifying the table headings and corresponding values:

```
//DISPLAY HEADINGS
cout.setf(ios::fixed);
cout.setf(ios::left);
cout.precision(3);
cout <<"\n\n\n\n"
        << setw(20) << "CURRENT"
        << setw(20) << "RESISTANCE"
        << setw(20) << "VOLTAGE" << endl;
cout << setw(20) << "-------"
        << setw(20) << "----------"
        << setw(20) << "-------"
        << endl;

//DISPLAY VALUES
cout << setw(20) << current
        << setw(20) << resistance
        << setw(20) << voltage << endl;
```

Here, the *left* flag has been set prior to writing both the headings and values so that both will be left justified within their respective output fields. This code generates the following output:

```
CURRENT     RESISTANCE      VOLTAGE
----------  --------------  -----------
0.001       4700.000        4.700
```

Be aware that once the output is set to left justification all output from that point on will be left justified. If you want to go back to right justification you must unset the *left* flag or set the *right* flag like this:

```
cout.unset(ios::left);
```

or

```
cout.setf(ios::right);
```

Generating Currency Output.   When generating currency output, you will always want to do three things:

❏ Specify fixed decimal output by setting the *fixed* flag.
❏ Force the output to always display the decimal point by setting the *showpoint* flag.
❏ Specify a precision of 2 decimal places by calling the *precision(2)* function.

These three tasks can be accomplished using the following code:

```
cout.setf(ios::fixed);
cout.setf(ios::showpoint);
cout.precision(2);
```

The only thing new here is the setting of the *showpoint* flag. The *showpoint* flag forces the decimal point to always be displayed along with any trailing 0's required to fulfill the decimal precision specification. This means that an output of two dollars appears as 2.00 and not just the number 2. Likewise an output of two dollars and fifty cents would appear as 2.50 and not just 2.5. The formatting functions and flags just discussed are summarized in Table 4.3.

 Quick Check

1. The file that must be included to use *cout* is the _____ header file.
2. The operator that must be employed to insert information into the *cout* stream is the _____ operator.
3. Write a *cout* statement to display your name as a fixed string of information.
4. Write a *cout* statement to display your name when it is stored in a string object called *name*.
5. The escape sequence that must be used to generate a CRLF is the _____.
6. The file that must be included to use the *setw()* field-width manipulator is the _____ header file.
7. Write a *cout* statement that will display the value of a floating-point variable called *number* left-justified within a field width of 10 columns and a precision of 3 decimal places.
8. Explain the difference between using a \n versus an *endl* within a *cout* statement.
9. Write the code necessary to display a variable called *grossPay* in proper currency format.

TABLE 4.3   FORMATTING FUNCTIONS AND FLAGS

Function/Flag	Description
setf()	Sets a formatting flag.
unsetf()	Unsets a formatting flag.
precision(n)	Sets decimal output to *n* decimal places.
fixed	Forces fixed decimal point output.
left	Forces left justification within field.
right	Forces right justification within field.
scientific	Forces exponential, *e*, output.
showpoint	Forces a decimal point to be displayed along with trailing 0's. (Used for currency outputs)
showpos	Forces a + sign output for positive values.

4.2   GETTING STUFF IN

A program must respond to a user in order to be really useful. If a program always does exactly the same thing, it will be boring and, for the most part, useless. You can draw a happy face without input, but you cannot play a game of hangman without it. If you think about it, almost every program you use depends on user input for direction. Whether you're playing a game of solitaire or surfing the Internet, your mouse clicks and keystrokes decide what happens.

Getting information into a program for processing is called *reading*. In most present-day systems, character information is read from one of two sources: from a keyboard or from a disk file. In this section, you will learn how to read information that is being entered via a keyboard by the system user.

Input is not as easy as output, so we have covered all the basic types of output first. The basic syntax for input in C++ is not complicated, but you will find that it has many little quirks that take some getting used to. Before you can collect input from the user, you must first decide what kind of input you want. This is important because *you must store the user's input in a variable.* This means that you need to decide on the data type that you expect to get from the user (e.g., numbers, characters, strings, etc.). After you have decided the type of data expected, you need to *prompt* the user for the data (i.e., you must tell the user with *cout* what he or she should enter). Once you have decided on the input variable data types and prompted the user, you are ready to actually read the data into a variable.

The primary C++ statement that we will use for reading keyboard data is the *cin* (pronounced "see-in") statement. Like *cout, cin* is a predefined stream object in C++ and is part of the *iostream.h* header file. The *cin* stream is an input stream attached, by default, to your system keyboard. Thus, as you enter information via the keyboard, it will flow into the *cin* stream.

Before you can understand how this statement works, you must know a little bit about how C++ "sees" a line of data. Suppose you enter a line of data as follows:

74 92 88↵

When typing in the foregoing data on a keyboard, you would type each number consecutively, separating the numbers with one or more spaces. As you typed the values, they are stored in the *cin* stream buffer.

> The *cin* **stream** flows, by default, from your system keyboard to your program. The *cin* **stream buffer** is a memory area where keystrokes are temporarily stored until read by your program.

At the end of a line, you will press the **ENTER** (↵) key. How do you suppose the system knows where one data item ends and another begins? You're right—the *white space* (blanks) between the data items separate one item from another. Next, how do you suppose the system knows where the line of data ends? Right again— by pressing the ↵ key you define the end of the line and enter a CRLF into the stream buffer. The stream buffer and its contents after the foregoing data entry operation are illustrated in Figure 4.6.

Now back to the *cin* object. The general format for using *cin* is as follows:

cin FORMAT

cin >> variable to be read;

Notice that the *cin* object is followed by the double right angle bracket *stream extraction operator*, >>, which is followed by the variable to be read. Notice, first of all, that the >> extraction operator used with *cin* is backwards from the << insertion operator used with *cout*. You will probably type this wrong a few times, and when you try to compile your code, the compiler will generate a syntax error and request that you fix it. Now, we say that the >> operator *extracts* a data item from the *cin* stream buffer. The input data item is then *assigned* to the variable listed in

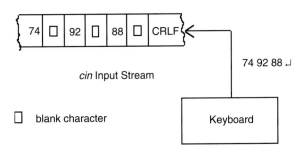

FIGURE 4.6   THE INPUT STREAM BUFFER AFTER ENTERING A LINE OF DATA.

the *cin* statement. Of course, the variable must be defined using a legal data type prior to using it in the *cin* statement.

> **DEBUGGING TIP**
>
> A common source of error when first writing *cout* and *cin* statements is to use the wrong operator. Remember that the << insertion operator is used to insert items in the *cout* stream, and the >> extraction operator is used to extract items from the *cin* stream.

Suppose, for example, that you have defined three integer variables called *score1, score2,* and *score3.* To read three scores into the system, you would insert three *cin* statements into your program, like this:

```
cin >> score1;
cin >> score2;
cin >> score3;
```

When C++ encounters the foregoing statements in your program, it halts execution until the user enters the required data. Now suppose the user enters the following via the system keyboard:

74 92 88↵

What do you suppose happens? You're right—the value 74 is extracted from the *cin* stream and assigned to *score1,* the value 92 is extracted and assigned to *score2,* and the value 88 is extracted and assigned to *score3.* Thus, you can think of the *cin* operation as an assignment operation. A value entered on the keyboard is extracted from the input stream using the >> operator and assigned to the variable listed in the *cin* statement. The contents of the stream buffer for these entries are shown in Figure 4.7(a).

The user might also have entered these same values on three separate lines, like this:

74 ↵
92 ↵
88 ↵

The contents of the buffer for these entries are shown in Figure 4.7(b). If the same three *cin* statements were to read these entries, the same variable assignments would occur. Look at the two streams in Figure 4.7 again. Notice that the first stream contains two blanks and one CRLF character, whereas the second stream contains no blanks and three CRLF characters. If the same variable assignments are made for both streams, what does this tell you about how the >> operator is extracting the stream data? The only possible conclusion is that the >> extraction operator has totally ignored both the blank and CRLF white space characters—it is only extracting non-white space character data.

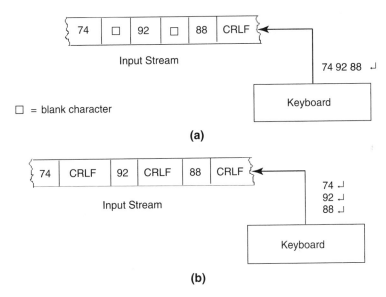

(a)

□ = blank character

(b)

FIGURE 4.7   **THE SAME VARIABLE ASSIGNMENTS WILL OCCUR FOR BOTH OF THESE TWO USER ENTRIES, BECAUSE THE >> STREAM EXTRACTION OPERATOR IGNORES ALL WHITE SPACE, INCLUDING CRLFS.**

PROGRAMMING NOTE

You can use the *cin* stream with the >> operator to read several variables as part of a single statement. For example, the statement

```
cin >> score1 >> score2 >> score3;
```

would allow you to read three user entries using a single *cin* statement. The values entered on the keyboard are assigned on a one-to-one basis to the variables listed in the *cin* statement. The assignment order is the order of the respective input data and variable listings.

Although this technique is acceptable, we suggest that, to prevent possible entry errors and confusion, you read only one variable at a time.

One other point: You should always generate a **prompt** to the screen using a *cout* statement prior to reading *each* variable, like this:

```
cout << "Enter an integer value for Score 1:" << endl;
cin >> score1;
cout << "Enter an integer value for Score 2:" << endl;
cin >> score2;
cout << "Enter an integer value for Score 3:" << endl;
cin >> score3;
```

Prompting for and reading one variable at a time also provides for better program readability and documentation.

Reading Mixed Data Types

The two cardinal rules that apply when reading any data are as follows:

1. All variables listed within the *cin* statement must be defined prior to their use in the statement.
2. The type of data entered for a given variable should match the data type defined for that variable.

By now, the first rule should be obvious. You cannot use a variable in a C++ program unless it has been previously defined in the program. The second rule needs to be explored a bit further. Consider the following program:

```
/*
THIS PROGRAM DEMONSTRATES THE cin OPERATION
*/

//PREPROCESSOR DIRECTIVES
#include <iostream.h>   //FOR cin AND cout

//MAIN FUNCTION
int main()
{
 //DEFINE INPUT VARIABLES
 int score1 = 0;
 double score2 = 0.0;

 //PROMPT AND READ USER DATA
 cout << "Enter a number:" << endl;
 cin >> score1;
 cout << "Enter a number:" << endl;
 cin >> score2;

 //RETURN
 return 0;
}//END main()
```

Now, suppose the user enters the following data when the *cin* statements are encountered:

```
Enter a number:
98.5↵
Enter a number:
78↵
```

What happens? Notice that the program defines *score1* as an integer and *score2* as a floating-point variable. However, the user has entered a decimal value for *score1* and an integer value for *score2*. Thus, C++ attempts to assign a decimal value (98.5) to an integer variable (*score1*). This is called a **type mismatch** and will result in an error in many strongly typed languages, like Pascal. However, C++ is not as strongly typed as some other languages. C++ actually assigns the integer portion of the first value to *score1* and the decimal portion of the first value to *score2*. Thus, *score1* takes on the value 98, and *score2* takes the value 0.5. The input value of 78 is not extracted from the stream and, therefore, remains in the stream buffer. This value would be read by any subsequent *cin* statement in the program. This clearly illustrates the reason you should define a variable so that it is the same data type as the data that are expected to be entered for that variable. In addition, the prompt should clearly state the type of data the user must enter. In this case, the first prompt should have directed the user to enter an integer value, and the second

DEBUGGING TIP

When you initially code a program, it is always wise to echo an input value to the display. This assures you that the program has performed the read operation and made the correct variable assignment. To echo an input value to the display, you simply insert a *cout* statement after the *cin* statement. Within the *cout* statement, you list the same variable that is listed within the *cin* statement. For instance, to echo the test scores in the foregoing program, you would add *cout* statements, like this:

```
/*
THIS PROGRAM DEMONSTRATES HOW TO ECHO
INPUT VARIABLES DURING PROGRAM DEVELOPMENT
*/

//PREPROCESSOR DIRECTIVES
#include <iostream.h>      //FOR cin AND cout

//MAIN FUNCTION
int main()
{
 //DEFINE INPUT VARIABLES
 int score1 = 0;
 double score2 = 0.0;

 //PROMPT AND READ/WRITE USER DATA
 cout << "Enter an integer value:" << endl;
 cin >> score1;
 cout << score1 << endl;                     //ECHO INPUT
 cout << "Enter a decimal value:" << endl;
 cin >> score2;                              //ECHO INPUT
 cout << score2 << endl;

 //RETURN
 return 0;
}//END main()
```

Once the program has been debugged and is completely operational, you can remove the echoing *cout* statements.

prompt should have directed the user to enter a decimal value. Otherwise, you are likely to obtain invalid data. Such a bug is often very difficult to track down.

Next, using the same program, suppose the user enters the following lines of data:

```
98↵
78↵
```

Now there is no problem here. But, how can this be, because the compiler assigns an integer value (78) to a floating-point variable (*score2*)? This is okay, because the integers are a subset of the real numbers. The compiler simply converts the integer value to the floating-point format. Thus, the integer value 78 is converted to the floating-point value 78.0 for storage within primary memory.

Reading Single-Character Data

Reading numeric data is straightforward, as long as you adhere to the two rules for reading data. However, there are several things that you will want to keep in mind when reading single character data using *cin*.

1. Only one character is read at a time.
2. *White space* (blanks, tabs, new lines, carriage returns, etc.) are ignored by *cin* when using the >> operator. However, white space can be read using different *cin* functions.
3. Numeric values can be read as characters, but each digit is read as a separate character.

Let's look at a simple program that illustrates most of these concepts. Consider the following:

```
/*
THIS PROGRAM DEMONSTRATES READING
OF CHARACTER DATA
*/

//PREPROCESSOR DIRECTIVES
#include <iostream.h>   //FOR cin AND cout

//MAIN FUNCTION
int main()
{
  //DEFINE INPUT VARIABLES AND INITIALIZE WITH BLANKS
  char grade1 = ' ';
  char grade2 = ' ';
  char grade3 = ' ';

  //READ/WRITE USER DATA
  cin >> grade1;
```

```
cout << grade1 << endl;
cin >> grade2;
cout << grade2 << endl;
cin >> grade3;
cout << grade3 << endl;

//RETURN
return 0;
}//END main()
```

The foregoing program defines three variables (*grade1, grade2, grade3*) as character variables, which are initialized with blanks. The program then reads the three character variables from the system keyboard and echoes the variables to the system display. Now, let's see what the program will do for several input cases.

Case 1:

User types in: A⏎
System displays: A

User types in: B⏎
System displays: B

User types in: C⏎
System displays: C

You see the output that you would expect. The compiler assigns a single input character to the respective character variable listed in the *cin* statement.

Case 2:

User types in: ABC⏎
System displays: A
                   B
                   C

Here, the user has entered the input characters *A, B,* and *C,* on a single line. Thus, all three characters are placed into the input stream buffer. The compiler still assigns the character *A* to *grade1*, the character *B* is to *grade2*, and the character *C* to *grade3*. Here's how it works: The user has placed three characters in the input stream. The first *cin* statement extracts only the first character (*A*), and the subsequent *cout* statement echoes the character to the display. As result, the character *A* is extracted from the stream, but the characters *B* and *C* remain. The second *cin* statement extracts the second character (*B*) from the stream, leaving the character *C* in the stream. The subsequent *cout* statement echoes *B* to the display. Finally, the third *cin* statement extracts the last character (*C*) from the stream. This character is then echoed to the display. Although the input assignments have worked as expected, a prompt prior to each *cin* statement to instruct the user to enter a single character would clarify how to enter the data and prevent any possible assignment errors.

Case 3:

User types in:	A B C↵
System displays:	A
	B
	C

Notice here that there are blanks between the *A* and *B* and the *B* and *C* characters. This white space is ignored by the >> operator. Thus, the compiler still makes the correct assignments to the respective variables.

Case 4:

User types in:	75 92 88↵
System displays:	7
	5
	9

In this case, the user has typed in three numeric test grades on a single line rather than letter grades. However, because the variables are defined as character variables, the system treats the digits as characters during the read operation. Each digit within a number is seen as a separate character. Thus, the character *7* is assigned to *grade1*, the character *5* is assigned to *grade2*, and the character *9* is assigned to *grade3*. The remaining data (*2 88*) are not extracted from the stream by the three *cin* statements, but still remain in the stream buffer. Of course, any subsequent *cin* statements would extract all or part of the remaining data. The lesson to be learned here is to always use numeric variables (integer or floating-point) to read numeric data. As you can see, data can easily be corrupted when using character variables to read numeric data.

Case 5:

User types in:	97.5 73 84↵
System displays:	9
	7
	.

Again, the user has typed in three numeric test scores, which are treated as character data by the program. Thus, the first three characters are assigned, and the remaining information is left in the input stream buffer. As you can see from the echo, the character *9* is assigned to *grade1*, the character *7* is assigned to *grade2*, and the decimal point is assigned to *grade3*. Again, generating a prompt prior to each *cin* statement clearly stating how much and what type of data to be entered would prevent many of the problems encountered here.

Using *get()* To Read Single Character Data.   From the previous discussion, it is quite obvious that the >> operator ignores white space characters. There will be times, however, when you will need to read and store non-white space as well as white space characters. The *iostream* class includes a function called *get()* for this purpose. The *get()* function will extract any single character, including white space, from the input stream. It is called using the *cin* object via the following statement format:

> ### *get( ) FORMAT*
>
> *cin.get*(*character variable*);

To call the *get()* function, you follow *cin* with a dot, **.** , which is followed by the *get()* function using a character variable as its argument. When called, *get()* extracts a single character from the input stream and assigns it to the character variable listed as its argument.

In one of the cases we considered earlier using the >> operator, the user entered three grades separated by blanks, like this:

    A B C⏎

How many total characters does this place in the stream buffer? You're right if you thought six characters. There are three non-white space characters, *A, B,* and *C,* and three white space characters, two blanks and a CRLF. (Remember, even though CRLF is two characters, C++ "sees" it as a single character. To read all these characters would require six calls to *get(),* as follows:

```
cin.get(char1);
cin.get(char2);
cin.get(char3);
cin.get(char4);
cin.get(char5);
cin.get(char6);
```

Of course, this assumes that the six variables, *char1–char6,* have been defined as character variables. What do you suppose the variable assignments would be? Well, let's use a *cout* member function called *put()* to write these character variables. The *put()* function inserts a single character into the output stream and is called by the *cout* object, like this:

> ### *put( ) FORMAT*
>
> *cout.put*(*character variable*);

To display the six characters just read by *get(),* we would call *put()* six times, as follows:

```
cout.put(char1);
cout.put(char2);
cout.put(char3);
cout.put(char4);
cout.put(char5);
cout.put(char6);
```

This would display the six characters just as they were entered by the user. Thus, the output would be

A B C⏎

Of course, you would not see the CRLF character, but it would force the cursor to the next line of the display. This should be proof enough that *get()* reads white space as well as non-white space characters.

EXAMPLE 4.7

There will be times when you want to "freeze" the display for the user until he/she takes some action, such as pressing the ENTER key. This can be accomplished by inserting a call to the *get()* function into your program, along with an appropriate prompt, at the point you want to freeze the output. Write the C++ code required to accomplish this task.

Solution

```
cout << "HELLO THERE! Press the ENTER key to continue" << endl;;
cin.get();
cout << "GOOD LOOKING!" << endl;
```

With this code, the message *HELLO THERE! Press the* ENTER *key to continue* is displayed, and program execution is halted by the *cin.get()* statement until the user presses the ENTER key. The *cin.get()* statement reads the CRLF produced by the ENTER key, and program execution continues, displaying the message *GOOD LOOKING!.* Notice that there is no argument provided for *get().* This is okay, because we do not need to store the CRLF entry in a variable in this situation.

As you can see, reading only one character at a time imposes a severe limitation on entering character data. A separate variable is required for each individual character to be read. Because most real-world character information appears in the form of strings, we need a way to read string data.

Reading String Data

You will have difficulties when trying to use the *cin* object with the >> operator to read string data that contains white space. Let's see what happens when we try to do it via the following program:

```
/*
THIS PROGRAM SHOWS HOW cin READS STRING DATA
USING THE >> OPERATOR
*/

//PREPROCESSOR DIRECTIVES
#include <iostream>     //FOR cin and cout
#include <string>       //FOR string CLASS
using namespace std;    //REQUIRED WHEN INCLUDING iostream

//MAIN FUNCTION
int main()
{
  string name = " ";                        //DEFINE STRING OBJECT
  cout << "Enter your name: " << endl; //PROMPT FOR NAME
  cin >> name;                              //READ STRING
  cout << name << endl;                     //WRITE STRING

  //RETURN
  return 0;
}//END main()
```

This program defines *name* as a string object. After the definition, a prompt is generated via a *cout* statement, and *name* is read via a *cin* statement. The user input is then echoed to the display via a *cout* statement. Here's how the program works:

> User types in: `Jane Doe⏎`
> System displays: `Jane`

What happened to Jane's last name? Well, when reading *string data,* the >> operator *terminates* the read operation whenever any white space is encountered. So, the variable *name* stores only the string *Jane.*

> When reading *string data,* the **>>** operator *terminates* the read operation whenever any white space is encountered.

Thus, when the >> operator "sees" the blank between the strings *Jane* and *Doe,* it terminates the read operation. The remaining input characters are not extracted from the stream. In fact, if another *cin* statement were to follow this one, it would read Jane's last name (*Doe*), because the user has already typed in the full name, thereby placing *Doe* in the stream buffer.

There are several ways around this dilemma. One way is to define a separate string object for each whole word to be entered. In this case, you could create a *firstName* object and a *lastName* object and use two *cin >>* statements to read in the first and last names, respectively. Another way is to use a function called *getline()* available in the Standard C++ Library *string* class.

Using *getline()* to Read Strings. Another, more preferred, solution to the white space dilemma is to use a member function of the standard *string* class called *getline()*. The *getline()* function is used in place of *cin* >> to read a string containing white space. This function will allow *cin* to read the entire string, including any white space. Here's the general format:

> ### READING STRINGS WITH getline( )
>
> *getline(input stream, string object, 'delimiting character');*

> **PROGRAMMING NOTE**
>
> There is also a *getline()* function in the *iostream.h* class, which is different from the *getline()* function in the *string* class. To prevent a conflict when using the *string* class *getline()* you must include the C++ *iostream* header file for *cin* and *cout* and *not* the *iostream.h* header file. When you include the ANSI/ISO *iostream* header file, make sure you add the *using namespace std* statement after your include statements.

The *getline()* function requires up to three arguments. The first argument is the input stream that will receive the string. This will always be *cin* for keyboard input, but it will be something different for file input. More about this later. The second argument is the string object identifier. This is the name of the string object defined to store the string. Finally, the delimiting character tells the *getline()* function when to terminate the read operation. The delimiting character terminates the string entry and is *not* stored as part of the string. The delimiting character will normally be \n so that the entry will terminate when the user enters a CRLF by pressing the ENTER key. If you do not specify a delimiting character, C++ assumes \n by default.

The *getline()* function reads characters into the string object, one at a time, until the specified delimiter is encountered. Once the delimiter is encountered, the function extracts it from the input stream and discards it so that it is not stored as part of the string. If no delimiting character is specified, its value defaults to the \n (CRLF) escape sequence character. Let's look at an example program:

```
/*
THIS PROGRAM SHOWS HOW TO USE getline() TO READ
STRING DATA
*/

//PREPROCESSOR DIRECTIVES
#include <iostream>     //FOR cin AND cout
#include <string>       //FOR string CLASS

using namespace std;//REQUIRED WHEN INCLUDING iostream
```

```
//MAIN FUNCTION
int main()
{
  string name = " ";                        //DEFINE STRING OBJECT
  cout << "Enter your name: " << endl;      //PROMPT FOR NAME
  getline(cin,name);                        //READ THE STRING
  cout << name << endl;                     //DISPLAY THE STRING

  //RETURN
  return 0;
}//END main()
```

The program works like this:

> User types in: Jane Doe↵
> System displays: Jane Doe

You see here that the string now holds the entire string, including the blank between the first and last names. Also notice that no delimiting character is specified for the *getline()* function. As a result, the ENTER key (CRLF) terminates the operation. However, the CRLF (\n) character is not stored as part of the string. This character was extracted from the stream and discarded by the *getline()* function.

EXAMPLE 4.8

Write a program that will read and write the user's name and address.

Solution

Obviously, the data to be entered will be string data. So, you must define several string objects to accommodate the input strings. How must the input information be partitioned? Should you define one string object for the user's name and another for his/her address? But, what if our program needs to access just the user's zip code? It might make more sense to break up the address into several string objects that could be individually accessed. So, let's define one object to store the user's name and then define four additional objects to store the user's street, city, state, and zip code, respectively. Then we will insert individual *getline()* statements to read and write the required information. Here's the program:

```
/*
THIS PROGRAM WILL READ AND WRITE THE USER'S
NAME, ADDRESS, AND PHONE NUMBER
*/

//PREPROCESSOR DIRECTIVES
#include <iostream>  //FOR cin AND cout
#include <string>    //FOR string CLASS

using namespace std; //REQUIRED WHEN INCLUDING iostream
```

```
//MAIN FUNCTION
int main()
{
//DEFINE STRING OBJECTS
string name = " ";          //USER NAME
string street = " ";        //USER STREET
string city = " ";          //USER CITY
string state = " ";         //USER STATE ABBREVIATION
string zip = " ";           //USER ZIP

//PROMPT USER AND READ/DISPLAY NAME AND ADDRESS STRINGS
cout << "Enter your name: ";
getline(cin,name);
cout << "Enter your street address: ";
getline(cin,street);
cout << "Enter your city: ";
getline(cin,city);
cout << "Enter your state: ";
getline(cin,state);
cout << "Enter your zip code: ";
getline(cin,zip);

//DISPLAY NAME AND ADDRESS STRINGS
cout << name << endl;
cout << street << endl;
cout << city << endl;
cout << state << endl;
cout << zip << endl;

//RETURN
return 0;
} //END main()
```

First, notice that a string object has been defined for each of the required strings. Once the string objects are properly defined, the program reads each string with a separate *getline()* statement and then writes each string with a separate *cout* statement. Notice that *endl*'s were not used at the end of the prompt statements. This leaves the cursor on the same line of the prompt for the subsequent user entry.

Here is what will happen when the program is executed:

```
Enter your name: Jane M. Doe↵
Enter your street: 999 Programmer's Lane↵
Enter your city: C++ City↵
Enter your state: WY↵
Enter your zip code: 12345↵
```

System displays:

```
Jane M. Doe
999 Programmer's Lane
C++ City
WY
12345
```

A Problem When Using *getline().*   Although *getline()* will work when reading consecutive string data, you will have trouble trying to use it to read a string variable after you have used *cin* to read a character variable or a numeric variable. For instance, suppose that you read the string variable *name* after you read the integer variable *number,* like this:

```
/*
THIS PROGRAM DEMONSTRATES THE PROBLEM OF
USING cin.getline() TO READ A STRING AFTER YOU
HAVE READ A NUMERIC VARIABLE
*/

//PREPROCESSOR DIRECTIVES
#include <iostream>                  //FOR cin and cout
#include <string>                    //FOR string CLASS

using namespace std;                 //REQUIRED WHEN INCLUDING iostream

//MAIN FUNCTION
int main()
{
 //DEFINE INPUT VARIABLES AND OBJECTS
 int number = 0;                //INTEGER VARIABLE
 string name = " ";            //STRING OBJECT

 //PROMPT USER AND READ/DISPLAY INPUT DATA
 cout << "Enter an integer: "; //PROMPT USER FOR INTEGER
 cin >> number;                //READ INTEGER
 cout << number << endl;       //DISPLAY INTEGER
 cout << "Enter a name: ";     //PROMPT USER FOR STRING
 getline(cin,name);            //READ STRING
 cout << name << endl;         //DISPLAY STRING

 //RETURN
 return 0;
}//END main()
```

When this program is executed, it seems as if C++ skips over the *getline()* statement. How could this be? Assume that the user enters the number *123* after the prompt. Now, think about what the input stream must look like at this point. The user typed in the value *123* and then pressed the ENTER key to enter the value. This places the value *123* along with a CRLF in the stream buffer as shown in Figure 4.8.

Now, the *cin >> number* statement extracts the value *123* from the stream, but does not extract the CRLF character (because it is white space), and it remains in

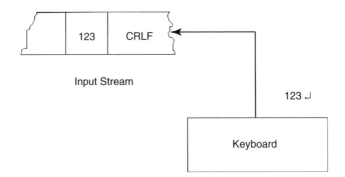

FIGURE 4.8 THE INPUT STREAM BUFFER AFTER ENTERING THE VALUE *123*.

the buffer. When the *getline(cin,name)* statement is executed, it reads the buffer and sees the CRLF character. By default, this is the delimiting character, so it reads the CRLF and terminates. Thus, the user never gets an opportunity to enter a name.

There are basically two ways around this problem. One way is to specify a different delimiting character in the *getline()* function. However, the user must enter this character to terminate the operation. This is not natural and does not make the program very user friendly.

A second method is to employ the *ws* (white space) I/O manipulator to read any white space prior to using *getline()*. The *ws* manipulator extracts any leading white space from the input stream. To use it, simply place a *cin >> ws* statement prior to the *getline()* statement in your program, like this:

```
/*
THIS PROGRAM DEMONSTRATES THE USE OF cin >> ws
TO CLEAR THE STREAM BUFFER OF WHITE SPACE
PRIOR TO USING getline() TO READ STRING DATA
*/

//PREPROCESSOR DIRECTIVES
#include <iostream>      //FOR cin and cout
#include <string>        //FOR string CLASS

using namespace std;     //REQUIRED WHEN INCLUDING iostream

//MAIN FUNCTION
int main()
{
 //DEFINE INPUT VARIABLES AND OBJECTS
 int number = 0;                  //INTEGER VARIABLE
 string name = " ";               //STRING OBJECT

 //PROMPT USER AND READ/DISPLAY INPUT DATA
 cout << "Enter an integer: "; //PROMPT USER FOR INTEGER
 cin >> number;                   //READ INTEGER
```

```
cout << number << endl;      //DISPLAY INTEGER
cout << "Enter a name: ";    //PROMPT USER FOR STRING
cin >> ws;                   //READ WHITE SPACE
getline(cin,name);           //READ STRING
cout << name << endl;        //DISPLAY STRING

//RETURN
return 0;
}//END main()
```

The statement *cin >> ws* extracts any remaining CRLF white space from the input stream buffer so that the *getline()* function does not terminate its execution prior to reading the string. The *ws* manipulator is included as part of the *iostream* header file.

PROGRAMMING TIP

Sometimes *getline()* will not wait for the user to input any data. What happens is that a CRLF character remains in the buffer from an earlier input operation. When this happens, *getline()* reads the CRLF and terminates. To avoid this problem, use the line *cin >> ws* (*ws* stands for *white space*) before the *getline()* statement. This is not required, and it is not always needed, but it never hurts anything either.

Quick Check

1. The operator that must be employed to extract data from the *cin* input stream is the _____ operator.
2. Write statements to prompt and read an integer variable called *value.*
3. Provide some examples of white space.
4. Write a statement to read a single white space character and store it in a variable called *whiteSpace.*
5. Write a statement to display the single white space character that was read in question 4.
6. True or false: When reading single-character data, *cin >>* will read only one character at a time.
7. When does the *cin* statement terminate when using the >> operator to read string data?
8. What function can be employed with *cin* to read string data, including white space?
9. Employ the *getline()* function to read a string and store it in an object called *myName.*
10. Explain why *cin >> ws* should be used prior to *getline()* when reading string data.

4.3   READING AND WRITING DISK FILES

To complete our discussion of I/O, we must discuss the basics of reading and writing disk files. At this time, it is only important that you understand how to read information into your program from a disk file and write program data to a disk file. You will learn more about manipulating disk files later, in Chapter 12. We will be processing files using the ANSI/ISO *fstream* header file. So, your compiler must be ANSI/ISO compatible to compile the code given in this section.

File Streams

In C++, all I/O is based on the concept of file streams.

> A *file stream* provides a channel for data to flow between your program and the outside world.

In particular, a file stream provides a channel for the flow of data from some source to some destination. Think about what happens when you are typing characters on the keyboard when prompted by a program. You think of the characters as flowing, or streaming, from the keyboard into the program through the input stream. Likewise, when your program generates a character display, you visualize the characters streaming from the program to the display via the output stream. C++ actually treats the keyboard and display as the default input and output files, respectively, of the system. So, what needs to be done to read and write a disk file is to create a separate file stream for the disk file and define an object for this stream. We will then use our file object to read and write the disk file just like we used the standard *cin* and *cout* objects to read from the keyboard and write to the monitor.

Classes: The Basis for C++ Files

The familiar *cin* and *cout* stream objects that you have been using in your programs for keyboard input and display output are objects of the *iostream* class. As you are aware, the *cin* and *cout* objects invoke predefined file streams. Thus, we say that *standard input* is read from the *cin stream* and *standard output* is written to the *cout stream*. When you include the *iostream.h* (or *iostream*) header file in your program, the *cin* and *cout* file streams are defined automatically. Of course, the only files that you can access conveniently with *cin* and *cout* are the keyboard and display files that are *attached* to these file streams.

When you create your own file stream for reading/writing disk files, the first thing you must do is define an object for one of the file classes: *ifstream, ofstream,* or *fstream.* These file stream classes are found in the *fstream* header file. Thus, you must include *fstream* in your program to use these classes.

File stream objects that are used exclusively for input are defined as objects of the *ifstream* class. Thus, the statement

```
ifstream fin("sample.txt");
```

defines *fin* as an input file stream object and *attaches* it to a physical disk file called *sample.txt* in the current working directory. This is called "opening a file." Your file stream object is a *logical* entity within your program, while the disk file is a *physical* entity in secondary storage. Thus, defining a file stream object opens a file which attaches, or connects, your logical file stream object to a physical disk file as illustrated by Figure 4.9.

Notice from the forgoing object definition that the physical disk file name is a string that is enclosed within parentheses after the file object name. The disk file name must adhere to the requirements of the operating system. File names such as *sample, sample.txt,* and *sample2.txt* are all legal file names for most operating systems. (*Note:* You don't have to add the *.txt* to the end of your file name, but it is recommended if using Windows so that it will open correctly when you want to view it.) You can also specify a path to locate the file. Examples of legal DOS/Windows paths might be *A:sample.txt, C:\\myDir\\sample.txt.* In the former case a drive designation is specified and in the later case, a directory path is specified for the hard drive. Notice that the C++ double backslash, \\, escape sequence must be used to separate the directory names. A single backslash will result in the file not being found. Unix does not have this requirement because the single forward slash, /, is used to separate directory names. If you do not specify a file path, C++ looks for the file in the current working directory.

When specifying DOS or Windows directory paths in C++, you must use the double backslash escape sequence, \\, and *not* the single backslash, \, to separate the directory names.

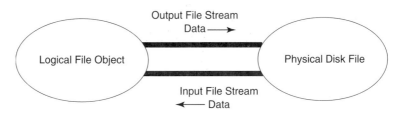

FIGURE 4.9 **THE *ifstream, ofstream,* AND *fstream* CLASSES ARE USED TO CREATE FILE STREAMS THAT ATTACH A LOGICAL PROGRAM OBJECT TO A PHYSICAL DISK FILE.**

The physical disk file name can be specified directly within double quotes (e.g., "*sample.txt*") or indirectly as a string object (e.g., *fileName*). However, the string object must call the *c_str()* function to convert the string object to a C-string. (A C-string is an array of characters and will be discussed in Chapter 9.) So, assuming that a disk file name is stored in a string object called *fileName,* the code required to open this file for input would be:

```
ifstream fin(fileName.c_str());
```

You use the *ofstream* class to define file stream objects that are used exclusively for output. Thus, the statement

```
ofstream fout("A:\\myDir\\sample.txt");
```

defines *fout* as an output file stream object and opens the *sample.txt* file located in the *myDir* directory on the *A:* drive, assuming a DOS or Windows operating system.

You can name your file objects anything you want. We have used *fin* and *fout* in the foregoing examples to be consistent with *cin* and *cout.*

Finally, you must use the *fstream* class when defining objects that will be used for both file input and output. The statement

```
fstream finout(fileName.c_str());
```

defines *finout* as both an input and output file stream object and opens the file whose name is contained in the string object *fileName.*

EXAMPLE 4.9

Write statements to open the following disk files:

a. A file stream called *read* that will read from a disk file called *myFile.txt* on the *A:* drive.

b. A file stream called *write* that will write to a disk file called *myFile.txt* in the current working directory.

c. A file stream called *readWrite* that will read and write a disk file called *myFile.txt* in a Windows hard-drive directory called *myDirectory.*

d. A file stream called *readWrite* that will read and write a disk file whose path is stored in a string object called *myFile.*

Solution

a. `ifstream read("A:myFile.txt");`

b. `ofstream write("myFile.txt");`

c. `fstream readWrite("C:\\myDirectory\\myFile.txt");`

d. `fstream readWrite(myFile.c_str());`

Processing a Disk File

Once a file is opened, it is ready for processing. By processing we mean that an input file will be read-from, an output file will be written-to, and a input/output file will be both read-from and written-to. We will process the file within an **if/else** statement like this:

```
if(!fileObject)
{
 cout << "This file cannot be opened" << endl;
 exit(1);
}
else
{
 //PROCESS THE FILE
}
```

The *if(!fileObject)* will check the file object to see if it was indeed opened without any problems. If not, the *cout* statement generates an error message and the *exit()* function exits the program. If no problems are encountered, the **else** will process the file. The **if/else** statement will be discussed in detail later, but you can see that the idea is pretty simple.

You read from a disk file using your input file stream object and the >> extraction operator, just as you do using the standard *cin* file stream object and the >> operator. For example, suppose that we have opened an input file, like this:

```
ifstream fin("sample.txt");
```

Here, the file stream object that we have created is called *fin*. To obtain a string of data from this file, all we need to do is apply the >> operator to our input object, like this:

```
fin >> fileString;
```

Of course, this statement assumes that *fileString* has been defined as a string object. Remember, however, that the >> operator will terminate when white space is encountered.

You write to a disk file using your output file stream object and the << insertion operator, just as you do using the standard *cout* file stream object and the << operator. Thus, if we open an output file object, like this:

```
ofstream fout("sample.txt");
```

we could write a string of data to this file using the statement

```
fout << fileString << endl;
```

Again, this assumes that the variable *fileString* has been defined as a string object.

EXAMPLE 4.10

Code a program to copy three strings of data from a disk file named *input.txt* to a file called *output.txt* located on the *A:* disk drive.

Solution

A file copy operation requires that we read one file and echo that input information to a second file. We will read the *input.txt* file and write to the *output.txt* file. First, we need to open two file streams. As in the past, let's call them *fin* and *fout*. Then, we will read using the *fin* file object and write using the *fout* file object. Here's the required code:

```
/*
EXAMPLE 4.10 (EX04_10.CPP)
THIS PROGRAM COPIES THREE STRINGS FROM ONE FILE TO ANOTHER
*/

//PREPROCESSOR DIRECTIVES
#include <fstream>  //FOR FILE I/O
#include <string>   //FOR string CLASS
#include <iostream> //FOR cin AND cout
#include <stdlib.h> //FOR exit()

using namespace std; //REQUIRED FOR fstream OR iostream

//MAIN FUNCTION
int main()
{
 //DEFINE STRING OBJECT
 string fileString = " ";

 //DEFINE FILE OBJECTS AND OPEN FILES
 ifstream fin("A:input.txt");   //DEFINE FILE INPUT OBJECT
 ofstream fout("A:output.txt"); //DEFINE FILE OUTPUT OBJECT

 //INPUT FILE OPEN OK? IF NOT, EXIT
 if(!fin)
 {
    cout << "The input file cannot be opened." << endl;
    exit(1);
 }//END IF

 //OUTPUT FILE OPEN OK? IF NOT, EXIT
 if(!fout)
 {
    cout << "The output file cannot be opened." << endl;
    exit(1);
```

```
}//END IF
else //STRINGS FROM INPUT FILE TO OUTPUT FILE
{
  fin >> fileString;              //READ FIRST STRING
  fout << fileString << endl; //WRITE FIRST STRING
  fin >> fileString;              //READ SECOND STRING
  fout << fileString << endl; //WRITE SECOND STRING
  fin >> fileString;              //READ THIRD STRING
  fout << fileString << endl; //WRITE THIRD STRING
}//END ELSE

//RETURN
return 0;
}//END main()
```

The first thing you should notice in this program is that the *fstream, string,* and *iostream* header files are included using the *#include* preprocessor directive. The *fstream* header file must be included in order to use the *fstream, ifstream,* and *ofstream* classes, required for file I/O. Notice that we have included *fstream* and *iostream* without the *.h* extension. This is required when using the ANSI/ISO *string* class. We have also added the *using namespace std* statement because we are including *fstream* and *iostream* without the *.h* extension. Of course, this program would not compile if your compiler is not ANSI/ISO compatible. The *string* header file must be included to use the *string* class, which is required to create a string object for reading and writing the files. Next, two file objects are defined for their respective classes and the files are opened. Notice that a path is specified to the *A:* disk drive for both files. The entire file path, including drive and folders (subdirectories) can be specified in the open statement. If no path is specified, C++ will use the current working directory to locate the files. After attempting to open the files, the file objects are tested to see if there were any problems using **if** statements. If there were, an error message is displayed. If no problems were encountered, the strings are read from the input file and written to the output file within the **else** part of the second **if** statement. The *fin >> fileString* statement reads a string of data from the *input.txt* disk file and places it in the string object called *fileString*. Of course, this assumes that the *input.txt* file has already been stored on a disk in the *A:* drive and that it contains three valid strings. Now, remember that, when reading string data, the >> operator terminates when white space is encountered. As a result, no blanks will be read as part of a given string. How can you read white space as part of a string? By using the *getline()* function in lieu of using the *cin >>* statement. The correct *getline()* statement would be *getline(fin,fileString)*. Notice that the file stream object, *fin,* is referenced rather than the *cin* keyboard stream object. The same rules apply when reading strings from a disk file using your own file stream object as when reading strings from the keyboard using the standard *cin* object.

Once a string is read, the *fout << fileString << endl* statement copies the string to the *output.txt* disk file. Notice that each output statement includes an *endl* manipulator to place a CRLF at the end of each string in the output file.

Finally, every time you open a file for output, it will erase anything that was in the file before you ran the program. Each time you run the program above, it first automatically deletes the *output.txt* file when it is opened. Reading a file does not affect the file contents. As a result, the *input.txt* file is not altered by the program, regardless of how many times it is run.

Example 4.11

Code a program that will read two integers from a file called *integers.txt* and write their sum to a file called *sum.txt*, both of which are to be stored on the *A:* drive of the system.

Solution

The major difference here is that we will be reading integer data rather than string data. Here's the solution:

```
/*
EXAMPLE 4.11 (EX04_11.CPP)
THIS PROGRAM READS TWO INTEGERS FROM ONE FILE AND WRITES
THEIR SUM TO ANOTHER FILE
*/

//PREPROCESSOR DIRECTIVES
#include <fstream>  //FOR FILE I/O
#include <iostream> //FOR cout
#include <stdlib.h> //FOR exit()

using namespace std; //REQUIRED WHEN INCLUDING fstream OR
iostream

//MAIN FUNCTION
int main()
{
 //DEFINE VARIABLES
 int integer1 = 0;       //FIRST INTEGER VARIABLE
 int integer2 = 0;       //SECOND INTEGER VARIABLE
 int sum = 0;            //SUM VARIABLE

 //DEFINE FILE OBJECTS AND OPEN FILES
 ifstream fin("A:integers.txt");     //DEFINE INPUT OBJECT
 ofstream fout("A:sum.txt");         //DEFINE OUTPUT OBJECT

 //INPUT FILE OPEN OK? IF NOT, EXIT
 if(!fin)
 {
   cout << "The input file cannot be opened" << endl;
   exit(1);
 }//END IF
 else    //READ FILE
 {
   //READ TWO INTEGERS FROM INPUT FILE
   fin >> integer1;      //READ FIRST INTEGER
   fin >> integer2;      //READ SECOND INTEGER
 }//END ELSE

 //SUM TWO INTEGERS
 sum = integer1 + integer2; //CALCULATE SUM
```

```
//OUTPUT FILE OPEN OK? IF NOT, EXIT
if(!fout)
{
   cout << "The output file cannot be opened" << endl;
   exit(1);
}//END IF
else    //WRITE FILE
{
 //WRITE SUM TO OUTPUT FILE
 fout << sum;           //WRITE SUM
}//END ELSE

//RETURN
return 0;
}//END main()
```

Here, we have defined three integer variables: two variables to store the two integer values to be read and a third variable to store their sum. The file objects are first defined and the two disk files are opened. Once the files are opened, the two integers are read from the *integers.txt* file by the *fin* object using the >> operator. Of course, this assumes that there is a valid *integers.txt* file already stored on a disk in the *A:* drive that contains two valid integers. Once the two integers are read, the sum is calculated and then written to the *sum.txt* file by the *fout* object and the << operator. That's all there is to it! Remember, once you create your own file objects for input or output and open the disk files, you simply apply all that you have learned about the standard *cin* and *cout* objects to your own input and output file objects, respectively.

Using Loops to Read and Process Files.   Although you have not studied loops yet, it is often advantageous to use a loop to read an input file so that you do not have to repeat the input statement for each data item in the file. In most cases, you will not even know how many data items are in the file. At this point, we will provide you with the code to use until Chapter 7, where you will study loops in detail.

Here's the general format for such a loop:

```
while (Read Data Item From Input File )
{ //BEGIN LOOP
     Process data item.
} //END LOOP
```

The loop says *while there is data in the input file to be read, read the data and process the data.* So, when the loop is executed, it will repeatedly read and process the file data items, one at a time, until an ***end-of-file marker*** is detected. All disk files contain an ***end-of-file marker***, called ***EOF***, to mark the end of a given file on the disk. When reading a disk file, the loop tests for the EOF marker and terminates the reading operations when it is detected.

Notice that the file read operation is placed within parentheses after the keyword **while** and the file processing operation(s) is placed within the body of the loop, which is *framed* using curly braces, {}. Let's look at an example.

EXAMPLE 4.12

Rewrite the program given in Example 4.10 to employ a loop to copy the *input.txt* file to the *output.txt* file.

Solution

Here's the revised code using a loop:

```
/*
EXAMPLE 4.12 (EX04_12.CPP)
THIS PROGRAM COPIES THREE STRINGS FROM ONE FILE TO ANOTHER
*/

//PREPROCESSOR DIRECTIVES
#include <fstream>  //FOR FILE I/O
#include <string>   //FOR string CLASS
#include <iostream> //FOR cin AND cout
#include <stdlib.h> //FOR exit()

using namespace std; //REQUIRED FOR fstream OR iostream

//MAIN FUNCTION
int main()
{
 //DEFINE STRING OBJECT
 string fileString = " ";

 //DEFINE FILE OBJECTS AND OPEN FILES
 ifstream fin("A:input.txt");    //DEFINE FILE INPUT OBJECT
 ofstream fout("A:output.txt"); //DEFINE FILE OUTPUT OBJECT

 //INPUT FILE OPEN OK? IF NOT, EXIT
 if(!fin)
 {
    cout << "The input file cannot be opened." << endl;
    exit(1);
 }//END IF

 //OUTPUT FILE OPEN OK? IF NOT, EXIT
 if(!fout)
 {
    cout << "The output file cannot be opened." << endl;
    exit(1);
```

```
}//END IF
else //LOOP TO COPY FILE DATA
{
    while(fin >> fileString) //READ STRING AND TEST FOR EOF
    {
        fout << fileString << endl; //WRITE STRING
    }//END WHILE
}//END ELSE

//RETURN
return 0;
} //END main()
```

Notice that the file read operation is placed within the loop as well as the file write operation. This is because we are simply reading a data item from the input file and echoing it to the output file as our processing operation. The loop will repeatedly read a string from the input file, then write the string to the output file until an end-of-file, EOF, marker is detected within the input file.

An advantage to using such a loop to read a file is that you often do not know how many data items a file contains. By using a loop, you do not need to know how many data items are in the file, because the loop will continue to read the file until the end of the file is reached.

There is much more to learn about file processing. For example, how can data within a file be appended or changed? These issues are too complex to deal with at

Quick Check

1. Which header file must be included to read/write disk files?
2. The class used to define input file objects is the _____ class.
3. The class used to define output file objects is the _____ class.
4. How do you test to see if there were any problems opening a file?
5. Write a statement to open a disk file in the current working directory called *data.txt* for processing by an input file object called *myInput*.
6. Write a statement to open a disk file stored on a disk in the *A:* drive called *results.txt* for processing by an output file object called *myResults*.
7. Assume that the file called *data.txt* in question 5 contains an unknown number of integers. Write the code required to read each integer in the file, multiply it by 10, and write the product to the *results.txt* file in question 6.
8. Combine all your answers to the preceding questions into a single C++ program that will accomplish the file processing tasks indicated.

this point, but are covered in Chapter 12 after you have the necessary background to deal with them. For now, you have enough information to perform simple read/write operations on files.

PROBLEM SOLVING IN ACTION: USER-FRIENDLY PROGRAMS

PROBLEM

As an overall program summary to the material presented in this chapter, let's write a user-friendly program that will calculate the monthly payment for an installment loan from different values of principle, interest rate, and term entered by the user. We will format a four-column table for principle, interest rate, term, and payment and underscore each column heading. Thus, the final program output will be a table showing the loan principle, interest rate, term, and monthly payment. In addition, we will display the program user's name and the date the program was run.

Let's first define the problem in terms of output, input, and processing as follows.

Defining the Problem

Output: The final program output must be a table showing the calculated monthly loan payment along with the loan principle, interest rate, and term used in the calculation. The user's name and date the program was run will be displayed above the table. In addition, user prompts should be provided on the monitor to direct the user to enter the required values.

Input: The input must be the user's name, date the program was run, and values for the loan principle, interest rate, and term.

Processing: $payment = principle * rate/(1 - (1+rate)^{-term})$
                where: *principle* is the amount of the loan.
                         rate is a monthly interest rate in decimal form.
                         term is the number of months of the loan.

Planning the Solution

The next step is to construct a set of algorithms from the problem definition. Now, try to identify the separate tasks that must be performed to solve the problem. First, the program must obtain the required data from the user. Once the data are entered, the program must calculate the payment. Finally, the program must display the results. Thus, we can identify three program tasks, or functions, as follows:

❑ Obtain the user's name, date of program run, loan principle, interest rate, and term from the user.

PROGRAMMING TIP

You must always strive to make your programs as user-friendly as possible. By a user-friendly program, we mean a program that is easy to use and does not confuse the user. Such a program should always include the following (at a minimum):

1. A program description message that tells the user what the program is going to do.
2. Prompting messages prior to any read operations. These user prompts must tell the user what information to enter and how to enter it in clear, unconfusing terms.
3. Output information that is well formatted and whose meaning is easily understood by the user.

❏ Calculate the monthly payment using the equation

$payment = principle * rate/(1 - (1+rate)^{-term})$

❏ Display the user's name, date the program was run, and table of results.

The problem solving diagram in Figure 4.10 shows the structure required for the program.

Because we are using the modular technique to design the program, we must employ stepwise refinement to develop the algorithms. The initial algorithm level, *main()*, will simply reflect the problem definition and call the individual subprogram functions, as follows:

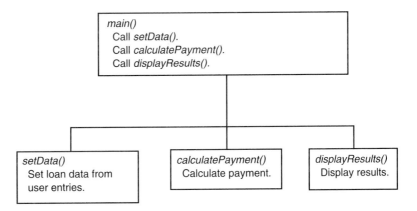

FIGURE 4.10   A PROBLEM-SOLVING DIAGRAM FOR LOAN PROBLEM.

Initial Algorithm

main()
BEGIN
    Call function to obtain the input data from the user.
    Call function to calculate the loan payment.
    Call function to display the results.
END.

The first level of refinement requires that we show a detailed algorithm for each subprogram module, or function. They are as follows:

First Level of Refinement

setData()
BEGIN
    Write a user prompt to enter the user's name.
    Read *name*.
    Write a user prompt to enter the date.
    Read *date*.
    Write a user prompt to enter the loan principle, or amount.
    Read *principle*.
    Write a user prompt to enter the annual interest rate of the loan.
    Read *rate*.
    Write a user prompt to enter the term of the loan, in months.
    Read *term*.
END.

calculatePayment()
BEGIN
    Calculate *decRate = rate/12/100*.
    Calculate *payment = principle * decRate/(1 − (1+decRate)$^{-term}$)*.
END.

displayResults()
BEGIN
    Display user's name and date of program run.
    Display table headings for principle, rate, term, and payment.
    Display the principle, rate, term, and payment values under the respective headings.
END.

Notice that *rate* is converted to a monthly value in decimal form. Why? Because the user entry is an annual value in percentage form; however, the payment calculation formula requires a monthly value in decimal form.

Coding the Program

Here is how the foregoing algorithms are translated into C++ code using a flat implementation:

```
/*
ACTION 4-1 (ACT04_01.CPP)
OUTPUT:      A TABLE MENU SHOWS THE LOAN AMOUNT, INTEREST,
             TERM, AND MONTHLY PAYMENT.
             USER PROMPTS AS NECESSARY.

INPUT:       LOAN AMOUNT, INTEREST RATE, AND TERM.

PROCESSING:  PAYMENT = PRINCIPLE * RATE/1-(1+RATE) -TERM

WHERE:       PRINCIPLE IS THE AMOUNT OF THE LOAN.
             RATE IS A MONTHLY INTEREST RATE IN DECIMAL
             FORM.
             TERM IS THE NUMBER OF MONTHS OF THE LOAN.
*/

//PREPROCESSOR DIRECTIVES
#include <iostream>      //FOR cin and cout
#include <string>        //FOR string CLASS
#include <math.h>        //FOR pow()

using namespace std;     //REQUIRED WHEN INCLUDING iostream

//MAIN FUNCTION
int main()
{
 //DEFINE AND INITIALIZE OBJECTS AND VARIABLES
 string name = " ";      //CUSTOMER NAME
 string date = " ";      //DATE OF REPORT
 double principle = 0.0; //LOAN PRINCIPLE
 int term = 0;           //TERM OF LOAN IN MONTHS
 double rate = 0.0;      //ANNUAL INTEREST IN PERCENT FORM
 double payment = 0.0;   //MONTHLY PAYMENT
 double decRate = 0.0;   //MONTHLY INTEREST IN DECIMAL FORM

 //DISPLAY PROGRAM DESCRIPTION MESSAGE
 cout << "\nThis program will calculate a monthly loan interest"
      << "\npayment, total loan interest, and total loan amount."
      << endl;
 //setData ()FUNCTION: SET VARIABLES TO DATA ENTERED BY USER
 cout << "\nPlease enter your name: ";
 cin >> ws;
 getline(cin,name);
 cout << "\nEnter the date in XX/XX/XX format: ";
 cin >> ws;
 getline(cin,date);
 cout << "\nEnter the amount of the loan: $";
 cin >> principle;
 cout << "\nEnter the duration of the loan in months: ";
 cin >> term;
 cout << "\nEnter the annual interest rate in percent: ";
 cin >> rate;
```

```
//calculatePayment() FUNCTION
decRate = rate/12/100;
payment = principle * decRate/(1-pow((1+decRate),-term));

//displayResults() FUNCTION
cout.setf(ios::fixed);
cout.setf(ios::showpoint);
cout.precision(2);
cout << endl << endl;
cout << "Name: " << name << endl;
cout << "Date: " << date << endl;
cout << "\n\n"
        << "LOAN AMOUNT"
        << "\tINTEREST RATE"
        << "\t\tTERM"
        << "\t\tPAYMENT" << endl;
cout << "-----------"
        << "\t-------------"
        << "\t\t----"
        << "\t\t-------" << endl;
cout << "$" << principle
        << "\t" << rate << "%"
        << "\t\t\t" << term << " Months"
        << "\t$" << payment << endl;

//RETURN
return 0;
}//END main()
```

Here is a sample of what the user would see when executing the program.

```
This program will calculate a monthly loan interest
payment, total loan interest, and total loan amount.

Please enter your name: Andrew C. Staugaard, Jr. ⏎
Enter the date in XX/XX/XX format: 05/25/99⏎

Enter the amount of the loan: $1000.00⏎
Enter the duration of the loan in months: 12⏎
Enter the annual interest rate in percent: 12⏎

Name: Andrew C. Staugaard, Jr.
Date: 05/25/99

LOAN AMOUNT   INTEREST RATE   TERM        PAYMENT
-----------   -------------   ---------   -------
      $1000           12.0%   12 Months   $88.85
```

Compare the program code to the corresponding output seen by the user. Make an effort to look at each of the coding details. You should pay particular attention to the following:

❑ The way in which the prompts are generated using *cout* without using *endl* so that the user's entry appears on the same line as the prompt.

❑ The assignment of the keyboard entry to a variable via *cin* and *getline()*.

❑ The conversion of the annual percentage rate entered by the user to a monthly decimal rate required by the payment formula.

❑ The payment calculation which uses a standard *pow()* function to raise *(1 + decRate)* to the *–term* power. More about this in the next chapter. However, notice that the *math.h* header file was included in the preprocessor section of the program to obtain this function.

❑ The formatting calls to *setf()* and *precision()*.

❑ The output table formatting using the \n and \t escape sequence characters. (*Note:* It is often a job of trial-and-error to finetune the output to get what you want.)

❑ The strategic placement of the % and $ symbols when required for clarity.

You now should have no trouble understanding this program with the material presented in this chapter. Now, make a serious effort to complete all of the questions and problems that follow. It is time to get your hands dirty and program your system to apply the program exercises that follow. This is where you will really begin learning how to program in C++.

CHAPTER SUMMARY

Getting information into your system is called *reading,* and getting information out of your system is called *writing.* The C++ statement used for reading is the *cin* statement or *getline()* function, and the statement used for writing is the *cout* statement.

Each *cout* statement must include a listing of the items to be written. The items in the listing must be separated by the << stream insertion operator. The *cout* statement can be used to write either fixed or variable information. Fixed numeric information is written by simply listing the numeric values within the *cout* item listing. When writing fixed character information, the information to be written must be enclosed within single quotes for single characters and double quotes for strings. When writing variable information, the variable identifier must be listed within the *cout* statement. To format an output, you must often include an I/O manipulator or escape sequence in the item listing. As an example, the *setw()* field-width manipulator must be included prior to the item to be written to adjust the item field width. The field-width manipulator value specifies the number of columns of output that will be allocated to the item being written. You must include the *iomanip.h* or *iomanip* file when using the *setw()* I/O manipulator. Examples of common escape sequence characters are \n (CRLF) and \t (tab). These characters are inserted into the output stream as single characters or as part of a string as needed. Finally, you should always use a layout chart to lay out your output and determine the correct field-width values.

For reading data in C++ you employ the *cin* input stream object or the *getline()* function. Like *cout*, *cin* is a predefined file stream object in C++. The *cin* statement must include a variable(s) to be read. Any variable listed within the *cin* statement must be defined prior to its use in the program. Moreover, the type of data entered for a given variable should match the data type defined for that variable. The >> stream extraction operator is used within the *cin* statement to extract data from the input stream and assign these data to the variable(s) listed in the *cin* statement. When reading single-character data, the >> operator ignores white space. However, you can call the *get()* function with *cin* to read single-character white space data.

When reading string data, the >> operator will terminate on white space. As a result, you should use the *getline()* function when reading strings. When using *getline()*, you must discard the CRLF remaining in the keyboard buffer from a prior read operation. To accomplish this, you can use a different delimiting character for *getline()* or the *ws* manipulator.

All program I/O is supported by files that operate on predefined classes in C++. For accessing disk files, you must use one of three classes: *ifstream, ofstream,* or *fstream,* all of which are located in the *fstream* header file. The *ifstream* class is used to perform input, or read, operations from disk files, the *ofstream* class is used to perform output, or write, operations to disk files, and the *fstream* class can be used to perform both read and write operations on disk files. These classes are used to define file objects and open disk files by attaching the logical file object to a physical disk file.

All disk files contain an *end-of-file marker,* called *EOF,* to mark the end of a given file on the disk. When reading a disk file, we use a read operation within a loop to instruct the compiler to look for the EOF marker and terminate the reading operations when it is detected.

User-friendly programs require interaction between the program and the user. At a minimum, a user-friendly program must do the following:

❏ Write a program description message to the user.

❏ Prompt the user prior to any read operations.

❏ Generate well-formatted outputs whose meanings are easily understood by the user.

QUESTIONS AND PROBLEMS

QUESTIONS

1. Indicate the output for each of the following:

a. `cout << "\n\n" << endl;`
b. `cout << setw(40) << "HELLO" << endl;`
c. `cout << setw(12) << -36.2 << endl;`
d. `cout << 3.75 << endl;`
e. `cout << '\n' << 1 << '\t' << 2 << '\t' << 3 << '\t' << 4 << endl;`
f. `cout << setw(20) << "My test score is: 97.6/n/n " << endl;`
g. `cout <<"\n\t\tTEST SCORE\t\t97.5" << endl;`
h. `cout <<"\n\t\tTEST SCORE\n\t\t97.5" << endl;`

2. Suppose that you define a constant as follows:

```
const char SPACE = ' ';
```

What will the following statement do?

```
cout << '\n' << setw(20) << SPACE << "HELLO" << endl;
```

3. What will the following statement do?

```
cout << '\n' << setw(20) << ' ' << "HELLO" << endl;
```

4. What is the difference between the output produced by the following two statements?

```
cout << "\n#\n#\n#" << endl;
cout << "\n###" << endl;
```

5. Consider the following program segment:

```
char a = ' ';
char b = ' ';
cin >> a;
cin >> b;
cout << a << b << endl;
```

What will be displayed for each of the following user entries?

   a. A
      B
   b. AB
   c. 3.14
   d. A B   (*Note:* There is a space between the *A* and the *B*.)

6. What header file must be included in order to use the *setw()* field-width manipulator?

7. What function must be used to obtain string data that includes white space?

8. Define an appropriate object and write statements to read and then display your school name. Make provision to include white space in your school name.

9. True or false: The *cin* object is used for reading disk files as well as keyboard data.

10. True or false: The *getline()* function stores the delimiting character as part of the string.

11. The default delimiting character for the *getline()* function is the _____ character.

12. At a minimum, what arguments must be provided when using *getline()* to read string data?

13. What is the relationship between *iostream, cin*, and *getline()?*

14. Write the code necessary to display the contents of a variable called *profit* in proper currency format.

15. Write the code necessary to force all subsequent output to be left justified.

16. Write the code necessary to undo the left justification specified in question 15.

17. True or false: C++ treats the two CR and LF characters as a single character within an input or output stream.

18. True or false: White space is discarded before it enters the *cin* stream.

19. Why is *getline()* unsafe for reading string data after it is used to read numeric or single character data?

20. Describe a method for solving the *getline()* problem referred to in question 19.

21. Write the code necessary to obtain a decimal output with three decimal places to the right of the decimal point.

22. What is a file stream?

23. Write statements to open the following disk file stream objects:
    a. A file stream called *fileIn* that will read a disk file called *myData.txt* located in the current working directory.
    b. A file stream called *fileOut* that will write to a file whose name is stored in a string called *fileName* located in the current working directory.

24. Why is it advantageous to use loops when reading and processing a disk file?

25. What should you do in order to make a program more user-friendly?

PROBLEMS

Least Difficult

1. Using the layout chart in Figure 4.3, write a program to display your first name in the middle of the monitor screen.

2. Using the layout chart in Figure 4.3, write a program to display your first name in the upper left-hand corner of the display using characters that are six lines high.

3. Write a program that will generate a rectangle whose center is located in the middle of the display. Construct the rectangle 8 lines high and 20 columns wide using X's.

4. Write a program that will generate the following output in the middle of the display:

```
STUDENT        SEMESTER AVERAGE
-------        ----------------
   1                 84.5
   2                 67.2
   3                 77.4
   4                 86.8
   5                 94.7
```

More Difficult

In the problems that follow, you will need to employ several arithmetic operations. In C++, a plus symbol (+) is used for addition, a minus symbol (−) is used for subtraction, a star symbol (*) is used for multiplication, and a slash symbol (/) is used for division.

5. Write a program to calculate simple interest on a $2000 loan for 2 years at a rate of 12.5 percent. Format your output appropriately, showing the amount of the loan, time period, interest rate, and interest amount. (*Note*: Set the *ios::showpoint* flag to assure proper dollars and cents format for currency output.)

6. Write a program that will prompt the user to enter any four-letter word. Then display the word backwards. (Keep it clean!)

7. Electrical power in a direct-current (dc) circuit is defined as the product of voltage and current. In symbols, *power = voltage × current.* Write a program to calculate dc power from a voltage value of 12 volts and a current value of 0.00125 ampere. Generate a tabular display of input and output values in decimal form.

8. Write a program that employs a loop to read a character file called *lowcase.txt* consisting of all lowercase characters. Convert the lowercase characters to uppercase by subtracting 32 from each character, and write the uppercase characters to a file called *upcase.txt*. (*Note*: You must create the *lowcase.txt* file using your ASCII text editor.)

9. Write a user-friendly program that will calculate power from voltage and current values entered by the user. In symbols, *power = voltage × current*. Generate a tabular display of input and output values in decimal form.

10. The rumor mill at the CPP∗Mart super-center is saying that employees are about to get a 5.5 percent raise. Write a user-friendly program for the employees that will allow them to determine their new annual as well as monthly gross salary if the rumor is true. Assume that the user will enter his/her current monthly salary. (*Note:* Set the *ios::showpoint* flag to assure proper dollars and cents format for currency output.)

Most Difficult

11. Write a user-friendly program that will calculate the weekly gross pay amount for an employee, given his/her rate of pay and number of hours worked. Assume the employee is part-time and, therefore, works less than 40 hours per week. Generate a display showing the employee's name, rate of pay, hours worked, and gross pay. Provide the appropriate display headings.

12. Write a user-friendly program to calculate the circumference and area of a circle from a user's entry of its radius. Generate a tabular display showing the circle's radius, circumference, and area. (*Note:* Circumference of a circle is calculated using the equation $2 \times pi \times r$ and the area of a circle is calculated using the equation $pi \times r^2$.)

13. Write a user-friendly program that will allow a student to calculate his/her test average from four test scores. Generate a display of the student's name, course name, individual test scores, and test average.

14. The "4 Squares" bowling team has four bowlers. On a given bowling night, each team member bowls three games. Write a program that will read the date, each bowler's name, and the individual game scores for each bowler. Using the input information, display a bowling report. The report should show the date at the top of the screen, and then a table showing each bowler's scores, total, and integer average.

15. Write a user-friendly program that will calculate the equivalent resistance of a series circuit from five resistances entered by the user. Generate a tabular display of input and output values in decimal form. (*Note:* The equivalent resistance of a series circuit is found by summing the individual resistances.)

16. Write a user-friendly program that will calculate the equivalent resistance from two parallel resistances entered by the user. Generate a tabular display of input and output values in decimal form. Use the following product over sum rule to calculate the equivalent resistance value:

$$R_{equiv} = (R_1 \times R_2) / (R_1 + R_2)$$

Observe the use of parentheses to group the quantities in this equation. Why do you suppose this is necessary?

17. Write a user-friendly program to act as an electronic cash register. The program must display a receipt showing four sales items, their price, a subtotal of the four sales items, the sales tax at a rate of 7 percent, the total amount due, the amount tendered, and the amount of change returned.

Example Output:

Fish Hooks	$1.29
Sinkers	$.98
Line	$7.45
Worms	$2.00
Subtotal	$11.72
Sales Tax	$.82
Total	$12.54
Amount Tendered	$20.00
Change	$7.46

GUI 101: Simple Windows I/O

Purpose
- To become familiar with general window behavior.
- To work with a C++ windows template.
- To understand event-driven programs.
- To introduce the OOP concept of behavior.
- To introduce the OOP concept of inheritance.
- To become familiar with message boxes and the *MessageBox()* function.
- To become familiar with text lines and the *TextOut()* function.
- To become familiar with simple character input.

INTRODUCTION

*A **graphical user interface**, or **GUI**,* is a window-based program whereby input and output are handled via ***graphical components.*** Components include message boxes, menus, buttons, checkboxes, text fields, and radio buttons, just to mention a few. Windowed programs are event-driven programs, whereby the flow of the program logic is dictated by events. These events usually are the result of a mouse action, such a clicking or movement, or a keyboard stroke.

In this module you will be acquainted with the topic of graphical user interfaces, or GUIs. This module will familiarize you with the C++ code that is required to generate a window and some simple GUI components. You will be asked to load a given program, execute the program, and exercise the GUI. In some cases, you will be asked to modify the program code and observe the effect on the GUI and its components. Don't worry about how to design your own GUIs yet—this is a topic for an advanced course in C++. For now, it is only important that you get acquainted with GUIs in general along with some GUI terminology and behavior. Of course, we hope you have some fun doing it.

All the code for this and succeeding C++ programs was developed with Visual C++, version 6.0, and might not compile with another compiler. At this time, you might want to go to Appendix C and familiarize yourself with this compiler, if you have not already done so. The prewritten C++ programs that you will use can be copied from the text CD or downloaded from the text Web site. (*Note:* You must disable the read-only file attribute in order to edit files copied from the text CD or downloaded from the text Web site).

PROCEDURE

1. Create a new *empty* "Win32 Application" project in Visual C++ (see Appendix C for instructions). Name the project *GUI101*. Once your application workspace has been created, add a file to the project and call it *GUI101.cpp*. Type in the following code for the *GUI101.cpp* file. You can copy the *GUI101.cpp* file from the text CD, or, if you are connected to the Internet, you can download the file *GUI101.cpp* from the text Web site and insert it into your workspace. If you type it in, you will have to type it exactly as it is shown.

```
/*
GUI101.CPP
THIS IS A WINDOW TEMPLATE THAT YOU WILL USE TO EXPERIMENT
WITH WINDOWS PROGRAMMING
*/


//PREPROCESSOR DIRECTIVES
#include <windows.h>

/*                              A                              */
/* * * * * * * * * * * * * * * * * * * * * * * * * * * * * * * * * * * */   Data Types
/*                 INSERT YOUR CONSTANTS HERE                  */

/* * * * * * * * * * * * * * * * * * * * * * * * * * * * * * * * * * * */
LRESULT CALLBACK WndProc(HWND, UINT, WPARAM, LPARAM);

int WINAPI WinMain(HINSTANCE hInstance, HINSTANCE
hPrevInstance, PSTR szCmdLine, int iCmdShow)
{
/*                              B                              */
/* * * * * * * * * * * * * * * * * * * * * * * * * * * * * * * * * * * */   Title Bar

   static TCHAR szAppName[]=TEXT("GUI101");

/* * * * * * * * * * * * * * * * * * * * * * * * * * * * * * * * * * * */
   HWND hwnd;
   MSG msg;
   WNDCLASS wndclass;

   wndclass.style=CS_HREDRAW|CS_VREDRAW;
   wndclass.lpfnWndProc=WndProc;
   wndclass.cbClsExtra=0;
   wndclass.cbWndExtra=0;
   wndclass.hInstance=hInstance;
   wndclass.hIcon=LoadIcon(NULL, IDI_APPLICATION);
   wndclass.hCursor=LoadCursor(NULL, IDC_ARROW);
      wndclass.hbrBackground=(HBRUSH)
      GetStockObject(WHITE_BRUSH);
   wndclass.lpszMenuName=NULL;
   wndclass.lpszClassName=szAppName;
```

```
    if(!RegisterClass(&wndclass))
    {
      MessageBox(NULL,TEXT("This program requires Windows NT!"),
               szAppName,MB_ICONERROR);
        return 0;
    }//END IF

    hwnd=CreateWindow(     szAppName,

/*                              C                            */
/***********************************************************/

                TEXT("GUI101"),

/***********************************************************/
                WS_OVERLAPPEDWINDOW,
                CW_USEDEFAULT,
                CW_USEDEFAULT,
                CW_USEDEFAULT,
                CW_USEDEFAULT,
                NULL,
                NULL,
                hInstance,
                NULL);

    ShowWindow(hwnd, iCmdShow);
    UpdateWindow(hwnd);

    while(GetMessage(&msg, NULL, 0, 0))
    {
     TranslateMessage(&msg);
     DispatchMessage(&msg);
    }//END WHILE

    return msg.wParam;
}//END WinMain()

LRESULT CALLBACK WndProc(HWND hwnd, UINT message,
                        WPARAM wParam, LPARAM lParam)
{
 HDC hdc;
 PAINTSTRUCT ps;
 RECT rect;

/*                              D                            */
/***********************************************************/
/*              INSERT YOUR VARIABLES HERE                  */

/***********************************************************/
```

```
switch(message)
{
case WM_CREATE:

 /*                              E                              */
 /* * * * * * * * * * * * * * * * * * * * * * * * * * * * * * * */
 /* INSERT CODE BETWEEN THE LINES BELOW */
 /* * * * * * * * * * * * * * * * * * * * * * * * * * * * * * * */


 /* * * * * * * * * * * * * * * * * * * * * * * * * * * * * * * */

          return 0;

     case WM_PAINT:
         hdc=BeginPaint(hwnd, &ps);

         GetClientRect(hwnd, &rect);

 /*                              F                              */
 /* * * * * * * * * * * * * * * * * * * * * * * * * * * * * * * */
 /* INSERT CODE BETWEEN THE LINES BELOW                        */
 /* * * * * * * * * * * * * * * * * * * * * * * * * * * * * * * */


 /* * * * * * * * * * * * * * * * * * * * * * * * * * * * * * * */
         EndPaint(hwnd, &ps);
         return 0;
 /*                              G                              */
 /* * * * * * * * * * * * * * * * * * * * * * * * * * * * * * * */
 /*         ADD OTHER CASES BETWEEN THE LINES BELOW            */
 /* * * * * * * * * * * * * * * * * * * * * * * * * * * * * * * */


 /* * * * * * * * * * * * * * * * * * * * * * * * * * * * * * * */
     case WM_DESTROY:
         PostQuitMessage(0);
         return 0;
     }//END SWITCH

     return DefWindowProc(hwnd, message, wParam, lParam);
     }//END WndProc
```

PROCEDURE (*CONTINUED*)

2. Compile the program. Find and correct any syntax errors that you might have created if you typed-in the program. You will probably have to try to compile it several times to work out any typos you might have made.

3. Run the program and you should observe the window shown in Figure 1.

4. Resize the window by grabbing and moving the window borders.

5. Click the button in the upper left-hand corner. A drop-down control menu should appear. Exercise the control menu by selecting the various menu items.

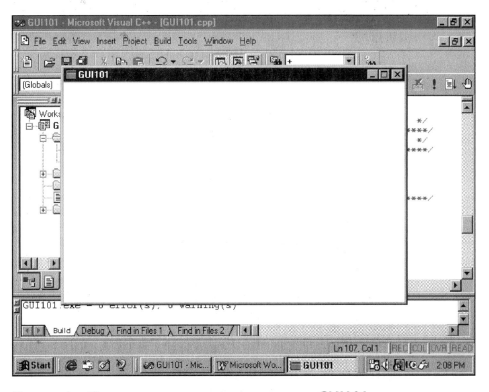

FIGURE 1   THE WINDOW GENERATED BY THE _GUI101.CPP_ PROGRAM IN A WINDOWS ENVIRONMENT.

6. Exercise the maximize and minimize buttons in the upper right-hand corner.

7. Click the close button (**X**) to close the window. You will now have to run the program again to get the window back.

8. Run the program again and see if you can identify the following components of the GUI:
   ❏ Title bar
   ❏ Title
   ❏ Control button and associated menu
   ❏ Maximize button
   ❏ Minimize button
   ❏ Restore button
   ❏ Close button

DISCUSSION

The window that you just exercised contains most of the basic components required for any window GUI. You observed a standard window that contained a title bar with title and window borders just like any other window. The window could be maximized, minimized, resized, and closed. These features provide the window **_behavior_** and are common to all windows. Any GUI we create will _inherit_ this basic look and behavior. One of the cornerstones of OOP is ***inheritance***. You inherit things, like standard window features, from other things that have already been developed. As a result, you do not have to reinvent the wheel. Through inheritance you can now use this template as the basis for all of your windows programs, so you will not have to type it in again.

PROCEDURE (*CONTINUED*)

9. You have probably seen ***message boxes*** before. Message boxes are those annoying little windows that pop up, usually with an error message of some kind. You have to click a button (e.g., *OK* or *Cancel*) to make it go away. You can put a message box at any place in your code using the *MessageBox()* function. For starters lets put it at point **E** in the windows program template. Close the *GUI101* window if you have not already done so. Then, type the following code at point **E** in the template:

```
MessageBox(hwnd,
          TEXT("This is the message that appears in"
              "the message box window"),
          TEXT("Message Title"),MB_OK);
```

10. Compile and run the program and you should observe the message box shown in Figure 2. Notice that the string within the first call to function *TEXT()* in the above code appears as the message within the box. The string within the second call to function *TEXT()* is the title that shows at the top of the message box.

11. Click *OK* in the message box and notice that our *GUI101* window opens.

12. Close the *GUI101* window.

13. Change the string argument values within the *TEXT()* function call. Run the program again, and notice that your message box reflects the changes.

14. Click the *OK* button and close the *GUI101* window.

15. The most interesting part of the *MessageBox()* function is the last argument in the function call. In the foregoing code, we sent the argument *MB_OK* to the function, so the message box only displayed one ***button*** labeled *OK*. We could have sent any of the following arguments to change the button label:

```
MB_OKCANCEL
MB_ABORTRETRYIGNORE
MB_YESNOCANCEL
MB_YESNO
MB_RETRYCANCEL
```

Try putting each of these as the last argument within the *MessageBox()* function in place of *MB_OK*. Run the program each time and watch what happens. Notice how the buttons and their labels change. Click on any of the buttons and notice that all the buttons have the same effect even though they say different things. In a more complex program, we may take different actions depending on which button is clicked. This is ***event -driven*** programming, since the program action depends of which event is generated through a mouse click.

16. Click a button and close the *GUI101* window.

17. You may have noticed that the left-most button is always the *default button*. In other words, when the message box appears, the button furthest to the left has a bold out-

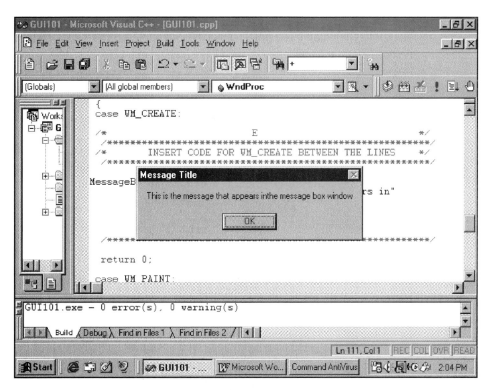

**FIGURE 2   THE MESSAGE BOX GENERATED BY THE *GUI101.CPP*
PROGRAM USING THE *MESSAGEBOX()* FUNCTION.**

line, and hitting the ENTER key or the space bar is equivalent to clicking on the button.
You can change that by adding a "|" and one of the following specifications to the button argument:

```
MB_DEFBUTTON1
MB_DEFBUTTON2
MB_DEFBUTTON3
```

If you don't add any of these specifications, then MB_DEFBUTTON1 is assumed
(i.e., the left-most button is the default). If you create a message box with two or three
buttons, then MB_DEFBUTTON2 will make the second button from the left the default button. Of course, to use MB_DEFBUTTON3, you need to create a message
box that has three buttons, and the right-most button will be the default. For example,
replace the last argument in the *MessageBox()* function with the following code:

```
MB_ABORTRETRYIGNORE|MB_DEFBUTTON3
```

18. Compile and run the program and notice that the *Abort, Retry,* and *Ignore* buttons appear where the *Ignore* button is the default.

19. Click a button and close the *GUI101* window.

20. There is one more thing you can do to customize a message box. Using the same
method that you are able to change the default button, you add an ***icon,*** or small
graphic, to the message box. Here are your choices (the ones that appear on the same
line are actually different names for the same icon):

```
MB_ICONHAND or MB_ICONERROR or MB_ICONSTOP
MB_ICONQUESTION
MB_ICONEXCLAMAION or MB_ICONWARNING
MB_ICONASTERISK or MB_ICONINFORMATION
```

For example, replace the last argument in the *MessageBox()* function with the following code:

```
MB_ABORTRETRYIGNORE|MB_DEFBUTTON3|MB_ICONQUESTION
```

21. Compile and run the program again and notice that a question mark icon appears within the message box. Also, the *Ignore* button is the default. Why?

22. Click a button and close the *GUI101* window.

23. Now, try creating your own message boxes using the *MessageBox()* function. Here are a few that you can try. Can you predict what they will do?

```
MessageBox(hwnd,
           TEXT("This is some information."),
           TEXT("Important Information"),
           MB_OK|MB_ICONINFORMATION);

MessageBox(hwnd,
           TEXT("How about this question?"),
           TEXT("Question"),
           MB_YESNO|MB_DEFBUTTON2|MB_ICONQUESTION);

MessageBox(hwnd,
           TEXT("LOOK OUT!!!!!"),
           TEXT("Oops"),
           MB_ABORTRETRYIGNORE|MB_DEFBUTTON2|MB_ICONERROR);
```

DISCUSSION

A message box is just what it says it is—a box that generates a message. The box has a title in the title bar at the top of the box window and a message within the window. In addition, the box includes one or more buttons that can be clicked to activate some other process. Message boxes are created using the *MessageBox()* function. The function allows for arguments that set the following attributes of the box:

Box title

Box message

Box buttons

Default button

Special icons

That's about the extent of message boxes. They are limited to popup messages. The next windows output function, *TextOut()*, can do much more.

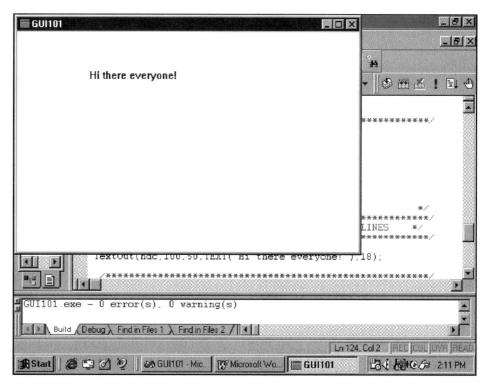

FIGURE 3   A LINE OF TEXT GENERATED BY THE *GUI101.CPP* **PROGRAM USING THE** *TextOut()* **FUNCTION.**

PROCEDURE (*CONTINUED*)

24. Close the *GUI101* window if you have not already done so.

25. The next function you will experiment with is the *TextOut()* function. Remove any *MessageBox()* statements from section **E** of the *GUI101* template and place the following statement in section **F** of the template.

```
TextOut(hdc,100,50,TEXT("Hi there everyone!"),18);
```

26. Compile and run the program and you should see a message within a window as shown in Figure 3.

DISCUSSION

The first argument sent to *TextOut()* is simply *hdc.* Just think of this as a requirement without worrying about what it means for now. The second argument, called the *x argument,* is the number of *pixels,* or picture elements, that the output string will be displaced from the left side of the window. The third argument, or *y argument,* is the number of pixels that the output string will be displaced from the top of the window. Most PC monitors support a screen size of 640 × 480 pixels. This

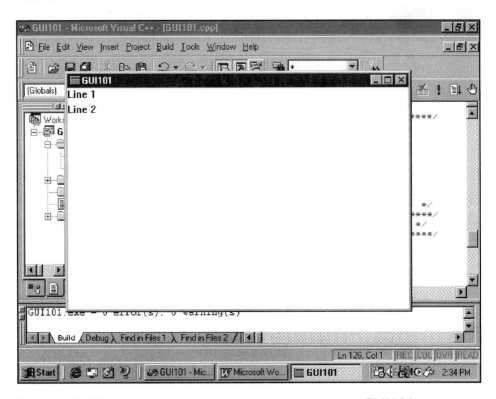

FIGURE 4   **TWO LINES OF TEXT GENERATED BY THE *GUI101.CPP*
PROGRAM USING TWO CALLS TO THE *TEXTOUT()* FUNCTION.**

means 640 pixels horizontally in the *x* direction and 480 pixels vertically in the *y* direction. The fourth argument contains the actual string that you want to appear within the window. The fifth and final argument is the length of the string that you want to display. Remember that a string's length is the number of characters in the string, including spaces and punctuation.

There are some limitations on the strings that you can display with the *TextOut()* function. You cannot display any of the escape characters except \" and \' for the double and single quotes. Also, remember when counting the number of characters that \" and \' count as only one character.

This raises the question of how to get another line. You have to use another *TextOut()* statement. In fact, you must use a separate *TextOut()* statement for each line of text.

PROCEDURE (*CONTINUED*)

27. Close the *GUI101* window if you have not already done so.

28. Replace the *TextOut()* statement in section **F** of your template with the following two statements:

```
TextOut(hdc,0,0,TEXT("Line 1"),6);
TextOut(hdc,0,20,TEXT("Line 2"),6);
```

29. Compile and run the program and you should observe the window shown in Figure 4. Notice that there are two lines of text output within the window, one line generated by each of the *TextOut()* functions that you placed within the template.

30. Close the *GUI101* window.

31. If you are too tired to count the length of the string, but not too tired to do a little extra typing, you can use the *lstrlen()* function to get the length of your string calculated for you by the compiler. The only problem with this method is that you have to type your string in twice. For example, replace the two *TextOut()* statements in section **F** of your template with the following two statements:

```
TextOut(hdc,0,0,TEXT("Line 1"), lstrlen(TEXT("Line 1")));
TextOut(hdc,0,20,TEXT("Line 2"), lstrlen(TEXT("Line 2")));
```

32. Compile and run the program and you should again observe the window shown in Figure 4. You see that that you get the same results that you obtained when using the actual number of string characters before. Notice that the actual string length argument is replaced by the *lstrlen()* in the foregoing code.

33. Close the *GUI101* window.

34. This next statement shows the value of using the *lstrlen()*. Add the following *TextOut()* statement in section **F** of your template. Use copy/paste on the string to expedite the statement entry.

```
TextOut(hdc,0,40,TEXT("Super-cali-fragil-istic-expi-alidocious"),
    lstrlen(TEXT("Super-cali-fragil-istic-expi-ali-docious")));
```

35. Compile and run the program and you should see a third text line displayed within the window.

36. Close the *GUI101* window.

37. You might want to play around with the various arguments of the *TextOut()* function. You might note that if you make the *x* and *y arguments* too large, your message will not appear on the screen. This is something you just have to be careful about for now.

38. Close the *GUI101* window if you have not already done so.

39. Remove any *TextOut()* statements from section **F** of the *GUI101* template.

40. Add the following statement to part **D** of the *GUI101* template:
```
static TCHAR keyString[2]=TEXT("\0");
```

41. Add the following code into part **G** of the template:

```
case WM_CHAR:
    keyString[0]=wParam;
    MessageBox(hwnd,keyString,TEXT("Key Pushed"),MB_OK);
    break;
```

42. Now, compile and run the program. You will see the empty *GUI101* window pop up.

43. Press the 'a' key. A message box window pops up as shown in Figure 5. Notice that the character 'a' appears in the message box.

44. Click *OK* or press the ENTER key. Press another key and observe the results. Each time you press a key, the message box will appear showing the key that you pressed.

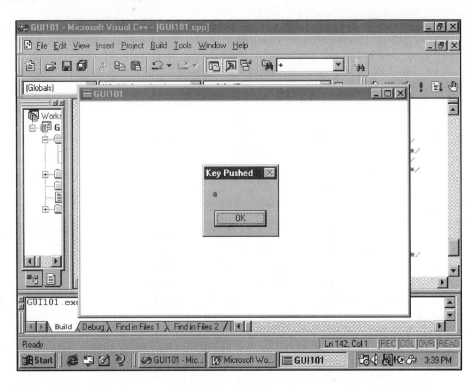

FIGURE 5 **A MESSAGE BOX CONTAINING THE KEYBOARD CHARAC-TER 'a' THAT YOU PRESSED.**

45. Remove the *case* statement that you added in part **G** of the template when you are finished.

DISCUSSION

We won't go into the details of how this works, but basically the *wParam* variable in the forgoing code contains the character that you pressed. This character is assigned to a string object called *keyString* to create a string that contains exactly one character: the one that you pressed. The *MessageBox()* function then uses the *keyString* object to display the character.

Windows input is an advanced topic and there are too many types of input to cover in this module, or this book for that matter. Hopefully you now have a "look and feel" for Windows programming. The rest of the text will concentrate on simple text I/O (*CUIs*), saving Windows I/O (*GUIs*) for a more advanced programming course.

Nuts and Bolts: Standard Stuff in C++

Chapter Objectives

When you are finished with this chapter, you should have a good understanding of the following:

- The standard arithmetic operators provided by C++.
- The order of precedence used for arithmetic operators in C++.
- The standard mathematical functions provided by the *math.h* header file.
- How to call the standard math functions.
- The increment/decrement operators in C++.
- Pre-increment/decrement versus post-increment/decrement when used within arithmetic expressions.
- Simple and compound assignment operators in C++.
- The use of trig functions in C++.

INTRODUCTION

In order for your programs to perform meaningful tasks, you must be familiar with several standard, or built-in, operators available to you in C++. The simplest of these are the arithmetic operators. By definition, an arithmetic operator generates a numeric result. Such operators are the topic of the first section of this short chapter. Pay particular attention to the division (/), modulus (%), and increment/decrement (++, −−) operators.

The second section deals with the C++ assignment operators. Assignment operators assign a value to a variable in memory. There are compound assignment operators in C++ that allow you to combine an arithmetic operation with the assignment operation.

In order to simplify the programming task, C++ employs several standard functions. These functions allow you to easily implement many common operations, such as square root, sine, and cosine, without writing special routines. Standard functions are discussed in the third section.

The chapter closes with three *Problem Solving in Action* case studies. Make sure you go through these problems in detail, since each focuses on a how to use the operations discussed in this chapter.

5.1 ARITHMETIC OPERATORS

You are now ready to begin learning how to write simple straight-line programs in C++. By a straight-line program, we mean a program that does not alter its flow; it simply executes a series of statements in a straight line, from beginning to end. In order for your programs to perform meaningful tasks, you must be familiar with several standard, or built-in, operators available to you in C++. The simplest of these are the standard arithmetic operators. By definition, an arithmetic operator generates a numeric result.

Arithmetic operators in C++ provide for the common add, subtract, multiply, and divide operations, as well as increment/decrement operations. The basic add, subtract, multiply, and divide operations can be performed on any numeric data type. Recall that the standard numeric data types in C++ are the integers and floats. In addition, you can perform arithmetic operations on character data in C++, because characters are represented as integers (ASCII) within the computer.

The five basic arithmetic operators and the C++ symbols used to represent those operators are listed in Table 5.1. The addition (+), subtraction (−), and multiplication (∗) operators are straightforward and do not need any further explanation. However, you might note that an asterisk (∗) is used for multiplication rather than a times symbol (×) so that the computer does not get multiplication confused with the character 'x'.

The division operator needs some special attention. This operator will generate a result that is the same data type of the operands used in the operation. Thus, if you divide two integers, you will get an integer result. If you *divide one or more*

TABLE 5.1   ARITHMETIC OPERATORS DEFINED IN C++

Operation	Symbol
Addition	+
Subtraction	–
Multiplication	*
Division	/
Modulus (remainder)	%

decimal floating-point values, you get a decimal result. Thus, 10 / 3 = 3 and 10.0 / 3 = 3.333333. Here, the former is integer division and generates an integer result. The latter is floating-point division and generates a floating-point result.

Finally, the modulus operator (%) simply generates the remainder that occurs when you divide two integer values. For example, the result of 5 % 3 is 2, 5 % 4 is 1, and 5 % 5 is 0.

PROGRAMMING NOTE

The modulus operator (%) is only defined for integers. So, what happens if you use a floating-point value with modulus? Well, consider the statement

```
cout << 6.0 % 3 << endl;
```

This statement produces an *illegal use of floating-point* error when compiled. The lesson to be learned here is never use the modulus operator with floating-point values, since you will get a compiler error.

Let's look at a couple of examples that illustrate the use of these operators. Example 5.1 shows several arithmetic operations on integers, and Example 5.2 deals with arithmetic operations on floating-point values.

EXAMPLE 5.1

What value will be returned as the result of each of the following operations?

   a. 3 * (–5)

   b. 4 * 5 – 10

   c. 10 / 3

   d. 9 % 3

   e. –21 / (–2)

   f. –21 % (–2)

   g. 4 * 5 / 2 + 5 % 2

Solution

   a. 3 * (−5) returns the value −15.

   b. 4 * 5 − 10 returns the value 10. Note that the multiplication operation is performed before the subtraction operation.

   c. 10 / 3 returns the value 3, because this is integer division.

   d. 9 % 3 returns the value 0, because there is no remainder.

   e. −21 / (−2) returns the integer quotient, 10.

   f. −21 % (−2) returns the remainder, −1.

   g. 4 * 5 / 2 + 5 % 2 = (4 * 5) / 2 + (5 % 2) = 20 / 2 + (5 % 2) = 10 + 1 = 11.

Notice that the multiplication, *, division, /, and remainder, %, operators are executed first, from left to right. The addition operator is executed last.

Aside from showing how the individual operators work, the foregoing example illustrates the priority, or ordering, of the operators. When more than one operator is executed within an expression, you must know the order in which they will be executed to determine the result. C++ executes the arithmetic operators in the following order:

   ❏ All operators within parentheses are performed first.

   ❏ If there are nested parentheses (parentheses within parentheses) the inner-most operators are performed first, from the inside out.

   ❏ The *, /, and % operators are performed next, from left to right within the expression.

   ❏ The + and − operators are performed last, from left to right within the expression.

This order of precedence is summarized in Table 5.2.

EXAMPLE 5.2

Evaluate each of the following expressions:

   a. 4.6 − 2.0 + 3.2

   b. 4.6 − 2.0 * 3.2

TABLE 5.2   ORDER OF PRECEDENCE FOR C++ ARITHMETIC OPERATORS

Operator(s)	Operation	Precedence
( )	Parentheses	Evaluated first, inside-out if nested, or left-to-right if same level.
*, /, or %	Multiply Divide Modulus	Evaluated second, left-to-right.
+, −	Add Subtract	Evaluated last, left-to-right.

c. $4.6 - 2.0 / 2 * 3.2$

d. $-3.0 * ((4.3 + 2.5) *2.0) -1.0$

e. $-21.0 / -2$

f. $-21.0 \% -2$

g. $10.0 / 3$

h. $((4 * 12) / (4 + 12))$

i. $4 * 12 / 4 + 12$

Solution

a. $4.6 - 2.0 + 3.2 = (4.6 - 2.0) + 3.2 = 2.6 + 3.2 = 5.8$

b. $4.6 - 2.0 * 3.2 = 4.6 - (2.0 * 3.2) = 4.6 - 6.4 = -1.8$

c. $4.6 - 2.0 / 2 * 3.2 = 4.6 - ((2.0 / 2) * 3.2) = 4.6 - (1.0 * 3.2) = 4.6 - 3.2 = 1.4$

d. $-3.0 * ((4.3 + 2.5) *2.0) -1.0 = -3.0 * (6.8 * 2.0) -1.0 = -3.0 * 13.6 - 1.0 =$
$-40.8 - 1.0 = -41.8$

e. $-21.0 / -2 = 10.5$

f. Compiler error, must be coded as –21 % –2. The solution would then be –1.

g. $10.0 / 3 = 3.333333$

h. $((4 * 12) / (4 + 12)) = 48 / 16 = 3$

i. $4 * 12 / 4 + 12 = 48 / 4 + 12 = 12 + 12 = 24$

Notice that we have used parentheses in the solutions for the preceding examples to indicate the order of the operations. As you can see, the parentheses clarify the expression. For this reason, we suggest that you always use parentheses

DEBUGGING TIP

Beginning programmers, and even experienced programmers for that matter, often forget that the C++ division operator produces an integer result if both of the operands are integers. For example, consider the problem of converting degrees Fahrenheit to degrees Celsius. The equation you all learned in high school for this is, $C = 5/9 \times (F - 32)$, where F is degrees Fahrenheit and C is degrees Celsius. Now, suppose you were to code this equation as you see it, as follows:

```
C = 5/9 * (F - 32);
```

What do you suppose would happen? You're right, the resulting value for C would always be 0, regardless of the value of F. (Why?) How could this be corrected? Yes, by coding either the numerator or denominator of the fractional constant as a floating-point value, like this:

```
C = 5.0/9 * (F - 32);
```

TABLE 5.3 INCREMENT AND DECREMENT
OPERATORS

Operation	Symbol
Increment	++
Decrement	--

DEBUGGING TIP

When using parentheses within an arithmetic expression, the number of left parentheses must equal the number of right parentheses. When coding your programs, always count each to make sure that this equality holds.

when writing arithmetic expressions. This way, you will always be sure of the order in which the compiler will execute the operators within the expression. Keep in mind, however, that the compiler will always execute the operators within parentheses from inside out, as shown in part d of Example 5.2. In particular, notice how the evaluation of part h of Example 5.2 differs from part i. The parentheses in part h force C++ to perform the division operation last, after the addition operation. In part i, the division operation is performed prior to the addition operation, generating a completely different result. This is why you should always use parentheses when writing expressions. It is better to be safe then sorry!

Increment and Decrement Operators

Many times in a program you will need to increment (add 1) or decrement (subtract 1) a variable. The increment and decrement operators shown in Table 5.3 are provided for this purpose.

Increment/decrement can be applied to both integer and floating-point variables, as well as character variables. An increment operation adds 1 to the value of a variable. Thus, $++x$ or $x++$ is equivalent to the statement $x = x + 1$. Conversely, a decrement operation subtracts 1 from the value of a variable. As a result, $--x$ or $x--$ is equivalent to the statement $x = x - 1$. As you can see, you can *pre*increment/*pre*decrement a variable, or *post*increment/*post*decrement a variable.

Here's a short example to illustrate increment/decrement:

EXAMPLE 5.3

Determine the output generated by the following program:

```
int x = 5;
int y = 10;
cout << "x = " << ++x << endl;
cout << "x = " << --x << endl;
cout << "y = " << (y = ++x - 2)<< endl;
```

```
x = 5;
cout << "y = " << (y = x++ - 2) << endl;
cout << "x = " << x << endl;

x = 0;
cout << "y = " << (y = x-- 2) << endl;
cout << "x = " << x << endl;
```

Solution

Here is the output that you will see on the monitor:

```
x = 6
x = 5
y = 4
y = 3
x = 6
y = -2
x = -1
```

Notice that the variable x is initialized with the value 5 at the start of the program. The first *cout* statement simply increments x to the value 6. The second *cout* statement then decrements x back to the value 5. Next, the third *cout* statement **preincrements** the value of x and then subtracts 2 from its value. We say that x is preincremented because the increment symbol appears before x and the increment operation is performed *before x is used in the expression*. Thus, the expression reduces to $y = x + 1 - 2 = 5 + 1 - 2 = 4$. Observe that the arithmetic operations are performed first, and then the result is assigned to y via the assignment operator. Thus, the value displayed by the *cout* statement is the value of y, or 4.

The fourth *cout* statement involves a *postincrement* operation on x. A postincrement operation is indicated by the increment symbol following x. So, what's the difference between a preincrement and a postincrement operation? Well, a preincrement operation increments the variable *before any expression involving the variable is evaluated.* On the other hand, a postincrement operation increments the variable *after any expression involving the variable is evaluated.* Now, looking at the fourth *cout* statement in the program, you find that x starts out with the value 5. Thus, the expression reduces to $y = x - 2 = 5 - 2 = 3$. *After* the expression is evaluated, x is incremented to the value 6, as shown by the next *cout* statement. Finally, the last two *cout* statements show the result of a postdecrement operation. Here, x is assigned the value 0 to be used in the expression. Thus, $y = 0 - 2 = -2$. *After* the expression is evaluated, the value of x is decremented to -1, as shown by the last output value.

From Example 5.3, you see that a variable can be preincremented or postincremented. Likewise, a variable can be predecremented or postdecremented. If a variable is preincremented or predecremented within an expression, the variable is incremented/decremented *before* the expression is evaluated. On the other hand, if a variable is postincremented or postdecremented within an expression, the variable is incremented/decremented *after* the expression is evaluated. To further illustrate this idea, consider the following:

```
a = 1;
b = ++a;
```

In this snippet of code, we have integer variables *a* and *b*. First, using the assignment operator, we set *a* to 1, then we set *b* = ++*a*. Since we are using preincrement, *a* is first incremented to 2, then *b* is set to 2. So, we end up with both *a* and *b* set to a value of 2. Now, consider the following:

```
a = 1;
b = a++;
```

This piece of code is similar. We first set *a* to 1. Then we set *b* to *a*++. This time, however, we are using postincrement, so *b* is set to the original value of *a* which is 1. After that, *a* is incremented. So, this time we end up with *a* set to 2 and *b* set to 1.

DEBUGGING TIP

There is often confusion about pre- versus postincrement/-decrement. Just remember that it doesn't matter *unless* the increment/decrement operation is part of an expression. Within an expression a preincrement/-decrement is executed *before* the expression is evaluated, while a postincrement/-decrement is executed *after* the expression is evaluated. As a further example, suppose we define two integer variables called *number* and *value*. Then the statements

```
++value;  and value++;
```

will produce the same value for *value*. However, the statements

```
number = ++value;  and  number = value++;
```

will produce two different values for *number*. Of course, the value of *value* would be incremented by 1 after executing any of the foregoing statements. To avoid potential problems, we suggest that you *do not* use ++ or −− within expressions, even within simple assignment and *cout* statements. Use the more readable and predictable longer form of adding or subtracting 1 from a variable. Only use ++ or −− when a variable is being incremented/decremented as a statement by itself.

Now, you can probably guess why Dr. Stroustrup chose to name his language C++. He simply *postincremented* the C language by *adding* OOP capability.

Quick Check

1. List the order in which C++ executes its arithmetic operators. Be sure to mention how parentheses are handled.

2. What can be said about x if x % 2 returns the value 0?

3. What can be said about y if y % 17 returns the value 0?

4. What is returned by the expression 1 / 2 % 5?

5. What is returned by the expression $(2 - ++x)$, assuming that x has the value 1 before the expression is evaluated?

6. What is returned by the expression $(2 - x++)$, assuming that x has the value 1 before the expression is evaluated?

7. Write a statement using the decrement operator that is equivalent to the statement $x = x - 1$.

8. True or false: The division operator will produce an integer result when either of the operands is an integer.

9. What is the difference between using the preincrement operator versus the postincrement operator on a variable when the variable is used as part of an expression?

10. What is the result of 10 / 100?

5.2   ASSIGNMENT OPERATORS

An assignment operator stores a value in memory. The value is stored at a location in memory that is accessed by the variable on the left-hand side of the assignment operator. As a result, a C++ assignment operator *assigns* the value on the right side of the operator to the variable appearing on the left side of the operator. Another way to say this is that the variable on the left side of the operator is *set* to the value on the right side of the operator. The C++ assignment operators are listed in Table 5.4.

First, let's say a word about the simple assignment operator, =. Although an equals symbol is used for this operator, you cannot think of it as equals. Here's

TABLE 5.4   ASSIGNMENT OPERATORS USED IN C++

Operation	Symbol	Example	Equivalent to
Simple assignment	=	*value* = 1	*value* = 1
Addition/assignment	+=	*value* += 1	*value* = *value* + 1
Subtraction/assignment	−=	*value* −= 1	*value* = *value* − 1
Multiplication/assignment	*=	*value* *= 2	*value* = *value* * 2
Division/assignment	/=	*value* /= 2	*value* = *value* / 2
Modulus/assignment (integers only)	%=	*value* %= 2	*value* = *value* % 2

why: Consider the statement $x = x + 1$. If you put this expression in an algebra exam, your professor would mark it wrong, because x cannot be equal to itself plus 1, right? However, in C++, this expression means *to add 1 to x, and then assign the resulting value back to x.* In other words, *set x to the value x + 1.* This is a perfectly legitimate operation. As you will soon find out, equals is a Boolean operator and uses two equals symbols, ==, in C++.

The compound assignment operators shown in Table 5.4 simply combine the assignment operator with an arithmetic operator. Suppose that we define x and y as integers; then the following holds:

x += y is equivalent to $x = x + y$

x −= y is equivalent to $x = x − y$

x *= y is equivalent to $x = x * y$

x /= y is equivalent to $x = x / y$

x %= y is equivalent to $x = x \% y$

As you can see, both the increment/decrement operators and the compound assignment operators provide a shorthand notation for writing arithmetic expressions. This shorthand notation takes a bit getting used to. These are simply syntactic shortcuts which you don't have to use. In fact, many instructors prefer the regular notation because it is more readable and less cryptic than the shorthand notation. Ask your instructors which notation they prefer.

Quick Check

1. Write an expression using the compound addition assignment operator that is equivalent to the expression $x = x + 5$.
2. Write an expression using the compound division assignment operator that is equivalent to the expression $x = x / 10$.
3. What is wrong with the expression $x = 10 / x$?
4. Why does the expression $x = x + 5$ make sense in C++, but not in your math class?
5. Write four different expressions that will increment the variable x in C++.

5.3   SOME STANDARD FUNCTIONS IN C++

In earlier chapters, you were introduced to several standard functions, such as *sqrt(), getline(), get(),* and so on. Standard operations such as these are so common in programming that C++ includes them as built-in functions. There are hundreds of standard functions available in the various C++ header files. The tables that follow list some of the more commonly used functions. We should caution you, however, that different versions of C++ have different standard functions available.

Compiler manufacturers are allowed to value-add nonstandard functions to their compilers to enhance their marketability. Only those functions specified in the ANSI/ISO standard will be common to all compilers and discussed in this text.

As you progress through this text, you will be using some of the functions that follow and we will discuss them in detail when the need arises to use them. As a result, do not worry about learning them now. Simply scan each table to get an idea of what functions are available. The tables that follow list the function, its header file, and a short description of its operation. Space does not permit a detailed listing of all the functions available in C++.

Conversion Functions

The conversion functions listed in Table 5.5 convert one type of data to another type, usually between integer and character data types.

Mathematical Functions

Mathematical functions perform an arithmetic operation. Since these functions require a numeric argument and return a numeric result, they are sometimes called numeric functions. Some standard mathematical functions are listed in Table 5.6. Most of these operations should be familiar to you from your background in mathematics. When using any of these functions in C++, you must make sure that the argument is the correct data type as specified by the function definition. In addition, any variable to which the function is assigned must be defined the same data type returned by the function.

Notice that the *math.h* header file also includes the standard trig operations. However, be careful when using these, because they *evaluate radians, not degrees.* For example, the statement

```
cout << sin(90 * 3.14159/180);
```

displays the value *1.0.*

Let's take a closer look at this last statement. First, you see that the *sin()* function is being called. The intent here is to display the sine of 90 degrees. However, notice from Table 5.6 that the *sin()* function requires radians, rather than degrees, as its argument. To convert degrees to radians, you must multiply the degrees by

TABLE 5.5   SOME STANDARD CONVERSION FUNCTIONS AVAILABLE IN C++

Function Name	Header File	Operation
toascii()	ctype.h	Converts a character to its ASCII value.
tolower()	ctype.h	Converts a character to lowercase.
toupper()	ctype.h	Converts a character to uppercase.

TABLE 5.6   SOME STANDARD MATHEMATICAL FUNCTIONS AVAILABLE IN C++

Function Name	Header File	Operation
abs()	math.h	Returns the absolute value of the argument.
acos()	math.h	Returns the arc cosine of the argument (radians).
asin()	math.h	Returns the arc sine of the argument (radians).
atan()	math.h	Returns the arc tangent of the argument (radians).
cos()	math.h	Returns the cosine of the argument (radians).
hypot(a,b)	math.h	Returns the hypotenuse of a right triangle whose sides are a and b.
log()	math.h	Returns the natural log of the argument.
log10()	math.h	Returns the base 10 log of the argument.
pow(x,y)	math.h	Returns x raised to the power of y.
pow10(y)	math.h	Returns 10 raised to the power of y.
rand()	stdlib.h	Generates a random number between 0 and $2^{15} - 1$.
srand()	stdlib.h	Initializes the random-number generator and should be used prior to rand().
sin()	math.h	Returns the sine of the argument (radians).
sqrt()	math.h	Returns the square root of the argument.
tan()	math.h	Returns the tangent of the argument (radians).

$\pi/180$. Thus, we multiply 90 by 3.14159/180 to convert 90 degrees to radians as required by the *sin()* function.

Make sure to check your C++ compiler on-line help for more functions available in the *math.h* header file as well as other standard functions available in C++.

> The standard trig functions in the C++ *math.h* header file evaluate radians, not degrees. Multiply degrees by 3.14159/180 within the trig function argument to convert degrees to radians.

A very common operation in application programs is that of generating a random number. C++ includes two functions in the *stdlib.h* header file called *srand()* and *rand()* for this purpose. The function *srand()* must be executed to set a starting point for the generation of a random number using the *rand()* function. The *srand()* function requires an argument called a *seed* value. A common seed value is 1. So, to generate a random number, call *srand(1)* followed by a call to *rand()* like this:

```
srand(1);
cout << rand() % 100;
```

The *rand() % 100* operation *scales* the value returned by *rand()* to produce a range of values between 0 and 99, inclusive. Of course, the random value would be displayed on by monitor by the *cout* object. Here you also see a common use for the modulus (%), operator to scale a value. Without scaling, the *rand()* function will generate a value between 0 and 32767. If we divide any value within this range by 100 and then take the remainder, we will always get a value between 0 and 99, right? For example, suppose that *rand()* generates a value of 32563. Then 32563 % 100 will be 63, which is between 0 and 99.

Quick Check

1. In order to use a standard function in your program, you must include its _____.
2. Explain how you can get an on-line description of a standard function using your compiler.
3. Write a statement to display the tangent of 45 degrees.
4. What header file must be included in your program so that the statement in question 3 will compile?
5. Write an expression using a function to convert 'a' to 'A'.
6. What header file must be included in your program so that the statement in question 5 will compile?
7. What range of values will be produced if the values generated by *rand()* are scaled by 10?

PROBLEM SOLVING IN ACTION: INVENTORY CONTROL

PROBLEM

Following is a partial inventory listing of items in the sporting goods department of the CPP*Mart super-center:

Item	Beginning Quantity	Units Sold This Month
Fishing line	132 spools	24 spools
Fish hooks	97 packages	45 packages
Sinkers	123 packages	37 packages
Fish nets	12 ea.	5 ea.

Write a program that will display a monthly report showing the item name, beginning quantity, units sold this month, ending quantity, and percent of quantity sold. The problem solution begins with the problem definition phase.

Defining the Problem

Output: The program must generate a monthly report of the item name, beginning quantity, units sold this month, ending quantity, and percent of quantity sold. Now is a good time to develop the output format. Suppose we use a tabular format, like this:

MONTH:

<u>ITEM</u> <u>BEGIN QTY</u> <u>UNITS SOLD</u> <u>ENDING QTY</u> <u>% SOLD</u>

Input: The sporting goods manager must enter the month of the report and inventory data shown in the above table, except for the ending quantity and % sold, which will be calculated by our program. Therefore, the program must be very user friendly.

Processing: The program must use the input information to calculate two things: the ending quantity and the percent sold. The ending quantity is found by simply subtracting the units sold from the beginning quantity, like this:

$$ending\ qty = begin\ qty - units\ sold$$

The percent sold is found by dividing the units sold by the beginning quantity and multiplying by 100%, like this:

$$\%\ sold = (units\ sold\ /\ begin\ qty) \times 100\%$$

Planning the Solution

We must now construct a set of algorithms from the problem definition. Using a modular program design, we will divide the problem into individual subproblems to solve the overall problem. There are three major tasks that follow directly from the problem definition:

❑ Obtain the inventory data for a given item from the user.
❑ Calculate the ending quantity and percent sold for the given item.
❑ Display the item report.

Because we do not yet have a way of telling C++ to automatically repeat a task, the first two tasks must be repeated for each item in the inventory. The diagram in Figure 5.1 shows the modular structure required for the program.

The initial algorithm level, *main()*, will reflect the foregoing analysis and call the individual function modules.

Initial Algorithm

main()
BEGIN
    Call function to set the inventory data for a given item from user entries.
    Call function to calculate the ending quantity and percent sold.
    Repeat last two calls for each inventory item.
    Call function to display the item report.
END.

In developing the algorithm, you would quickly realize that the processing is the same for each sales item. As a result, we have used a single *repeat* statement rather than actually repeating the algorithm statements three more times. This has been done to make the algorithm more efficient.

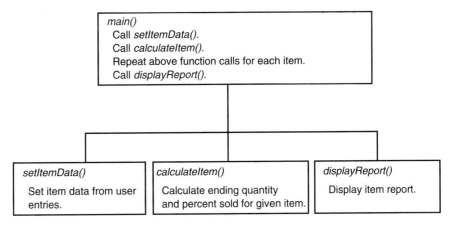

FIGURE 5.1 **A PROBLEM-SOLVING DIAGRAM FOR THE INVENTORY PROBLEM.**

The first level of refinement requires that we show a detailed algorithm for each task, or function, that we have identified. They are as follows:

First Level of Refinement

> *setItemData()*
> BEGIN
> > Write a user prompt to enter the item name.
> > Read *item*.
> > Write a user prompt to enter the beginning quantity.
> > Read *begin qty*.
> > Write a user prompt to enter the number of units sold.
> > Read *units sold*.
> END.

> *calculateItem()*
> BEGIN
> > Calculate *ending qty = begin qty – units sold*.
> > Calculate *% sold = (units sold / begin qty) × 100%*.
> END.

> *displayReport()*
> BEGIN
> > Display *item, begin qty, units sold, ending qty,* and *% sold* for each item.
> END.

Given our problem definition, the foregoing collection of algorithms is straightforward. The first two functions must be executed for each of the items in the inventory. The last function is executed to display the composite report. The *setItemData()* function prompts and reads the item information from the user and assigns it to the item variables. The *calculateItem()* function will make the required calculations. Finally, the *displayReport()* function will display the item report.

Now the job is to code these algorithms in C++. With your present knowledge of C++, coding most of these algorithms should not present a problem. But what about the repeat statement at the end of the *main()* function algorithm? Well, notice that this statement requires that you go back and repeat many of the previous statements over and over until all the items are processed. Such a repeating operation is called an **iteration,** or **looping,** operation. To date, you do not have the C++ tools to perform such an operation. So, we will have to repeat all of the processing steps for each of the sales items in the inventory. In Chapter 7 you will learn how to perform iterative operations in C++, thus making the code much more efficient.

Here's the flat implementation of the foregoing algorithms:

Coding the Program

```
/*
ACTION 5-1 (ACT05_01.cpp)

OUTPUT:      A MONTHLY REPORT OF THE
             ITEM NAME, BEGINNING QUANTITY,
             UNITS SOLD THIS MONTH, ENDING
             QUANTITY, AND PERCENT OF QUANTITY SOLD

INPUT:       MONTH OF REPORT, ITEM NAME, BEGIN QTY.
             UNITS SOLD THIS MONTH

PROCESSING:  THE PROGRAM MUST CALCULATE TWO THINGS:
             ENDING QUANTITY AND THE PERCENT SOLD

*/

//PREPROCESSOR DIRECTIVES
#include <iostream>          //FOR cin AND cout
#include <string>            //FOR string CLASS

using namespace std; //REQUIRED WHEN INCLUDING iostream

//MAIN FUNCTION
int main()
{
   //DEFINE AND INITIALIZE MONTH OBJECT
   string month = " ";            //MONTH OF REPORT

   //DEFINE AND INITIALIZE ITEM 1 OBJECTS AND VARIABLES
   string item1 = " ";         //SALES ITEM NAME
   double beginQty1 = 10.0;   //BEGINNING QUANTITY
   double unitsSold1 = 5.0;   //NUMBER OF UNITS SOLD
   double endQty1 = 0;        //ENDING QUANTITY
   double percentSold1 = 0.0;//PERCENT OF SALES
```

```cpp
//DEFINE AND INITIALIZE ITEM 2 OBJECTS AND VARIABLES
string item2 = " ";        //SALES ITEM NAME
double beginQty2 = 0.0;    //BEGINNING QUANTITY
double unitsSold2 = 0.0;   //NUMBER OF UNITS SOLD
double endQty2 = 0;        //ENDING QUANTITY
double percentSold2 = 0.0;//PERCENT OF SALES

//DEFINE AND INITIALIZE ITEM 3 OBJECTS AND VARIABLES
string item3 = " ";        //SALES ITEM NAME
double beginQty3 = 0.0;    //BEGINNING QUANTITY
double unitsSold3 = 0.0;   //NUMBER OF UNITS SOLD
double endQty3 = 0;        //ENDING QUANTITY
double percentSold3 = 0.0;//PERCENT OF SALES

//DEFINE AND INITIALIZE ITEM 4 OBJECTS AND VARIABLES
string item4 = " ";        //SALES ITEM NAME
double beginQty4 = 0.0;    //BEGINNING QUANTITY
double unitsSold4 = 0.0;   //NUMBER OF UNITS SOLD
double endQty4 = 0;        //ENDING QUANTITY
double percentSold4 = 0.0;//PERCENT OF SALES

//DISPLAY PROGRAM DESCRIPTION MESSAGE
cout << "\n\nDear Sporting Goods Manager\n"
     << "You will be asked to enter four sales items, one at\n"
     << "a time. With each item you will be asked to enter\n"
     << "the item name, beginning quantity, and quantity\n"
     << "sold this month. The computer will print a monthly\n"
     <<"inventory report for the sales items." << endl;

//SET MONTH FROM USER ENTRY
cout << "\nPlease enter the month in of this report: ";
cin >> month;

//SET ITEM 1 DATA FROM USER ENTRY
cout << "\nPlease enter the item name: ";
cin >> ws;
getline(cin,item1);
cout << "Please enter the beginning quantity of " << item1 << ": ";
cin >> beginQty1;
cout << "Please enter the quantity of " << item1 << " sold in "
     << month << ": ";
cin >> unitsSold1;

//CALCULATE ENDING QUANTITY AND PERCENT SOLD FOR ITEM 1
endQty1 = beginQty1 - unitsSold1;
percentSold1 = unitsSold1 / beginQty1 * 100;

//SET ITEM 2 DATA FROM USER ENTRY
cout << "\nPlease enter the item name: ";
cin >> ws;
```

```
    getline(cin,item2);
cout << "Please enter the beginning quantity of " << item2 << ": ";
cin >> beginQty2;
cout << "Please enter the quantity of " << item2 << " sold in "
     << month << ": ";
cin >> unitsSold2;

//CALCULATE ENDING QUANTITY AND PERCENT SOLD FOR ITEM 2
endQty2 = beginQty2 - unitsSold2;
percentSold2 = unitsSold2 / beginQty2 * 100;

//SET ITEM 3 DATA FROM USER ENTRY
cout << "\nPlease enter the item name: ";
cin >> ws;
getline(cin,item3);
cout << "Please enter the beginning quantity of " << item3 << ": ";
cin >> beginQty3;
cout << "Please enter the quantity of " << item3 << " sold in "
     << month << ": ";
cin >> unitsSold3;

//CALCULATE ENDING QUANTITY AND PERCENT SOLD FOR ITEM 3
endQty3 = beginQty3 - unitsSold3;
percentSold3 = unitsSold3 / beginQty3 * 100;

//SET ITEM 4 DATA FROM USER ENTRY
cout << "\nPlease enter the item name: ";
cin >> ws;
getline(cin,item4);
cout << "Please enter the beginning quantity of " << item4 << ": ";
cin >> beginQty4;
cout << "Please enter the quantity of " << item4 << " sold in "
     << month << ": ";
cin >> unitsSold4;

//CALCULATE ENDING QUANTITY AND PERCENT SOLD FOR ITEM 4
endQty4 = beginQty4 - unitsSold4;
percentSold4 = unitsSold4 / beginQty4 * 100;

//DISPLAY REPORT HEADER INFORMATION
cout << "\n\nMONTH: " << month << endl;
cout << "\n\n\nITEM\tBEGIN QTY\tUNITS SOLD\tENDING QTY"
     << "\t% SOLD" << endl;
cout << "----\t---------\t---------\t---------\t-----" << endl;

//DISPLAY ITEM REPORT
cout << item1 << "\t" << beginQty1 << "\t\t" << unitsSold1
     << "\t\t" << endQty1 << "\t\t" << percentSold1 << endl;
cout << item2 << "\t" << beginQty2 << "\t\t" << unitsSold2
     << "\t\t" << endQty2 << "\t\t" << percentSold2 << endl;
```

```
  cout << item3 << "\t" << beginQty3 << "\t\t" << unitsSold3
       << "\t\t" << endQty3 << "\t\t" << percentSold3 << endl;
  cout << item4 << "\t" << beginQty4 << "\t\t" << unitsSold4
       << "\t\t" << endQty4 << "\t\t" << percentSold4 << endl;

//RETURN
return 0;
}//END main()
```

Using the sales data provided, this program will print the following inventory report:

```
MONTH: May
```

ITEM	BEGIN QTY	UNITS SOLD	ENDING QTY	%SOLD
Fishing Line	132	24	108	18.18
Fish Hooks	97	45	52	46.39
Sinkers	123	37	86	30.08
Fish Nets	12	5	7	41.67

Again, notice how a whole block of C++ code is repeated four times to process the four sales items. Wouldn't it be nice to simply code the processing steps once and then tell the computer to repeat these steps the required number of times? Such a repeating operation would make our coding much more efficient, wouldn't it?

You should be able to understand the above C++ code, given the material presented up to this point in the text. However, there are a couple of small, but important, points that need some discussion. First, notice that there is a separate set of variables for each sales item. Would it be possible to use just one set of variables for all the sales items? Well, that depends on the problem definition. The problem definition requires a composite monthly report. If we were to use just one set of variables, the report for a given item would have to be displayed before the same set of variables could be used for the next item. But then the prompts required to get the next item data would appear on the display before its report could be displayed. In other words, we could not generate a composite table of results using just one set of variables. We must use a separate set of variables for each item to store all the item results before generating the report. Second, look at the *percentSold* calculation in the program. Notice that it is obtained by dividing the *unitsSold* by the *beginQty* and multiplying by 100. Now, you see that in the variable definition section at the top of the program that both *unitsSold* and *beginQty* are defined as double floating-point values. Well, why couldn't they be defined as integers, because both will always be whole number values, right? The reason that you can't define them as integers is that if you divide two integers using the / operator, you will get an integer result. Thus, if the units sold were 10 and the beginning quantity were 100, the *integer* quotient would be $10 / 100 = 0$. As a result, the *percentSold* would be 0, which is obviously incorrect. So, the solution is to define *unitsSold* and *beginQty* as floating-point values. Then dividing the two will yield a floating-point result. Using the preceding values, you would get $10 / 100 = 0.1$, resulting in a correct value of 10% sold.

PROBLEM SOLVING IN ACTION: DATA COMMUNICATIONS

PROBLEM

In the field of data communications, binary digital computer data are converted to analog sine-wave data for transmission over long distances via the telephone network. Hardware devices that perform this operation are called **modems.** As you know, digital data is composed of binary 1's and 0's. On the other hand, analog data is composed of sine waves. Thus a modem converts binary 1's and 0's to a series of sine waves for communication over the telephone system. Since binary data are represented using sine waves, the study of data communications often requires the analysis of a sine wave. One such analysis is to find the amplitude, in volts, of a sine wave at any given point in time. This is called the **instantaneous value** of the sine wave and is found using the equation

$$v = V_{peak} \sin(2\pi f t)$$

where

v is the instantaneous voltage at any point in time t on the waveform, in volts.

V_{peak} is the peak amplitude of the waveform, in volts.

π is the constant 3.14159.

f is the frequency of the waveform, in kilohertz.

t is the time, in milliseconds, for v.

Write a program to find the instantaneous voltage value of the sine wave in Figure 5.2. Have the user enter the peak voltage in volts, the frequency in kilohertz, and the time in milliseconds.

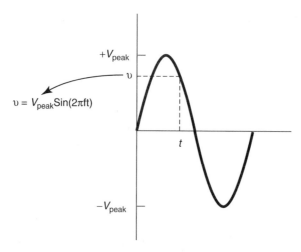

FIGURE 5.2   A SINE WAVE FOR THE DATA COMMUNICATIONS PROBLEM.

Defining the Problem

Output: The program must display the instantaneous voltage value, v, resulting from the previous equation.

Input: The user must enter the following information:

- ❏ The peak amplitude of the waveform, V_{peak}, in volts.
- ❏ The frequency of the waveform, f, in kilohertz.
- ❏ The point in time, t, in milliseconds for which the instantaneous voltage must be calculated.

Processing: The program must calculate the instantaneous voltage value using the equation $v = V_{peak} \sin(2\pi f t)$

Planning the Solution

Using the modular approach to solving this problem, we will divide the problem into three subproblems that reflect the problem definition. The three major tasks that follow directly from the problem definition are

- ❏ Set the values for V_{peak}, f, and t from user entries
- ❏ Calculate the instantaneous voltage.
- ❏ Display the instantaneous voltage value, v, resulting from the calculation.

Here are the respective algorithms:

Initial Algorithm

    main()
    BEGIN
       Call function to set the values for V_{peak}, f, and t.
       Call function to calculate the instantaneous voltage.
       Call function to display the instantaneous voltage value, v.
    END.

First Level of Refinement

    setData()
    BEGIN
       Write a user prompt to enter the peak amplitude of the waveform, V_{peak}, in volts.
       Read V_{peak}.
       Write a user prompt to enter the frequency of the waveform, f, in kilohertz.
       Read f.
       Write a user prompt to enter the time, t, in milliseconds.
       Read t.
    END.

calculateVoltage()
BEGIN
     Calculate $v = V_{peak} \sin(2\pi ft)$.
END.

displayVoltage()
BEGIN
     Write the instantaneous voltage value, v.
END.

Coding the Program

The flat implementation of the above set of algorithms follows:

```
/*
ACTION 5-2 (ACT05_02.CPP)

OUTPUT:      THE PROGRAM MUST DISPLAY
             THE INSTANTANEOUS VOLTAGE VALUE, V,
             RESULTING FROM THE ABOVE EQUATION.

INPUT:       THE USER MUST ENTER THE FOLLOWING:
             THE PEAK AMPLITUDE OF THE WAVEFORM, Vpeak,
             IN VOLTS.
             THE FREQUENCY OF THE WAVEFORM, F,
             IN KILOHERTZ.
             THE POINT IN TIME, T, IN MILLISECONDS FOR WHICH
             THE INSTANTANEOUS VOLTAGE MUST
             BE CALCULATED.

PROCESSING:  THE PROGRAM MUST CALCULATE THE
             INSTANTANEOUS VOLTAGE VALUE.
*/

//PREPROCESSOR DIRECTIVES
#include <iostream.h>   //FOR cin AND cout
#include <math.h>       //FOR sin()

//DEFINE CONSTANT
const double PI = 3.14159;

//MAIN FUNCTION
int main()
{
//DEFINE VARIABLES
 double V_Peak = 0.0;      //PEAK VOLTAGE IN VOLTS
 double f = 0.0;           //FREQUENCY IN KILOHERTZ
 double t = 0.0;           //TIME IN MILLISECONDS
 double v = 0.0;           //INSTANTANEOUS VOLTAGE IN VOLTS

 //DISPLAY PROGRAM DESCRIPTION MESSAGE
 cout << "This program will display the instantaneous voltage\n"
```

```
        << "value of an AC signal. You must enter the following\n"
        << "three quantities: " << endl << endl;

    cout << "\tPeak voltage of the signal, V_Peak.\n\n"
        << "\tFrequency of the signal, f.\n\n"
        << "\tThe point in time, t, for which the voltage\n"
        << "\tmust be calculated. " << endl << endl;

    //SET DATA VARIABLES FROM USER ENTRIES
    cout << "Enter the peak signal voltage in volts: V_Peak = ";
    cin >> V_Peak;
    cout << "Enter the signal frequency in kilohertz: f = ";
    cin >> f;
    cout << "Enter the time in milliseconds: t = ";
    cin >> t;

    //CALCULATE INSTANTANEOUS VOLTAGE VALUE
    v = V_Peak * sin(2 * PI * f * t);

    //DISPLAY INSTANTANEOUS VOLTAGE VALUE
    cout.setf(ios::fixed);
    cout.precision(4);
    cout << "\n\nThe instantaneous voltage at " << t
        << " milliseconds is\n"
        << v << " volts." << endl;

    //RETURN
    return 0;
}//END main()
```

It's probably a good idea to take a closer look at some of the features of this program. Here is what you will see on the display after the program has been run:

```
This program will display the instantaneous voltage
value of an AC signal. You must enter the following
three quantities:

    Peak voltage of the signal, V_Peak.

    Frequency of the signal, f.

    The point in time, t, for which the voltage
    must be calculated.

Enter the peak signal voltage in volts: V_Peak = 10↵

Enter the signal frequency in kilohertz: f = 1↵

Enter the time in milliseconds: t = .125↵

The instantaneous voltage at 0.1250 milliseconds is
7.0711 volts.
```

As you can see, the program description message describes the purpose of the program. In addition, it tells the user what values must be entered and identifies the variables to be used for the entered values. Another observation from the above program output is that the user must enter the waveform frequency in kilohertz and the time in milliseconds. These are typical units found in data communications. Notice that the user prompts indicate this entry requirement.

The calculation of the output voltage, v, is performed with the following program statement:

```
v = V_Peak * sin(2 * PI * f * t);
```

The equation does not have to be altered to accommodate f in kilohertz and t in milliseconds, because the product of these two units cancel each other out (10^{+3} cancels 10^{-3}). Another thing you see from the program statement is the use of the word *PI* to represent the value 3.14159. As you can see, this identifier is defined as a constant at the beginning of the program. One final point: The *sin()* function in C++ is defined to evaluate angles in *radians*. Fortunately, the quantity ($2 * PI * f * t$) produces radians and not degrees. If the value to be evaluated by the *sin()* function is in degrees, it must be converted to radians to obtain a correct result. To use the *sin()* function, you see that the *math.h* header file has been included at the beginning of the program.

PROBLEM SOLVING IN ACTION: A TECHNICAL CHALLENGE: POLAR AND RECTANGULAR COORDINATES

PROBLEM

Many times in physics and engineering problems, you are required to convert between rectangular and polar coordinates. This is especially true in vector analysis. The vector diagram in Figure 5.3 summarizes the conversion process.

As you can see, a vector can be represented in one of two ways.

1. Polar coordinate:

$$M \angle \theta$$

   where

   M is the magnitude, or length, of the vector.

   θ is the angle the vector makes with the horizontal axis.

2. Rectangular coordinate:

$$x + jy$$

   where

   x is the real axis, or horizontal coordinate, for the tip of the vector.

   y is the imaginary axis, or vertical coordinate, for the tip of the vector.

   $j = \sqrt{-1}$, an imaginary number

Using right-angle trigonometry, you can convert between polar and rectangular coordinates. The conversion equations are shown in the figure. Let's write a C++ program that will convert from polar to rectangular coordinates using values supplied by the user. (A program to convert from rectangular to polar is left as a problem for you at the end of the chapter.)

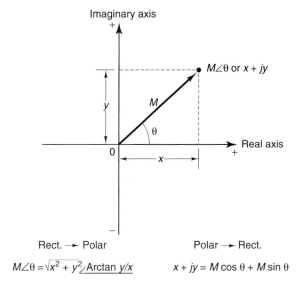

Rect. → Polar

$$M\angle\theta = \sqrt{x^2 + y^2}\angle\text{Arctan } y/x$$

Polar → Rect.

$$x + jy = M\cos\theta + M\sin\theta$$

FIGURE 5.3   POLAR/RECTANGULAR CONVERSION.

Defining the Problem

Output: The output will be in tabular form, showing the input polar coordinate and the corresponding rectangular coordinate. The polar coordinate will be displayed in the format $M @ \theta$. The values of M and θ will be displayed as variables, and the @ symbol will be displayed as a fixed character. The rectangular coordinate will be displayed using the format $x + jy$. The values of x and y will be displayed as variables using two decimal places. The + symbol and j character will be displayed as fixed character information.

Input: The user must enter the magnitude of the vector and the angle it makes with the horizontal axis, in degrees.

Processing: The program must calculate x and y as follows:

$$x = M\cos\theta$$

$$y = M\sin\theta$$

Planning the Solution

Using the foregoing problem definition, an appropriate set of algorithms is as follows:

Initial Algorithm

   main()
   BEGIN
       Call function to set the polar coordinates from user entries.
       Call function to calculate the rectangular coordinate.

Call function to display the input polar coordinate and calculated rectangular coordinate.

END.

First Level of Refinement

setData()
BEGIN

Write a user prompt to enter the vector magnitude, *M*.
Read *M*.
Write a user prompt to enter the vector angle, *Angle,* in degrees.
Read *Angle*.

END.

calculateRectangular()
BEGIN

Calculate $x = M \cos (Angle)$.
Calculate $y = M \sin (Angle)$.

END.

displayResults()
BEGIN

Write the table headings.
Write the polar coordinate, *M @ Angle*.
Write the rectangular coordinate $x + jy$.

END.

Coding the Program

Following this set of algorithms, the flat program implementation is as follows:

```
/*
ACTION 5-3 (ACT05_03.CPP)
OUTPUT:          THE OUTPUT WILL BE IN TABULAR FORM, SHOWING
                 THE INPUT POLAR COORDINATE AND THE
                 CORRESPONDING RECTANGULAR COORDINATE.
                 THE POLAR COORDINATE WILL BE DISPLAYED
                 IN THE FORMAT M @ ANGLE.
                 THE VALUES OF M AND ANGLE WILL BE DISPLAYED
                 AS VARIABLES AND THE @ SYMBOL WILL
                 BE DISPLAYED AS A FIXED CHARACTER.
                 THE RECTANGULAR COORDINATE WILL
                 BE DISPLAYED USING THE FORMAT X + JY.
                 X AND Y WILL BE DISPLAYED AS VARIABLES USING
                 TWO DECIMAL PLACES. THE + SYMBOL AND
                 J CHARACTER WILL BE DISPLAYED AS
                 FIXED CHARACTER INFORMATION.
```

```
INPUT:              THE USER MUST ENTER THE MAGNITUDE, M,
                    OF THE VECTOR AND ITS ANGLE.

PROCESSING:         THE PROGRAM MUST CALCULATE X AND Y AS
                    FOLLOWS:
                    X = M * COS (ANGLE)
                    Y = M * SIN (ANGLE)
                    THE ANGLE MUST BE CONVERTED
                    TO RADIANS DURING THE CALCULATION.
*/

//PREPROCESSOR DIRECTIVES
#include <iostream.h> //FOR cin AND cout
#include <iomanip.h>  //FOR setw()
#include <math.h>     //FOR sin(), cos()

//DEFINE CONSTANT
const double PI = 3.14159;

//MAIN FUNCTION
int main()
{

    //DEFINE VARIABLES
    double x = 0.0;     //RECTANGULAR X-COORDINATE
    double y = 0.0;     //RECTANGULAR Y-COORDINATE
    double M = 0.0;     //POLAR MAGNITUDE
    double Angle = 0.0;//POLAR ANGLE

    //DISPLAY PROGRAM DESCRIPTION MESSAGE
    cout << "This program will convert polar vector coordinates\n"
         << "to rectangular vector coordinates. " << endl << endl;

    //SET POLAR COORDINATE VALUES FROM USER
    cout << "Enter the magnitude of the vector: M = ";
    cin >> M;
    cout << "Enter the vector angle in degrees: Angle = ";
    cin >> Angle;

    //CALCULATE RECTANGULAR COORDINATE
    x = M * cos(PI/180 * Angle); //(PI/180 * Angle) CONVERTS
                                 //DEGREES TO RADIANS
    y = M * sin(PI/180 * Angle);

    //DISPLAY POLAR AND RECTANGULAR VALUES TO USER
    cout << "\n\n\n" << setw (25) << "POLAR COORDINATE"
         << setw(40) << "RECTANGULAR COORDINATE " << endl;
    cout << setw(25) << "----------------"
         << setw(40) << "----------------------" << endl << endl;
    cout.setf(ios::fixed);
    cout.precision(2);
```

```
            cout << setw(10) << M << " @ " << setw(6) << Angle << " degrees"
                 << setw(23) << x << " + j" << y << endl;

        //RETURN
        return 0;
    }//END main()
```

This program will generate the following display when executed:

```
This program will convert polar vector coordinates
to rectangular vector coordinates.

Enter the magnitude of the vector: M = 5↵

Enter the vector angle in degrees: Angle = 53.13↵

POLAR COORDINATE        RECTANGULAR COORDINATE
5 @ 53.13 degrees       3 + j4
```

You should now have the knowledge required to write such a program. One thing that you should note is the conversion from degrees to radians within the *cos()* and *sin()* functions. You must multiply the *Angle* by the quantity (*PI*/180) to get radians. Remember that the *cos()* and *sin()* functions will only evaluate radians, not degrees.

CHAPTER SUMMARY

Arithmetic operators available in C++ include the common add, subtract, multiply, and divide operators that can be performed on any numeric data type. Addition, subtraction, multiplication, and division are basically the same for both the integer and floating-point data types. However, when you divide two integers, you will get an integer result. If you need a floating-point result, at least one of the operands must be defined as a floating-point value. The modulus (%) operator generates an integer division remainder and, therefore, is defined for integers only and will generate a compile error if used with floating-point values.

There are increment/decrement operators defined in C++. The increment operator, ++, adds one to a variable, and the decrement operator, ––, subtracts one from a variable. You can preincrement/-decrement a variable or postincrement/-decrement a variable. There's a big difference when the increment/decrement is used as part of an expression to be evaluated by C++. A preincrement/-decrement operation on a variable is performed *before* the expression is evaluated, and a postincrement/-decrement operation is performed on the variable *after* the expression is evaluated.

The simple assignment operator in C++ is the = operator. A value on the right side of the = operator is assigned to a variable on the left side of the operator. There are compound assignment operators, such as +=, *=, and so on, that combine an arithmetic operation with the assignment operation. These operators are used as a form of shorthand notation within a C++ program.

Finally, the various C++ header files include several standard functions that can be used to perform common tasks. There are mathematical functions and conversion functions, just to mention a couple of categories.

QUESTIONS AND PROBLEMS

QUESTIONS

1. What value will be returned for each of the following integer operations:
   a. `4 - 2 * 3`
   b. `-35 / 6`
   c. `-35 % 6`
   d. `-25 * 14 % 7 * -25 / -5`
   e. `-5 * 3 + 9 - 2 * 7`
   f. `(-13 / 2) % 6`

2. Evaluate each of the following expressions:
   a. `0.5 + 3.75 / 0.25 * 2`
   b. `2.5 - (1.2 + (4.0 - 3.0) * 2.0) + 1.0`
   c. `6.0e-4 * 3.0e+3`
   d. `6.0e-4 / 3.0e+3`

3. Evaluate each of the following expressions, assuming that any whole numbers are represented using a 2-byte integer:
   a. `5.0 - (6.0 / 3)`
   b. `200 * 200`
   c. `5 - 6 / 3`
   d. `(5 - 6) / 3`
   e. `1 + 25 % 5`
   f. `-33000 + 2000`

4. Evaluate each of the following expressions:
   a. `int i = 0;`
       `int j = 10;`
       `++i + j++;`
   b. `double k = 2.5;`
       `k-- * 2;`
   c. `char character = 'a';`
       `++character;`
   d. `int x = 1;`
       `int y = -1;`
       `int z = 25;`
       `++x + ++y - --z;`

5. Explain how to get information on how to use a standard function available in your compiler.

6. Determine the value returned by the following functions. Use your compiler reference manual or on-line help feature to make sure that you understand how the function operates.
   a. `abs(-5)`
   b. `sin(1.57)`
   c. `log(2.73)`
   d. `log10(100)`
   e. `pow(2,5)`
   f. `pow10(3)`
   g. `cos(0)`
   h. `toascii(' ')`
   i. `tolower('A')`
   j. `toupper('A')`

PROBLEMS

Least Difficult

1. Write a program that will allow a user to convert a temperature in degrees Fahrenheit to degrees Celsius using the following relationship:

$$C = 5/9 \times (F - 32)$$

2. Write a program that will allow a user to convert a measurement in inches to centimeters.

3. Write a simple test program that will demonstrate what happens when you use an illegal argument within a function. For example, what happens when you use a character argument in an arithmetic function?

4. Write a program that will allow a user to find the hypotenuse of a right triangle using the Pythagorean theorem. (*Hint:* Try using the *hypot()* function in the *math.h* header file.)

5. Write a program to solve the following equation for *x*:

$$3x - 5y + 2 = 35$$

Assume that values for *y* will be entered by the user.

More Difficult

6. Write a program to convert from rectangular to polar coordinates. Generate a tabular output of the rectangular versus polar coordinate.

7. The kinetic energy of a moving object is found using the equation

$$K = (1/2) (mv^2)$$

where

   K is the kinetic energy, in kg/s.

   m is the mass, in kilograms.

   v is the velocity, in m/s.

Write a program that accepts inputs of mass and velocity of an object and determines its kinetic energy.

8. Here is the inventory and price list of the Health and Beauty Aids department in Ma and Pa's General Store.

Item	Price
Grandma's Lye Soap	0.49
Bag Balm	1.29
Chicken Soup	0.29
Liniment	2.35
Baking Soda	0.63

Ma and Pa want to run a "big" sale and reduce all Health and Beauty Aid items by 5 percent. Write Ma and Pa a program that will display a listing of all the Health and Beauty Aid items showing the regular and sale price. Assume that Ma or Pa will enter the preceding price list.

9. Revise the program in problem 8 to allow Ma or Pa to enter any percentage sales discount.

10. Workers at the CPP∗Mart super-center just received a 5.5% pay increase retroactive for seven months. Write a program that accepts the employee name, employee number, and current annual salary. The program must then display the employee's name, number, amount of retroactive pay due, the new annual salary and new monthly salary in a tabular format.

Most Difficult

11. Revise the program in problem 8 to read the item names and prices from a disk file called *prices.txt* located on a disk in the *A:* drive. Generate the report on your system monitor. (*Note:* You must create a *prices.txt* text file on you're *A:* disk drive with your editor that contains the item names and prices given in the table in problem 8.)

12. Ma and Pa were so elated with the programs you have written so far that they want to expand their computer operations to the payroll department. Write Ma and Pa a payroll program that will calculate Herb's (their only employee) net pay given the following information:

   Employee's name

   Number of weekly hours worked

   Hourly rate of pay

   FICA (7.15%)

   Federal withholding (28%)

   State withholding (10%)

Assume that Ma or Pa will only be required to enter the first three items when running the program. Generate a report using the following format:

       Employee Name: XXXXXXXXXXXXXXXXXXXXXXXX

Rate of Pay:	$XXX.XX
Hours Worked:	XX.XX
Gross Pay:	$XXXX.XX
Deductions:	
FICA:	$XXX.XX
Fed. Withholding:	XXX.XX
State Withholding:	XXX.XX
Total Deductions:	$XXX.XX
Net Pay:	$XXXX.XX

13. The diagram in Figure 5.4 illustrates how triangulation is used to find the distance to an object. Here's the idea: Two triangulating devices are positioned a certain distance apart, and both devices get a "fix" on an object as shown in the figure. The two triangulating devices and the object form a triangle whose one leg, *d,* and two angles $\theta 1$ and $\theta 2$ are known. The third angle is easily found by subtracting the two known angles from 180 degrees. The distance from each triangulating device to the object is then found using the Law of Sines, which states

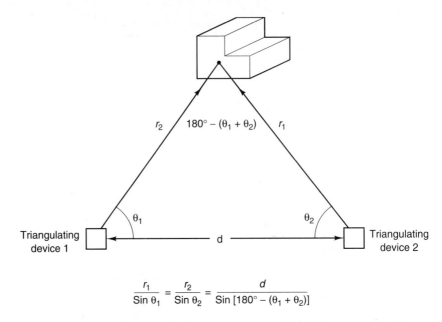

$$\frac{r_1}{\text{Sin } \theta_1} = \frac{r_2}{\text{Sin } \theta_2} = \frac{d}{\text{Sin } [180° - (\theta_1 + \theta_2)]}$$

FIGURE 5.4 A TRIANGULATION DIAGRAM FOR PROBLEM 13.

$$r_1 / \sin \theta_1 = r_2 / \sin \theta_2 = d / \sin[180 - (\theta_1 + \theta_2)]$$

Write a program to find the distance that the object is from each triangulation device. Assume that the user will enter the distance (d) between the devices and the two angles (θ_1 and θ_2) that the object makes with the triangulating devices.

GRAPHICS 101: SIMPLE GRAPHICS

Purpose

- To become familiar with simple windows graphics.
- To learn how to draw points, or pixels, of different colors.
- To understand RGB colors.
- To learn how to draw lines.
- To learn how to draw rectangles.
- To learn how to draw ellipses.

INTRODUCTION

In this module, you will experiment with graphical components. These components include pixels, lines, rectangles and ellipses. They are created in windows by using functions available in the *windows.h* header file. You will use the windows template from the *GUI* module as a shell for your graphics code. You will modify the code and observe the effect on the graphics generated by the template. Now, let's have some fun.

PROCEDURE: PIXELS

1. Load your *GUI101* project code, which includes the windows template. Make sure that you have removed any code added to the template in the *GUI101* module. If the project is not available, go back to the *GUI101* module at the end of Chapter 4 and repeat step 1 of the procedure.

2. The most basic windows graphics function is *SetPixel()*. All other graphics are represented by groups of pixels; therefore, you could actually draw every other graphic discussed in this module using the *SetPixel()* function, but you probably wouldn't want to, because there are additional functions for these other graphics. Place the following statement in section **F** of the windows template.

```
SetPixel(hdc,5,10,RGB(0,0,0));
```

3. Compile and run the program. You should see the *GUI101* window and, if you look real close, you should see a dot in the upper left-hand quadrant of the window. This is a single pixel created by the *SetPixel()* function.

4. Close the *GUI101* window.

5. Look at the *SetPixel()* function code. The second and third arguments are the *x*- and *y*-coordinates for the pixel location within the window. Change these values,

recompile, and rerun the program. The pixel location will change according to the *x*- and *y*-coordinate values that you entered.

6. Close the *GUI101* window.

7. Notice from the code that the *RGB()* function is called as the last argument of the *SetPixel()* function. *RGB* means *Red*, *Green*, *Blue*. These are the three primary colors used by your monitor to create color graphics. Any color can be created by combining these three primary colors. The strength of each color is controlled by a value between 0 and 255. The color values are the arguments for the *RGB()* function. The forgoing code created a black pixel because the *RGB* color values were 0,0,0. What color pixel would be created for the following *RGB* values?

255,0,0
0,255,0
0,0,255
255,255,255

Change the *RGB* function arguments to each of these values. Compile, and run the program for each value. Were you right? The first value produces a red pixel, the second a green pixel, the third value a blue pixel, and the fourth value a white pixel. Of course, you couldn't see the white pixel because all the other pixels in the window are also white.

DISCUSSION

A pixel, or picture element, is a small unit of screen measurement. The size of a pixel varies depending on your screen *resolution*. The screen resolution is determined by how many pixels your monitor screen contains. Typically, your screen will be 640 × 480 pixels, 800 × 600 pixels, or 1024 × 768 pixels.

All graphics functions require an *x*- and *y*-coordinate, measured in pixels, as arguments to locate the graphic. Remember that the *x*-coordinate is the distance from the left side of the window, and a *y*-coordinate is the distance from the top of the window. The number and meaning of these coordinates differs with the graphic function being used. For instance, to draw a pixel you specify the *x*- and *y*-coordinates of the pixel to draw, but to draw a line you specify the *x*- and *y*- coordinates of the beginning point, then you specify the *x*- and *y*-coordinates of the end point.

PROCEDURE (*CONTINUED*) LINES

8. Close the *GUI101* window if you have not already done so.

9. Place the following two statements into section **F** of the template.

```
MoveToEx(hdc,0,0,NULL);
LineTo(hdc,100,100);
```

10. Compile and run the program. You should see at line running from the upper left-hand corner of the window down towards the middle of the window.

11. Close the *GUI101* window.

12. It takes two functions to draw a line. First, you need to set where to draw the line from using *MoveToEx()*, then you specify where to draw the line to using *LineTo()*. The numeric arguments in each function provide the *x*- and *y*-coordinate values for the function. Change the coordinate arguments, then recompile and run the program observing the effect on the line being drawn.

13. Close the *GUI101* window.

14. Replace any code in section **F** of the template with the following:

```
MoveToEx(hdc,0,0,NULL);
LineTo(hdc,100,100);
LineTo(hdc,300,50);
```

15. Compile and run the program and you should see the two connected lines shown in Figure 1.

16. Close the *GUI101* window.

17. Add the following two lines of code to the code already in section **F** of the template:

```
MoveToEx(hdc,0,50,NULL);
LineTo(hdc,200,50);
```

18. Compile and run the program and you should see the lines shown in Figure 2.

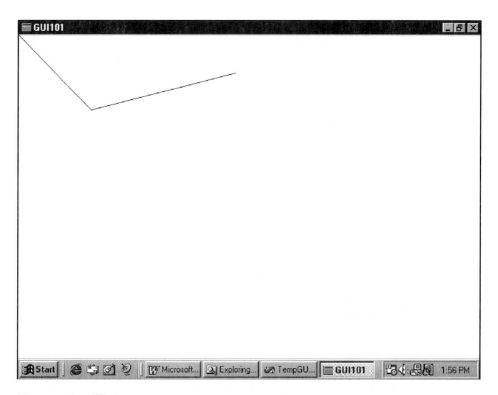

FIGURE 1   TWO CONNECTED LINES ARE DRAWN USING TWO CALLS TO FUNCTION *LINETO()*, AFTER A CALL TO *MOVETOEX()*.

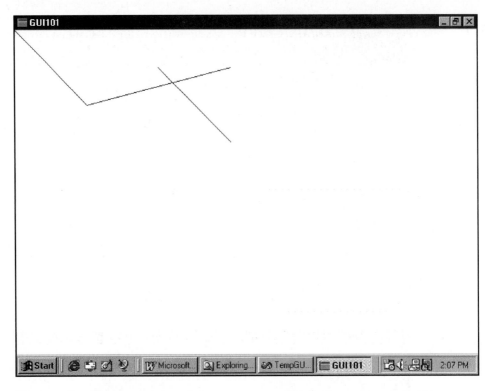

FIGURE 2 **TWO UNCONNECTED LINES REQUIRES TWO CALLS TO**
MOVETOEX(), EACH FOLLOWED BY A CALL TO LINETO().

DISCUSSION

It takes two functions to draw a line. First you need to set where to draw the line from using *MoveToEx()*, then you specify where to draw the line to using *LineTo()*. The numeric arguments in each function provide the *x*- and *y*-coordinate values for the function. For example, the statement *MoveToEx(hdc,0,0,NULL)* says that the line will start at *x*- and *y*-coordinate values of 0 [i.e., (0,0)]. The function requires *hdc* as the first argument, then the *x*-coordinate of the starting point, the *y*-coordinate of the starting point, and the word *NULL* in all capital letters. Notice that there is no reference to color in this call. The line will always be black. (*Note:* It is possible to change the color, but this is beyond the scope of this module.)

If you want to draw a second line connected to the first, you don't have to call *MoveToEx()* again—the endpoint of the previous line will be the starting point of the second line. You just insert a second *LineTo()* function immediately after the first. The *MoveToEx()* function is like picking up a pen and putting the tip at a place on the paper, and the *LineTo()* function is like dragging the point of the pen over the paper to another spot to make the line. If you draw a second straight line without picking up the pen, you will have two connected lines. If you draw a second line after picking up the pen and setting it at a different starting point, you will get two unconnected lines.

PROCEDURE *(CONTINUED)* RECTANGLES AND ELLIPSES

19. Close the *GUI101* window if you have not already done so.

20. Replace any code in section **F** of the template with the following:

```
Rectangle(hdc,100,100,400,200);
```

21. Compile and run the program. You should see a rectangle inside the *GUI101* window.

22. Close the *GUI101* window.

23. Add the following statement to section **F** of the template, below the *Rectangle()* statement:

```
Ellipse(hdc,100,100,400,200);
```

24. Compile and run the program. You should see an ellipse inside the rectangle as shown in Figure 3. Notice that the ellipse just touches all four sides of the rectangle. Also notice that the arguments of *Rectangle()* and *Ellipse()* are identical in this example.

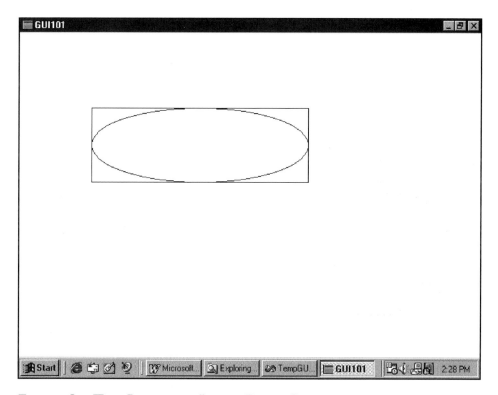

FIGURE 3   **T**HE *R*ECTANGLE*()* AND *E*LLIPSE*()* FUNCTION ARGUMENTS ARE THE SAME. **Y**OU CAN THINK OF THE *E*LLIPSE*()* ARGUMENTS AS DEFINING A BOUNDING RECTANGLE, INSIDE OF WHICH AN ELLIPSE WILL BE DRAWN.

DISCUSSION

The *Rectangle()* and *Ellipse()* functions take identical arguments. The first argument is, once again, *hdc*. You can think of the next four arguments in a couple of different ways. If you want, you can think of them as the x- and y-coordinates of the top left and bottom right corners of the rectangle. You can also think of them as the x-coordinate of the leftmost vertical line, the y-coordinate of the topmost horizontal line, the x-coordinate of the rightmost vertical line, and the y-coordinate of the bottommost horizontal line, respectively. These are the four lines that make up the rectangle.

The example above draws a rectangle with the top left point (100,100) (i.e., x value 100 and y value 100) and the bottom left point (400,200). The rectangle is 300 pixels wide and 100 pixels tall.

The *Ellipse()* function is similar to *Rectangle()*. Once again, the first argument is *hdc,* and once again, the next four arguments can be interpreted a couple of ways. We can view them as the left-most x point that the ellipse touches, the top-most y point that it touches, the right-most x point that it touches, and the bottom-most y point that it touches, respectively. The other way to look at it is as the definition of the rectangle that the ellipse fits into, barely touching the center of all four walls as you can see from Figure 3. Said another way, you can think of the *Ellipse()* arguments as defining a *bounding rectangle,* inside of which an ellipse will be drawn. The bounding rectangle actually drawn in Figure 3 is the one that you must imagine is there when you are drawing an ellipse by itself.

PROCEDURE (*CONTINUED*)

25. Close the *GUI101* window if you have not already done so.

26. Change the order of the two statements in section **F** as follows:

```
Ellipse(hdc,100,100,400,200);
Rectangle(hdc,100,100,400,200);
```

27. Compile and run the program again. Where did the ellipse go? The answer is simple—it is underneath the rectangle. The figures are actually solid rather than transparent. They are filled with white, but they are still filled. Anything that is drawn first will be covered up by the second graphic.

28. Close the *GUI101* window.

29. Try moving the ellipse over a little by changing the *Ellipse()* statement to:

```
Ellipse(hdc,150,100,450,200);
```

30. When you run the above code, you should see the right side of the ellipse poking out from beneath the rectangle. You need to be careful about the order in which you draw your graphics. For instance, if you want to draw a smiling face using ellipses for the head and the eyes, draw the head first otherwise it will cover the eyes. By the way, how do you suppose you would use the *Ellipse()* function to draw a circle?

31. Draw a smiling face using ellipses for the head, eyes, and mouth and connecting lines for the nose.

32. Now, its time to have some fun! Make up your own graphics using the functions discussed in this module. Here are some more graphic functions that you might want investigate. Consult your online help or compiler manuals for their descriptions.

Chord()
FillRect()
FrameRect()
InvertRect()
Pie()
Polygon()
PolyPolygon()
RoundRect()

DECISIONS, DECISIONS, DECISIONS

■ Chapter Contents

Chapter Objectives

When you are finished with this chapter, you should have a good understanding of the following:

- The common Boolean relational operators and logical operators used in C++.
- The C++ decision control structures of **if**, **if/else**, and **switch**.
- How to read and write Boolean data.
- How to compare strings.
- Nested **if** and **if/else** structures.
- How to test for invalid user entries in a program.
- When to use the **break** and **default** options in a **switch** statement.
- How to write menu-driven programs.
- How functions are used to pass data within a program.

INTRODUCTION

At the basic level of any programming language are three fundamental patterns called *control structures*. A control structure is simply a pattern for controlling the flow of a program module. The three fundamental control structures of a programming language are *sequence*, *decision* (sometimes called *selection*), and *iteration*. The sequence control structure is illustrated in Figure 6.1. As you can see, there is nothing fancy about this control structure, because program statements are executed sequentially, one after another, in a straight-line fashion. This is called *straight-line programming* and is what you have been doing in C++ up to this point.

> A *control structure* is a pattern for controlling the flow of a program module. The three fundamental control structures of any programming language are *sequence*, *decision*, and *iteration*.

The second two control structures, decision and iteration, allow the flow of the program to be altered, depending on one or more Boolean conditions. The decision control structure is a decision-making control structure. It is implemented in C++ using the **if**, **if/else**, and **switch** statements. These are the topics of this chapter. The iteration control structure is a repetition control structure. It is implemented in C++ using the **while**, **do/while**, and **for** statements. These operations are discussed in the next chapter. Both the decision and iteration control structures force the computer to make decisions based on the result of a Boolean test condition. So, lets first explore the Boolean operators available in C++.

6.1   BOOLEAN OPERATORS

The real intelligence of a computer comes from its ability to make decisions. All computer decisions, no matter how complex, reduce to Boolean decisions because of the digital nature of the CPU. A Boolean decision is one that is based on a Boolean result of true or false. That's pretty simple, right? Remember, no matter how complex or sophisticated a digital computer system seems to be, it is only making simple Boolean decisions: on or off, 1 or 0, true or false. Decisions in a computer program are made by testing one condition against another, such as *if x < y*. Here, the condition of *x* is tested against the condition of *y*. If *x* is in fact less than *y*,

FIGURE 6.1   **THE SEQUENCE CONTROL STRUCTURE IS A SERIES OF SEQUENTIAL STEP-BY-STEP STATEMENTS.**

the test result is true. However, if the value of *x* is greater than or equal to the value of *y*, the test is false. Thus, the result of such a test will be a Boolean result of true or false.

To test conditions within a program, you will use a Boolean operator. In C and C++, a logical false is equated to a 0, and a logical true is equated to a 1. (Actually, *any nonzero* value is considered true when applied to a Boolean operation in C++.) Boolean operators in C++ can be categorized as either *relational* or *logical* operators.

> The C and C++ languages equate a Boolean value of false to 0 and a Boolean value of true to a non-zero value, usually 1.

Relational Operators

Relational operators allow two quantities to be compared. The six common relational operators available in C++ are listed in Table 6.1. The relational operators in Table 6.1 can be used to compare any two variables or expressions. In general, you should only compare data of the same data type. This means that integers should be compared to integers, floating-point to floating-point, and characters to characters. The one exception to this rule is that floating-point values can be compared to integers, because any integer can be expressed as a floating-point value. In all cases, the operation generates a Boolean result of true or false. Let's look at some examples.

EXAMPLE 6.1

Evaluate the following relational operations:

  a.   5 == 5
  b.   0.025 >= 0.333
  c.   3 != 3
  d.   −45.2 < −3

TABLE 6.1   THE SIX RELATIONAL OPERATORS USED IN C++

Mathematical Symbol	C++ Operator	Meaning
=	==	Equal to
≠	!=	Not equal to
<	<	Less than
≤	<=	Less than or equal to
>	>	Greater than
≥	>=	Greater than or equal to

    e. 'A' < 'Z'

    f. $x = 25, y = -10$

       $x <= y$

Solution

    a. true', because 5 equals 5.

    b. false, because 0.025 is not greater than or equal to 0.333.

    c. false, because 3 equals 3.

    d. true, because −45.2 is less than −3.

    e. true, because C++ is actually comparing the ASCII value of 'A' to the ASCII value of 'Z'.

    f. false, because the value assigned to x (25) is not less than or equal to the value assigned to y (−10).

Relational operators can also be combined with arithmetic operators, like this:

$$5 + 3 < 4$$

Now the question is: How does the computer evaluate this expression? Does it perform the addition operation or the relational operation first? If it performs the addition operation first, the result is false. However, if it performs the relational operation first, 3 is less than 4 and the result is true. As you might suspect, the addition operation is performed first, and then the relational operation. Consequently, the result is false, because 8 is not less than 4. Remember, when relational operators are combined with arithmetic operators within an expression, the *relational operators are always performed last.*

EXAMPLE 6.2

Both arithmetic and relational operators can be part of an output statement to evaluate an expression. Determine the output generated by the following program:

```
/*
EXAMPLE 6-2 (EX06_02.cpp)
*/

//PREPROCESSOR DIRECTIVES
#include <iostream.h>   //FOR cout

//MAIN FUNCTION
int main()
{
   cout << (3 + 4 == 7) << endl;
   cout << ('J' > 'K') << endl;
   cout << (3 * 10 % 3 - 2 > 20 / 6 + 4) << endl;

   //RETURN
   return 0;
}//END main()
```

Solution

The output generated by the above program segment is

```
1
0
0
```

The first output line is true, because the sum 3 + 4 is equal to 7. Notice that C++ displayed a 1 for the Boolean value of true. The result of 'J' > 'K' is false (0) because the ASCII value for 'J' is not greater than the ASCII value for 'K'. Finally, the result of the last expression is false (0). Here, the evaluation process goes like this:

$$(((3 * 10) \% 3) - 2) > ((20 / 6) + 4) =$$
$$((30 \% 3) - 2) > (3 + 4) =$$
$$0 - 2 > 7 =$$
$$-2 > 7 =$$
$$0 \text{ (false)}$$

Notice that the multiplication operation is performed first, followed by the % and / operations, from left to right. Then the addition/subtraction operations are performed, and finally the greater-than operation is performed.

DEBUGGING TIP

To avoid execution problems, it is not a good idea to use the == or != operators to test floating-point values. Rather, you should use <, >, <=, or >= when testing floating-point values because of the way that the computer represents floating point values in memory. Unless you have infinite precision, two floating-point values cannot, theoretically, ever be equal.

You can also compare string objects using the Boolean relational operators. For example, suppose we define two string objects like this:

```
string myName = "Andy";
string yourName = "Sandy";
```

Then, to compare these two objects for equality you would use the equals, ==, operator like this:

```
myName == yourName
```

Of course, the result would be false, because the two strings are not equal.

String objects can also be compared using the relational operators. However, the objects must be defined as objects of the ANSI/ISO *string* class.

Logical Operators

Logical operators also generate Boolean results. The three logical operators used in C++ are given in Table 6.2. The C++ ANSI/ISO standard allows you to use the operation names when performing logic operations. As an alternative (and a necessity when using old compilers), you see from the table that the exclamation symbol (!) is used for **NOT**, the double vertical bar symbols (||) for **OR**, and the double ampersand symbols (&&) for **AND**. In an ANSI/ISO compatible compiler, the words **NOT**, **OR**, and **AND** are keywords.

TABLE 6.2   LOGICAL OPERATORS USED
IN C++

Operation Name	Symbol
NOT	!
OR	||
AND	&&

The **NOT** (!) operator is used to negate, or invert, a Boolean value. Because there are only two possible Boolean values (true and false), the negation of one results in the other. For example, suppose we define a Boolean variable A. Then the variable A can take on only two values, true or false. If A is true, then **NOT** A is false. Conversely, if A is false, then **NOT** A is true. This operation can be shown using a *truth table*. A truth table simply shows the result of a logic operation on a Boolean value. Here is the truth table for the simple **NOT** operation:

A	$!A$ (**NOT** A)
true	false
false	true

The **OR** operator is applied to multiple Boolean values. For instance, suppose that A and B are both defined as Boolean variables. Then A and B can be either true (nonzero) or false (zero). The **OR** operator dictates that if either A or B is true, the result of the operation is true. Another way to say this is that "*any* true results in true." In terms of a truth table,

A	B	$A \| B$ (A **OR** B)
true	true	true
true	false	true
false	true	true
false	false	false

Notice from the table that A **OR** B is true whenever A is true *or* B is true. Of course, if both A and B are true, the result is true.

The **AND** operator also operates on multiple Boolean values. Here, if A and B are Boolean variables, then the expression A **AND** B is true only when both A and B are both true. Another way to say this is that "*any* false results in false." In terms of a truth table

A	B	A && B (A **AND** B)
true	true	true
true	false	false
false	true	false
false	false	false

The Boolean logical operators can also be applied to logical expressions. For example, consider the following:

$$(-6 < 0) \ \&\& \ (12 > = 10)$$

Is this expression true or false? Well, $-6 < 0$ is true and $12 > = 10$ is true. Since the && means **AND**, the expression must be true. How about this one?

$$((3 - 6) == 3) \ || \ (\ !(2 == 4))$$

You must evaluate both sides of the expression. If either side is true, then the result is true, because the || symbol means **OR**. On the left side, $3 - 6$ is equal to -3, which is not equal to 3. Thus, the left side is false. On the right side, $2 == 4$ is false, but $!(2 == 4)$ must be true, because the ! means **NOT** and **NOT**$(2 == 4)$ is **NOT** false, which is true. Consequently, the right side of the expression is true. This makes the result of the **OR**ing operation true.

Observe in the two foregoing expressions that parentheses are used to define the expressions being operated upon. Remember to do this whenever you use a logical operator to evaluate two or more expressions. In other words, *always* enclose the things you are **OR**ing and **AND**ing within parentheses.

You will see in the next section how these logical operators are used to make decisions that control the flow of a program. For example, using the **AND** operator, you can test to see if two conditions are true. If both conditions are true, the program will execute a series of statements, while skipping those statements if one of the test conditions is false.

PROGRAMMING NOTE

You should be aware that the single vertical bar, |, and single ampersand symbol, &, also have meaning to C++. So, always be sure to use two vertical bars, ||, and two ampersand symbols, &&, when you code the logical **OR** and **AND** tests, respectively.

Quick Check

1. Operators that allow two values to be compared are called _____ operators.
2. What is the difference between the = operator and the == operator in C++?
3. What value is generated as a result of the following operation?

    $$4 > 5 - 2$$

4. What value is generated as a result of the following operation?

    $$(5 \mathrel{!=} 5) \mathbin{\&\&} (3 == 3)$$

5. How do you test string objects for equality or inequality?

PROBLEM SOLVING IN ACTION: BOOLEAN LOGIC

PROBLEM

A common Boolean logic operator that is not available in C++ is the NAND (NOT AND) operation. Given two variables, A and B, the NAND operation is defined as follows:

A	B	A NAND B
true	true	false
true	false	true
false	true	true
false	false	true

Notice that the NAND operation is simply the opposite of the AND operation. In symbols, A NAND B = NOT(A AND B). Write a C++ program that will display the NAND result of two logical values entered by the user. Let's begin by defining the problem in terms of output, input, and processing.

Defining the Problem

Output: The program must display the logical result of the NAND operation as defined by its truth table.

Input: The user must enter logical values for the input variables, A and B.

Processing: Although the NAND operation is not available in C++, you can implement it by using the NOT and AND operators, like this:

$$A \text{ NAND } B = \text{NOT}(A \text{ AND } B)$$

Because this is a relatively simple problem, we do not need to divide the problem into smaller subproblems. Rather, we will develop a single algorithm from the problem definition. Now, the problem definition requires us to prompt the user to enter two Boolean values for A and B and apply the foregoing relationship to generate a Boolean result. However, there is one minor difficulty. *You cannot read Boolean values directly from the keyboard.* Instead, you must read character information, test the information for true or false, and then make an assignment to the variables, A and B. Here's an algorithm that will do the job.

Planning the Solution

BEGIN
    Write a program-description message.
    Write a prompt to enter a logical value of 'T' for true or 'F' for false.
    Read *entry*.
    If *entry* is 'T' then
        Assign true to A.
    Else
        Assign false to A.
    Write a prompt to enter a logical value of 'T' for true or 'F' for false.
    Read *entry*.
    If *entry* is 'T' then
        Assign true to B.
    Else
        Assign false to B.
    Assign NOT(A AND B) to NAND.
    Write NAND.
END.

The algorithm shows that a character ('T' or 'F') is read in and then tested to see if it is a 'T' or 'F'. An assignment is then made to the Boolean variable, depending on the test. If the character is a 'T', then true is assigned to the Boolean variable; else false is assigned to the variable. This testing operation is called an **if/else** operation, for obvious reasons. You will learn more about this in the next section. Once the proper Boolean values have been assigned, the NAND operation is performed, and the result is displayed. Here's the program.

Coding the Program

```
/*
ACTION 6-1 (ACT06_01.CPP)

OUTPUT: THE PROGRAM MUST DISPLAY THE
LOGICAL RESULT OF THE NAND OPERATION

INPUT: THE USER MUST ENTER BOOLEAN VALUES FOR
THE INPUT VARIABLES, A AND B.

PROCESSING: A NAND B = NOT (A AND B) = ! (A && B)
*/
```

```
//PREPROCESSOR DIRECTIVES
#include <iostream.h>        //FOR cin AND cout

//MAIN FUNCTION
int main()
{

//DEFINE VARIABLES
char entry = ' ';                       // USER ENTRY
bool NAND = false;                      // RESULT OF NAND OPERATION
bool A = false;                         // BOOLEAN VALUE
bool B = false;                         // BOOLEAN VALUE

//DISPLAY PROGRAM DESCRIPTION MESSAGE
cout << "\nThis program will generate a NAND (not AND) result\n"
     << "from two bool values that you must enter. "
     << endl << endl;

//GET USER INPUT FOR FIRST BOOLEAN VARIABLE
cout << "Enter a Boolean value (T for TRUE or F for FALSE)" << endl;
cin >>  entry;

//TEST USER INPUT FOR TRUE OR FALSE AND
//MAKE BOOLEAN ASSIGNMENT
if ((entry == 'T') || (entry == 't'))
   A = true;
else
   A = false;

//GET USER INPUT FOR SECOND BOOLEAN VARIABLE
cout << "Enter a Boolean value (T for TRUE or F for FALSE)" << endl;
cin >>  entry;

//TEST USER INPUT FOR TRUE OR FALSE AND
//MAKE BOOLEAN ASSIGNMENT
if ((entry == 'T') || (entry == 't'))
   B = true;
else
   B = false;

//DETERMINE NAND RESULT
NAND = !(A && B);

//TEST NAND RESULT FOR TRUE OR FALSE AND DISPLAY RESULT
if (NAND == true)
   cout << "\n\nThe NAND result is:  TRUE" << endl;
else
   cout << "\n\nThe NAND result is:  FALSE" << endl;
```

```
//RETURN
   return 0;
} //END main()
```

This program will generate the *NAND (NOT AND)* result, given two Boolean values entered by the user. One thing you will notice is that the variables (*A* and *B*) are defined as variables of the data type **bool.** You must create an enumerated data type if you are using a older non-ANSI/ISO compatible compiler. Of course, if you have an ANSI/ISO compatible compiler, it contains the **bool** data type. Next you see that the variables (*A* and *B*) are assigned TRUE *if* the user enters a 'T' or 't'; *else* the variables are assigned FALSE. Notice also that the logical **OR** operator, ||, is employed to test for either a 't' or 'T' input character in order to make the appropriate assignment. Once the variable assignments are made, the *NAND* expression is evaluated and assigned to the Boolean variable *NAND*. Don't worry about the **if/else** statement syntax now, because it is covered in the next few sections. At this time, it is only important that you understand the program logic. Next, you see the statement *NAND = !(A && B)* used to determine the *NAND* result by employing the **NOT** (!) and **AND** (&&) operators. Finally, the Boolean value of *NAND* is displayed. Remember, however, that C++ will display a 0 for false and a 1 for true. This is why another **if/else** statement is used to display the word *TRUE* or *FALSE*. This is the reason for the final **if/else** statement.

6.2   THE if STATEMENT

The operation of the **if** statement is illustrated by the diagram in Figure 6.2.

The diamond symbol in Figure 6.2 is used to denote a Boolean decision operation, while the rectangles are used to denote processing statements. Observe that the flow of the program is altered, depending on the result of a test expression. The **if** test can be true or false. If the test expression is true, the **if** statements are executed. However, if the result of the test is false, the **if** statements are bypassed and the program flow continues. This is known as a ***decision-making***, or ***selection***, operation, because the program selects, or decides, between one of two possible routes, depending on the conditions that are tested. In summary, the **if** operation

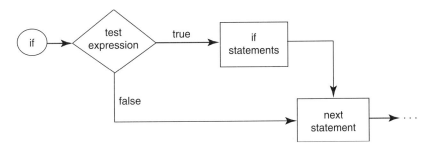

FIGURE 6.2   THE FLOW OF THE IF OPERATION.

can be stated in words like this: "If the test is true, execute the **if** statements." Of course, this implies that if the test is false, the **if** statements are not executed and are then bypassed.

Before we look at the C++ format for the **if** statement, let's take a closer look at the test expression. The test expression is a conditional test. This means that one or more conditions are tested to generate a true or false result. To test a single condition, you will use the relational Boolean operators of ==, !=, <, >, <=, and >=. For instance, a typical test might be *if (x == y)*. Here, the single condition, *x == y*, is tested. If *x* does in fact equal *y*, the result of the test is true, and the **if** statements will be executed. If *x* does not equal *y*, the **if** statements are bypassed, and the next sequential statement is executed.

To test multiple conditions, you must use the Boolean logical operators of **OR** and **AND**. For example, a test such as *if ((x != y) && (a < b))* tests two conditions. If *x* does not equal *y* *and* if *a* is less than *b*, the test result is true, and the **if** statements will be executed. On the other hand, if *x* equals *y* *or* if *a* is *greater than or equal to b*, then the **if** statements are bypassed.

The C++ format for the **if** statement is as follows:

---

*if **STATEMENT FORMAT***

if *(test expression)*
{
  statement 1;
  statement 2;
    •   //COMPOUND STATEMENT
    •
    •
  statement n;
} //END IF

First, notice the overall structure of this format. The word **if** and its associated test expression are written on the first line of the statement. The word **if** is a keyword in C++. The test expression follows the **if** keyword and *must* be enclosed within parentheses. The first line is followed by the statements that will be executed if the test is true. This statement block is *framed* by curly braces. A left curly brace, {, signals the beginning of the statement block, and a right curly brace, }, denotes the end of the block. Notice that the beginning curly brace is placed on a separate line, directly below the keyword **if**. The ending curly brace is placed on a separate line, immediately after the last statement in the block and in the same column as the beginning brace. In addition, you should always indent all the block statements two or three spaces in from the curly braces for readability. When this structure is part of a complex program, there is no question which statements belong to the **if** operation. If there is more than one statement to be executed within this block, the entire group of statements is referred to as a ***compound statement***. When a compound statement is encountered within a C++ program, the entire group of statements is treated like a single statement. Compound statements must always be framed with curly braces. However, framing is optional when there is only a single statement within the block.

Finally, look at the punctuation syntax of the **if** statement. Notice that there is no semicolon after the test expression in the first line. However, each statement within the statement block is terminated by a semicolon.

PROGRAMMING NOTE

Framing of statements within the **if** control structure using left and right curly braces, { }, is *always* required when there is more than one statement, but optional when there is only a single statement. However, framing is a good habit to get into, even when there is only a single statement. This way, if you need to add a statement later on, you will not forget to add the framing.

DEBUGGING TIP

A common error when coding an "equals" test in an **if** statement is to use the assignment symbol, =, rather than the Boolean equals test symbol, ==. Thus, the statement **if** (x = y) will always cause a compiler error and must be corrected to **if** (x == y).

DEBUGGING TIP

A common error when coding an **if** statement is to place a semicolon on the first line, after the test expression, like this

```
if (x == y);
    cout << "This statement will always execute." << endl;
```

This is a very difficult error to find, because it does not generate a compiler error. What happens is that the compiler "sees" two separate statements. The first statement simply compares the value of *x* to the value of *y* and generates a Boolean result that is not used for anything. The next statement is the *cout* statement. So, it's as if no condition is tested at all. The *cout* statement will always be executed.

It's probably a good idea to look at some example exercises and programs at this time to get a "feel" for the **if** operation.

EXAMPLE 6.3

Determine the output for each of the following program segments. Assume that x and y have the following assignments prior to the execution of *each* **if** operation:

```
x = 2;
y = 3;
```

a.
```
if (x < y)
{
    cout << "x = " << x << endl;
    cout << "y = " << y << endl;
}//END IF
```

b.
```
if (x != 0)
    cout << "The value of x is nonzero." << endl;
```

c.
```
if (x < y)
{
    temp = y;
    y = x;
    x = temp;
    cout << "x = " << x  << endl;
    cout << "y = " << y  << endl;
}//END IF
```

d.
```
if ((x < y) && (y != 10))
{
    sum = x + y;
    cout << "x = " << x  << endl;
    cout << "y = " << y << endl;
    cout << "sum = " << sum << endl;
}//END IF
```

e.
```
if ((x > y) || (x - y < 0))
{
    ++x;
    --y;
    cout << "x = " << x << endl;
    cout << "y = " << y << endl;
}//END IF
```

f.
```
if ((x > y) || (x * y < 0))
{
    ++x;
    --y;
    cout << "x = " << x << endl;
    cout << "y = " << y << endl;
}//END IF
cout << "x = " << x << endl;
cout << "y = " << y << endl;
```

g.
```
if (x % y == 0)
    cout << "x is divisible by y." << endl;
    cout << "x is not divisible by y." << endl;
```

Solution

a. The value of *x* is less than the value of *y*. Thus, the output is

```
x = 2
y = 3
```

b. Here, the test is on the value of *x*. If *x* is zero, the test is false. When *x* is a nonzero value, the test is true and the *cout* statement is executed, producing an output of

```
The value of x is nonzero.
```

c. The value of *x* is less than *y*, so the compound statement is executed and the output is

```
x = 3
y = 2
```

Notice that the values of *x* and *y* have been swapped using a temporary variable called *temp*. Why is this temporary variable required?

d. The value of *x* is less than *y* *and* the value of *y* is not equal to 10. As a result, the two values are added and the output is

```
x = 2
y = 3
sum = 5
```

e. Here, the value of *x* is not greater than the value of *y*, but *x* − *y* is less than 0. Thus, the test result due to the **OR** (||) operator is true, and the compound statement is executed, resulting in an output of

```
x = 3
y = 2
```

Notice that the compound statement increments *x* and decrements *y*.

f. This time the test is false. Thus, the **if** statements are bypassed. As a result, the values of *x* and *y* remain unchanged, and the output is

```
x = 2
y = 3
```

g. This is a tricky one. Here, the test is false, because *y* does not divide evenly into *x*. So, what happens? There are no curly braces framing the block, so the compiler takes only the first *cout* statement to be the **if** statement. As a result, the first *cout* statement is bypassed, and the second one is executed to produce an output of

```
x is not divisible by y.
```

Remember, the logical flow of the program always goes to the next statement outside the **if** when the test is false. What would happen if the test expression were true? In this case, both *cout* statements would be executed, generating an output of

```
x is divisible by y.
x is not divisible by y.
```

But, this logic doesn't make sense. You want only one of the *cout* statements executed, not both. To solve this dilemma, we need a different decision control structure called the **if/else** control structure. The **if/else** control structure is discussed next.

Quick Check

1. True or false: The logical opposite of greater-than is only less-than.

2. True or false: When a test expression in an **if** statement evaluates to true, the related **if** statements are bypassed.

3. What is wrong with the following **if** statement?
   ```
   if (x = y)
       cout << "Is there is a problem here?" << endl;
   ```

4. What Boolean operator must be employed to test if all conditions are true?

5. What Boolean operator must be employed to test if one or more of several conditions is true?

6. For what values of *x* will the *cout* statement in the following code be skipped?
   ```
   if(x > 50)
       cout << "Skip me" << endl;
   ```

6.3   THE if/else STATEMENT

The operation of the **if/else** statement is illustrated by the diagram in Figure 6.3. Here, you see that there are two sets of statements that can be executed, depending on whether the test expression is true or false. If the test result is true, the **if** statements are executed. Conversely, if the test result is false, the **else** statements are executed. In words, "If the test expression is true, then execute the **if** statements; otherwise, execute the **else** statements." As compared to the **if** operation, you could say **if/else** is a two-way decision process, and **if** is a one-way decision process.

The C++ format for the **if/else** operation is as follows:

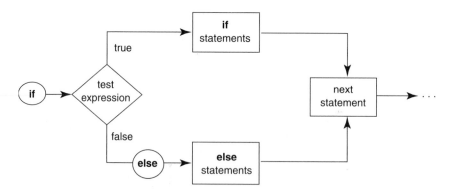

FIGURE 6.3   THE FLOW OF THE IF/ELSE OPERATION.

> ### if/else STATEMENT FORMAT
>
> **if** *(test expression)*
> {
>   *statement 1;*
>   *statement 2;*
>   •   //COMPOUND STATEMENT
>   •
>   •
>   *statement n;*
> } //END IF
> **else**
> {
>   *statement 1;*
>   *statement 2;*
>   •   //COMPOUND STATEMENT
>   •
>   •
>   *statement n;*
> } //END ELSE

As you can see, the **else** option is included after the **if** statement. If the test expression is true, the **if** statements are executed, and the **else** statements are ignored. However, if the test expression is false, the **if** statements are ignored, and the **else** statements are executed.

A few words about syntax: First, observe that both the **if** and **else** statements are *framed* using curly braces. However, you can eliminate the curly braces in either section when only a single statement is required. Second, notice the indentation scheme. Again, such a scheme makes your programs self-documenting and readable.

EXAMPLE 6.4

Determine when the **if** statements will be executed and when the **else** statements will be executed in each of the following program segments.

a.
```
if (x < y)
     sum = x + y;
else
     difference = x - y;
```

b.
```
if (x != 0)
   sum = x + y;
else
   difference = x - y;
```

c.
```
if (x = 0)
   sum = x + y;
else
   difference = x - y;
```

d.
```
if ((x < y) && (2*x - y == 0))
   sum = x + y;
else
   difference = x - y;
```

e.
```
if ((x < y) || (2*x - y == 0))
   sum = x + y;
else
   difference = x - y;
```

f.
```
if (x > 2*y)
   sum = x + y;
   product = x * y;
else
   difference = x - y;
```

Solution

a. The **if** statement is executed when x is less than y, and the **else** statement is executed when x is greater than or equal to y. Remember, the opposite of less than is greater than *or equal to*.

b. The **if** statement is executed when x is nonzero. The **else** statement is executed when the value of x is zero.

c. This is a syntax error, because the Boolean test is coded as $x = 0$ and must be coded as $x == 0$.

d. This segment employs the Boolean && (**AND**) operator. Here, the **if** statement is executed when the value of x is less than the value of y *and* the value of $2x - y$ is equal to zero. The **else** statement is executed when the value of x is *greater than or equal to* the value of y *or* the value of $2x - y$ is not equal to zero.

e. This segment employs the Boolean || (**OR**) operator. Here, the **if** statement is executed when the value of x is less than the value of y *or* the value of $2x - y$ is equal to zero. The **else** statement is executed when the value of x is *greater than or equal to* the value of y *and* the value of $2x - y$ is not equal to zero.

f. This segment of code will not compile because of a *dangling*, or *misplaced*, **else**. This means that the compiler "sees" the **else** all by itself because it cannot associate it with an **if** statement. The **if** statements must be framed in this example to eliminate the dangling **else**. When the **if** statements are framed, they will be executed when the value of x is greater than the value of $2y$. The **else** statement will execute when the value of x is *less than or equal to* the value of $2y$.

DEBUGGING TIP

Always remember to frame your **if/else** statements with curly braces, { }, when you have more than one statement to execute. If the braces are missing, only the first statement will execute. This could cause an error that is very difficult to find. For example, consider the following:

```
if (x < y)
    --x;
    cout << "x is less than y" << endl;
else
    cout << "x is greater than or equal to y" << endl;
```

Here, the compiler "sees" three separate statements, one of them illegal. The first statement is the **if** statement that decrements the value of x if the test is true. The second statement is a *cout* statement. Even though this statement is indented under the **if**, the compiler does *not* consider it to be part of the **if** statement, because it is not framed as part of the **if**. The only statement that the compiler recognizes as part of the **if** is the --x statement. This is a logic error and would not be caught by the compiler. Finally, the **else** is all by itself and, therefore, is referred to as a **dangling**, or **misplaced**, **else**. An **else** must *always* be associated with a corresponding **if**. This is a syntax error and would be caught by the compiler. The dangling **else** problem often occurs when improper framing is used within nested **if/else** logic. Nested **if/else** logic will be disucussed in the next section.

Comparing Strings

The *string* class allows you to compare string objects just like comparing any of the primitive data types. As an example, consider the following:

```
string s1 = "Andy";
string s2 = "Janet";
if (s1 < s2)
    cout << "String s1 is less than string s2" << endl;
else
    cout << "String s1 is not less than string s2" << endl;
```

The comparison test actually subtracts the individual ASCII values of the two strings one character at a time from left to right until an unequal condition occurs or it runs out of characters. Here, the string *Andy* is less than the string *Janet*, since the character *A* is less than the character *J* in the ASCII table.

If you are just interested in string equality, use the equals, ==, operator like this:

```
if (s1 == s2)
    cout << "The strings are equal" << endl;
else
    cout << "The strings are not equal" << endl;
```

Quick Check

1. Why does the following pseudocode need an **else** statement?

    If *today* is Friday

        Write "It's pay day."

    Write "It's not pay day."

2. True or false: Framing with curly braces is always required when an **if** or **else** statement section has more than one statement.

3. When comparing two strings, C++ actually performs a _____ operation on the strings.

4. True or false: An **else** must always be associated with a corresponding **if**.

5. True or false: Objects of the *string* class are compared using the Boolean relational operators just like any other primitive data type variables.

6.4   NESTED ifs

Until now, you have witnessed one-way and two-way decisions using the **if** and **if/else** statements, respectively. You can achieve additional decision options by using nested **if** statements. A nested **if** statement is simply an **if** statement within an **if** statement. To illustrate this idea, consider the diagram in Figure 6.4. Here, a temperature is being tested to see if it is within a range of 0 to 100 degrees Celsius. If it

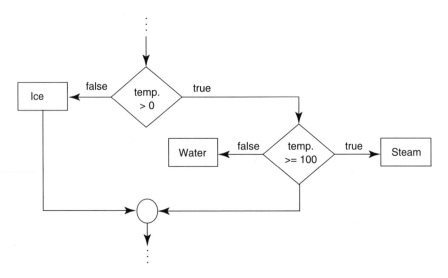

FIGURE 6.4   A NESTED IF OPERATION.

is within this range, you get water. However, if it is outside the range, you get steam or ice, depending on whether it is above or below the range, respectively.

Let's follow through the diagram. The first test-expression operation checks to see if the temperature is greater than 0 degrees. If the test result is false, the temperature must be less than or equal to 0 degrees, resulting in ice. However, if the test result is true, a second test is made to see if the temperature is greater than or equal to 100 degrees. If this test result is true, you get steam. However, if this second test result is false, you know that the temperature must be somewhere between 0 degrees and 100 degrees, resulting in water. Notice how the second test is *nested* within the first test. The first test result must be true before the second test is performed.

Let's develop a program to implement the nested decision-making operation illustrated in Figure 6.4. We begin with the problem definition.

Defining the Problem

Output: The word "WATER", "STEAM", or "ICE".
Input: Temperature in degrees Celsius from the user keyboard.
Processing: Determine if the temperature constitutes water, steam, or ice.

Now for the algorithm. Here is one that will work.

Planning the Solution

```
BEGIN
    Write a program description message.
    Write a user prompt to enter the temperature in degrees Celsius.
    Read temperature.
    If temperature > 0
      If temperature > = 100
        Write "STEAM."
      Else
        Write "WATER."
    Else
      Write "ICE."
END.
```

This algorithm is constructed by simply following the diagram in Figure 6.4. Notice how the second **if/else** operation is nested within the first **if/else** operation. If the *temperature* is not greater than 0 degrees, the nested **if** operation is not performed. However, if the *temperature* is greater than 0, the nested **if** operation is performed to see if the *temperature* results in steam or water.

To code the program, you simply follow the algorithm, like this:

Coding the Program

```
/*
OUTPUT:         DISPLAY THE WORD "STEAM", "ICE", OR "WATER",
                DEPENDING ON TEMPERATURE TO BE ENTERED
                BY THE USER.
```

```
INPUT:          A CELSIUS TEMPERATURE FROM THE USER.

PROCESSING: TEST TEMPERATURE VALUE AGAINST
                A RANGE OF 0 TO 100 DEGREES CELSIUS.
*/

//PREPROCESSOR DIRECTIVES
#include <iostream.h>   //FOR cin AND cout

//MAIN FUNCTION
int main()
{
   //DEFINE VARIABLE
   double temperature = 0.0;   //TEMPERATURE VALUE FROM USER

   //DISPLAY PROGRAM DESCRIPTION MESSAGE TO USER
   cout << "This program will evaluate a temperature to see if\n"
           "it produces ice, water, or steam. " << endl << endl;

   //GET THE TEMPERATURE FROM USER
   cout << "Enter a temperature in degrees Celsius: ";
   cin >> temperature;

   //TEST IF TEMPERATURE IS  WATER, STEAM, OR ICE
   if (temperature > 0)
       if (temperature >= 100)
           cout << "STEAM" << endl;
       else
           cout << "WATER" << endl;
   else
       cout << "ICE" << endl;

   //RETURN
   return 0;
} //END main()
```

Notice how the program flow can be seen by the indentation scheme. However, you do not see any curly brace pairs framing the **if** or **else** blocks. Remember that you do not need to frame a code block when it consists of only a single statement. But, you say that the first **if** block looks as if it consists of several statements. Well, the first **if** block contains a single **if/else** statement. Because the compiler sees this as a single statement, it does not need to be framed. Of course, if you are in doubt, it does no harm to frame the block, like this:

```
if (temperature > 0)
{
   if (temperature >= 100)
       cout << "STEAM" << endl;
   else
       cout << "WATER" << endl;
} //END IF TEMP > 0
else
  cout << "ICE" << endl;
```

PROGRAMMING NOTE

There are different ways to construct nested **if/else** logic. For example, some might see the algorithm logic as follows:

> If *temperature* <= 0
>   Write "ICE"
> Else
>   If *temperature* > = 100
>   Write "STEAM."
>   Else
>   Write "WATER."

Here you see the inner **if/else** operation nested inside of the outer **else** operation. This logic will also accomplish the required decision task. Both methods are correct and adhere to good programming style. We will refer to this method as the **if-else-if-else** form and the earlier method as the **if-if-else-else** form. It's often a matter of personal choice and how you view the logic of the problem. However, as a general guideline, the **if-else-if-else** form should be used when a number of different conditions need to be satisfied before a given action can occur, and the **if-if-else-else** form should be used when the same variable is being tested for different values and a different action is taken for each value. This latter reason is why we first chose to use the **if-if-else-else** form. Notice also that indentation is extremely important to determine the nested logic.

EXAMPLE 6.5

Determine when "Red," "White," and "Blue" will be written in each of the following program segments.

a.
```cpp
if (x < y)
    if (x == 0)
        cout << "Red" << endl;
    else
        cout << "White" << endl;
else
    cout << "Blue" << endl;
```

b.
```cpp
if (x >= y)
    cout << "Blue" << endl;
else
    if (x == 0)
        cout << "Red" << endl;
    else
        cout << "White" << endl;
```

c.
```cpp
if ((x < y) && (x == 0))
    cout << "Red" << endl;
if ((x < y) && (x != 0))
    cout << "White" << endl;
if (x >= y)
    cout << "Blue" << endl;
```

Solution

All three segments of code will produce the same results. "Red" will be written when the value of x is less than the value of y and the value of x is zero. "White" will be written when the value of x is less than the value of y and the value of x is not equal to zero. "Blue" will be written when the value of x is greater than or equal to the value of y, regardless of whether or not the value of x is zero. Desk-check the logic of each code segment to verify that they all produce the same results.

EXAMPLE 6.6

Convert the following series of **if** statements to nested **if/else** statements using the **if-else-if-else** form and the **if-if-else-else** form.

```
if (year == 1)
    cout << "Freshman" << endl;
if (year == 2)
    cout << "Sophomore" << endl;
if (year == 3)
    cout << "Junior" << endl;
if (year == 4)
    cout << "Senior" << endl;
if (year > 4)
    cout << "Graduate" << endl;
```

Solution

a. To convert to the **if-else-if-else** form, we use the logic that if the year is greater than 4, then we know to write "Graduate"; else we test to see if the year is greater than 3. If the year was not greater than 4 but is greater than 3, its value must be 4, so we write "Senior"; else we test to see if the year is greater than 2. If it passes this test, you know that the year was not greater than 4 and not greater than 3 but is greater than 2, so its value must be 3, and we write "Junior". We continue this logic to produce "Sophomore" and "Freshman" for year values of 2 and 1, respectively. Here's the resulting code:

```
if (year > 4)
    cout << "Graduate" << endl;
else
    if (year > 3)
        cout << "Senior" << endl;
    else
        if (year > 2)
            cout << "Junior" << endl;
        else
            if (year > 1)
                cout << "Sophomore" << endl;
            else
                cout << "Freshman" << endl;
```

b. To convert to the **if-if-else-else** form, we use the logic that if the year is greater than 1, we test to see if the year is greater than 2, then 3, then 4. If it passes all of these tests, we know to write "Graduate". However, if the year was not greater than 1 in the first test, we know to write "Freshman", which forms the **else** part of the first **if** test. Next, if the year is greater than 1, but fails the second **if** test (>2), we know to write "Sophomore", which forms the **else** part of the second **if** test. This logic continues to produce "Junior" and "Senior" for year values of 3 and 4, respectively. Here's the resulting code:

```
if (year > 1)
    if (year > 2)
        if (year > 3)
            if (year > 4)
                cout << "Graduate" << endl;
            else
                cout << "Senior" << endl;
        else
            cout << "Junior" << endl;
    else
        cout << "Sophomore" << endl;
else
    cout << "Freshman" << endl;
```

Quick Check

1. Explain why indentation is important when operations are nested.
2. True or False: Any given **else** always goes with the closest **if**.

Consider the following pseudocode to answer questions 3–6:

    If *value* < 50
        If *value* > –50
            Write "Red"
        else
            Write "White"
    else
        Write "Blue"

3. What range of values will cause *Red* to be written?
4. What range of values will cause *White* to be written?
5. What range of values will cause *Blue* to be written?
6. Convert the **if-if-else-else** logic to **if-else-if-else** logic.

6.5   THE switch STATEMENT

This last category of decision enables the program to select one of many options, or *cases*. The operation of the **switch** statement is illustrated by the diagram in Figure 6.5. The selection of a particular case is controlled by a matching process. A *selec-*

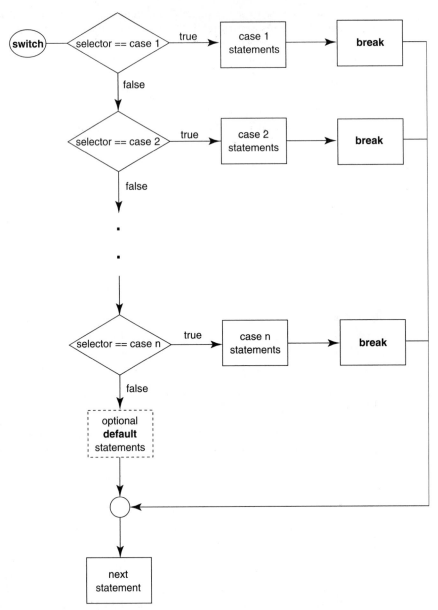

FIGURE 6.5 THE FLOW OF THE SWITCH OPERATION.

tor variable is first evaluated to produce a value. The selector value is then compared to a series of cases. If the selector value matches one of the case values, the corresponding case statements are executed. If no match is made, the program simply continues in a straight-line fashion, with the first statement following the **switch** statement. Here's the C++ format for **switch**:

switch STATEMENT FORMAT

switch *(selector variable)*
{
   case *case 1 value* : *case 1 statements;*
                    break;
   case *case 2 value* : *case 2 statements;*
                    break;
                  •
                  •
                  •
   case *case n value* : *case n statements;*
                    break;
} //END SWITCH

The format requires the selector variable to follow the keyword **switch**. The selector variable must be enclosed within parentheses and must be an integral data type. By an *integral data type*, we mean a data type that is stored as an integer. This basically means that the selector variable must be defined as either an integer or a character. Defining the selector variable as a floating-point variable or string object will cause a compile error.

DEBUGGING TIP

When coding a **switch** statement, the selector variable and case values must be the same data type. Only the integral data types (integer or character) are allowed. Any other data type will cause a compiler error.

The **switch** syntax requires the use of curly braces to open and close the **switch** block of **case** statements as shown. The **switch** block is comprised of several cases that are identified using the keyword **case**. An integral case value must be supplied with each case for matching purposes. The **switch** statement attempts to match the value of the selector variable to a given case value. If a match occurs, the corresponding **case** statements are executed. Note that a colon separates the case value from the **case** statements. A given **case** statement block can be any number of statements in length and does not require framing with curly braces. However, the keyword **break** is often inserted as the last statement in a given **case** statement block. If **break** is not used, any subsequent cases will be executed after a given **case** match has occurred until a **break** is encountered. This may be desirable at times, especially when multiple case values are to "fire" a given set of **case** statements. Again, the idea behind the **switch** statement is easy, if you simply think of it as a matching operation. Some examples should demonstrate this idea.

Suppose the selector variable is the letter grade you made on your last quiz. Assuming that the variable *letterGrade* is defined as a character variable, a typical **switch** statement might go something like this:

```
switch (letterGrade)
{
    case 'A' : cout << "Excellent" << endl;
              break;
    case 'B' : cout << "Superior" << endl;
              break;
    case 'C' : cout << "Average" << endl;
              break;
    case 'D' : cout << "Poor" << endl;
              break;
    case 'F' : cout << "Try again" << endl;
              break;
} //END SWITCH
```

Here, the selector variable is *letterGrade*. The case values are 'A', 'B', 'C', 'D', and 'F'. The value of the selector variable is compared to the list of case values. If a match is found, the corresponding **case** statements are executed. For instance, if the value of *letterGrade* is 'B', the code generates an output of

```
Superior
```

Now, suppose you leave out the keyword **break** in each of the previous cases, like this:

```
switch (letterGrade)
{
    case 'A' : cout << "Excellent" << endl;
    case 'B' : cout << "Superior" << endl;
    case 'C' : cout << "Average" << endl;
    case 'D' : cout << "Poor" << endl;
    case 'F' : cout << "Try again" << endl;
} //END SWITCH
```

This time, assuming that *letterGrade* has the value 'B', the code generates an output of

```
Superior
Average
Poor
Try Again
```

As you can see from the output, case 'B' was matched and its **case** statement executed. However, all of the **case** statements subsequent to case 'B' were also executed. Surely, you can see the value of using **break** in this application.

Are there times where you might want to eliminate the **break** command? Of course! Consider the following **switch** statement:

```
switch (letterGrade)
{
    case 'a' :
    case 'A' : cout << "Excellent" << endl;
              break;
```

```
              case 'b' :
              case 'B' : cout << "Superior" << endl;
                         break;
              case 'c' :
              case 'C' : cout << "Average" << endl;
                         break;
              case 'd' :
              case 'D' : cout << "Poor" << endl;
                         break;
              case 'f' :
              case 'F' : cout << "Try again" << endl;
                         break;
        } //END SWITCH
```

Here, multiple case values need to fire the same **case** statement. So, if *letterGrade* has the value 'b', then a match is made with case 'b'. No **break** is part of this case, so the next sequential case is executed, which will write the word "Superior". Because case 'B' contains a **break**, the **switch** statement is terminated after the output is generated.

What happens if no match occurs? As you might suspect, all the cases are bypassed, and the next sequential statement appearing after the **switch** closing brace is executed.

The default Option

The last thing we need to discuss is the use of the **default** option within a **switch** statement. The **default** option is normally employed at the end of a **switch** statement, like this:

---

default OPTION FORMAT

switch *(selector variable)*
{
   case *case 1 value : case 1 statements;*
                    break;
   case *case 2 value : case 2 statements;*
                    break;
                 •
                 •
                 •
   case *case n value : case n statements;*
                    break;
   default: *default statements;*

} //END SWITCH

The **default** option allows a series of statements to be executed if no match occurs within the **switch**. On the other hand, if a match does occur, the **default** statements are skipped. This provides a valuable protection feature within your program. For instance, suppose that you ask the user to enter a letter grade to be used in a **switch** statement. But, what if the user presses the wrong key and enters a character that is not a valid case value? You can use the **default** option to protect against such invalid entries, like this:

```
switch (letterGrade)
{
    case 'a' :
    case 'A' : cout << "Excellent" << endl;
            break;
    case 'b' :
    case 'B' : cout << "Superior" << endl;
            break;
    case 'c' :
    case 'C' : cout << "Average" << endl;
            break;
    case 'd' :
    case 'D' : cout << "Poor" << endl;
            break;
    case 'f' :
    case 'F' : cout << "Try again" << endl;
            break;
    default  : cout << "No match was found for the ENTRY "
                    << letterGrade << endl;
} //END SWITCH
```

Here, the **default** statement is executed if *letterGrade* is anything other than the listed case characters. For example, if the user entered the character 'E' for *letterGrade*, the foregoing **switch** statement would produce an output of

```
No match was found for the ENTRY E
```

You will find that the **default** option in the **switch** statement is extremely useful when displaying menus for user entries.

EXAMPLE 6.7

A **switch** statement is simply a convenient way to code a series of **if** statements. Convert the following series of **if** statements to a single **switch** statement that employs the **default** option.

```
if (year == 1)
    cout << "Freshman" << endl;
if (year == 2)
    cout << "Sophomore" << endl;
if (year == 3)
    cout << "Junior" << endl;
if (year == 4)
    cout << "Senior" << endl;
else
    cout << "Graduate" << endl;
```

Solution

All that needs to be done to convert a series of **if** statements to a single **switch** statement is to use the **if** test variable as the selector variable and the **if** test values as cases within the **switch**. Here's the converted code:

```
switch (year)
{
    case 1: cout << "Freshman" << endl;
            break;
    case 2: cout << "Sophomore" << endl;
            break;
    case 3: cout << "Junior" << endl;
            break;
    case 4: cout << "Senior" << endl;
            break;
    default: cout << "Graduate" << endl;
}//END SWITCH
```

Notice how the **default** option is used to write "Graduate". You know to write "Graduate" if no match is made to the previous four cases, right? So, the **else** part of the last **if** test is converted to the **default** in the **switch** statement.

PROGRAMMING NOTE

Be aware that a **switch** statement can only be used to code simple equality tests and *not* relational tests. For instance, you cannot use a **switch** statement to determine if a test score is within a range of values. You must use nested **if/else** logic for such an application.

 ## Quick Check

1. The selection of a particular case in a **switch** statement is controlled by a _____ process.
2. Suppose that you have *n* cases in a switch statement and there are no **break** statements in any of the cases. What will happen when a match is made on the first case?
3. True or false: There are never any times when a case should not contain a **break** statement.
4. A statement that can be inserted at the end of a **switch** statement to protect against invalid entries is the _____ statement.
5. A common application for a **switch** statement is_____.

PROBLEM SOLVING IN ACTION: MENU-DRIVEN PROGRAMS

PROBLEM

The **switch** statement is often used to create menu-driven programs. We're sure you have seen a menu-driven program. It's one that asks you to select different options during the execution of the program. For instance, suppose you must write a menu-driven consumer loan calculator program that will allow the user to determine several things about a loan. The idea will be to generate a menu similar to the one shown in Figure 6.6 that gives the user four options as follows:

❑ An option to calculate monthly loan payments.
❑ An option to calculate the total interest of the loan.
❑ An option to calculate the total amount of the loan.
❑ An option to quit the program.

We will assume that the user will enter the amount of the loan, the annual interest rate of the loan, and the term of the loan. The program should reject invalid entries.

Defining the Problem

Output: A program menu that prompts the user to select a monthly payment, total interest, or total loan amount calculation option.
The monthly loan payment, total loan interest, or total loan amount, depending on the program option that the user selects.
Invalid entry messages as required.

Input: A user response to the menu (P, I, T, or Q).
If P is selected: User enters the loan amount, interest rate, and term.
If I is selected: User enters the loan amount, interest rate, and term.
If T is selected: User enters the loan amount, interest rate, and term.
If Q is selected: Terminate program.

```
This program will calculate a monthly loan
payment, total loan interest, or total loan amount.


        Enter P to get monthly payment
        Enter I to get total loan interest
        Enter T to get total loan amount
        Enter Q to quit

    Please enter your choice:
```

FIGURE 6.6   A MENU FOR THE CONSUMER LOAN CALCULATOR PROBLEM.

Processing:	Calculate the selected option as follows:

Case P: *payment = principle * rate/(1 − (1+rate)$^{-term}$)*
Case I: *interest = term * payment − principle*
Case T: *total = principle + interest*
Case Q: Quit the program.
where: *principle* is the amount of the loan.
        rate is a monthly interest rate in decimal form.
        term is the number of months of the loan.

Planning the Solution

Using a modular program design, we will divide the problem into individual sub-problems to solve the overall problem. Two major tasks follow directly from the problem definition:

- ❏ Display the menu and read the user choice.
- ❏ Perform the chosen calculation and display the results.

First, the program must display a menu of choices to the user. The user will enter his or her choice from the menu, and, depending on this choice, one of three calculations will be made to determine the required quantity. The problem-solving diagram in Figure 6.7 illustrates the design.

Notice that there are now three levels to solving the problem. At the first level, *main()*, a function is called to display the menu and get the user choice. The *displayMenu()* function accomplishes this task and *returns* the user choice back to *main()* as indicated on the diagram. Function *main()* will then *pass* the choice to a

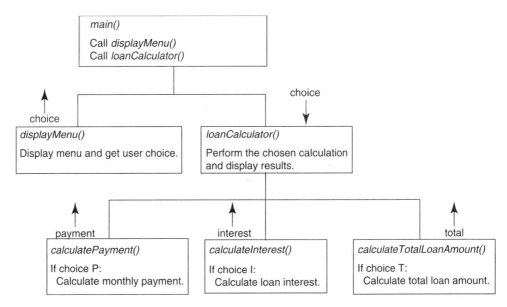

FIGURE 6.7   A PROBLEM-SOLVING DIAGRAM FOR THE LOAN PROBLEM.

function called *loanCalculator()*, which will call one of three functions, depending on the choice, to perform the required calculation. This is the first time you have seen the *passing* of data between functions. This concept is central to both structured and object-oriented program design and the use of functions. From the problem solving diagram you see that the user choice, *choice*, is *passed* from the *displayMenu()* function back to its calling function, *main()*. Then, when *main()* calls the *loanCalculator()* function, *choice* is passed from *main()* to *loanCalculator()*. The *loanCalculator()* function will then use *choice* to determine which calculation function to call. Finally, each of the calculation functions will *return* the value it calculates back to the *loanCalculator()* function.

The initial algorithm reflects *main()*, which is used to call the *displayMenu()* and *loanCalculator()* functions, as follows:

Initial Algorithm

main()
BEGIN
      Call the *displayMenu()* function.
      Call the *loanCalculator()* function.
END.

The first level of refinement shows the contents of the *displayMenu()* and *loanCalculator()* functions, as follows:

First Level of Refinement

displayMenu()
BEGIN
      Display a program menu that prompts the user to choose a monthly payment (P), total interest (I), total loan amount (T), or quit (Q) option.
      Read *choice*.
      Return *choice*.
END.

loanCalculator()
BEGIN
      Case P: Call function *calculatePayment()* and display payment.
      Case I: Call function *calculateInterest()* and display interest.
      Case T: Call function *calculateTotalLoanAmount()* and display total loan amount.
      Case Q: Quit the program.
      Default: Write an invalid entry message and ask the user to select again.
END.

The *displayMenu()* function simply displays the menu and reads the user's choice. Notice that a *Return* statement is used to indicate that the function returns *choice* to the function which called it, *main()*. The The *loanCalculator()* function calls the required calculation function and displays the result, depending on the user's choice. In addition, the *loanCalculator()* function terminates the program if the user chooses to quit and writes an invalid entry message if the user's choice does not reflect one of the choice options.

Now, we need a second level of refinement to show the contents of the calculation functions. Here it is.

Second Level of Refinement

calculatePayment()
BEGIN
> Write a prompt to enter the amount of the loan.
> Read *principle*.
> Write a prompt to enter the annual interest rate.
> Read *rate*.
> Write a prompt to enter the term of the loan.
> Read *term*.
> If *rate* <= 0 OR *rate* > 100
>> Write an invalid entry message.
> Else
>> Calculate *rate = rate/12/100*.
>> Calculate *payment = principle * rate/(1−(1+rate)$^{-term}$)*.
>> Return *payment*.

END.

calculateInterest()
BEGIN
> Write a prompt to enter the amount of the loan.
> Read *principle*.
> Write a prompt to enter the annual interest rate.
> Read *rate*.
> Write a prompt to enter the term of the loan.
> Read *term*.
> If *rate* <= 0 OR *rate* > 100
>> Write an invalid entry message.
> Else
>> Calculate *rate = rate/12/100*.
>> Calculate *payment = principle * rate/(1−(1+rate)$^{-term}$)*.
>> Calculate *interest = term * payment − principle*.
>> Return *interest*.

END.

calculateTotalLoanAmount()
BEGIN
> Write a prompt to enter the amount of the loan.
> Read *principle*.
> Write a prompt to enter the annual interest rate.
> Read *rate*.
> Write a prompt to enter the term of the loan.

Read *term*.
If *rate* <= 0 OR *rate* > 100
    Write an invalid entry message.
Else
    Calculate *rate = rate/12/100*.
    Calculate *payment = principle * rate/(1−(1+rate)$^{-term}$)*.
    Calculate *interest = term * payment − principle*.
    Calculate *total = principle + interest*.
    Return *total*.
END.

Each calculation function obtains the data required for the respective calculation. First, notice that each function employs an **if/else** statement to protect against an invalid interest rate entry. We will reject any interest rate that is less than or equal to 0 percent or greater than 100 percent as being invalid. If the interest rate is invalid, the user is notified. Otherwise, the function makes the respective calculation and *returns* the result. Notice also that the annual percentage interest rate must first be converted to a monthly decimal value for use in the subsequent payment calculation. Finally, you see that each function *returns* the result of its calculation to its calling function.

Coding the Program

At this time, we will code the solution using a flat implementation. However, remember what you have learned here, because in Chapter 8 we will employ structured programming to modularize the coded solution into the functions. Here is the flat implementation of the foregoing program design:

```
/*
ACTION 6-2 (ACT06_02.CPP)
OUTPUT: A PROGRAM MENU THAT PROMPTS THE USER TO SELECT A
        MONTHLY PAYMENT, TOTAL INTEREST, OR TOTAL LOAN AMOUNT
        CALCULATION OPTION.
        INVALID ENTRY MESSAGES AS REQUIRED.
        THE MONTHLY LOAN PAYMENT, TOTAL LOAN INTEREST,
        OR TOTAL LOAN AMOUNT, DEPENDING ON THE PROGRAM OPTION THAT THE
        USER SELECTS.
        INVALID ENTRY MESSAGES AS REQUIRED.

INPUT: A USER RESPONSE TO THE MENU (P, I, T, OR Q).
       IF P IS SELECTED: USER ENTERS THE LOAN AMOUNT, INTEREST
       RATE, AND TERM.
       IF I IS SELECTED: USER ENTERS THE LOAN AMOUNT, INTEREST
       RATE, AND TERM.
       IF R IS SELECTED: USER ENTERS THE LOAN AMOUNT, INTEREST
       RATE, AND TERM.
       IF Q IS SELECTED: TERMINATE PROGRAM.

PROCESSING: CALCULATE THE SELECTED OPTION AS FOLLOWS:
       CASE P: PAYMENT = PRINCIPLE * RATE/(1 - (1+RATE) -TERM)
       CASE I: INTEREST = TERM * PAYMENT - PRINCIPLE
```

```
        CASE T: TOTAL = PRINCIPLE + INTEREST
        CASE Q: QUIT THE PROGRAM.

        WHERE: PRINCIPLE IS THE AMOUNT OF THE LOAN.
        RATE IS A MONTHLY INTEREST RATE IN DECIMAL FORM.
        TERM IS THE NUMBER OF MONTHS OF THE LOAN.
*/

//PREPROCESSOR DIRECTIVES
#include <iostream.h>    //FOR cin AND cout
#include <math.h>        //FOR pow()

//MAIN FUNCTION
int main()
{
  //DEFINE AND INITIALIZE VARIABLES
char choice = 'Q';               //USER MENU ENTRY
double payment = 0.0;            //MONTHLY PAYMENT
double interest = 0.0;           //TOTAL INTEREST FOR LIFE OF LOAN
double total = 0.0;              //TOTAL LOAN AMOUNT
double principle = 0.0;          //LOAN AMOUNT
double rate = 0.0;               //INTEREST RATE
int term = 0;                    //TERM OF LOAN IN MONTHS


//SET OUTPUT FORMAT
cout.setf(ios::fixed);
cout.setf(ios::showpoint);
cout.precision(2);

//DISPLAY PROGRAM DESCRIPTION MESSAGE
cout << "This program will calculate a monthly loan\n"
     << "payment, loan interest, or loan amount." << endl;

//displayMenu() FUNCTION
cout  << "\n\n\t\t\tEnter P to get monthly payment"
      << "\n\t\t\tEnter I to get total loan interest"
      << "\n\t\t\tEnter T to get total loan amount"
      << "\n\t\t\tEnter Q to quit" << endl;

cout << "\n\n\tPlease enter your choice:   ";

//READ USER CHOICE
cin >> choice;

//loanCalculator() FUNCTION
switch (choice)
{
    case 'p':  //calculatePayment() FUNCTION
    case 'P' : cout << "\nEnter the amount of the loan: $";
               cin >> principle;
```

```cpp
                    cout << "\nEnter the duration of the loan in months: ";
                    cin >> term;
                    cout << "\nEnter the annual interest rate in percent: ";
                    cin >> rate;

                    //CHECK FOR INVALID ENTRY
                    if ((rate <= 0) || (rate > 100))
                        cout << "\n\nThis is an invalid entry. Please"
                             << " run the program again." << endl;
                    else
                    {
                        rate = rate/12/100;
                        payment = principle * rate/(1 - pow((1+rate), -term));
                        cout << "\n\nThe monthly payment is $"
                             << payment << endl;
                    }//END ELSE
                    break;

        case 'i': //calculateInterest() FUNCTION
        case 'I' :cout << "\nEnter the amount of the loan: $";
                  cin >> principle;
                  cout << "\nEnter the duration of the loan in months: ";
                  cin >> term;
                  cout << "\nEnter the annual interest rate in percent: ";
                  cin >> rate;
                  //CHECK FOR INVALID ENTRY
                  if ((rate <= 0) || (rate > 100))
                      cout  << "\n\nThis is an invalid entry. Please"
                            << " run the program again." << endl;
                  else
                  {
                      rate = rate/12/100;
                      payment = principle * rate/(1-pow((1+rate), -term));
                      interest = term * payment - principle;
                      cout << "\n\nThe total interest is $"
                           << interest << endl;
                  }//END ELSE
                  break;

        case 't': //calculateTotalLoanAmount() FUNCTION
        case 'T':cout << "\nEnter the amount of the loan: $";
                 cin >> principle;
                 cout << "\nEnter the duration of the loan in months: ";
                 cin >> term;
                 cout << "\nEnter the annual interest rate in percent: " ;
                 cin >> rate;
                 //CHECK FOR INVALID ENTRY
                 if ((rate <= 0) || (rate > 100))
                 cout  << "\n\nThis is an invalid entry. Please"
                       << " run the program again." << endl;
```

```
              else
              {
                rate = rate/12/100;
                payment = principle * rate/(1-pow((1+rate), -term));
                interest = term * payment - principle;
                total = principle + interest;
                cout << "\n\nThe total loan amount is $" << total
                      << endl;
              }//END ELSE
              break;

case 'q': //QUIT THE PROGRAM
case 'Q': cout << "Program terminated" << endl;
          break;

//DISPLAY INVALID ENTRY MESSAGE
default : cout << "\n\nThis is an invalid entry. Please"
              << " run the program again." << endl;
 } //END SWITCH

 //RETURN
 return 0;
} //END main()
```

First, notice how the functions from our design are embedded into this flat implementation. The comments show the location of our functions. Now look at the program closely, and you will find that it incorporates most of the things that you have learned in this chapter. In general, you will find a **switch** statement that contains a **default** option. In addition, notice the **if/else** statements embedded within each **case**. In particular, you should observe the beginnings and endings of the various sections, along with the associated indentation and commenting scheme. As you can see, the program is very readable and self-documenting.

Now for the details. There are eight cases, two for each user-selected option. Notice that the first case in each option allows the user to enter a lowercase character. These cases do not have a **break** statement and, therefore, permit the program to *fall through* to the uppercase character case. This is done to allow the user to enter either a lower- or an uppercase character for each option. Notice that there is a **break** statement at the end of each uppercase case to terminate the **switch** once the case statements are executed.

If the user enters an invalid character from the main menu, the **default** statement is executed, which displays an error message and asks the user to run the program again. Likewise, if the user enters an invalid interest rate within a given case, it is caught by the **if/else** statement, which displays an error message and asks the user to run the program again. As you can see, we have used the **if** part of the **if/else** to catch the invalid entry and the **else** part to proceed with the calculation if the entry is valid. This logic is typical of the way that many programs are written.

```
This program will calculate a monthly loan
payment, loan interest, or loan amount.


                    Enter P to get monthly payment
                    Enter I to get total loan interest
                    Enter T to get total loan amount
                    Enter Q to quit

           Please enter your choice: p↵

Enter the amount of the loan: $1000↵

Enter the duration of the loan in months: 12↵

Enter the annual interest rate in percent: 12↵


The monthly payment is $88.85
```

FIGURE 6.8 **A SCREEN SHOT PRODUCED FROM
THE** *ACTION06_02* **C++ PROGRAM.**

Finally, notice how that standard *pow()* function is to make the payment calculation.

The screen-shot in Figure 6.8 shows the menu generated by the program as well as a sample case execution.

STYLE TIP

As you begin to frame more operations using curly braces, it is often difficult to determine what a closing curly brace is closing. The indentation scheme helps, but a commenting technique is also used. When several closing curly braces appear in succession, you should insert a comment after the brace, as shown at the end of the foregoing program, to indicate what a given brace is closing. Commenting helps both you and anyone reading your program to readily see the program framing.

CHAPTER SUMMARY

Boolean operators are those that generate a logical result of true or false. The two categories of Boolean operators in C++ are relational and logical operators. Relational operators allow two quantities to be compared. These operators include ==, !=, >, <, <=, and >=. Logical operators perform logic operations on Boolean values to generate a Boolean result. The standard logical operators available in C++ are **NOT** (!), **OR** (||), and **AND** (&&). Boolean operators are used within your program to test conditions as part of the decision and iteration control structures in C++.

In this chapter, you learned about the decision-making, or selection, control structure available in C++. These include the **if**, **if/else**, and **switch** statements. Each of these operations alters the flow of a program, depending on the result of a Boolean test expression or matching condition.

The **if** statement executes its statements *if* its test expression is true. If the test result is false, the **if** statements are bypassed and the program continues in a straight-line fashion. The **if** statement can be a single-line statement or a compound statement composed of a series of single-line statements. When using a compound statement, you must frame the entire statement block within curly braces.

The **if/else** statement consists of **if** statements and **else** statements. If the associated test expression is true, the **if** statements are executed; otherwise, the **else** statements are executed when the test result is false. Thus, you could say that **if/else** is a two-way decision operation. Again, compound statements can be used within the **if** or **else** statements; however, they must be framed within curly braces. Additional selection options can be achieved using nested **if** or **if/else** statements.

The **switch** statement achieves decision using a matching process. Here, the value of an integral selector variable is compared to a series of case values. If the selector value matches one of the case values, the corresponding **case** statements are executed until a **break** statement is encountered or the **switch** statement terminates. If no match is made, the program simply continues in a straight-line fashion. In addition, C++ provides a **default** option with the **switch** statement. When using the **default** option, the **default** statements are executed if no match is made. However, if a match does occur, the corresponding **case** statements are executed, and the **default** statements are skipped. Remember, you must always frame the body of the **switch** statement using curly braces.

QUESTIONS AND PROBLEMS

QUESTIONS

1. Evaluate each of the following relational operations:
   a. `7 != 7`
   b. `-0.75 <= -0.5`
   c. `'m' > 'n'`
   d. `2 * 5 % 3 - 7 < 16 / 4 + 2`
   e. `"Andy" == "Andy"`
   f. `"Andy" < "andy"`

2. Determine the output generated by the following (Remember, for Boolean operations, C++ translates false to 0 and true to non-zero, usually 1.):
   a. `cout << (!(1 || 0)) << endl;`
   b. `cout << ((2 - 5/2 * 3) <= (8 % 2 - 6)) << endl;`
   c. `cout << (1 && 0) << endl;`
   d. `cout << (1 || 0) << endl;`

3. The ANSI/ISO C++ standard specifies the *exclusive OR*, **XOR** logic operator. The standard provides for the keyword **XOR** or an alternative caret, ^, symbol to be used as syntax for this operator. Given any two Boolean variables, *A* and *B*, here is how the **XOR** operator is defined:

A	B	A **XOR** B
true	true	false
true	false	true
false	true	true
false	false	false

Do you see a pattern in the table that gives a hint to how **XOR** works? Well, the **XOR** operator will always produce a true result if there is an odd number of true variables. Now for the question: Which of the following logical expressions will produce the **XOR** operation?

a. NOT A OR NOT B
b. (A AND NOT B) OR (NOT A AND B)
c. NOT(A AND NOT B) OR (NOT A AND B)
d. NOT(NOT A AND NOT B)

4. What standard logical operation is performed by the expression in question 3d?

5. Develop a truth table for the following logical expression:

NOT A OR NOT B

6. Which of the following is equivalent to the logic operation in question 5?
a. !(A && B)
b. !(A || B)
c. !A && !B
d. None of these

7. Prove or disprove via truth tables that

NOT A AND NOT B == NOT(A AND B)

8. When will x be written as a result of the following **if** statement?

```
if ((x <= 0) && (x % 5 == 0))
   cout << x << endl;
```

9. Convert the single **if** statement in question 8 into two nested **if** statements.

10. Consider the following program segment:

```
cout << "Enter a value for x:   ";
cin >> x;
cout << "Enter a value for y:   ";
cin >> y;
if x > 0
{
   if y > 0
      --y;
}//END IF x > 0
else
   ++x;
```

a. Are there any syntax errors in this code? If so, where are they?
b. Assuming any syntax errors are corrected, when will y be decremented?
c. Assuming any syntax errors are corrected, when will x be incremented?

11. Consider the following segment of code:

```
cout << "Enter a value for x: ";
cin >> x;
cout << "Enter a value for y: ";
cin >> y;
```

```
if (x > 0)
{
   if (y > 0)
      --y;
else
   ++x;
}//END IF x > 0
```

a. Are there any syntax errors in this code? If so, where are they?

b. Assuming any syntax errors are corrected, when will *y* be decremented?

c. Assuming any syntax errors are corrected, when will *x* be incremented?

12. True or false: You must always frame the body of a **switch** statement.

13. Which **if** does the **else** belong to in the following code segment?

```
if (x > 0)
   if (y > 0)
      --y;
else
   ++x;
```

14. True or false: When using a **switch** statement in C++, a no-match condition results in an error.

15. Consider the following segment of code:

```
if (x >= 0)
   if (x < 10)
   {
       y = x * x;
       if (x <= 5)
          x = sqrt(x);
   }//END IF x < 10
   else
         y = 10 * x;
else
      y = x * x * x;
cout << "x = " << x << endl;
cout << "y = " << y << endl;
```

What will be displayed by the program for each of the following initial values of *x*?

a. x = 0;

b. x = 4;

c. x = -5;

d. x = 10;

16. Consider the following **switch** statement:

```
x = 2;
switch (power)
{
   case 0 :  cout << '1' << endl;
             break;
   case 1 :  cout << x << endl;
             break;
   case 2 :  cout << x * x << endl;
             break;
```

```
case 3 :   cout << x * x * x << endl;
             break;
case 4 :   cout << x * x * x * x << endl;
             break;
default : cout << "No match exists for this power." << endl;
} //END SWITCH
```

What will be displayed by the code for each of the following values of *power*?

a. power = 0;
b. power = 1;
c. power = 2;
d. power = 3;
e. power = 4;

17. Consider the following nested **switch** statements:

```
switch (x)
{
  case 2 :
  case 4 :
  case 6 :   switch (y)
               {
                 case 1 :
                 case 2 :
                 case 3 :  x = x + y;
                             break;
                 case -1 :
                 case -2 :
                 case -3 : x = x - y;
                             break;
               }//END SWITCH y
               break;
  case 1 :
  case 3 :
  case 5 :   switch (y)
               {
                 case 2 :
                 case 4 :
                 case 6 : x = x * y;
                             break;
                 case -1 :
                 case -4 :
                 case -6 : x = y * y;
                             break;
               }//END SWITCH y
               break;
} //END SWITCH x
cout << "x = " << x << endl;
cout << "y = " << y << endl;
```

What will be displayed by the code for each of the following values of *x* and *y*?

a. x = 4;
   y = -2;
b. x = 3;
   y = 6;

c. x = 1;
 y = -4;
d. x = 7;
 y = -2;
e. x = 2;
 y = 5;

PROBLEMS

Least Difficult

1. A dimension on a part drawing indicates that the length of the part is 3.00 ±0.25 inch. This means that the minimum acceptable length of the part is 2.75 inches and the maximum acceptable length of the part is 3.25 inches. Write a program to display "ACCEPTABLE" if the part is within tolerance or "UNACCEPTABLE" if the part is out of tolerance. (*Note:* In Chapter 2, problem 5, you developed an algorithm for this problem. Why not use this algorithm to code the C++ program?)

2. Use your algorithm from problem 10 in Chapter 2 to code a program that will find the roots of a quadratic equation.

3. Write a program that will display two integer values in numerical order, regardless of the order in which they are entered.

4. Write a program that will calculate weekly gross pay for an employee, given the employee's hourly rate and hours worked. Assume that overtime is paid at "time and a half" for any hours worked in excess of 40 hours.

5. Write a program that will display the corresponding name of a month for an integer entry from 1 to 12. Protect for invalid entries.

6. Write a program to generate a truth table for a NOR operation. A NOR operation is a **NOT OR** operation. Thus,

$$A \text{ NOR } B = \textbf{NOT}(A \textbf{ OR } B)$$

Assume that logical values for A and B will be entered by the user.

More Difficult

7. Employ nested **if/else** statements to convert a numerical grade to a letter grade according to the following scale:

90–100   : A

80–89   : B

70–79   : C

60–69   : D

Below 60 : F

8. Electrical power, in watts, of a direct-current (dc) circuit is defined as the product of voltage and current. In symbols,

$$P = V \times I$$

where

P is power, in watts.

V is voltage, in volts.

I is current, in amperes.

Write a menu-driven program that will allow a technician to find dc power, voltage, or current, given the other two values. Protect against invalid entries.

9. Write a program that will determine monthly credit card interest when interest is charged at a rate of 18 percent for the first $500 of balance and 12 percent for any balance amount over $500. Assume that the user will enter the account number, customer name, and current balance. Display a statement in a businesslike format.

Most Difficult

10. Ma and Pa are at it again. This time they need a program that will project the profit of their sporting goods department. The items in the department are coded with a 1, 2, or 3, depending on the amount of profit for the item. An item with a profit code of 1 produces a 10-percent profit, a code of 2 produces a 12-percent profit, and a code of 3 generates a 15-percent profit. Write a program that will project the profit of the following inventory:

Item	Quantity	Price	Profit Code
Fishing Line	132 spools	$3.95	1
Fish Hooks	97 packages	$0.89	2
Sinkers	123 packages	$0.49	2
Fish Nets	12 ea.	$8.75	1
Spinner Baits	256 ea.	$2.49	3
Jigs	49 ea.	$0.29	3

The program should generate a report of the item, quantity, expected profit in dollars per item, and total expected profit for all items.

11. Besides getting a regular salary, Herb also receives a commission on what he sells at Ma and Pa's General Store. His commission is based on the total dollar sales he makes in one week according to the following schedule:

Sales	Commission (%)
Below $250	0
$250–$499	5
$500–$1000	7.5
Over $1000	10

Write Ma and Pa a program that will determine Herb's sales commission from a user entry of his weekly sales. The program should display the total sales dollars and corresponding sales commission in dollars.

12. The value of y is defined as follows:

$$y = x^2 + 2x - 3 \quad \text{if} \quad -3 <= x <= 2$$
$$y = 5x + 7 \quad \text{if} \quad 2 < x <= 10$$
$$y = 0 \quad \text{if} \quad x < -3 \text{ or } x > 10$$

Write a program that will find y, given a user entry for x.

13. Write a menu-driven program that will allow the user to convert between the following units.
   1. Degrees Fahrenheit to degrees Celsius.
   2. Degrees Celsius to degrees Fahrenheit.
   3. Inches to centimeters.
   4. Centimeters to inches.
   5. Pounds to kilograms.
   6. Kilograms to pounds.

   Provide for invalid user entries.

14. The *Foo.com* company has come up with an early retirement incentive program based on years of service according to the following schedule:

20 years or more:	$50,000.00 bonus
15 to 20 years:	$25,000.00 bonus
10 to 15 years:	$15,000.00 bonus
5 to 10 years:	$10,000.00 bonus

Less than 5 years: $0

Write a program using nested **if/else** logic that will determine the correct retirement bonus for an employee. Assume that the employee will enter his/her number of years of service.

SE101: Software Engineering: History and Overview

Objectives

When you are finished with this module, you should have a good understanding of the following:

- The importance of software engineering.
- The purpose of software engineering.
- The six major steps of the software development life cycle.

INTRODUCTION

There is a story about the new *Foo.com* company, whose programmers developed an accounting software system. Although the accounting system performed most tasks without any problems, the programmer's did not test the customer billing software for the case when a customer's account balance was $0.00. So, at the end of each month, the system would automatically send a statement requesting a minimum payment of $0.00 to each customer with a $0.00 balance. When a customer would complain, the *Foo.com* customer service department instructed the customer to simply send a check for $0.00 to avoid penalties and bad credit reports. (Of course, you could probably imagine how this went over with the customer!) Several customers did as instructed and sent their checks for $0.00. One day, the *Foo.com* accounting department received a call from their bank, complaining that the checks they deposited for $0.00 totally crashed their banking system! Of course, the accounting department, along with the customer relations department, immediately requested their programmers to fix the problem.

This type of problem often occurs when problem solving and software development is left completely to programmers, without direction from experienced software engineers, sometimes called systems analysts. Such scenarios are not uncommon in today's world. In most cases, the problems they create are not catastrophic and are corrected with little loss. But, what if such a software "glitch" occurred in our national defense system or the laser system that is performing surgery on your eye? This is where software engineering comes into play. Software engineering is an attempt to solve problems *before* they happen. Specifically, software engineering is a discipline whose goal is to produce error-free software that considers all the what-if scenarios, is cost-effective, and meets all the client's needs. The term *software engineering* was coined in 1967 by NATO to describe software development as an engineering process which attempts to head-off problems through engineering-like activities *before* the software is released to the client.

The renowned computer scientist Grace Hopper stated in her 1988 address to the ACM conference in Atlanta, that we *must* put the systems analyst back into the software development cycle. She further stated that we must walk all the way around a problem, considering all the what-if scenarios. Like, in the foregoing story, what if the customer's balance is $0.00? She also stressed that the human being must be kept within the processing loop, citing what happened to the stock market in October 1987 when we human beings were left out of the trading loop. In October 1987, the market crashed over 1000 points in a few seconds through accelerated computer trading. As a result, the Securities and Exchange Commission (SEC), has since stipulated that all computer trading must cease after any market swing of 200 points or more, thus placing we humans back in the loop. Fortunately, most of the computer industry took her words of wisdom seriously and have since placed more emphasis on software engineering.

> **Software engineering** is a discipline whose goal is to produce error-free software that considers all the what-if scenarios, is cost-effective, and meets all the client's needs.

THE SOFTWARE LIFE CYCLE

Software engineering is concerned with the entire life of a software project, often referred to as the software life cycle, from initial problem definition through the eventual retirement of the software. The software life cycle is formalized by a set of phases which describe a logical process used by software engineers to develop fault-free, cost-effective software that meets all the client's needs. Most texts identify six phases to the life cycle as follows:

- ❏ Survey phase
- ❏ Analysis phase
- ❏ Design phase
- ❏ Construction phase
- ❏ Maintenance phase
- ❏ Retirement phase

The Survey Phase

This phase is sometimes called the *feasibility* phase or the *requirements* phase. The primary purpose of this phase is to investigate the problems, opportunities, and directives that might have triggered the need for a software solution to a problem. Its purpose is to determine what the client *needs*, not what the client *wants*. In addition, the software engineer/analyst attempts to define the scope, size, and preliminary timetable for the project. And finally the engineer must answer the question: "Is the project both technically and economically feasible?"

> The primary purpose of the survey phase is to investigate the problems, opportunities, and directives that might have triggered the need for a software solution to a problem.

The survey phase usually begins with a series of meetings between the engineering team and the major players and users within the client organization. Interviews are then scheduled with key client personnel. These interviews can be structured with pre-planned, closed-ended questions, or non-structured with open-ended questions which encourage the interviewee to speak out. Simple questionnaires can also be used to ascertain information about the needs of the client. The engineering team will also perform a preliminary look at the various manual and automated forms that are used within the target area of the project.

The outcome of this phase will be an initial feasibility report addressing the project scope and timetable and conclude with a go/no-go recommendation.

The Analysis Phase

The analysis phase, sometimes called the *study* phase, is a continuation of the survey phase. Most engineers agree that this phase is probably the most important phase in the software development life cycle, since it attempts to model and formalize the current system. Notice we said the *current* system and *not* the future system. The current system might be a manual or an automated system. In order to develop a new system, the engineer must completely understand the current system. Modeling the current system provides the analyst with a more thorough understanding of the problems, opportunities, and directives that created the system request. The analysis phase also attempts to define the requirements and priorities for a new or improved system.

> The purpose of the analysis phase is to model the current system, whether it be a manual or automated system, and to determine *what* the new or improved system is supposed to do. It also attempts to define the requirements and priorities for a new or improved system.

Further interviews, observations and questionnaires are conducted. The results are formalized using a visual (graphical) modeling technique, depending on whether a structured or object-oriented analysis is being performed. **Structured analysis** uses **logical data flow diagrams** (**LDFDs**) to model the flow of data within the current system. A LDFD is a graphic that shows the logical movement of data within the system and the processes being performed on that data without regard to the physical software or hardware devices that are operating on the data. ***Object-oriented analysis (OOA)*** employs use-case and class modeling to describe the current as well as future system in terms of existing objects and new or modified objects. A ***CASE (Computer-Aided Systems Engineering) tool*** is often used to generate the required graphics with either the structured or object-oriented approach. CASE tools are software products that automate the phases of the software development life cycle. Both structured analysis and object-oriented analysis will be explored in future software engineering modules in this book.

At this point, some engineers might employ a ***rapid prototype***, especially for simple projects. A rapid prototype is a quickly-built software package that models the target system. Fourth generation languages, such as Microsoft Access, are often used for this purpose. The idea is to allow the client users to experiment with the prototype system, while the engineers observe, ask questions, and record their observations. A rapid prototype allows the engineers and the client to quickly agree on what the software should do, since it resembles the basic functionality of the target system.

The outcome of the analysis phase is a comprehensive ***systems requirements statement*** which includes the graphical models, prototypes, and supporting documentation such as interview, observation and questionnaire summaries. A refined timetable as well as another go/no-go recommendation is also normally included in the document.

The Design Phase

The purpose of the design phase is to determine *how* the new system is to satisfy the client's needs. Thus the engineer must convert the analysis requirements statement to a specification for a new or modified system.

> The purpose of the design phase is to determine *how* the new system is to satisfy the client's needs. Thus the engineer must convert the analysis requirements statement to a specification for a new or modified system.

Here, alternative solutions are first identified and evaluated based on technical, economical, and schedule feasibility. Alternative solutions often include doing nothing, modifying the current system, buying canned software, or developing new software, or some combination of these. Based on the alternative analysis, a target solution is recommended to the client and, if acceptable, the actual system design begins.

The design of new software can be a ***structured design*** or an ***object-oriented design (OOD)***. A structured design requires formalization of the new process models in the form of ***physical data flow diagrams (PDFDs)***. A PDFD depicts actual physical entities of the proposed system such as a "C++ *xyz* function," not just logical entities like a process as in the LDFD of the analysis phase. Structured design also employs ***entity relationship diagrams (ERDs)*** to formalize data relationships in order to build any required system databases. An object-oriented design requires formalization of detailed class and class interaction diagrams. Again, a CASE tool is used to automate the design process, whether it be a structured or object-oriented design. In addition to the graphical design, algorithms are developed for the various processes defined for the system. System prototypes are again often employed to get user feedback on input and output design specifications.

The outcome of the design phase is a system specification consisting of the alternative analyses, system recommendation, graphical models and algorithms for the proposed system, prototypes, and a refined timetable. A final cost-benefit analysis is sometimes included to determine if the proposed system is still economically feasible. Of course, the engineer also makes another go/no-go recommendation at this point.

The Construction Phase

The construction phase, sometimes called the *implementation* phase, is pretty straightforward. This is when the various design components are coded and tested individually, then integrated together and tested as a system. The system components will include the classes (OOP), processes (algorithms), databases, and interfaces specified in the design phase. In addition, the system must be fully documented in terms of user and reference manuals.

> The purpose of the construction phase is to code and test the individual system components as well as the complete integrated system.

The outcome of this phase is a completed software system, ready for delivery to the client.

The Maintenance Phase

The maintenance phase is where any future changes and enhancements to the system are made. Two types of maintenance are *corrective maintenance* and *enhancement maintenance*. Corrective maintenance is the removing of any software bugs found by the system developers or the user, without requiring any changes to the software specification developed in the design phase. Enhancement maintenance involves updating the software with new or improved features. When enhancements are made, the software specifications are changed first, then the changes are implemented by changing or adding the system code. By the way, studies have shown that over the complete life cycle of the system, the maintenance phase accounts for over 50 percent of the total cost of the system.

> The purpose of the maintenance phase is to perform both corrective and enhancement maintenance on the system until it is retired.

The Retirement Phase

The retirement phase is when the system software is "retired" from service. However, even a human retiree might do some work at a part-time job, right? So do software systems, since various components of the system might be used in newer systems, especially with object-oriented systems that employ inheritance. Some say that old systems never die, they just keep getting enhanced or converted. We have thought for years that the old COBOL and RPG systems would retire, but they haven't done so yet. Rather than getting retired, they get converted using a newer paradigm and language, like object-orientation using C++ or Java.

You should now have a good overall perspective of software engineering and its role in the software life cycle. Future modules will address both the structured and object-oriented software engineering paradigms in more detail.

LOOPING OPERATIONS: ITERATION

Chapter Objectives

When you are finished with this chapter, you should have a good understanding of the following:

- Pretest, posttest, and fixed repetition iteration control structures.
- The C++ iteration control structures of **while**, **do/while**, and **for**.
- How to detect an infinite loop condition.
- How to desk-check a loop for the correct number of iterations and termination.
- How to initialize product and sum variables.
- How to construct a sentinel controlled loop for data entry.
- How to construct loop-controlled menu-driven programs.
- How to test for invalid user entries in a program using loops.
- When to use the **break** and **continue** options in a loop statement.

- Nested loop structures.
- Down-to loop structures.
- When to use one C++ loop structure over another.

INTRODUCTION

In Chapter 6, you learned about the decision control structure. It is now time to explore the third and final control structure employed by C++: *iteration*. Iteration simply means doing something repeatedly. In programming, this is called *looping* because the iteration control structure causes the program flow to go around in a loop. Of course, there must be a way to get out of the loop, or the computer would loop forever! Such a situation is called an *infinite loop*, for obvious reasons. To prevent infinite looping, all iteration control structures test a condition to determine when to exit the loop. *Pretest* loops test a condition before each loop is executed. *Posttest* loops test a condition after each loop iteration. And, finally, *fixed repetition* loops cause the loop to be executed a predetermined number of times.

The three iteration control structures employed by C++ are the **while**, **do/while**, and **for**. As you will learn in this chapter, each provides a means for you to perform repetitive operations. The difference between them is found in the means by which they control the exiting of the loop. The **while** is a pretest loop, the **do/while** is a posttest loop, and the **for** is a fixed repetition loop. Let's begin our discussion with the **while** loop.

7.1   THE while LOOP

You can see from Figure 7.1 that the **while** loop is a pretest loop because a Boolean test is made *before* the loop body can ever be executed. If the test expression is true, the loop body is executed. If the test expression is false the loop body is bypassed, and the next sequential statement after the loop is executed. As long as the test expression is true, the program continues to go around the loop. In other words, the loop is repeated *while* the test expression is true. To get out of the loop,

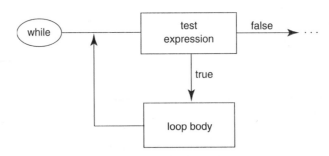

FIGURE 7.1   THE WHILE LOOP OPERATION.

something must change within the loop that makes the test expression false. If such a change does not take place, you have an infinite loop. In addition, the diagram shows that *if the test expression is false the first time it is encountered, the loop body will never be executed.* This is an important characteristic of the **while** control structure.

The C++ format for the **while** statement is as follows:

---

while *STATEMENT FORMAT*

while (*test expression*)
{
   statement 1;
   statement 2;
     •
     •   *//LOOP BODY*
     •
   statement n;
} *//END WHILE*

The first line of the statement contains the keyword **while** followed by a test expression within parentheses. To test a single condition, you will often use the Boolean operators of ==, !=, <, >, <=, >=, and !. To test multiple conditions, you must use the logical operators of **OR** (||) and **AND** (&&). Notice that the loop body is framed using curly braces. This forms a compound statement, which consists of the individual loop body statements. An indentation scheme is also used so that the loop body can be easily identified. Finally, you should be aware that the loop body does not have to be framed if it consists of only a single statement. However, the CPU will execute just this single statement during the loop. Any additional statements are considered to be outside the loop structure. Let's see how the **while** loop works by looking at a few simple examples.

DEBUGGING TIP

Always remember to frame the body of a loop with curly braces, { }, if it contains more than one statement. For example, consider the following:

```
count = 0;
while (count < 10)
   cout << count;
   ++count;
```

The body of this loop obviously consists of two statements, as shown by the indentation. However, the loop body is not framed. As a result, you have an infinite loop. (Why?)

EXAMPLE 7.1

What will be displayed by the following segments of code?

a.

```
int number = 5;
int sum = 0;
while (number > 0)
{
 sum += number;
 --number;
} //END WHILE
cout << "The sum is " << sum << endl;
```

Here, the ***loop control variable,*** *number,* is first assigned the value 5, and the variable *sum* is assigned the value 0. The **while** loop body will be executed as long as *number* is greater than 0. Observe that each time the loop is executed, the value of *number* is added to *sum.* In addition, the value of *number* is decremented by 1. Let's desk-check the code by tracing through each iteration to see what is happening, keeping track of the values of *number* and *sum* after each iteration:

1st Iteration:	*sum* is 5
	number is 4
2nd Iteration:	*sum* is 9
	number is 3
3rd Iteration:	*sum* is 12
	number is 2
4th Iteration:	*sum* is 14
	number is 1
5th and Final Iteration:	*sum* is 15
	number is 0

The looping stops here because the value of *number* is zero. As a result, the loop body is bypassed and the *cout* statement is executed, producing a display of

```
The sum is 15
```

In summary, you could say that the program segment computes the sum of integers from 1 through 5.

DEBUGGING TIP

Always initialize a variable that is accumulating a sum to 0. On the other hand, always initialize a variable that is accumulating a product to 1 *not* 0. What will be the result if such a product variable is initialized to 0?

b.

```
int sum = 0;
while (number > 0)
{
   sum += number;
   --number;
} //END WHILE
cout << "The sum is " << sum << endl;
```

What has been changed in this segment of code versus the previous segment in part a? Well, notice that the loop control variable, *number,* has not been initialized prior to the loop test. As a result, *number* will initially have some arbitrary value from memory. This condition will result in an indeterminate number of looping iterations, often producing an infinite loop for all practical purposes.

> ### DEBUGGING TIP
>
> Make sure the loop control variable always has a meaningful value prior to entering the **while** loop statement. The **while** loop is a pretest loop and, therefore, must have a legitimate value to test the first time the loop test is executed.

c.

```
int number = 5;
int sum = 0;
while (number > 0)
{
 if (number % 2 != 0)
     sum += number;
 --number;
} //END WHILE
cout << "The sum is " << sum << endl;
```

Here, an **if** statement has been included within the loop so that *number* is added to *sum* only if *number* is odd. Why will the calculation be performed when *number* is odd? Well, the remainder of any odd number divided by 2 is 1, right? Since 1 is not equal to 0, the test is true and *number* is added to *sum.* If *number* is even, the remainder operation generates a 0 result. This makes the **if** test false and the calculation statement is bypassed. This program segment computes the sum of odd integers from 1 through 5, resulting in a display of

```
The sum is 9
```

d.

```
int number = 5;
int sum = 0;
while (number > 0)
{
 if (number % 2 == 0)
     sum += number;
 --number;
} //END WHILE
cout << "The sum is " << sum << endl;
```

This time, the program computes the sum of even integers from 1 through 5, because *number* is added to *sum* only if *number* is even. (Why?) As a result, the display is

```
The sum is 6
```

e.

```
int maxNumber = 5;
int number = 0;
double sum = 0;
while (number != maxNumber)
  sum += number;
cout << "The average of the first " << maxNumber
     << "positive integers is :  " << sum/maxNumber << endl;
```

This is an infinite loop. Notice that the loop is executed as long as *number* and *maxNumber* are not equal. The initial value of *number* is 0, and the initial value of *maxNumber* is 5. However, these values are never changed within the loop. Thus, number is always not equal to *maxNumber,* resulting in an infinite loop. No display is generated, and with many systems you must turn off the computer in order to get out of the loop. To correct this problem, you must change the loop control variable somewhere within the loop so that the loop test will eventually become false. In this segment of code, you need to increment *number* within the body of the loop, like this:

```
int maxNumber = 5;
int number = 0;
double sum = 0;
while (number != maxNumber)
{
 ++number;
 sum += number;
} //END WHILE
cout << "The average of the first " << maxNumber
     << " positive integers is :  " << sum/maxNumber << endl;
```

The loop will now produce a result of

```
The average of the first 5 positive integers is:   3.0
```

By the way, why was *sum* defined as a floating-point value?

f.

What would happen if *number* were incremented by 2 in part e? This modification would also result in an infinite loop, because the value of *number* would skip over the value of *maxNumber* and the two would always be unequal.

DEBUGGING TIP

Remember, an infinite loop is the result of a logical error in your program. **The compiler will not detect an infinite loop condition.** For this reason, you should always **desk-check** your loop structures very closely prior to coding and execution. A little time desk-checking will save you a lot of time at the keyboard.

g.

```
bool positive = true; //DEFINE BOOLEAN FLAG VARIABLE
                      //ASSUMES ANSI/ISO STANDARD
int number = 0;
int sum = 0;
while (positive == true)
{
  cout << "\nEnter an integer value: ";     //GET A NUMBER
  cin >> number;
  if (number < 0)     //SET FLAG TO FALSE IF NUMBER < 0
  {
      positive = false;
      cout << "Loop terminated" << endl;
  }//END IF
```

```
        else                    //ADD NUMBER TO SUM AND DISPLAY
        {
          sum = sum + number;
          cout << "The sum is now: " << sum << endl;
        }//END ELSE
      }//END WHILE
```

This is an example of a ***flag-controlled loop.*** A ***flag*** is a Boolean variable that is used to control the flow of a program. We first initialize the flag to **true**, then change it to **false** when a given event has occurred within the program. Here, we have started out by defining a variable for the **bool** data type (ANSI/ISO standard) called *positive*. The variable *positive* is then initialized to the value **true**. The loop will continue to execute as long as the value of *positive* remains **true**. With each iteration, the program will display the sum of the integers entered by the user. However, when the user enters a negative number, *positive* is set to **false**, and the loop will terminate. Why? Here is a typical output produced by the loop:

```
        Enter an integer value: 1↵
        The sum is now 1

        Enter an integer value: 2↵
        The sum is now 3

        Enter an integer value: 3↵
        The sum is now 6

        Enter an integer value: −1↵
        Loop terminated
```

Data Entry Using while

There are many situations in which you will want to use a looping operation to read data. One common example is to read a sequence of characters. The idea is to read a single data element, such as a character, each time the loop is executed. Then break out of the loop when the character sequence is terminated. For instance, consider the following program:

```
//DEFINE PERIOD CONSTANT
const char PERIOD = '.';

//DEFINE VARIABLES
char inChar = ' ';          //USER ENTRY VARIABLE
int charCount = 0;          //CHARACTER COUNT
cout << "Enter several characters, pressing ENTER after each\n"
     << "entry. Terminate the input with a period. " << endl;
cin >> inChar;              //READ A CHARACTER

//COUNT AND READ CHARACTERS WHILE != PERIOD
while (inChar != PERIOD)    //CHARACTER A PERIOD?
{
```

```
      ++charCount;                //INCREMENT CHARACTER COUNT
      cin >> inChar;              //READ A CHARACTER
   } //END WHILE

   //DISPLAY CHARACTER COUNT
   cout << "The number of characters entered was " << charCount << endl;
```

The general idea of this program is to read a sequence of characters, one character at a time, until a period, '.', is encountered. The period is called a *sentinel value,* because it ends the character sequence but is not part of the legally defined sequence. The input variable is *inChar.* The **while** loop is executed as long as *inChar* is not equal to a period. With each iteration, a counter (*count*) is incremented to count the number of characters that were entered before the period. Here is what you will see when the program is executed:

```
      Enter several characters, pressing ENTER after each
      entry. Terminate the input with a period.
      a↵
      b↵
      c↵
      d↵
      .↵
      The number of characters entered was 4
```

Here the user has entered five characters, including the sentinel. The program counts the number of characters entered, excluding the sentinel value.

Now, let's look at the program a bit closer. First, notice that a character is read just prior to the **while** statement because the **while** statement tests the variable *inChar* to see that it is not a period. Without the first read operation, *inChar* would not have a value and, therefore, could not be tested. Remember that the variable being tested in the **while** statement must always have a value prior to the first test. This is a common source of error when writing **while** loops. Why didn't the program count the period? The loop is broken and *count* is not incremented for the period character.

A *sentinel-controlled* loop is a loop that terminates when a given sentinel value is entered by the user.

Programming Tip

When using a sentinel-controlled loop, always provide a prompt that instructs the user what to enter as the sentinel value. The prompts for data entry must continually remind the user of the sentinel value in a clear, unambiguous manner. Never use a sentinel value that the user could confuse with the normal data items being entered.

Quick Check

1. True or false: A **while** loop repeats until the test expression is true.
2. True or false: The **while** loop is a posttest loop.
3. What is wrong with the following code?
   ```
   int x = 10;
   while (x > 0)
     cout << "This is a while loop." << endl;
     --x;
   ```
4. Correct the code in question 3.
5. How many times will the following loop execute?
   ```
   int x = 1;
   while (x <= 0)
   {
        cout << "How many times will this loop execute?"
            << endl;
        ++x;
   }//END WHILE
   ```
6. How many times will the following loop execute?
   ```
   int x = 1;
   while (x >=0)
   {
        cout << "How many times will this loop execute?"
            << endl;
        ++x;
   }//END WHILE
   ```

7.2 THE do/while LOOP

The flow of the **do/while** loop can be seen in Figure 7.2.

If you compare Figure 7.2 to the flow of **while** in Figure 7.1, you will find that the test is made at the end of the loop, rather than the beginning of the loop. This is the main difference between the **while** and the **do/while** loops. Because the **do/while** is a posttest loop, *the loop body will always be executed at least once.* To break the loop, the test expression must become false. Thus, if the test condition is initially true, something must happen within the loop to change the condition to false; otherwise, you have an infinite loop. Here's the required C++ syntax:

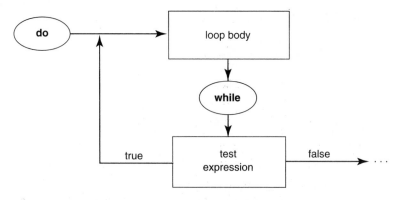

FIGURE 7.2   THE DO/WHILE LOOP OPERATION.

DO/WHILE STATEMENT FORMAT

do
{
    statement 1;
    statement 2;
       •
       •   *//LOOP BODY*
       •
    statement n;
}//END DO/WHILE
while (*test expression*);

This format shows that the operation must begin with the single keyword **do**. This is followed by the loop body, which is followed by the keyword **while** and the test expression enclosed within parentheses. You must always frame the loop body with curly braces if it contains multiple statements. However, no framing is required when there is only a single loop statement within the body of the loop. In addition, notice that there is no semicolon after the keyword **do** in the first line, but a semicolon is required after the test expression in the last line. Look at the program segments in Example 7.2, and see if you can predict their results.

EXAMPLE 7.2

What will be displayed by the following segments of code?

   a.

```
int number = 5;
int sum = 0;
```

```
do
{
 sum += number;
 --number;
}//END DO/WHILE
while (number > 0);
cout << "The sum is " << sum << endl;
```

In this segment, the value of *number* is initially set to 5, and the value of *sum* to 0. Each time the loop is executed, the value of *number* is added to *sum*. In addition, the value of *number* is decremented by 1. The looping will end when *number* has been decremented to 0. The resulting display is

```
The sum is 15
```

Notice that this **do/while** loop computes the sum of integers 1 through 5, as did the **while** loop in Example 7.1a.

b.

```
int number = 0;
int sum = 0;
do
{
 sum += number;
 ++number;
}//END DO/WHILE
while (number != 5);
cout << "The sum is " << sum << endl;
```

In this segment, both *number* and *sum* are initially 0. Again, you might suspect that the loop computes the sum of the integers 1 through 5. But, it actually computes the sum of integers 1 through 4. Why? Notice that *number* is incremented after the *sum* is calculated. Thus, when *number* increments to 5, the loop is broken, and the value 5 is never added to *sum*. The resulting display is

```
The sum is 10
```

How would you change the loop to sum the integers 1 through 5? One way is to change the test expression to *while(number != 6)*. Another, more preferred, way is to reverse the two loop statements so that *number* is incremented prior to the *sum* calculation.

c.

```
int maxNumber = 5;
int number = 0;
double total = 0;
do
{
 --number;
 total += number;
}//END DO/WHILE
while (number != maxNumber);
cout.setf(ios::fixed);
cout.setf(ios::showpoint);
cout.precision(2);
cout << "The average of the first " << maxNumber
     << "positive integers is :  " << total/maxNumber << endl;
```

In this segment, *maxNumber* begins with the value 5, and both *number* and *total* are initialized to 0. The loop is broken when the value of *number* equals the value of *maxNumber*. How many times will the loop execute? If you said "five," you are wrong! Notice that *number* is decremented each time the loop is executed. Theoretically, the loop will execute an infinite number of times. However, because the range of integers in C++ is often from –32768 to 32767, the loop will execute 65,531 times. How did we get this figure? Well, 32768 loops will have executed when *number* reaches –32768. The next looping operation will decrement *number* to 32767. It then takes 32762 loops to decrement *number* to 5. Note that 32768 + 1 + 32,762 = 65,531. Of course, this is infinite for all practical purposes!

d.

```
int maxNumber = 5;
int number = 0;
double total= 0;
do
{
   ++number;
   total += number;
}//END DO/WHILE
while (number != maxNumber);
cout.setf(ios::fixed);
cout.setf(ios::showpoint);
cout.precision(2);
cout << "The average of the first " << maxNumber
     << "positive integers is :  "  << total/maxNumber << endl;
```

Here, the loop in part c has been corrected so that the value of *number* is incremented by 1 with each iteration. When *number* reaches 5, it equals the value of *maxNumber,* and the loop is broken. The resulting display is

```
The average of the first 5 positive integers is:  3.00
```

e.

```
const  char PERIOD = '.'; //DEFINE PERIOD CONSTANT
char inChar = ' ';         //DEFINE USER ENTRY VARIABLE
int charCount = 0;         //DEFINE CHAR COUNTER

cout << "\nEnter several characters, pressing ENTER after each\n"
     << "entry. Terminate the input with a period." << endl;
do
{
   ++charCount;
   cin >> inChar;
}//END DO/WHILE
while (inChar != PERIOD); //CHARACTER A PERIOD?
   cout << "The number of characters entered was " <<  --charCount << endl;
```

This program segment shows how a sentinel value can be employed to break a **do/while** loop. Notice that each iteration reads a single character from the keyboard until the period key is pressed. When this operation was performed using a **while** loop, you had to read the first character prior to the loop structure, so there was an initial value to test. This is because the Boolean test is made at the beginning of **while**. On the other hand, a **do/while** loop performs the Boolean test at the end of the loop. As a result, you do not have to read the first character prior to the loop structure, because the loop body will always be executed at least once and *inChar* will have a legitimate value before the loop test is made.

Now, look at the *cout* statement. The value being displayed is *--charCount*. Why? Observe that *charCount* will be incremented, even for the last loop iteration that reads the period sentinel value. Therefore, *charCount* must be decremented to get the correct number of characters entered, excluding the sentinel value. This is required because of the posttest nature of **do/while**.

Assuming the user enters the string "abcd.", the display would be

```
Enter several characters, pressing ENTER after each
entry. Terminate the input with a period.
a⏎
b⏎
c⏎
d⏎
.⏎
The number of characters entered was 4
```

PROBLEM SOLVING IN ACTION: LOOP-CONTROLLED MENU-DRIVEN PROGRAMS

PROBLEM

In the last chapter, you saw that the **switch** statement is used to create menu-driven programs. It is often desirable to allow the user to select a menu option, perform the task associated with that option, then return to the menu to select another option without terminating the program until a quit option is chosen. Such a program would require the menu to be displayed repeatedly until the quit option is chosen. This is an ideal application for looping. We will encase our menu within a loop so that the menu and associated tasks will keep repeating until the user chooses to terminate the program. We will apply this technique to the menu-driven loan program developed in the last chapter. Let's revisit the problem.

Defining the Problem

Output:	A program menu that prompts the user to select a monthly payment, total interest, or total loan amount calculation option.
	The monthly loan payment, total loan interest, or total loan amount, depending on the program option that the user selects.
	Invalid entry messages as required.
Input:	A user response to the menu (P, I, T, or Q).
	If P is selected: User enters the loan amount, interest rate, and term.
	If I is selected: User enters the loan amount, interest rate, and term.
	If T is selected: User enters the loan amount, interest rate, and term.
	If Q is selected: terminate program.
Processing:	Calculate the selected option as follows:

Case P: *payment = principle * rate/(1 - (1+rate)$^{-term}$)*

Case I: *interest = term * payment - principle*

Case T: *total = principle + interest*

Case Q: terminate program.

where: *principle* is the amount of the loan.

                rate is a monthly interest rate in decimal form.

                term is the number of months of the loan.

Planning the Solution

Using the program design developed in the last chapter, we divided the problem into two subproblems to solve the overall problem. They were:

❏ Display the menu and read user choice.
❏ Perform the chosen calculation and display results.

The problem-solving diagram for this solution is shown again in Figure 7.3.

Recall that there were three levels to solving the problem. At the first level, *main()*, a function is called to display the menu and get the user choice. The *displayMenu()* function accomplishes this task and sends the user choice back to *main()*, as indicated on the diagram. Function *main()* will then send the choice to a function called *loanCalculator()*, which will call one of three functions, depending on the choice, to perform and return the required calculation. Now, the process description requires that we add a loop control feature to the program. Here is the revised set of algorithms through the first level of refinement:

Initial Algorithm

main()
BEGIN
    do
           Call *displayMenu()* function.
           Call *loanCalculator()* function.
    while *choice* ≠ 'q' AND *choice* ≠ 'Q'
END.

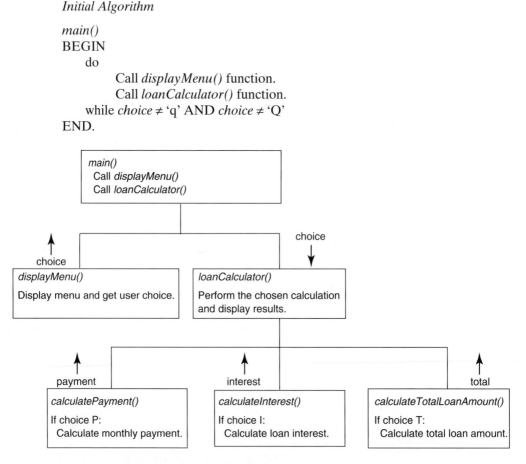

FIGURE 7.3 **A PROBLEM-SOLVING DIAGRAM FOR THE LOAN PROBLEM.**

First Level of Refinement

displayMenu()
BEGIN
> Display a program menu that prompts the user to choose a monthly payment (P), total interest (I), total loan amount (T), or quit (Q) option. Read *choice*.

END.

loanCalculator()
BEGIN
> Case P: Call function *calculatePayment()* and display payment.
>
> Case I: Call function *calculateInterest()* and display interest.
>
> Case T: Call function *calculateTotalLoanAmount()* and display total loan amount.
>
> Case Q: Terminate program.
>
> Default: Write an invalid entry message and ask the user to select again.

END.

Notice that the loop control feature is added to the initial algorithm level, *main()*. The *displayMenu()* and *loanCalculator()* algorithms at the first level of refinement have not changed much from our earlier solution. So, let's focus on the loop control in *main()*. Now, recall that the *displayMenu()* function obtains the user's menu choice. If the user enters a 'q' *or* 'Q' to quit the program, the loop will break, and the program terminates. But, is there something wrong here? We said if the "user enters a 'q' or 'Q' to quit the program…"; however, the loop test employs the AND operation. So, why have we used the Boolean AND operation rather than the OR operation to perform this test? This is a classic candidate for desk-checking the algorithm logic *before* coding the program. Ask yourself: "When will the loop break?" Any C++ loop breaks when the condition being tested is false, right? Remember that the result of an AND operation is false when any one of its conditions is false. As a result, the loop will break when *choice* is a 'q' *or* a 'Q'. The loop will continue when both sides of the AND operation are true. Therefore, the loop will continue as long as *choice* is not a 'q' *and choice* is not 'Q'. Isn't this what we want to do? What would happen if you mistakenly used the OR operation in the foregoing loop test? An OR operation produces a true result when any one of its conditions is true. One of these conditions would always be true, because *choice* cannot be both a 'q' and a 'Q'. The result of this oversight would be an infinite loop.

Another point needs to be made here. This application is a classic candidate for a **do/while** loop rather than a **while** loop, because you always want the menu to be displayed at least once to allow for a user choice.

Now that we have desk-checked our loop control logic, we are ready to code the program.

DEBUGGING TIP

A common mistake when developing loop control logic is to use an OR operation rather than an AND operation, or vice versa. This mistake almost always results in an infinite loop. The lesson to be learned here is to *always* desk-check your loop control logic before coding the program.

Coding the Program

Here is the flat implementation of the foregoing program design:

```
/*
ACTION 7-1 (ACT07_01.CPP)
OUTPUT: A PROGRAM MENU THAT PROMPTS THE USER TO SELECT A
        MONTHLY PAYMENT, TOTAL INTEREST, OR TOTAL LOAN AMOUNT
        CALCULATION OPTION.
        INVALID ENTRY MESSAGES AS REQUIRED.
        THE MONTHLY LOAN PAYMENT, TOTAL LOAN INTEREST,
        OR TOTAL LOAN AMOUNT, DEPENDING ON THE PROGRAM OPTION THAT THE
        USER SELECTS.
        INVALID ENTRY MESSAGES AS REQUIRED.

INPUT: A USER RESPONSE TO THE MENU (P, I, T, OR Q).
       IF P IS SELECTED: USER ENTERS THE LOAN AMOUNT, INTEREST RATE, AND TERM.
       IF I IS SELECTED: USER ENTERS THE LOAN AMOUNT, INTEREST RATE, AND
       TERM.
       IF R IS SELECTED: USER ENTERS THE LOAN AMOUNT, INTEREST RATE, AND
       TERM.
       IF Q IS SELECTED: TERMINATE PROGRAM.

PROCESSING: CALCULATE THE SELECTED OPTION AS FOLLOWS:
       CASE P: PAYMENT = PRINCIPLE * RATE/(1 - (1+RATE) -TERM)
       CASE I: INTEREST = TERM * PAYMENT - PRINCIPLE
       CASE T: TOTAL = PRINCIPLE + INTEREST
       CASE Q: QUIT THE PROGRAM.
       WHERE: PRINCIPLE IS THE AMOUNT OF THE LOAN.
       RATE IS A MONTHLY INTEREST RATE IN DECIMAL FORM.
       TERM IS THE NUMBER OF MONTHS OF THE LOAN.
*/

//PREPROCESSOR DIRECTIVES
#include <iostream.h>    //FOR cin AND cout
#include <math.h>        //FOR pow()

//MAIN FUNCTION
int main()
```

```cpp
{
 //DEFINE AND INITIALIZE VARIABLES
char choice = 'Q';         //USER MENU ENTRY
double payment = 0.0;      //MONTHLY PAYMENT
double interest = 0.0;     //TOTAL INTEREST FOR LIFE OF LOAN
double total = 0.0;        //TOTAL LOAN AMOUNT = PRINCIPLE + INTEREST
double principle = 0.0;    //LOAN AMOUNT
double rate = 0.0;         //INTEREST RATE
int term = 0;              //TERM OF LOAN IN MONTHS

//SET OUTPUT FORMAT
cout.setf(ios::fixed);
cout.setf(ios::showpoint);
cout.precision(2);
//DISPLAY PROGRAM DESCRIPTION MESSAGE
cout << "This program will calculate a monthly loan\n"
     << "payment, total loan interest, or total loan amount." << endl;

//MENU LOOP - DO UNTIL ENTRY 'q' OR 'Q'
do
{

    //displayMenu() FUNCTION
    cout  << "\n\n\t\t\tEnter P to get monthly payment"
          << "\n\t\t\tEnter I to get total loan interest"
          << "\n\t\t\tEnter T to get total loan amount"
          << "\n\t\t\tEnter Q to quit" << endl;
    cout << "\n\n\tPlease enter your choice:   ";

    //READ USER CHOICE
    cin >> choice;

    //loanCalculator() FUNCTION
    switch (choice)
    {
        case 'p': //calculatePayment() FUNCTION
        case 'P' :cout << "\nEnter the amount of the loan: $";
                  cin >> principle;
                  cout << "\nEnter the duration of the loan in months: ";
                  cin >> term;
                  cout << "\nEnter the annual interest rate: ";
                  cin >> rate;

                  //CHECK FOR INVALID RATE
                  while ((rate <= 0) || (rate > 100))
                  {
                   //DISPLAY INVALID ENTRY MESSAGE
                   cout << "\n\nThis is an invalid entry." << endl;
                   cout << "\nEnter the annual interest rate: ";
                   cin >> rate;
                  }//END WHILE
```

```
                        //CALCULATE AND DISPLAY PAYMENT
                        rate = rate/12/100;
                        payment = principle * rate/(1 - pow((1+rate), -term));
                        cout << "\n\nThe monthly payment is $" << payment << endl;
                        break;

            case 'i':  //calculateInterest() FUNCTION
            case 'I' : cout << "\nEnter the amount of the loan: $";
                        cin >> principle;
                        cout << "\nEnter the duration of the loan in months: ";
                        cin >> term;
                        cout << "\nEnter the annual interest rate: ";
                        cin >> rate;

                        //CHECK FOR INVALID RATE
                        while ((rate <= 0) || (rate > 100))
                        {
                         //DISPLAY INVALID ENTRY MESSAGE
                         cout << "\n\nThis is an invalid entry." << endl;
                         cout << "\nEnter the annual interest rate: ";
                         cin >> rate;
                        }//END WHILE

                        //CALCULATE AND DISPLAY INTEREST
                        rate = rate/12/100;
                        payment = principle * rate/(1-pow((1+rate), -term));
                        interest = term * payment - principle;
                        cout << "\n\nThe total interest is $" << interest << endl;
                        break;

            case 't':  //calculateTotalLoanAmount() FUNCTION
            case 'T':  cout << "\nEnter the amount of the loan: $";
                        cin >> principle;
                        cout << "\nEnter the duration of the loan in months: ";
                        cin >> term;
                        cout << "\nEnter the annual interest rate: ";
                        cin >> rate;

                        //CHECK FOR INVALID RATE
                        while ((rate <= 0) || (rate > 100))
                        {
                         //DISPLAY INVALID ENTRY MESSAGE
                         cout << "\n\nThis is an invalid entry." << endl;
                         cout << "\nEnter the annual interest rate: ";
                         cin >> rate;
                        }//END WHILE

                        //CALCULATE AND DISPLAY TOTAL
                        rate = rate/12/100;
                        payment = principle * rate/(1-pow((1+rate), -term));
                        interest = term * payment - principle;
```

```
                total = principle + interest;
                cout << "\n\nThe total loan amount is $" << total << endl;
                break;

        case 'q': //QUIT THE PROGRAM
                case 'Q': cout << "Program terminated" << endl;
                break;

        //DISPLAY INVALID ENTRY MESSAGE
        default : cout << "\n\nThis is an invalid entry. Please"
                        << " select again." << endl;
      } //END SWITCH
    }//END WHILE
    while ((choice != 'q') && (choice != 'Q'))

    //RETURN
    return 0;
} //END main()
```

The major change here is the **do/while** loop control feature that we added in our solution planning. Notice how the conditional loop test is coded at the end of the program. The entire test must be within parentheses. The variable *choice* is tested twice; both tests must be enclosed within parentheses. The results of both tests are combined via the Boolean AND (&&) operation.

> ### Debugging Tip
>
> A common mistake when coding a compound Boolean test on a variable is to forget to code it so that each side of the compound test produces a Boolean result. For example, suppose that we coded the foregoing loop test as
>
> ```
>         while (choice != 'q' && 'Q');
> ```
>
> This code will always produce a compiler error, because the right side of the AND operation does not produce a Boolean result. It might make sense for you to code it this way, but it doesn't make sense to the compiler!

We have added another feature to the program which uses a **while** loop to check for invalid user entries. Notice how the *rate* is obtained from the user. The *rate* is read using a *cin* statement, then a **while** loop test is made see if the *rate* is less than or equal to 0 or greater than 100. If it is, the body of the loop executes displaying an invalid entry message and requiring the user to enter another value for *rate*. The **while** loop will force the user to enter a value which is between 0 and 100, exclusive, because the loop will not terminate until the user does so. This is a classic example of where you would use a **while** loop rather than a **do/while** loop. You must use the **while** loop because you do not want the loop to execute at all if the user enters a *rate* that is within the specified range. Of course, because the **while** loop is a pretest loop, you must obtain a value for *rate* before the loop test is made, right?

Using a **while** loop like this to force a user to enter correct data is a much better technique than using an **if/else** statement as we did in the last chapter. Of course, we didn't have the **while** loop at our disposal in the last chapter, did we?

Use a **while** loop to force a user to enter correct data rather than an **if/else** statement. Remember, however, to read the data once before the loop so that the loop has a legitimate value to test the first time. Then, within the body of the loop display an invalid entry message and read the data again. The loop will not terminate until the user enters the correct data.

Quick Check

1. True or false: A **do/while** repeats until the loop test is true.
2. True or false: The **do/while** loop is a posttest loop.
3. What is wrong with the following code?

   ```
   int x = 10;
   do
      cout << "This is a do/while loop" << endl;
   while (x > 0);
   ```

4. Correct the code in question 3.
5. How many times will the following loop execute?

   ```
   int x = 1;
   do
      cout << "This is a do/while loop" << endl;
      ++x;
   while (x <= 0);
   ```

6. How many times will the following loop execute?

   ```
   int x = 1;
   do
   {
      cout << "This is a do/while loop" << endl;
      ++x;
   }//END DO/WHILE
   while (x >=0);
   ```

7.3   THE for LOOP

The **for** loop is called a *fixed repetition* loop because the loop is repeated a fixed number of times. You would use it in place of a **while** or **do/while** loop when it is known in advance, by you or the program, exactly how many times the loop must repeat itself.

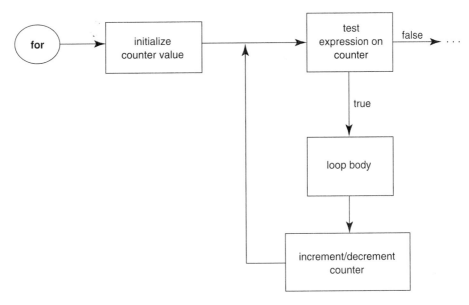

FIGURE 7.4 THE FOR LOOP OPERATION.

You can see from Figure 7.4 that the first thing that takes place before the loop body is executed is the initialization of a loop counter. Initialization means setting a counter variable to some initial, or beginning, value. A test expression is then executed to test the counter value. If the result of this test is true, the loop body is executed. Each time the loop body is executed, the counter value must be incremented or decremented. The test expression is evaluated again before the loop body is executed another time. The loop is repeated as long as the result of the test expression is true. In other words, the counter is incremented/decremented, tested, and the loop is repeated *until* the test expression is false. When this occurs, the loop body is not executed again, and the loop is broken. Control of the program then goes to the next sequential statement following the loop.

Here's the C++ syntax:

for *STATEMENT FORMAT*

for (int *counter* = *initial value; counter test expression;*
    increment/decrement counter)
{
  statement 1;
  statement 2;
       •
       •   *//LOOP BODY*
       •
  statement n;
} *//END FOR*

The statement begins with the keyword **for**. This is followed by *three* separate statements: an *initialization* statement, a Boolean *test expression,* and an *increment/decrement* statement, all enclosed within a single set of parentheses. The loop counter is initialized by assigning an initial value to the counter variable. The counter variable will almost always be an **int** but can be any simple data type, except a floating-point type. The counter variable can be defined before the **for** statement or within the **for** statement as part of the initialization step, like this:

```
for (int count = 1; ...
```

The test expression is used to test the value of the loop counter against some predetermined value. The loop body will be executed until the result of the test expression becomes false.

The increment/decrement statement is used to change the value of the loop counter so that the test expression becomes false after a fixed number of iterations. If the value of the loop counter is never changed, you have an infinite loop. It is important to note that the increment/decrement statement is not executed until *after* the loop body is executed in a given iteration. Thus, *if the initial test expression is true, the loop body will be executed at least once.* However, *if the initial test expression is false, the loop body is never executed.* This means that the **for** loop acts very much like the **while** loop. In fact, a **for** loop and a **while** loop are really one and the same looping structure, just coded differently. Think about it! Finally, notice from the above format that the loop body is framed within the curly braces. This is always required when there is more than one loop statement. The framing can be eliminated when there is only a single loop statement.

One last point about the loop counter variable: *Never* alter the counter variable within the body of the loop. The counter variable can be used within the body of the loop, but its value should not be altered. In other words, never use the counter variable on the left side of the assignment symbol (=) within the loop.

DEBUGGING TIP

A common programming error is to increment the loop counter inside a **for** loop like this:

```
for (int count = 0; count != 5; ++count)
{
  cout << count;
  ++count;
}
```

This code will not produce a compiler error, but will produce an infinite loop! Why? Because *count* is incremented twice during each loop thereby skipping completely over the value 5 and creating an infinite loop condition. The lesson to be learned here is *don't mess with the loop counter inside a for loop.*

EXAMPLE 7.3

What will be displayed by the following segments of code?

a.

```
for (int count = 1; count != 11; ++count)
    cout << count << endl;
```

The loop counter variable, *count,* ranges from 1 to 11. How many iterations will there be? Eleven, right? Wrong! The *++count* statement increments the value of *count* <u>after</u> each loop iteration. When the value of *count* reaches 11, the test expression is false and the loop is broken. As a result, there is no eleventh iteration. With each loop iteration, the *cout* statement displays the value of *count,* like this:

```
1
2
3
4
5
6
7
8
9
10
```

DEBUGGING TIP

When desk-checking a loop, always check the *loop boundaries.* The loop boundaries occur at the initial and final value of the loop control variable. Checking these values will help prevent *off-by-one* errors, where the loop executes one time more or one time less than it is supposed to. Also, when desk-checking a loop, try to imagine circumstances where the loop might execute 0 times, 1 time, or *n* times.

b.

```
for (int count = 10; count != 0; --count)
    cout << count << endl;
```

Here, the value of *count* ranges from 10 to 0. The *--count* statement decrements the value of *count* after each loop iteration. When the value of *count* reaches zero, the loop is broken. This type of loop is sometimes referred to as a "down-to" loop. The output generated by this loop is

```
10
9
8
7
6
5
4
3
2
1
```

c.

```
int sum = 0;
for (int count = 0; count != 5; ++count)
{
    sum = sum + count;
    cout << "The sum in the first iteration is " << sum << endl;
    ++count;
}//END FOR
```

This is an infinite loop! Notice that the loop counter is incremented within the body of the loop. What actually happens is that the loop counter is incremented twice, once within the body of the loop by the increment statement and then automatically by the **for** statement. As a result, the value of *count* skips over the value 5, creating an infinite loop. The lesson to be learned here is this: *Never change a* **for** *loop counter within the body of the loop.*

d.

```
for (int count = -5; count < 6; ++count)
    cout << count << endl;
```

Here, *count* ranges from −5 to 6. Because the loop is broken when *count* reaches 6, the *cout* loop statement is executed for values of *count* from −5 to 5. How many times will the loop be executed? Ten, right? Wrong! There are eleven integers in the range of −5 to 5, including 0. As a result, the loop is executed eleven times to produce an output of

```
-5
-4
-3
-2
-1
0
1
2
3
4
5
```

e.

```
cout << "\n\tNumber\tSquare\tCube" << endl;
cout << "\t------\t------\t------" << endl;
for (int count = 1; count < 11; ++count)
    cout << '\t'<< count << '\t' << count * count
         << '\t' << count * count * count << endl;
```

This **for** loop is being used to generate a table of squares and cubes for the integers 1 through 10. Notice how the counter variable *count* is squared and cubed within the *cout* loop statement. However, observe that at no time is the value of *count* altered within the loop. The resulting display is

Number	Square	Cube
1	1	1
2	4	8
3	9	27
4	16	64
5	25	125
6	36	216

7	49	343
8	64	512
9	81	729
10	100	1000

f.
```
for (char character = 'A'; character <= 'Z'; ++character)
   cout << character;
```

The counter variable in this loop is the character variable *character*. Recall that the character data type is ordered so that 'A' is smaller than 'Z'. Notice that the test expression, *character* <= 'Z' forces the loop to execute for the last time when the value of *character* is 'Z'. Consequently, the loop is executed 26 times as *character* ranges from 'A' to 'Z'. The value of *character* is displayed each time using a *cout* statement to produce an output of

```
ABCDEFGHIJKLMNOPQRSTUVWXYZ
```

g.
```
const int MAXCOUNT = 100;
double sum = 0.0;
double average = 0.0;
for (int count = 1; count <= MAXCOUNT; ++count)
     sum = sum + count;
average = sum / MAXCOUNT;
cout << "\nThe average of the first " << MAXCOUNT
     << " positive integers is:  " << average << endl;
```

Here, the counter value is being added to the floating-point variable *sum* each time through the loop. Thus, the loop adds all the positive integers within the defined range of the counter variable. The range of *count* is from 1 to *MAXCOUNT*. Notice that *MAXCOUNT* has been defined a constant with a value of 100. Therefore, *count* will range from 1 to 100 + 1, or 101. However, because the loop is broken when *count* reaches the value 101, this value is never added to *sum*. This results in a summing of all integers within the range of 1 to *MAXCOUNT*. After the loop is broken, the value of *sum* is divided by *MAXCOUNT* to calculate the *average* of all integers from 1 to 100. Here's what you would see:

```
The average of the first 100 positive integers is: 50.5
```

Notice that the variable *sum* was defined as a floating-point value, so that the division operator, /, produces a floating-point quotient. If both *sum* and *MAXCOUNT* were defined as integer values, the division operator would produce an erroneous integer result of 50. Also, you should be aware that constants like *MAXCOUNT* are often used as shown here for the initial or final counter values in a **for** loop. The reason is this: If the constant value needs to be changed for some reason, you need to change it in only one place, at the beginning of the program within the constant definition. This changes its value any place it is used within the program.

h.
```
const int MAXCOUNT = 100;
for (int i = 1; i <= MAXCOUNT; ++i)
{
   if (i % 17 == 0)
        cout << "The value " << i << " is divisible by 17." << endl;
} //END FOR
```

An **if** statement is used in this loop to determine when the counter value, *i*, is divisible by 17. Thus, the loop displays all the values between 1 and *MAXCOUNT* (100) that are divisible by 17. Do you understand how the test expression is working in the **if** statement? Here is what you would see when it is executed:

```
The value 17 is divisible by 17.
The value 34 is divisible by 17.
The value 51 is divisible by 17.
The value 68 is divisible by 17.
The value 85 is divisible by 17.
```

PROGRAMMING TIP

Suppose that a loop must execute *n* times and you create a loop control variable called *count*. In C++, if the loop control variable begins with the value 0, the loop test would use the *less than* (<) operator, like this: *count < n*. If the application requires you to begin the loop control variable with the value 1, the test would use the *less than or equal to* (<=) operator, like this: *count <= n*. When the application does not require otherwise, it is standard practice to initialize C++ loop control variables with the value 0 and use the *less than* test.

Nested Loops

Many applications require looping operations within loops. This is called **nested looping.** To get the idea, think about the seconds, minutes, and hours of a 12-hour digital timer. Isn't each a simple counter? The seconds count from 0 to 59, the minutes from 0 to 59, and the hours from 0 to 11. For every 60 seconds, the minutes counter is incremented. Likewise, for every 60 minutes, the hours counter is incremented. Thus, the seconds count is "nested" within the minutes count, and the minutes count is "nested" within the hours count. Here's how a digital timer might be coded in a C++ program using nested **for** loops:

```
//DISPLAY HEADINGS
cout << " \t\t\tHours\tMinutes\tSeconds" << endl;

//START TIMER
for (int hours = 0; hours < 12; ++hours)
    for (int minutes = 0; minutes < 60; ++minutes)
        for (int seconds = 0; seconds < 60; ++seconds)
        {
            cout << "\t\t\t\t\t\t\r";          //BLANK DISPLAY
            cout << "\t\t\t" << hours << '\t'
                 << minutes                    //DISPLAY TIME
                 << '\t' << seconds << '\r';
        } //END SECONDS LOOP
```

As you can see, the seconds **for** loop is part of the minutes loop, which is part of the hours loop. The *outer* **for** loop begins by initializing the *hours* counter to 0. The statement within this loop is another **for** loop that begins by initializing the *minutes* counter to 0. This leads to the seconds loop, where the *seconds* counter is initialized to 0. Once the *seconds* counter is initialized, the seconds loop is executed 60 times, as *seconds* ranges from 0 to 59. Each time the seconds loop is executed, the *hours, minutes,* and *seconds* count values are displayed. After the seconds loop is executed 60 times, the *minutes* count is incremented, and the seconds loop is entered again and executed 60 more times.

So, the seconds loop is executed 60 times for each iteration of the minutes loop. Likewise, because the minutes loop is nested within the hours loop, the minutes loop is executed 60 times for each iteration of the hours loop. After 60 iterations of the minutes loop (3600 iterations of the seconds loop), the *hours* count is incremented and displayed. The hours loop is not broken until it has been executed 12 times, from 0 to 11. Of course, this requires $12 \times 60 = 720$ iterations of the minutes loop and $12 \times 60 \times 60 = 43{,}200$ iterations of the seconds loop. We say that the seconds loop is the *innermost* loop, and the hours loop is the *outermost* loop. It is important to observe that the index of an outer loop controls how many times its inner loop statement is entered. For instance, since the hours loop executes 12 times, the minutes loop statement is entered 12 times. Since the minutes loop executes 60 times, the seconds loop statement is entered 60 times.

Notice that *no* framing is required for the hours and minutes loops because the hours loop consists of a single **for** statement, which is the minutes loop, and the minutes loop consists of a single **for** statement, which is the seconds loop. An indentation scheme becomes important here, because it is the indentation that really shows the nesting. The seconds loop requires framing because it consists of two *cout* statements. The first *cout* statement "blanks" the output values prior to displaying the time values in the second *cout* statement. Blanking is required so that

---

DEBUGGING TIP

A common error when coding a **for** loop is to place a semicolon at the end of the **for** statement like this:

```
for(int count = 1; count <= 5; ++count);
    cout << "Hello World" << endl;
```

Here, the programmer obviously wanted to display *Hello World* down the screen five times. However, the string is only displayed once. Why? Because the semicolon at the end of the **for** statement terminates the statement and the *cout* statement is seen as a single statement all by itself. The **for** loop actually executes five times but does not do anything since it has no statement section. It just sits there and "spins its wheels."

There might be an application where this is desirable within a program. Can you think of one? How about creating time delays within a program? You could simply use a very large final test value and force the program to loop enough times to create a noticeable delay. Of course, the precise amount of delay would depend on your system performance, right?

the time values appear correctly on the screen. Notice that the \r escape sequence is employed in both *cout* statements so that a given output overwrites the previous output.

To make the digital timer work, the *seconds* counter must be incremented precisely once every second. This requires a time-delay routine within the seconds loop to slow down the seconds count accordingly. This will be an exercise at the end of the chapter. Can you think of how you might use a **for** loop to do nothing but create a time delay?

Aside from counting, nested **for** loops are commonly used in graphics applications for line drawing, pattern drawing, and graphing things like histograms.

Before we leave the topic of nested loops, you should be aware that **while** and **do/while** loops can also be nested. You will find examples of this in the questions at the end of the chapter.

Down-to for Loops

In most of the **for** loops you have seen so far, the loop counter has been incremented from some initial value to some final value. You can also begin the loop counter at some value, then decrement it down to a final value. Such a loop is called a ***down-to loop,*** for obvious reasons. The digital timer program segment could be easily revised to employ down-to loops, like this:

```
//DISPLAY HEADINGS
cout << "\t\t\tHours\tMinutes\tSeconds" << endl;

//START TIMER
for (int hours = 12; hours; --hours)
    for (int minutes = 60; minutes; --minutes)
        for (int seconds = 60; seconds; --seconds)
        {
          cout << "\t\t\t\t\t\r"; //BLANK DISPLAY
          cout << "\t\t\t" << hours << '\t'
               << minutes           //DISPLAY TIME
               << '\t' << seconds << '\r';
        } //END SECONDS LOOP
```

The differences here are that the initial and final values of the respective loop counters have been changed so that the timer counts down from 11:59:59 and times out when the count reaches 00:00:00. The test expressions are simply the counter values, and the counters are being decremented rather than incremented. When a given counter value reaches zero, the loop test becomes false and the respective loop is broken. The net effect is still the same: There are 60 iterations of the seconds loop for each iteration of the minutes loop and 60 iterations of the minutes loop for each iteration of the hours loop. Of course, the timer counts down rather than counting up as in the previous program.

Quick Check

1. List the three things that must appear in the first line of a **for** loop structure.
2. True or false: The loop counter in a **for** loop is altered after the loop body is executed in a given iteration.
3. True or false: A **for** loop can always be replaced by a **while** loop, because both are basically the same looping structure, just coded differently.
4. How many times is the following loop executed?

   ```
   for (int x = 0; x > 0; ++x)
      cout << "How many times will this loop execute?" << endl;
   ```
5. How many times is the following loop executed?

   ```
   for (int x = 0; x <= 10; ++x)
      cout << "How many times will this loop execute?" << endl;
   ```
6. When must the body of a **for** loop be framed?
7. Suppose that you have two nested loops. The inner loop executes five times and the outer loop executes ten times. How many total iterations are there within the nested loop structure?
8. In a down-to loop, the loop counter is always _____.

7.4   THE break AND continue OPTIONS

The **break** and **continue** statements can be used to alter the execution of predefined control structures, such as loops, when certain conditions occur. In general, the **break** statement is used to immediately terminate a loop, and the **continue** statement is used to terminate a single loop iteration.

The break Statement

You observed the use of the **break** statement within the **switch** statement in the last chapter. Recall that the **break** statement forced the **switch** statement to terminate. The same is true when you use the **break** statement inside a loop structure. When C++ executes the **break** statement within a loop, the loop is immediately terminated, and control is passed to the next statement following the loop. The **break** statement is usually used as part of an **if** statement within the loop to terminate the loop structure if a certain condition occurs. The action of the **break** statement within a **while** loop can be illustrated like this:

THE **break** *OPTION*

while (*test expression*)
{
   statement 1;
   statement 2;
        •
        •
        •

   if (*test expression*)
    break;   //TERMINATE LOOP
        •
        •

   statement n;
} //END WHILE
Next statement after **while;**

Consider the following program segment:

```
int number = 1;            //LOOP CONTROL VARIABLE
while (number < 11)
{
 if (number == 5)
      break;
 cout << "In the while loop, number is now:  " << number << endl;
 ++number;
} //END WHILE

cout << "The loop is now terminated and the value of number is:  "
     << number << endl;
```

This **while** loop employs a **break** statement to terminate the loop when *number* reaches the value of 5. Here is what you would see as a result of the loop execution:

```
In the while loop, number is now:  1
In the while loop, number is now:  2
In the while loop, number is now:  3
In the while loop, number is now:  4
The loop is now terminated and the value of number is:  5
```

As you can see, even though the final value of *number* is 5, the *cout* statement within the loop is not executed when *number* reaches 5 because the **break** statement forces the loop to terminate for this value. Normally, you would not break out of a loop as a result of a natural loop counter value. Doing so would indicate that you have coded your loop test incorrectly. This was done only to illustrate how the **break** statement works. You will use the **break** statement primarily to break out of a loop when the potential for an infinite loop exists. Such an application could be to interrupt the digital timer loops given in the last section as the result of a user entry to stop the timer.

The continue Statement

You have not seen the use of the **continue** statement before this, because it is used primarily to terminate a single iteration within a loop if a certain condition occurs. Like the **break** statement, the **continue** statement is normally employed within a loop as part of an **if** statement. We can illustrate the operation of **continue** within a **for** loop, like this:

THE* continue *OPTION

for (*counter = initial value; counter test expression;***
    *increment/decrement counter***)**
{
    statement 1;
    statement 2;
        •
        •
    if (*test expression***)**
        continue;   //TERMINATE THIS ITERATION
        •
        •
    statement n;
} //END FOR
Next statement after **for;**

Here you see that when the **if** statement test expression is true, the **continue** statement is executed, forcing the current iteration to terminate. It is important to remember that *only the current iteration is terminated* as the result of **continue**. All subsequent iterations will be executed, unless, of course, they are terminated by executing a **break** or **continue**. The following program segment demonstrates how **continue** works:

```
for(int number = 1;number < 11; ++number)
{
    if (number == 5)
            continue;
    cout << "In the while loop, number is now: " << number
            << endl;
} //END FOR
cout << "The loop is now terminated and the value of number is:  "
    << number << endl;
```

Here is the result of executing the program segment:

```
In the for loop, number is now:  1
In the for loop, number is now:  2
In the for loop, number is now:  3
In the for loop, number is now:  4
In the for loop, number is now:  6
In the for loop, number is now:  7
In the for loop, number is now:  8
In the for loop, number is now:  9
In the for loop, number is now:  10
The loop is now terminated and the value of number is:   10
```

You see here that the fifth iteration is skipped because of the execution of the **continue** statement. All subsequent iterations are performed, and the loop is broken naturally when *number* reaches the value of 11.

PROGRAMMING TIP

We *strongly* urge you to only use a **break** or **continue** statement within a loop as a last resort. If your loops are well thought-out, there should be very few times that you would need to use **break** or **continue.** If you find yourself using **break** or **continue** too often, you might not be thoroughly thinking through the loop logic. Overuse of **break** and **continue** makes the program logic hard to follow.

Quick Check

1. The statement that will cause only the current iteration of a loop to be terminated is the _____ statement.
2. The **break** and **continue** statements are normally used as part of a(n) _____ statement within a loop structure.
3. How many times will the following loop execute?

```
x = 0;
while (x <10)
{
  cout << "How many times will this loop execute?" << endl;
  if (x > 0)
      break;
  ++x;
} //END WHILE
```

PROBLEM SOLVING IN ACTION: PARALLEL RESISTOR CIRCUIT ANALYSIS

PROBLEM

Let's close this chapter by writing several programs that will allow a user to find the total resistance of a circuit for any number of resistors in parallel, as shown in Figure 7.5. We will solve the problem three different ways, using each of the three iteration control structures discussed in this chapter. First, let's define the problem in terms of output, input, and processing. Suppose you are working for an industrial firm and you are assigned to write a program that will allow an engineer to find the total equivalent electrical resistance of a resistive circuit for any number of resistors in parallel.

A simple way to find the equivalent resistance of the circuit is to use the *product-over-sum rule*. To use this rule, you start with the first two resistor values (R_1 and R_2) and calculate an equivalent resistance, like this:

$$R_{equiv} = (R_1 \times R_2) / (R_1 + R_2)$$

Notice that the equivalent resistance for the two resistances is found by dividing their product by their sum. Thus, the rule is called the product-over-sum rule.

Next, the equivalent value obtained from this calculation is used with the third resistor value (R_3) to find a new equivalent, like this:

$$R_{equiv} = (R_{equiv} \times R_3) / (R_{equiv} + R_3)$$

Then, this equivalent value is used with the fourth resistor value (R_4) to calculate a new equivalent value, as follows:

$$R_{equiv} = (R_{equiv} \times R_4) / (R_{equiv} + R_4)$$

This process of calculating a new equivalent resistance value from the old one continues until all the resistor values in the circuit have been used. Notice that the same basic calculation must be *repeated* several times. Such a repetition operation would always suggest a loop structure in your program.

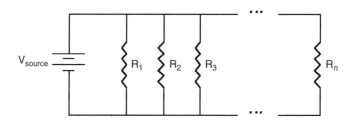

FIGURE 7.5   THE SOLUTION OF A GENERAL PARALLEL RESISTOR CIRCUIT IS A CANDIDATE FOR ITERATION.

Now, do you suppose that you can develop a program to perform the required task? Remember that the program must find the equivalent resistance of any number of resistors in parallel. Let's first define the task at hand in terms of output, input, and processing.

Defining the Problem

Output: The program must first prompt the user to enter the number of resistors in the parallel circuit. A prompt will then be generated to enter each resistor value separately. The final output will be a display of the equivalent parallel resistance.

Input: The number of resistors in the circuit and the individual resistor values.

Processing: Each time a resistor value (R) is entered, the equivalent parallel resistance (R_{equiv}) will be recalculated using the product-over-sum rule, as follows:

$$R_{equiv} = (R_{equiv} \times R) \; / \; (R_{equiv} + R)$$

Now, using this problem definition, we are ready for the algorithm. Let's first employ the **while** iteration control structure to repeatedly calculate the equivalent parallel resistance each time a resistor value is entered.

Planning the Solution

So as not to distract from concentrating on iteration, we will not stepwise refine the problem solution. Rather, we will employ a flat solution to the problem.

BEGIN
    Write a program-description message.
    Write a user prompt to enter the number of resistors in the circuit.
    Read *number*.
    Set *count* = 0.
    While (*count* < *number*)
        Set *count* = *count* + 1.
        Write prompt to enter resistor # *count*.
        Read *R*.
        If *count* == 1 Then
           Set R_{equiv} = *R*.
        Else
           Calculate R_{equiv} = ($R_{equiv} \times R$) / ($R_{equiv} + R$).
    Write R_{equiv}.
END.

As you can see, this is a rather simple algorithm employing the **while** control structure. Each time the loop is executed, an additional resistor value is entered, and the equivalent resistance of the circuit is calculated. You probably are wondering why the **if/else** statement is used within the loop. Well, the first resistor value is entered the first time through the loop. Because *count* = 1 during this first iteration, the **if** of the **if/else** statement is executed, and R_{equiv} is set to this first resistor value. In subsequent iterations, the **else** is executed to calculate R_{equiv} using the product-over-sum rule. Without setting R_{equiv} to the first resistor value the first time through the loop, R_{equiv} would have no beginning value for subsequent calculations, and the results would be unpredictable.

So, you say to set the value of R_{equiv} equal to zero prior to the loop. But, this will result in the numerator of the product-over-sum equation being zero, which makes the value of R_{equiv} zero in each loop iteration. The easiest solution is to set R_{equiv} to the value of the first resistor during the first loop iteration. Then, the value of R_{equiv} is recalculated with each subsequent loop iteration. Of course, if there is only one resistor in the circuit (*number* = 1), the loop is executed only once with the value of R_{equiv} being set to this single resistor value.

Notice also that a counter (*count*) must be initialized to 0 prior to the loop. The value of *count* must then be incremented with each loop iteration to prevent an infinite loop. The looping continues until the value of *count* equals the number of resistors in the circuit (*number*). When this happens, the loop statements are not executed again and the equivalent resistance is displayed.

Following the algorithm, you can easily code a C++ program, like this:

Coding the Program

```
/*
ACTION 7-2 (ACT07_02.CPP)
THIS PROGRAM WILL FIND THE EQUIVALENT RESISTANCE FOR ANY
NUMBER OF RESISTORS IN A PARALLEL CIRCUIT
*/

//PREPROCESSOR DIRECTIVE
#include <iostream.h> //FOR cin AND cout

//MAIN FUNCTION
int main()
{
   //DEFINE VARIABLES
   int count = 0;         //LOOP COUNTER
   int number = 0;        //NUMBER OF RESISTORS IN CIRCUIT
   double R_equiv = 0.0; //RESISTANCE OF CIRCUIT IN OHMS
   double R = 0.0;        //INDIVIDUAL RESISTANCE VALUES IN OHMS

   //WRITE PROGRAM DESCRIPTION MESSAGE AND GET NUMBER
   //OF PARALLEL RESISTORS
   cout << "\nThis program will calculate the equivalent resistance\n"
        << "of any number of parallel resistors." << endl << endl;
   cout << "Enter the number of resistors in the parallel circuit:  ";
   cin >> number;

   //CALCULATE EQUIVALENT RESISTANCE USING WHILE
   while (count < number)
   {
        ++count;
        cout << "Enter the value for resistor #" << count << ": ";
        cin >> R;
        if (count == 1)
```

```
        R_equiv = R;
    else
        R_equiv = (R_equiv * R) / (R_equiv + R);
} //END WHILE

//DISPLAY EQUIVALENT RESISTANCE
cout.setf(ios::fixed);
cout.precision(2);
cout << "The equivalent resistance for the parallel circuit is:   "
    <<  R_equiv << " ohms" << endl;
} //END main()
```

Here is what you would see on the display when this program is executed:

```
This program will calculate the equivalent resistance
of any number of parallel resistors.

Enter the number of resistors in the parallel circuit:   3↵
Enter the value for resistor #1: 10↵
Enter the value for resistor #2: 12↵
Enter the value for resistor #3: 15↵
The equivalent resistance for the parallel circuit is:   4.00 ohms
```

Next, suppose you want to use the **do/while** control structure to perform the same task. Remember the major difference is that the **do/while** loop statements are always executed at least once.

Planning the Solution

BEGIN
    Write a program-description message.
    Write a user prompt to enter the number of resistors in the circuit.
    Read *number*.
    Set *count* = 0.
    Do
        Set *count* = *count* + 1.
        If *number* == 0 Then
          Break
        Write prompt to enter resistor # *count*.
        Read *R*.
        If *count* == 1 Then
          Set R_{equiv} = *R*.
        Else
          Calculate $R_{equiv} = (R_{equiv} \times R) / (R_{equiv} + R)$.
    While (*count* < *number*).
    Write R_{equiv}.
END.

Here you can see that the only difference between this algorithm and the previous **while** algorithm is the addition of an **if** statement that will cause the loop to break if the user enters a value of zero for the number of resistors in the circuit.

Remember that a **do/while** loop is always executed at least once. Therefore, the loop must be broken and no calculation performed if there are no resistors in the circuit. This is an ideal application for the use of a **break** statement within a **do/while** loop. We did not need to use this option with the **while** loop. (Why?) Here's the resulting program.

Coding the Program

```
/*
ACTION 7-2 (ACT07_2b.CPP)
THIS PROGRAM WILL FIND THE EQUIVALENT RESISTANCE FOR ANY
NUMBER OF RESISTORS IN A PARALLEL CIRCUIT
*/

//PREPROCESSOR DIRECTIVE
#include <iostream.h> //FOR cin AND cout

//MAIN FUNCTION
int main()
{
  //DEFINE VARIABLES
  int count = 0;          //LOOP COUNTER
  int number = 0;         //NUMBER OF RESISTORS IN CIRCUIT
  double R_equiv = 0.0; //RESISTANCE OF CIRCUIT IN OHMS
  double R = 0.0;         //INDIVIDUAL RESISTANCE VALUES IN OHMS

  //WRITE PROGRAM DESCRIPTION MESSAGE AND GET NUMBER
  //OF PARALLEL RESISTORS
  cout << "\nThis program will calculate the equivalent resistance\n"
     << "of any number of parallel resistors." << endl << endl;
  cout << "Enter the number of resistors in the parallel circuit:  ";
  cin >> number;

  //CALCULATE EQUIVALENT RESISTANCE USING DO/WHILE
  do
  {
    if (number == 0)     //BREAK IF NUMBER IS ZERO
       break;
    ++count;
    cout << "Enter the value for resistor #" << count << ": ";
    cin >> R;
    if (count == 1)
       R_equiv = R;
    else
       R_equiv = (R_equiv * R) / (R_equiv + R);
  }//END DO/WHILE
  while (count < number);

  //DISPLAY EQUIVALENT RESISTANCE
  cout.setf(ios::fixed);
  cout.precision(2);
```

```
cout << "The equivalent resistance for the parallel circuit is:   "
     <<  R_equiv << " ohms" << endl;

//RETURN
return 0;
}//END main()
```

The output of this program is the same as that of the **while** loop program.

Finally, let's rewrite the algorithm and code a program to employ the **for** iteration control structure. Remember that with the **for** structure, the loop is executed a fixed number of times as the loop counter ranges from its initial to final value. So, why not set the initial counter value to 1 and make a test against the number of resistors in the parallel circuit? Here's the idea in the form of an algorithm:

Planning the Solution

> BEGIN
>> Write a program-description message.
>> Write a user prompt to enter the number of resistors in the circuit.
>> Read *number*.
>> For *count* = 1 to *number*
>>> Write prompt to enter resistor # *count*.
>>> Read *R*.
>>> If *count* == 1 then
>>>> Set $R_{equiv} = R$.
>>> Else
>>>> Calculate $R_{equiv} = (R_{equiv} \times R) / (R_{equiv} + R)$.
>> Write R_{equiv}.
> END.

Here, the loop executes as *count* ranges from 1 to *number*. The counter is incremented and tested as part of the *For* loop control structure. Notice that the pseudocode statement used to express the *For* loop structure is as follows:

For count = 1 to number

This common way to pseudocode a *For* loop structure is quite different from the C++ code, which is:

```
for(int count = 1; count <= number, ++count)
```

The pseudocode indicates that *count* starts at 1 and goes up to *number*. We say that the incrementing of *count* and the testing of *count* against *number* are ***implicit***, or understood, within this pseudocode statement. However, the incrementing of *count* and the testing of *count* against *number* must be ***explicit***, or specified, within the C++ statement.

Now, here's the coded program:

Coding the Program

```
/*
ACTION 7-2 (ACT07-2c.CPP)
THIS PROGRAM WILL FIND THE EQUIVALENT RESISTANCE FOR ANY
```

```
NUMBER OF RESISTORS IN A PARALLEL CIRCUIT
*/

//PREPROCESSOR DIRECTIVE
#include <iostream.h>       //FOR cin AND cout

//MAIN FUNCTION
int main()
{
//DEFINE VARIABLES
int number = 0;         //NUMBER OF RESISTORS IN CIRCUIT
double R_equiv = 0.0; //RESISTANCE OF CIRCUIT IN OHMS
double R = 0.0;         //INDIVIDUAL RESISTANCE VALUES IN OHMS

//WRITE PROGRAM DESCRIPTION MESSAGE AND GET NUMBER
//OF PARALLEL RESISTORS
cout << "\nThis program will calculate the equivalent resistance\n"
     << "of any number of parallel resistors." << endl << endl;
cout << "Enter the number of resistors in the parallel circuit:  ";
cin >> number;

//CALCULATE EQUIVALENT RESISTANCE USING FOR
for(int count = 1; count <= number; ++ count)
{
    cout << "Enter the value for resistor #" << count << ": ";
    cin >> R;
    if (count == 1)
        R_equiv = R;
    else
        R_equiv = (R_equiv * R) / (R_equiv + R);
}//END FOR

//DISPLAY EQUIVALENT RESISTANCE
cout.setf(ios::fixed);
cout.precision(2);
cout << "The equivalent resistance for the parallel circuit is:  "
     << R_equiv << " ohms" << endl;

  //RETURN
  return 0;
}//END main()
```

Again, notice how the algorithm statement *For count = 1 to number* is coded in C++ as *for (int count = 1; count <= number; ++count)*. The value of *count* is first initialized to 1. Then, to allow *count* to range from 1 to *number,* the test must be *count <= number.* This allows the final iteration to occur when the value of *count* equals the value of *number* and forces the loop to break when the value of *count* exceeds the value of *number.* Of course, the value of *count* is incremented as part of the **for** statement. Do we need a **break** statement here to terminate the program if the user enters a 0 for *number?* The answer is no. (Why?) The output of this program is the same as that for the previous two programs.

DEBUGGING TIP

When desk-checking a loop, always check the *loop boundaries*. The loop boundaries occur at the initial and final value of the loop control variable. Checking these values will help prevent *off-by-one* errors, where the loop executes one time more or one time less than it is supposed to.

CHAPTER SUMMARY

In this chapter, you learned about the three iteration control structures employed by C++: **while**, **do/while**, and **for**. The **while** is a pretest looping structure, the **do/while** a posttest looping structure, and the **for** a fixed repetition looping structure. As a result, the following general guidelines should be considered when deciding which looping structure to use in a given situation:

❑ Use **while** whenever there is a possibility that the loop statements will not need to be executed.

❑ Use **do/while** when the loop statements must be executed at least once.

❑ Use **for** when it can be determined exactly how many times the loop statements must be executed. Thus, if the number of loop iterations is predetermined by the value of a variable or constant, use a **for** loop.

The **break** and **continue** statements can be used to interrupt loop iterations. Execution of the **break** statement within a loop forces the entire loop structure to terminate immediately and pass control to the next statement following the loop structure. Execution of the **continue** statement within a loop terminates only the current loop iteration.

QUESTIONS AND PROBLEMS

QUESTIONS

1. Name the three iteration control structures employed by C++.

2. Which iteration control structure(s) will always execute the loop at least once?

3. Which iteration control structure(s) evaluates the test expression before the loop is executed?

4. Which iteration control structure(s) should be employed when it can be determined in advance how many loop repetitions there should be?

5. What will the following loop do?

```
while (count < 10)
   cout << "Hello" << endl;
```

6. Explain the difference between the execution of **break** and **continue** within a loop.

In questions 7 to 17, determine the output generated by the respective program segment. Assume that the appropriate header files have been included.

7. `int A = 1;`
`   while (17 % A != 5)`

```
   {
    cout << A << "   " << 17 % A << endl;
    ++A;
   }//END WHILE
8. int B = 2;
   do
   {
    cout << B << "   " << B / 5 << endl;
    B *= 2;
   }//END DO/WHILE
   while (B != 20);
9. int B = 2;
   do
   {
    cout << B << "   " << B / 5 << endl;
    B *= 2;
   }//END DO/WHILE
   while (B != 32);
10. int number = 1;
    int product = 1;
    do
    {
     ++number;
     product *= number;
    }//END DO/WHILE
    while (number < 5);
    cout << "The product is:  " << product << endl;
11. int count = -3;
    while (count < 3)
    {
     if (count == 0)
       continue;
     cout << count << '\t';
     ++count;
    }//END WHILE
12. int count = -3;
    while (count < 3)
    {
     ++count;
     if (count == 0)
       continue;
     cout << count << '\t';
    }//END WHILE
13. int count = -3;
    while (count < 3)
    {
     ++count;
     if (count == 0)
       break;
     cout << count << '\t';
    }//END WHILE
```

14.
```
cout << "Angle\tSin\tCos" << endl;
cout << "----\t---\t---" << endl;
const double PI = 3.14159;
cout.setf(ios::fixed);
cout.precision(3);
for (int angle = 0; angle < 91; angle += 5)
 cout << angle << '\t' << sin(angle * PI/180)
       << '\t' << cos(angle * PI/180) << endl;
```

15.
```
for (int row = 1; row < 6; ++row)
 {
 for (int col = 1; col < 11; ++col)
  cout << row << ',' << col << '\t';
 cout << endl;
}//END FOR
```

16.
```
int count = 0;
const int MAXCOUNT = 5;
while (count < MAXCOUNT)
 {
 for (int i = 1; i < MAXCOUNT + 1; ++i)
  cout << i;
 cout << endl;
 ++count;
}//END WHILE
```

17.
```
int const MAXCOUNT = 5;
int times = 3;
do
 {
 int count = 0;
 while (count < MAXCOUNT)
  {
  for (int j = 1; j < count + 1; ++j)
     cout << j;
  ++count;
  cout << endl;
  }//END WHILE
  cout << endl;
  --times;
}//END DO/WHILE
while (times != 0);
```

18. When will the following loop terminate?
```
bool flag = true;          //DEFINE BOOLEAN VARIABLE
                           //ASSUMES ANSI/ISO STANDARD
int number = 0;            //INPUT VARIABLE
int sum = 0;               //SUM VARIABLE
char query = 'N';          //CONTINUE QUERY

while (flag == true)
{
   cout << "Enter an integer value: ";
   cin >> number;
```

```
        cout << "Want to continue (y/n)?" << endl;
        cin >> query;
        if ((query == 'n') || query == 'N'))
        {
            flag = false;
            cout << "Loop terminated" << endl;
        }//END IF
        else
        {
          sum = sum + number;
            cout << "The sum is now " << sum << endl;
        }//END ELSE
    }//END WHILE
```

PROBLEMS

Least Difficult

1. Write a program that will compute the average of any number of test scores using a **while** loop. Assume that the test scores will be entered by the user.

2. Revise the program in problem 1 to employ a **do/while** loop.

3. Revise the program in problem 1 to employ a **for** loop.

4. Write a C++ program that will find the equivalent resistance of any number of resistors in series. Employ the **while** control structure and assume that the resistor values will be entered by the user. (*Note:* The equivalent resistance of a series circuit is simply the sum of the individual resistors the circuit.)

5. Revise the program in problem 4 to employ the **do/while** control structure.

6. Revise the program in problem 4 to employ the **for** control structure.

7. Using the formula $C = 5/9(F - 32)$, generate a Celsius conversion table for all *even* temperatures from 32 degrees to 212 degrees Fahrenheit.

More Difficult

8. Write a C++ program that will ask the user for a number, then display a box of asterisks whose dimension is the number entered. Place the routine within a loop that allows the user to repeat the task until he or she wants to quit.

9. Write a program that will calculate the mean ($\bar{x}$) and standard deviation (σ) of a series of numbers. The mean of a series of numbers is the same as the average of the numbers. The standard deviation of a series of numbers is found using the following formula:

$$\sigma = \sqrt{\frac{(x_1 - \bar{x})^2 + (x_2 - \bar{x})^2 + ... + (x_n - \bar{x})^2}{n}}$$

10. Some programming languages, like BASIC, allow you to use a STEP command within a **for** statement, like this:

FOR *counter = initial value* TO *final value* STEP *n*

The STEP command allows the loop counter to increment by some value (*n*), other than the value 1, with each loop iteration.

Write a **for** loop in C++ that will emulate this STEP operation. Provide for user entry of any desired step value. To demonstrate its operation, use your step loop to display every fifth integer, from 1 to 100.

11. To make the digital timer program given in this chapter work properly, you must insert a time delay within the seconds loop so that the seconds counter is incremented precisely once every second. To do this, you can insert a **for** loop that simply decrements a large counter, like this:

```
for(long int timer = 40000000; timer > 0; --timer);
```

This loop will not do anything but waste time because it is terminated by the semicolon at the end of the line. However, the amount of time delay is dependent on the initial counter value and the clock speed of your system CPU. Insert such a delay loop into the timer program given in this chapter, and, by trial and error, determine a counter value that will provide a one-second delay for your system. Compile, execute, and observe the program output. (*Note:* If you have a super-fast computer, you might need to nest two or more time delay loops.)

12. Using the ideas you saw in the digital timer program in this chapter, write a C++ program to display the output of a 4-bit binary counter. A 4-bit binary counter simply counts in binary from 0000 to 1111. The first count value is 0000, the second is 0001, the third is 0010, and so on, until it reaches the final count value of 1111. Insert a delay in the program so that the counter increments once every 2 seconds. Change the delay value and observe the effect on the count frequency. (*Hint:* You will need four nested loops, one for each bit within the count value.)

13. The subway system in C++ City, USA has three fee classifications: student (17 years old or less), adult, and senior (65 years old or more). Write a program that counts how many of each fee classification rode the subway on a given day. Assume that the subway conductor has a laptop PC that runs your program. The conductor enters the age of each customer as the subway is under way. Your user instructions tell the conductor to enter a sentinel value of –1 at the end of the day to terminate the entry process. After the sentinel value is entered, the program must display the number of customers in each fee category.

14. In Chapter 6, you wrote a program for Ma and Pa's Sporting Goods department that would calculate expected profit based on profit codes for each item in the department. The items in the department are coded with a 1, 2, or 3, depending on the amount of profit for the item. An item with a profit code of 1 produces a 10 percent profit, a code of 2 produces a 12 percent profit, and a code of 3 generates a 15 percent profit. Rewrite the program to allow the user to enter sales item information until the user decides to quit. The required sales item information includes an item description, quantity on hand, price, and profit code. For example, a typical entry dialog might appear as follows:

Enter Item Name: **Fishing Line** ↵

Enter Quantity on Hand: **125** ↵

Enter Price: **5.25** ↵

Enter Profit Code: **1** ↵

Have another item to enter? (y/n) **y** ↵

The program should generate a tabular report of the item, quantity, expected profit in dollars per item, and total expected profit for all items at the end of the report.

15. Write a program that will obtain any two integers between 2 and 10 from the user and display a multiplication a table. For example, if the user enters the values 4 and 5, the table would be:

1	2	3	4	5
2	4	6	8	10
3	6	9	12	15
4	8	12	16	20

16. Write a tax program that will figure depreciation using the *straight-line* method. With the straight-line method, the cost of the item is depreciated each year by $1/n$, where n is the number of years to depreciate. Assume that the user will enter the original cost of the item and the number of years to depreciate the item. The program should display a table showing the depreciated value at the end of each year, the amount depreciated for each year, and the total accumulated depreciation at the end of each year.

Most Difficult

17. Write a program that will determine the value of a bank account balance that is compounded monthly. Assume that the user will enter the beginning balance, annual interest rate, and number of years to compound. As an example, suppose that the beginning balance was $1000 and the annual interest rate is 12 percent. Then, at the end of the first month, the balance would be $1010. At the end of the second month, the balance would be $1020.10, and so on. Notice that at the end of each month, the interest is added to the old balance to form a new balance that will be used in the next month's calculation.

18. Ma and Pa have asked you to write a program for their Bass Boat department. The program is to read the price of the boat from the user and, using an interest rate of 1 percent per month, display a table showing the monthly payment, amount of principle, amount of interest, and remaining loan balance for each month over the number of months specified by the user.

19. Write a program that will find the equivalent resistance of a series-parallel circuit of any arbitrary configuration. A series-parallel circuit is one in which there are both series and parallel resistor connections. (*Hint:* When combining resistors in such a circuit, you must start with the last resistor, at the end of the circuit, and work toward the first resistor, at the beginning of the circuit.)

20. Write a program that employs a **while** loop to read a file called *scores.txt* on the *A:* drive that contains an unknown number of test scores. Display the scores along with their average.

SE102: SOFTWARE PARADIGMS

Objectives

When you are finished with this module, you should have a good understanding of the following:

- The concept of a paradigm.
- The history of software paradigms.
- The idea behind the structured paradigm.
- The idea behind the object-oriented paradigm.
- The software development life-cycle applied using the structured versus the object-oriented paradigm.

INTRODUCTION

When the chief information officer (CIO) of *Foo.com* heard about the problems in their billing software, he became *so upset* that he summoned together his programmers. With his past experience as a programmer and systems analyst, he just could not believe that his programmers did not follow the software development life-cycle. As a result, he directed all of them to learn about the life-cycle and how it must be applied using a modern programming paradigm. Many of them decided to take a course in software engineering or systems analysis/design at their local university to learn the latest software engineering techniques.

In this module, you will find out what they learned about different programming paradigms and how the life-cycle differs when applied to these paradigms. Then, in future *SE* modules, you will follow their analysis and design of a new billing system.

A HISTORICAL PERSPECTIVE

First, we should define what we mean by a "paradigm." Webster defines a paradigm as "a pattern, example, or model." Another way to say it is that a ***paradigm*** is a way of thinking of things. In religion, for example, there is the Jewish paradigm, the Christian paradigm, the Islamic paradigm, among others. In software engineering, there are primarily two ways of thinking of things, using the structured paradigm or the object-oriented paradigm. Prior to these paradigms there was no software engineering at all. The way of thinking of things, or paradigm, was to built-it and fix-it without any formal analysis or design specifications. The idea was to solve the problem at the keyboard, test it, and fix it until the client was satisfied.

This approach will probably work to solve simple problems using small programs, but is totally unworkable for today's complex problems requiring complex software solutions. Remember folks, all the simple problems have been solved! Today's problems are extremely complex, requiring thousands and even millions of lines of code. The built-it, fix-it model just doesn't cut the mustard when dealing with today's real world problems. This is why this book is striving to teach you good software development techniques, even though the problems you are solving are relatively simple and could be solved at the keyboard using the build-it, fix-it approach. The intent of this book is to get you into good software development habits so that you will be able to deal with the complex problems that you will encounter in the real world. This short module will provide an overview and comparison of the two most common paradigms in use today: the structured paradigm and the object-oriented paradigm. Then, later modules will explore these two paradigms in more detail, from a software engineering perspective.

A *paradigm* is a model that provides a way of thinking of things.

In the mainframe days of the 1960s, it became clear that the build-it, fix-it paradigm was not sufficient to manage the increasing complexity of software systems. Many programs written in these days resulted in "spaghetti code" which became totally unreadable, and therefore, impossible to maintain. How can you deal with complexity? One way is to break a complex problem down into smaller subproblems which are more manageable than the original complex problem. Then employ teams of programmers to solve the individual subproblems. This is the essence of the structured paradigm which was developed in the early 1970s to deal with ever-increasing complexity.

The *structured paradigm* employs a top/down functional decomposition methodology that breaks the original complex problem down into smaller, more manageable subproblems.

As complexity continued to increase exponentially during the 1970s and early 1980s it became apparent that the structured paradigm needed to be replaced. This realization led to the object-oriented paradigm which was developed in the late 1980s and early 1990s. The object-oriented paradigm employs objects and object interaction to attack complex problems in a natural way, like we humans tend to think about things. So, both paradigms are attempts to deal with the increasing complexity of the software projects and resulting systems. When we talk about software complexity, we usually associate it with the number of lines of code required to solve a problem. The structured paradigm was developed to handle systems with hundreds and thousands of lines of code. But when systems begin to grow beyond

100,000 lines of code, the structured paradigm becomes inadequate to manage the increased complexity. The object-oriented paradigm was developed to manage systems with hundreds of thousands and even millions of lines of code. Yes, some of today's software products require millions of lines of code! We feel that it is important that you know both paradigms so that you can deal with either when needed. In fact, you will find that the object-oriented paradigm contains many elements of its predecessor, the structured paradigm.

> The **object-oriented paradigm** employs objects and object interaction to attack complex problems in a natural way, like we humans tend to think about things.

THE STRUCTURED VERSUS THE OBJECT-ORIENTED PARADIGM

The primary difference between the structured paradigm and the object-oriented paradigm is that the structured paradigm is either *data-oriented* or *action-oriented,* but not both. In the structured paradigm, the program data structures are designed and coded separately, but working in conjunction with, the program algorithms (functions). In the object-oriented paradigm, the program data structures and related algorithms are combined into well-defined independent units called objects. Objects represent the application system more naturally because they reflect the way we humans think about the system. For example, consider an ATM machine. We don't think of the data (money) it contains separately from the operations, or actions, that it performs on the data. We look at it as one *encapsulated* and independent unit that dispenses its data (money) in connection with a related action, such as a withdrawal.

In the *SE101* module, you were introduced to the software development life-cycle in general. There are minor, but important, differences when the life-cycle is applied using the structured versus the object-oriented paradigm. Here are the general life-cycle phases we discussed in *SE101*:

- ❐ *Survey phase.*
- ❐ *Analysis phase.*
- ❐ *Design phase.*
- ❐ *Construction phase.*
- ❐ *Maintenance phase.*
- ❐ *Retirement phase.*

The general phases are still the same, but let's consider one additional level of refinement. Here is a refinement of the life cycle when applied to the structured paradigm:

❏ *Survey phase.*
Initial feasibility study and report.

❏ *Analysis phase.*
Detailed analysis of the current system using logical DFDs to produce a requirements statement that specifies what the new system is supposed to do.

❏ *Design phase.*
Determination of how the new system is to satisfy the client's needs through physical DFDs and functional decomposition. Also, the writing of any algorithms required for the functions.

❏ *Construction phase.*
Code the data structures and algorithms separately then combine.

❏ *Maintenance phase.*
Perform corrective and enhancement maintenance.

❏ *Retirement phase.*

Now, here is the life-cycle when applied to the object-oriented paradigm:

❏ *Survey phase.*
Initial feasibility study and report.

❏ *Analysis phase.*
Detailed analysis of the current system to produce a requirements statement that specifies what the new system is supposed to do.
Identification of the system objects.

❏ *Design phase.*
Determination of how the new system is to satisfy the client's needs by constructing object interaction and class diagrams.

❏ *Construction phase.*
Code the data and related algorithms together as objects.

❏ *Maintenance phase.*
Perform corrective and enhancement maintenance.

❏ *Retirement phase.*

The major differences that you see if you compare the two cycles is that the analysis phase is extended in the object-oriented paradigm to include identification of the objects, thus addressing the software structure, or *architecture,* of the system early during the analysis phase, *before* the design phase. In the structured paradigm, the system architecture is not addressed until the design phase when the functional decomposition takes place. Since the object-oriented paradigm addresses the system architecture during the analysis phase, the design phase deals with the required object interaction to satisfy the client's needs. This approach introduces the primary system component, the object, earlier in the life-cycle and makes for an easier transition from the analysis to the design phase, thus managing complexity in a more natural and cohesive way.

Also, notice that in the construction phase, the data structures and algorithms are coded separately then combined using the structured paradigm. However, in the object-oriented paradigm, the data structures and related algorithms are coded together to form the program objects. The objects are then combined in an application program as specified by the object interaction which was determined in the design phase. Again, this makes for an easier transition from the design phase to the construction phase.

Now that you are familiar with the fundamental differences between the two paradigms, future *SE* modules will deal with the details of each as related to software engineering.

FUNCTIONS IN-DEPTH

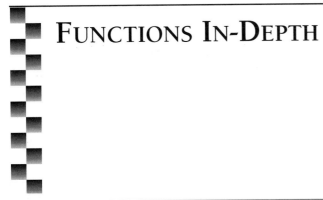

Chapter Contents

Chapter Objectives

When you are finished with this chapter, you should have a good understanding of the following:

- The concept of recursion.
- The concept of a stack and how it is employed by a compiler to perform recursive function calls.
- How to construct your own functions in C++.

- The difference between a non-void function and a void function.
- How to call non-void versus void functions.
- How to develop function interfaces.
- The significance of a function interface.
- The scope, or visibility, of a variable.
- The difference between an argument and a parameter.
- Overloaded functions and the concept of polymorphism.

INTRODUCTION

In Chapter 2, you were introduced to structured design using stepwise refinement and structured programming using C++ functions. In the last few chapters, we have developed top/down structured program designs, but have employed a flat implementation when coding these designs. As a result, we have been coding C++ programs that consist of one main section defined by function *main()*. It is now time to learn how to code structured designs using a structured C++ program that employs functions. As you know, functions are the basis for structured programming in the C++ language. In addition, functions provide the only method of communicating with objects in object-oriented programming. So this chapter is crucial to your learning of both structured programming and object-oriented programming in the C++ language.

You have already used built-in, or predefined, functions in your programs. All of these functions are part of the various header files included with C++. Now it is time to develop your own functions and employ them to create modular, well-structured C++ programs as well as your own classes and objects later on when you study object-oriented programming. Functions that you create for your own use in a program are called ***programmer-defined*** functions.

> A ***programmer-defined function*** is a block of statements, or a subprogram, that is written to perform a specific task required by you, the programmer.

A function is given a name and ***called***, or ***invoked***, using its name each time the task is to be performed within the program. The code that calls, or invokes, a function is often referred to as the ***calling program***.

Up to this point, you have employed one function, *main()*, within a single program. However, commercial programs are actually written as a collection of functions in the case of structured programming, or classes that contain functions in the case of object-oriented programming. Writing a program as a collection of functions has several advantages, as follows:

❐ Functions eliminate the need for duplicate statements within a program. Given a task to be performed more than once, the statements are written just once for the function. Then, the function is called each time the task must be performed.

❐ Functions make the program easier to design, since the program behaviors (algorithms) are modularized as individual functions, whose combined execution solves the problem at hand.

❐ Functions make the program easier to code and test, since you can concentrate on a single function at a time, rather than one big *main()* function.

❐ Functions allow for *software reusability*, where existing functions can be reused to create new programs.

❐ Functions make the program more clear and readable, thus making the program easier to maintain.

❐ And most important, the use of functions provides the basis for us to construct classes in object-oriented programming.

In C++, the function can be made to serve two roles. A function can be made to return a single value to the calling program. This type of function is referred to as a *non-void* function in C++. Functions can also be written to perform specific tasks or return multiple values to the calling program. These functions are called *void* functions in C++.

This chapter will close with a discussion of a very powerful language capability known as ***recursion***. Recursion is a process whereby an operation keeps "cloning" itself until a terminating condition is reached. Although the process of performing recursion is rather complex, it is relatively simple for the programmer, because most of the work is done by the compiler. Many problems are recursive in nature, such as calculating compound interest, among others.

8.1   NON-VOID FUNCTIONS

You have already had some experience with functions that return a single value in C++. Recall the standard functions that you learned about in Chapter 5, such as *sqrt()*, *sin()*, and *cos()*, just to mention a few. However, suppose you want to perform some operation that is not a predefined function in C++, such as cube. Because C++ does not include any standard function for the cube operation, you could code the operation as a statement in your program, like this:

```
cube = x * x * x;
```

Then, you insert this statement into your program each time the value of *x* must be cubed. However, wouldn't it be a lot easier simply to insert the command *cube(x)* each time *x* is to be cubed, where C++ knows what to do just as it knows how to execute *sqrt(x)*? You can do this by defining your own *cube()* function. Such a function is called a ***programmer-defined function***, for obvious reasons.

A programmer-defined function is a subprogram that, when invoked, performs some task or returns a single value that replaces the function name wherever the name is used in the calling program. Thus, if *cube()* is a programmer-defined function that will cube a value, say, *x*, the statement *cout << cube(x)* will invoke the function and cause the cube of *x* to be displayed. Now you need to learn how to create such programmer-defined functions.

Here is the format that you must use when defining your own non-void functions:

NON-VOID FUNCTION FORMAT

//FUNCTION HEADER
return data type function name (parameter list)

{ *//BEGIN FUNCTION STATEMENT BLOCK*

    //LOCAL VARS
    local variables should go here

    //FUNCTION STATEMENTS or BODY
    function statement #1;
    function statement #2;
        •
        •
        •
    function statement #n;
    return *value;*
} *//END FUNCTION STATEMENT BLOCK*

The non-void function format consists of four main components: a *function header* line, any *local variables* required by the function, a *statement section*, and a *return statement*.

The Function Header

The *function header* provides the data *interface* for the function.

> A *function header*, or *interface*, is a statement that forms a common boundary between the function and its calling program.

This idea is illustrated by Figure 8.1. Notice that the header dictates what data the function will *accept* from the calling program and what data the function will *return* to the calling program. When developing function headers, your perspective needs to be relative to the function. You must ask yourself two things:

1. What data must the function *accept* from the calling program in order to perform its designated task?

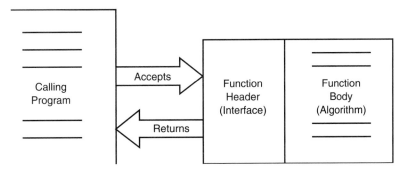

FIGURE 8.1 **THE FUNCTION HEADER FORMS THE INTERFACE BETWEEN THE CALLING PROGRAM AND THE FUNCTION.**

2. What data, if any, must the function *return* to the calling program in order to fulfill its designated task?

In general, the function header consists of the following three parts:

❐ The data type of the value to be returned by the function, if any.

❐ The name of the function.

❐ A parameter listing.

The Return Data Type.   The return type can be **void** or non-void. A **void** return type indicates that that function does not return anything. On the other hand, if a function is non-void, the return type indicates the type of data the function will return. A non-void function, such as our *cube()* function, will *always return a single value*. Thus, the return type will be any of the primitive data types discussed earlier, such as **int**, **double**, **char**, and so on. For example, suppose that a *cube()* function returns the cube of an integer. Because the cube of an integer is an integer, the function will return an integer value. As a result, the return type must be **int** or **long** and specified in the function header, like this:

```
long cube(parameter listing)
```

On the other hand, if our *cube()* function were to cube a floating-point value, the return type would have to be **float** or **double**, and the header would look like this:

```
double cube(parameter listing)
```

A non-void function always returns a single value. You can think of this value as replacing the function name wherever the name appears in a calling program. For example, the statement *cout << cube(2)* is actually seen as the statement *cout << 8*. The value that replaces the function name in the calling program, 8 in this example, is referred to as the ***return value***.

The Function Name.   The function name can be any legal identifier in C++. However, the function name *should not* begin with an underscore symbol because some debuggers always place an underscore symbol in front of the function name if an error is found in the function. The function name should be a verb or a verb phrase in mixed lower- and uppercase. Like a variable name, the first letter of the name should be lowercase and the first letter of any subsequent word uppercase. The function name should be descriptive of the operation that the function performs, just as *cube* describes the cubing of a value. You will use this name when you call, or invoke, the function within your calling program.

Three things to remember:

1. The function name can never be used as a variable *inside of the function*. In other words, the following statement inside the *cube()* function will generate an error:

```
cube = x * x * x;
```

There is one exception to this rule called **recursion**, which will be discussed later.

2. The function name can never be used on the left side of the assignment symbol *outside of the function*. Therefore, the following statement will cause an error in the calling program:

```
cube = x * x * x;
```

3. All logical *paths* within a non-void function must always lead to a **return** statement. Thus, if you have an **if/else** statement within the function and the **if** leads to a **return** statement, the **else** must also lead to a **return** statement.

DEBUGGING TIP

A non-void function *must always* return a value, or a compiler error will result. So, regardless of the path of execution a non-void function takes, it must lead to a **return** statement.

The Parameter Listing. The function parameter listing includes variables, called **parameters**, that will be *passed* from the calling program and evaluated by the function. Think of a parameter as a function variable, waiting to receive a value from the calling program when the function is called. To determine the function parameters, ask yourself: What data must the function *accept* to perform its designated task? Suppose that our *cube()* function will cube integer values. Then, the function must accept an integer value from the calling program and return an integer value to the calling program. Thus, our *function interface* can be described as follows:

Function *cube()*:	Cubes an integer.
Accepts:	An integer value.
Returns:	An integer value.

Let's designate *x* as the integer variable that the function will accept. In C++, a given parameter must be specified in the function header by indicating its data type followed by its identifier. As a result, the appropriate parameter listing for the *cube()* function would be *(int x)*. Putting everything together, the complete header would be

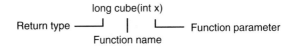

Notice that we have used an **int** for the integer parameter type and **long** for the integer return type. Why? Because cubing will always generate a result of more magnitude than the value being cubed.

If the *cube()* function were to cube floating-point values, the appropriate header would be

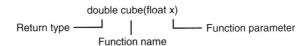

Here, we have used **double** as the return type and **float** as the parameter type. (Why?)

EXAMPLE 8.1

Suppose you want to write a programmer-defined function to calculate the voltage in a dc circuit using Ohm's law. Write an appropriate function header.

Solution

Let's call the function *calculateVoltage*, because this is what the function must do each time the function is called.

To develop the function header, we will treat the function like a black box and ask ourselves the following two questions: (1) What data must the function *accept* from the calling program in order to perform the application task? (2) What must it *return* to the calling program? The answers to these questions will dictate the function header, or interface. To answer the first question, think about what the function must evaluate. In order to calculate voltage using Ohm's law, the function must evaluate two things: current and resistance. So let's use the words *current* and *resistance* as our parameters. Of what data type should the parameters be? The obvious choice is floating-point, because you want to allow the function to evaluate decimal values of current and resistance. Thus, the function must accept a floating-point value of *current* and a floating-point value of *resistance*.

Next, you must decide what data the function must *return* to the calling program. Because the function is evaluating floating-point values, it makes mathematical sense that the returned value should also be a floating-point value. Now, the function interface can be described as follows:

Function *calculateVoltage()*:   Calculates voltage using Ohm's law.

Accepts: A floating-point value for *current* and a floating-point value for *resistance*.

Returns: A floating-point value for *voltage*.

Once you have decided what the function accepts and returns, the function header is easily constructed in C++ syntax as follows:

```
double calculateVoltage(double current, double resistance)
```

Notice that we have chosen to use **double** rather than **float** to assure adequate precision.

The Statement Section

The statement section, or body, of the function includes those operations that the function must perform to return a value to the calling program. This is where you will code your function algorithm. Look at the general format for a programmer-defined function again. As you can see, the entire statement section is framed with curly braces. After the opening curly brace, you should begin the statement section by defining any variables that will be used within the function. Any variables listed here are called *local*, because they are defined only for local use within the function itself. Local variables have no meaning outside of the function in which they are defined. *You do not duplicate any of your function parameters here.* You list only additional variables that the function might require during its execution. A common example of a local variable is a loop counter that is employed as part of a **while, do/while,** or **for** loop within the function. Actually, you can define local variables anyplace within the function as long as they are listed prior to their use. However, good style dictates that they be defined at the beginning of the statement section of the function.

> **CAUTION**
>
> Do not confuse local variables with function parameters. A local variable is defined after the opening brace of a function for use within that function. A function parameter is defined in the function header as a place holder for argument values passed to the function when the function is called. It is used within the function to supply data from the calling program to the function.

The executable statements of the function follow any local definitions. Remember, any logical path within a non-void function must lead to a **return** statement. The **return** statement is used when a single value must be returned to the calling program. So, if our *cube()* function must return the cube of *x*, an appropriate **return** statement would be

```
return x * x * x;
```

Combining the function header and statement section for the cube function will give us the complete function as follows:

```
long cube(int x)
{
  return x * x * x;
}//END cube()
```

Obviously, this is a relatively simple function that doesn't require any local variables or executable statements other than the **return** statement.

EXAMPLE 8.2

Complete the *calculateVoltage()* function whose header was developed in Example 8.1.

Solution

Ohm's law requires the function to multiply current by resistance to get voltage. Thus, the only statement required in the function is a **return** statement that will return the product of current and resistance. By putting it all together, the complete function becomes

```
double calculateVoltage(double current, double resistance)
{
   return current * resistance;
}//END calculateVoltage ()
```

DEBUGGING TIP

A common source of error in coding a non-void function is to make an assignment to the function name within the function, as follows:

```
double voltage(double current, double resistance)
{
   return voltage = current * resistance;
}//END voltage()
```

This will always cause a compiler error, because you are attempting to return the function name. You must return a value, which, in this case, is the product of *current* and *resistance*.

EXAMPLE 8.3

Write a function to return the sum of all integers from 1 to some maximum integer value, called *max*. The function must obtain the value of *max* from the calling program.

Solution

Let's call this function *calculateSum()*. Now, the function must *accept* an integer value, called *max*, from the calling program. Because the function is to sum all the integers from 1 to *max*, it must return an integer value. Thus, our function interface can be described as follows:

Function *calculateSum()*:	Sums all integers from 1 to *max*.
Accepts:	An integer value, *max*.
Returns:	An integer value.

Using this information, the function header becomes

```
int calculateSum(int max)
```

The next step is to determine if there are any local variables required by the function statements. You can use a **for** loop to calculate the sum of integers from 1 to *max*. However, the **for** statement requires a counter variable. This is a classic application for a local variable. Let's call this local counter variable *count*. Next, you also need a temporary variable within the **for** loop to keep a running subtotal of the sum each time the loop executes. Let's call this local variable *subTotal*. Using these ideas, the complete function becomes

```
int calculateSum(int max)
{
    int subTotal = 0;    //TEMP SUBTOTAL VARIABLE
    for (int count = 1; count <= max; ++count)
        subTotal = subTotal + count;
    return subTotal;
}//END calculateSum ()
```

Notice that *subTotal* is defined as a local variable for the function and *count* is defined locally inside the **for** loop.

Calling a Non-Void Function

You call, or invoke, a non-void function just about anywhere in your program just as you call many of the standard functions in C++. For example, you can call a non-void function by using an assignment operator or a *cout* statement, like this:

```
y = cube(2);
or
cout << cube(2);
```

In both cases, the *argument* value 2 is *passed to* the function to be cubed. Thus, in our *cube()* function, the parameter x takes on the argument value 2. The function will return the cube of 2, which is 8. With the assignment statement, the variable y will be assigned the value 8, and the *cout* statement causes the value 8 to be displayed on the monitor.

Here are two other ways that our *cube()* function can be called:

```
int a = 2;
y = cube(a);
```

or

```
cout << cube(a);
```

In these cases, the function is cubing the variable argument a, where a has been previously assigned the value 2. Thus, the value of a, or 2, is passed to the function. In our *cube()* function, the parameter x takes on the argument value of a. Notice that the parameter variable is x, while the function argument variable is a. Is this a problem? No, parameter and argument names can be and often are different.

Functions can also be called as part of arithmetic expressions or relational operations. For instance, our *cube()* function can be called as part of an arithmetic expression, like this:

```
int a = 2;
y = 1 + cube(a) * 2;
```

What will be assigned to *y*? Well, C++ evaluates the *cube()* function first to get 8, then performs the multiplication operation to get 16, and finally adds 1 to 16 to get 17.

You also can use functions as part of relational operations, like this:

```
if (cube(a) >= 27)
```

When will the relationship be true? When *a* is greater than or equal to 3, right? When *a* is greater than or equal to 3, *cube(a)* is greater than or equal to 27. Just remember the *value returned by a non-void function replaces the function name wherever the name is used in the calling program.*

PROGRAMMING NOTE

You will normally call non-void functions within your program using an assignment statement, a *cout* object, or as part of an arithmetic operation. Remember to think of the function call as a *value*. That is, a value replaces the function call where it appears in the program. Ask yourself: "Does a *value* make sense here?" For example, the following statements all make sense, because a value can easily be substituted for the function call:

```
result = cube(a);
cout << cube(a);
solution = 2 * cube(a) + 5;
```

On the other hand, the following statement would not make sense and would cause a compile error, because the compiler sees just a single value coded as an executable statement.

```
cube(a);
```

Arguments Versus Parameters

Some terminology is appropriate at this time. In the foregoing *cube()* example, the variable *a* used in the calling program is called an **argument**. The corresponding variable *x* used in the function header is called a **parameter**.

Arguments are values/variables used within the function call, and **parameters** are variables used within the function header that receive the argument values.

Thus, we say that the parameter in our *cube()* function, *x*, takes on the value of the argument, *a*, used in the function call. Here are some things that you will want to remember about arguments and parameters:

❏ Argument variables must be defined in the calling program. This will be function *main()*, unless functions are calling other functions.

❏ The data type of the corresponding arguments and parameters should be the same.

❏ Parameters are place holders for the argument values during the execution of the function. Parameters are always listed in the parameter section of the function heading.

❏ The number of arguments used during the function call must be the same as the number of parameters listed in the function heading, except when default parameters are used. Default parameters will be discussed shortly.

❏ The correspondence between arguments and parameters is established on a one-to-one basis according to the respective listing orders.

❏ Although the argument and parameter variables often have different variable names, they can be the same. When this is the case, the respective argument variables must still be defined in the calling program and must also appear in the parameter listing of the function.

DEBUGGING TIP

Always remember to check that the number and data types of the arguments in a function call match the number and data types of the parameters in the function header on a one-to-one basis, according to their respective listing orders. Each argument in the function call *must* correspond to one and only one parameter in the function header, and the respective ordering *must* be the same. You will always get a compiler error if the number of arguments does not match the number of parameters, unless default parameters are employed. However, you will often not get a compiler error if their data types do not match or the respective ordering is different. The result here will be garbage, and its source might be very difficult to locate.

The names of the arguments do not have to match the names of the parameters and often do not match. For instance, suppose we have a function interface as follows:

```
double foo(int a, int b, int c)
```

Then, a function call of

```
value = foo(x,y,z);
```

is perfectly legal. Here, *a* takes on the value of *x*, *b* takes on the value of *y*, and *c* takes on the value of *z* within the body of the function. Of course, the argument variables *x, y*, and *z* must be defined as **int** prior to the function call.

Quick Check

1. List four advantages of using functions within a C++ program.
2. The four major components of a non-void function are: _____, _____, _____ and _____.
3. All logical paths in a non-void function must lead to a _____ statement.
4. What two things must be considered when developing a function interface?
5. What is the purpose of the function header in a C++ program?
6. List the three parts of a function header.
7. A function variable, waiting to receive a value from the calling program, is called a _____.
8. What is the twofold purpose of a **return** statement?
9. Explain the difference between an argument in a calling program and a parameter in a function header.
10. Write an interface for a non-void function called *calculatePayment()* that will return a monthly loan payment, given the loan amount, interest rate, and term.
11. Write a statement to call the function in question 10.

8.2   VOID FUNCTIONS

Functions that do not return a single value to the calling program are often written to return multiple values or perform some specific task. These are called *void* functions.

> A *void function* is a function that returns multiple values or performs some specific task, rather than returning a single value to the calling program.

When a function is not returning a single value to the calling program, you must use the keyword **void** as the return data type. In addition, these functions may or may not require parameters. When no parameters are required, you simply leave the parameter listing blank to indicate to the compiler that the function does not need to receive any values from the calling program. Functions that do not return a value or do not require any parameters are the simplest type of functions in C++. For example, suppose that you want to write a function that will display the following header on the monitor each time it is called:

NAME   STREET   ADDRESS   STATE   CITY   ZIP
_____   _____   _____   _____   ____   ___

Let's call this function *displayHeader()*. To develop the function header, ask yourself what the function must *accept* to perform its designated task and what it must *return*. In this case, the function is simply displaying constant header information and does not need to accept any data from the calling program or return any data to the calling program. Thus, our function interface can be described as follows:

Function *displayHeader()*:	Displays fixed header information.
Accepts:	Nothing.
Returns:	Nothing.

Using this information, the header becomes

```
void displayHeader()
```

Look at the function header and you will see the keyword **void** used as the function return type. The keyword **void** used here indicates to the compiler that there is no return value. Furthermore, notice that there are no parameters required by this function, because the parameter listing is left blank. In other words, the function does not return a value and does not require any arguments to evaluate. It simply performs a given task, in this case displaying a header. To display the header, all you need is a *cout* statement in the body of the function. Putting everything together, the function becomes

```
void displayHeader()
{
 cout << "\tNAME\tSTREET ADDRESS\tCITY\tSTATE\tZIP"
      << "\n\t____\t_____\t_____\t_____\t_____" << endl;
}//END displayHeader()
```

Finally, you do not see a **return** statement at the end of the function, because no single value is being returned by the function.

PROGRAMMING NOTE

You should be aware that any function, upon completion, always returns control back to the calling program. Non-void functions return a value along with control, while void functions only return control to the calling program when they are finished executing.

Calling Void Functions

How would you call a void function in your program? Simple; just use the function name as a statement within the calling program each time the function must be called, like this:

```
displayHeader();
```

No arguments are listed in the function call, because no arguments need to be evaluated by the function. That's all there is to it!

PROGRAMMING NOTE

When calling a void function, simply list the function name and required arguments as a single statement within your program. *Do not* call a void function with an assignment operator or *cout* object as you do non-void functions. The following calls of *displayHeader()* would, at best, cause a compiler error,

```
header = displayHeader(); //ERROR
cout << displayHeader();  //ERROR
```

The correct call is simply

```
displayHeader();
```

EXAMPLE 8.4

Write a function called *display()* that could be used to display a name, address, and telephone number obtained from the calling program. Write a statement to call the *display()* function.

Solution

The first chore in writing a function is to write the function interface. To do this, you must decide what the function accepts and returns. Here is a description of the required interface:

Function *display()*:   Displays a name, address, and telephone number obtained from the calling program.

Accepts: Three strings representing a name, address, and telephone number.

Returns: Nothing.

To pass a string to a function, you simply define a string object in the function parameter listing. Our function requires that three strings be passed to it. Thus, the function interface becomes:

```
void display(string nam, string addr, string ph)
```

Notice that the function return type is **void**. (Why?) Once the function interface is determined, the function body is developed. This function only requires *cout* statements. Thus, the complete function then becomes:

```
void display(string nam, string addr, string ph)
{
   cout << nam << endl;
   cout << addr << endl;
   cout << ph << endl;
} //END display()
```

How do you suppose this function will be called? Suppose we define three string objects in *main()* like this:

```
string name = "Andrew C. Staugaard, Jr.";
string address = "C++ City, USA";
string phone = "(123) 456-7890";
```

Then, to call the function you simply use the string identifiers as arguments as follows:

```
display(name, address, phone);
```

Notice that the string object identifiers in the function call are different from those used in the parameter listing. Is there a problem here? No! In fact, the argument identifiers used in a function call are often different from the identifiers employed in the function parameter listing. This allows the function parameters to be more general, as you will see shortly. The only requirement is that the number and types of the arguments be the same and that they be listed in the same respective order as the function parameters.

PROGRAMMING NOTE

Is it possible to place a **return** statement within a **void** function to return control to the calling program? Yes! For instance, consider the following function:

```
void processIfEven(int value)
{
// IS value ODD?
if (value % 2 == 1)
    return;                //VALUE IS ODD, RETURN CONTROL

else                       //VALUE IS EVEN, PROCESS VALUE
{
    //PROCESS value
        .
        .
        .
    }//END else
}//END processIfEven()
```

This function will only process the value that it receives if *value* is even. If *value* is odd, control is *returned* to the calling program via the **return** statement.

Value Versus Reference Parameters

The preceding *displayHeader()* function did not require any parameter listing, because it did not need to receive any arguments from the calling program to evaluate. When parameters are required for evaluation by the function, they must be listed in the function interface in one of two ways: as ***value parameters*** or as ***reference parameters***.

Value Parameters. You have been using value parameters up to this point in this chapter. Value parameters allow for *one-way communication* of data from the calling program to the function. This concept is illustrated in Figure 8.2a.

A ***value parameter*** provides for one-way communication of data from the calling program to the function.

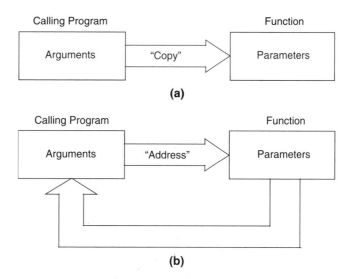

FIGURE 8.2   PASSING PARAMETERS (A) BY VALUE AND (B) BY REFERENCE.

Observe that the argument values in the calling program are passed (by value) to the parameters in the function. Another way to think of it is that the parameter receives a *copy* of the argument value. When the function operates on a value parameter, it is operating on a copy, rather than the original value in the calling program. Thus, the argument value in the calling program is protected from being accidentally changed by the function. The important thing to remember when using value parameters is that any manipulation of the parameters within the function does not affect the argument values used for the function call. For instance, consider the following function:

```
void passByValue(int x,int y)
{
 //INCREMENT AND DECREMENT PARAMETERS
 ++x;
 --y;

 //DISPLAY PARAMETER VALUES
 cout << "x = " << x << endl;
 cout << "y = " << y << endl;
}//END passByValue()
```

Here, the parameters *x* and *y* are value parameters. Notice that, within the function, the value of *x* is incremented and the value of *y* is decremented. Then, the resulting values are displayed using *cout* statements. Now, suppose the above function is called by the following program:

```
int main()
{
 //DEFINE ARGUMENT VARIABLES
 int a = 0;
 int b = 0;
```

```
//CALL FUNCTION
passByValue(a,b);

//DISPLAY ARGUMENT VALUES
cout << "a = " << b << endl;
cout << "a = " << b << endl;

//RETURN
return 0;
}//END main()
```

First, notice how the function is called. Because it is a void function, it is simply a statement in the calling program. The function name is listed, followed by the required arguments within parentheses. The arguments are *a* and *b*, because they are listed in the function call. When the function call is executed, the value of *a* is passed to the value parameter *x*, and the value of *b* is passed to the value parameter *y*. Another way to say this is that *x* receives a copy of *a* and *y* receives a copy of *b*. Notice that before the function call, the calling program initializes both *a* and *b* to the value 0. As a result, both *x* and *y* receive the value 0 from the calling program. The function then increments the value of *x*, decrements the value of *y*, and displays the new values of *x* and *y*. However, the operations on *x* and *y* have no effect on the arguments (*a* and *b*) in the calling program because the function is only working on copies of *a* and *b*, not the variables themselves. The values of *a* and *b* remain 0. Notice that after the function call, *main()* displays the values of *a* and *b*. What would you see on the display by executing the program? Well, the *passByValue()* function displays *x* and *y*, then *main()* displays *a* and *b*. Therefore, the resulting display is

```
x = 1
y = -1
a = 0
b = 0
```

Reference Parameters.   Reference parameters differ from value parameters in that they provide two-way communication between the calling program and the function, as illustrated in Figure 8.2b.

> A **reference parameter** provides two-way communication of data between the calling program and function.

Observe the two-way communication path: The argument values are passed to the parameters in the function, and then the parameter values are passed back to the arguments. This allows the function to change the argument values in the calling program. Recall that a *value parameter* is simply a copy of the argument value; therefore, any operations on the parameter within the function have no effect on its original argument value. On the other hand, a *reference parameter* represents the *address* in memory of the argument variable. As a result, any changes made to the reference parameter within the function will change what's stored at that address. This obviously changes the original value of the argument variable in the calling program.

To create a reference parameter, you simply insert an ampersand, &, prior to the appropriate parameter identifiers in the function heading. Let's change our preceding example to use reference parameters, as follows:

```
void passByReference(int &x,int &y)
{
 //INCREMENT AND DECREMENT PARAMETERS
 ++x;
 --y;

 //DISPLAY PARAMETER VALUES
  cout << "x = " << x << endl;
  cout << "y = " << y << endl;
}//END passByReference()
```

The major change here is to insert an ampersand prior to *x* and *y* in the function heading. Of course, the function name has also been changed to reflect the new application. What would you see on the display as a result of executing the following program?

```
int main()
{
  //DEFINE ARGUMENT VARIABLES
  int a = 0;
  int b = 0;

  //CALL FUNCTION
  passByReference(a,b);

  //DISPLAY ACTUAL ARGUMENT VALUES
  cout << "a = " << a << endl;
  cout << "b = " << b << endl;

  //RETURN
  return 0;
}//END main()
```

Because *x* and *y* are now reference parameters and not value parameters, any operations that affect *x* and *y* within the function will also affect the values of the arguments, *a* and *b*, used in the function call. Here are the values displayed by the program:

```
x = 1
y = -1
a = 1
b = -1
```

As you can see, the new values of *x* and *y* are passed back to *a* and *b*, respectively. We use that term "passed back" to describe the action. However, remember that nothing is actually being passed back, because the function is simply operating on the addresses of the argument variables, *a* and *b*.

EXAMPLE 8.5

What will be displayed as a result of the following program?

```
//MAIN FUNCTION
int main()
{
  //DEFINE ARGUMENT VARIABLES
  int a = 0;
  int b = 0;

  //CALL FUNCTION
  displayParameters(a,b);

  //DISPLAY ARGUMENT VALUES
  cout << "a = " << a << endl;
  cout << "b = " << b << endl;

  //RETURN
  return 0;
}//END main()

/*******************************************************
THIS FUNCTION DEMONSTRATES THE USE OF VALUE
VERSUS REFERENCE PARAMETERS
*******************************************************/
void displayParameters(int &x, int y)
{
//INCREMENT AND DECREMENT PARAMETERS
  ++x;
  --y;

//DISPLAY PARAMETER VALUES
  cout << "x = " << x << endl;
  cout << "y = " << y << endl;
} //END displayParameters()
```

Solution

Here you see an entire program that incorporates a function. The function is located immediately following the closing brace of function *main()*. The function is then called within the statement section of *main()* by simply listing its name followed by a listing of the required arguments. Notice that the arguments (*a* and *b*) are defined as integer variables in *main()*. Now look at the function heading. The parameters are *x* and *y*. Both are integers; however, *x* is a reference parameter, whereas *y* is a value parameter. Observe the use of the ampersand prior to *x*. This defines *x* as a reference parameter. However, a comma follows *x*, ending this definition. Then, *y* is defined separately as a value parameter (no ampersand). As a result, *x* receives the *address* of *a*, whereas *y* receives a *copy* of *b*. Here's what you would see on the display:

```
x = 1
y = -1
a = 1
b = 0
```

Notice that the value of *a* is the same as the value of *x*, indicating that the function operation on *x* also operated on *a*; whereas the value of *b* is different from the value of *y*, indicating that the function operation on *y* had no affect on *b*.

EXAMPLE 8.6

Write a function called *exchange()* that will accept two integer variables from the calling program and return the variables with their values exchanged.

Solution

This is an ideal application for reference parameters because, to exchange the variable values, the exchange process within the function must change the original variable values in the calling program. So, the function must accept two integer variables and return the same two variables with their values exchanged. Here's a description of the function interface:

Function *exchange()*:	Exchanges the values of two integer variables.
Accepts:	Two integer variables.
Returns:	The same two integer variables that were accepted.

Because the function must return the same two integer variables that it accepts, both will be reference parameters. Let's label the parameters *variable1* and *variable2*. The function interface then becomes

```
void exchange(int &variable1, int &variable2)
```

Notice the use of the ampersand to indicate that the parameters are reference parameters. Because *variable1* and *variable2* are reference parameters, the values of the argument variables used in the function call will be exchanged. Now, to exchange the two variable values within the function, you must create a temporary local variable so that one of the values is not lost. Using this idea, the complete function is

```
void exchange(int &variable1, int &variable2)
{
   //DEFINE TEMPORARY LOCAL VARIABLE
   int temp;

   //EXCHANGE VARIABLE VALUES
   temp = variable1;
   variable1 = variable2;
   variable2 = temp;
}//END exchange()
```

To call this function in a program, you simply list the function name and provide two argument variables to be exchanged, like this:

```
exchange(a,b);
```

Of course, *a* and *b* must be defined and initialized with values within the calling program, somewhere prior to this function call.

> **CAUTION**
>
> Although functions that employ reference parameters might have a **void** return type, they are, in fact, returning values to the calling program via the reference parameters. Do not get the idea of the function return type confused with the idea of returning values via reference parameters. They are two different things.

Locating Functions Within Your Program

As you can see from Example 8.5, programmer-defined functions are located just after the closing brace of function *main()*. There is no limit on the number of programmer-defined functions that can be used in a program. To call a function that returns a single value, you must insert the function name where you want the value to be returned. To call a void function, you simply list its name as a statement within the calling program. Of course, in both cases, any arguments required by the function must be listed within parentheses after the function name when it is called. In addition, the number of arguments used in the function call must be the same as the number of parameters defined in the respective function header.

The placement of functions in a C++ program is summarized in Figure 8.3. Here you see that each function must have a *prototype* located before *main()*. Function prototypes are discussed in the next section. Also the code for each function is

```
function1() prototype;
function2() prototype;
int main()
{
    Call function1();
    Call function2();
} //END main()

function1() Implementation
    function1()
    {
        _____
        _____

        _____
    } //END function1()

function2() Implementation
    function2()
    {
        _____
        _____

        _____
    } //END function2()
```

FIGURE 8.3 FUNCTIONS ARE USUALLY PLACED AFTER *main()* **IN A C++ PROGRAM.**

placed below *main()*. The function code in its entirety (header and body) is referred to as the *function implementation*.

Notice the block structure of the overall program. Function *main()* forms the overall outer program block, and the programmer-defined functions form the inner blocks that are nested within function *main()* via the function calls. This is why C++ can be called a *block-structured language*. From now on, when we develop C++ programs, we will attempt to divide the overall programming problem into a group of simpler subproblems whose combined solution solves the original problem. How will these subproblems be coded? You've got it—as functions! This is the essence of structured programming and top-down software design.

Quick Check

1. What must be used as the return data type when a function does not return a single value to the calling program?
2. One-way communication of data from the calling program to a function is provided via _____ parameters.
3. Two-way communication of data between the calling program and a function is provided via _____ parameters.
4. To specify a reference parameter in a function header, you must use the _____ symbol prior to the parameter identifier.
5. Where is the body of a function normally located in a C++ program?

8.3   FUNCTION PROTOTYPES

You undoubtedly noticed the presence of a *function prototype* in Figure 8.3. A *function prototype*, sometimes referred to as a *function declaration*, is a *model* of the *interface* to the function that can be used by the compiler to check calls to the function for the proper number of arguments and the correct data types of the arguments.

A *function prototype* is a model of the interface to the function used by the compiler to check for the correct number and types of arguments during the function call.

Prototyping forces the compiler to perform additional data-type checking of your function calls, thus aiding in the detection of programming errors associated with function calls. For example, if a function expects to receive an integer value and the programmer tries to pass it a string, the compiler can detect the error because C++ requires that the function prototype be specified prior to the function call. Because prototyping forces the compiler to check for errors during compile time, it does not affect the size or speed of the run-time program. Although it takes the compiler slightly longer to perform this error-checking task, any errors detected via prototyping can save hours of debugging time had prototyping not been employed. For these reasons, function prototypes are required by the C++ language. You should be aware, however, that function prototyping is optional in the C language. As a result, the C++ language is considered more strongly typed than the C language.

In the foregoing definition of a prototype, you see it provides a model of the interface to the function. Well, the function interface is the function header; therefore, the function prototype is simply a copy of the function header used by the compiler to verify the calls to the function. Thus, the prototype dictates what types of data the function will accept from the calling program and what types of data the function will return to the calling program.

You see from Figure 8.3 that the function prototypes are located just prior to function *main()*, after the preprocessor directives. The function prototype can be nothing more than a copy of the function header followed by a semicolon, like this:

```
void displayStudentData(int number, double average, char grade);
```

Here, the prototype tells the compiler that the function *displayStudentData()* will not be returning a value to the calling program (**void**). In addition, *displayStudentData()* expects to receive three arguments when it is called. The first argument will be interpreted as an integer, the second as a floating-point value, and the third as a character. If the function is called with more than or a fewer number of arguments than the number of parameters listed in the prototype, the compiler will generate an error, unless default parameters are specified. If the function is called with arguments that belong to different data types than those listed in the prototype, the arguments will be treated as if they were the respective data types listed in the parameter listing. Here is a program that uses the *displayStudentData()* function whose prototype was shown above:

```
//PREPROCESSOR DIRECTIVE
#include <iostream.h> //FOR cin AND cout

//FUNCTION PROTOTYPE
void displayStudentData(int number, double average, char grade);

int main()
{
  displayStudentData(5, 85.6, 'B');

  //RETURN
  return 0;
} //END main()
```

```
/********************************************************
THIS FUNCTION WILL DISPLAY A STUDENT's AVERAGE AND
GRADE
********************************************************/
void displayStudentData (int number, double average, char grade)
{
   cout.setf(ios::fixed);
   cout.precision(1);
   cout << "There are " << number << " tests, resulting "
        << "in an average of " << average << " and a grade of "
        << grade << '.' << endl;
} //END displayStudentData()
```

The output generated by this program is

```
There are 5 tests, resulting in an average of 85.6 and a grade of B.
```

As you can see, the arguments in the function call were passed to *displayStudentData()* and used to construct the *cout* statement. If more or fewer arguments had been used in the function call, a compiler error would have been the result. But what would happen if the argument data types were not the same as those listed in the prototype? Consider this function call:

```
displayStudentData('B', 'A', 67);
```

This call would not produce a compiler error, because the number of parameters is correct. However, the compiler would interpret the first parameter as an integer, the second as a floating-point value, and the third as a character value. As a result, the output generated by the function call would be

```
There are 66 tests, resulting in an average of 65.0 and a grade of C.
```

Do you see what happened? The function used the integer equivalent of the character 'B' for the first parameter, the floating-point equivalent of the character 'A' for the second parameter, and the character equivalent of the integer 67 for the third parameter. Of course, these equivalencies are derived from the ASCII character code. So, the lesson here is to make sure that the argument data types match the parameter data types, or you may get unpredictable results.

Look at the *displayStudentData()* function prototype again, and you will see that it is just a copy of the function header. Because of this, prototypes are easily coded into your program by using the copy/paste feature of your editor. Once you code a function, simply mark the function header and copy/paste it to the prototype area just prior to function *main()*. Don't forget to add a semicolon at the end of the prototype, because the copied function header will not have one.

You may also list your function prototypes without any parameter identifiers, like this:

```
void displayStudentData(int, double, char);
```

After all, the compiler is not interested in the parameter names, it is only interested in the number of parameters and their data types. One final point: If you forget to include a prototype for a function you will get the familiar *prototype expected* error when you compile your program. You will also get this error if you forget to include a header file for a standard function in your program because prototypes for the standard functions in C++ are included in the respective function header files.

DEBUGGING TIP

Remember that a semicolon must terminate a function prototype. You will get a *declaration syntax error* message during compilation if it is missing. However, there must *not* be a semicolon at the end of a function header. You will get a *declaration terminated incorrectly* error message during compilation if it is present.

Default Parameters

When a parameter has a default value, the parameter assumes its default value when no argument is supplied for that parameter in the function call.

A *default parameter* is a function parameter that is assigned a default value in either the function prototype or the function header, but not both.

Consider the following program:

```
//PREPROCESSOR DIRECTIVES
#include <iostream.h>  //FOR cin AND cout

//FUNCTION PROTOTYPE
int volume(int length, int width = 5, int height = 2);

//MAIN FUNCTION
int main()
{
  //DEFINE FUNCTION ARGUMENT VARIABLES
  int  l = 10;          //LENGTH
  int w = 15;           //WIDTH
  int h = 12;           //HEIGHT

  //FUNCTION CALLS
  cout << "The volume for this function call is:  " << volume(l,w,h)
       << endl << endl;
  cout << "The volume for this function call is:  " << volume(l,w)
       << endl << endl;
```

```
   cout << "The volume for this function call is:  " << volume(1)
        << endl << endl;
   cout << "The volume for this function call is:  " << volume(3,3,3)
        << endl << endl;

   //RETURN
   return 0;
} //END main()


//FUNCTION IMPLEMENTATION
int volume(int length, int width, int height)
{
   cout << "The parameters for this function call are: " << length << ", "
        << width << ", " << height << endl;
   return  length * width * height;
}//END volume()
```

Here you see a prototype for function *volume()* where the *width* and *height* parameters are assigned default values of 5 and 2, respectively. Looking at the function implementation, you see that the function simply writes its parameter values and returns the product of these values. Now, look at the function calls in the body of *main()*. Notice how the function is called several times, each time with a different set of arguments. Here is what you would see on your monitor after executing this program:

```
The parameters for this function call are:  10, 15, 12
The volume for this function is:  1800

The parameters for this function call are:  10, 15, 2
The volume for this function call is:  300

The parameters for this function call are:  10, 5, 2
The volume for this function call is:  100

The parameters for this function call are:  3, 3, 3
The volume for this function call is:  27
```

The first time the function is called, all three arguments are supplied by the way of the three variables *l*, *w*, and *h*, which are initialized to 10, 15, and 12, respectively, in *main()*. The second time the function is called, only *l* and *w* are supplied as function arguments. Because the *height* argument is not supplied, the compiler inserts the default *height* value of 2 for this argument. Thus, the returned volume is $10 \times 15 \times 2$, or 300. In the third call, only the value of *l* is supplied as a function argument, and the compiler inserts the default values of 5 and 2 for the *width* and *height* arguments, respectively. This results in a volume value of $10 \times 5 \times 2$, or 100. Finally, in the last function call, all three arguments are hard-coded into the call, and the resulting volume is $3 \times 3 \times 3$, or 27.

Here are some things that you will want to remember when using default parameters:

❑ Default parameter values are supplied by the compiler in a function call when an argument is not provided in the call for a given parameter.

❑ Default values can be provided in either the function prototype or function header, *but not both.*

❑ Once you assign a default value to a parameter in either a function prototype or header, all the remaining parameters must have default values. So, if a default value is specified for parameter *n*, then default parameters must also be specified for parameters *n* + 1, *n* + 2, and so on.

❑ The default values for a given parameter must be the correct data type for that parameter.

Function Overloading

The idea of function overloading is important to programming in C++. When a function is overloaded, it is designed to perform differently when it is supplied with a different number of arguments or argument data types. In other words, the same function exhibits different *behavior* with a different number of arguments or argument data types. Thus, a given function might *behave* one way when supplied one argument and an entirely different way when supplied two arguments. For example, consider the following program:

```
//PREPROCESSOR DIRECTIVE
#include <iostream.h> //FOR cin AND cout

//FUNCTION PROTOTYPES
int calculateArea(int);
int calculateArea(int, int);
double calculateArea(double);

//MAIN FUNCTION
int main()
{
  //DEFINE FUNCTION ARGUMENT VARIABLES
  int side = 3;
  int length = 4;
  int width = 5;
  double radius = 6.25;

  //FUNCTION CALLS
  cout <<"The area of the square is: " << calculateArea(side) << endl;
  cout <<"The area of the rectangle is: " << calculateArea(length,width) << endl;
  cout <<"The area of the circle is: " << calculateArea(radius) << endl;

  //RETURN
  return 0;
} //END main()

//THIS FUNCTION FINDS THE AREA OF A SQUARE
int calculateArea(int s)
```

```
{
  return s * s;
} //END calculateArea(int)

//THIS FUNCTION FINDS THE AREA OF A RECTANGLE
int calculateArea(int l, int w)
{
  return l * w;
} //END calculateArea(int,int)

//THIS FUNCTION FINDS THE AREA OF A CIRCLE
double calculateArea(double r)
{
   return 3.14159 * r * r;
} //END calculateArea(double)
```

Look at the function prototyping section. The first thing you see are three different prototypes for *calculateArea()*. In the first prototype, *calculateArea()* requires a single integer argument and returns an integer value. In the second prototype, *calculateArea()* requires two integer arguments and returns an integer value. In the third prototype, *calculateArea()* requires a single floating-point argument and returns a floating-point value. Looking at the function implementations at the bottom of the program, you find that the single function *calculateArea()* is implemented three different times to do three different things. The way *calculateArea()* will *behave* is determined by the number and types of the arguments supplied when it is called. If a single integer argument is provided when *calculateArea()* is called, it will return the area of a square. If two integer arguments are supplied in the call, *calculateArea()* will return the area of a rectangle, which is not square. However, if a single floating-point argument is supplied in the call, *calculateArea()* will return the area of a circle. Here is the result of the program execution:

```
The area of the square is:   9
The area of the rectangle is:   20
The area of the circle is:   122.718
```

Obviously, you could say that *calculateArea()* is *overloaded* with work, because it is performing three different tasks, depending on the number and data types of the arguments used in its call. Overloading is used where the tasks are very similar, differing only in the number of arguments required by the function or the data types of the arguments. Without overloading, you would have to invent different names for each similar task instead of just one, thus requiring you and your program users to remember all of them.

Function overloading is related to the concept of **polymorphism**, which is one of the cornerstones of object-oriented programming, as you will find out later. We are introducing it here so that you understand the concept. You will see how it is applied when you learn about OOP in a later chapter. By the way, function overloading is not possible in the C language.

Quick Check

1. What is the primary purpose of a function prototype?
2. Where is a function prototype located in a C++ program?
3. True or false: Parameters listed in a function prototype can be listed only by data type, without any corresponding identifiers.
4. True or false: Default parameters can appear in either the function prototype or function header, but not both.
5. True or false: Once a default parameter is specified in a function prototype, the remaining parameters in the parameter listing must be default parameters.
6. When overloading a function, what determines how the function will behave?

PROBLEM SOLVING IN ACTION: PROGRAMMING WITH FUNCTIONS

PROBLEM

In previous chapters, we developed a loop-controlled, menu-driven loan program. However, although we developed a modular design, we have employed a flat implementation when coding the design. It is now time to do it right and employ modular programming via functions to implement the modular design. Here is the problem definition that we developed earlier:

Defining the Problem

Output: A program menu that prompts the user to select a monthly payment, total interest, or total loan amount calculation option.

The monthly loan payment, total loan interest, or total loan amount, depending on the program option that the user selects.

Invalid entry messages as required.

Input: A user response to the menu (P, I, T, or Q).

If P is selected: User enters the loan amount, interest rate, and term.

If I is selected: User enters the loan amount, interest rate, and term.

If T is selected: User enters the loan amount, interest rate, and term.

If Q is selected: Terminate program.

Processing: Calculate the selected option as follows:

Case P: $payment = principle * rate/(1 - (1+rate)^{-term})$

Case I: $interest = term * payment - principle$

Case T: $total = principle + interest$

Case Q: Terminate program.

where: *principle* is the amount of the loan.

rate is a monthly interest rate in decimal form.

term is the number of months of the loan.

Planning the Solution

The problem-solving diagram we developed earlier is shown again in Figure 8.4. Now, here is the set of algorithms we developed earlier:

Initial Algorithm

> main()
> BEGIN
>   do
>   Call *displayMenu()* function.
>   Call *loanCalculator()* function.
>   while *choice* ≠ 'q' AND *choice* ≠ 'Q'
> END.

First Level of Refinement

> displayMenu()
> BEGIN
>   Display a program menu that prompts the user to choose a monthly payment (P), total interest (I), total loan amount (T), or quit (Q) option.
>   Read *choice*.
> END.

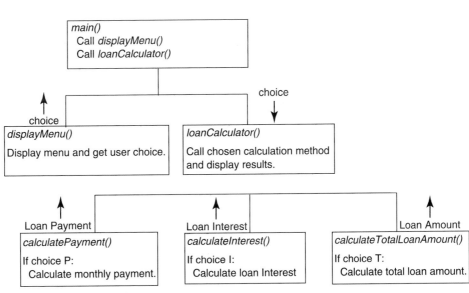

FIGURE 8.4   A PROBLEM-SOLVING DIAGRAM FOR THE LOAN PROBLEM.

loanCalculator()
BEGIN
    Case P: Call function *calculatePayment()* and display payment.
    Case I: Call function *calculateInterest()* and display interest.
    Case T: Call function *calculateTotalLoanAmount()* and display total loan
              amount.
    Case Q: Terminate program.
    Default: Write an invalid entry message and ask the user to select again.
END.

Coding the Program

Now, to implement the design, we need to construct the functions. The main task here is to develop the function interfaces, or headers. To do this, we must develop a problem definition for *each* function. The problem definition developed earlier addresses output, input, and processing for the overall application program, *main()*. This is still needed to define the problem for the program as a whole. However, to construct the function interfaces, we must address problem definition from the perspective of the function. In other words, we must consider the output, input, and processing of each individual function. The *input* to the function is what the function must *accept* in order to perform its designated task, the *output* from the function is what the function *returns*, and the *processing* is the task, or algorithm, the function will perform.

We will start with the *displayMenu()* function. You must ask yourself two questions: 1) "What does the function need to *accept* (input) to perform its designated task?" and 2) "What does the function need to *return* (output) to the calling program?" The task of the *displayMenu()* function is to display the menu and return the user's choice to its calling function, *main()*. Thus, this function does not need to accept anything from *main()* to perform its task but needs to return a single value to *main()*, which is the user's menu choice. This is shown in the problem solving diagram by the variable *choice* coming out of *displayMenu()*. Notice that nothing is going into this function. Here is the problem definition from the perspective of this function:

    Function *displayMenu()*:   Display menu and get user entry.
    Accepts: Nothing.
    Returns: Menu choice obtained from user.

The function definition describes the function interface. The first decision you need to make is whether to use a void function or a non-void function. Use a non-void function if the function produces a single value that is returned to the calling program. Use a void function if the function returns *more than* one value or does not return anything to the calling program. In other words, if the problem-solving diagram indicates that a single value is being produced by the function, use a non-void function. If the problem solving diagram indicates that more than one value or

TABLE 8.1   FUNCTION RETURN TYPE

Returns	Return Data Type
A single value	non-void type
Nothing	void
Multiple values	void

nothing is being returned by the function, use a void function. These guidelines are summarized in Table 8.1. Because our *displayMenu()* function accepts nothing, but returns the user's menu choice, it must be a non-void function. So, the return type must be **char**, because the user's choice will be a character from the menu.

Next, we must decide the function parameters. Table 8.2 provides the guidelines for determining whether a given parameter must be a value or a reference parameter.

TABLE 8.2   FUNCTION PARAMETERS

Accepts/Returns	Parameter
Nothing accepted	none
Accepts without returning (one-way)	value
Accepts and returns (two-way)	reference

No parameters are required for *displayMenu()*, because it does not accept anything. Thus, the function interface is simply

```
char displayMenu()
```

DEBUGGING TIP

When deciding what a function must accept, you only include those items that need to be accepted from the *calling program*. Since *choice* is entered by the user, and not received from the calling program, it is not a parameter in the foregoing *displayMenu()* function.

Now, we simply place the *displayMenu()* code developed earlier inside the function. Here is the complete function:

```
char displayMenu()
{
  //DEFINE LOCAL CHOICE VARIABLE
  char choice = 'Q';
```

```
        cout  <<  "\n\n\t\t\tEnter P to get monthly payment"
              <<  "\n\t\t\tEnter I to get total loan interest"
              <<  "\n\t\t\tEnter T to get total loan amount"
              <<  "\n\t\t\tEnter Q to quit" << endl;

        cout  <<  "\n\n\tPlease enter your choice:   ";

        //READ USER CHOICE
        cin >> choice;

        //RETURN CHOICE
        return choice;
      } //END displayMenu()
```

Notice that our *choice* variable is now defined as a local variable inside the function. In addition, a **return** statement is placed at the end of the function to return *choice* to its calling function, *main()*.

Next, let's develop the *loanCalculator()* function. We begin by developing the function interface. From the problem-solving diagram, it is easy to see the following:

Function *loanCalculator()*:	Perform chosen calculation and display results.
Accepts:	Menu entry, *choice*, obtained from *main()*.
Returns:	Nothing.

From the interface description, it is easy to see that we must use a void function, because nothing is returned by the function. Even though the function is displaying the result, it *is not* returning any values to its calling function, *main()*. However, this function needs to accept the menu choice from *main()*. This means that we need a function parameter. The required parameter is a character, so the function interface becomes

```
        void loanCalculator(char choice)
```

Now, inserting our switch statement code into the body of the function, the complete function becomes:

```
//LOAN CALCULATION FUNCTION
void loanCalculator(char choice)
{
  switch (choice)
  {
   case 'p':   //CALL calculatePayment() FUNCTION
   case 'P':   cout << "The monthly loan payment is $"
                    << calculatePayment() << endl;
               break;

   case 'i':   //CALL calculateInterest() FUNCTION
   case 'I' :  cout << "The monthly loan payment is $"
                    << calculateInterest() << endl;
               break;
```

```
case 't':    //CALL calculateTotalLoanAmount() FUNCTION
case 'T':    cout << "The monthly loan payment is $"
                  << calculateTotalLoanAmount() << endl;
             break;

case 'q':    //TERMINATE PROGRAM
case 'Q':    cout << "Program terminated." << endl;
             break;

             //DISPLAY INVALID ENTRY MESSAGE
 default :   cout << "\n\nThis is an invalid entry." << endl;
 } //END SWITCH
}//END loanCalculator()
```

Notice that the body of the function employs our earlier **switch** statement, which acts on the user choice, *choice*, received as a parameter from the calling function, *main()*. Next, you see that each **case** calls another function as part of a *cout* statement to calculate the required loan payment, interest, or total loan amount, depending on the value of *choice*. Each function will return a single value of monthly payment, interest, or total loan amount, depending on which **case** is executed. Does this give you a hint as to what type of functions these will be (void or non-void)? Finally, notice that there is no **return** statement in our *loanCalculator()* function, because it is a void function.

Next, here are the interface descriptions for each of the loan functions:

Function *calculatePayment()*:	Get loan principle, rate, and term from user and calculate the loan payment.
Accepts:	Nothing.
Returns:	Loan payment.
Function *calculateInterest()*:	Get loan principle, rate, and term from user and calculate the loan interest.
Accepts:	Nothing.
Returns:	Loan interest.
Function *calculateTotalLoanAmount()*:	Get loan principle, rate, and term from user and calculate the total loan amount.
Accepts:	Nothing.
Returns:	Loan amount.

Each of these functions will have the same interface, except, of course, for the function name. Each function will be a non-void function, because a single value is being produced and returned by the function. No parameters are required, because none of the functions need to accept any data from the calling function, *loanCalculator()*. You are probably thinking each function needs the three unknown quantities in order to make the required calculation, right? However, these quantities will be obtained from the user within each of the functions and not from the *loanCalculator()* calling function. As a result, these values are *not* passed to any of the functions. Here are the resulting function interfaces:

```
double calculatePayment()
double calculateInterest()
double calculateTotalLoanAmount()
```

Now, here is each complete function implementation:

```cpp
//CALCULATE PAYMENT FUNCTION
double calculatePayment()
{
 //DEFINE LOCAL VARIABLES
 double principle = 0.0; //LOAN PRINCIPLE
 double rate = 0.0;      //ANNUAL INTEREST RATE
 int term = 0;           //TERM OF LOAN IN MONTHS

 //GET LOAN DATA FROM USER
 cout << "\nEnter the amount of the loan: $";
 cin >> principle;
 cout << "\nEnter the duration of the loan in months: ";
 cin >> term;
 cout << "\nEnter the annual interest rate: ";
 cin >> rate;

 //CHECK FOR INVALID RATE
 while ((rate <= 0) || (rate > 100))
 {
   //DISPLAY INVALID ENTRY MESSAGE
   cout << "\n\nThis is an invalid entry. " << endl;
   cout << "\nEnter the annual interest rate: ";
   cin >> rate;
 }//END WHILE

 //CALCULATE PAYMENT
 rate = rate/12/100;
 return principle * rate/(1-pow((1+rate),-term));
}//END calculatePayment()

//CALCULATE INTEREST FUNCTION
double calculateInterest()
{
 //DEFINE LOCAL VARIABLES
 double payment = 0.0;    //MONTHLY PAYMENT
 double principle = 0.0; //LOAN PRINCIPLE
 double rate = 0.0;      //ANNUAL INTEREST RATE
 int term = 0;           //TERM OF LOAN IN MONTHS

 //GET LOAN DATA FROM USER
 cout << "\nEnter the amount of the loan: $";
 cin >> principle;
 cout << "\nEnter the duration of the loan in months: ";
 cin >> term;
 cout << "\nEnter the annual interest rate: ";
 cin >> rate;
```

```
//CHECK FOR INVALID RATE
while ((rate <= 0) || (rate > 100))
{
 //DISPLAY INVALID ENTRY MESSAGE
 cout << "\n\nThis is an invalid entry. " << endl;
 cout << "\nEnter the annual interest rate: ";
 cin >> rate;
}//END WHILE

 //CALCULATE INTEREST
 rate = rate/12/100;
 payment = principle * rate/(1-pow((1+rate),-term));
 return term * payment - principle;
}//END calculateInterest()

//CALCULATE TOTAL LOAN AMOUNT FUNCTION
double calculateTotalLoanAmount()
{
 //DEFINE LOCAL VARIABLES
 double payment = 0.0;  //MONTHLY PAYMENT
 double interest = 0.0;  //TOTAL INTEREST FOR LIFE OF LOAN
 double principle = 0.0; //LOAN PRINCIPLE
 double rate = 0.0;      //ANNUAL INTEREST RATE
 int term = 0;           //TERM OF LOAN IN MONTHS

 //GET LOAN DATA FROM USER
 cout << "\nEnter the amount of the loan: $";
 cin >> principle;
 cout << "\nEnter the duration of the loan in months: ";
 cin >> term;
 cout << "\nEnter the annual interest rate: ";
 cin >> rate;

 //CHECK FOR INVALID RATE
 while ((rate <= 0) || (rate > 100))
 {
  //DISPLAY INVALID ENTRY MESSAGE
  cout << "\n\nThis is an invalid entry. " << endl;
  cout << "\nEnter the annual interest rate: ";
  cin >> rate;
 }//END WHILE

  //CALCULATE TOTAL LOAN AMOUNT
  rate = rate/12/100;
  payment = principle * rate/(1-pow((1+rate),-term));
  interest = term * payment - principle;
  return principle + interest;
}//END calculateTotalLoanAmount()
```

Notice that each function obtains the data required for the calculation from the user. The interest rate value is tested. If invalid, a loop is entered which writes an invalid entry message and continues to iterate until the user enters a valid interest rate.

We are now ready to combine everything into a complete program. Here it is:

```
/*
ACTION 8-1 (ACT08_01.CPP)
OUTPUT: A PROGRAM MENU THAT PROMPTS THE USER TO SELECT A
        MONTHLY PAYMENT, TOTAL INTEREST, OR TOTAL LOAN AMOUNT
        CALCULATION OPTION.
        INVALID ENTRY MESSAGES AS REQUIRED.
        THE MONTHLY LOAN PAYMENT, TOTAL LOAN INTEREST,
        OR TOTAL LOAN AMOUNT, DEPENDING ON THE PROGRAM OPTION THAT THE
        USER SELECTS.
        INVALID ENTRY MESSAGES AS REQUIRED.

INPUT:  A USER RESPONSE TO THE MENU (P, I, T, OR Q).
        IF P IS SELECTED: USER ENTERS THE LOAN AMOUNT, INTEREST RATE, AND TERM.
        IF I IS SELECTED: USER ENTERS THE LOAN AMOUNT, INTEREST RATE, AND TERM.
        IF R IS SELECTED: USER ENTERS THE LOAN AMOUNT, INTEREST RATE, AND TERM.
        IF Q IS SELECTED: TERMINATE PROGRAM.

PROCESSING:  CALCULATE THE SELECTED OPTION AS FOLLOWS:
        CASE P:    PAYMENT = PRINCIPLE * RATE/(1 - (1+RATE) -TERM)
        CASE I:    INTEREST = TERM * PAYMENT - PRINCIPLE
        CASE T:    TOTAL = PRINCIPLE + INTEREST
        CASE Q:    QUIT THE PROGRAM.

        WHERE: PRINCIPLE IS THE AMOUNT OF THE LOAN.
               RATE IS A MONTHLY INTEREST RATE IN DECIMAL FORM.
               TERM IS THE NUMBER OF MONTHS OF THE LOAN.
*/

//PREPROCESSOR DIRECTIVES
#include <iostream.h> //FOR cin AND cout
#include <math.h>     //FOR pow()

//FUNCTION PROTOTYPES
char displayMenu();
void loanCalculator(char choice);
double calculatePayment();
double calculateInterest();
double calculateTotalLoanAmount();

//MAIN FUNCTION
int main()
{
  //DEFINE VARIABLES
  char choice = 'Q';  //USER MENU ENTRY
```

```cpp
//DISPLAY PROGRAM DESCRIPTION MESSAGE
cout << "\nThis program will calculate a monthly loan interest\n"
     << "payment, total loan interest, or total loan amount." << endl;

//MENU CONTROL LOOP
do
{
 choice = displayMenu();
 loanCalculator(choice);
 } //END DO/WHILE
while ((choice != 'q') && (choice != 'Q'));

 //RETURN
 return 0;
}//END main()

//DISPLAY MENU FUNCTION
char displayMenu()
{
 //DEFINE LOCAL CHOICE VARIABLE
 char choice = 'Q';

 cout  << "\n\n\t\t\tEnter P to get monthly payment"
       << "\n\t\t\tEnter I to get total loan interest"
       << "\n\t\t\tEnter T to get total loan amount"
       << "\n\t\t\tEnter Q to quit" << endl;

 cout  << "\n\n\tPlease enter your choice:  ";

  //READ USER CHOICE
  cin >> choice;

  //RETURN CHOICE
  return choice;
 } //END displayMenu()

//LOAN CALCULATION FUNCTION
void loanCalculator(char choice)
{
 switch (choice)
 {
 case 'p':  //CALL calculatePayment() FUNCTION
 case 'P':  cout << "The monthly loan payment is $"
                 << calculatePayment() << endl;
            break;

 case 'i':  //CALL calculateInterest() FUNCTION
 case 'I':  cout << "The monthly loan payment is $"
                 << calculateInterest() << endl;
            break;
```

```
        case 't': //CALL calculateTotalLoanAmount() FUNCTION
        case 'T': cout << "The monthly loan payment is $"
                       << calculateTotalLoanAmount() << endl;
                  break;

        case 'q': //TERMINATE PROGRAM
        case 'Q': cout << "Program terminated." << endl;
                  break;

                  //DISPLAY INVALID ENTRY MESSAGE
        default : cout << "\n\nThis is an invalid entry." << endl;
     } //END SWITCH
}//END loanCalculator()

//CALCULATE PAYMENT FUNCTION
double calculatePayment()
{
  //DEFINE LOCAL VARIABLES
  double principle = 0.0;    //LOAN PRINCIPLE
  double rate = 0.0;         //ANNUAL INTEREST RATE
  int term = 0;              //TERM OF LOAN IN MONTHS

  //GET LOAN DATA FROM USER
  cout << "\nEnter the amount of the loan: $";
  cin >> principle;
  cout << "\nEnter the duration of the loan in months: ";
  cin >> term;
  cout << "\nEnter the annual interest rate: ";
  cin >> rate;

  //CHECK FOR INVALID RATE
  while ((rate <= 0) || (rate > 100))
  {
   //DISPLAY INVALID ENTRY MESSAGE
   cout << "\n\nThis is an invalid entry." << endl;
   cout << "\nEnter the annual interest rate: ";
   cin >> rate;
  }//END WHILE

  //CALCULATE PAYMENT
  rate = rate/12/100;
  return principle * rate/(1-pow((1+rate),-term));
}//END calculatePayment()

//CALCULATE INTEREST FUNCTION
double calculateInterest()
{
  //DEFINE LOCAL VARIABLES
  double payment = 0.0;    //MONTHLY PAYMENT
  double principle = 0.0; //LOAN PRINCIPLE
  double rate = 0.0;       //ANNUAL INTEREST RATE
  int term = 0;            //TERM OF LOAN IN MONTHS
```

```
  //GET LOAN DATA FROM USER
  cout << "\nEnter the amount of the loan: $";
  cin >> principle;
  cout << "\nEnter the duration of the loan in months: ";
  cin >> term;
  cout << "\nEnter the annual interest rate: ";
  cin >> rate;

  //CHECK FOR INVALID RATE
  while ((rate <= 0) || (rate > 100))
  {
    //DISPLAY INVALID ENTRY MESSAGE
    cout << "\n\nThis is an invalid entry." << endl;
    cout << "\nEnter the annual interest rate: ";
    cin >> rate;
  }//END WHILE

  //CALCULATE INTEREST
  rate = rate/12/100;
  payment = principle * rate/(1-pow((1+rate),-term));
  return term * payment - principle;
}//END calculateInterest()

//CALCULATE TOTAL LOAN AMOUNT FUNCTION
double calculateTotalLoanAmount()
{
  //DEFINE LOCAL VARIABLES
  double payment = 0.0;    //MONTHLY PAYMENT
  double interest = 0.0;   //TOTAL INTEREST FOR LIFE OF LOAN
  double principle = 0.0;  //LOAN PRINCIPLE
  double rate = 0.0;       //ANNUAL INTEREST RATE
  int term = 0;            //TERM OF LOAN IN MONTHS

  //GET LOAN DATA FROM USER
  cout << "\nEnter the amount of the loan: $";
  cin >> principle;
  cout << "\nEnter the duration of the loan in months: ";
  cin >> term;
  cout << "\nEnter the annual interest rate: ";
  cin >> rate;

  //CHECK FOR INVALID RATE
  while ((rate <= 0) || (rate > 100))
  {
    //DISPLAY INVALID ENTRY MESSAGE
    cout << "\n\nThis is an invalid entry." << endl;
    cout << "\nEnter the annual interest rate: ";
    cin >> rate;
  }//END WHILE

  //CALCULATE TOTAL LOAN AMOUNT
  rate = rate/12/100;
```

```
   payment = principle * rate/(1-pow((1+rate),-term));
   interest = term * payment - principle;
   return principle + interest;
}//END calculateTotalLoanAmount()
```

One of the first things you see at the top of the program are the function proto-types. These are simply copied from the function headers with a semicolon added to the end of each. Remember that C++ requires a prototype for each function so that it can check the correctness of the function calls. Next, you should be impressed by the simplicity of function *main()*. All that needs to be done here is to write a program description message and call our two functions within a program control loop. Most of the real work of the program is being done within the functions. The rest of the program contains each of the functions that we discussed earlier.

> **DOCUMENTATION NOTE**
>
> It's a good idea to include any program documentation that you have created within the program listing. Then, anyone looking at the listing can readily see the program design through the problem definitions and algorithms, without having to go through the code. We suggest that our students place the appropriate interface description and algorithm for each function in comments, just prior to the function in the program code. This means that the original problem definition and initial algorithm should be placed in comments just prior to *main()*. Then, each function interface description and algorithm should be placed in comments just prior to the respective function code. This way, there are no doubts about what the various parts of the program are doing.

8.4 SCOPING-OUT VARIABLES AND CONSTANTS— BLOCK STRUCTURE

In the last two sections, you observed the use of local variables.

> A *local variable* is a variable that is defined within a specific block of code, such as a function.

A local variable is created for use only within a function block and has no mean-ing outside of the respective function. Don't get local variables confused with the function parameters listed in the function header. Local function variables are de-fined after the opening brace of a function, and parameters are defined in the func-tion header. Defining variables locally supports the concept of ***modularity***.

To realize the importance of modularity, suppose that you are a member of a programming team that must develop the software to solve a very complex indus-trial problem. The easiest way to solve any complex problem is to divide the problem into simpler, more manageable subproblems. Then, solve the subproblems and combine their solutions in order to solve the overall complex problem. This is called ***modular design***. Using the modular design approach, your team leader divides the complex programming problem into simpler subproblems and then asks each member of the team to write a function to solve a given subproblem. How does this relate to the use of local variables? Well, you can write your function using any local variables you wish, without worrying that another team member might use the same local variables. Even if two team members use the same local variable identifiers, the functions will still execute independently when they are combined in the main program. This allows a modular team approach to software design, something that is not available in nonstructured languages like BASIC. The functions act as modular building blocks to form the overall program.

The Scope of Variables

We say that a local variable defined in a function is said to have ***block scope***, because it is available only within the function block in which it is defined.

> The ***scope*** of a variable refers to the largest block in which a given variable is accessible.

A term often associated with scope is ***visibility***. You could say that the visibility of a local variable is the block in which it is defined. Look at the following code to get the idea.

```
//FUNCTION PROTOTYPES
void function1();
void function2();

//MAIN FUNCTION
int main()
{
 int x0; //LOCAL TO main();

 //RETURN
 return 0;
}//END main()

void function1()
{
 int x1; //LOCAL TO function1()
}//END function1()

void function2()
{
 in x1; //LOCAL TO function2()
}//END function2()
```

Here, *x0* has block scope, because it is defined local to *main()* and therefore is visible only in *main()* and cannot be accessed by *function1()* or *function2()*. How could it be accessible to the other functions? By passing it as an argument to any function that needs it, right? How about *x1*? Here, *x1* is defined inside of *function1()* and, therefore, is local to this function and cannot be used by any other function, including *main()*. Finally, notice that the variable *x1* is also defined in *function2()* as a local variable. Is there a problem here, because *x1* is also defined in *function1()*? No! The local variable *x1* in *function2()* is independent of the variable *x1* defined in *function1()*. Because *x1* is defined locally in *function2()*, any operations on *x1* within this function will not affect the *x1* in *function1()*. It's as if they are two separate variables.

In summary, we could make the following statements concerning the scope of the variables in the foregoing program.

- ❏ The *x0* variable defined in *main()* is visible to *main()*, but not visible to *function1()* or *function2()*.
- ❏ The *x1* variable defined in *function1()* has a block scope of *function1()*.
- ❏ The *x1* variable defined in *function2()* has a block scope of *function2()*.
- ❏ The *x1* variable defined is *function1()* is completely separate from the *x1* variable defined in *function2()*.

Always define your variables as locally as possible within a given function block. If variables need to be shared among functions, pass them.

The Scope of Constants

The general rule for defining constants is just the opposite of defining variables— you should *define constants as globally as possible*. To do this, you define them prior to *main()*. Defining constants globally allows all functions access to a given constant. Moreover, constants are not always constant. Remember the *POSTAGE* and *SALES_TAX* constants we used in Chapter 3? These constants are subject to change over a period of time. When they must be changed, you only need to make a change in one place in the program if they are defined globally. However, if they are defined locally, a change must be made in each function in which they are defined.

Quick Check

1. Where must a constant that has global scope be placed in a C++ program?
2. A local variable has _____ scope.
3. How can a variable defined in *main()* be accessed by a function in the same program?

PROBLEM SOLVING IN ACTION: PROGRAMMING WITH FUNCTIONS

In Chapter 3, we employed stepwise refinement to design a solution for a bank account application. We coded the solution using a flat implementation because, at that time, you did not know how to implement a design using C++ functions. Let's revisit this application with our newly gained knowledge of functions.

Here's the problem statement again:

PROBLEM

Your local bank has contracted you to design a C++ application program that will process savings account data for a given month. Assume that the savings account accrues interest at a rate of 12 percent per year and that the user must enter the current account balance, amount of deposits, and amount of withdrawals. Develop a problem definition, set of algorithms, and C++ program to solve this problem.

Here is how we defined the overall problem in terms of output, input, and processing:

Defining the Problem

Output:	The program must display a report showing the account transactions and balance for a given savings account in a given month.
Input:	To process a savings account, you need to know the initial balance, amount of deposits, amount of withdrawals, and interest rate. We will assume that these values will be entered by the program user, with the exception of the interest rate, which will be coded as a constant.
Processing:	The program must process deposits and withdrawals and calculate interest to determine the monthly balance.

This will serve as our problem definition for the initial algorithm, *main()*.

Planning the Solution

Next, using stepwise refinement we constructed the problem solving diagram in Figure 8.5 along with the following set of related algorithms.

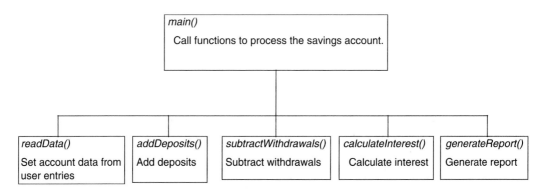

FIGURE 8.5   A PROBLEM-SOLVING DIAGRAM FOR THE BANKING PROBLEM.

Initial Algorithm

main()
BEGIN
    Call function to obtain the transaction data from user.
    Call function to add the account deposits.
    Call function to subtract the account withdrawals.
    Call function to calculate the account interest.
    Call function to generate the account report.
END.

First Level of Refinement

readData()
BEGIN
    Write a prompt to enter the current account balance.
    Read *balance*.
    Write a prompt to enter the monthly deposits.
    Read *deposits*.
    Write a prompt to enter the monthly withdrawals.
    Read *withdrawals*.
END.

addDeposits()
BEGIN
    Calculate *balance = balance + deposits*.
END.

subtractWithdrawals()
BEGIN
    Calculate *balance = balance − withdrawals*.
END.

addInterest()
BEGIN
    Calculate *balance = balance + (balance * interest)*.
END.

generateReport()
BEGIN
    Write *balance*.
    Write *deposits*.
    Write *withdrawals*.
END.

With our new-found knowledge of functions, we can modify the problem-solving diagram, as shown in Figure 8.6. Notice what has been added. First, the box at the

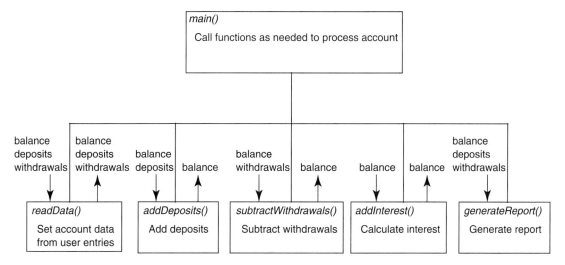

FIGURE 8.6   AN EXPANDED PROBLEM-SOLVING DIAGRAM SHOWS DATA ITEMS FLOWING TO/FROM THE BANK ACCOUNT FUNCTIONS.

top is labeled *main()* and simply calls the individual functions in the order that they are needed to solve the problem. Second, data items being passed to/from the functions are shown on the lines connecting *main()* to the functions. Items the function accepts are shown to the left of the connecting line, and items the function returns are shown to the right of the line, as follows:

❏ If a given data item goes one way into the function, it is a value parameter.

❏ If a given data item goes one way out of the function, it is a return value.

❏ If a given data item goes two ways in and out of the function, it is a reference parameter.

To construct the expanded diagram, you must consider a problem definition for each function by describing the function interface in terms of what it accepts and returns. Let's begin with the *readData()* function.

Function *readData()*:	Obtain current account balance, deposits, and withdrawals from the user.
Accepts:	Variable *placeholders* for balance, deposits, and withdrawals.
Returns:	Balance, deposits, and withdrawals.

The *readData()* function must obtain user entries and return them to the calling program, *main()*. As a result, the function must accept a variable *placeholder* for each user entry. Think of a variable placeholder as an empty bucket being passed from *main()* to the function. The function will fill the bucket with the variable values entered by the user and pass it back to *main()* so that the variable values can be passed on to the other functions.

The interface description is represented on the diagram in Figure 8.6 by showing the variables *balance*, *deposits*, and *withdrawals* going both into and out of the *readData()* function module. This means that all three must be reference parameters, resulting in a function interface of

```
void readData(double &balance, double &deposits, double &withdrawals)
```

The *addDeposits()* function interface can be described as follows:

Function *addDeposits()*: Add deposits to the current balance.

Accepts: The current account balance and deposits.

Returns: A new account balance.

This function requires that the function receive the current account balance and deposits in order to calculate and return the new account balance. As a result, *balance* and *deposits* are accepted by the function, *balance* is then changed by adding *deposits*, and *balance* is returned to *main()*, as shown in the diagram. Notice that *balance* is going two ways, into the function and out of the function, whereas *deposits* is going only one way into the function. This means that *balance* must be a reference parameter, and *deposits* must be a value parameter. Therefore, the resulting function interface must be

```
void addDeposits(double &balance, double deposits)
```

The *subtractWithdrawals()* function must receive the current account balance and withdrawals, subtract the withdrawals, and return the new account balance. With this information, its interface can be described as follows:

Function *subtractWithdrawals()*: Subtract withdrawals from the current balance.

Accepts: The current account balance and withdrawals.

Returns: A new account balance.

The diagram illustrates this information by showing *balance* going two ways into the function and out of the function, whereas *withdrawals* is going only one way, into the function. Thus, *balance* must be a reference parameter, and *withdrawals* must be a value parameter. The resulting function interface is

```
void subtractWithdrawals(double &balance, double withdrawals)
```

Next, the *addInterest()* function must receive the account balance, calculate the monthly interest, and return the balance. We will assume that the interest rate is a global constant. This function can be described as follows:

Function *addInterest()*: Add monthly interest to account balance.

Accepts: The current account balance.

Returns: A new account balance.

Here, the account balance is accepted by the function, changed by adding the monthly interest, and returned to *main()* by the function. Transcribing this information to the diagram, you find that *balance* goes into and out of the *addInterest()* function module. The resulting interface is

```
void addInterest(double &balance)
```

Finally, the *generateReport()* function must receive the account balance, deposits, and withdrawals in order to generate the required account report. This function can, therefore, be described as follows:

Function *generateReport()*:   Generate account report.

Accepts: The current account balance, deposits, and withdrawals.

Returns: Nothing.

In order to generate the account report, the function must receive the account balance, deposits, and withdrawals from *main()*. However, these values are not being modified and returned; they are just being displayed as part of the report by the function. Thus, the diagram indicates *balance*, *deposits*, and *withdrawals* going only one way, into the function module. This means that they all must be value parameters, right? The resulting function interface is

```
void generateReport(double balance, double deposits, double withdrawals)
```

Make sure that you see how the interface description for each function is illustrated on the problem-solving diagram and how the diagram is translated directly into the foregoing C++ interface code. If a given data item only comes out of the function, it is a return value. Observe that there are no variables that only come out of any of the functions. As a result, all of the functions have return types of **void**. If a given item only goes into the function, it is a value parameter. If a given item goes both into and out of a function, it is a reference parameter and must be preceded by an ampersand symbol in the prototype.

Finally, using the function interfaces, algorithms, and combining everything, we get the following code:

Coding the Program

```
/**************************************************************************
ACTION 8-2 (ACT08_02.CPP)
THIS PROGRAM WILL PROCESS A BANKING ACCOUNT
**************************************************************************/

//PREPROCESSOR DIRECTIVE
#include <iostream.h>  //FOR cin AND cout

//DEFINE GLOBAL INTEREST CONSTANT
const double INTEREST = 0.01; //CURRENT MONTHLY INTEREST RATE

//FUNCTION PROTOTYPES
void readData(double &balance, double &deposits, double &withdrawals);
void addDeposits(double &balance, double deposits);
void subtractWithdrawals(double &balance, double withdrawals);
void addInterest(double &balance);
void generateReport(double balance, double deposits, double withdrawals);
```

```cpp
//MAIN FUNCTION
int main()
{
   //DEFINE FUNCTION ARGUMENT VARIABLES
  double balance = 0.0;          //ACCOUNT BALANCE
  double deposits = 0.0;         //MONTHLY DEPOSITS
  double withdrawals = 0.0;      //MONTHLY WITHDRAWALS

   //DISPLAY PROGRAM DESCRIPTION MESSAGE
  cout << "This program will generate a banking report based"
       << "on information entered by the user" << endl << endl;

  //CALL FUNCTIONS
  readData(balance,deposits,withdrawals);
  addDeposits(balance,deposits);
  subtractWithdrawals(balance,withdrawals);
  addInterest(balance);
  generateReport(balance,deposits,withdrawals);

  //RETURN
  return 0;
} //END main()

//THIS FUNCTION GETS THE MONTHLY ACCOUNT
//INFORMATION FROM THE USER
void readData (double &balance, double &deposits, double &withdrawals)
{
  cout << "Enter the account balance:  $";
  cin  >> balance;
  cout << "Enter the deposits this month:  $";
  cin >> deposits;
  cout << "Enter the withdrawals this month:  $";
  cin >> withdrawals;
} //END readData()

//THIS FUNCTION ADDS THE MONTHLY DEPOSITS
//TO THE ACCOUNT BALANCE
void addDeposits(double &balance, double deposits)
{
  balance = balance + deposits;
} //END addDeposits()

//THIS FUNCTION SUBTRACTS THE MONTHLY WITHDRAWALS
//FROM THE ACCOUNT BALANCE
void subtractWithdrawals(double &balance, double withdrawals)
{
 balance = balance - withdrawals;
} //END subtractWithdrawals()

//THIS FUNCTION ADDS MONTHLY INTEREST
//TO THE ACCOUNT BALANCE
```

```
void addInterest(double &balance)
{
  balance = balance + (balance * INTEREST);
} //END addInterest()

//THIS FUNCTION DISPLAYS THE MONTHLY ACCOUNT REPORT
void generateReport(double balance, double deposits, double withdrawals)
{
  //FORMAT OUTPUT IN DOLLARS AND CENTS
  cout.setf(ios::fixed);
  cout.setf(ios::showpoint);
  cout.precision(2);

  //DISPLAY ACCOUNT REPORT
  cout << "The account balance is currently:  $" << balance << endl;
  cout << "Deposits were  $" << deposits << endl;
  cout << "Withdrawals were  $" << withdrawals << endl;
} //END generateReport()
```

That's it! You should now have the knowledge to understand all facets of this problem, from the structured design to the structured C++ program.

8.5   RECURSION

The C++ language supports a very powerful process called *recursion*.

Recursion is a process whereby an operation calls itself until a terminating condition is reached.

A recursive function is a function that calls itself. That's right, with the power of recursion, a given function can actually contain a statement that calls, or invokes, the same function, thereby calling itself. By calling itself, the function actually "clones" itself into a new problem which is one step closer to a terminating condition. A recursive function keeps calling, or cloning, itself until the terminating condition is reached.

To get the idea of recursion, consider a typical compound interest problem. Suppose you deposit $1000 in the bank at a 12 percent annual interest rate, but it is compounded monthly. What this means is that the interest is calculated and added to the principle on a monthly basis. Thus, each time the interest is calculated, you get interest on the previous month's interest. Let's analyze the problem a bit closer.

Your initial deposit is $1000. Now, the annual interest rate is 12 percent, which translates to a 1 percent monthly rate. Because interest is compounded monthly, the balance at the end of the first month will be

$$\text{month 1 balance} = \$1000 + (0.01 \ \times \ \$1000) \ = \$1010$$

As you can see, the interest for month 1 is $0.01 \times \$1,000$, or $10.00. This interest amount is then added to the principle ($1,000) to get a new balance of $1010. Using a little algebra, the same calculation can be made like this:

$$\text{month 1 balance} = 1.01 \times \$1000 = \$1010$$

Now, how would you calculate the interest for the second month? You would use the balance at the end of the first month as the principle for the second month calculation, right? So, the calculation for month 2 would be

$$\text{month 2 balance} = 1.01 \times \$1010 = \$1020.10$$

For month 3, the calculation would be

$$\text{month 3 balance} = 1.01 \times \$1020.10 = \$1030.30$$

Do you see a pattern? Notice that to calculate the balance for any given month, you must use the balance from the previous month. In general, the calculation for any month becomes

$$balance = 1.01 \times previous\ balance$$

Let's let *balance(n)* represent the balance of any given month, *n*, and *balance(n − 1)* the previous month's balance. Using this notation, the balance for any month, *balance(n)* is

$$balance(n) = 1.01 \times balance(n - 1)$$

Let's use this relationship to calculate what your balance would be after four months. Here's how you must perform the calculation:
First, the balance for month 4 is

$$balance(4) = 1.01 \times balance(3)$$

However, to find *balance(4)* you must find *balance(3)* like this:

$$balance(3) = 1.01 \times balance(2)$$

Then *balance(2)* must be found like this:

$$balance(2) = 1.01 \times balance(1)$$

Finally, *balance(1)* must be found like this:

$$balance(1) = 1.01 \times balance(0)$$

Now, you know that *balance(0)* is the original deposit of $1000. This is really the only thing known, aside from the interest rate. Therefore, working backwards, you get

$$balance(1) = 1.01 \times \$1000 = \$1010$$

$$balance(2) = 1.01 \times \$1010 = \$1020.10$$

$$balance(3) = 1.01 \times \$1020.10 = \$1030.30$$

$$balance(4) = 1.01 \times \$1030.30 = \$1040.60$$

This is a classic example of recursion, because in order to solve the problem, you must solve the previous problem condition using the same process, and so on, until you encounter a known condition (in our case, the initial $1000 deposit). This known condition is called a ***terminating condition***. Thus, a recursive operation is an operation that calls itself until a terminating condition is reached. Likewise, a recursive function is one that calls, or invokes, itself until a terminating condition is reached.

Now, suppose we wish to express the preceding compound interest calculation as a recursive function. The mathematical expression would be

$$balance(0) = 1000 \text{ and } balance(n) = 1.01 \times balance(n-1) \text{ (for } n > 0)$$

This mathematical expression can be expressed in pseudocode form, like this:

> If n is 0
>> $balance(n) = 1000$
>
> Else
>> $balance(n) = 1.01 \times balance(n-1)$

Notice that the terminating condition is tested first. There must *always* be a test for a terminating condition. If the terminating condition exists, the cloning process is halted and the return substitution process begins; otherwise, another recursive call is made to the function.

Next, let's assume the we use a variable called *deposit* to represent the initial deposit and a variable called *rate* to represent the annual interest rate. Then, our balance could be calculated using recursion, as follows:

> If n is 0
>> $balance(n) = deposit$
>
> Else
>> $balance(n) = (1 + rate / 12 / 100) \times balance(n-1)$

If a programming language supports recursive operations, a software function can be coded directly from the above algorithm. Because C++ employs the power of recursion, the C++ function is

```
double balance(double deposit, int month, double rate)
{
  if (month == 0)
    return deposit;
  else
    return (1 + rate / 12 / 100) * balance(deposit,month - 1,rate);
} //END balance()
```

Here, the deposit, number of months to compound, and annual interest rate are listed as parameters for the function because these values are needed by the function to perform the balance calculation. That's all there is to it! This function will calculate the balance at the end of any month, *month*, passed to the function. Notice how the function calls itself in the **else** clause. Here's how it works. When the computer encounters the recursive call in the **else** clause, it must temporarily delay the calculation to evaluate the recursive function call just as we did as part of the compounded interest calculation. When it encounters the **else** clause a second time, the function calls itself again, and keeps calling itself each time the **else** clause is executed until the terminating condition is reached. When this happens, the **if** clause is executed (because *month* is zero), and the recursive calling ceases.

Now, let's insert this function into a program to calculate compounded interest, as follows:

```
//PREPROCESSOR DIRECTIVE
#include <iostream.h>  //FOR cin AND cout

//FUNCTION PROTOTYPE
double balance(double deposit, int month, double rate);

//MAIN FUNCTION
int main()
{

   //DEFINE VARIABLES
   double deposit = 0.0;  //INITIAL DEPOSIT
   double rate = 0.0;     //ANNUAL INTEREST RATE
   int month = 0;         //NUMBER OF MONTHS AFTER INITIAL
                          //DEPOSIT TO DETERMINE BALANCE

   //GET  DEPOSIT, NUMBER OF MONTHS, AND INTEREST RATE
   cout << "Enter the initial deposit:  $";
   cin >> deposit;
   cout << "Enter the number of months to compound:  ";
   cin >> month;
   cout << "Enter the annual interest rate:  ";
   cin >> rate;

   //SET FIXED OUTPUT AND PRECISION
   cout.setf(ios::fixed);
   cout.precision(2);

   //DISPLAY RESULTS, MAKING RECURSIVE FUNCTION CALL
   cout << "\n\nWith an initial deposit of $" << deposit
        << " and an interest rate of " << rate
        << "% \nthe balance at the end of " << month
        << " months would be $" << balance(deposit,month,rate)
        << endl ;
   //RETURN
   return 0;
} //END main()

/*
THIS RECURSIVE FUNCTION WILL CALCULATE A BANK BALANCE
BASED ON A MONTHLY COMPOUNDED INTEREST RATE
*/
double balance(double deposit, int month, double rate)
{
   if (month == 0)
```

```
       return deposit;
   else
       return (1 + rate / 12 / 100) * balance(deposit,month - 1,rate);
} //END balance()
```

This program prompts the user to enter the deposit, number of months to compound, and the current annual interest rate. These values are passed to the function. Once the user enters the required values, the recursive calls are made, and the program will write the ending balance. Here is a sample of the program output:

```
Enter the initial deposit:  $1000↵

Enter the number of months to compound:  4↵

Enter the annual interest rate:  12↵

With an initial deposit of $1000 and an interest rate of 12%
the balance at the end of 4 months would be $1040.60
```

During any recursive call, all information required to complete the calculation after the recursive call is saved by the computer in a memory area called a **stack**. As the recursive calls continue, information is saved on the memory stack until the terminating condition is reached. Then the computer works backward from the terminating condition, retrieving the stack information to determine the final result. The process that the computer goes through is identical to what we did when working the compound interest problem and is illustrated in Figure 8.7. The values shown in the figure assume a $1000 initial deposit and an interest rate of 12 percent per year, compounded monthly. Notice that the last thing placed into the stack is the first thing retrieved from the stack when recursion begins to "unwind." This

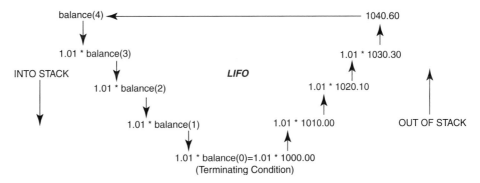

FIGURE 8.7 **AS RECURSION WINDS UP, CALCULATION INFORMATION IS PLACED INTO A MEMORY STACK UNTIL A TERMINATING CONDITION IS REACHED. RECURSION THEN UNWINDS BY RETRIEVING THE CALCULATION INFORMATION OUT OF THE STACK AND USING SUBSTITUTION TO GENERATE THE FINAL RESULT.**

principle is known as *last-in-first-out*, or **LIFO**. All stacks operate using the LIFO principle. Stacks and LIFO are discussed in detail later in this text.

> ### CAUTION
>
> A word of caution: A recursive function must always reach a terminating condition. If it does not, the function will keep calling itself forever, resulting in a memory over-flow run-time error. (Why?)

EXAMPLE 8.7

Write a recursive C++ function to find the sum of all integers from 1 to some number, n.

Solution

Think about this operation for a minute. Isn't it a classic recursive operation? To find the sum of integers 1 to, say, 5, couldn't you add 5 to the sum of integers from 1 to 4? Then, to find the sum of integers from 1 to 4, you add 4 to the sum of integers from 1 to 3, and so on, right? Expressed in symbols,

$$sum(5) = 5 + sum(4)$$
$$sum(4) = 4 + sum(3)$$
$$sum(3) = 3 + sum(2)$$
$$sum(2) = 2 + sum(1)$$
$$sum(1) = 1$$

Notice that $sum(1)$ is the terminating condition, because its value is known. Now, translating this process to a recursive function, you get

$$sum(1) = 1 \text{ and } sum(n) = n + sum(n-1) \text{ (for } n > 1)$$

This function can be expressed in pseudocode, like this:

> If n is 1
> $sum(n) = 1$
> Else
> $sum(n) = n + sum\ (n-1)$

The recursive C++ function is then coded directly from the algorithm as

```
int sum(int n)
{
 if (n == 1)
     return 1;
 else
     return n + sum(n - 1);
} //END sum()
```

Although recursion is a very powerful feature of any language, you should be aware that it is not always the most efficient method of solving a problem. Whenever we talk about computer efficiency, we must consider two things: *execution speed* and *memory usage*. When using recursion, the computer must keep track of each recursive call in a stack so that it can work backward to obtain a solution. This requires large amounts of both memory and time. As a result, a recursive solution to a problem may not always be the most efficient solution. *All* recursive problems can also be solved nonrecursively using iteration. For instance, consider the sum of integers from 1 to *n* done recursively in Example 8.7. This problem can be solved using an iterative function, like this:

```
int sum(int n)
{
  int subTotal = 0;        //SUM SUBTOTAL
  for (int count = 1; count <= n; ++count)
      subTotal = subTotal + count;
  return subTotal;
} //END sum()
```

So, why use recursion? Probably the main reason is that many recursive solutions are much simpler than iterative solutions. In addition, there are some problems in data structures, such as binary trees and graphs, where recursion isn't a mere convenience, it is essential to keep the code manageable. Here are two guidelines that should help you decide when to use recursion:

1. Consider a recursive solution only when a *simple* iterative solution *is not* possible.

2. Use a recursive solution only when the execution and memory efficiency of the solution is within acceptable limits, considering the system limitations.

 Quick Check

1. True or false: There is no way that a C++ function can call itself.
2. Explain why we can describe recursion as a "winding" and "unwinding" process.
3. What terminates a recursive function call?
4. A factorial operation, *factorial(n)*, finds the product of all integers from 1 to some positive integer *n*. Thus, 5! = 5 × 4 × 3 × 2 × 1. Write the pseudocode required to find *factorial(n)*, where *n* is any integer. (*Note:* By definition, *factorial(1)* = 1.)
5. True or false: An advantage of recursion is that it does not require a lot of memory to execute.
6. True or false: All recursive problems can also be solved using iteration.
7. Recursion employs a memory data structure called a _____ to save information between recursive calls.
8. Stacks operate on the _____ principle.

CHAPTER SUMMARY

In this chapter, you learned how to write and use functions in C++. All programmer-defined functions to be used in *main()* are defined after the closing brace of *main()*. The function is defined by writing a function header, which includes the function return type, the function name, and a parameter listing. The body, or statement section, of the function then follows the function header. Unlike the C language, the C++ language requires that each function have a prototype. The function prototypes must be listed prior to *main()* and must include the return data type of the function, the function name, and a listing of the parameter data types. Prototypes are used by the compiler to check for the proper number of arguments when the function is called. Functions in C++ can be made to return a single value to the calling program, multiple values to the calling program, or perform some specific task. When a function is designed to return a single value to the calling program, the value returned replaces the function name wherever the name is used in the calling program. Thus, the function name can appear as part of an assignment operation, a *cout* statement, an arithmetic operation, or a test statement. When a function is designed to return multiple values or perform a specific task, the function is called by using the function name (followed by a list of arguments) as a statement in the program.

Arguments are data passed to the function when the function is called. Parameters are defined within the function header and take on the value(s) of the arguments when the function is called. Furthermore, parameters can be passed between the calling program and function by value or reference. When passing parameters by value, the arguments in the calling program are not affected by operations on the parameters within the function. When passing parameters by reference, the arguments in the calling program will reflect any changes to the parameters within the function. Thus, passing parameters by value is one-way communication of data from the calling program to the function. Passing parameters by reference is two-way communication of data from the calling program to the function and back to the calling program. In C++, reference parameters are defined using an ampersand (&) prior to the parameter name in the function heading.

The scope of a constant or variable refers to the largest block in which it is visible. Variables always should be defined as locally as possible, whereas constants should be defined as globally as possible.

A recursive function is a function that calls itself until a terminating condition is reached. There must always be a terminating condition to terminate a recursive function call; otherwise, a run-time error will occur. Recursive operations are performed as part of an **if/else** statement. The terminating condition forms the **if** clause, and the recursive call is part of the **else** clause of the statement. All recursive operations also can be performed using iteration. Because recursion eats up time and memory as compared to iteration, you should consider recursion only when a simple iterative solution is not possible and when the execution and memory efficiency of the solution are within acceptable limits.

QUESTIONS AND PROBLEMS

QUESTIONS

1. What three things must be specified in a function header?

2. Explain the difference between an argument and a parameter.

3. Which of the following are invalid function headings? Explain why they are invalid.
   a. `double average(num1, num2)`
   b. `int largest(x,y : int)`
   c. `double smallest(double a,b)`
   d. `void result(string s)`

4. Write the appropriate headings for the following functions:
   a. Inverse of *x*: 1/*x*
   b. *tan (x)*
   c. Convert a decimal test score value to a letter grade.
   d. Convert degrees Fahrenheit to degrees Celsius.
   e. Compute the factorial of any integer *n* (*n!*)
   f. Compute the average of three integer test scores.

5. True or false: When a function does not have a return data type, you must indicate this with the keyword **null**.

6. Explain the difference between a value parameter and a reference parameter.

7. When passing a parameter to a function by reference,
   a. The argument takes on the parameter value.
   b. The parameter takes on the argument value.
   c. The argument reflects any changes to the parameter after the function execution.
   d. a and b
   e. b and c
   f. a and c

8. When using an assignment operator to call a function, the function must include a _____ statement.

9. Which of the following are invalid function prototypes? Explain why they are invalid.
   a. `void printHeader();`
   b. `int error(double num1, char num2);`
   c. `void readData(&int amount, char date);`
   d. `double average(int number, double total)`
   e. `char sample(int, char, double);`

10. True or false: A variable defined in *main()* has visibility in all functions called by *main()*.

11. Which of the following are value parameters and which are reference parameters?
    a. `char prob_a(char &a, char &b, double x, int y);`
    b. `int prob_b(int num1, int num2, int num3, double &avg);`
    c. `double prob_c(int, double, char &);`

12. Write the appropriate headers for the following functions:
    a. A function called *sample()* that must return a floating-point value and receive an integer, a floating-point value, and a character (in that order) when it is called.
    b. A function called *skip()* that will cause the cursor to skip a given number of lines where the number of lines to skip is obtained from the calling program.

    c. A function called *swap()* that will swap the values of two integer variables obtained from the calling program and return the swapped values to the calling program.

    d. A function called *hypot()* that will return the hypotenuse of a right triangle, given the values of the two sides from the calling program.

13. Write prototypes for the functions in question 12.

14. Write C++ statements that will call the four functions in question 12.

15. Given the following function,

```
void swap(int &x, int &y)
{
    int temp;
    temp = x;
    x = y;
    y = temp;
} //END swap()
```

determine the output for each of the following segments of code that call function *swap()*.

```
a. a = 2;
   b = 10;
   cout << "a = " << a << "  b = " << b << endl;
   swap(a,b);
   cout << "a = " << a << "  b = " << b << endl;
b. a = 20;
   b = -5;
   cout << "a = " << a << "  b = " << b << endl;
   if (a < b)
       swap(a,b);
   else
       swap(b,a);
   cout << "a = " << a << "  b = " << b << endl;
c. num1 = 1;
   num2 = 5;
   for (int count = 5; count; --count)
   {
       swap(num1,num2);
       cout << "num1 = " << num1 << "  num2 = " << num2 << endl;
       ++num1;
       --num2;
   } //END FOR
```

16. What is the visibility of a local variable?

17. What is meant by the scope of a variable?

18. True or false: Constants should be defined as globally as possible.

19. True or false: Variables should be defined as locally as possible.

20. A local variable has _____ scope.

21. Suppose that a function must have access to a variable defined in *main()*. How must this be accomplished?

22. Explain recursion.

23. When should you consider a recursive solution to a problem?

PROBLEMS

Least Difficult

Write functions to perform the following tasks:

1. Convert a temperature in degrees Fahrenheit to degrees Celsius.
2. Find x^y, where x is a real value and y is an integer value.
3. Calculate *tangent*(θ), for some angle θ in degrees.
4. Find the inverse ($1/x$) of any real value x.
5. Find the maximum of two integer variables.
6. Find the minimum of two integer variables.
7. Find $n!$ using iteration.
8. Find $n!$ using recursion.
9. Examine a range of values, and return the Boolean value true if a value is within the range and false if the value is outside of the range.
10. Find your bank balance at the end of any given month for some initial deposit value and interest rate. Define the number of months, deposit, and interest rate variables in *main()* and pass them to your function.
11. Display your name, class, instructor, and hour. To display your name, class, and instructor, the function must accept a string object. To make the function accept a string, you simply provide a string object as a parameter in your function interface. For example, suppose that you define a string object in *main()* to hold your name, as follows:

    ```
    string name = "Andy";
    ```

    To receive this string object from *main()*, you simply repeat the string object definition in your function interface, like this:

    ```
    void display(string name, …
    ```

    Of course, parameters for the instructor's name, class name, and class hour must be added to the interface. To call the function, simply pass the required string objects as arguments to the method like this:

    ```
    display(name, …
    ```

12. Swap, or exchange, any two floating-point values.
13. Compare some new floating-point value to a maximum value obtained from the calling program. Replace the maximum value with the new value if the new value is greater than the maximum value. Use the function that you developed in problem 12 for the exchange operation.
14. Cause the cursor on the display to skip a given number of lines, where the number of lines to be skipped is passed to the function.

More Difficult

In problems 15–18, write three independent functions for each problem, as follows:

❏ *One function to read the required input values.*
❏ *A second function to perform the required calculations using the input values from the first function.*
❏ *A third function to display the results of the second function.*

15. Revise the payroll program you developed for Ma and Pa in problem 12 of Chapter 5 to employ functions. Recall that the payroll program will calculate Herb's net pay given the following information:

Employee's name

Number of weekly hours worked

Hourly rate of pay

FICA (7.15%)

Federal withholding (28%)

State withholding (10%)

Ma or Pa will be required to enter only the first three items when running the program. The program must generate a report using the following format:

Employee Name: XXXXXXXXXXXXXXXXXXXXX

Rate of Pay:	$XXXXX
Hours Worked:	XXXXX
Gross Pay:	$XXXXX
Deductions:	
FICA	$XXXXX
Federal withholding	$XXXXX
State withholding	$XXXXX
	————
Total Deductions	$XXXXX
Net Pay:	$XXXXX

16. Find the height at which the ladder in Figure 8.8 makes contact with the wall, given the length of the ladder and the distance the base of the ladder is from the wall.

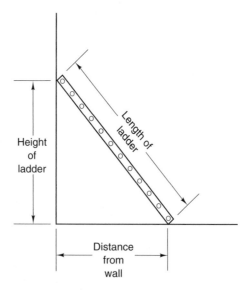

FIGURE 8.8   A LADDER FOR PROBLEM 16.

Most Difficult

17. Table 8.3 provides the 2001 federal income tax schedule for single tax payers. Write a program that calculates the federal income tax, given the taxable income from the user. Use three functions: one to obtain the taxable income from the user, one to calculate the income tax, and one to display the taxable income and corresponding income tax.

18. McCPP's coffee shop sells expresso coffee for $1.25 a cup, bagels for $1.50 and Danish pastries for $2.25. Write a cash register program to compute a customer's bill. Use functions to obtain the quantity of each item ordered, calculate the subtotal of the bill, calculate the total cost of the bill, including a 7 percent sales tax, and display an itemized bill as follows:

Item	Quantity	Price
Coffee	3	$3.75
Bagels	2	$3.00
Danish	1	$2.25
Sub total		$9.00
Sales Tax		$ .63
Total		$9.63

19. A Fibonacci sequence of numbers is defined as follows:

$$F_0 = 0$$

$$F_1 = 1$$

$$F_n = F_{n-1} + F_{n-2}, \text{ for } n > 1$$

This says that the first two numbers in the sequence are 0 and 1. Then, each additional Fibonacci number is the sum of the two previous numbers in the sequence. Thus, the first 10 Fibonacci numbers are

$$0, 1, 1, 2, 3, 5, 8, 13, 21, 34$$

Here, we say that the first number occupies position 0 in the sequence, the second number position 1 in the sequence, and so on. Thus, the last position in a 10-number sequence is position 9.

TABLE 8.3   2001 FEDERAL TAXABLE INCOME RATES FOR SINGLE TAXPAYERS

If the amount on Form 1040 line 38, is: Over —	But not over	Enter on Form 1040, line 39		of the amount over -
$ 0	$24,650		15%	$ 0
24,650	59,750	3,697.50 +	28%	24,650
59,750	124,650	13,525.50 +	31%	59,750
124,650	271,050	33,644.50 +	36%	124,650
271,050		86,348.50 +	39.6%	271,050

Develop a program that employs a recursive function to generate a Fibonacci sequence of all numbers up to some position n entered by the user.

20. Develop a program that employs an iterative function to generate a Fibonacci sequence of all numbers up to some position n entered by the user.

21. Measure the amount of time it takes each of the programs in problems 19 and 20 to generate a Fibonacci sequence of 50 elements. What do you conclude about the efficiency of recursion versus iteration? Why does the recursive program take so long?

SE103: THE STRUCTURED PARADIGM

Objectives

When you are finished with this module, you should have a good understanding of the following:

- Structured analysis and design.
- Context diagrams.
- Logical data flow diagrams.
- Physical data flow diagrams.
- The difference between a logical and a physical data flow diagram.
- Functional decomposition diagrams.

INTRODUCTION

At the direction of their CIO, the *Foo.com* programmers took a course in software engineering at their local university. After learning about the general software development life-cycle, they applied the life-cycle using both the structured paradigm and the object-oriented paradigm. This *SE* module provides an overview of their structured analysis and design, while the next *SE* module looks at their object-oriented analysis and design.

STRUCTURED ANALYSIS

From *SE101*, you learned that the purpose of the analysis phase is to model the current system, whether it be a manual or automated system, to determine *what* the new or improved system is supposed to do. This analysis is done by studying the current system and documenting the system relative to the flow of data within the system using graphical models called *logical data flow diagrams*, or *LDFDs*. Graphical CASE tools are used to produce the LDFDs. Since the structured paradigm is a top/down approach to problem solving, the data flow diagrams produced by structured analysis take on a top/down hierarchy of several levels. At the top level is the *context* diagram. The context diagram shows the entire system as *one* process and the *external entities* with which the system must interact. An external entity is a person, organization, or system that interacts with the system being studied. Thus, a context diagram defines the boundaries of the system. The context diagram developed by the *Foo.com* programmers for their billing system is shown in Figure 1.

> A *context diagram* shows the entire system as one process and what external entities with which the system must interact. Thus, a context diagram defines the boundaries of the system.

At this level, only one process represents the system being analyzed. Notice that the process symbol is a rounded rectangle. At the top of the rectangle is the level of the process. The context diagram is always labeled as level 0, because it is at the top of the process hierarchy. The external entities are represented with a standard, non-rounded, rectangle. As you can see, the *Foo.com* billing system interacts with four external entities—the customer, management, credit agency, and the customer services system. The external entities depict the input and output to and from the system, thereby defining the scope and boundary of the system. The data flows

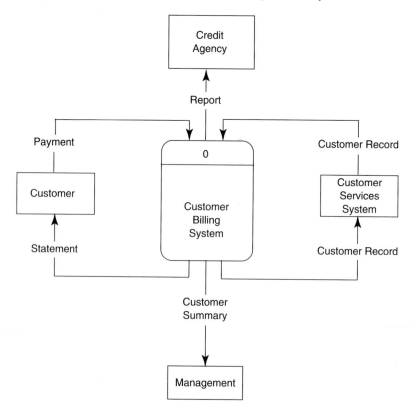

FIGURE I   THE CONTEXT DIAGRAM PRODUCED BY THE FOO.COM PROGRAMMERS, FOR THEIR BILLING PROCESS.

to/from the system process are shown using arrows, labeled with the data/information that they represent.

Next, using a classic structured approach, the context diagram is refined to one or more levels. The *Foo.com* programmers identified four processes within the billing system, as shown in Figure 2.

The process refinements should be self-explanatory. Notice, however, that each process has a key number associated with it. In addition, you can see here that a *data store* is central to the entire system. A data store can be a manual location to store data, such as a file cabinet, or an automated location such as a disk file or database. We don't really care during the analysis, we are only concerned with modeling the *current* system and how/where data moves within this system. As you can see the LDFD represents a data store with an open-ended rectangle.

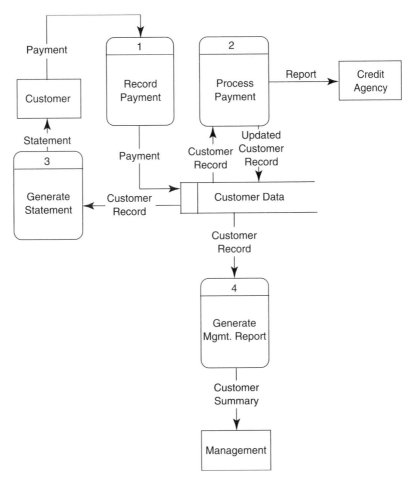

**FIGURE 2 THE FIRST LEVEL OF REFINEMENT FOR THE
FOO.COM BILLING PROCESS.**

Since this problem is relatively simple, the processes do not need any more levels of refinement. If they did, we would simply expand any processes needing further refinement. The labeling technique would be consistent with the refinement. So, if process 1 needed refinement, we would refine it into processes 1.1, 1.2, 1.3, and so on. If further refinement of process 1.2, for example, was needed, we would refine it into processes 1.2.1, 1.2.2, 1.2.3, and so on. Hopefully, you can visualize the top/down hierarchy inherent in the structured paradigm.

Now, its on to see how the *Foo.com* programmers performed their system design.

STRUCTURED DESIGN

During the structured design phase the engineers must determine how the new system is to satisfy the client's needs through a physical DFD and a functional decomposition diagram. Algorithms are also developed for any functions identified during in the functional decomposition diagram.

One of the first tasks at this phase is to convert the logical DFD developed in the analysis phase to a physical DFD. Remember, a logical DFD only depicts the logical processing and storage of data, without regard to *how* the data are to be processed or stored. A physical DFD addresses the *physical* things, like programs, files, and database tables that are used to process and store the data. So, the *Foo.com* programmers took their logical DFD from Figure 2 and converted it to the physical DFD shown in Figure 3.

Here you see that each data flow, process, and data store has been labeled with the *physical* way in which it will be implemented in the *new* system. The data flows are labeled with the form in which the data will take. In addition, if the data flow involves a data store, it is shown as a *read*, *write*, or *update* operation depending on its action on the data store involved.

The processes will be labeled according to who or what will be implementing the process in the new system. If the process is a manual process, it is be labeled with the title of the person performing the process as in process 1 of Figure 3. If the process is a automated process, it is labeled with the type of software unit performing the process, as in processes 2, 3, and 4 of Figure 3.

The data stores are labeled according to the type of data storage unit being proposed. A manual data store will usually be labeled as a file cabinet. An automated data store might be labeled as a disk file or database table.

The physical DFD leads directly to a functional decomposition diagram, as shown in Figure 4.

Look familiar? Notice that the functional decomposition diagram looks very much like the problem-solving diagrams that we have been developing during our case studies. Here you see each function identified by its process number, as well as the major tasks to be performed within each function. Notice that process 1 from Figure 3 is not included here because it is a manual process.

The final task is to translate each function identified in the functional decomposition diagram to an algorithm. Here are the algorithms developed by the *Foo.com* programming team.

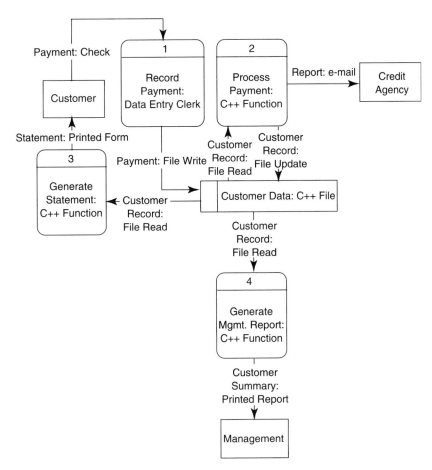

FIGURE 3 **THE FIRST LEVEL OF REFINEMENT FOR THE**
FOO.COM BILLING PROCESS.

processPayment()
BEGIN
    While (read customer record from customer file)
        Subtract *payment* from *balance*.
        Calculate *interest* and add to *balance*.
        If *payment* late or *payment* < *minimumPayment*
            Generate report to credit agency.
            Add late charge to *balance*.
            Set *minimumPayment* to 10 % of *balance*.
        If *balance* == 0
            Set *minimumPayment* to 0.
        Else
            Set *minimumPayement* to 5% of *balance*.
END.

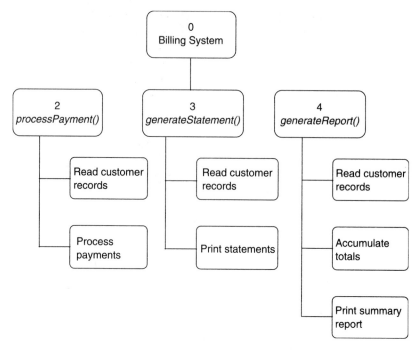

FIGURE 4   A FUNCTIONAL DECOMPOSITION DIAGRAM DEVELOPED FROM THE PHYSICAL DFD IN FIGURE 3.

generateStatement()
BEGIN
    While (read customer record from customer file)
        Write *balance, minimumPayment,* and *interest* to customer statement.
        Print customer statement.
END.

generateReport()
BEGIN
    While (read customer record from customer file)
        Add *balance* to *balanceTotals.*
        Add *interest* to *interestTotals.*
        If *payment* late
            Increment *latePayments* counter.
        If *payment* < *minimumPayment*
            Increment *lowPayments* counter.
    Write *balanceTotals, interestTotals, latePayments,* and *lowPayments* to summary report.
    Print summary report.
END.

In each of the algorithms you see that a *while* loop is required to read the customer records from the customer file. Each customer record is processed within the *while* loop. Look at the logic in the *processPayment()* algorithm and you will see that the *Foo.com* programmers now have solved the $0.0 balance problem that they created when they first attempted to "design the system at the keyboard" using the build-it, fix-it paradigm. They now have a system that has been fully analyzed, designed, and documented.

You should now have a good idea of what goes on during the analysis and design phases of the software life-cycle using the structured paradigm. Be aware, however, that an alternative solution analysis, feasibility analysis, database design, prototyping, and other activities also take place during the structured design phase. We have only scratched the surface here with the major tasks directly related to the program design.

The next *SE* module will discuss how the life-cycle is applied using the object-oriented paradigm.

ONE-DIMENSIONAL ARRAYS

Chapter Contents

Chapter Objectives

When you are finished with this chapter, you should have a good understanding of the following:

- How to define one-dimensional arrays in C++.
- How to initialize an array with elements.

- How to access one-dimensional arrays using direct assignment, reading/writing, and loops.
- How to use character arrays to process C-strings.
- How to pass arrays to functions.
- How to pass individual array elements to functions.
- How to search an array for a given element.
- How to sort an array.

INTRODUCTION

This chapter will introduce you to a very important topic in any programming language: *arrays*. The importance of arrays cannot be overemphasized, because they lend themselves to so many applications.

> An *array* is an indexed data structure that is used to store data elements of the same data type.

Arrays simply provide an organized means for locating and storing data, just as the post office boxes in your local post office lobby provide an organized means of locating and storing mail. This is why an array is referred to as a *data structure*. The array data structure can be used to store just about any type of data, including integers, floats, characters, arrays, pointers, and objects. In addition, arrays are so versatile that they can be used to implement other data structures, such as stacks, queues, linked lists, and binary trees. In fact, in some languages, like FORTRAN, the array is the only data structure available to the programmer, because most other structures can be implemented using arrays.

9.1   THE STRUCTURE OF AN ARRAY

An array is a data structure. In other words, an array consists of data elements that are organized, or structured, in a particular way. This array data structure provides a convenient means of storing large amounts of data in primary, or user, memory. There are both one-dimensional and multidimensional arrays. In this chapter, you will learn about one-dimensional arrays. Then, in a later chapter, you will literally expand this knowledge into multidimensional arrays.

To get the idea of an array, look at the illustration in Figure 9.1. Here you see a single row of post office boxes as you might find in any common post office lobby. As you know, each box has a post office (P.O.) box number. In Figure 9.1, our P.O. box numbers begin with 0 and go up to some finite number N. How do you locate a given box? By using its P.O. box number, right? However, the P.O. box number

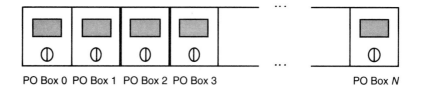

PO Box 0 PO Box 1 PO Box 2 PO Box 3   PO Box *N*

FIGURE 9.1 A ONE-DIMENSIONAL ARRAY IS LIKE A ROW OF POST OFFICE BOXES.

has nothing to do with what's inside the box. It is simply used to locate a given box. Of course, the contents of a given box is the mail delivered to that box. The reason the postal service uses the P.O. box method is that it provides a convenient, well-organized method of storing and accessing the mail for its postal customers. An array does the same thing in a computer program; it provides a convenient, well-organized method of storing and accessing data for you, the programmer. By the way, how many post office boxes are there in Figure 9-1? Because the first box number is 0 and the last is *N*, there must be *N* + 1 boxes.

You can think of a one-dimensional array, like the one shown in Figure 9.2, as a row of post office boxes. The one-dimensional array consists of a single row of storage locations, each labeled with a number called an **index**. Each index location is used to store a given type of data. The data stored at a given index location is referred to as an array **element**. Thus, a one-dimensional array is a sequential list of storage locations that contain individual data elements that are located, or accessed, via indices.

The two major components of any array are the elements stored in the array and the indices that locate the stored elements. Don't get these two array components confused! Although array elements and indices are related, they are completely separate quantities, just as the contents of a P.O. box is something different from its P.O. box number. With this in mind, let's explore array elements and indices a bit further.

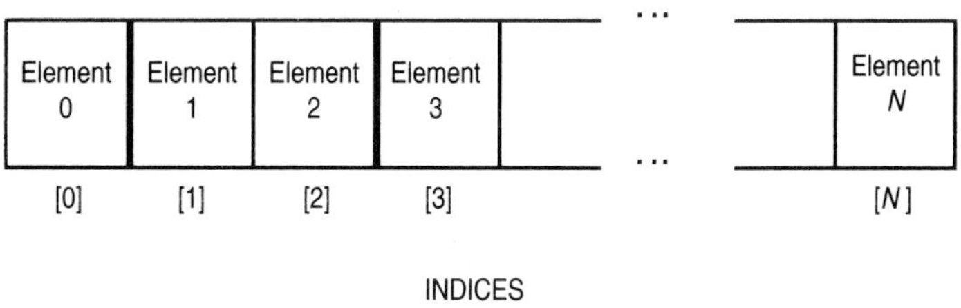

Element 0	Element 1	Element 2	Element 3		...	Element *N*
[0]	[1]	[2]	[3]			[*N*]

INDICES

FIGURE 9.2 A ONE-DIMENSIONAL ARRAY, OR LIST, IS A SEQUENTIAL LIST OF STORAGE LOCATIONS THAT CONTAIN DATA ELEMENTS THAT ARE LOCATED VIA INDICES.

The Array Elements

The elements of an array are the data stored in the array. These elements can be any type of data that you have seen so far. Thus, a given array can store integer elements, floating-point elements, character, and Boolean elements. In addition to these standard data-type elements, an array can also be used to store enumerated data elements. In fact, the elements in an array even can be other arrays. However, there is one major restriction that applies to the array elements: *The elements in a given array all must be of the same data type.*

As you will see shortly, you must define arrays in a C++ program. Part of the definition is to specify the type of the elements that the array will store. Once a given array is defined for a certain data type, only elements of that type should be stored in that array.

The Array Indices

The array indices locate the array elements. In C++, the compiler automatically assigns integer indices to the array element list beginning with index 0. So, the first element of the array in Figure 9.2 is located at index 0, and the last element is located at index N. The indices begin with 0 and go to N, so there must be $N + 1$ elements in the array, right? Also, because this is a one-dimensional array, sometimes called a **list**, we say that it has a **dimension** of $1 \times (N + 1)$, meaning that there is one row of $N + 1$ elements. The dimension of an array indicates the size of the array, just as the dimension of a piece of lumber indicates its size.

Quick Check

1. The two major components of an array are the _____ and _____ .

2. True or false: The elements within a given array can be any combination of data types.

9.2 DEFINING ONE-DIMENSIONAL ARRAYS IN C++

All arrays in C++ must be defined. In order to define an array, you must specify three things:

1. The data type of the array elements.
2. The name of the array.
3. The size of the array.

Here's the general format:

ONE-DIMENSIONAL ARRAY FORMAT

element data type array name **[***number of array elements***];**

The first thing you see in the definition is the data type of the array elements. The array data type is followed by the array identifier, or name, which is followed by the number of elements that the array will store enclosed within square brackets, [ ]. A semicolon terminates the definition. For instance, the following defines an array of 10 characters whose name is *characters[]*. Notice that we will place double brackets, [], after the array name when referring to an array so that it can be distinguished from a primitive variable.

```
char characters[10];
```

EXAMPLE 9.1

Write definitions for the following arrays:

a.   An array called *integers[]* that will store 10 integers.

b.   An array called *floats[]* that will store five floating-point values.

c.   An array called *characters[]* that will store 11 characters.

d.   An array called *class[]* that will store the grades of 25 students. Assume the grades A, B, C, D, and F are defined in an enumerated data type called *grades*.

e.   What index locates the last element in each of the above arrays?

Solution

a.   ```int integers[10];```

b.   ```double floats[5];```

c.   ```char characters[11];```

d.   ```enum grades {F, D, C, B, A};```
      ```grades class[25];```

e.   The index that locates the last element in each of the above arrays is one less than the defined size of the array.

In each of the preceding definitions, the element data type is listed first, followed by the array identifier, followed by the size of the array enclosed in square brackets. Each definition should be fairly obvious, except perhaps the *class[]* array definition. In this definition, the data type of the array is the enumerated data type called *grades*, which must be defined prior to the array definition. So, we would say that the *class[]* array can store elements whose data type is *grades*. Thus, the elements that can be stored in the *class* array are limited
      ```

to the enumerated data type elements of F, D, C, B, and A. Take note that these are not considered characters by the compiler, but rather elements of an enumerated data type called *grades*.

Initializing Arrays

Before leaving this section, you need to know how to initialize arrays at the time they are defined. Arrays, like variables, can be initialized when they are created. The initializing values can be supplied for any array, wherever the array is defined in the program. Let's consider some example array definitions to illustrate how arrays can be initialized.

```
int integers[3] = {10,20,30};
```

In this definition, an integer array of three elements has been defined. The three integer elements have been initialized to the values 10, 20, and 30, respectively. Notice the syntax. The array definition is followed by an assignment operator, which is followed by the initialization values enclosed within curly braces. Here is what you would see if you inspected the array using a debugger:

DEBUGGER RESULTS

Inspecting *integers* [ ]
```
        [0]    10
        [1]    20
        [2]    30
```

As you can see, the first initialization value, 10, is placed at index 0 of the array, the value 20 is placed at index 1, and the value 30 is placed at the last index position, which is 2. Now, what do you suppose happens if you were to provide fewer initialization values than there are positions in the array? Well, suppose you define the array like this:

```
int integers[3] = {10,20};
```

Here is what you would find when inspecting the array using a debugger:

DEBUGGER RESULTS

Inspecting *integers* [ ]
```
        [0]    10
        [1]    20
        [2]    00
```

As you can see, the compiler has initialized the last position of the array with zero. Zero is the default initialization value for integer arrays when not enough values are supplied to fill the array.

The next obvious question is: What happens if you supply too many initialization values? For instance, suppose you define the array like this:

```
int integers[3] = {10,20,30,40};
```

In this case, you will get a compiler error stating, *too many initializers*. One way to solve this problem is to increase the size of the array. Another, more preferred, way is to define the array without any specified size, as follows:

```
int integers[] = {10,20,30,40};
```

With this definition, the compiler will set aside enough storage to hold all the initialization values. Here is what you would see if you inspected this array definition using a debugger:

DEBUGGER RESULTS

Inspecting *integers* [ ]

```
[0]    10
[1]    20
[2]    30
[3]    40
```

Next, let's consider character arrays. Suppose that you define a character array of size 5, like this:

```
char characters[5] = {'H','E','L','L','O'};
```

Again you see that the initialization values are enclosed in curly braces after an assignment operator. Here is what a debugger would reveal:

DEBUGGER RESULTS

Inspecting *characters* [ ]

```
[0]    'H'
[1]    'E'
[2]    'L'
[3]    'L'
[4]    'O'
```

You see here that the five initialization characters are placed in the array starting at index zero and ending at the last index position, 4. What happens if you supply fewer initialization characters than are required to fill the array? Suppose that you define the array this way:

```
char characters[5] = {'H','E'};
```

The contents of the array would now be as follows:

DEBUGGER RESULTS

Inspecting *characters* [ ]

       [0]   'H'
       [1]   'E'
       [2]   '\0'
       [3]   '\0'
       [4]   '\0'

This time, the compiler has inserted a null terminator character as the default character to fill the array. The ***null terminator*** character, '\0', is a special character used to terminate a string of characters. More about this later. On the other hand, if you supply too many characters, the compiler will generate a *too many initializers* error message. Again, the safe way to handle this problem is to let the compiler determine the array size to fit the number of initialization values.

Here is a summary of the foregoing discussion:

❏ Integer, floating-point, and character arrays are initialized by using an assignment operator after the array definition, followed by a listing of the individual initializing values within curly braces.

❏ Too few initializing values will result in default values (zeros for integer and floating-point arrays, and null terminators for character arrays) being inserted in the extra array positions.

❏ Too many initializing values will result in a compiler error.

❏ If no size is specified in the array definition, the compiler will create just enough storage to hold the initialization values.

Quick Check

1. Define an array called *testScores[ ]* that will store up to 15 test scores.
2. What is the dimension of the array in question 1?
3. What is the index of the first element of the array in question 1?
4. What is the index of the last element of the array in question 1?
5. Define an array called *thisSemester[ ]* that will store elements of an enumerated type called *courses*, which includes the courses that you are taking this semester.
6. Suppose that the index of the last element in an array is [25]. How many elements will the array store?
7. Define an array and initialize it with the integer values –3 through +3.
8. What is the dimension of the array that you defined in question 7?
9. Show the contents of the following array:
```
char language[5] = {'C','+','+'};
```

9.3   ACCESSING ARRAYS

Accessing the array means to insert elements into the array for storage or to get stored elements from the array.

Placing Elements into One-Dimensional Arrays

There are basically three major ways to place, or *insert*, elements into an array: by using a *direct assignment* statement, by *reading from the keyboard*, or by using *loops*.

Direct Assignment.   Here's the general format for inserting an element into an array using a direct assignment:

> ### DIRECT ASSIGNMENT FORMAT (INSERTING ARRAY ELEMENTS)
>
> *array name* **[***index***]** = *element value;*

Using the following array definitions,

```
char characters[6];
int integers[3];
```

direct assignments might go something like this:

```
characters[0] = 'H';
characters[5] = ' ';
integers[0] = 16;
integers[2] = -22;
```

In each of these instances, an element is placed in the first and last storage positions of the respective array. The character *H* is placed in the first position of the *characters[]* array, and a blank character is placed in the last position of this array. Recall that the first position of an array is always [0], and the last array position is always one less than the array size. The integer 16 is placed in the first position of the *integers[]* array, and the integer −22 placed in the last position of this array.

Observe that the respective array name is listed, followed by the array index within brackets. An assignment operator (=) is then used, followed by the element to be inserted. The data type of the element being inserted should be the same as the data type defined for the array elements; otherwise, you could get unpredictable results when working with the array elements.

> ### DEBUGGING TIP
>
> Remember that C++ array indices are integer values. This means that any specified index is converted to its integer equivalent. For instance, you can specify an index as a character, like this: *array['A'];* however, C++ sees this as *array[65],* because the integer equivalent of the character 'A' is 65 from the ASCII code. Likewise, you can specify an index using a floating-point value, like this: *array[1.414];* however, C++ sees this as *array[1],* because the integer portion of 1.414 is 1. Enumerated data elements can also be used as indices, because the compiler equates enumerated elements to integers, according to the listing order of the enumerated data type declaration. To avoid confusion and potential problems, we suggest that you always use integer values for your indices, unless the application specifically dictates otherwise.

Keyboard Entry.   You can also use the *cin* object to insert array elements from a keyboard entry, like this:

```
cin >> characters[1];
cin >> integers[0];
```

Here, the user must type the respective array element value on the keyboard and press the **ENTER** key to execute each statement. A character should be entered for the first *cin* statement and an integer for the second *cin* statement. (Why?) The character entered from the keyboard will be stored in the second position (index [1]) of the *characters[]* array, whereas the integer entered from the keyboard will be stored in the first position (index [0]) of the *integers[]* array.

Using Loops.   The obvious disadvantage to using direct assignments to insert array elements is that a separate assignment statement is required to fill each array position. You can automate the insertion process by using a loop structure. Although any of the three loop structures (**while**, **do/while**, **for**) can be employed, the **for** structure is the most common. Here's the general format for using a **for** loop:

> ### *INSERTING INTO A ONE-DIMENSIONAL ARRAY USING A FOR LOOP*
>
> **for** *(int index = 0; index < array size; ++index)*
>   *assign or read to array[index]*

Consider the following program:

```
//PREPROCESSOR DIRECTIVE
#include <iostream.h> //FOR cin AND cout
```

```
//DEFINE ARRAY SIZE
const int SIZE = 10;

int main()
{
  int sample[SIZE];          //DEFINE INTEGER ARRAY

  cout << "Enter a list of " << SIZE << " elements and press"
          "the ENTER key after each entry." << endl;
  for (int i = 0; i < SIZE; ++i)
    cin >> sample[i];

//RETURN
  return 0;
} //END main()
```

First, you see a global constant called *SIZE* defined. Notice where *SIZE* is used in the program. It is the array-size value and the final counter value in the **for** loop. Using a constant like this allows you to change the size of the array easily. Here, the array size is 10 elements. To change the size of the array, you only need to make a change one place in the program under the constant definition.

Next, look at the array definition. The array *sample[]* is defined locally as an array of integer elements. The user is told to *Enter a list of SIZE (where SIZE is 10) values and press the **ENTER** key after each entry.* Once this prompt is displayed, the program enters a **for** loop. The loop counter variable is *i*, which ranges from 0 to *SIZE.* When the loop counter reaches the value of *SIZE,* the loop is broken, because the loop test is *i < SIZE.* It is important to use the less than (<) test here rather than the *less than or equal to* (<=) test; otherwise, the loop will execute one too many times. (Why?) The loop counter is employed as the index value for the array. With each loop iteration, a single *cin* statement is executed to insert an element into the array at the respective position specified by the loop counter, *i.*

Let's analyze the *cin* statement. First, the identifier *sample* is listed with the loop counter variable *i* as the array index in brackets. What does *i* do with each loop iteration? It increments from 0 to *SIZE,* right? As a result, the first loop iteration reads a value into *sample*[0], the second iteration reads a value into *sample*[1], and so on, until the last loop iteration reads a value into the last array position *sample*[*SIZE* − 1]. When the loop counter increments to the value of *SIZE* at the end of the last loop iteration, the loop is broken and no more elements are inserted into the array. That's all there is to it! The array is filled!

You can also use loops for assigning values to array elements. For instance, using the foregoing definitions, consider this loop:

```
for (int i = 0; i < SIZE; ++i)
    sample[i] = 2 * i;
```

This time, the array elements are assigned twice the loop counter value with each loop iteration. What values are actually inserted into the array? How about the 10 even integers from 0 through 18?

Copying Elements from One-Dimensional Arrays

When copying an array element, we simply *copy* its value to a variable. The element remains stored in the array until it is replaced by another value using an insertion operation. As with insertion, you can copy array elements using one of three general methods: *direct assignment, writing to the display,* or *looping.*

Direct Assignment to a Variable. Copying array elements using assignment statements is just the reverse of inserting elements using an assignment statement. Here's the general format:

DIRECT ASSIGNMENT FORMAT (EXTRACTING ARRAY ELEMENTS)

variable = *array name*[*index*];

As an example, suppose we make the following definitions:

```
const int SIZE = 10;
int sample[SIZE];
int x;
```

As you can see, the array *sample[]* consists of 10 integer elements. Now, assuming the array has been filled, what do you think the following statements do?

```
x = sample[0];
x = sample[SIZE - 1];
x = sample[3] * sample[5];
x = 2 * sample[2] - 3 * sample[7];
```

The first statement assigns the element stored in the first array position to the variable *x*. The second statement assigns the element stored in the last array position to the variable *x*. The third statement assigns the product of the elements located at indices [3] and [5] to *x*. Finally, the fourth statement assigns two times the element at index [2] minus three times the element at index [7] to *x*. The last two statements illustrate how arithmetic operations can be performed using array elements.

In all of the foregoing cases, the array element values are not affected by the assignment operations. The major requirement is that *x* should be defined as the same data type as the array elements so that you don't get unexpected results.

As a final example, consider these assignment statements:

```
sample[0] = sample[SIZE - 1];
sample[1] = sample[2] + sample[3];
```

Can you determine what will happen here? In the first statement, the first array element is replaced by the last array element. Is the last array element affected? No, because it appears on the right side of the assignment operator. In the second case, the second array element at index [1] is replaced by the sum of the third and fourth array elements at indices [2] and [3]. Again, the third and fourth array elements are not affected by this operation, because they appear on the right side of the assignment operator.

Displaying Array Elements.   The *cout* object can be used to display array elements. Let's use the same array to demonstrate how to write array elements. Here's the array definition again:

```
const int SIZE = 10;
int sample[SIZE];
```

Now what do you suppose the following statements will do?

```
cout << sample[0] << endl;
cout << sample[SIZE - 1] << endl;
cout << sample[1] / sample[2] << endl;
cout << sqrt(sample[6]) << endl;
```

The first statement will display the element contained at index [0] of the array. The second statement will display the last element of the array, located at index [*SIZE* – 1]. The third statement will divide the element located at index [1] by the element located at index [2] and display the integer quotient. Finally, the fourth statement will display the square root of the element located at index [6]. None of the array element values is affected by these operations.

Using Loops.   As with inserting elements into an array, copying array elements using loops requires less coding, especially when copying multiple elements. Again, any of the loop structures can be used for this purpose, but **for** loops are the most common.

Consider the following program:

```
//PREPROCESSOR DIRECTIVE
#include <iostream.h> //FOR cin AND cout

//DEFINE ARRAY SIZE
const int SIZE = 10;

int main()
{
 int sample[SIZE];              //DEFINE INTEGER ARRAY
 for (int i = 0; i < SIZE; ++i)
   sample[i] = i * i;
 for (i = 0; i < SIZE; ++i)
   cout << sample[i] << '\t';

 //RETURN
 return 0;
} //END main()
```

Here again, the array is defined locally as an array of *SIZE* (10) integer values. The array name is *sample[]*. Notice that the loop counter variable *i* is used as the array index in both **for** loops. The first loop will fill the array locations with the square of the loop counter. Then, the second loop will display each of the array elements located from index [0] to index [*SIZE* – 1]. A *cout* statement is used to display the array elements horizontally across the face of the display. Notice also that each time an element is displayed, a tab is written after the element to separate it from the next sequential element. Here is what you would see on the display:

0	1	4	9	16	25	36	49	64	81

DEBUGGING TIP

Be careful not to specify an array index that is out of range. Such an index would be one that is less than zero or greater than the maximum index value. For example, suppose that you define an array like this:

```
const int SIZE = 10;
char array[SIZE];
```

A common mistake using this definition would be to attempt to access the element *array[SIZE]*. However, remember that array indices in C++ begin with 0; therefore, *SIZE* specifies one position beyond the maximum index value of the array. The maximum index value in this array is *SIZE* – 1. In a loop situation, the following loop statement would create the same problem:

```
for (int i = 0; i <= SIZE; ++i)
        cout << array[i];
```

Again, the last loop iteration specifies an array index of *SIZE*, which is out of the index range. To prevent this error, the test must be *i* < *SIZE* or *i* <= *SIZE* – 1.

When an array index is out of range, you *will not* get a compiler error. At best, you will get garbage. At worst, you might destroy something in memory that is required by your program or operating system, resulting in a program or system crash. Errors such as this are very difficult to locate. So, be safe and make sure that your indices are always within their specified range.

Quick Check

1. Write a **for** loop that will fill the following array from user entries:
   ```
   char characters[15];
   ```
2. Write a **for** loop that will display the contents of the array in question 1, separated by tabs.

9.4 ARRAYS OF CHARACTERS: C-STRINGS

As you know, a string is simply a collection of characters. When operating on strings, you must keep in mind that you are still operating with individual characters. This is why the C language requires you to hold strings in character arrays. The C language does not support the C++ *string* class, because C does not have any object-oriented classes. It is important that you learn about these so-called *C-strings* just in case you need to store and manipulate strings without having the handy C++ *string* class at your disposal.

Figure 9.3 illustrates how strings are stored in memory using a C-string. As you can see, each individual character is placed in a 1-byte memory cell. The collection of cells holding the string is an array of characters.

The last position in the C-string array always contains the character '\0' to terminate the string. This '\0' character is referred to as a **null terminator** character. The null terminator tells the compiler where the string ends in memory.

As you see from Figure 9.3, the character 'C' is located at position [0] of the array, and the null terminator is located at position [8] of the array. Notice that the array requires nine cells to store an eight-character string because of the null-terminator requirement.

> C-stings are stored in character arrays where the last element of the string is always the '\0' null terminator character. The array size must always be one greater than the maximum string size to allow room for the null terminator character.

A C-string is stored in an array of characters. So, to define a C-string variable, you must define a character array. There are two ways to do this: 1) define a character array of a specified size and initialize it with a null terminator string, "\0", or 2) define a character array without a specified size and initialize it with a given string value. Here are the required formats:

C-STRING DEFINITION WITH A SPECIFIED SIZE

char *variable identifier[maximum size of string + 1]* = **"\0"**;

*C-STRING DEFINITION WITHOUT
A SPECIFIED SIZE*

char *variable identifier[ ]* = *"string value"*;

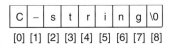

C	–	s	t	r	i	n	g	\0
[0]	[1]	[2]	[3]	[4]	[5]	[6]	[7]	[8]

**FIGURE 9.3   C-STRINGS ARE STORED IN CHARACTER ARRAYS THAT
ARE TERMINATED BY A NULL TERMINATOR.**

In the first case, the compiler must know the maximum size of the string, plus 1. The size must be specified so that the compiler knows how much memory to set aside to store the string. You must specify a size that is one greater than the maximum anticipated string size to allow room for the null terminator character. The array is then initialized with a string of null terminators, "\0". This will place null terminators in *all of the array positions.*

In the second case, you do not need to specify a string size, because the compiler can determine how much memory to set aside from the initializing string. A maximum string size can be specified; however, it must be at least as large as the length of the initializing string, plus 1.

EXAMPLE 9.2

Define a C-string array called *dayOfWeek[]* to hold any of the days in a week. Define the array by specifying its maximum size. Then rewrite the definition without a size specification.

Solution

```
char dayOfWeek[10] = "\0";
```

With this definition, the array variable *dayOfWeek[]* can be used to represent the entire day of the week word (*Sunday, Monday, Tuesday,* etc.). Why did we choose 10 as the maximum length of the string? Because the longest day of the week word is *Wednesday,* which has 9 characters. However, you must leave room for the null terminator character, making the size of the string 10.

You can eliminate the size specification and initialize the array to the largest possible string, *Wednesday,* with the following definition:

```
char dayOfWeek[] = "Wednesday";
```

With this definition, the string *Wednesday* is stored in memory and located by the identifier *dayOfWeek[].* The compiler automatically inserts the null terminator character after the last character, *y.* Why would you create a potential problem if the string were initialized with any other day of the week? If the string were initialized with any other day of the week, it could not store the longest string, *Wednesday.* This is the inherent danger in using C-strings. If the array is not big enough to store the string during an operation, the compiler will attempt to store it anyway, often writing the string data over other important data in memory. The results can be garbage at best or a system crash at worst.

EXAMPLE 9.3

Suppose that you must write a program to store a user's name and address. Choose appropriate string identifiers and define C-string arrays to represent this information.

Solution

You must define several character arrays to accommodate the strings. How must the strings be partitioned? Should you define one character array for the user's name and another for his/her address? But, what if our program needs to access just the zip code? It might make more sense to break up the address into several character arrays that could be individually accessed. So, let's define one character array to store the user's name and then define four character arrays to store the user's street, city, state, and zip code, respectively. But, what size should we make each of these arrays? You have to accommodate the maximum length that each of these string might be. If you are not sure, it is better to overestimate, rather than underestimate its size. Here are the array definitions that we came up with:

```
char name[31] = "\0";  //USER NAME
char street[31] = "\0";//USER STREET
char city[21] = "\0";  //USER CITY
char state[3] = "\0";  //USER STATE ABBREVIATION
char zip[11] = "\0";   //USER ZIP
```

First, notice the array sizes. We have defined each array size to be *one* character longer than the maximum anticipated string size. This is to leave room for the '\0' null terminator character. The *name[]* array size is 31 to allow for a 30 character string plus the null terminator. Likewise, the *street[]* array size is 31 to allow for a maximum string size of 30. The *state[]* array is 3 bytes long to provide for a two-character state abbreviation along with the null terminator character. And finally, the *zip[]* array will allow for a 10 character zip code plus the null terminator. This will permit a zip code such as *65686-0148* to be stored in this array.

Next, notice that each string is initialized with a null terminator string, "\0". This fills-up each array with null terminators. This will prevent output of random memory data, and a likely program crash, should the string values not be changed within the program and subsequently displayed on the monitor.

PROGRAMMING NOTE

It is always good practice to initialize C-strings with the null terminator string, "\0". Initializing a C-string with "\0" will fill-up the character array with null terminator characters. This will prevent output of random memory data, and a likely program crash, should the string values not be changed within the program and subsequently written to the monitor. During an output operation, the compiler begins with the first character, then writes each successive array character to the screen until it encounters the null terminator character. If no null terminator character is encountered, the compiler just continues to write random memory information, resulting in garbage output at best or a system crash at worst.

Reading and Writing C-Strings

The *iostream.h* header file contains a function called *getline()* that can be used to read C-strings. This is a different function from the *getline()* function provided by the C++ *string* class and it is called differently. The C-string *getline()* function is called by the *cin* object. Because *getline()* is a member function of the *iostream.h* class, *cin* can call upon *getline()* to read an entire line, including any white space. Here's the general format:

READING C-STRINGS WITH getline()

***cin.getline**(array ident., array size, 'delimiting character'**)**;

> The C-string *getline()* function is called differently than the C++ *string* class *getline()* function.

The C-string *getline()* function requires a maximum of three arguments. The first argument is the character array identifier. This is the name of the character array defined to store the string. The second argument is the size of the array into which the string will be read. Remember, the size of the largest string that can be read into this array is actually one less than the array size to leave room for the '\0' null terminator character. The *getline()* function automatically inserts the null terminator as the last string character. Finally, the delimiting character tells the *getline()* function when to terminate the read operation. The delimiting character terminates the string entry and is not stored as part of the string.

The *getline()* function reads characters into the array, one at a time, until the specified delimiter is encountered. Once the delimiter is encountered, the function extracts it from the input stream and discards it so that it is not stored as part of the string. If no delimiting character is specified, its value defaults to the \n (CRLF) escape sequence character. Let's look at an example program:

```
/*
THIS PROGRAM SHOWS HOW TO USE getline() TO READ
C-STRING DATA
*/

//PREPROCESSOR DIRECTIVE
#include <iostream.h> //FOR cin AND cout

const int SIZE = 31;          //DEFINE ARRAY SIZE CONSTANT

//MAIN FUNCTION
int main()
{
  char name[SIZE] = "\0";     //DEFINE CHARACTER ARRAY
  cout << "Enter your name: " ;//PROMPT FOR NAME
  cin >> ws;
  cin.getline(name,SIZE);     //READ THE NAME STRING
  cout << name << endl;       //DISPLAY THE NAME STRING

  //RETURN
  return 0;
}//END main()
```

The program works like this:

```
User types in: Jane Doe↵
System displays: Jane Doe
```

If you were to use your debugger to display the *name* array, you would see this:

DEBUGGER RESULTS

```
name
[0]    'J'
[1]    'a'
[2]    'n'
[3]    'e'
[4]    ' '
[5]    'D'
[6]    'o'
[7]    'e'
[8]    '\0'
[9]    '\0'
[10]   '\0'
 .
 .              (null terminators left over from array
 .              initialization)
[30]
```

You see here that the array holds the entire string, including the blank between the first and last names. Also notice that no delimiting character is specified for the *getline()* function. As a result, the **ENTER** key (CRLF) terminates the operation. However, the CRLF (\n) character is not stored as part of the string in the array. This character was extracted from the stream and discarded by the *getline()* function. We have also included the statement *cin >> ws* to eliminate any leading white space from the buffer prior to reading the string. This is always good practice. Do you see how the call of *getline()* here differs from how it was called when using the C++ *string* class? Here, to read a C-string, the call is *cin.getline(name,SIZE)*, whereas the call would be *getline(cin,name)* to read a string using the C++ *string* class. Of course, the later assumes that *name* is defined as an object of the *string* class and *not* as a character array.

Finally, notice that the *cout* object is used to display the string contents using the character array variable name, just like any other variable.

EXAMPLE 9.4

Write a program that will read and write the user's name and address using the C-strings defined in Example 9.3.

Solution

Once the C-string arrays are defined we can use individual *cin.getline()* and *cout* statements to read and write the string. Here's the program:

```
/*
EXAMPLE 9-4 (EX09_04.CPP)
THIS PROGRAM WILL READ AND WRITE THE USER'S
```

```
NAME AND ADDRESS
*/

//PREPROCESSOR DIRECTIVE
#include <iostream.h>        //FOR cin AND cout

//MAIN FUNCTION
int main()
{
 //DEFINE CHARACTER ARRAYS
  char name[31] = "\0";    //USER NAME
  char street[31] = "\0";  //USER STREET
  char city[21] = "\0";    //USER CITY
  char state[3] = "\0";    //USER STATE ABBREVIATION
  char zip[11] = "\0";     //USER ZIP

 //PROMPT USER AND READ/DISPLAY NAME AND ADDRESS STRINGS
  cout << "Enter your name: ";
  cin >> ws;
  cin.getline(name,31);
  cout << "Enter your street address: ";
  cin >> ws;
  cin.getline(street,31);
  cout << "Enter your city: ";
  cin >> ws;
  cin.getline(city,21);
  cout << "Enter your state: ";
  cin >> ws;
  cin.getline(state,3);
  cout << "Enter your zip code: ";
  cin >> ws;
  cin.getline(zip,11);

 //DISPLAY NAME AND ADDRESS STRINGS
  cout << name << endl;
  cout << street << endl;
  cout << city << endl;
  cout << state << endl;
  cout << zip << endl;

 //RETURN
  return 0;

} //END main()
```

Once the character arrays are properly defined, the program reads each string with a separate *cin.getline()* statement and then writes each string with a separate *cout* statement.
Here is what will happen when the program is executed:

User types in:

```
Jane M. Doe↵
999 Programmer's Lane↵
C++ City↵
WY↵
12345↵
(000)123-4567↵
```

System displays:

```
Jane M. Doe
999 Programmer's Lane
C++ City
WY
12345
(000)123-4567
```

C-String Functions

There are several standard C-string functions available in the *string.h* header file that are used to manipulate C-strings. Notice that we said *string.h* and not *string* header file. These functions, listed in Table 9.1, provide some of the more common C-string manipulation routines.

A string function of special interest is the *strcpy()* function. This function should be used when assigning strings to C-string array variables. As an example, consider the following string variable definition:

```
char name[31] = "\0";
```

Now, suppose that you wish to assign a string value to the *name[]* string. The following statement *will not* compile:

```
name = "Gayle";
```

Why won't this work? It worked fine when using the C++ *string* class, right? The reason that direct assignment will not work with C-strings is that an array variable name is actually a memory address. Thus, you are attempting to assign a character string value to an address value. This is called a **type mismatch** and will not compile. To assign string data, you *must* use the *strcpy()* function to copy the string value into the string storage area, like this:

```
strcpy(name,"Gayle");
```

Of course, you must include the *string.h* header file in the program for this statement to compile.

TABLE 9.1 SOME C-STRING FUNCTIONS AVAILABLE IN *string.h*

Function Name	Header File	Operation
strcat()	string.h	Appends one string to another.
strcmp()	string.h	Compares two strings.
strlen()	string.h	Returns length of a string.
strcpy()	string.h	Copies a string.

The string compare function, *strcmp()*, should be used when comparing C-strings rather than Boolean relational operators because Boolean relational operators are not reliable when comparing C-strings. Let's see what happens when the following program is executed:

```
//PREPROCESSOR DIRECTIVES
#include <iostream.h> //FOR cout
#include <string.h>   //FOR strcmp()

//MAIN FUNCTION
int main()
{
  cout << strcmp("Janet","Janet") << endl;
  cout << ("Janet" == "Janet") << endl;
  cout << strcmp("JANET","Janet") << endl;;
  cout << strcmp("Janet","JANET") << endl;

 //RETURN
 return 0;
}//END main()
```

This program first uses the *strcmp()* function to compare the string *Janet* to the string *Janet*. The second line of the program also compares *Janet* to *Janet* using the == Boolean relational operator. If you look up the operation of *strcmp(),* you will find that it returns a 0 if the two strings are equal, a negative value if the first string argument is less than the second string argument, and a positive value if the first string is greater than the second string. How are the two strings compared? Well, recall that each character in the string is represented by an ASCII value. The *strcmp()* function actually *subtracts* the individual ASCII values one character at a time from left to right until an unequal condition occurs or it runs out of characters. If all the characters in the two strings are the same, the result of subtracting character-by-character is zero. If a given character in the first string is larger than the corresponding character in the second string, the subtraction result is positive. If a given character in the first string is smaller than the corresponding character in the second string, the subtraction result is negative. Here is the output produced by the program:

```
0
0
-32
 32
```

Notice that the output of the first statement is 0, correctly indicating that, according to the *strcmp()* function, the two strings are equal. However, the output of the second statement, which uses the Boolean relational operator == , is also 0. As you know, this means false, thereby erroneously indicating that the two strings are unequal. In the third statement, the *strcmp()* function generates a negative value of −32, correctly indicating that *JANET* is less than *Janet,* according to the ASCII code. Finally, in the last statement, the *strcmp()* function generates a positive value of 32, correctly indicating that *Janet* is greater than *JANET*. Why the values –32 and 32? Only the compiler designers know the answer to this question, since it does not matter what the values are, only that a negative or positive value be returned by *strcmp()* when the strings are unequal.

Now, suppose that you want to compare two C-strings as part of an **if** statement. If the two strings are equal, the *strcmp()* function returns a 0. But, a 0 in an **if** statement is interpreted by the compiler as a Boolean value of false, right? As a result, you must use the **NOT** operator (!) to invert the logic to get the results you want. For example, suppose that we have two C-strings called *string1* and *string2*. We want to write the words *The strings are equal* when, in fact, they are equal. To do this, we must use an **if** statement with the *strcmp()* function like this:

```
if(!strcmp(string1,string2))
   cout << "The two strings are equal" << endl;
```

Remember, that *strcmp()* returns a 0 if the two strings are equal. This 0 is interpreted within the **if** statement to be false. So we must apply the **NOT** (!) operator to invert the logic to get the desired result. How would the compiler interpret the value returned by *strcmp()* if the two strings were unequal? Well, if the strings are unequal, *strcmp()* returns a non-zero value (positive or negative). This value is interpreted as true in the above **if** statement because it is a non-zero value.

Maybe now you are beginning to see the advantages of using the C++ *string* class rather than C-strings in a C++ program. Of course, your compiler must support the *string* class, else you are forced to use C-strings.

Quick Check

1. Given a C-string of up to 25 characters. What array size must be specified in the C-string definition?
2. Define a C-string array called *course[]* that will be initialized to a string value of *Data Structures*.
3. Define a C-string array called *month[]* to store the months of the year.
4. Write a statement to store the month of *May* in the C-string array you defined in question 3.
5. Write a statement that uses *getline()* function to read a month from the user and store it in the array you defined in question 3.
6. Write a statement to display the user entry in question 5.
7. Why is it good practice to always initialize a string with null terminators, when no other initializing string is required?
8. Write an **if** statement to display *The two strings are unequal* if two C-strings, called *s1* and *s2*, are in fact unequal.

9.5 PASSING ARRAYS AND ARRAY ELEMENTS TO FUNCTIONS

You can pass an entire array to a function or pass single array elements to a function. The important thing to remember is that to pass the entire array, you must pass the address of the array. In C and C++, *the array name is the address of the first element (index [0]) of the array.* Let's begin by looking at the required function header. Here is typical prototype for passing a one-dimensional array to a function:

```
void weird(char array[SIZE]);
```

Looking at the prototype, you see that the function does not return a value. There is one character parameter called *array[SIZE].* The single set of square brackets after the parameter identifier indicates that the parameter is a one-dimensional array with a size of *SIZE.* When passing arrays to a function, the function must know how large an array to accept. Now, the array identifier references the address of the array, so the array is passed *by reference* to the function. Thus, any operations on the array within the function will affect the original array contents in the calling program. Also, because the array name references the address of the array, no ampersand symbol, &, is required to pass the array by reference. In fact, the use of an ampersand prior to the array parameter will cause a compile error.

Next, to call this function and pass the array, you simply use the following statement:

```
weird(name);
```

Of course, this call assumes that *name* is the array name in the calling program. (Remember that the actual argument identifier and the formal parameter identifier *can be* different.) The call to *name* references the address of the array, so the array address is passed to the function rather than a copy of the array. Thus, any operations on the array within the function will affect the original array elements. Here's a complete program:

```
//PREPROCESSOR DIRECTIVE
#include <iostream.h>   //FOR cin AND cout

//DEFINE ARRAY SIZE
const int SIZE = 3;

 //FUNCTION PROTOTYPE
void weird(char array[SIZE]);

//MAIN FUNCTION
int main()
{
  //DEFINE CHARACTER ARRAY
  char name[SIZE];

  //FILL name ARRAY WITH CHARACTERS
  name[0] = 'I';
```

```
  name[1] = 'B';
  name[2] = 'M';

  //DISPAY name ARRAY
  cout << "The contents of name[] before weird() is:  " << endl;
  for(int i = 0;i < SIZE;++i)
    cout << name[i];

  //CALL FUNCTION weird()
  weird(name);

  //DISPLAY name ARRAY
  cout << "\n\nThe contents of name[] after weird() is:  " << endl;
  for(i = 0;i < SIZE;++i)
    cout << name[i];

  //RETURN
  return 0;
} //END main()

//THIS FUNCTION DECREMENTS EACH OF THE ARRAY ELEMENTS
void weird(char array[SIZE])
{
  for (int i = 0; i < SIZE; ++i)
    --array[i];
} //END weird()
```

The array *name[]* is defined as an array of characters and filled using direct assignment with the characters 'I', 'B', 'M' in *main()*. The characters stored in the array are displayed on the monitor using a **for** loop. Then, the function *weird()* is called using the array name, *name,* as its argument. This passes the address of the array to function *weird(),* where each of the elements in the array is decremented. What do you suppose the user will see on the monitor after executing the program? This is why things are "weird."

```
The contents of name[] before weird() is:
IBM

The contents of name[] after weird() is:
HAL
```

The point here is that the decrement operation within the function affected the original array elements. Thus, the string *IBM* was converted to the sring *HAL.* Is there anything weird here? Recall that HAL was the artificially intelligent computer in the book and movie *2001: A Space Odyssey.* Is there a message here or is this just a coincidence? You will have to ask the author, Arthur Clarke, to find out.

One final point: You *cannot* pass the entire array by value to a function. If you do not want operations within the function to affect the array elements, you should pass the array to the function, make a temporary local copy of the array within the function, and then operate on this temporary array. For example, suppose that we have a function called *foo()* that accepts an integer array called *integers[]*. If *foo()* must process the array elements without affecting the original array contents, the code might be:

```
void foo(int integers[SIZE])
{
 //DEFINE LOCAL ARRAY
 int temp[SIZE];

 //MAKE LOCAL COPY
 for(int index = 0; index < SIZE; ++index)
    temp[index] = integers[index];

 //PROCESS temp[]
   .
   .
   .
}//END foo()
```

Here you see that a local array called *temp[]* defined as the same size as the *integers[]* array. A **for** loop then copies the *integers[]* array to the *temp[]* array. Processing would then continue on the *temp[]* array elements without affecting the *integers[]* array elements.

Passing Individual Array Elements to Functions

You pass individual array elements by value or by reference to a function just like you pass any primitive data element to a function. Look at the following function prototype:

```
void passByValue(int arrayElement);
```

The header says that the function does not return any value and expects to receive an integer value from the calling program. To pass a single array element to the function, you simply list the array name and provide the index of the element to pass as the function argument. For example, to pass the first element of an integer array called *integers[]* to the *passByValue()* function, the call would be:

```
passByValue(integers[0]);
```

Notice that the argument in the function call is *integers[0]*. This will cause a copy of the element stored at index [0] in the *integers[]* array to be passed to the function by value. The function expects to receive a single integer value and we are passing a single integer value—the value stored in *integers[0]*. Since we are passing by value, any operations on this element within the function will not affect the element value in the original *integers[]* array. If you want the element to reflect any operations within the function, you must pass it by reference using the ampersand symbol in the function prototype, like this:

```
void passByReference(int &arrayElement);
```

Now, any call to the function will pass the address of the element to the function, thereby passing the element by reference. The following program illustrates how array elements can be passed by value or reference.

```
//PREPROCESSOR DIRECTIVE
#include <iostream.h> //FOR cin AND cout

//DEFINE ARRAY SIZE
const int SIZE = 3;

//FUNCTION PROTOTYPES
void passByValue(int arrayElement);
void passByReference(int &arrayElement);

//MAIN FUNCTION
int main()
{
 int integers[SIZE];
 integers[0] = 10;
 integers[1] = 20;
 integers[2] = 30;
 cout << "Element at integers[0] before passByValue is:   "
      << integers[0] << endl;
 passByValue(integers[0]);
 cout << "Element at integers[0] after passByValue is:   "
      << integers[0] << endl;

 cout << "Element at integers[0] before passByReference is:   "
      << integers[0] << endl;
 passByReference(integers[0]);
 cout << "Element at integers[0] after passByReference is:   "
      << integers[0] << endl;

 //RETURN
 return 0;
} //END main()

void passByValue(int arrayElement)
{
 ++arrayElement;
} //END passByValue()

void passByReference(int &arrayElement)
{
 ++arrayElement;
} //END passByReference()
```

The output produced by the program reflects the effect of the two functions on the array element.

```
Element at integers[0] before passByValue is:   10
Element at integers[0] after passByValue is:   10
```

```
Element at integers[0] before passByReference is:   10
Element at integers[0] after passByReference is:   11
```

Notice that *passByValue()* does not affect the array element value, whereas *passByReference()* does affect the array value.

Study the last two programs to make sure that you understand how entire arrays and individual array elements are passed to functions.

EXAMPLE 9.5

Write a program that uses an array to store a maximum of 25 test scores and calculate their average. Use one function to fill the array with the scores, a second function to calculate the average, and a third function to display all the scores along with the calculated average.

Solution

We will begin in true structuring style and develop the interfaces for the required functions. Let's call the three functions *setScores()*, *average()*, and *displayResults()*. Now, the *setScores()* function must obtain the test scores from the user and place them in an array. Thus, the function must accept the entire array structure and return the entire array containing the test scores. This leads to the following function interface description:

Function *setScores()*:	Obtains test scores from user and places them in an array.
Accepts:	A placeholder for the number of test scores to be entered by the user and the test scores array of size *SIZE*.
Returns:	The number of test scores the user entered and the test scores array filled with scores entered by the user.

The function interface requires that it must accept and return the entire array structure. Let's assume that the test scores will be decimal values and, therefore, require a floating-point array. By using these ideas, the function prototype becomes

```
void setScores (int &number, double scores[SIZE]);
```

From here, writing the function is easy. We will employ a *cin* statement within a **for** loop in the function body to fill the array with the test scores. Here's the entire function:

```
void setScores (int &number, double scores[SIZE])
{
 cout << "How many scores do you want to average?" << endl;
 cin >> number;
 cout << "Enter each score, and press ENTER after each entry." << endl;
 for (int i = 0; i < number; ++i)
 {
   cout << "Enter score #" << i + 1 << ":   ";
   cin >> scores[i];
 } //END FOR
} //END setScores()
```

Within the function body you see that the user is prompted to enter the number of test scores and each individual score. The scores are entered and placed in the array via a *cin* statement within a **for** loop. Notice that the value the user enters for *number* is employed to terminate the **for** loop. Also notice that number is a reference parameter. As a result, it will be returned to the calling program for use by other functions.

Next, a function called *average()* must be written to average the test scores in the array. This function must accept the array to obtain the test scores and return a single floating-point value that is the average of the scores. So, the function interface description is as follows:

Function *average():*	Computes the average of the test scores.
Accepts:	The number of test scores to average and the test score array of size *SIZE*.
Returns:	A single value that is the average of the test scores.

This time, the array must be passed to the function and the function must return a single value. Therefore, the function prototype becomes

```
double average(int number, double scores[SIZE]);
```

The body of the function simply adds up all the test scores in the array and divides by their number. Here is the complete function:

```
double average(int number, double scores[SIZE])
{
  double total = 0.0;
  for (int i = 0; i < number; ++i)
    total += scores[i];
  return total/number;
} //END average()
```

There are two local function variables defined: *total* and *i*. The variable *total* will act as a temporary variable to accumulate the sum of the scores, and the variable *i* is the loop counter variable. The variable *total* is first initialized to 0. Then the loop is used to obtain the array elements, one at a time, and to add them to *total*. Observe that the loop counter (*i*) acts as the array index within the loop. Thus, the array elements, from index [0] to [*number* – 1], are sequentially copied with each loop iteration and added to *total*. The last test score is located at index [*number* – 1]. Once the loop calculates the sum total of all the test scores, a **return** statement is used to return the calculated average.

Finally, the *displayResults()* function must display the individual test scores obtained from the user along with their average. To do this, we must pass the array to the function to obtain the test scores. Here's the function description:

Function *displayResults():*	Displays the individual test scores and their average.
Accepts:	The number of scores to display and the test scores array of size *SIZE*.
Returns:	Nothing.

To display the average, we will simply call the *average()* function within this function as part of a *cout* statement. The entire function then becomes

```
void displayResults(int number, double scores[SIZE])
{
  cout << endl << endl;
  cout << "test scores" << endl;
  cout << "---------" << endl;
  cout.setf(ios::fixed);
  cout.precision(2);
```

```
        for (int i = 0; i < number; ++i)
            cout << scores[i] << endl;
        cout << "\nThe average of the above scores is:  "
                << average(scores) << endl;
    } //END displayResults()
```

Again, a **for** loop is employed to display the individual test scores. Notice how the *average()* function is called in the final *cout* statement to calculate the test average.

Now, putting everything together, we get the following program:

```
/*
EXAMPLE 9-5 (EX09_05.CPP)
THIS PROGRAM WILL CALCULATE A TEST AVERAGE
FROM SCORES ENTERED BY THE USER INTO AN ARRAY
*/

//PREPROCESSOR DIRECTIVE
#include <iostream.h>        //FOR cin AND cout

//GLOBAL CONSTANT
const int SIZE = 25;//MAXIMUM NUMBER OF SCORES

//FUNCTION PROTOTYPES
void setScores (int &number, double scores[SIZE] );
double average(int number, double scores[SIZE]);
void displayResults(int number, double scores[SIZE]);

//MAIN FUNCTION
int main()
{
 //DEFINE NUMBER OF SCORES VARIABLE AND TEST SCORES ARRAY
  int number = 0;           //ACTUAL NUMBER OF SCORES
  double scores[SIZE];      //ARRAY DEFINITION

  //CALL FUNCTION TO GET SCORES AND DISPLAY RESULTS
  setScores(number, scores);       //CALL FUNCTION setScores()
  displayResults(number, scores); //CALL FUNCTION displayResults()
} //END main()

/* * * * * * * * * * * * * * * * * * * * * * * * * * * * * * * * * * * * * * * * * * * * *
THIS FUNCTION WILL GET THE SCORES FROM THE USER
AND PLACE THEM INTO THE SCORES ARRAY
* * * * * * * * * * * * * * * * * * * * * * * * * * * * * * * * * * * * * * * * * * * * */
void setScores (int &number, double scores[SIZE])
{
   cout << "How many scores do you want to average?" << endl;
   cin >> number;
   cout << "Enter each score, and press ENTER after each entry." << endl;

   for (int i = 0; i < number; ++i)
   {
     cout << "Enter score #" << i + 1 << ":   ";
     cin >> scores[i];
   } //END FOR
} //END setScores()
```

```
/****************************************************************
THIS FUNCTION WILL CALCULATE THE AVERAGE OF THE
SCORES IN THE ARRAY
****************************************************************/
double average(int number, double scores[SIZE])
{
  double total = 0.0;
  for (int i = 0; i < number; ++i)
   total += scores[i];
  return total/number;
} //END average()


/****************************************************************
THIS FUNCTION DISPLAYS THE ARRAY SCORES AND THE
FINAL SCORE AVERAGE
****************************************************************/
void displayResults(int number, double scores[SIZE])
{
  cout << endl << endl;
  cout << "test scores" << endl;
  cout << "----------" << endl;
  cout.setf(ios::fixed);
  cout.precision(2);
  for (int i = 0; i < number; ++i)
     cout << scores[i] << endl;
  cout << "\nThe average of the above scores is:   "
          << average(number, scores) << endl;
} //END displayResults()
```

As you can see, a global constant (*SIZE*) is first defined. This will be the maximum number of elements in the array. After the global constant is defined, the three function prototypes are listed. Now, look at the statement section of *main()*. Are you surprised at its simplicity? Function *main()* is relatively short, because all the work is done in the other functions. All *main()* does is call the two other functions in the order that they are needed. You see that at the beginning of *main()*, a variable called *number* is defined to hold the actual number of test scores entered by the user. This value will be passed to and from the functions as needed. Then, the array, called *scores[]*, is defined as an array of *SIZE*, or 25, floating-point elements. The array name is *scores,* so this identifier must be used when accessing the array. After the array is defined, the *setScores()* function is called, followed by the *displayResults()* function. Observe that, in both cases, both *number* and the array, *scores[],* are passed to the function by listing their names as the function arguments. The function *setScores()* is first called to obtain the scores from the user and to insert them into the array. Next, the function *displayResults()* is called. Again, the number of scores, *number,* and the test scores array, *scores[],* are passed to the function by listing their respective names as arguments in the function call. This function displays the test scores from the array and calls the *average()* function to calculate the test average.

You now have all the ingredients you need to write programs using the versatile one dimensional array. Next, you will learn how to search an array for a given element value as well as sort the elements in an array. What follows are some classic searching and sorting algorithms that are important for you to learn, regardless of the programming language that you are using. Of course, we will implement these classic algorithms using the C++ language.

Quick Check

1. True or false: An array name is the address of index [1] of the array.

2. Write a prototype for a function called *sample()* that must alter the following array:

        char characters[15];

   Assume that the function does not return any values except the altered array.

3. Write a prototype for a function called *test()* that will alter a single array element in the array defined in question 2.

4. Write a statement that will call the function prototyped in question 3 to alter the element stored at index [5] of the array defined in question 2.

PROBLEM SOLVING IN ACTION: SEARCHING AN ARRAY USING SEQUENTIAL SEARCH

Many applications require a program to search for a given element in an array. Two common algorithms used to perform this task are **sequential**, or **serial**, **search**, and **binary search**. Sequential search is commonly used for unsorted arrays, and binary search is used on arrays that are already sorted. You will learn about both of these searching techniques in this chapter.

PROBLEM

Develop a function that can be called to sequentially search an array of integers for a given element value and return the index of the element if it is found in the array.

Defining the Problem

Because we are dealing with a function, the problem definition will focus on the function interface. As a result, we must consider what the function will accept and what the function will return. Let's call the function *seqSearch()*. Now, from the problem statement, you find that the function must search an array of integers for a given element value. Thus, the function needs two things to do its job: (1) the array to be searched, and (2) the element for which to search. These will be our function parameters. Do these need to be value or reference parameters? The function will not be changing the array or the element being searched for, right? Therefore, the parameters will be value parameters.

Next, we need to determine what the function is to return to the calling program. From the problem statement, you see that the function needs to return the index of the element being searched for if it is found in the array. All array indices in C++ are integers, so the function will return an integer value. But, what if the element being searched for is not found in the array? We need to return some integer value that will indicate this situation. Because array indices in C++ range from

0 to some finite positive integer, let's return the integer –1 if the element is not found in the array. Thus, we will use –1 to indicate the "not-found" condition, because no array index in C++ can have this value. Here is the function interface description:

Function *seqSearch()*:	Searches an integer array for a given element value.
Accepts:	An array of integers and the element for which to search.
Returns:	The array index of the element if found, or the value –1 if the element is not found.

The preceding function interface description provides all the information required to write the function interface. Here it is:

```
int seqSearch(int array[SIZE], int element)
```

The interface dictates that the function will accept two things: (1) an array of *SIZE* integer elements, and (2) an integer value, called *element,* that will be the value for which to search.

The next task is to develop the sequential search algorithm.

Planning the Solution

Sequential search does exactly what it says: It *sequentially* searches the array, from one element to the next, starting at the first array position and stopping when either the element is found or it reaches the end of the array. Thus, the algorithm must test the element stored in the first array position, then the second array position, then the third, and so on until the element is found or it runs out of array elements. This is obviously a repetitive task of testing an array element, then moving to the next element and testing again, and so on. Consider the following algorithm that employs a **while** loop to perform the repetitive testing operation:

seqSearch() Algorithm

seqSearch()
BEGIN
  Set *found* = false.
  Set *index* = first array index.
  While (*element* is not *found*) AND (*index* <= last array index)
    If (*array*[*index*] == *element*) Then
      Set *found* = true.
    Else
      Increment *index*.
  If (*found* == true)
    Return *index*.
  Else
    Return –1.
END.

The idea here is to employ a Boolean variable, called *found,* to indicate if the element was found during the search. The variable *found* is initialized to false, and a variable called *index* is initialized to the index of the first element in the array. Notice the **while** loop test. Because of the use of the **AND** operator, the loop will continue as long as the element is not found *and* the value of *index* is less than or equal to the last index value of the array. Another way to say this is that the loop will repeat until the element is found *or* the value of *index* exceeds the last index value of the array. Think about it!

Inside the loop, the value stored at location [*index*] is compared to the value of *element,* received by the function. If the two are equal, the Boolean variable *found* is set to true. Otherwise, the value of *index* is incremented to move to the next array position.

When the loop terminates, either the element was found or not found. If the element was found, the value of *found* will be true, and the value of *index* will be the array position, or index, at which the element was found. Thus, if *found* is true, the value of *index* is returned to the calling program. If the element was not found, the value of *found* will still be false from its initialized state, and the value –1 is returned to the calling program. That's all there is to it!

Coding the Program

Here is the C++ code that reflects the foregoing algorithm:

```
/*
ACTION 9-1 (ACT09_01.CPP)
SEQUENTIAL SEARCH FUNCTION
*/

int seqSearch(int array[SIZE], int element)
{
  bool found = false;              //INITIALIZE found TO FALSE
  int i = 0;                       //ARRAY INDEX VARIABLE

//SEARCH ARRAY UNTIL FOUND OR REACH END OF ARRAY
  while ((!found) && (i < SIZE))
  {
    if (array[i] == element)   //TEST ARRAY ELEMENT
      found = true;            //IF EQUAL, SET found TO TRUE
    else                       //ELSE INCREMENT ARRAY INDEX
      ++i;
  } //END WHILE

//IF ELEMENT FOUND, RETURN ELEMENT POSITION IN ARRAY
//ELSE RETURN -1.
  if (found)
    return i;
  else
    return -1;
} //END seqSearch()
```

There should be no surprises in this code. At the top of the function, you see the header that is identical to the function interface developed earlier. The variable *found* is defined as Boolean variable and set to false. We will use the variable *i* as our array index variable. This variable is defined as an integer and set to the first array index, 0. Remember that arrays in C++ always begin with index 0. The **while** loop employs the **AND** (&&) operator to test the values of *found* and *i*. The loop will repeat as long as the element is not found (!*found*) and the value of *i* is less than the size of the array, *SIZE*. Remember that when the size of the array is *SIZE*, the last array index is *SIZE* – 1. So, when *i* exceeds the maximum array index, *SIZE* – 1, the loop breaks. When the loop is broken, the value of *found* is tested. If *found* is true, the value of *i* is returned; if *found* is false, the value –1 is returned to indicate that the element was not found in the array.

PROBLEM SOLVING IN ACTION: SORTING AN ARRAY USING INSERTION SORT

To sort an array means to place the array elements in either ascending or descending order from the beginning to the end of the array. Many common algorithms are used for sorting: *insertion sort, bubble sort, selection sort, quick sort, merge sort,* and *heap sort,* just to mention a few. In a data structures course, you will most likely learn about and analyze all of these sorting algorithms. In this chapter, we will develop the *insertion sort* algorithm and code it as a function in C++.

PROBLEM

Develop a function that can be called to sort an array of characters in ascending order using the *insertion sort* algorithm.

Defining the Problem

Again, we will code the algorithm as a C++ function, so the problem definition will focus on the function interface, leading us to the function prototype. Let's call our function *insertSort()*. Think about what *insertSort()* needs to do its job. It must receive an unsorted array of characters and return the same array as a sorted array, right? Does it need anything else? No, additional data are not required by the function, because the only thing being operated upon is the array itself.

What about return values? Does the function need to return a single value or a set of values? The function does not return any single value, but must return the sorted array. Therefore, the return type of the function must be **void**, and the array must be a reference parameter, right? Remember that when arrays are passed to C++ functions, they are always treated as reference parameters because the array name represents an address in memory. So, here's our *insertSort()* function interface description:

Function *insertSort()*:	Sorts an array of characters in ascending order.
Accepts:	An unsorted array of characters.
Returns:	A sorted array of characters.

From the preceding description, the function interface is easily coded as

```
void insertSort(char array[SIZE])
```

The interface says that *insertSort()* will receive a character array of size *SIZE*. The return type is **void**, because no single value is returned. However, because the entire array is being passed to the function, any sorting operations on the array within the function will be reflected in the calling program. Now for the insertion sort algorithm.

Planning the Solution

Before we set up the algorithm, let's see how insertion sort works. Look at Figure 9.4. We will assume that we are going to sort a five-character array in ascending order. Before getting into the details, look at the figure from top to bottom and from left to right. The unsorted array is shown at the top of the figure, and the sorted array is shown at the bottom of the figure. Notice that highlighting is employed in the figure to show the sorting process from top to bottom. As we proceed from the unsorted array at the top, the highlighting decreases, showing the portion of the array that is unsorted, until the entire array is sorted at the bottom of the figure.

The top-to-bottom sequence shows that we will make four passes through the array to achieve the sorted array shown at the bottom of the figure. With each pass, an element is placed into its sorted position *relative to the elements that occur before it* in the array. The first pass begins with the first element, 'E', sorted as indicated by the fact that it is not highlighted. The single character 'E' is considered to be sorted by itself, because it does not have any elements preceding it. Thus, the task in this first pass is to sort the second element, 'D', relative to the character 'E' that precedes it.

The second pass begins with the characters 'D' and 'E' sorted. The task in this pass is to sort the third character, 'C', relative to these two characters. In the third pass, the elements 'C', 'D', and 'E' are sorted, and the task is to sort the character 'B' relative to these characters. Remember, in each pass, the task is to sort the first character of the unsorted portion of the array relative to the characters that precede it in the sorted portion of the array. The process continues until all the characters are sorted, as shown at the bottom of the figure. With each pass, you are essentially repeating what was done in the previous pass. As a result, you can identify a repetitive process, from pass to pass, from the top to the bottom of the figure. This repetition will result in a loop structure in our algorithm.

Now, the question is: What happens during each pass to eventually sort the entire array? During each pass, the first element in the unsorted (highlighted) portion of the array is examined by comparing it to the sorted sequence of elements that precede it. If this element is less than the element preceding it, the two elements are exchanged. Once the element is exchanged with its predecessor, it is compared with its new predecessor element. Again, if it is less than its predecessor, the two elements are exchanged.

This process is repeated until one of two things happens: (1) the element is greater than or equal to its predecessor, or (2) the element is in the first position of the array (index [0]). In other words, the left-to-right compare/exchange process

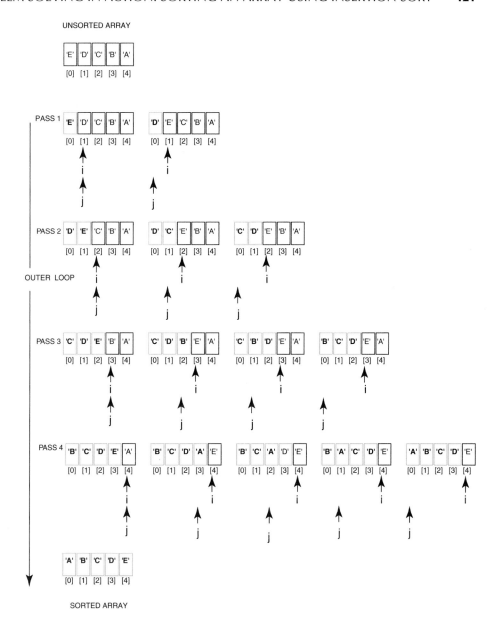

FIGURE 9.4 INSERTION SORT IS A NESTED REPETITION PROCESS.

shown in Figure 9.4 ceases when the element under examination has been *inserted* into its proper position in the sorted portion of the array. This compare/exchange process represents repetition from left to right in the figure and will result in another loop structure in our algorithm. So, we can identify two repetitive processes in the figure: one from top to bottom and one from left to right. How are the two repetitive processes related? It seems that for each top-to-bottom pass through the array, the compare/exchange process is executed from left to right. Thus, the left-to-right process must be nested within the top-to-bottom process. This will be reflected in our algorithm by two loop structures: one controlling the left-to-right compare/exchange process that must be nested inside a second loop controlling the top-to-bottom process. Look at the figure again to make sure that you see this nested repetition. Now that you have an idea of how insertion sort works, here is the formal algorithm:

insertSort() **Algorithm**

insertSort()
BEGIN
  Set *i* = second array index.
  While (*i* <= last array index)
    Set *j* = *i*.
    While (((*j* > first array index) AND (*array*[*j*] < *array*[*j* – 1]))
        Exchange *array*[*j*] and *array*[*j* – 1].
        Decrement *j*.
      Increment *i*.
END.

The variables *i* and *j* in the algorithm correspond to the *i* and *j* shown in Figure 9.4. The variable *i* controls the outer loop, and *j* controls the inner loop. Notice that *i* begins at the second array index. Why not the first array index? Because the first element in the array is always sorted relative to any preceding elements, right? So, the first pass begins with the second array element. The first statement in the outer loop sets *j* equal to *i*. Thus, both *i* and *j* locate the first element in the unsorted portion of the array at the beginning of each pass. Now, the inner loop will exchange the element located by *j*, which is *array*[*j*], with its predecessor element, which is *array*[*j* – 1], as long as *j* is greater than the first array index *and* element *array*[*j*] is less than element *array*[*j* – 1]. Once the exchange is made, *j* is decremented. This forces *j* to follow the element being inserted into the sorted portion of the array. The exchanges continue until either there are no elements preceding element *array*[*j*] that are less than element *array*[*j*] or the element is inserted into the first element position.

Once the inner loop is broken, element *array*[*j*] is inserted into its correct position relative to the elements that precede it. Then, another pass is made by incrementing the outer loop control variable *i*, setting *j* to *i*, and executing the inner loop again. This nested looping process continues until *i* is incremented past the last array position.

Study the preceding algorithm and compare it to Figure 9.4 until you are sure that you understand *insertSort()*. Now for the C++ code.

Coding the Program

We have already developed the *insertSort()* function interface. The algorithm is easily coded as a function in C++, like this:

```
/*
ACTION 9-2  (ACT09_02.CPP)
INSERTION SORT FUNCTION
*/

//EXCHANGE FUNCTION
void exchange(char &x, char &y)
{
 char temp;                              //CREATE TEMPORARY VARIABLE
 temp = x;                              //SET temp TO x
 x = y;                                 //SET x TO y
 y = temp;                              //SET y TO temp
} //END exchange()

//INSERTION SORT FUNCTION
void insertSort(char array[SIZE])
{
 int i;                                 //OUTER LOOP CONTROL VARIABLE
 int j;                                 //INNER LOOP CONTROL VARIABLE
 i = 1;                                 //SET i TO SECOND ARRAY INDEX
 while (i < SIZE)                       //MAKE SIZE - 1 PASSES THRU ARRAY
 {
  j = i;                                //j LOCATES FIRST ELEMENT
                                        //OF UNSORTED ARRAY
  while ((j > 0) && (array[j] < array[j - 1])) //COMPARE/EXCHANGE

  {
     exchange(array[j], array[j - 1]);
     --j;                               //MAKE j FOLLOW INSERT ELEMENT
  } //END INNER WHILE
  ++i;                                  //MAKE i LOCATE FIRST ELEMENT OF
                                        //UNSORTED PORTION

 }  //END OUTER WHILE
}  //END insertSort()
```

Here you see two functions coded in C++. Recall that the *insertSort()* algorithm requires an exchange operation. A function called *exchange()* has been coded to accomplish this task. Notice that this function has two reference parameters that are characters. Thus, the function receives two characters that are exchanged by using a temporary local variable (*temp*) within the function. The exchanged characters are sent back to the calling program via the reference parameters. Of course, the calling program will be our *insertSort()* function.

The *insertSort()* code should be straightforward from the algorithm that we just analyzed. Study the code and compare it to the algorithm. You will find that they are identical from a logical and structural point of view. You might notice how the *exchange()* function is called within *insertSort()*. The array elements *array[j]* and *array[j − 1]* are passed to the function. These elements are simply characters, right? So, the function receives two characters and exchanges them. The respective characters in the array reflect the exchange operations, because *exchange()* employs reference parameters.

PROBLEM SOLVING IN ACTION: SEARCHING AN ARRAY USING RECURSION (BINARY SEARCH)

In this problem, we will develop another popular searching algorithm, called *binary search*. The binary search algorithm that we will develop will employ recursion, although it can also be done using iteration. One of the major differences between binary search and sequential search is that binary search requires that the array be sorted prior to the search, whereas sequential search does not have this requirement. If, however, you have a sorted array to begin with, binary search is much faster than sequential search, especially for large arrays. For example, if you were to apply sequential search to an array of 1000 integers, the sequential search algorithm would make an *average* of 500 comparisons to find the desired element. Even worse, if the desired element is in the last array position, sequential search will make 1000 comparisons to find the element. On the other hand, a binary search would require a maximum of 10 comparisons to find the element, even if it is in the last array position! Of course, you must pay a price for this increased efficiency. The price you must pay is that of a more complex algorithm. So, when searching a sorted array, the advantage of sequential search is simplicity, whereas the advantage of binary search is efficiency.

PROBLEM

Develop a C++ function that can be called to search a sorted array of integers for a given element value and return the index of the element if it is found in the array. Employ a recursive binary search to accomplish this task.

We will be developing a C++ function, so our problem definition will again focus on the function interface. However, before we can consider the function interface, we must see how a recursive binary search works, because the search algorithm will dictate our function parameters. So, let's first deal with the algorithm and then develop the function interface.

Planning the Solution

Binary search represents a natural recursive operation. Remember that the idea behind recursion is to divide and conquer. You keep dividing a problem into simpler subproblems of exactly the same type, or cloning itself, until a terminating condition occurs. This is not the same as top/down software design, which divides problems into simpler subproblems. The difference with recursion is that the sub-problems are clones of the original problem. For example, suppose that you are searching for a name in a telephone book. Imagine starting at the beginning of the telephone book and looking at every name until you found the right one. This is exactly what sequential search does. Wouldn't it be much faster, on the average, to open up the book in the middle? Then, determine which half of the book contains the name that you are looking for, divide this section of the book in half, and so on, until you obtain the page on which the desired name appears. Here is an algorithm that describes the telephone book search just described

A Recursive Telephone Book Search Algorithm

teleSearch()
BEGIN
    If (the telephone book only contains one page)
        Look for the name on the page.
    Else
        Open the book to the middle.
        If (the name is in the first half)
            teleSearch(first half of the book for the name).
        Else
            teleSearch(second half of the book for the name).
END.

Do you see how this search is recursive? You keep performing the same basic operations until you come to the page that contains the name for which you are looking. In other words, the *teleSearch()* algorithm keeps calling itself in the nested **if/else** statement until the correct page is found. The reason that this is called a *binary* search process is that you must divide the book by 2 (*bi*) each time the algorithm calls itself.

Now, let's see how this process can be applied to searching an array of integers. We will call our recursive binary search function *binSearch()* and will develop our algorithm in several steps. Here is the first-level algorithm.

binSearch() Algorithm: First Level

binSearch()
BEGIN
    If (the array has only one element)
        Determine if this element is the element being searched for.
    Else
        Find the midpoint of the array.
        If (the element is in the first half)
            binSearch(first half).
        Else
            binSearch(second half).
END.

Notice how this algorithm is almost identical to the *teleSearch()* algorithm. Here, the recursive searching process continues until the array is reduced to one element that is tested against the element for which we are searching. Do you see how the search keeps calling itself until the terminating condition occurs? Although this algorithm provides the general binary search idea, we need to get more specific in order to code the algorithm. To do this, we must ask ourselves what data *binSearch()* needs to accomplish its task. Well, like sequential search, it needs an array to search and the element for which to search, right? However, sequential search deals with one array of a given size, whereas binary search needs to deal with arrays of different sizes as it keeps dividing the original array in half. Not only are these arrays of different sizes, but the first and last indices of each half are different. As a result, we must provide *binSearch()* with the boundaries of the array that it is dealing with at any given time. This can be done by passing the first and last indices of the given array to the function. Let's call these indices *first* and *last*.

We are now ready to write the function-interface description:

Method *binSearch():*	Searches a sorted array of integers for a given value.
Accepts:	An array of integers, an element for which to search, the first index of the array being searched, and the last index of the array being searched.
Returns:	The array index of the element, if found, or the value –1 if the element is not found.

This description gives us enough information to write the C++ function interface, as follows:

```
int binSearch(int array[], int element, int first, int last)
```

Here, *binSearch()* will return an integer value that represents the index of the element being searched for. Again, you will see that the value –1 will be returned if the element is not found in the array. The function receives the integer array being searched (*array[]*), the element being searched for (*element*), the first index of the array being searched (*first*), and the last index of the array being searched (*last*).

The next problem is to determine what the value of *first* and *last* will be for any given array during the search. Well, remember that we must divide any given array in half to produce two new arrays each time a recursive call to *binSearch()* is made. Given any array where the first index is *first* and the last index is *last,* we can determine the middle index, like this:

$$mid = (first + last) / 2$$

By using this calculation, the first half of the array begins at *first* and ends at *mid* –1, and the second half of the array begins at *mid* + 1 and ends at *last*. This idea is illustrated in Figure 9.5.

But, notice that neither half of the array contains the middle element. By using this technique, the two halves do not make a whole, right? So, before the split is made, suppose that we test the middle element to see if it is the element that we are looking for. The following test will do the job:

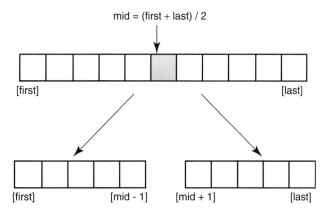

FIGURE 9.5   RECURSIVE BINARY SEARCH REQUIRES THAT AN ARRAY BE DIVIDED IN HALF WITH EACH RECURSIVE CALL.

If $(array[mid] == element)$

Return *mid*.

If this test is true prior to the split, we have found the element that we are looking for, and we can cease the recursive calls. Otherwise, the element stored in *array[mid]* is not the element that we are looking for, and this array position can be ignored during the rest of the search. If this is the case, we will split the array and continue the recursive process. However, we have just added a second terminating condition to our recursive algorithm. Here are the two terminating conditions that we now have:

1. The array being searched has only one element.
2. *array[mid] == element.*

Either of these terminating conditions will cause the recursive calls to cease. Now, let's consider the first terminating condition more closely. How do we know if the array being searched has only one element? Well, as the recursive calls continue without finding the element, the array will eventually be reduced to a single element. If this is the element that we are looking for, the test *If array[mid] == element* will be true, and the recursive calls will stop. If this is not the element that we are looking for, the value of *first* will become greater than the value of *last* on the next split. Why? Because if you think about the splitting action of the algorithm, you will realize that each recursive call causes *first* to increase and *last* to decrease. Thus, if the element is not in the array, the value of *first* will eventually become larger than the value of *last*. So we can use this idea to test for the element not being in the array, as well as use it for a terminating condition. Thus, we will replace the original terminating condition with the following statement:

If $(first > last)$

Return -1

If this condition occurs, the value –1 is returned, indicating that the element was not found, and the recursive calls cease.

Now, let's apply this knowledge to a second-level algorithm. Here it is:

binSearch() Algorithm: Second Level

> *binSearch(array, element, first, last)*
> BEGIN
>   If (*first* > *last*)
>   Return –1.
>   Else
>   Set *mid* = (*first* + *last*) / 2.
>   If (*array*[*mid*] == *element*)
>   Return *mid*.
>   Else
>   If (the element is in the first half)
>   *binSearch(array, element, first, mid – 1)*.
>   Else
>   *binSearch(array, element, mid + 1, last)*.
> END.

It is much clearer now that our algorithm is performing recursion, because you see the function calling itself in either one of two places, depending on which half of the split array the element is likely to be found. Also, observe where the two terminating conditions are tested. If, at the beginning of any recursive call, *first* > *last*, the element is not in the array, and the recursive calls cease. In addition, if, after calculating *mid*, we find the element at *array[mid]*, the recursive calls cease. In both cases, the function has finished executing, and a value is returned to the calling program. The last thing our algorithm needs is a way to determine if the element being searched for is likely to be in the first half or the second half of the split array. Here is where the requirement for a sorted array comes in. If the array is sorted, the element will likely be in the first half of the array when *element* < *array[mid]*; otherwise, the element is likely to be in the second half of the array. Notice that we are using the term "likely." We cannot guarantee that the element is in either half, because it might not be in the array at all! All we can do is to direct the search to that half where the element is likely to be, depending on the sorted ordering of elements. So, we can now complete our algorithm using this idea. Here is the final algorithm:

binSearch() Algorithm

> *binSearch(array, element, first, last)*
> BEGIN
> If (*first* > *last*)
>   Return –1.
> Else
>   Set *mid* = (*first* + *last*) / 2.
>   If (*array*[*mid*] == *element*)
>   Return *mid*.

> Else
>   If (*element* < *array*[*mid*])
>   *binSearch(array, element, first, mid – 1)*.
>   Else
>   *binSearch(array, element, mid + 1, last)*.
> END.

Notice how ***elegant*** the algorithm is. By elegant, we mean that the rather complicated binary search process is reduced to just a few statements. You *know* there is a lot going on here, but recursion allows us to express all of this processing in just a few statements. As you can see, recursive algorithms often provide simple solutions to problems of great complexity, where an equivalent iterative solution might be rather complex. This is not always the case, because some recursive solutions are impractical relative to speed and memory efficiency. Remember the rule of thumb when considering recursion: Consider a recursive solution to a problem only when a simple iterative solution is not possible. You should be aware that binary search has a relatively simple iterative solution. You will code this solution for one of the problems at the end of the chapter.

Coding the Program

The required C++ function now can be easily coded from the final algorithm. Here it is:

```
/*
ACTION 9-3  (ACT9_03.CPP)
THIS FUNCTION SEARCHES AN INTEGER ARRAY USING RECURSIVE
BINARY SEARCH
*/

int binSearch(int array[], int element, int first, int last)
{
    int mid;                              //ARRAY MIDPOINT
    if (first > last)                     //IF ELEMENT NOT IN ARRAY
        return -1;                        //RETURN -1, ELSE CONTINUE
    else
    {
        mid = (first + last) / 2;         //FIND MIDPOINT OF ARRAY
        if (element == array[mid])        //IF ELEMENT IS IN ARRAY[MID]
            return mid;                   //RETURN MID
        else                              //ELSE SEARCH APPROPRIATE HALF
            if (element < array[mid])
                return binSearch(array, element, first, mid - 1);
            else
                return binSearch(array, element, mid + 1, last);
    } //END OUTER ELSE
} //END binSearch()
```

You should not have any trouble understanding this code, because it reflects the function interface and algorithm just developed. The only difference here is that the recursive calls on *binSearch()* must be part of a **return** statement. Remember that C++ requires that all execution paths of a nonvoid function lead to a **return** statement.

9.6 THE STL VECTOR CLASS

The C++ Standard Template Library, or STL, contains a class called *vector* that can be used to build and manipulate one-dimensional arrays. The *vector* class is defined in the *vector* header file. Thus to use it, you must include the *vector* header file at the beginning of your program. Some of the functions available in the *vector* class are listed in Table 9.2

Let's demonstrate how to use the *vector* class via the following program:

```
//PREPROCESSOR DIRECTIVES
#include <vector>        //FOR vector CLASS
#include <algorithm>     //FOR sort()
#include <iostream.h>    //FOR cin AND cout

//MAIN FUNCTION
int main()
{

   //DEFINE VECTORS
   vector<int> v1(10,0);  //INTEGER VECTOR, SIZE 10, INITIALIZED TO 0s
   vector<int> v2;        //INTEGER VECTOR, NO SIZE, NO INITIAL VALUES

   //PLACE RANDOMVALUES IN v1
   srand(1);
   for(int i = 0; i < v1.size(); ++i)
       v1[i] = rand()%100;

   //DISPLAY FIRST RANDOM VALUE IN v1
   cout << "\nThe first vector value is " << v1.front() << endl;

   //DISPLAY LAST RANDOM VALUE IN v1
   cout << "\nThe last vector value is " << v1.back() << endl;
```

TABLE 9.2   FUNCTIONS AVAILABLE IN THE **STL** VECTOR CLASS

Function Prototype	Purpose
void begin()	Places iterator at beginning of the vector.
vector data type back()	Returns, but does not remove, the last element of the vector.
bool empty()	Returns true if vector is empty.
void end()	Places iterator at end of the vector.
vector data type front()	Returns, but does not remove, the first element of the vector.
void pop_back()	Removes, but does not return, the last element of the vector.
void push_back(element)	Places *element* at the end of the vector.
int size()	Returns the number of elements in the vector.

```
//DISPLAY ALL RANDOM VALUES IN v1 BEFORE SORTING
cout << "\nVector v1 before sorting: " << endl;
for(i = 0; i < v1.size(); ++i)
    cout << v1[i] << '\t';

//SORT v1
sort(v1.begin(),v1.end());

//DISPLAY ALL RANDOM VALUES IN v1 AFTER SORTING
cout << "\nVector v1 after sorting: " << endl;
for(i = 0; i < v1.size(); ++i)
    cout << v1[i] << '\t';;

//COPY v1 INTO v2
v2 = v1;

//DISPLAY v2 COPY
cout << "\nThe contents of vector v2 are: " << endl;
for(i = 0; i < v1.size(); ++i)
    cout << v2[i] << '\t';

  //RETURN
    return 0;
}
//END main()
```

We have highlighted the vector-related code in bold so that you can quickly see what's going on. First, you see that the *vector* class has been included in the pre-processor section of the program. Also, we have included the *algorithm* class. This class has been included because it contains a *sort()* function that will allow us to sort a vector. At the beginning of *main()* you see two vector objects defined, *v1* and *v2*. Notice the syntax. The statement *vector<int> v1(10,0)* defines *v1* as a vector (array) of integers, *<int>*, with a size of 10 initialized with all zeros, *(10,0)*. The statement *vector<int> v2* defines *v2* as a vector of integers with no predefined size or initializing value. So, when defining a vector object, you must first list the *vector* class, followed by the data type of the elements enclosed within angle brackets, *<>*. The object name follows the data type specification. You can then list the number of vector elements and an initializing value if desired. Since *vector* is a template class, you can define a vector object to store any type of elements you want. This is one of the purposes of a template. Templates allow you to develop generic classes and functions for arbitrary data types. For example, we can create a vector of strings in the same application program using the definition *vector<string> v*.

> **Templates** allow you develop generic classes and functions for arbitrary data types.

Once the vector objects are defined, the program employs a **for** loop to fill *v1* with random values, just as you would fill an array. The standard *srand()* and *rand()* functions are used for this purpose. However, notice in the loop test that the *size()* function is called by *v1* to return the size of the vector and provide the loop termination value. Next, the *front()* function is called by *v1* to return the first element in the vector, followed by a call to the *back()* function to return the last element in the vector.

The entire vector is then displayed using a **for** loop the same as you would display the contents of an array, except that the *size()* function is called in the loop test to return the size of the vector.

Next, the *sort()* function is called to sort the vector. The *sort()* function requires two **iterator** arguments which define the range of values to sort. An iterator is a pointer used to traverse the elements in the vector. The arguments *(v1.begin(),v1.end())* tell the *sort()* function to start at the beginning of the *v1* vector and stop at the end of the *v1* vector. Notice how the *begin()* and *end()* functions of the *vector* class are used here. That's all there is to it, the vector is sorted! Once sorted, the vector is displayed again using a **for** loop.

Lastly, vector *v1* is assigned to vector *v2* using the standard assignment operator. Try doing that using arrays! The fact is, C++ does not support direct assignment of array variables. To do it, you must use a loop. However, the *vector* class supports such operations. In fact, you can also use the Boolean relational operators of ==, !=, <, >, <=, and >= to compare two vectors. This is one advantage to using the *vector* class. Now, once the assignment is made, the contents of vector *v2* are displayed with a **for** loop.

Here is a sample run of the program:

```
The first vector value is 41

The last vector value is 64

Vector v1 before sorting:
41   67   34   0   69   24   78   58   62   64

Vector v1 after sorting:
0    24   34   41   58   62   64   67   69   78

The contents vector v2 are:
0    24   34   41   58   62   64   67   69   78
```

Quick Check

1. True or false: To use the vector class, you must include the *vector.h* header file in your program.
2. What is the purpose of a template in C++?
3. Define a vector called *myVector* of 5 strings, initialized to blanks.
4. Write a **for** loop to fill the vector defined in question 3 from user entries.
5. Write a **for** loop to display the vector defined in question 3.
6. Write a statement to sort the vector defined in question 3.
7. What header files must be included for the code in questions 3–6 to compile?

You might want to consult your compiler online help or reference manuals for more information on the *vector* and *algorithm* classes. We just don't have the time or space to completely discuss all the features of these versatile classes here.

CHAPTER SUMMARY

An array is an important data structure used to locate and store elements of a given data type. The two components of any array are the elements that are stored in the array and the indices that locate the stored elements. Array elements can be any given data type, and array indices are always integers ranging from [0] to [*SIZE* – 1], where *SIZE* is the number of elements that the array will store.

There are both one-dimensional arrays and multidimensional arrays. A one-dimensional array, or list, is a single row of elements. It has dimensions of $1 \times n$, where *n* is the number of elements in the array. In C++, the maximum index in any dimension is the size of the dimension (*n*) minus 1.

Arrays are defined in C++ by specifying the element data type, the array name, and the size of the array. To access the array elements, you must use direct assignment statements, read/write statements, or loops. The **for** loop structure is the most common way of accessing multiple array elements.

Searching and sorting are common operations performed on arrays. **Sequential search** is an iterative search that looks for a given value in an array by sequentially comparing the value to the array elements, beginning with the first array element, until the value is found in the array or until the end of the array is reached. **Binary search** is a recursive process whereby the array is repeatedly divided into two (bi) smaller arrays until the search item is found or not found.

Many real-world applications require that information be sorted. There are several common sorting algorithms, including **insertion sort, bubble sort, selection sort**, and **quick sort**. All of these algorithms operate on arrays. The insertion sort algorithm is an iterative process that inserts a given element in the array in its correct place relative to the elements that precede it in the array. You will be acquainted with bubble sort and selection sort in the chapter problems.

The ANSI/ISO Standard Template Library, or STL, contains the *vector* class that allows you to easily create and manipulate one-dimensional arrays. The *vector* class is a template class contained in the *vector* header file. To define a vector object, you must include the *vector* header file in your program, then define an object for the *vector* class, specifying the element data type and an optional vector size and initializing value.

QUESTIONS AND PROBLEMS

QUESTIONS

1. What three things must be specified in order to define an array?

Use the following array definition to answer questions 2–7.
```
char characters[15];
```

2. What is the index of the first array element?

3. What is the index of the last array element?

4. Write a statement that will place the character 'Z' in the third cell of the array.

5. Write a statement that will display the last array element.

6. Write the code necessary to fill the array from keyboard entries. Make sure to prompt the user before each character entry.

7. Write a loop that will display all the array elements vertically on the screen.

8. Show the contents of the following array:

```
int integers[5] = {1,2,3};
```

9. Show the contents of the following array:

```
char characters[5] = {'C','+','+'};
```

10. What is wrong with the following C-string array definition?

```
char OOPs[3] = "C++";
```

How would you correct the problem in this definition?

11. True or false: Strings cannot be used in a C++ program without the *string* class.

12. What is wrong with the following array definition?

```
int numbers[4] = {0,1,2,3,4};
```

13. Given the following array definition,

```
int values[10];
```

write a statement to place the product of the first and second array elements in the last element position.

Use the following array definition to answer questions 14–18:

```
const int SIZE = 4;
char myString[SIZE] = "C++";
```

14. Write the prototype for a function called *stringLength()* that will receive the entire array and return the length of the string.

15. Write a prototype for a function called *stringElement()* that will receive a single element of the string so that any operation on that element within the function *will not* affect the element value within the array.

16. Write a statement to call the function in question 15 and pass the first element of the array to the function.

17. Write a prototype for a function called *changeElement()* that will receive a single element of the string so that any change to that element within the function will *change* the element value in the array.

18. Write a statement to call the function in question 17 and pass the second element of the array to the function.

19. In general, what element position will be returned by the sequential search function developed in this chapter if there are multiple occurrences of the element in the array?

20. Write a definition for a C-string array called *myString[]* that will store strings of no more than 25 characters in length. Be sure to initialize the array with null terminators.

21. Write a statement to read a string from the keyboard and place it in the C-string array defined in question 20.

22. Revise the *insertSort()* algorithm to sort the array in descending order.

23. Define a floating-point vector called *floatVector* to store up to *SIZE* floating-point values, initialized to zeros.

24. Write the code required to display the values stored in the vector you defined in question 23.

Problems

Least Difficult

1. Write a program to fill an array with all the odd integers from 1 to 99. Write one function to fill the array and another function to display the array, showing the odd integers across the screen separated by commas.

2. Write a function to read the user's name from a keyboard entry and place it in a C-string array. Write another function to display the user's name stored in the array. Test your functions via an application program.

3. Write a program to read a list of 10 character elements from a keyboard entry and display them in reverse order. Use one function to fill the list with the entered elements and another function to display the list.

4. Write a program that uses six C-string arrays to store the user's name, street address, city, state, zip code, and telephone number. Provide one function to fill the arrays and another to display the array contents using proper addressing format.

5. Write and test a program that will create a vector of strings, fill the vector from user entries, display the vector, sort the vector, and display the sorted vector.

More Difficult

6. Write a program to test the *seqSearch()* function developed in this chapter. Use the *srand()* and *rand()* functions available in *stdlib.h* to fill an array with random integer values prior to applying *seqSearch()*. A call to *srand(1)* must be made first to initialize the random number generator. Then, a call to *rand()* will return an integer value between 0 and RAND_SIZE, where RAND_SIZE is defined by your compiler. For example, the following code will generate 10 random integers between 0 and 99:

```
srand(1);
for (int i = 0; i < 10 ; ++i)
 cout << rand() % 100 << endl;
```

The *srand()* function is called first with an argument value of 1 to initialize the random number generator so that the same 10 numbers are not generated each time the loop is executed. The % 100 operation *scales* the value returned by *rand()* to produce a range of values between 0 and 99.

Most Difficult

7. Here is the pseudocode for an iterative version of *binary search:*

binarySearch()
BEGIN
    Set *found* = false.
    Set *first* = first array index.
    Set *last* = last array index.

```
While ( !found AND first <= last)
    Set mid = (first + last) / 2.
    If (element == array[mid])
        Set found = true.
    Else
        If (element < array[mid])
            Set last = mid – 1.
        Else
            Set first = mid + 1.
    If (found)
        Return mid.
    Else
        Return –1.
END.
```

Binary search is much more efficient than sequential search, but the array must be sorted before binary search will work. Thus, prior to calling the binary search algorithm, you must call a sorting function to sort the array. You can use the insertion sort function developed in this chapter for this purpose. Code the binary search algorithm as a C++ function to search for a given element in an integer array. Write an application program to test the function.

8. Another common iterative sorting algorithm is ***bubble sort***. Here's the algorithm:

```
bubbleSort()
BEGIN
    Set passes = 1.
    Set exchange = true.
    While (passes < number of array elements) AND (exchange == true)
        Set exchange = false.
        For index = (first array index) To (last array index – passes)
            If array[index] > array[index + 1]
                swap(array[index], array[index + 1]).
                Set exchange = true.
        Set passes = passes + 1.
END.
```

The bubble sort algorithm makes several passes through the array, comparing adjacent values during each pass. The adjacent values are exchanged if the first value is larger than the second value. The process terminates when *SIZE* – 1 passes have been made (where *SIZE* is the number of elements in the array) or when no more exchanges are possible.

Your job is to code the previous algorithm as a C++ function called *bubbleSort()*. In addition, you will have to code a *swap()* function that can be called by the *bubbleSort()* function to exchange two array elements as shown in the algorithm. Write your functions to sort a character array. Incorporate them into a program that will test the sorting procedure.

9. Another common iterative sorting algorithm is **selection sort.** The algorithm goes like this:

selectSort()
BEGIN
    For *index1* = (first array index) To (last array index)
      Set *position* = *index1.*
      Set *smallest* = *array*[*position*].
      For *index2* = (*index1* + 1) To (last array index)
        If *array*[*index2*] < *smallest*
          Set *position* = *index2.*
          Set *smallest* = *array*[*position*].
      Set *array*[*position*] = *array*[*index1*].
      Set *array*[*index1*] = *smallest.*
END.

As with bubble sort, selection sort makes several passes through the array. The first pass examines the entire array and places the smallest element in the first array position. The second pass examines the array beginning at the second element. The smallest element in this array segment is found and placed in the second array position. The third pass examines the array beginning at the third element, finds the smallest element in this array segment, and places it in the third element position. The process continues until there are no more array segments left.

Your job is to code the previous algorithm as a C++ function called *selectSort()*. Write your function to sort a character array. Then use it in a program that will test the sorting procedure.

10. Write a program that will take an *unsorted* integer array and find the location of the maximum value in the array. (*Hint:* Copy the array into another array and sort this second array to determine its maximum value. Then search the original array for this value.)

CLASSES AND OBJECTS IN DEPTH

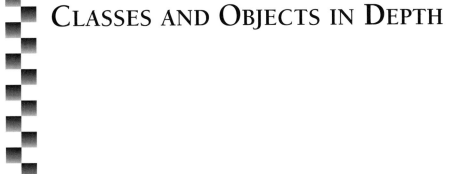

Chapter Contents

Chapter Objectives

When you are finished with this chapter, you should have a good understanding of the following:

- UML class diagrams.
- How to construct your own C++ classes and objects.
- Classes at the abstract as well as the implementation level.
- Encapsulation and information hiding.
- Private versus public class members.

- Constructor and access functions.
- Overloaded constructor functions.
- Scoping inside functions.
- How to develop your own class header files.
- How to develop multi-file C++ programs.

INTRODUCTION

This chapter will introduce you to the important topic of object-oriented programming (OOP) and is intended to prepare you for further study of the topic. This means that you will need to study OOP further to become a competent object-oriented programmer.

Recall that C++ was first created to add OOP ability to the C language. With OOP, you construct complex programs from simpler program entities called *objects*, which are real instances, or specimens, of abstract *classes*. Object-oriented programs are organized as a collection of objects that cooperate with each other. Thus, OOP employs objects, rather than algorithms, as the fundamental building blocks for program development.

Object-oriented programming facilitates the extension and reuse of general-purpose classes in other applications with minimal modification to the original code. Although this can be accomplished with ordinary functions in algorithmic programming, OOP provides an important feature called *inheritance*, which is a mechanism for deriving new classes from existing ones. As a result, classes are related to each other to create a hierarchy of classes through inheritance. This inheritance feature also allows new applications to *inherit* code from existing applications, thereby making the programming chore much more productive.

In summary, the goals of OOP are to improve programmer productivity by managing software complexity via the use of classes and their associated objects that provide for reusable code via the class inheritance feature.

Up to this point, you have been learning how to construct programs using a structured top/down approach. Although the overall design of any software is a top/down process, writing object-oriented programs requires a different approach. You create object-oriented programs from the inside out by expanding on classes through the use of inheritance. For example, you might approach a banking problem by creating a bank account class that defines the basic data that all accounts must contain (account number, balance, etc.) as well as the fundamental operations that are performed on bank accounts (deposit, withdrawal, etc.). This basic bank account class can then be expanded using inheritance into classes that define specific types of bank accounts, such as checking accounts, interest bearing checking accounts, savings accounts, and so on.

There are four concepts central to OOP: *encapsulation with information hiding*, *inheritance*, *polymorphism*, and *dynamic binding*. In this chapter, you will be exposed to the idea of encapsulation and information hiding. The next chapter is devoted entirely to inheritance. The concepts of polymorphism and dynamic binding are beyond the scope of this text and, as a result, will only be covered lightly in the next chapter.

Object-oriented programming has its own unique terminology. Be sure to grasp the terminology as you progress through the chapter. A glossary of OOP terms is provided at the end of this text for quick reference.

In this chapter, we will apply ***Unified Modeling Language***, or ***UML***, as a design tool when developing our classes. There is a learning module on UML at the end of the chapter. You should read this module when instructed to do so within the first section of the chapter.

10.1   CLASSES AND OBJECTS

A thorough understanding of classes and objects is essential to developing object-oriented code. You have been working with some standard C++ classes and objects, like the *string* class, since Chapter 3, so you should now have a good feeling for the class/object concept. It is now time to learn how to create your own classes and objects that provide all the ADT characteristics of the standard classes. Before we get into the details, let's reinforce your class/object knowledge with a real-world example of how they might be used in a commercial program.

The Idea of Classes and Objects

For now, you can think of a class as a model, or pattern, for its objects. If you have used a word processor, you are aware that most word processing programs include templates for business letters, personal letters, interoffice memos, press releases, etc. (*Note*: Be aware that OOP uses the term *template* in a different sense than it is used here in word processing.) The idea is to first open one of the built-in general-purpose template files when you want to generate, let's say, an interoffice memo. An example of such a template is provided in Figure 10.1.

InterOffice Memo	
To:	Recipient
From:	Sender
Date:	May 16, 2001
Subject:	The Subject of the Memo
CC:	

FIGURE 10.1   **A *CLASS* CAN BE THOUGHT OF AS A MODEL, OR PATTERN, LIKE THIS MEMO TEMPLATE IN A WORD PROCESSOR.**

InterOffice Memo

To:	All C++ Students
From:	Prof. Andrew C. Staugaard, Jr.
Date:	May 16, 2001
Subject:	Classes and Objects

This memo represents an object of the class shown in Figure 10.1. The class provides a general framework from which objects are created. It is important that you understand this concept.

CC:
Your Instructor

FIGURE 10.2 **AN** *OBJECT* **IS A PARTICULAR INSTANCE, OR SPECIMEN, OF A CLASS, AS THIS MEMO IS AN INSTANCE OF THE MEMO TEMPLATE OF FIGURE 10.1.**

As you can see, the template provides the accepted interoffice memo formatting, the memo type style, and any fixed information, such as headings and the date. Using this template, you fill in all the *object* information required for the memo, including the text of the memo as shown in Figure 10.2.

In other words, you provide the details that might make one memo different from another. You can think of a class as the memo template and the actual memo that you generate as an object of that template. Different memos made from the same memo template would represent unique objects of the same class. The class template provides the framework for each of its object memos. All the object memos would have the same general format and type style defined by the class template but would have different text information defined by a given object memo. You could load in another template file, let's say for a business letter, that would represent a different class. Then using this template, you could construct different object business letters from the business letter template.

The word *class* in OOP is used to impart the notion of classification. Objects defined for a class share the fundamental framework of the class. Thus, the class is common to the set of objects defined for it. In the preceding example, the interoffice memo template defines the characteristics that are common to all interoffice memos created by the word processor. In fact, many current word processing programs employ classes and objects for this purpose. A given class provides the foundation for creating specific objects, each of which shares the general *attributes*, or *characteristics*, and *behavior* of the class.

A class provides the foundation for creating specific objects, each of which shares the general **attributes**, or **characteristics**, and **behavior** of the class.

As you can see from this example, classes and objects are closely related. In fact, it is difficult to discuss one without the other. The important difference is that a class is only an ***abstraction***, or pattern, whereas an object is a real entity. The interoffice memo class is only an abstraction for the real memo object that can be physically created, printed, and mailed. As another example, think of a class of fish. The fish class describes the general characteristics and behavior of all fish. However, the notion of a fish only provides an abstraction of the real thing. To deal with the real thing, you must consider specific fish objects such as a Charlie the tuna, or my goldfish Skippy, and so on. A fish, in general, behaves as you would expect a fish to behave, but a particular *instance* of a fish has its own unique behavior and personality.

Classes

In order to completely understand the nature of a class, we must consider two levels of definition: the ***abstract*** level and the ***implementation*** level.

The Abstract Level.   The abstract level of a class provides the outside view of the class, without concern for the inner structure and workings of the class. Here's how we define a class at the abstract level.

> At the abstract level, a ***class*** can be described as an *interface* that defines the behavior of its objects.

An ***interface*** is something that forms a common boundary, or barrier, between two systems. The interface for a class is provided by its functions. The function interfaces of a class define how data must be presented to the class. At the abstract level, all you need to be concerned about are the function interfaces and not the inner workings of the class. A good analogy to this idea would be the postal system. You do not have to know how the postal system works to mail a letter and get it to its destination. All you need to know is how to present the required data (address and a stamp) and place the letter in a mailbox. The postal system defines how the letter must be addressed (data presentation) just as the function interfaces of a class define how data must be presented to the class. The class functions also define the behavior of the class through their designated operations. In this way, we say a class defines the behavior common to all of its objects. By behavior, we mean how an object of a given class acts and reacts when it is accessed via one of its functions.

The abstract view of a class as an interface provides its *outside* view while hiding its internal structure and behavioral details. Thus, an object of a given class can be viewed as a black box, as shown in Figure 10.3. As you can see, the operation, or function, interface provides a communications channel to and from the class object. The application program generates an operation request to the object, and the object responds with the desired result. The interface dictates *what* must be supplied

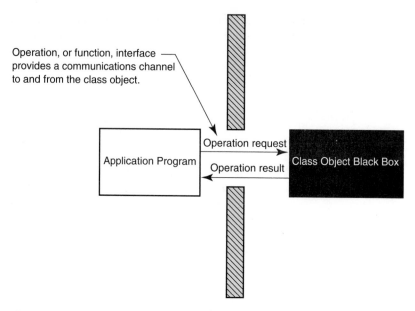

Operation, or function, interface provides a communications channel to and from the class object.

Application Program

Operation request

Operation result

Class Object Black Box

FIGURE 10.3 AT THE ABSTRACT LEVEL, A CLASS IS AN INTERFACE THAT DEFINES THE BEHAVIOR OF ITS OBJECTS.

to the object and *how* the object will respond. As a result, a class, through its operation interfaces, defines how its objects will behave. At the client application level, you treat the class object as a black box because you do not care about what goes on inside the object. All you care about is how to work with the object.

The Implementation Level.   The class implementation provides its *inside* view, showing the secrets of its data organization and function implementations. As a result, the class implementation reveals the secrets of its behavior, because it is primarily concerned with the operations that define the abstract level, or interface.

> At the implementation level, a *class* is a syntactical unit that describes a set of data and related operations that are common to its objects.

The implementation of a class consists of two types of *members*: 1) *data members* and 2) *function members*. Any item declared in a class is called a class *member*. Consequently, to implement a class we create data members and function members.

The Data Members.   The data members of the class provide the class attributes, or characteristics. The data members of the class are usually the variables defined within the class. We say that these members are *private* because they are *accessible* *only by the function members declared for the class*. This means that the data members can be changed only by the function members in the class.

The Function Members.   The function members of the class consist of functions that operate on the data members of the class. These functions are usually *public* because they can be accessed anywhere within the scope of a given class. In other words, function members can be called from outside the class, as long as the class is visible at the time of access. As you might suspect, it is the public function members that form the interface and exhibit the behavior of the class objects.

There is nothing special about public member functions, except that they are used to operate on the data members of the class. The important thing to remember is that *no functions outside a given class can access the private data members of the class*.

The Class Declaration.   The implementation level of a class can be clearly seen by its declaration format, as follows:

CLASS DECLARATION FORMAT

class *name*
{
//FUNCTION MEMBERS
public:
 function 1 prototype;
  function 2 prototype;

•
•
•

 function n prototype;

//DATA MEMBERS
private:
data type variable 1;
data type variable 2;
•
•
•
data type variable n;
};*//END CLASS*

The declaration begins with the keyword *class,* followed by the class name. The class name should be a noun or a noun phrase that is descriptive of its purpose. The first letter of each word within the name should be capitalized. The entire class declaration is enclosed in a set of curly braces. Normally, the public section of the class is declared first using the keyword *public* followed by a colon and a listing of the public members. The private section of the class is declared second using the keyword *private* followed by a colon and a listing of the private members of the class. You might see the public and private sections reversed in some texts; however, we will always declare the public section first, to emphasize the fact that the public member functions are the important aspect of the class, because they define the class behavior and its interface.

To declare a function as a member of a class, you list the function prototype. The function members of the class are called *instance functions.* An instance function is a function that will be available to any given object of the class. The entire function implementation is provided after the class declaration. You just list the function prototype in the class declaration.

The data members of the class consist of *private instance variables.* An instance variable is a variable that will be created for any given object of the class. A private member of a class is visible only within that class and, therefore, can only be accessed by functions within the class. Functions can also be private but then they are only accessible within the class and cannot be called outside the class. Such functions are referred to as *utility functions,* since they are often used within the class to perform housekeeping, or utility, operations.

DEBUGGING TIP

A common error when coding a class is to forget to add the required semicolon after the closing brace of the class. This will always cause a compiler error that can be very difficult to find.

The **public** class functions form the interface to the class and are accessible from outside the class. Public functions are used to provide access to and manipulate the private class members. A **private** class member is only accessible within the class by functions of the same class.

Encapsulation and Information Hiding

Encapsulation is simply the idea of packaging things together in a well-defined programming unit. A record or table in a database program is encapsulated because it is a collection of data that are combined into a well-defined unit, the record or table. The class in C++ obviously provides for encapsulation by packaging both functions and data into a single class unit.

Encapsulation means to package data and/or operations into a single well-defined programming unit.

The idea of encapsulation can be enhanced with ***information hiding.***

> ***Information hiding*** means that there is a binding relationship between the information, or data, and its related operations so that operations outside the encapsulated unit cannot affect the information inside the unit.

With information hiding, there is a *binding* relationship between the information and the operations that are performed on that information. The class provides for information hiding in C++. The public functions provide the class interface that is accessible from outside the class, and the private data members provide the information that is accessible only from within the class itself. Only the functions declared for the class can operate on the private class members. Thus, the private data members of a class provide the information hiding. Without encapsulation and information hiding, there is no such binding relationship. In programming languages that do not support information hiding, you define data structures and the code that operates on those data structures separately. Then, you place both in a single source code file while attempting to treat the data and code as separate modules within the file. Although such an approach seems reasonable, it can create problems. Because there is no defined, or explicit, binding relationship between the data and the code, another programmer could write functions to access and inadvertently change the data.

For instance, suppose that you are writing a program for a bank that calculates bank account interest. To write such a program, you would define an account balance variable, among others, and write functions to change the balance based on deposits, withdrawals, interest earned, and so on. These functions would be written according to the policies dictated by the bank—and the government, for that matter. Would you want another programmer to be able to write functions that would affect the account balances differently than yours? Even worse, would you want the transactions of one account to affect the balance of another account? Of course not!

With information hiding, you can truly separate the account data and the functions operating on those data into two separate categories, private and public but bind them tightly together in an encapsulated class unit. Only public functions can operate on the private account data. This means that outside functions written by another programmer cannot corrupt the data. Thus, only the operations that you have defined for a given type of account can be applied to that type of account and no others. In addition, these same operations applied to one account cannot affect another account of the same type. The class dictates the data format and legal operations for all accounts of a given type. Then, individual accounts of the same type are created as objects of the account class. A class in C++ inherently enforces information hiding.

There is a cost, however. You must use a function call to access the private data. This reduces the efficiency of the code slightly. On the other hand, using the compiler to enforce the rules that relate data to code can pay off in a big way when it comes time to debug a large program. In addition, object-oriented code is much easier to maintain because the classes and their objects closely match the application. Finally, once object-oriented code is developed for a given application program, it can be easily reused in another program that has a similar application. Consider a windows program. All windowing programs employ the same window classes. To create a new windows application program, you simply *inherit* the general window classes and customize them to the new application.

The ideas of encapsulation and information hiding are not new. Only languages like Ada, Modula II, C++, and Java, which easily and efficiently provide for encapsulation and information hiding, are new. These concepts have been around as long as computers. Common examples of information hiding include those data and routines that are part of BIOS to control a PC keyboard, monitor, and file access. Also, the file handling routines built into most operating systems employ information hiding. Imagine what would happen if you could inadvertently corrupt these data and routines (system crash, lost unrecoverable files, etc.). You can use these built-in routines just by knowing how to operate them but you cannot get at the inner workings of the routines. Likewise, you can operate your CD player via its controls without worrying about the inner workings of the player. Imagine what might happen if a non-technical user could get to the inner workings of your CD player. This is why it is so important to think of a class in the abstract sense of an interface.

You should be aware that some texts equate encapsulation with information hiding. However, remember that encapsulation does not necessarily relate to information hiding. Each language permits various parts of a programming entity to be accessible to the outside world. Those parts that are not visible to the outside world represent the information hiding aspect of encapsulation. COBOL records, for example, are encapsulated and permit all member data to be visible and manipulated by outside operations and, therefore, do not provide any information hiding. C++ classes are encapsulated, but in addition, provide information hiding through the private members of the class.

Now, let's declare our first class. Suppose you are working for a bank, and they want you to convert an old COBOL program to a C++ application program. The program is a savings account program that contains an account number, account balance and account interest rate. The operations within that program allow the user to add deposits, subtract withdrawals, add interest, and report the current balance.

The first thing you should do when writing an object-oriented program is to develop a problem statement and look for the nouns and verbs within the statement. The nouns will suggest classes as well as data members for those classes. The verbs will suggest functions, or interfaces, for the classes. Here is the foregoing problem statement again, with the applicable noun and verb phases underlined.

Convert an old COBOL program to a C++ application program. The program is a savings account program that contains an account number, account balance and account interest rate. The program allows the user to add deposits, subtract withdrawals, add interest, and return the current balance.

Now, there are four noun phrases: *savings account, account number, account balance,* and *account interest.* Do you see a hierarchy within these? Of course, the main noun phrase is *savings account.* The other three, *account number, account balance* and *account interest,* are part of the *savings account,* right? Thus, the class will be a savings account class, which includes data members of account number, account balance and account interest.

The four verb phrases within the problem statement are: *add deposits*, *subtract withdrawals*, *add interest*, and *return balance*. Each of these phrases suggests an action to be performed on the account data and therefore will form the function members of the class. So, here is the class specification:

Class: *SavingsAccount*

Function Members: *addDeposit()*

subtractWithdrawal()

addInterest()

getBalance()

Data Members: *accountNumber*

balance

interestRate

> The **Unified Modeling Language,** or **UML,** is a technique for analyzing and designing object-oriented software. Read the UML module at the end of this chapter for an introduction to the UML before going on, if you have not already done so.

Now, let's consider the function interfaces. The *addDeposit()* and *subtractWithdrawal()* functions both need to accept an amount from outside the class to add or subtract from the account *balance*. These functions will not return anything because they are simply operating on the private member, *balance*. This gives us enough information to write the UML interface descriptions as follows:

```
+addDeposits(in amount:double)
+subtractWithdrawals(in amount:double)
```

Remember what this means? Both functions are public, as indicated by the + sign, and both functions accept (*in*) a double floating-point value as a parameter. Nothing is returned by either function, indicated by the lack of any return type after the parameter listing.

Next, the *addInterest()* function will simply operate on the private account *balance* member using the private *interestRate* member. Thus, no parameters or return types are required. In OOP, when function members of a class operate directly on private data members of the same class, you *do not* pass the member data to the functions as you do in structured programming. Therefore, the resulting UML description is simply:

```
+addInterest()
```

Finally, the job of the *getBalance()* function is to return the value of *balance* outside the class. Remember, because *balance* is a private class member, you must use a function to obtain its value. Does *getBalance()* need any parameters? No, because *balance* is class member and, therefore, does not have to be passed. Any of the class functions have direct access to the private class members. Thus the UML description is:

```
+getBalance():double
```

This says that *getBalance()* is a public function , +, that does not require any parameters, *()*, and returns a double, *:double*.

Finally, the UML descriptions of the private members are:

```
-accountNumber:int
-balance:double
-interestRate:double
```

As you can see, each is a private member, as indicated by the – symbol. The *accountNumber* will be an integer, while the *balance* and *interestRate* members will be double floating-point values.

We now have addressed all the class members. The resulting UML class diagram is shown in Figure 10.4.

Once you develop the UML class diagram showing all the class members, the class can be coded directly from the diagram, as follows:

```
class SavingsAccount
{
public:
 void addDeposit(double amount);     //ADD DEPOSIT
```

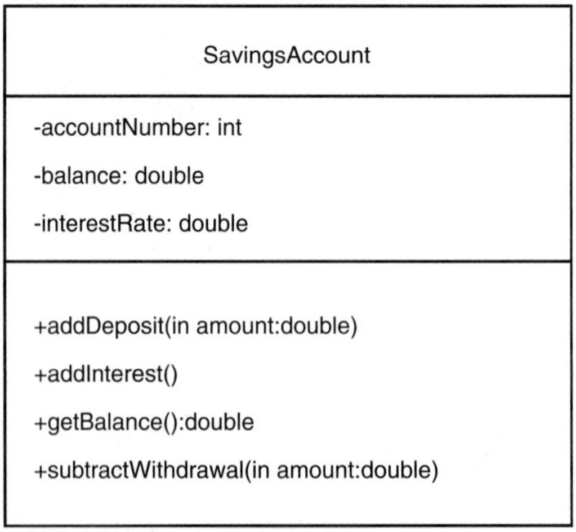

SavingsAccount
-accountNumber: int -balance: double -interestRate: double
+addDeposit(in amount:double) +addInterest() +getBalance():double +subtractWithdrawal(in amount:double)

FIGURE 10.4   THE *SAVINGSACCOUNT* CLASS CONSISTS OF PUBLIC *ADDDEPOSIT(), SUBTRACTWITHDRAWAL(), ADDINTEREST(),* AND *CURRENTBALANCE()* FUNCTIONS THAT FORM THE CLASS INTERFACE, OR BOUNDARY AND PRIVATE *ACCOUNTNUMBER, BALANCE* AND *INTERESTRATE* MEMBERS WHICH ARE HIDDEN INSIDE THE CLASS.

```
   void addInterest();    //ADD MONTHLY INTEREST
   double getBalance();   //RETURN BALANCE
   void subtractWithdrawal(double amount);//SUBTRACT WITHDRAWAL

 private:
   int accountNumber;     //ACCOUNT NUMBER
   double balance;        //ACCOUNT BALANCE
   double interestRate;   //MONTHLY INTEREST RATE
 }; //END SavingsAccount
```

The class declaration begins with the keyword **class,** followed by our class name, *SavingsAccount*. Next, you find a listing of the public member functions of the class following the keyword **public.** Note that only the function prototypes are listed, not the full implementations. Each prototype has been coded directly from the UML class diagram. (*Note:* the UML requires that function members be specified after the data members in a class diagram. However, we will place the public function members before the private data members when coding a C++ class.) This class contains five public function members. All the functions operate on the private data members. The *addDeposit()* function adds an amount received from the calling program to the account balance. The amount to be added must be supplied as an argument when the function is called. The *addInterest()* function calculates a new balance from the current private member values and, therefore, does not require any parameters. The *getBalance()* function returns the value of the account balance to the calling program. Again, because of encapsulation, this is the only way the *balance* can be accessed for reporting purposes. The *subtractWithdraw()* function subtracts an amount received from the calling program from the account balance. The amount to be subtracted must be supplied as an argument when the function is called.

Finally, you find a listing of the private class members following the keyword **private.** There are three private members: *accountNumber*, *balance* and *interestRate*. As the UML diagram shows, the *accountNumber* is an integer, while the *balance* and *interestRate* are floating-point members. That's all there is to it! See how everything is nice and tight within the class structure. The class data define the attributes of the class while the class functions define the class behavior.

EXAMPLE 10.1

Develop a UML class diagram and code a class declaration for a rectangle class that consists of the rectangle length and width with functions to return the area and perimeter of the rectangle.

Solution

The rectangle class requires two public functions, one to calculate the area and another to calculate the perimeter of the rectangle. Let's call them *area()* and *perimeter()*. The two private members must be the rectangle length and width, so let's call them *length* and *width*.

Now, how about the function interfaces? Well, both functions need the private rectangle length and width members to perform their task. Thus, because they are private members, they do not have to be passed, right? What about return values? Each function must return its calculated value outside the class so *area()* will return the area of the rectangle and *perimeter()* will return the perimeter of the rectangle. The resulting function interfaces can be described as follows:

Function *area()*: Returns the area of a rectangle.

Accepts: Nothing

Returns: Area

Function *perimeter()*: Returns the perimeter of a rectangle.

Accepts: Nothing

Returns: Perimeter

Notice that both functions do not receive data from outside the class. The rectangle length and width are private members of the class and, therefore, do not need to be passed to the functions. Because the private data and public functions are so tightly bound within the class, you *do not pass the private data to or from the public functions as you would in structured programming*. We now have enough information to write the UML descriptions as follows:

```
+area():double
+perimeter():double
```

Next, the two private members are *length* and *width*. We will define these as double floating-point variables. We now have enough information to construct the UML class diagram shown in Figure 10.5.

The class is then coded directly from the diagram as follows:

```
class Rectangle
{
  public:
    double area();       //RETURN AREA
    double perimeter();  //RETURN PERIMETER

  private:
    double length;       //RECTANGLE LENGTH
    double width;        //RECTANGLE WIDTH
}; //END Rectangle
```

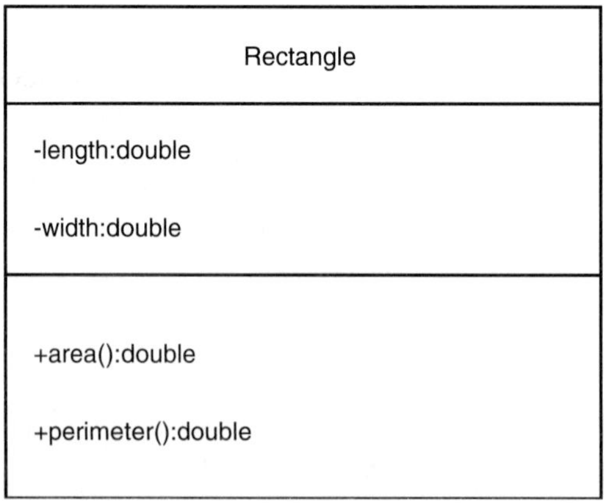

Rectangle
-length:double
-width:double
+area():double
+perimeter():double

FIGURE 10.5 A UML CLASS DIAGRAM FOR THE *RECTANGLE* CLASS.

PROGRAMMING NOTE

Remember, when function members of a class operate directly on private data members of the class, you *do not* pass the member data to/from the functions. The reason is that the function and data members are so tightly bound within the class that passing of class data is not necessary.

Objects

You should now have a pretty good handle on what an object is. Here is a technical definition for your reference.

An **object** is an instance, or specimen, of a given class. An object of a given class has the structure and behavior defined by the class that is common to all objects of the same class.

An object is a real thing that can be manipulated in a program. An object must be defined for a programmer-defined class to use the class, just as an object must be defined for the standard *string* class to use the class. An object defined for a class has the structure and behavior dictated by the class which are common to all objects defined for the class. You see from the foregoing definition that an object is an *instance* of a class. The word *instance* means an example or specimen of something. In this case, you could say that an object is an example or specimen of a class. If you have a class of dogs, then my dog *Randy* is an example or specimen of a dog. The same idea applies between C++ objects and classes.

Defining Objects.   You define an object for a class just as you define a variable for a primitive type. When the object is defined, memory is allocated to store the class for which the object is defined. Many different objects can be defined for a given class with each object made up of the data described by the class and responding to functions defined by the class. However, the private member data are hidden from one object to the next, even when multiple objects are defined for the same class. Objects are usually nouns. This means that they are persons, places, or things, like a *box* object for a *Rectangle* class, a *myAccount* object for a *SavingsAccount* class, a *myMemo* object for a *Memo* class, and so on. Notice that the object names begin with a lowercase letter, while the class names begin with an uppercase letter. This will allow us to distinguish between classes and objects in our code. Now, here is the required object definition format:

FORMAT FOR DEFINING CLASS OBJECTS

class name object name;

When defining objects, you simply list the object name after the class name. You will normally define objects separate from the class declaration because the object definition will appear in an application program, whereas the class declaration will appear in a header file. More about this later.

EXAMPLE 10.2

Create a *box* object for a class called *Rectangle* and a *myAccount* object for a class called *SavingsAccount*.

Solution

The *box* object definition is

```
Rectangle box;
```

The *myAccount* object definition is

```
SavingsAccount myAccount;
```

Quick Check

1. What do we mean when we say that a class defines the behavior of its objects?
2. True or false: Encapsulation ensures information hiding.
3. True or false: Private class members can be accessed only via public member functions.
4. Combining data with the functions that are dedicated to manipulating the data so that outside operations cannot affect the data is known as _____.
5. True or false: You must always pass private data to a public function of the same class, if the function needs the data to complete its designated operation.
6. Information hiding is provided by the _____ section of a class.
7. The behavioral secrets of a class are revealed at the _____ level.
8. Define an object called *myTruck* for a class called *Truck*.
9. Define an object called *myCar* for a class called *Automobile*.

10.2 MEMBER FUNCTIONS

The member functions in a class provide the interface to the class objects. Recall that to include a function as part of a class declaration, you simply list the function prototype in the public section of the class. The body of the function, or **implementation,** is given separately from the class declaration.

> A function **implementation** is the definition of the function that includes the function header and the body of the function.

Here is the general format required to implement a function when the function is part of a C++ class:

> **FORMAT FOR A FUNCTION IMPLEMENTATION**
>
> *return type class name :: function name* (*parameter listing*)
> {
>
> *//BODY OF FUNCTION GOES HERE*
>
> }*//END FUNCTION*

As an example, remember that earlier we declared a class called *SavingsAccount* that included a function called *addDeposit()*. The *addDeposit()* function was used to add a deposit amount received by the function to the private class member *balance*. Here is the class declaration again:

```
class SavingsAccount
{
public:
 void addDeposit(double amount);          //ADD DEPOSIT
 void addInterest();                      //ADD MONTHLY INTEREST
 double getBalance();                     //RETURN BALANCE
 void subtractWithdrawal(double amount);  //SUBTRACT WITHDRAWAL

private:
 int accountNumber;                       //ACCOUNT NUMBER
 double balance;                          //ACCOUNT BALANCE
 double interestRate;                     //MONTHLY INTEREST RATE
}; //END SavingsAccount
```

The important thing to remember is that the class declaration shows only the function prototypes that define the class interface. The details of how a given function works are provided in the function implementation. Here is the implementation for the *addDeposit()* function:

```
void SavingsAccount :: addDeposit(double amount)
{
 balance = balance + amount;
} //END initialize()
```

Look closely at the function header and you will see a double colon, **::,** separating the class name and the function name. The double colon is called the **scoping** *operator.* To implement a function as part of a class, you *must* include the scoping operator in the function header to tell the compiler that the function is part of a class. In other words, the foregoing function header tells the compiler that *the addDeposit() function has scope within the SavingsAccount class.* Once the function header is properly coded using the scoping operator, the body of the function is coded within curly braces just like any other function body.

> ### DEBUGGING TIP
>
> A common error when coding the implementation of a function member of a class is to place the function return type after the scoping operator like this:
>
> ```
> SavingsAccount :: void addDeposit(double amount)
> ```
>
> This seems to make sense because the return type is part of the function header, but such an oversight will always generate a compiler error. The correct syntax is to code the function return type before the class name, like this:
>
> ```
> void SavingsAccount :: addDeposit(double amount)
> ```

EXAMPLE 10.3

Write function implementations for the following *Rectangle* class:

```
class Rectangle
{
 public:
    double area();       //RETURN AREA
    double perimeter(); //RETURN PERIMETER

 private:
    double length;    //RECTANGLE LENGTH
    double width;     //RECTANGLE WIDTH
}; //END Rectangle
```

Solution

The *area()* function must calculate and return the area of the rectangle, resulting in an implementation of

```
double Rectangle :: area()
{
 return length * width;
} //END area()
```

The *perimeter()* function needs to calculate and return the perimeter of the rectangle. Here is the appropriate implementation:

```
double Rectangle :: perimeter()
{
 return 2 *(length + width);
} //END perimeter()
```

In the above member function implementations, you see the scoping operator employed to tell the compiler the class scope of the function. In addition, notice that each function operates using the private members of the class.

Constructor Functions

> A **constructor** is a special class function that is used to initialize an object automatically when the object is defined.

Although a constructor is a function used to initialize an object, it is often used to allocate dynamic memory, open files, and generally get an object ready for processing. You might have noticed in the foregoing class declarations that we did not initialize the private data members of the classes. This is because you will get a syntax error if you try to do so. A class is a *declaration* and does not reserve storage. As a result, we cannot store an initial value for a class data member. We can only store a value for a data member when an object is *defined* for the class. Recall that defining an object reserves storage. This is where a constructor comes in. A constructor will initialize the data members each time an object is defined for the class. To do this, the constructor is called automatically when an object is defined.

Here are the rules governing the creation and use of constructors:

- ❐ The name of the constructor must be the same as the name of the class.
- ❐ The constructor cannot have a return type, not even **void.**
- ❐ The constructor can have default parameters.
- ❐ A class cannot have more than one constructor; however, the constructor can be overloaded.
- ❐ Overloaded constructors with default parameters can cause ambiguity problems for the compiler.
- ❐ Constructors should not be developed for tasks other than to initialize an object for processing.

To illustrate how to set up a constructor, consider a modified *SavingsAccount* class declaration as follows:

```
class SavingsAccount
{
public:
 //CONSTRUCTOR
 SavingsAccount(int num, double bal, double rate);

 void addDeposit(double amount);      //ADD DEPOSIT
 void addInterest();                  //ADD MONTHLY INTEREST
```

```
    double getBalance();                //RETURN BALANCE
    void subtractWithdrawal(double amount); //SUBTRACT WITHDRAWAL
  private:
    int accountNumber;                  //ACCOUNT NUMBER
    double balance;                     //ACCOUNT BALANCE
    double interestRate;                //MONTHLY INTEREST RATE
};  //END SavingsAccount
```

This is the declaration for the *SavingsAccount* class that we developed earlier, with one big difference: It includes a constructor. Aside from the comment, you can recognize the constructor because it has the same name as the class and does not have any return type, not even **void.** The format of the *SavingsAccount()* constructor header is illustrated in Figure 10.6.

Once the constructor is declared in the class declaration, it must be implemented. Here is how the *SavingsAccount()* constructor might be implemented:

```
    SavingsAccount:: SavingsAccount(int num, double bal, double rate)
    {
     accountNumber = num;
     balance = bal;
     interestRate = rate;
    } //END SavingsAccount()
```

The implementation shows that the three private class members *accountNumber,* *balance,* and *interestRate,* are being initialized to the values received by the constructor parameters *num, bal,* and *rate,* respectively.

Now, the next question is: How is the constructor called? The reason for using a constructor over a regular function to initialize an object is that the constructor is called automatically when an object is defined. So, let's define two objects for the *SavingsAccount* class and therefore automatically call the constructor.

```
    SavingsAccount myAccount(1234,1000.00,12.0);
    SavingsAccount yourAccount(5678,2532.50,10.5);
```

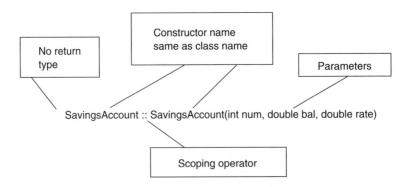

FIGURE 10.6 THE FORMAT OF THE *SAVINGSACCOUNT* CLASS CONSTRUCTOR HEADER

Here, *myAccount* and *yourAccount* are defined as objects of the *SavingsAccount* class. Notice that three argument values are passed to each object. As an example, *myAccount* object receives the argument values (1234,1000.00,12.0). What do you suppose happens with these arguments? You're right, the argument values are passed to the constructor, which is automatically called to set the *accountNumber*, *balance*, and *interestRate* to 1234, 1000.00, and 12.0, respectively. So, the idea is to list the constructor arguments in parentheses after the object name when the object is defined. This passes the arguments to the constructor, which is automatically called to perform its initializing task.

Default Parameters for Constructors.   Like any other function, a constructor can have default parameters. Recall that a default parameter is used when no arguments are supplied for that parameter. The default parameter values *must be supplied in the constructor function prototype*. This means that the default parameter values must be present in the class declaration. Here is our *SavingsAccount* class again with default parameters inserted into the constructor prototype:

```
class SavingsAccount
{
public:
 //CONSTRUCTOR
 SavingsAccount(int num = 0, double bal = 0.0, double rate = 0.0);

 void addDeposit(double amount);        //ADD DEPOSIT
 void addInterest();                    //ADD MONTHLY INTEREST
 double getBalance();                   //RETURN BALANCE
 void subtractWithdrawal(double amount); //SUBTRACT WITHDRAWAL

private:
 int accountNumber;          //ACCOUNT NUMBER
 double balance;             //ACCOUNT BALANCE
 double interestRate;        //MONTHLY INTEREST RATE
}; //END SavingsAccount
```

Now, when we define our objects, like this,

```
        SavingsAccount myAccount;
        SavingsAccount yourAccount(1234,2532.50,10.5);
```

the *myAccount* object will have its private members initialized to the default parameter values (0,0.0,0.0), and the *yourAccount* object will have its private members set to the constructor argument listing (1234,2532.50,10.5). Notice that no argument values are present in the *myAccount* object definition. When this is the case, the compiler will substitute the default values for any missing parameters.

Overloaded Constructors.   Any function, even a constructor, can be overloaded. In fact, constructors are almost always overloaded in object-oriented programs. Recall from Chapter 8 that an overloaded function is one that performs different tasks depending on the number and/or type of arguments that it receives. Here is our earlier *Rectangle* class with an overloaded constructor:

```
class Rectangle
{
public:
   //CONSTRUCTOR FOR A SQUARE  RECTANGLE
   Rectangle(double s);

   //CONSTRUCTOR FOR A NONSQUARE RECTANGLE
   Rectangle(double 1, double w);

   double area();          //RETURN AREA
   double perimeter();     //RETURN PERIMETER

private:
   double length;          //RECTANGLE LENGTH
   double width;           //RECTANGLE WIDTH
}; //END Rectangle
```

You are probably thinking that there are two constructors in the foregoing declaration. No, there is a single constructor called *Rectangle()*, which is overloaded. You can tell that the *Rectangle()* constructor is overloaded, because it has two different sets of parameters.

Now, let's look at the constructor implementations. Here they are:

```
//IMPLEMENTATION OF SQUARE CONSTRUCTOR
Rectangle :: Rectangle(double s)
{
 length = width = s;
} //END Rectangle()

//IMPLEMENTATION OF NONSQUARE CONSTRUCTOR
Rectangle :: Rectangle(double 1, double w)
{
 length = 1;
 width = w;
} //END Rectangle()
```

There are two implementations of this constructor, because it is overloaded. The first implementation is for a square and the second for a non-square rectangle. The square implementation sets the *length* and *width* members of the rectangle equal to the same value, *s*, that is received when the constructor is called. The non-square implementation sets the *length* and *width* to two different values, *l* and *w*, when the constructor is called. What determines which implementation is used? If the constructor is called with a single argument, the square implementation is executed. If the constructor is called with two arguments, the non-square implementation is executed. How is the constructor called? Of course, by defining objects for the class. Here is a sample object definition:

```
Rectangle  square(1);
Rectangle  box(2,3);
```

Here, two objects, *square* and *box*, are defined. In addition, a single argument of (1) is passed to the *square* object, and a double argument of (2,3) is passed to the *box* object. What do you suppose happens? When the *square* object is defined, the first constructor implementation is executed, setting the *length* and *width* of the *square* object to the same value, 1. When the *box* object is defined, the second constructor implementation is executed, setting the *length* to 2 and the *width* to 3.

> ### CAUTION
>
> When overloading a constructor and using default values, you can easily create *ambiguity* as to which constructor implementation should be executed. Such ambiguity *always* results in a compiler error.

Be careful to prevent ambiguity when using default values with overloaded constructors. For example, suppose we would have declared the *Rectangle* class as follows:

```
//THIS CLASS DECLARATION CREATES AMBIGUITY
class Rectangle
{
public:
  //CONSTRUCTOR FOR A SQUARE  RECTANGLE
  Rectangle(double s = 0.0);

  //CONSTRUCTOR FOR A NONSQUARE RECTANGLE
  Rectangle(double l = 0.0, double w = 0.0);

  double area();      //RETURN AREA
  double perimeter(); //RETURN PERIMETER

private:
  double length;      //RECTANGLE LENGTH
  double width;       //RECTANGLE WIDTH
}; //END Rectangle
```

Then we define our objects like this:

```
Rectangle  square;
Rectangle  box;
```

When this code is compiled, the compiler will generate an *ambiguity* error message. Why? Because the compiler doesn't know which constructor implementation to execute. Does it execute the implementation containing one parameter or the implementation containing two parameters? For this reason, it is wise not to use default parameters with an overloaded constructor. Obviously, there can never be an ambiguity problem with non-overloaded constructors, because there is only one implementation for the constructor.

Scoping Inside of Functions

When using a constructor, or any class function for that matter, a problem can occur when the private member names are the same as the function parameter names. For instance, suppose that we declare a simple *Circle* class that contains a private member called *radius*. You then decide to use the *radius* name as a parameter for the constructor. Here is the appropriate class declaration:

```
class Circle
{
public:
 Circle(double radius = 0.0); //CONSTRUCTOR
private:
 double radius;                //CIRCLE RADIUS
}; //END Circle
```

There is nothing wrong with this declaration. The problem arises in the constructor implementation. Consider the following implementation:

```
//CONSTRUCTOR IMPLEMENTATION
Circle :: Circle(double radius)
{
    radius = radius;
} //END Circle()
```

The implementation will compile; however, it will initialize *radius* to garbage! Look at the statement within the implementation and you will see ambiguity in the use of the *radius* name. It appears that *radius* is being assigned to itself. How does the compiler know what *radius* to use? Is *radius* the variable defined as the private class member, or is *radius* the value received by the constructor, or both? We must tell the compiler that the *radius* on the left side of the assignment operator is the private class member and the *radius* on the right side of the assignment operator is the value received by the constructor. There are two ways to solve this problem: 1) by using the scoping operator, or 2) by using the **this** pointer.

The Scoping Operator Revisited.   You were introduced to the double colon scoping operator, ::, when you learned how to code the header of a member function implementation. The scoping operator simply defines the scope of something. In the case of a function header, it is used to tell the compiler that the function belongs to a certain class and therefore has class scope. The scoping operator can also be used inside of a function to define the scope of a variable. Using the scoping operator, we can fix the previous ambiguity problem by coding the *Circle()* constructor implementation as follows:

```
//CONSTRUCTOR IMPLEMENTATION
Circle :: Circle(double radius)
{
 Circle :: radius = radius;
} //END Circle()
```

The addition of the scoping operator in the constructor statement tells the compiler that the *radius* on the left side of the assignment operator belongs to the *Circle* class. Therefore, the *radius* on the right side of the assignment operator must be the function parameter. Now there is no ambiguity between the two *radius* names.

The "this" Pointer

> A **pointer** is a direct program reference to an actual physical address in memory. You will study pointers in a future chapter.

All the member functions of a class carry with them an invisible pointer, called **this,** that points to the object that called the function. (Pointers will be discussed in detail later.) Although the pointer is invisible, it can be used to prevent ambiguity problems like the one in the foregoing *Circle()* constructor. Here is how the **this** pointer can be employed in the constructor implementation to solve an ambiguity problem:

```
//CONSTRUCTOR IMPLEMENTATION
Circle :: Circle(double radius)
{
 this -> radius = radius;
} //END Circle()
```

The compiler knows that **this** points to the object that called the constructor, and it knows what class the object belongs to. As a result, *this –> radius* references the private member *radius* of the *Circle* class. Now there is no ambiguity between the two *radius* names.

PROGRAMMING TIP

A simple solution to the use of duplicate names in a program is to make sure that you employ different names to avoid any ambiguity if possible. For instance, the radius of a circle could be named *radius, rad,* or *r,* depending on where it is used in the program. Thus, the *Circle()* constructor could be coded like this:

```
//CONSTRUCTOR IMPLEMENTATION
Circle :: Circle(double r)
{
 radius = r;
} //END Circle()
```

This represents much better overall programming style and is less confusing to anyone looking at the code.

EXAMPLE 10.4

Develop a UML class diagram and declare a *Point* class that defines an (x,y) coordinate for a cursor position on the monitor. Provide a constructor to initialize the coordinate when an object is defined for *Point*. The default coordinate should be (0,0). Include a function, called *plot()*, as part of the class that will display the string "C++" at the (x,y) coordinate location. Finally, code a statement to define an object, *p*, of the *Point* class, and initialize this object to point to the middle of the monitor screen. Also, write a statement to call the *plot()* function.

Solution

From the problem description the class must contain two private data members, *x* and *y*, along with two public functions: a constructor called *Point()* to initialize the (x,y) values and a function called *plot()* to plot a string at the coordinate location specified by the *x* and *y* data members. First, let's address the function interfaces. The *Point()* constructor function must initialize the (x,y) values. We must use a default coordinate of (0,0), but we will also allow the constructor to receive a different set of coordinate values when an object is defined. Thus, our constructor interface can be described as follows:

Function *Point()*:   Initializes the (x,y) coordinate values.

Accepts: A value for *x* and a value for *y*.

Returns: Nothing.

In terms of UML, the representation of this function would be:

```
+Point(in x:int = 0, in y:int = 0)
```

Remember what this representation means? Well, the + means that *Point()* is a public class member. It has two parameters, *x* and *y*, which are both being accepted (*in*) by the function. Both parameters are *int* and the default value for both is a 0. There is no return value, because this function is a constructor.

Next, the *plot()* function must display a string at a position on the screen specified by the private *x* and *y* values. Since *x* and *y* are members of the class, they are not passed to the function. Also, the function is not returning any values outside the class, because it is simply writing to the monitor. The appropriate interface description is simply:

```
+plot()
```

The corresponding UML class diagram is shown in Figure 10.7. Now, the class can be coded directly from the UML diagram, like this:

```
//Point CLASS DECLARATION
class Point
{
public:
 Point(int x = 0, int y =0); //CONSTRUCTOR
 void plot();                //PLOT POINT(X,Y)

private:
 int x;                      //X-COORDINATE
 int y;                      //Y-COORDINATE
}; //END Point
```

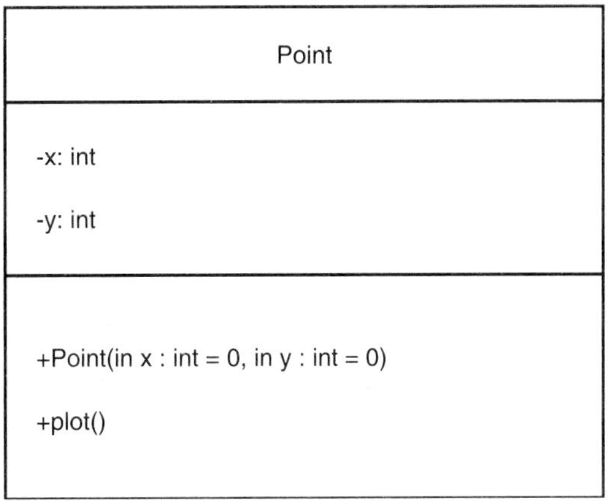

Point
-x: int -y: int
+Point(in x : int = 0, in y : int = 0) +plot()

FIGURE 10.7   A UML CLASS DIAGRAM FOR THE *POINT* CLASS.

This declaration should be straightforward. The *Point* class consists of two private integer members, *x* and *y*, that will form the coordinate. A constructor function is included to initialize the *x* and *y* values and provide a default coordinate of (0,0). The *plot()* function will use the *x* and *y* member values to position the cursor at an (*x,y*) coordinate on the screen and display the string "C++". To see how the functions work, we need to develop their implementations. Here they are:

```
//CONSTRUCTOR IMPLEMENTATION
Point :: Point(int x, int y)
{
 this -> x = x;
 this -> y = y;
} //END Point()

//PLOT IMPLEMENTATION
void Point :: plot()
{
 for(int i = 0; i < y; ++i)    //MOVE CURSOR DOWN y LINES
  cout << endl;
 for ( i = 0; i < x; ++i)      //MOVE CURSOR OVER x LINES
  cout << ' ';
 cout << "C++" << endl;        //DISPLAY "C++"
} //END plot()
```

The constructor implementation applies the **this** pointer to prevent ambiguity between the *x,y* class members and the *x,y* constructor parameters. The *plot()* implementation uses the *x,y* class members within **for** loops to position the cursor at the (*x,y*) position on the monitor. Once the cursor is positioned, the final *cout* statement displays the string "C++" at the cursor position.

A statement to define an object, *p*, of the *Point* class and initialize *p* to point to the middle of the screen is

```
Point  p(40,12);
```

This statement defines *p* and calls the constructor to initialize the (*x,y*) coordinate to (40,12), which is the approximate middle of the screen. The following statement will call the *plot()* function to move the cursor to the (*x,y*) coordinate position and display the string.

```
p.plot();
```

To call a non-constructor function, you simply list the object, a dot, and then the function name with any required arguments. Of course, the *plot()* function doesn't require any arguments, because it operates directly on the private members of the object. However, the function could be easily modified to display any string passed as a parameter to the function, right?

Access Functions

Remember that the only way to access the private members of an object are with a member function. Even if we simply want to examine the private members of an object, we need to use a public function that is declared within the same object class. Such a function needs to return only the private member(s) to the calling program. Access functions are used for this purpose.

> An **access function,** sometimes called a **get function,** is a function that returns only the values of the private members of an object.

Let's revisit one of our *Rectangle* class declarations, adding access functions to it, as follows:

```
class Rectangle
{
public:
    Rectangle(double l=0.0, double w=0.0); //CONSTRUCTOR
    double perimeter();                     //RETURN PERIMETER
    double area();                          //RETURN AREA
    double getLength();                     //GET LENGTH
    double getWidth();                      //GET WIDTH

private:
    double length;           //RECTANGLE LENGTH
    double width;            //RECTANGLE WIDTH
}; //END Rectangle.
```

Two new member functions called *getLength()* and *getWidth()* have been added here to return the *length* and *width* private member values, respectively. The only purpose of an access function is to return the value of a private member, so the implementation requires only a **return** statement, as follows:

```
//IMPLEMENTATION OF LENGTH ACCESS FUNCTION
double Rectangle :: getLength()
```

```
{
 return length;
} //END getLength()

//IMPLEMENTATION OF WIDTH ACCESS FUNCTION
double Rectangle :: getWidth()
{
 return width;
} //END getWidth()
```

When either of these implementations is executed, the respective private member value is returned to the calling program. So, if we define *box* to be an object of *Rectangle*, you can call either access function using dot notation to examine the private members. For instance, to display the member values of *box*, the access functions could be called as part of *cout* statements, like this:

```
cout << "The length of the box is:  " << box.getLength() << endl;
cout << "The width of the box is:  " << box.getWidth() << endl;
```

Messages

A *message* is a call to a member function.

The term ***message*** is used for a call to a member function with the idea that when we are calling a member function, we are sending a message to the object. The object responds to the calling program by sending back return values. This idea is illustrated in Figure 10.8. As you will see shortly, objects communicate with each other using messages.

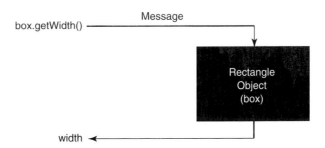

FIGURE 10.8 MESSAGES ARE THE MEANS OF COMMUNICATING WITH AN OBJECT.

To generate a message to an object, you must call one of its member functions. You call a member function by using the dot operator. The required format is

SENDING A MESSAGE USING THE DOT OPERATOR

object name • function name (*argument listing*);

Here is our *Rectangle* class again with all the features that we have added up to this point:

```
class Rectangle
{
public:
 Rectangle(double l = 0.0, double w = 0.0);   //CONSTRUCTOR
 double perimeter();                          //RETURN PERIMETER
 double area();                               //RETURN AREA
 double getLength();                          //GET LENGTH
 double getWidth();                           //GET WIDTH
private:
 double length;                              //RECTANGLE LENGTH
 double width;                               //RECTANGLE WIDTH
}; //END Rectangle()
```

Let's define three *Rectangle* objects called *box1*, *box2*, and *box3*. Here are the required definitions:

```
Rectangle box1(2,3);    //box1 OBJECT DEF
Rectangle box2(3,4);    //box2 OBJECT DEF
Rectangle box3;         //box3 OBJECT DEF
```

Next, let's send messages to all the functions of the three boxes using *cout* statements. We will use a separate *cout* statement for each message so that you can easily observe the required syntax. Here are the messages:

```
cout << "The length of box1 is:  " << box1.getLength() << endl;
cout << "The width of box1 is:  " << box1.getWidth()<< endl;
cout << "The perimeter of box1 is:  " << box1.perimeter()<< endl;
cout << "The area of box1 is:  " << box1.area()<< endl << endl;

cout << "The length of box2 is:  " << box2.getLength()<< endl;
cout << "The width of box2 is:  " << box2.getWidth()<< endl;
cout << "The perimeter of box2 is:  " << box2.perimeter()<< endl;
cout << "The area of box2 is:  " << box2.area() << endl << endl;

cout << "The length of box3 is:  " << box3.getLength()<< endl;
cout << "The width of box3 is:  " << box3.getWidth()<< endl;
cout << "The perimeter of box3 is:  " << box3.perimeter()<< endl;
cout << "The area of box3 is:  " << box3.area()<< endl << endl;
```

Observe that each group of four *cout* statements deals with a different box object. Each group sends messages to its respective object via the dot operator. That's all there is to it!

Putting Everything Together in a Complete Program

We now have all the ingredients to build a complete program. Here it is:

```cpp
#include <iostream.h>  //FOR cin AND cout

//Rectangle CLASS DECLARATION
class Rectangle
{
public:
 Rectangle(double l = 0.0, double w = 0.0); //CONSTRUCTOR
 double perimeter();                     //RETURN PERIMETER
 double area();                          //RETURN AREA
 double getLength();                     //GET LENGTH
 double getWidth();                      //GET WIDTH

private:
 double length;                          //RECTANGLE LENGTH
 double width;                           //RECTANGLE WIDTH
}; //END Rectangle()

//MAIN FUNCTION
int main()
{
 //DEFINE OBJECTS
 Rectangle box1(2,3);                    //box1 OBJECT DEF
 Rectangle box2(3,4);                    //box2 OBJECT DEF
 Rectangle box3;                         //box3 OBJECT DEF

 //DISPLAY LENGTH, WIDTH, PERIMETER, AND AREA OF BOX OBJECTS
 cout << "The length of box1 is:  " << box1.getLength() << endl;
 cout << "The width of box1 is:  " << box1.getWidth()<< endl;
 cout << "The perimeter of box1 is:  " << box1.perimeter()<< endl;
 cout << "The area of box1 is:  " << box1.area()<< endl << endl;

 cout << "The length of box2 is:  " << box2.getLength()<< endl;
 cout << "The width of box2 is:  " << box2.getWidth()<< endl;
 cout << "The perimeter of box2 is:  " << box2.perimeter()<< endl;
 cout << "The area of box2 is:  " << box2.area() << endl << endl;

 cout << "The length of box3 is:  " << box3.getLength()<< endl;
 cout << "The width of box3 is:  " << box3.getWidth()<< endl;
 cout << "The perimeter of box3 is:  " << box3.perimeter()<< endl;
 cout << "The area of box3 is:  " << box3.area()<< endl << endl;
 //RETURN
 return 0;
} //END main()
```

```
//CONSTRUCTOR IMPLEMENTATION
Rectangle :: Rectangle(double l, double w)
{
 length = l;
 width =  w;
} //END Rectangle()

//IMPLEMENTATION OF perimeter() FUNCTION
double Rectangle :: perimeter()
{
 return 2 * (length + width);
} //END perimeter()

//IMPLEMENTATION OF area() FUNCTION
double Rectangle :: area()
{
  return length *  width;
} //END area()

//IMPLEMENTATION OF getLength() FUNCTION
double Rectangle :: getLength()
{
  return length;
} //END getLength()

//IMPLEMENTATION OF getWidth() FUNCTION
double Rectangle :: getWidth()
{
 return width;
} //END getWidth()
```

You see that our program includes the *Rectangle* class declaration, which includes five public function members and two private data members. The functions consist of a constructor with default values, two access functions, and two functions that return the perimeter and area of the rectangle. Three objects are defined for the *Rectangle* class within *main()*, and then messages are sent to the objects by calling all their respective functions. Here is the output from the program:

```
The length of box1 is:   2
The width of box1 is:   3
The perimeter of box1 is:   10
The area of box1 is:   6

The length of box2 is:   3
The width of box2 is:   4
The perimeter of box2 is:   14
The area of box2 is:   12

The length of box3 is:   0
The width of box3 is:   0
```

```
The perimeter of box3 is:  0
The area of box3 is:  0
```

This program summarizes most of what has been covered in the last two sections. Before going on, study the program to make sure that you understand everything in it. Many important OOP concepts are demonstrated here.

Quick Check

1. The operator employed in a function header that designates the function as being a member of a given class is the _____ operator.
2. The complete definition of a member function, which includes the function header and body, is called the function _____.
3. Write a header for a member function called *wheels()* that will return the number of wheels from a class called *Truck*.
4. A member function that is used specifically to initialize class data is called a _____.
5. How do you know which member function in a class is the constructor function?
6. True or false: The return type of a constructor function is optional.
7. How do you call a class constructor?
8. All member functions of a class carry with them a built-in pointer to the object that called the function, which is called _____.
9. How do you call a non-constructor member function of a class?
10. A member function that returns only a value of a private class member is called a(n) _____ function.
11. Why is the term "message" used for a call to a member function?

PROBLEM SOLVING IN ACTION: BUILDING PROGRAMS USING CLASSES AND OBJECTS

Professional baseball has heard about C++, and they have hired you to write a simple program for their pitchers. The program must store the pitcher's name, team, wins, losses, winning percentage, and earned run average (ERA). In addition, a provision must be provided for the user to enter a given pitcher's stats as well as display a given pitcher's stats. Develop such a program using classes and objects.

The first thing to be done when developing an object-oriented program is to identify the nouns and verbs in the problem statement. Remember, the nouns suggest private data for the class and the verbs suggest functions for the class. Here is the problem statement again with the important nouns and verbs underlined:

The program must store the pitcher's _name, team, wins, losses, winning percentage_, and _ERA_. In addition, provision must be provided for the user to _enter_ a given *pitcher's data as well as <u>display</u> a given pitcher's data. Develop such a program using classes and objects.*

From the nouns and verbs, we develop a class specification as follows:

Class: *Pitcher*
    Function Members: *setStats()*
                            getStats()
    Data Members: *name*
                    team
                    wins
                    losses
                    winPercent
                    era

After analyzing the class members, a UML diagram can be constructed as shown in Figure 10.9. Notice how the UML diagram dictates that the constructor will initialize all the private members, with the exclusion of *winPercent* which will be calculated by the private *calculateWinPercent()* function shown at the bottom of the diagram. More about this shortly.

Now, we are ready to code the class. Here it is:

```
class Pitcher
{
 //PUBLIC MEMBERS
 public:
```

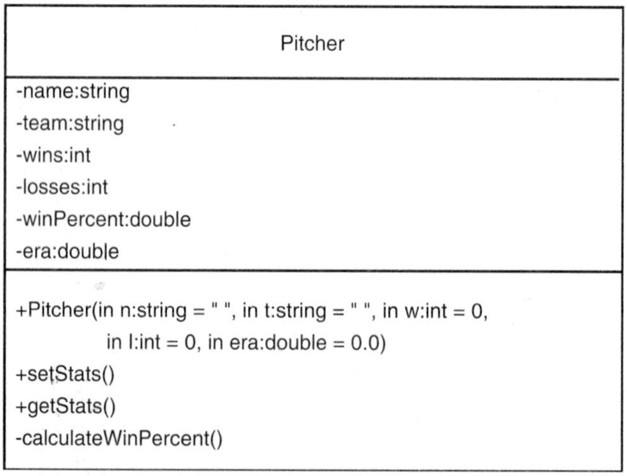

Pitcher
-name:string
-team:string
-wins:int
-losses:int
-winPercent:double
-era:double
+Pitcher(in n:string = " ", in t:string = " ", in w:int = 0,
in l:int = 0, in era:double = 0.0)
+setStats()
+getStats()
-calculateWinPercent()

FIGURE 10.9   A UML CLASS DIAGRAM FOR THE *PITCHER* CLASS.

```
//CONSTRUCTOR THAT INITIALIZES ALL PITCHER DATA EXCEPT WIN %
Pitcher(string n = " ",string t = " ", int w = 0, int l = 0, double era = 0.0);

//SET PITCHER STATS TO USER ENTRIES
void setStats();

//GET AND DISPLAY STATS
void getStats();

//PRIVATE MEMBERS
private:
    string name;            //PITCHER'S NAME
    string team;            //PITCHER'S TEAM
    int wins;               //NUMBER OF WINS
    int losses;             //NUMBER OF LOSSES
    double winPercent;      //WIN PERCENTAGE
    double era;             //EARNED RUN AVERAGE
    //UTILITY FUNCTION TO CALCULATE winPercent
    void calculateWinPercent();
}; // END Pitcher CLASS
```

First, look at the function members of the class. The first thing you see is a constructor. The constructor defines default parameters for each of the data members, except the winning percentage. Thus, you have the option of providing no arguments when defining an object for the class, or providing initializing values for each argument. If you do not supply any arguments, the default values will be used. If you supply arguments, the argument values are assigned to their respective data members. The remaining public members are the *setStats()* and *getStats()* function members that will obtain the pitcher stats from the user and display the pitcher stats, respectively.

Next, look at the data members of the class. Here you see all the data members that we found in the problem statement. In addition, you see a private function member called *calculateWinPercent()*.This function calculates the winning percentage using the *wins* and *losses* data members. Such a function is called a ***utility function*** and must be called within a public function. This is an ideal application for a utility function, because it will only be called within the class to calculate the *winPercent* data member and does not need to be called from outside the class. You will see that our constructor function and *setStats()* function both call this function to initialize the *winPercent* data member.

Now, here are the function implementations:

```
//CONSTRUCTOR THAT INITIALIZES ALL PITCHER DATA EXCEPT
//WIN %
Pitcher :: Pitcher(string n,string t, int w, int l,
                   double era)
{
    name = n;
    team = t;
    wins = w;
    losses = l;
```

```
        this -> era = era;
        calculateWinPercent();
}//END Pitcher(string,string,int,int,double)

//SET PITCHER STATS TO USER ENTRIES
void Pitcher :: setStats()
{
        //PROMPT AND READ PITCHER STATS
        cout << "Enter the pitcher's name: ";
        cin >> ws;
        getline(cin,name);
        cout << "Enter the pitcher's team: ";
        cin >> ws;
        getline(cin,team);
        cout << "Enter the number of wins for " << name << ": ";
        cin >> wins;
        cout << "Enter the number of losses for " << name << ": ";
        cin >> losses;
        cout << "Enter the era " << name << ": ";
        cin >> era;
        calculateWinPercent();
}//END setStats()

//GET AND DISPLAY STATS
void Pitcher :: getStats()
{
        cout << "\nPitcher name: " << name << endl;
        cout << "\tTeam: " << team << endl;
        cout << "\tNumber of wins: " << wins << endl;
        cout << "\tNumber of losses: " << losses << endl;
        cout << "\tWinning percentage: " << winPercent << endl;
        cout << "\tERA: " << era << endl;
}//END getStats()

void Pitcher :: calculateWinPercent()
{
        if ((wins + losses) == 0)
          winPercent = 0.0;
        else
          winPercent = (double)wins/(wins + losses) * 100;
//TYPE CASTING
}//END calculateWinPercent
```

As you can see, the constructor does its job of initializing the private data members. In particular, notice how the constructor calls the private *calculateWinPercent()* function to initialize the winning percentage. The next function, *setStats()*, prompts the user and reads the user entries for the private members. Again, notice that the *calculateWinPercent()* function is called to determine *winPercent* member value after the *wins* and *losses* have been set by the user. The *getStats()* function simply displays the pitcher data stored by the private data members of the class.

Now, look at the *calculateWinPercent()* function. Since this is a private function it cannot be called from outside the class and must be called by a public function member of the class. You see that it contains an **if/else** statement. Why? Because if both *wins* and *losses* were zero, a run-time error would occur and the program would crash. So, the **if/else** statement protects against division by zero. Last, you see something that you have not seen before. The statement

```
winPercent = (double)wins/(wins + losses) * 100;  //TYPE CAST
```

includes what is called a ***type cast.*** A type cast temporarily converts data of one type to a different type. The type cast is created by the code (`double`) in the preceding statement. Without the type cast to double, the calculation would always be 0. Why? Because *wins* and *losses* are both integers. When you divide two integers, you get an integer. Since (`wins + losses`) will always be greater than *wins*, integer division will always give you a result of 0. The type cast forces a double floating-point result, which is what we need for our *winPercent* member. Remember this little trick, because it often comes in handy. We should caution you, however, that type casting should only be used when really necessary as in the above application. If you find yourself doing a lot of type casting, then you have probably not data-typed your variables properly when they were defined. This is why we have not discussed type casting until now.

PROGRAMMING NOTE

A ***type cast*** converts data of one type to a different type, temporarily. You can convert data of one type to another type by preceding the data variable/expression with the type to convert to within parentheses like this: (`double`). The conversion is not permanent, since it is only in effect for the statement in which it resides. Type casting should be used sparingly, when a legitimate need for its use arises. Too much type casting within a program indicates a problem in the way in which the program variables have been typed when they were defined.

Now, the last thing to do is to create an application program to exercise our *Pitcher* class. Here is the complete program:

```
/*
ACTION 10-1(ACT10_01.CPP)
*/

//PREPROCESSOR DIRECTIVES
#include <iostream> //FOR cin AND cout
#include <string>   //FOR string CLASS

using namespace std;  //REQUIRED WHEN INCLUDING iostream

//PITCHER CLASS DECLARATION
class Pitcher
{
```

```
//PUBLIC MEMBERS
public:

//CONSTRUCTOR THAT INITIALIZES ALL PITCHER DATA EXCEPT WIN %
Pitcher(string n = " ",string t = " ", int w = 0, int 1 = 0,
        double era = 0.0);

//SET PITCHER STATS TO USER ENTRIES
void setStats();

//GET AND DISPLAY STATS
void getStats();

//PRIVATE MEMBERS
private:
  string name;           //PITCHER'S NAME
  string team ;          //PITCHER'S TEAM
  int wins;              //NUMBER OF WINS
  int losses;            //NUMBER OF LOSSES
  double winPercent;     //WIN PERCENTAGE
  double era;            //EARNED RUN AVERAGE

  //UTILITY FUNCTION TO CALCULATE winPercent
  void calculateWinPercent();
}; // END Pitcher CLASS

//MAIN FUNCTION
int main()
{
  //DEFINE PITCHER OBJECT
  Pitcher JohnSmoltz;

  //CALL PITCHER FUNCTIONS
  JohnSmoltz.setStats();
  JohnSmoltz.getStats();

  //RETURN
  return 0;

}//END main()

//PITCHER CLASS FUNCTION IMPLEMENTATIONS

//CONSTRUCTOR THAT INITIALIZES ALL PITCHER DATA EXCEPT
//WIN %
Pitcher :: Pitcher(string n,string t, int w, int 1, double era)
{
    name = n;
    team = t;
    wins = w;
    losses = 1;
    this -> era = era;
```

```
        calculateWinPercent();
}//END Pitcher(string,string,int,int,double)


//SET PITCHER STATS TO USER ENTRIES
void Pitcher :: setStats()
{
    //PROMPT AND READ PITCHER STATS
    cout << "Enter the pitcher's name: ";
    cin >> ws;
    getline(cin,name);
    cout << "Enter the pitcher's team: ";
    cin >> ws;
    getline(cin,team);
    cout << "Enter the number of wins for " << name << ": ";
    cin >> wins;
    cout << "Enter the number of losses for " << name << ": ";
    cin >> losses;
    cout << "Enter the era " << name << ": ";
    cin >> era;
    calculateWinPercent();
}//END setStats()


//GET AND DISPLAY STATS
void Pitcher :: getStats()
{
    cout << "\nPitcher Name: " << name << endl;
    cout << "\tTeam: " << team << endl;
    cout << "\tNumber of wins: " << wins << endl;
    cout << "\tNumber of losses: " << losses << endl;
    cout << "\tWinning percentage: " << winPercent << endl;
    cout << "\tERA: " << era << endl;
}//END getStats()


void Pitcher :: calculateWinPercent()
{
   if ((wins + losses) == 0)
      winPercent = 0.0;
   else
      winPercent = (double)wins/(wins + losses) * 100;  //TYPE CASTING
}//END calculateWinPercent
```

The application program is called *act10_01.cpp*. Notice that a *JohnSmoltz* object is defined for our *Pitcher* class inside of *main()*. The default initializing values will be used because no arguments are provided with the object definition. The *John Smoltz* object is then used to call the *setStats()* and *getStats()* functions to allow the user to enter the pitcher data and display the data, respectively. That's it! Now you are ready to build your own object-oriented programs.

This case study summarizes most of what has been covered in the last two sections. Before going on, study the program to make sure that you understand everything in it. Many important OOP concepts are demonstrated here.

10.3 MULTIFILE PROGRAM CONSTRUCTION

Up to this point, we have been working with relatively simple C++ programs for learning purposes. Commercial programs, on the other hand, can get very complex, involving several thousand lines of code. Remember what to do when tackling a complex problem? You're right, divide it into simpler sub-problems, the old "divide-and-conquer" strategy. The same is true when building a large program. Rather than placing everything into a single source file and compiling/linking this file into an executable file, we place different parts of the program in separate files, edit them separately, compile them separately, and then link them all together to create the executable file. This is the way the pros do it!

From the beginning, you have included header files in your C++ programs. These header files primarily provide interfaces to the standard functions and objects used in your program. The C and C++ languages were developed around the idea of using many separate files for a programming project and linking them together to create the executable file. There are several reasons for this approach. First, it allows you to create smaller, more manageable files. This facilitates a team approach to software development. Each team member writes, debugs, and compiles his/her own part of the project code independent of the other team members. When all the individual files are completed, they are linked to create a common executable program.

Second, programs made of separately compiled files are easier to maintain. When changes need to be made to the program, only those files affected by the change need to be modified and recompiled. In many cases, the unaffected files do not need to be recompiled.

Third, you can hide any important proprietary parts of the program code from another programmer by only providing the user with the binary object code for those parts. What really makes one C++ program different from another are the member function implementations. So, suppose that you provide the class declarations to the user as a *.cpp* source file and the function implementations as a *.obj* object file. The class declaration provides a listing of all the data members as well as the function prototypes. The function prototypes provide the required interface to an object of that class. This is all any good programmer needs to know to use the class. He or she does not need to know how the functions are implemented. The function implementations can be compiled into a binary object file and supplied to the programmer. The programmer can then include the class declaration file in his/her application program and link it along with the function implementation object file to create the final executable file. This encourages programmers to write object-oriented code that can be reused in other programs and shared with other programmers without compromising confidentiality. This idea is illustrated in Figure 10.10.

You should be aware of the rules for what must be recompiled and linked if things change in the class declaration header file or the function implementation file. If the *.h* class declaration header file is modified, then *every .cpp* source file that includes the header file must be recompiled. On the other hand, if the *.cpp* function implementation file is modified, then only this file must be recompiled. In either case, the entire application project must be relinked.

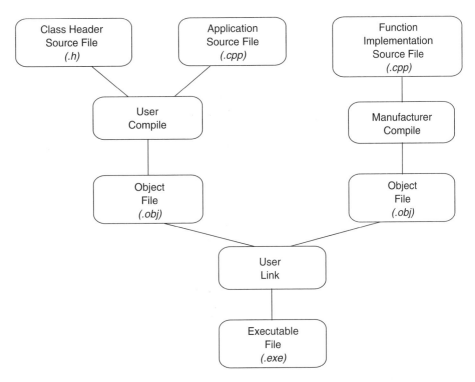

FIGURE 10.10   **OBJECT INTERFACES CAN BE MADE PUBLIC BY
SUPPLYING OTHER PROGRAMMERS WITH THE CLASS
HEADER FILES AS SOURCE CODE, WHILE HIDING
THE FUNCTION IMPLEMENTATIONS IN OBJECT FILES.**

PROBLEM SOLVING IN ACTION: BUILDING A MULTIFILE C++ PROGRAM

C++ compilers and commercial programs are constructed using the multifile concept. The software manufacturers provide you with all the standard header files that include the function prototypes as source code, but do not supply you with the source code for the function implementations. Thus, you cannot alter and possibly corrupt the standard function implementations.

Most C++ compilers allow you to build your own multifile programs. In this problem, you will see how a typical C++ compiler allows you to build multi-file programs through the use of its *project manager.* When using the project manager, you specify all the files required to build an application program. This information is kept in a *project file.*

A *project file* identifies the files that need to be compiled and linked to create a given executable program.

You can add or delete files to and from your project, view/edit individual files in the project, and set options for a file in the project. When working with program files in the project, the project manager automatically updates the information kept in the project file and identifies those files that need to be recompiled and linked to produce an executable program. If a given program file is altered, only that file is recompiled by the project manager. This saves program development time.

As an example, let's build a project out of the *Rectangle* program that we developed at the end of the last section. We will place the *Rectangle* class declaration in a separate file called *rectangl.h*, like this:

```
//rectangl.h HEADER FILE

//Rectangle CLASS DECLARATION
class Rectangle
{
public:
  Rectangle(double l = 0.0, double w = 0.0); //CONSTRUCTOR
  double perimeter();                        //RETURN PERIMETER
  double area();                             //RETURN AREA
  double getLength();                        //GET LENGTH
  double getWidth();                         //GET WIDTH

private:
  double length;                             //RECTANGLE LENGTH
  double width;                              //RECTANGLE WIDTH
}; //END Rectangle
```

Next, we will place all the function implementations in a separate file called *rectangl.cpp*, like this:

```
//rectangl.cpp IMPLEMENTATION FILE


#include "rectangl.h"   //FOR Rectangle CLASS

//CONSTRUCTOR IMPLEMENTATION
Rectangle :: Rectangle(double l, double w)
{
  length = l;
  width =  w;
} //END Rectangle()

//IMPLEMENTATION OF perimeter() FUNCTION
double Rectangle :: perimeter()
{
  return 2 * (length + width);
} //END perimeter()

//IMPLEMENTATION OF area() FUNCTION
double Rectangle :: area()
{
  return length *  width;
} //END area()
```

```
//IMPLEMENTATION OF getLength() FUNCTION
double Rectangle :: getLength()
{
 return length;
} //END getLength()

//IMPLEMENTATION OF getWidth() FUNCTION
double Rectangle :: getWidth()
{
 return width;
} //END getWidth()
```

The first executable statement that you see in this file is a preprocessor directive that includes the *rectangl.h* class declaration header file. This directive is required so that the *rectangl.cpp* file can be compiled to produce a *rectangl.obj* file. The file will not compile unless the class header file is included, because without it, the compiler doesn't know the class declaration from which the functions are derived. Notice that double quotes are employed around the header file name. This tells the compiler to look for the file in the system working directory. This is where a source file that you have developed will most likely be located.

PROGRAMMING NOTE

Whenever you include a *standard* header file in your program, you must specify the header file name within double angle brackets, like this: <*filename.h*>. When you write *your own* header files and place them in the working directory, you must specify the header file name within double quotes, like this: "*filename.h*".

Finally, you will write a separate application file. Let's call this file *myProg.cpp*. Here it is:

```
//myProg.cpp APPLICATION FILE

#include "rectangl.h" //FOR Rectangle CLASS
#include <iostream.h> //FOR cin AND cout
int main()
{
 //DEFINE OBJECTS
 Rectangle box1(2,3);          //box1 OBJECT DEF
 Rectangle box2(3,4);          //box2 OBJECT DEF
 Rectangle box3;               //box3 OBJECT DEF

 //DISPLAY LENGTH, WIDTH, PERIMETER, AND AREA OF BOX OBJECTS
 cout << "The length of box1 is:  " << box1.getLength() << endl;
 cout << "The width of box1 is:  " << box1.getWidth()<< endl;
 cout << "The perimeter of box1 is:  " << box1.perimeter()<< endl;
 cout << "The area of box1 is:  " << box1.area()<< endl << endl;
```

```
cout << "The length of box2 is:  " << box2.getLength()<< endl;
cout << "The width of box2 is:  " << box2.getWidth()<< endl;
cout << "The perimeter of box2 is:  " << box2.perimeter()<< endl;
cout << "The area of box2 is:  " << box2.area() << endl << endl;

cout << "The length of box3 is:  " << box3.getLength()<< endl;
cout << "The width of box3 is:  " << box3.getWidth()<< endl;
cout << "The perimeter of box3 is:  " << box3.perimeter()<< endl;
cout << "The area of box3 is:  " << box3.area()<< endl << endl;

//RETURN
return 0;
} //END main()
```

Here is where the objects are defined for the program. In addition, function *main()* appears here along with any other functions that are part of the application program. This file must also include the *rectangl.h* header file, because it won't compile unless the compiler knows the class declaration for which the objects are being defined.

Now we have three separate files: *rectangl.h*, *rectangl.cpp*, and *myProg.cpp*. At this point, you could compile the *rectangl.cpp* function implementation file to produce a *rectangl.obj* object file. Then, compile the *myProg.cpp* application file and link it with the *rectangl.obj* object file to produce an executable program called *myProg.exe*. This would require separate compiling and linking steps. However, there is an easier way using a project manager. Once a project file is open, you can add and delete files to and from the project. For this project, you will simply add the *rectangl.h* header file, the *myProg.cpp* application file and the *rectangl.cpp* implementation file. Figure 10.11 depicts the composition of our project file. (*Note:* Some compilers require you to add the header file to the project, like Microsoft's Visual C++, while other compilers do not have this requirement, like C++Builder by Borland/Inprise. In the later case, the project manager references the header file through its *#include* directives within the application and implementation files.)

Once the project is built, you simply compile the project file. When the project file is compiled, it will automatically perform the compiling and linking steps required to produce an executable file called *myProg.exe*. In addition, if there are any errors in any of the files that make up the project, the project manager will open the file in error for editing. Once the error is corrected, you can attempt to compile the project again from that point. Furthermore, at any time, you can edit and compile any of the component files independently of the project file.

After building a project, you can open the project at any time. When a given project is opened, the compiler will load the files that are part of that project so that they can be viewed and altered if necessary. When a project is recompiled, the project manager only compiles those files that have been changed, resulting in reduced compile time.

At this point, it might be a good idea to build, compile, and execute your own project for the *Rectangle* program, using your compiler's project manager.

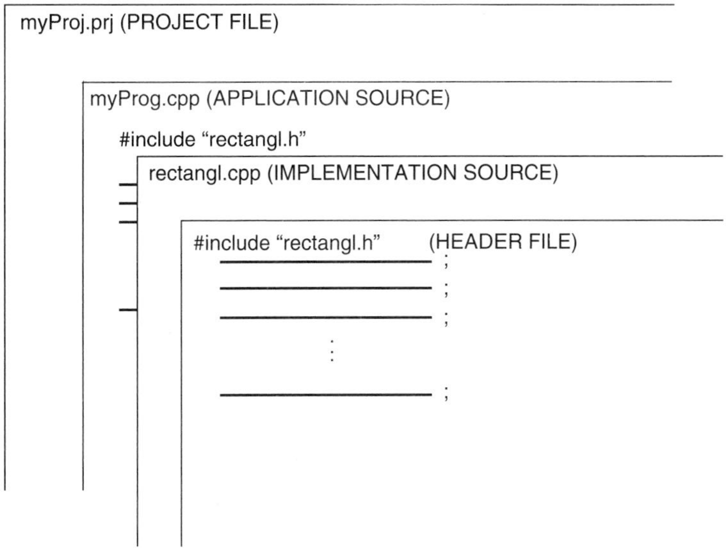

myProj.prj (PROJECT FILE)

myProg.cpp (APPLICATION SOURCE)

#include "rectangl.h"

rectangl.cpp (IMPLEMENTATION SOURCE)

#include "rectangl.h"   (HEADER FILE)
_____ ;
_____ ;
_____ ;

⋮

_____ ;

**FIGURE 10.11   A PROJECT FILE INCLUDES ALL THE
PROGRAM FILES NEEDED TO CREATE
AN EXECUTABLE APPLICATION FILE.**

Quick Check

1. State three reasons for using the multifile approach for developing software.
2. What file(s) in a C++ software project provide the interfaces to the class objects?
3. Why might a software manufacturer not supply you with the member function implementation source code?
4. A file that identifies the files that need to be compiled and linked to create an executable program is the _____ file.
5. When building a C++ project, which files must be referenced in the project manager using your compiler?

CHAPTER SUMMARY

Object-oriented programs are developed from the inside out by expanding on simple classes. The fundamental components of any object-oriented program are the class and its objects. At the abstract level, a class can be described as an interface, because it defines the behavior common to all of its objects. At the implementation level, a class is a programming construct that describes a set of data and related operations that are common to its objects. The abstract level provides an outside view of a class, whereas the implementation level provides the inside view of the class, disclosing its behavioral secrets. At the implementation level, a class is comprised of public and private members. The private class members are hidden from the outside, because they can only be accessed using the public member functions. This provides for information hiding within the class.

Encapsulation is the idea of packaging things together in a well-defined programming unit. A record or table in a database is encapsulated, because it consists of a collection of data members. A class in C++ is also encapsulated, because it consists of a collection of data members and related functions. However, a record does not provide information hiding, whereas a C++ class does provide information hiding through its private members.

An object is an instance, or specimen, of a class. Thus, an object of a given class has the structure and behavior defined by the class. The functions defined for a given class are called member functions. There are various types of member functions, including constructor functions and access functions. The member functions provide a means of communication with the object via messages. Messages are sent to an object by calling the member functions that perform a given task on the hidden object data. The object responds via the values returned by the member functions.

Object-oriented programs are normally constructed using a multifile approach. Class declarations are placed in separate header files. All the member function implementations for a given class are placed in a separate file that includes the class header file. Finally, the application program is placed in a separate file that includes all the class header files. The individual files are edited and compiled separately, then linked together to form an executable file. This facilitates a team approach to software development and makes such programs easier to maintain. Moreover, the user can be supplied the source code of the class header files and the object code of the function implementation files. This encourages reuse of the object-oriented code while protecting the implementation of that code from corruption by the user. Most C++ compilers include a project manager that facilitates the multifile approach to building programs.

Questions and Problems

Questions

1. Define the following OOP terms:

Class at the abstract level

Class at the implementation level

Encapsulation

Information hiding

Object

Instance

Member

Function implementation

Get function

Constructor

Access function

Utility function

Overloaded constructor

Message

2. What are the two major sections that make up a class declaration?

3. What is the scope of a private class member?

4. What is the scope of a public class member?

5. The concept of combining data with a set of operations that are dedicated to manipulating the data so tightly that outside operations cannot affect the data is called _____.

6. A computer window can be considered an object of a window class. What data and operations might be part of this object?

7. Where are function prototypes placed in an object-oriented program?

8. True or false: The abstract definition for a class provides the inside view of the class.

9. What is meant by the term "behavior" relative to a class object?

10. Why are classes *declared* and objects *defined*?

11. True or false: Utility functions are declared as **private** functions.

12. True or false: A class is an interface.

13. OOP provides an important feature called _____, which is a mechanism for deriving new classes from existing ones.

14. A member function that simply displays the values of class data members is called a _____ function.

15. What is the purpose of a constructor?

16. How do you provide default values for the private data members of a class?

17. Suppose that a member function called *foo()* is part of a class called *Student*. The prototype for the *foo()* function is

```
void foo();
```

a. Write a header line for the function implementation.

b. Write a statement to call the *foo()* function for the object *isaacNewton* of the *Student* class.

Use the following class declaration to answer questions 18–25:

```
class Student
{
public:
   Student(string nam = " ",      //CONSTRUCTOR
           string maj = " ",
           string num = " ",
           double gpa = 0.0);
   void setData();                //SET DATA FROM USER ENTRIES
   void getData();                //ACCESS STUDENT DATA
```

```
private:
  string name;                      //STUDENT NAME
  string major;                     //STUDENT MAJOR
  int studentNumber;                //STUDENT NUMBER
  double gpa;                       //STUDENT GPA
}; //END Student
```

18. What is the name of the constructor function?

19. Write a statement to define John Doe as a student object that will be initialized to the default values in the constructor.

20. Jane Doe (student #456) is a Computer Science major with a gpa of 3.58. Write a statement to define Jane Doe as a student object that will be initialized to the proper data values.

21. Write an implementation for the *Student()* function.

22. Write an implementation for the *setData()* function that will allow the user to enter the data values from the keyboard.

23. Write a statement that will allow the user to initialize the Jane Doe object from the keyboard.

24. Write an implementation for the *getData()* function, assuming that this function will display the student data.

25. Write a statement that will display the data in the John Doe student object.

26. True or false: A constructor may have default parameters.

27. Suppose that you have a class called *Circle*. What will be the corresponding constructor name?

28. When are constructors normally used in a C++ object-oriented program?

29. Given the following function implementation

```
Dogs :: Dogs(int legs)
{
  legs = legs;
} //END Dogs()
```

a. What special type of function is this?
b. What problem would the compiler encounter when attempting to compile this implementation?
c. Rewrite the implementation using the scoping operator to correct any problems.
d. Rewrite the implementation using the **this** pointer to correct any problems.

30. What operator is used to send a message to an object?

31. Explain why you should use a multi-file approach when developing C++ programs.

32. Suppose that you want to develop a commercial object-oriented program whereby you provide other programmers with the function interfaces while hiding their implementations. Explain how such a program would be organized and supplied to the programming community.

33. Explain the rules for recompiling and relinking when things are modified in a class header file or a function implementation file for a given application.

PROBLEMS

Least Difficult

1. Develop a class to store a person's name and address. The address should be divided into separate strings of street, city, state, and zip code. In addition, provision must be provided for the user to enter a given person's name and address as well as display a given person's data.

2. Write an application program that contains the class you developed in problem 1 and defines an object to test the class functions. Compile and execute your program.

3. Professional basketball has heard about C++ and they have hired you to write a program for their players' statistics. The program must store the player's name, team, total points scored, number of games played, average points per game, number of assists, number of rebounds, and average field goal percentage. In addition, provision must be provided for the user to enter a given player's stats as well as display a given player's stats. Develop the required program using classes and objects.

More Difficult

4. Ma and Pa were reading the latest issue of *Wired* and ran across an article on OOP. They were so excited that they contracted you to write an object-oriented payroll program. They want the program to include an *Employee* class to store the employee's name, hourly rate, and hours worked. The class is to have operations that perform the following tasks:

❐ An operation to initialize the hourly rate to a minimum wage of $6.00 per hour and the hours worked to 0 when an employee object is defined.

❐ An operation to obtain the employee's name, hourly rate, and hours worked from the user.

❐ An operation to return weekly pay, including overtime pay, where overtime is paid at a rate of time-and-a-half for any hours worked over 40.

❐ An operation to display all the employee information, including the employee's pay for a given week.

Declare the class as part of a header file called *employe.h*.

5. Write the implementations for the functions in problem 4 and place them in a file called *employe.cpp*.

6. Write an application program that defines an object for the class declared in problem 4 and tests the functions in problem 5. Place this program in a file called *pay.cpp*.

7. Build a project from the files created in problems 4 to 6. Compile, debug, and run the project file.

Use the multifile approach when writing your programs to solve the following problems.

8. Create an invoice class that contains all the information necessary to process one line of an invoice. Assume that the invoice must include the following data and functions:

Data:

Quantity Ordered

Quantity Shipped

Part number

Part Description

Unit Price

Extended Price (Quantity Ordered * Unit Price)

Sales Tax Rate

Sales Tax Amount

Shipping

Total

Functions:

❏ A function to initialize all the data items to 0, except the Sales Tax Rate, which should be initialized to 5%.

❏ A function to allow the user to initialize all the data items from the keyboard.

❏ A function to calculate the extended price of the item.

❏ A function to calculate the sales tax amount of the item.

❏ A function to calculate the total amount of the invoice.

❏ A function to display the invoice data with header information in a businesslike format.

Most Difficult

9. A stack ADT is ideal to implement using a class, because it must include the stack data elements as well as the functions that operate on those elements in a tightly bound manner. As a result, object-oriented programming is perfect for implementing stacks. Here is a declaration for a *Stack* class:

```
class Stack
{
public:
    Stack();                //CONSTRUCTOR INITIALIZES TOP TO -1
    void clearStack();      //CLEAR STACK BY SETTING TOP TO -1
    bool emptyStack();      //CHECKS FOR EMPTY STACK
    bool fullStack();       //CHECKS FOR FULL STACK
    void push(char c);      //PLACE ELEMENT ON TOP
    char pop();             //REMOVE ELEMENT FROM TOP

private:
    char data[SIZE];        //CHARACTER ARRAY TO HOLD THE STACK
    int top;                //top LOCATES TOP ELEMENT OF STACK
}; //END Stack
```

This stack can hold *SIZE* character elements as seen by the character array declaration within the class. An integer member called *top* is declared to access the top element of the stack. Thus, *top* provides the array index of the top element in the stack. The stack is empty when *top* is –1 and the stack is full when *top* is *SIZE* – 1. Write the stack function implementations according to the following criteria:

❏ *Stack()* is a constructor function that initializes *top* to –1.

❏ *clearStack()* sets *top* to –1.

❏ *emptyStack()* tests to see if *top* = –1.

❏ *fullStack()* tests to see if *top* = *SIZE* – 1 .

❏ *push()* checks to see if the stack is full by calling the *fullStack()* function. Then it must increment *top* and place a character element in the array at the index pointed to by *top*.

❏ *pop()* checks to see if the stack is empty by calling the *emptyStack()* function. If the stack is not empty, it returns the character element located at the array index pointed to by *top* and decrements *top*.

Write an application program to completely test your stack class.

10. Write a 12-hour clock program that declares a *Clock* class to store hours, minutes, seconds, A.M., and P.M. Provide functions to perform the following tasks:

❐ Set hours, minutes, seconds to 00:00:00 by default.

❐ Initialize hours, minutes, seconds, A.M., and P.M. from user entries.

❐ Allow the clock to tick by advancing the seconds by one and at the same time correcting the hours and minutes for a 12-hour clock value of A.M. or P.M.

❐ Display the time in hours:minutes:seconds A.M./P.M. format.

Write an application program that allows the user to set the clock and tick the clock at 1-second intervals while displaying the time.

SE104: THE OBJECT-ORIENTED PARADIGM USING UML

Objectives

When you are finished with this module, you should have a good understanding of the following:

- The basics of object-oriented analysis and design using the **Unified Modeling Language**, or **UML**.
- A brief history of the UML.
- Use-case modeling.
- Use-case diagrams.
- Use-case scenarios.
- Object identification using noun extraction.
- Object interaction diagrams.
- Class diagrams and corresponding UML notation.

INTRODUCTION

In the *SE103* module, you learned about the structured analysis and design performed by the *Foo.com* programmers on their billing system. In this module, you will learn about their object-oriented analysis/design. We should mention that we cannot do object-oriented analysis and design justice in just one short module. The intent here is to give you a "look and feel" for it using a simple example. Only the basic concepts and procedures employed by this paradigm will be covered here. You will need to take advanced courses in object-oriented analysis and design to become a competent software engineer.

We will implement the object-oriented analysis/design paradigm using the *Unified Modeling Language (UML)*. So, let's begin this module with an introduction to UML.

UNIFIED MODELING LANGUAGE, UML

The Unified Modeling Language, or UML, is *not* a computer language per se. The word "language" is used to mean a notation, or syntax. Furthermore, you see the word "modeling" in UML. This means that the UML is a *language*, or notation, for *modeling* systems. More specifically, the UML provides techniques to specify, visualize, construct, and document systems. The UML can be used for non-software business system modeling as well as software system modeling.

A Little History

The UML was developed at Rational Software Corporation when three pioneers of object-oriented engineering joined forces to "unify" their methods to produce an industry standard for object-oriented system modeling. These three pioneers are Grady Booch, Jim Rumbaugh, and Ivar Jacobson. Booch developed his *Booch Technique* at Rational, Rumbaugh developed his *Object Modeling Technique*, or *OMT*, at General Electric, while Jacobson developed his methodology, called *Object-Oriented Software Engineering*, or *OOSE*, at his Objectory company. All three methodologies were gaining popularity and, in fact, began evolving independently towards each other. So, it just made sense to combine their efforts to produce a common methodology that would become an industry standard. Rumbaugh joined Booch at Rational in 1994 and began to develop what they called the *Unified Methodology*, or *UM*. In 1995, Jacobson joined the effort to merge his OOSE method into UM. The resulting effort, named the UML, is widely becoming an industry standard for modeling object-oriented systems. You can get more information on the UML by going to the *UML Resource Center* within the Rational Web site at www.rational.com.

OBJECT-ORIENTED ANALYSIS, OOA

Remember from the *SE102* module how object-oriented analysis, or OOA, differs from structured analysis? Well, one of the goals of OOA is to identify the objects of the proposed system, thus addressing the software structure, or architecture, of the system early during the analysis phase, *before* the design phases. The structured paradigm does not address the software architecture until the design phase during functional decomposition. To identify the system objects, and thus perform the object-oriented analysis, you perform the following tasks:

- ❑ Develop *use-case* models of the system.
- ❑ Write *scenarios* for the use-cases.
- ❑ Extract the nouns from the use-case scenarios.
- ❑ Identify object candidates from the foregoing noun extraction.

Use-Case Modeling

A *use-case* model attempts to graphically depict the system users, called *actors*, and actions, called *use-cases*. It also defines the system boundaries. Remember from structured analysis, that the system boundaries were defined using a context diagram. So, to begin, the *Foo.com* programmers employed their billing system context diagram shown again in Figure 1.

From the context diagram, the programmers identified three actors: the customer, management, and the customer services system. An *actor* represents anything that must interact with the system. An actor can be a person, an organization,

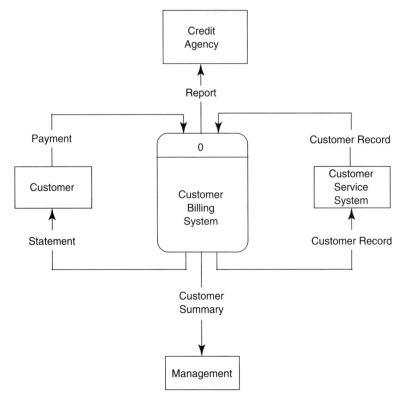

FIGURE 1   **THE CONTEXT DIAGRAM PRODUCED BY THE *FOO.COM* PROGRAMMERS FOR THEIR BILLING PROCESS.**

or another system. Actors usually initiate a system activity. Here, the customer actor is a person that initiates an activity by sending a payment to the system. The manangement actor represents an individual or organization that initiates an activity by making a request for a customer summary report. The customer service system actor is another system that interacts with the billing system by providing customer information.

An ***actor*** represents anything that must interact with the system. An actor can be a person, an organization, or another system.

Once the actors are identified from the context diagram, the engineer must attempt to define the actions, called ***use-cases***, performed by the system as the result of requests by the actors. A ***use-case*** represents a pattern of behavior exhibited by the system as the result of a dialogue between the system and an actor. The collection of all the system use-cases specifies all the ways in which to *use* the system.

A ***use-case*** represents a pattern of behavior exhibited by the system as the result of a dialogue between the system and an actor. The collection of all the system use-cases specifies all the ways in which to use the system.

Use-cases are created by examining the actors and defining everything a given actor can do with the system. The *Foo.com* programmers created two use-cases for their billing system: *make payment,* which is initiated by the customer actor and *request summary,* which is initiated by the management actor. No use-case was defined for the customer services actor, since its only purpose is to supply customer records to the system. The resulting ***use-case diagram*** is shown in Figure 2.

Here you see the UML symbols used for the actors, use-cases, and interaction. The actors are placed outside the system and the use-cases within the system, thus defining the system boundary. The lines between the actors and use-cases simply depict the actor interaction with one or more use-cases.

Use-Case Scenarios

Remember that each use-case represents a system behavior. Thus, the next task is to define this behavior via a ***use-case scenario***. A use-case scenario is simply the sequence of tasks that are performed for each use-case behavior.

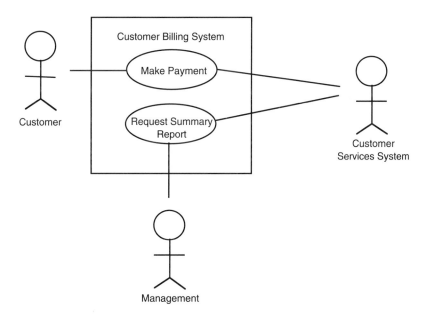

FIGURE 2   THE USE-CASE DIAGRAM PRODUCED BY THE *FOO.COM* PROGRAMMERS FOR THEIR BILLING PROCESS.

A *use-case scenario* is the sequence of tasks that are performed for a given use-case.

Here are the scenarios developed by the *Foo.com* programmers for their two use-cases.

Make Payment Scenario

1. Receive payment on customer account.
2. Customer record is read from customer services system.
3. Payment is subtracted from customer balance.
4. Customer interest is calculated and added to customer balance.
5. Payment is checked for late payment.
6. Payment is checked for less than minimum payment.
7. Customer balance is checked for $0.00 and minimum payment is calculated.
8. Customer statement is printed.

Request Summary Report Scenario

1. Receive summary report request from management.
2. Customer record is read from customer services system.
3. Customer balance is added to total balance for all customers.
4. Customer interest is added to total interest for all customers.
5. If payment was late, increment late payments.
6. If payment was less then minimum payment, increment low payments.
7. Summary report is printed.

Take a close look at each scenario so that you are familiar with each use-case behavior. The next step is to extract the nouns from the scenarios.

Noun Extraction

A noun is a word in a sentence which is a subject of a verb in the same sentence. Usually, a noun represents a person, place, or thing, but can also represent an action, such as *fishing*, a quality, such as *beauty*, or an idea, such as *love*. Nouns suggest potential objects within the system. All that needs to be done here is to underline the nouns in each use-case scenario, then compile a list of the nouns which where identified. Here are the use-cases again, showing the nouns underlined by the *Foo.com* programmers.

Make Payment Scenario

1. Receive payment on customer account.
2. Customer record is read from customer services system.
3. Payment is subtracted from customer balance.
4. Customer interest is calculated and added to customer balance.
5. Payment is checked for late payment.
6. Payment is checked for less than minimum payment.
7. Customer balance is checked for $0.00 and minimum payment is calculated.
8. Customer statement is printed.

Request Summary Report Scenario

1. Receive summary report request from management.
2. Customer record is read from customer services system.
3. Customer balance is added to total balance for all customers.
4. Customer interest is added to total interest for all customers.
5. If payment was late, increment late payments.
6. If payment was less than minimum payment, increment low payments.
7. Summary report is printed.

The nouns are then extracted and placed in noun extraction table which shows the potential system objects as follows:

NOUN EXTRACTION (POTENTIAL OBJECT LIST)

Customer account

Payment

Customer record

Customer services system

Customer balance

Customer interest

Late

Late payment

Minimum payment

Customer statement

Summary report

Management

Total balance

Total interest

Late payments

Low payments

Object Identification

The last step in the OOA is to identify object candidates from the noun extraction process. To accomplish object identification, you must eliminate any nouns that meet the following criteria:

- ❑ Synonyms (words of similar meaning).
- ❑ Nouns outside the system boundary.
- ❑ Abstract nouns that represent an action (*fishing*), a quality (*beauty*), or an idea (*love*).
- ❑ Nouns that are attributes of other higher-level object candidates.
- ❑ Nouns that are interface items, such as something coming from an actor.

Here is a table that the *Foo.com* programmers developed which lists all the nouns from the foregoing noun extraction table and shows which are potential object candidates and which are not, along with the reason why a given noun is not an object candidate:

Accept as Object ?	Potential Object	Reason for Not Accepting
✓	Customer account	
	Payment	Interface item
	Record	Part of file or database
	Customer services system	Outside boundary
	Customer balance	Attribute of customer account
	Customer interest	Attribute of customer account
	Late	Abstract noun
	Late payment	Attribute of customer account
	Minimum payment	Attribute of customer account
	Customer statement	Attribute of customer account
✓	Summary report	
	Management	Outside boundary
	Total balance	Attribute of summary report
	Total interest	Attribute of summary report
	Late payments	Attribute of summary report
	Low payments	Attribute of summary report

Notice that two object candidates have been identified: a customer account object and a summary report object. Do you understand why the other nouns are not object candidates from the reasons given? That's it! The potential system objects have been identified and the OOA is complete.

OBJECT-ORIENTED DESIGN, OOD

The purpose of the OOD is to determine how the new system is to satisfy the client's needs by the construction of object interaction and class diagrams, as well as other UML tools such as sequence and collaboration diagrams. In this module we will discuss two of these tasks, as follows:

❑ Construction of object interaction diagrams for the system objects identified in the OOA phase.

❑ Construction of class diagrams for each object identified in the OOA phase.

Object Interaction

Object interaction diagrams are used to show the ***relationships*** among the system objects. If two objects need to "talk" there must be a relationship between them. Object relationships are determined by examining the use-case diagram and scenarios developed in the OOA phase. The object interaction diagram developed by the *Foo.com* programmers for their billing system is shown in Figure 3.

Here, you see both objects represented by rectangles. The divisions within each object rectangle, called ***compartments***, will become apparent when you see the class diagrams shortly. With UML, a bi-directional line between two objects represents a relationship. The relationship shown in Figure 3 is called an ***association***, because it represents a pathway of communication between two objects. The association in Figure 3 is labeled to show how many objects on each side of the association participate in the relationship. This is called ***multiplicity***. Each end of the association is labeled. In our billing system the *SummaryReport* object end of the association is labeled with a **1**, while the *CustomerAccount* end of the association is labeled with a **1..***. This means that one (1) *SummaryReport* object will communicate with one or more (**1..***) *CustomerAccount* objects. Thus, a *SummaryReport* object must interact with one or more *CustomerAccount* objects to prepare its report. There are other possible association labels, such as ***roles*** and ***aggregations***. These are beyond the scope of both our simple billing system example and this book.

Another type of relationship is an ***inheritance*** relationship which shows how one object shares the structure and behavior of another object. You will see this relationship in a later chapter.

Once the interaction diagram is complete, it is time to construct the class diagrams.

Class Diagrams

Remember that a class provides a model for its objects. It defines the attributes and behavior common to all of this objects. A class diagram shows both the private data members which provide the attributes of the class and function members which provide the class behavior. Thus, using UML, a class diagram consists of two compartments, one for the private data members, and one for the function members.

FIGURE 3   THE OBJECT INTERACTION DIAGRAM PRODUCED BY THE *FOO.COM* PROGRAMMERS FOR THEIR BILLING PROCESS.

Here are the UML class diagrams developed by the *Foo.com* programmers for their billing system:

```
┌─────────────────────────────────────────┐
│            CustomerAccount                │
├─────────────────────────────────────────┤
│ -accountNumber:string                     │
│ -balance:double                           │
│ -interest:double                          │
│ -minPayment:double                        │
│ -latePayment:bool                         │
│ -lessThanMin:bool                         │
├─────────────────────────────────────────┤
│ +setCustData()                            │
│ +subtractPayment(in payment:             │
│                       double)             │
│ +addInterest()                            │
│ +checkLatePayment()                       │
│ +checkMinPayment()                        │
│ +calculateMinPayment()                    │
│ +getInterest():double                     │
│ +getBalance():double                      │
│ +getLatePayment():bool                    │
│ +getLessThanMin():bool                    │
│ +printStatement()                         │
└─────────────────────────────────────────┘
```

```
┌─────────────────────────────────────────┐
│             SummaryReport                 │
├─────────────────────────────────────────┤
│ -accountNumber:string                     │
│ -totalBalance:double                      │
│ -totalInterest:double                     │
│ -latePayments:int                         │
│ -lowPayments:int                          │
├─────────────────────────────────────────┤
│ +addTotalBalance()                        │
│ +addTotalInterest()                       │
│ +checkLatePayment()                       │
│ +checkLowPayment()                        │
│ +printReport()                            │
└─────────────────────────────────────────┘
```

First, notice that the data members are placed in the first compartment of the class, while the function members are placed in the second compartment. Next, notice that each member is labeled with a minus (–) or a plus (+) symbol. A minus symbol is used to denote a private member, while a plus symbol is used to denote a public class member. Notice that all the data members are private, while all the function members are public in these classes.

Looking at the data members in the first compartment, you see the member name, followed by a colon, followed by the data type or class of the data value. Looking at the function members in the second compartment, you find the function name, followed by a parameter listing. If parameters are required, they are listed as *in*, *out*, or *inout*. followed by the parameter name, followed by a colon, followed by the data type or class of the parameter value. For instance, in the *subtractPayment()* function you see a single parameter specified as *in payment : double*. This means that the function will accept (*in*) a parameter whose name is *payment* and is a *double* floating-point value. A specification of *out* would signify that the parameter is being returned by the function. A specification *inout* would signify that the parameter is being accepted and returned by the function as in the case of a reference parameter. The default label is *in* if none is specified.

If the function is a non-void function, a colon follows the parameter listing, followed by the return data type, as in the *getInterest()* and *getBalance()* functions shown.

That completes the object-oriented analysis and design performed by the *Foo.com* programmers for their billing system. The only thing they now have to do is to write individual algorithms for the class functions and code the classes and the application program. However, they must still study more about object-oriented software engineering, because there is much more to learn. A more complex problem would have required a more in-depth analysis and design, employing **collaboration diagrams** and **sequence diagrams** as well as other activities. You and they have just been exposed to "the tip of the iceberg" with this simple example.

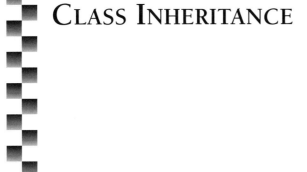

CLASS INHERITANCE

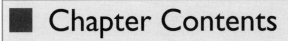

Chapter Contents

Chapter Objectives

When you are finished with this chapter, you should have a good understanding of the following:

- The concepts of inheritance, polymorphism, and dynamic binding.
- Why inheritance is important to object-oriented programming.
- Class hierarchies and families.
- How to build class families within C++ header files.
- The IS-A relationship between a derived class and its base class.
- The difference between a private, protected, and public class member.
- How to use a Venn diagram to represent a class family.
- The difference between static and dynamic binding.
- The difference between overloaded functions and virtual functions.

INTRODUCTION

One of the most important properties of object-oriented programming is ***inheritance***. In fact, some believe that a program that doesn't employ inheritance is not an object-oriented program.

Inheritance is that property of object-oriented programming that allows one class, called a **derived class,** to share the structure and behavior of another class, called a **base class.**

The natural world is full of inheritance. All living things inherit the characteristics, or traits, of their ancestors. Although you are different in many ways from your parents, you are also the same in many ways because of the genetic traits that you have inherited from them. In object-oriented programming, inheritance allows newly created classes to inherit members from existing classes. These new ***derived,*** or ***child,*** classes will include their own members and members inherited from the ***base***, or ***parent,*** class. So, you can view a collection of classes with common inherited members as a ***family*** of classes, just like the family that you belong to. Classes are related to each other through inheritance. Such inheritance creates a class hierarchy.

In this chapter, we will first explain why inheritance is important and then illustrate its use via a practical example. Finally, we will discuss two more important aspects of OOP: ***polymorphism*** and ***dynamic binding.***

11.1 WHY USE INHERITANCE?

One reason to use inheritance is that it allows you to reuse the code from a previous programming project without starting from scratch to reinvent the code. Many times the code developed for one program can be reused in another program. Although the new program might be slightly different from the old, inheritance allows you to build on what was done previously. Why reinvent the wheel?

Another reason for using inheritance is that it allows you to build a ***hierarchy*** among classes. The classes that include those things that are most commonly inherited are at the top of the hierarchy, just as your ancestors are at the top of your genetic family hierarchy. Take a banking situation, for example. A general bank account class is used to define variables, such as an account number and account balance, and member functions, such as deposit, that are common to all bank accounts. Then, classes that define different types of bank accounts, such as checking and savings, can all be derived from the bank account ***base*** class. This way, they will inherit the account number and balance members as well as the deposit function of the general bank account class. Although the derived classes may have their own unique members, they all include the bank account base class as part of their structure. Thus, a general bank account class would be at the top of a banking class

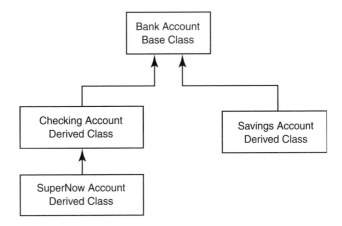

hierarchy. This idea is illustrated by the UML hierarchy diagram in Figure 11.1. The arrows point from the derived class to the base class.

Be aware that some object-oriented languages, like Java, refer to a base class as a *superclass* and a derived class as a *subclass.*

In fact, the left side of the hierarchy diagram in Figure 11.1 shows two levels of inheritance. The *BankAccount* class is inherited by both the *Checking* class and the *Savings* class. In addition, the *Checking* class is inherited by the *SuperNow* class, since this is a special type of checking account that accrues interest. Notice that the *SuperNow* class inherits the *BankAccount* class indirectly through the *Checking* class. A family of classes related like this is referred to as a ***class hierarchy***.

PROGRAMMING TIP

The important link between a derived class and its base class is the IS-A link. The IS-A relationship must exist if inheritance is used properly. For instance, a checking account IS-A bank account. A super-now account IS-A checking account. However, a savings account IS **NOT** A checking account; it IS-A banking account. Thus, a savings account should *not* be derived from a checking account, but a more general bank account class. Always consider the IS-A link when creating inheritance. If there is no IS-A relationship, inheritance should not be used.

Quick Check

1. A parent class is called a _____ class in C++.
2. A child class is called a _____ class in C++.
3. A collection of classes with common inherited members is called a _____.
4. List at least two reasons for using inheritance.
5. True or false: The proper use of inheritance would allow a line class to be derived from a point class.
6. True or false: The proper use of inheritance would allow a pixel class to be derived from a point class.
7. True or false: The proper use of inheritance would allow a pickup truck class to be derived from a truck class.

11.2 DECLARING AND USING DERIVED CLASSES

A derived class is declared using the following format:

> ### FORMAT FOR DECLARING DERIVED CLASSES
>
> **class** *derived class* **: public** *base class*
> {
> *Derived Class Member Functions*
>
> *Derived Class Member Data*
> }; //END CLASS

Let's illustrate inheritance via the classes of bank accounts shown in Figure 11.1. Look at the figure again. You see that the *Checking* and *Savings* classes are derived from the *BankAccount* base class, and the *SuperNow* class is derived from the *Checking* class. Here is how we will set up the various account classes:

BankAccount Class

The *BankAccount* class is at the top of the hierarchy diagram and, therefore, will be the base class for the entire family. It will contain member data and functions that are common to all types of bank accounts. The structure of this class will be as follows:

❑ *Function Members*
  ❑   A function to make deposits.

❐ A function to access the account number.

❐ A function to access the account balance.

❐ *Data Members*

    ❐ An account number.

    ❐ An account balance.

Checking Account Class

The *Checking* account class will inherit the *BankAccount* class members. In addition, it will contain the following members:

❐ *Function Members*

    ❐ A constructor function to initialize the *Checking* account data members.

    ❐ A function that will cash a check by receiving a check amount and debit the account balance accordingly.

❐ *Data Members*

    ❐ A minimum balance value that will dictate when a per-check charge is to be made.

    ❐ A value that will be charged on each check cashed when the account balance is less than the minimum required balance.

SuperNow Checking Account Class

A super-now acount is simply an interest-bearing checking account. As a result, this class will inherit the *Checking* account class members and, therefore, will also inherit the *BankAccount* class members. In addition, the *SuperNow* account class will contain the following members:

❐ *Function Members*

    ❐ A constructor function to initialize the *SuperNow* checking account data members.

    ❐ A function that will credit interest to the account if the balance is above the required minimum.

❐ *Data Members*

    ❐ An annual interest rate value that is credited to the account balance on a monthly basis, if the account balance remains above a minimum required level.

Savings Account Class

The *Savings* account class is derived from the original *BankAccount* base class. In addition to the *BankAccount* class members, the *Savings* account class will contain the following:

❐ *Function Members*

    ❐ A constructor function to initialize the *Savings* account data members.

❑ A function that will credit interest to the account.

❑ A function that will debit the account for a withdrawal.

❑ *Data Members*

❑ An annual interest rate value that is credited to the account balance on a monthly basis.

Now, we begin our program construction by developing the UML *BankAccount* class diagram shown in Figure 11.2.

The data members of the class are *acctNum* and *balance*. Notice that they are designated as ***protected members*** by the leading # symbol.

A ***protected member*** of a class is a member that is accessible to both the base class and any derived classes of the base class in which it is declared. Thus, a protected member of a base class is accessible to any descendent class within the class family, but not accessible to things outside the class family.

You could say that a protected member of a base class has accessibility that is somewhere between that of a private member and a public member. If a member is a private member of a base class, it is *not* accessible to a derived class. However, a protected member of a base class is accessible to any derived classes. On the other hand, a protected member is "protected" from being accessed outside of the class family, thereby preserving information hiding within the family.

The three public functions are *deposit()*, *getAcctNum()*, and *getBalance()*. The *deposit()* function will be used to make a deposit to the account. The *getAcctNum()* and *getBalance()* functions are access functions that are used to retrieve the account number and balance, respectively. You might be wondering why there is no

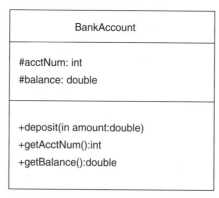

FIGURE 11.2 THE UML CLASS DIAGRAM FOR THE *BANKACCOUNT* BASE CLASS.

constructor function to initialize the data members of the class. Well, when inheritance is used properly, there are no objects created for the base class. When no objects are created for a class, the class is called an ***abstract class.*** An abstract class never needs a constructor, because there will be no objects created for it. Only the derived classes will have objects, and the constructors will be placed in each of the derived classes. These constructors will be used to initialize the data members inherited from the base class. You will see how this works shortly.

> An ***abstract class*** is a base class for which objects will never be created

The class declaration is now easily coded from the UML diagram, as follows:

```
//BANK ACCOUNT HEADER FILE (account.h)

#ifndef ACCOUNT_H
#define ACCOUNT_H

//BANK ACCOUNT BASE CLASS DECLARATION
class BankAccount
{
public:
    void deposit(double amount); //ADD DEPOSIT
    int getAcctNum();            //RETURN ACCOUNT NUMBER
    double getBalance();         //RETURN ACCOUNT BALANCE

protected:
    int acctNum;                 //ACCOUNT NUMBER
    double balance;              //ACCOUNT BALANCE
}; //END BankAccount
#endif
```

Here, you see that the class declaration is provided in a header file called *account.h.* Next, you see three preprocessor directives: *#ifndef* and *#define* at the beginning of the file and *#endif* at the end of the file. These directives are required because this header file will be included in several additional files. The specific purpose of these directives will be discussed shortly. Looking at the *BankAccount* class declaration, you see that it contains the three function members and two data members shown in its UML diagram. Finally, notice that the *acctNum* and *balance* data members are declared as protected members using the keyword **protected.**

Next, we develop an implementation file, called *account.cpp,* for the base class, as follows:

```
//ACCOUNT IMPLEMENTATION FILE (account.cpp)

#include "account.h"   //FOR BankAccount CLASS
```

```
//IMPLEMENTATION FOR deposit() FUNCTION
void BankAccount :: deposit(double amount)
{
 balance += amount;
} //END deposit()


//IMPLEMENTATION FOR getAcctNum() FUNCTION
int BankAccount :: getAcctNum()
{
 return  acctNum;
} //END getAcctNum()


//IMPLEMENTATION FOR getBalance() FUNCTION
double BankAccount :: getBalance()
{
 return  balance;
} //END getBalance()
```

The function implementations shown in this file should be self-explanatory.

Now, let's declare our first derived class. This class, called *Checking,* will be derived from the *BankAccount* class. The UML diagram in Figure 11.3 describes the class. Here you see two protected data members, *minimum* and *charge,* as well as two public functions, the *Checking()* constructor function and the *cashCheck()* function.

The UML class diagram leads to the C++ code, as follows:

```
//CHECKING ACCOUNT HEADER FILE (checking.h)

#ifndef CHECKING_H
#define CHECKING_H

#include "account.h"    //FOR BankAccount CLASS
```

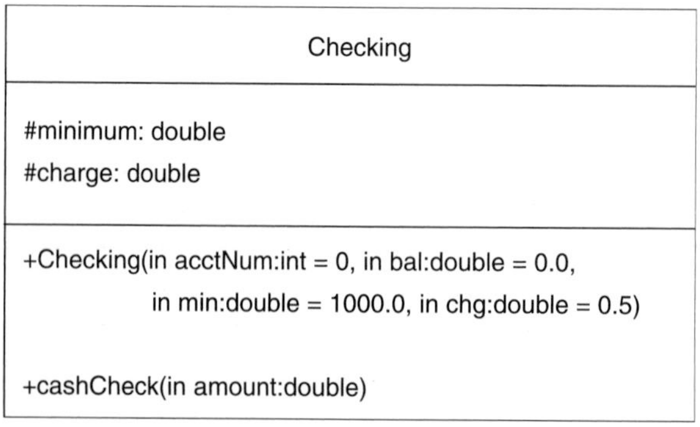

Checking
#minimum: double #charge: double
+Checking(in acctNum:int = 0, in bal:double = 0.0,   in min:double = 1000.0, in chg:double = 0.5) +cashCheck(in amount:double)

FIGURE 11.3   THE UML CLASS DIAGRAM FOR THE *CHECKING* DERIVED CLASS.

```
//CHECKING ACCOUNT DERIVED CLASS DECLARATION
class Checking:public BankAccount
{
public:
  Checking(int acctNum = 0000,
              double bal = 0.0,        //CONSTRUCTOR
              double min = 1000.0,
              double chg = 0.5);
  void cashCheck(double amt);          //CASH A CHECK

protected:
  double minimum;                      //MINIMUM BALANCE TO
                                       //AVOID CHECK CHARGE
  double charge;                       //PER-CHECK CHARGE
}; //END Checking
#endif
```

Again, the *Checking* class declaration is coded as a header file. The header file name is *checking.h*. Looking at the class declaration, you see that the *Checking* class is derived from the *BankAccount* class. This is indicated by the colon between the derived class (*Checking*) and the base class (*BankAccount*) in the class declaration. The base class header file (*account.h*) must be included in this file to make the declaration. Furthermore, notice the use of the keyword **public** prior to the base class name. This designation makes the *BankAccount* class a public base class to the derived *Checking* class.

> A **public base class** allows all public members of the base class to be public in the derived class.

When a base class is designated as **public** in the derived class declaration, the inherited members of the public base class maintain their access level in the derived class. Thus, the inherited protected members remain protected, and the inherited public members remain public in the derived class. In our example, the public members of the *BankAccount* class are the *deposit()*, *getAcctNum()*, and *getBalance()* functions. The use of the keyword **public** prior to the base class name, *BankAccount*, in the derived *Checking* class declaration makes all of these functions public to the *Checking* class just as if they were declared as part of the public section of the *Checking* class. Without the use of the keyword **public,** the public functions of the *BankAccount* class would *not* be accessible to any program using an object of the *Checking* class. In other words, without the base class being public, an application program could not call any of the base class functions via a derived class object.

For example, suppose an application program defines an object called *JohnDoe* for the *Checking* derived class, like this:

```
Checking JohnDoe;
```

If the *BankAccount* base class is not made public, then a message to its *getBalance()* function via the *JohnDoe* object would cause a compiler error. Thus, the statement

```
JohnDoe.getBalance();
```

would not compile, because *getBalance()* is not public for *Checking*.

Now, back to the *Checking* class declaration. Two member functions are declared for the *Checking* class: *Checking()* and *cashCheck()*. The *Checking()* function is a constructor that is used to initialize all four data members of the class. (Why does this class have four data members, when only two are shown in the foregoing declaration?) Notice that each data member has a default value. The *cashCheck()* function is used to debit the account balance by cashing a check.

You see that the *Checking* class has two protected members, *minimum* and *charge*. The *minimum* data member will be used to store a minimum balance value, whereby no per-check charge is made if the account balance is above the stored minimum value. The *charge* data member will be used to store a per-check charge for writing checks if the account balance is less than *minimum*. Notice that both *minimum* and *charge* are designated as protected members, because they will be inherited by the *SuperNow* class (see Figure 11.1).

Of course, because *Checking* is derived from *BankAccount*, the protected *BankAccount* class members, *acctNum* and *balance*, are inherited by the *Checking* class. Thus, *Checking* actually has four data members, *acctNum* and *balance*, which are inherited from *BankAccount*, as well as *minimum* and *charge*, which are declared in *Checking*.

PROGRAMMING TIP

You will avoid confusion about when to use the keywords **private, protected,** and **public** relative to inheritance if you remember the following points:

- Use the keyword **private** when declaring a member of a class if you *do not* want the member of the class to be inherited by another class. A **private** class member is only accessible by **public** functions of the *same* class.

- Use the keyword **protected** when declaring a member of a class if you want to allow access to the member by a derived class. A protected member will be accessible within all descendent classes of the class in which it is declared but not outside of its descendent classes.

- Use the keyword **public** when declaring a *member* if you want the member to be accessible anywhere the class is visible. Of course, data members should never be declared **public;** otherwise, the whole purpose of information hiding is defeated.

- Use the keyword **public** when declaring a *derived class* if you want the public members of the base class to be public for the derived class.

The **private, protected,** and **public** options are provided in C++ to provide flexibility during inheritance. With the proper use of these options, you can specify precisely which class members are to be inherited by other classes. If you *do not* want a member of a class inherited, declare it as **private.** If you *do* want a member of a class inherited, declare it as **protected** or **public.**

Next, we need to construct an implementation file for the *Checking* class. Let's call the file *checking.cpp*. Here it is:

```
//CHECKING IMPLEMENTATION FILE (checking.cpp)
#include "checking.h" //FOR Checking CLASS
#include <iostream.h> //FOR cout

//IMPLEMENTATION FOR Checking() CONSTRUCTOR
Checking :: Checking (int num, double bal, double min, double chg)
{
 acctNum = num;
 balance = bal;
 minimum = min;
 charge = chg;
} //END Checking()

//IMPLEMENTATION FOR cashCheck() FUNCTION
void Checking :: cashCheck (double amt)
{
 if (amt > balance)                      //TEST FOR OVERDRAW
   cout << "Cannot cash check, account overdrawn." << endl;
 else                                    //CASH CHECK
   if (balance < minimum)                //DEBIT BALANCE WITH
       balance -= amt + charge;          //CHECK AMOUNT AND CHARGE
   else                                  //DEBIT BALANCE WITH
       balance -= amt;                   //CHECK AMOUNT
} //END cashCheck()
```

As you can see, the *Checking()* constructor function sets the values of *acctNum*, *balance*, *minimum*, and *charge* from values received by the function when an object is defined for the class. Recall that a class constructor is automatically called when an object is defined for the class. Of course, if values are not provided in the object definition, the data members are initialized to their respective default values. The *cashCheck()* function receives an amount (*amt*) from the calling object and generates an error message if this amount exceeds the account balance. Otherwise, the check is cashed, and the account balance is debited accordingly. Notice that a check-cashing charge is applied if the amount of the check is less than the required minimum balance.

Looking back at Figure 11.1, you see that a *SuperNow* class is derived from the *Checking* class. A super-now account is one where you get interest on your checking account if you maintain a minimum balance. In addition, no per-check charge is made if the balance stays above the minimum. This is a perfect place to declare a derived class of the *Checking* class, because the *SuperNow* class can inherit the *minimum* and *charge* data members as well as the *cashCheck()* function of the *Checking* class. The UML diagram in Figure 11.4 describes this class.

So, let's develop a header file for the *SuperNow* class from the UML diagram and call it *supernow.h*. Here's one that will work:

```
//SUPER-NOW ACCOUNT HEADER FILE (supernow.h)
#include "checking.h" //FOR Checking CLASS
```

SuperNow
−interestRate: double

+SuperNow(in acctNum:int = 0, in bal:double = 0.0,
        in min:double = 1000.0, in chg:double = 0.5,
        in rate:double 12.0)
 	
+addInterest()

FIGURE 11.4 **THE UML CLASS DIAGRAM FOR THE *SUPERNOW* DERIVED CLASS.**

```
//SUPER-NOW ACCOUNT DERIVED CLASS DECLARATION
class  SuperNow:public Checking
{
public:
 SuperNow(int acctNum = 0,
          double bal = 0.0,      //CONSTRUCTOR
          double min = 5000.0,
          double chg = 0.5,
          double rate = 12.0);
 void addInterest();            //ADD INTEREST TO BALANCE

private:
 double interestRate;           //ANNUAL INTEREST RATE
}; //END SuperNow
```

First, you see that the *checking.h* header file is included, because the *SuperNow* class is derived from this class. The *SuperNow* class declaration uses the keyword **public** so that the public functions of *Checking* are inherited by *SuperNow*. There are two additional functions declared for this class: the *SuperNow()* constructor function, which initializes the data members of the class; and the *addInterest()* function, which will credit the account balance with interest at a rate specified by the *interestRate* data member.

The only data member unique to this class is *interestRate*, which specifies the annual interest rate to be applied to the account. However, through inheritance, there are four additional data members. What are they? *acctNum* and *balance* are inherited from the *BankAccount* class via the *Checking* class, and *minimum* and *charge* are inherited directly from the *Checking* class. Here is the implementation file for the class:

```
//SUPER-NOW IMPLEMENTATION FILE (supernow.cpp)

#include "supernow.h" //FOR SuperNow CLASS
```

```
//IMPLEMENTATION FOR SUPER-NOW CONSTRUCTOR
SuperNow :: SuperNow (int num,
                      double bal,
                      double min,
                      double chg,
                      double rate)
{
 acctNum = num;
 balance = bal;
 minimum = min;
 charge = chg;
 interestRate = rate;
} //END SuperNow()

//IMPLEMENTATION FOR addInterest() FUNCTION
void SuperNow :: addInterest()
{
 double interest;
 if (balance >= minimum)
 {
   interest = balance * (interestRate/12/100);
   balance += interest;
 } //END IF
} //END addInterest()
```

The file is called *supernow.cpp*. As you can see, the *SuperNow()* constructor function initializes all class data members. The *addInterest()* function adds monthly interest to the account if the account balance is greater than or equal to the minimum required balance.

The last class that we need to declare is the *Savings* account class. The UML diagram in Figure 11.5 describes this class.

The header file for the *Savings* class will be called *savings.h* and coded from the UML diagram, as follows

```
//SAVINGS ACCOUNT HEADER FILE (savings.h)
#include "account.h" //FOR BankAccount CLASS

//SAVINGS ACCOUNT DERIVED CLASS DECLARATION
class Savings: public BankAccount
{

public:
  Savings( int acctNum = 0,
           double bal = 0.0,      //CONSTRUCTOR
           double rate = 12.0);
  void addInterest();             //ADD INTEREST TO BALANCE
  void withdraw(double amt);      //SUBTRACT WITHDRAWAL

private:
 double interestRate;            //ANNUAL INTEREST RATE
}; //END Savings
```

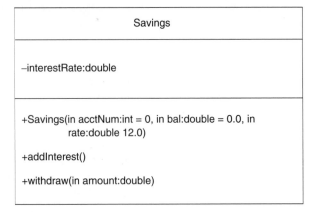

FIGURE 11.5 **THE UML CLASS DIAGRAM FOR THE *SAVINGS* DERIVED CLASS.**

There are three additional functions defined for the *Savings* class. The *Savings()* constructor function is used to initialize the class data members. The *addInterest()* function is used to credit the account balance with monthly interest earnings. The *withdraw()* function is used to debit the account balance when a savings withdrawal is made. Moreover, because the *Savings* class is derived from the *BankAccount* class, it inherits the *deposit()* function.

The *Savings* class also inherits the *acctNum* and *balance* data members from the *BankAccount* class. In addition, an *interestRate* data member is defined for this class. The *interestRate* data member will store an annual savings account interest rate value.

Here is the associated implementation file:

```
//SAVINGS IMPLEMENTATION FILE (savings.cpp)
#include "savings.h" //FOR Savings CLASS

//IMPLEMENTATION FOR Savings() CONSTRUCTOR
Savings :: Savings(int num, double bal, double rate)
{
 acctNum = num;
 balance = bal;
 interestRate = rate;
} //END Savings()

//IMPLEMENTATION FOR withdraw() FUNCTION
void Savings :: withdraw(double amt)
{
 balance -= amt;
} //END withdraw()

//IMPLEMENTATION FOR addInterest() FUNCTION
void Savings :: addInterest()
{
```

```
    double interest;
    interest = balance * (interestRate/12/100);
    balance += interest;
}  //END addInterest()
```

The function implementations should be self-explanatory by now. Notice, however, that this *addInterest()* function differs from the *addInterest()* function in the *SuperNow* class. The *Savings* class *addInterest()* function does not depend on a minimum balance, whereas the *SuperNow* class *addInterest()* function does.

We can use the **Venn diagram** shown in Figure 11.6 to summarize the bank account class family. Notice how the class inheritance patterns can be seen by the intersections between the classes. You might have studied Venn diagrams in an algebra course and wondered what practical application they had. Now, you can tell your math professor you have found a "real world" application for a Venn diagram.

Finally, we need an application file to exercise our class family. Here is one that will demonstrate most of the family features:

```
//BANKING APPLICATION FILE (banking.cpp)

//PREPROCESSOR DIRECTIVES
#include "account.h"    //FOR BankAccount CLASS
#include "checking.h"   //FOR Checking CLASS
#include "supernow.h"   //FOR SuperNow CLASS
#include "savings.h"    //FOR Savings CLASS
#include <iostream.h>   //FOR cin AND cout

//MAIN FUNCTION
int main()
{
   //DEFINE BANKING ACCOUNT OBJECTS
   Checking BjarneStroustrup1(0001);
   SuperNow JohnMcCarthy1(0002);
```

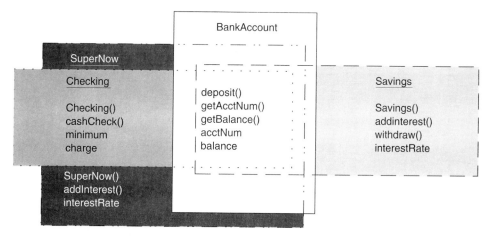

FIGURE 11.6   A VENN DIAGRAM OF THE BANK ACCOUNT CLASS FAMILY.

```
    Savings GraceHopper1(0003);
    Checking GraceHopper2(0004);

    //MONTHLY CHECKING ACCOUNT TRANSACTIONS
    BjarneStroustrup1.deposit(1500);
    BjarneStroustrup1.cashCheck (500.00);
    BjarneStroustrup1.cashCheck (500.00);
    BjarneStroustrup1.cashCheck (700.75);
    BjarneStroustrup1.cashCheck (200.00);
    GraceHopper2.deposit(2500);
    GraceHopper2.cashCheck(25.75);
    GraceHopper2.cashCheck(75.25);

    //MONTHLY SUPER-NOW ACCOUNT TRANSACTIONS
    JohnMcCarthy1.deposit(2000.00);
    JohnMcCarthy1.cashCheck(200.00);

    //MONTHLY SAVINGS ACCOUNT TRANSACTIONS
    GraceHopper1.deposit(2000.00);
    GraceHopper1.withdraw(350);

    //MONTHLY REPORT OF ACCOUNT BALANCES
    cout.setf(ios::fixed | ios::showpoint);
    cout.precision(2);
    JohnMcCarthy1.addInterest();
    GraceHopper1.addInterest();
    cout << "\t\t\tAccount balances" << endl << endl;
    cout << "Account Number:   "
         << BjarneStroustrup1.getAcctNum()
         << "\tBjarne Stroustrup:   $"
         << BjarneStroustrup1.getBalance() << endl;

    cout << "Account Number:   "
         << JohnMcCarthy1.getAcctNum()
         << "\tJohn McCarthy:   $"
         << JohnMcCarthy1.getBalance() << endl;

    cout << "Account Number:   "
         << GraceHopper1.getAcctNum()
         << "\tGraceHopper:   $"
         << GraceHopper1.getBalance() << endl;
    cout << "Account Number:   "
         << GraceHopper2.getAcctNum()
         << "\tGraceHopper:   $"
         << GraceHopper2.getBalance() << endl;

    //RETURN
    return 0;
} //END main()
```

The application file is called *banking.cpp* and begins by including all of the class header files. The class header files must be included because the respective class objects are defined in this application file. Looking at function *main()* within the file, you see that several objects are defined for the various banking account classes. The object name corresponds to the customer name. A suffix is added to the customer name so that the same customer can have more than one bank account. For instance, you see that *GraceHopper1* is a checking account object, and *GraceHopper2* is a savings account object. Notice also that a unique account number is specified when each object is defined. As a result, the customer account number in the base class is initialized with this value. All other data members will take on their respective default values, because only the account number value is specified during the object definition.

Next, monthly transactions are listed for each type of account. Can you determine what should happen in each transaction? Finally, a monthly balance report of each account is generated on the display monitor. What will be the balance for each account at the end of the month, using the indicated transactions in the order that they appear?

A project file is needed to efficiently develop such a program in C++. For this program, the project file would reference all the *.h* header files, all the *.cpp* implementation files and the *.cpp* application file.

Single Versus Multiple Inheritance

Up to this point, we have been dealing with single inheritance. Actually, two types of inheritance are possible: ***single inheritance*** and ***multiple inheritance.*** Single inheritance occurs when the inherited class members can be traced back to a single parent class. The type of inheritance depicted back in Figure 11.1 is single inheritance. Multiple inheritance occurs when the inherited class members can be traced back to more than one parent class. As an example of multiple inheritance, consider the *iostream.h* header file that you have been including in your programs to use the *cout* and *cin* objects. The *iostream.h* header file declares the *iostream* class. This class is derived from two parent classes: *istream* and *ostream*. The *istream* class provides the members necessary for formatted input, and the *ostream* class provides the members necessary for formatted output.

As a result of multiple inheritance, the *iostream* class inherits both the required input and output members. In addition, the *istream* and *ostream* classes are derived from a single class called *ios*. The *ios* base class provides file operations common to both input and output and maintains internal flags used by *istream* and *ostream*. Single inheritance allows both *istream* and *ostream* to inherit these common members. The UML diagram in Figure 11.7 illustrates the *ios* family hierarchy. Here, we have single inheritance from *ios* to *istream/ostream* and multiple inheritance from *istream/ostream* to *iostream*.

Using *#ifndef* : An Implementation Detail

To close this section, we need to discuss the *#ifndef* preprocessor directive as promised earlier. You observed the use of this directive along with the *#define* and *#endif* directives in the *BankAccount* and *Checking* class declarations. These

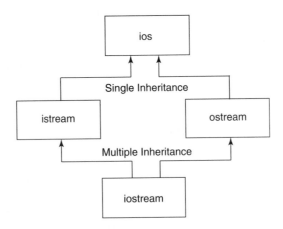

FIGURE 11.7 SINGLE INHERITANCE EXISTS BETWEEN THE *IOS* CLASS AND THE *ISTREAM*/*OSTREAM* CLASSES. MULTIPLE INHERITANCE OCCURS BETWEEN THE *ISTREAM*/*OSTREAM* CLASSES AND THE *IOSTREAM* CLASS.

classes are base classes, so they need to be included as header files in more than one file. For example, *account.h* is included in *checking.h*, *savings.h*, and *banking.cpp* files. Because *account.h* provides the declaration for the *BankAccount* class, the compiler sees multiple declarations for this class via the multiple include directives. It's as if you defined a variable several times in a single source file. Such an oversight causes a *multiple declaration for...* compiler error. The *BankAccount* class must be included in multiple files for inheritance purposes, so you must tell the compiler that you are only declaring it once. This is the purpose of the *#ifndef* directive. So, always use the following format when declaring base classes in C++:

> ### *DECLARING BASE CLASSES IN C++*
>
> **#ifndef** *HEADER FILE NAME_H*
> **#define** *HEADER FILE NAME _H*
>
> *BASE CLASS DECLARATION*
>
> **#endif**

Consult your compiler reference library if you need more information on the *#ifndef* directive.

Quick Check

1. True or false: When declaring a derived class, the derived class is listed first followed by a colon and the base class.

2. True or false: A public base class allows its public members to be used by any of its derived classes.

3. True or false: A protected base class member is protected from any use by the derived classes of that base class.

4. When base class header files are included in multiple implementation and application files, you must use the _____ directive to avoid *multiple declaration* compile errors.

5. What would be wrong with deriving the *Savings* class from the *SuperNow* class in the program discussed in this section?

6. What type of inheritance occurs when all the inherited members in a family can be traced back to more than one parent class?

11.3   POLYMORPHISM AND DYNAMIC BINDING

In the Chapter 10 introduction, we stated that there were four concepts central to OOP: encapsulation with information hiding, inheritance, polymorphism, and dynamic binding. We have thoroughly explored the first two. For completeness, we will now briefly discuss the latter two concepts of polymorphism and dynamic binding.

Polymorphism

The term "polymorphic" is Greek and means "of many forms." Polymorphism is associated with functions as indicated in the following definition:

> A **polymorphic** function is one that has the same name for different classes of the same family, but has different implementations, or behavior, for the various classes.

As you can see, polymorphism allows functions of the same name to behave differently within a class family. You have just seen an example of a polymorphic function in our bank account class family. Can you identify which function it is from the class header files? You're right if you thought the *addInterest()* function. Notice that this function is defined in both the *SuperNow* and *Savings* classes. The function interface is identical in both classes; however, the implementation is different in each class. In effect, we are hiding alternative operations behind the common *addInterest()* interface. This means that the two objects defined for these classes will respond to the common operation, *addInterest()*, in different ways. Languages that do not support polymorphism, such as Pascal and C, require large switch/case statements to implement this effect.

Polymorphism allows objects to be more independent, even though they are members of the same class family. Moreover, new classes can be added to the family without changing existing ones. This allows systems to evolve over time, meeting the needs of a changing application. Consider a word processing program where the system is required to print many different types of documents. Recall from Chapter 10 that many such programs employ classes to define the structure and behavior of a given type of document. Each document class will have a *print()* function to print a specific document in its correct format. Such a function would be a polymorphic function, because it would have a common interface, but behave differently for different document objects.

Polymorphism is accomplished using overloaded functions or ***virtual functions.*** Overloaded functions were discussed earlier in Chapters 8. However, virtual functions are something new. The difference between the two has to do with the different techniques that are used by C++ to call the function. Overloaded functions are called using ***static binding***, and virtual functions are called using ***dynamic binding***.

Dynamic Versus Static Binding

Binding relates to the actual time when the code for a given function is attached, or bound, to the function.

> ***Dynamic***, or ***late***, ***binding*** occurs when a polymorphic function is defined for several classes in a family but the actual code for the function is not attached, or bound, until execution time. A polymorphic function that is dynamically bound is called a ***virtual*** function.

Dynamic binding is implemented in C++ through ***virtual functions.*** With dynamic binding, the selection of code to be executed when a virtual function is called is delayed until execution time. This means that when a virtual function is called, the executable code determines at run time which version of the function to call. Remember, virtual functions are polymorphic and, therefore, have different implementations for different classes in the family.

As an example of dynamic binding consider what happens when you double-click a mouse. The double-clicking action generates an *event,* which calls upon a poloymorphic function. If you double-click on a file folder, a directory listing opens. If you double-click on an application icon, a program is executed. If you double-click on a document, a word processing program is launched and the document is opened. So, the double-clicking event resulted in a different behavior each time. This is polymorphism and it surely happens at execution time.

> ***Static binding*** occurs when a polymorphic function is defined for several classes in a family and the actual code for the function is attached, or bound, at compile time. Overloaded functions are statically bound.

Static binding, on the other hand, occurs when the function code is "bound" at compile time. This means that when a nonvirtual function is called, the compiler determines at compile time which version of the function to call. Overloaded functions are statically bound, whereas virtual functions are dynamically bound. With overloaded functions, the compiler can determine which function to call based on the number of and data types of the function arguments. However, virtual functions have the same interface within a given class family. Therefore, pointers must be used during run time to determine which function to call. Any ideas on how this is accomplished? (*Hint:* Remember that each function can be traced to its correct class via its calling object's unique ***this*** pointer.) Fortunately, you don't have to worry about how the binding is accomplished, because this is taken care of automatically by the compiler.

> A ***pointer*** is a direct program reference to an actual physical address in memory. Languages that allow the use of pointers, such as C and C++, provide more flexibility for the programmer, because the programmer can create a pointer to point to anything in memory, even the operating system memory. But, of course, this could be very hazardous to your system if not used properly. You will study pointers in a later chapter.

You should be aware that virtual functions are most often declared in a base class in C++ using the keyword **virtual.** When a function is declared as a virtual function in a base class, the compiler knows that the base class implementation might be overridden in a derived class. The base class implementation is overridden by defining a different implementation for the same function in a derived class. If the base class implementation is not overridden in a given derived class, then the base class implementation is available to the derived class.

Quick Check

1. True or false: A virtual function is polymorphic.
2. True or false: All polymorphic functions are virtual functions.
3. True or false: The virtual function interface is identical for each version of the function in a given class family.
4. Overloaded functions are _____ bound.
5. Virtual functions are _____ bound.
6. The implementation code for a dynamically bound function is determined at _____.

CHAPTER SUMMARY

Inheritance is an important property of object-oriented programming that allows one class, called a derived class, to share the structure and behavior of another class, called a base class. The derived class should always be related to its base class via the IS-A relationship. There is both single inheritance and multiple inheritance. Single inheritance occurs when the inherited class members can be traced to a single base class. Multiple inheritance occurs when the inherited class members can be traced back to more than one base class. You control the amount of class member inheritance by designating the members as private, protected, or public in the class declarations.

Polymorphism has to do with functions that have the same name, but different behavior within a class family. Polymorphism allows functions to be more independent and class families to be more flexible. Overloaded functions and virtual functions are polymorphic. Overloaded functions are statically bound to their code during compile time, whereas virtual functions are dynamically bound to their code during run time.

QUESTIONS AND PROBLEMS

Questions

1. Define the following terms:

     Base class

     Derived class

     Inheritance

     Single inheritance

     Multiple inheritance

     IS-A

     Polymorphism

     Dynamic binding

     Static binding

2. Suggest several real-world applications for the use of inheritance.

3. What relationship must be considered between a potential derived class and its base class when developing inheritance?

4. Given a base class called *Point,* write the class declaration header line for a derived class called *Pixel.* Assume that the functions in *Point* are to be public in *Pixel.*

5. Explain how a protected class member differs from a private class member and a public class member.

6. When should you use the keyword **public** in a derived class declaration?

7. When should you use the **#***ifndef* directive in a class header file?

8. Why is a virtual function polymorphic?

9. Explain the difference between static binding and dynamic binding.

PROBLEMS

Least Difficult

1. Determine the output generated by the application program (*banking.cpp*) given in this chapter.

2. Code the class header and implementation files for the banking program given in this chapter. Then, write your own application program to exercise the class family in different ways. See if you can predict the results of your banking transactions.

More Difficult

3. Add a *DebitCard* class to the *BankAccount* class family developed in this chapter. The *DebitCard* class should inherit the *BankAccount* class directly. Provide functions to debit monthly charges from the account balance. Write an application program to exercise a *DebitCard* object and report the balance due.

Most Difficult

4. Declare a *ResistorCircuit* base class that contains the following members:

Function Members

❑ A set function that will allow the user to enter the resistor values and the number of resistors in the circuit.

❑ A get function that will display the resistor values along with the equivalent resistance of the circuit.

Data Members

❑ The resistor values stored in an array.

❑ The number of resistors in the circuit.

❑ The equivalent resistance of the circuit.

5. Declare two derived classes called *SeriesCircuit* and *ParallelCircuit* that inherit the *ResistorCircuit* class declared in problem 4. Provide the following functions in these derived classes:

SeriesCircuit: A function to calculate the equivalent resistance of a series circuit.

ParallelCircuit: A function to calculate the equivalent resistance of a parallel circuit.

6. Write an application program that defines a series resistance object and a parallel resistance object from the classes declared in problems 4 and 5. Include statements in the program that will exercise the object functions to calculate circuit resistance of the respective objects.

7. Create a persons family of classes. Think of the persons that make up your institution. For example, a student is a person, a staff member is a person, a faculty member is a person, and an administrator is a person (some of the time). Each of these persons have common as well as unique attributes and behaviors. For instance, both a student and a faculty member have a name and address. However, a student has a GPA, while a faculty member has a rank.

Build, compile, and test your persons family using an application program. Be creative and try different things—this is when you really learn how to program in C++, as well as any other language for that matter.

8. Declare an *Insurance* base class that contains the following members:

Class: *Insurance*

Function Members

❏ A set function that will allow the user to enter the values of the data members.

❏ A get function that will display the data member values.

Data Members

❏ An insurance account number.

❏ An insurance policy number.

❏ The name of the insured.

❏ Annual premium.

9. Declare two derived classes called *Automobile* and *Home* that inherit the *Insurance* base class declared in problem 8. Provide the following members in these derived classes:

Class: *Automobile*

Function Members

❏ Set and get functions for the specific automobile data members.

Data Members

❏ Make of automobile.

❏ Model of automobile.

❏ Automobile VIN number.

❏ Amount of liability coverage

❏ Amount of comprehensive coverage.

❏ Amount of collision coverage.

Class: *Home*

Function Members

❏ Set and get functions for the specific home data members.

Data Members

❏ House square footage.

❏ Amount of dwelling coverage.

❏ Amount of contents coverage.

❏ Amount of liability coverage

10. Write an application class that defines an automobile and home insurance object from the classes declared in problems 8 and 9. Include statements in the program that will exercise the object functions.

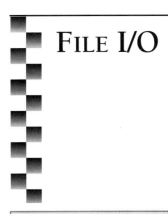

FILE I/O

■ Chapter Contents

Chapter Objectives

When you are finished with this chapter, you should have a good understanding of the following:

- The concept of streams and the role they play in communicating with I/O devices.

- How to use the C++ files stream classes to create, or open, disk files.

- How to write, read, append, and change disk files.

- How to overload *cin* and *cout* for file I/O.

- How to determine character and word boundaries in a file.

INTRODUCTION

All the data types and structures you have learned about so far have provided a means of organizing and storing data in primary memory. However, recall that primary memory is relatively small and, more importantly, volatile. In other words, when the system is turned off or power is lost for any reason, all information stored in primary memory goes to "bit heaven." The obvious solution to this problem is to store any long-term data in secondary memory, because secondary memory is non-volatile.

In Chapter 4, you learned how to read and write disk files. In this chapter, you will expand on this knowledge and learn how to create and manipulate your own disk files in C++. A file provides a means of storing information in a convenient and organized manner in secondary memory, such as magnetic disk. There are two basic types of files in C++: character, or text, files and binary files. Text files are used to store ASCII data, such as that produced by a text editor. Binary files are used to store executable code, such as that of a compiled program. In this chapter, we will discuss input and output of text files. We will also focus on the ANSI/ISO *fstream* header file, not *fstream.h*. If you do not have an ANSI/ISO compatible compiler, you can substitute *fstream.h* for *fstream*. Of course, those programs that use the *string* class will not compile unless you have an ANSI/ISO compatible compiler. To make these compile, you need to replace the *string* class objects with C-string array variables.

12.1   FUNDAMENTAL CONCEPTS AND IDEAS

> A *file* is a data structure that consists of a sequence of data items.

A file is a *sequence* of data items. This means that the data items are arranged within the file sequentially, or serially, from the first item to the last item. As a result, when accessing files, the file data items must be accessed in a sequential manner from one item to the next. A common analogy for a file is an audio cassette tape. Think of the songs on the tape as the file data items. How are they stored on the tape? You're right, sequentially from the first song to the last. How must you access a given song? Right again, by sequencing forward or backward through the tape until the desired song is found. Thus, like a cassette tape, a file is a sequential, or serial, storage medium. This makes file access relatively slow as compared to other random-access storage mediums.

You might be tempted to think of a file as a one-dimensional array, but there are some important differences. First, files provide a means for you to store information within a program run as you do with arrays. But, unlike arrays, files also allow you to store information between program runs. Second, many compilers require you to access the file data items in sequence, starting with the first file item.

You cannot jump into the middle of a file as you can an array to access a given item. However, C++ does provide a means of semirandom direct access using the *seek* operations. More about this later. Third, files are not declared with a specific dimension as are arrays. Once you declare a file, its size is theoretically unlimited. Of course, the file size is actually limited by the amount of storage space available in secondary memory, such as a disk.

In Chapter 4, you learned that all C++ file I/O is based on the concept of file streams.

> A *file stream* provides a channel for data to flow between your program and the outside world.

In particular, a file stream provides a channel for the flow of data from some source to some destination. Think about what happens when you are typing characters on the keyboard when prompted by a program. You can think of the characters as flowing, or streaming, from the keyboard into the program. Likewise, when your program generates a character display, you can easily visualize the characters streaming from the program to the display.

Classes Provide the Basis for C++ Files

The familiar *cin* and *cout* stream objects that you have been using in your programs for keyboard input and display output are objects of the *iostream* class. As you are aware, the *cin* and *cout* objects invoke predefined file streams. Thus, we say that *standard input* is read from the *cin stream* and *standard output* is written to the *cout stream*. When you include the *iostream.h* (or *iostream*) header file in your program, the *cin* and *cout* file streams are defined automatically. Of course, the only files that you can access conveniently with *cin* and *cout* are the keyboard and display files that are *attached* to these file streams.

When you create your own file stream for reading/writing disk files, the first thing you must do is define an object for one of the file classes: *ifstream*, *ofstream*, or *fstream*. These file stream classes are found in the *fstream* header file. Thus, you must include *fstream* in your program to use these classes.

Class inheritance provides the basis for C++ file streams. A UML hierarchy diagram of the C++ file class family is provided in Figure 12.1. Above the dashed line in Figure 12.1, you find the classes declared in *iostream*, and below the line, you see the classes declared in *fstream*. Notice that the *fstream* class is derived from the *iostream* class. File streams that you will define for disk I/O are referred to as **named** file streams.

Creating File Streams in C++: The File Stream Definition

Let's review how to create your own file streams in C++. When you create your own file stream for reading/writing disk files, the first thing you must do is define an object for one of the file classes: *ifstream*, *ofstream*, or *fstream*. These file stream

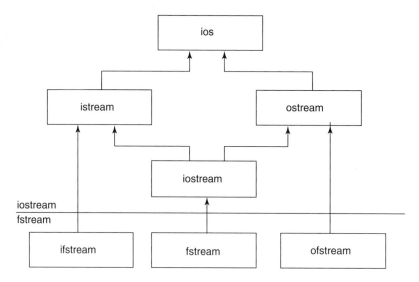

FIGURE 12.1   THE FILE CLASS HIERARCHY IN C++.

classes are found in the *fstream* header file. Thus, you must include *fstream* in your program to use these classes.

File stream objects that are used exclusively for input are defined as objects of the *ifstream* class. Thus, the statement

```
ifstream fin("sample.txt");
```

defines *fin* as an input file stream object and *attaches* it to a physical disk file called *sample.txt* in the current working directory. This is called "opening a file." Your file stream object is a *logical* entity within your program, while the disk file is a *physical* entity in secondary storage. Thus, defining a file stream object opens a file which attaches, or connects, a logical file stream object to a physical disk file as illustrated by Figure 12.2.

Notice from the foregoing object definition that the physical disk file name is a string that provides a constructor argument for the object. The *ifstream* class con-

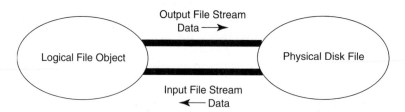

FIGURE 12-2   THE FILE STREAM CLASSES ARE USED TO CREATE FILE STREAMS THAT ATTACH A LOGICAL PROGRAM OBJECT TO A PHYSICAL DISK FILE.

structor automatically opens the file name specified as the constructor argument. All the *fstream* classes also have a ***destructor*** that automatically ***closes*** the file when the object is no longer visible within the program. A ***destructor*** is the counterpart of a constructor and is used to *clean up* an object after it is no longer needed, as in closing a file stream object file. Closing a file disconnects the logical file object from the physical disk file.

> A ***destructor*** is the counterpart of a constructor and is used to *clean up* an object after it is no longer needed, as in closing a file stream object file. Closing a file disconnects the logical file object from the physical disk file.

The disk file name must adhere to the requirements of the operating system. File names such as *sample*, *sample.txt*, and *sample2.txt* are all legal file names for most operating systems. (*Note*: You don't have to add the *.txt* to the end of your file name, but it is recommended if using Windows so that it will open correctly when you want to view it.) You can also specify a path to locate the file. Examples of legal DOS/Windows paths might be *"A:sample.txt"*, *"C:\\myDir\\sample.txt"*. In the former case, a drive designation is specified, and in the latter case, a directory path is specified for the hard drive. Notice that the C++ double backslash, \\, escape sequence must be used to separate the directory names. A single backslash will result in the file not being found. Unix does not have this requirement because the single forward slash, /, is used to separate directory names. If you do not specify a file path, C++ looks for the file in the current working directory.

> When specifying DOS or Windows directory paths in C++, you must use the double backslash escape sequence, \\, and *not* the single backslash, \, to separate the directory names.

The physical disk file name can be specified directly within double quotes (i.e., *"sample.txt"*) or indirectly as a string object (i.e., *fileName*). However, the string object must call the *c_str()* function to convert the string object to a C-string. So, assuming that a disk file name is stored in a string object called *fileName*, the code required to open this file for input would be:

```
ifstream fin(fileName.c_str());
```

You use the *ofstream* class to define file stream objects that are used exclusively for output. Thus, the statement

```
ofstream fout("A:\\myDir\\sample.txt");
```

defines *fout* as an output file stream object and opens the *sample.txt* file located in the *myDir* directory on the *A:* drive, assuming a DOS or Windows operating system.

You can name your file objects anything you want. We have used *fin* and *fout* in the foregoing examples to be consistent with *cin* and *cout*.

Finally, you must use the *fstream* class when defining objects that will be used for both file input and output. The statement

```
fstream finout(fileName.c_str());
```

defines *finout* as both an input and output file stream object and opens the file whose name is contained in the string object *fileName*.

EXAMPLE 12.1

Write statements to open the following disk files:

  a. A file stream called *read* that will read from a disk file called *myFile.txt* on the A: drive.

  b. A file stream called *write* that will write to a disk file called *myFile.txt* in the current working directory.

  c. A file stream called *readWrite* that will read and write a disk file called *myFile.txt* in a Windows hard drive directory called *myDirectory*.

  d. A file stream called *readWrite* that will read and write a disk file whose path is stored in a string object called *myFile*.

Solution

  a. `ifstream read("A:myFile.txt");`
  b. `ofstream write("myFile.txt");`
  c. `fstream readWrite("C:\\myDirectory\\myFile.txt");`
  d. `fstream readWrite(myFile.c_str());`

 ## Quick Check

1. True or false: A file is a random-access data structure.
2. A channel where data can flow between your C++ program and the outside world is called a _____.
3. Standard output in C++ is written to the _____ file stream.
4. What class is used in C++ to perform input, or read, operations from disk files?
5. True or false: The *iostream* class is derived using multiple inheritance.
6. Write a statement to define *myFile* as an output file stream object and attach it to a file called *data.txt* located in a subdirectory called *temp* on the hard drive.
7. Write a statement to define *yourFile* as an input/output file stream object and attach it to a file named *ASCII.txt* located on a disk in the A: drive.

12.2 ACCESSING FILE INFORMATION

Before getting into specific file access routines, let's take a minute to discuss the more important overall concept of file access.

The File Window

Files can be thought of as a means for a program to communicate with the "outside world." Information can be read into the program by placing it in a file and having the program read that file. In the same way, the program can write information to the outside world by writing to a file. As you know, C++ treats the user keyboard as an input file and the display monitor as an output file. Now, the question is: "How does your program communicate with the file?" The answer is: "Through something called a *file window*, sometimes called a *file pointer*." In other words, your program "sees" the outside file data items through something called a file window. This concept is illustrated by Figure 12.3.

In Figure 12.3, the file consists of a sequence of characters. To access a given character, the window must be positioned over that character so that it can be "seen." Once the window is positioned over the desired character, information can be read from, or written to, that character item position within the file through the window.

When you open a file, a window is automatically created to access the file data items. Consequently, the window is the link between the program and the file data items.

File Operations

Now that you know how a file is created and structured, you need to learn about some general operations that will allow you to work with files. The following discussion will center on C++. We should caution you, however, that file operations in C differ somewhat from file operations in C++, because file operations in C++ are structured around classes. As a result, there are operations available in C++ that are not available in C, and a program written in C++ might not compile in C.

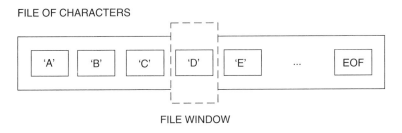

FILE OF CHARACTERS

FILE WINDOW

FIGURE 12.3 **FILE DATA ITEMS ARE ACCESSED THROUGH A FILE WINDOW.**

It is probably best to look at a comprehensive example in order to learn how to access C++ files. Let's begin by developing our own class that will be used specifically for file access. We will include member functions in the class that allow us to perform the following common file-access routines:

- ❏ Initialize a private data member with a disk file name entered by the user.
- ❏ Write, or create, a new file.
- ❏ Read and display an existing file.
- ❏ Append an existing file.
- ❏ Change an existing file.

Here is the class declaration:

```
//files.h  FOR FILES CLASS

#ifndef FILES_H
#define FILES_H

//PREPROCESSOR DIRECTIVES
#include <fstream>        //FOR FILE STREAM BASE CLASS
#include <string>         //FOR string CLASS
#include <iostream>       //FOR cin AND cout
#include <stdlib.h>       //FOR exit()

using namespace std;      //REQUIRED WHEN INCLUDING fstream OR iostream

class Files : public fstream
{
public:
  void setName();         //SETS THE DISK FILE NAME
  void writeFile();       //WRITES DATA TO USER DISK FILE
  void readFile();        //READS USER DISK FILE
  void appendFile();      //APPENDS USER DISK FILE
  void changeFile();      //CHANGES USER DISK FILE DATA

private:
  string fileName;        //USER DISK FILE NAME
}; //END Files
#endif
```

First, you see that the *fstream* header file is included prior to the class declaration. The *fstream* header file is included because it contains all the file stream class declarations that we need to define file objects.

Our class declaration provides for a single private data member called *fileName*. This *fileName* string will be used to store the name of the disk file being attached to our file stream objects. Four public functions are part of the class to provide the file-access routines previously listed. Our *Files* class declaration will be stored in a header file called *files.h*.

Next, we need to develop an implementation file for each of the member functions. Let's take them in order, beginning with the *setName()* function.

Obtaining a Disk File Name from the User. The *setName()* function simply obtains a physical disk file name from the user and initializes the *fileName* member of our *Files* class to the string entered by the user. Here's the implementation:

```
//setName.cpp IMPLEMENTATION FILE FOR setName() FUNCTION

//PREPROCESSOR DIRECTIVE
#include "files.h"      //FOR files CLASS

void Files :: setName()
{
//GET THE FILE NAME FROM USER TO
//INITIALIZE FILE NAME DATA MEMBER
   cout << "What file name do you want to use?\n"
        << "Note:  Make sure your file name is "
        << "compatible with your operating system" << endl;
   cin >> fileName;
} //END setName()
```

The opening comment indicates that the *setName()* implementation is stored in a file called *setName.cpp*. The *files.h* file must be included in this file, because *files.h* contains our *Files* class declaration, of which *setName()* is a member. The body of the implementation is straightforward, and you should not have any trouble understanding it at this point.

Writing, or Creating, a New File. Next, we need to develop an implementation for the *writeFile()* function. This function must accomplish the task of creating a new file if it doesn't already exist, or completely rewriting an existing file with new data items. Here are the general file operations required to accomplish this task:

❒ Define an output file stream object and open a disk file.

❒ Get the new file data items from the user and write them to the file.

We will place the *writeFile()* implementation in the following *write.cpp* file:

```
//write.cpp  IMPLEMENTATION FILE FOR writeFile()

//PREPROCESSOR DIRECTIVE
#include "files.h"  //FOR files CLASS

void Files :: writeFile()
{
  //LOCAL STRING OBJECT
  string line = " "; //line BUFFER

  //DEFINE OUTPUT FILE OBJECT AND OPEN FILE
  ofstream fout(fileName.c_str());

  //FILE OK?
  if (!fout)
  {
    cerr << "This file cannot be opened." << endl;
```

```
     exit(1);
  }//END IF
 else
 {
    //GET FILE STRINGS FROM USER AND WRITE TO FILE
    cout << "Enter a string or DONE when finished:" << endl;
    cin >> line;
    while (line != "DONE")
    {
       fout << line << endl;
       cout << "Enter a string or DONE when finished:" << endl;
       cin >> line;
    }//END WHILE
  }//END ELSE
}//END writeFile()
```

First, notice that each of the major operations that need to be performed in this implementation is commented so that it can be easily identified in the code. The code begins by including the header file that is needed in this implementation. Of course, our class header file (*files.h*) must be included, because *writeFile()* is a member function of our *Files* class. Before anything can be done with a file, a file stream object must be defined and opened. The object is called *fout* and is defined for the *ofstream* class, which is inherited via our *Files* class. The *ofstream* class is used here because *writeFile()* only writes information to the file. The constructor argument needed in the object definition is the physical disk file name that will be attached to the *fout* stream object. Recall that our *setName()* function obtains the disk file name from the user and sets the *fileName* member of the class to the user entry. Our file object has access to *fileName* because *fileName* is a member of our *Files* class. Notice that a call is made to *c_str()* to convert the string object to a C-string which is required by the constructor.

After the file object is defined, an **if** statement is inserted to determine if the file was, in fact, opened without any problems. (Can you think of any problem that might occur when opening a file?) If, for any reason, the file stream cannot be opened, the file stream object will return a value of zero. If a value of zero is returned, an error message is displayed via the *cerr* object, and the program is aborted via the *exit()* function. The *cerr* object does basically the same thing as *cout*. However, the *cerr* object is usually employed for file operations rather than *cout*, because some programs might attach *cout* to a file other than the standard display monitor file. You will see an example of this shortly. The *exit()* function is found in the *stdlib.h* header file and causes the program to abort and return to the operating system. In addition, *exit()* closes any files that were previously opened by the program. We have used an *exit()* function argument of 1, because a non-zero argument means an abnormal termination, whereas an argument of 0 means a normal termination.

The next section of code gets the file data items from the user and writes them to the file. Here, we are obtaining character strings from the user via the *cin* object and storing them in a local string object called *line*. Once a string is obtained from the user, it is written to our *fout* file stream object using the familiar << insertion operator. We say that the << operator "inserts" the string into the file stream. In our case, the string contained in *line* is inserted into the *fout* file stream. In addition to the string contained in *line*, an *endl* is inserted into the stream to produce a carriage return/line feed (CRLF) as a delimiter to separate the strings within the file. Notice that the user read and file write operations are both part of a **while** loop that iterates once for each item the user has to enter. The loop breaks when the user enters the string "DONE". Here is what the file looks like on disk, assuming the strings "Andy", "Janet", and "Ron" were written to the file. Notice that *endl* produced two characters on the disk, a carriage return (CR) character and a line feed (LF) character. The file is terminated by an end-of-file (EOF) marker character.

```
A n d y CR LF J a n e t CR LF R o n CR LF EOF
```

Reading and Displaying an Existing File. The next implementation we need to deal with is the *readFile()* implementation. The operations that must be performed here are as follows:

❒ Define an input file stream object and open a disk file.
❒ Read the file data items and display them to the user.

We will store this implementation in a separate file called *read.cpp*, as follows:

```
//read.cpp IMPLEMENTATION FILE FOR readFile()
//PREPROCESSOR DIRECTIVE
#include "files.h"      //FOR Files CLASS

void Files :: readFile()
{
  //LOCAL STRING OBJECT
  string line = " ";            //LINE BUFFER

  //DEFINE fin FILE OBJECT AND OPEN FILE
  ifstream fin(fileName.c_str());

  //FILE OK?
  if (!fin)
  {
     cerr << "This file cannot be opened." << endl;
     exit(1);
  }//END IF
  else
  {
     //READ A LINE, TEST FOR EOF, AND DISPLAY LINE
     while(fin >> line)
        cout << line << endl;
  }//END else
}//END readFile()
```

You see that our *files.h* file is again included in this file, because the *readFile()* function is part of our *Files* class. The file stream object is called *fin* and is defined for the *ifstream* class. The *ifstream* class is used, because all we will do is read a file. The file stream is opened and attached to the disk file name stored in *fileName*. Again, an error message is generated, and the program aborted if, for some reason, the file stream cannot be opened.

The first character string is read via a *fin >> line* statement within the loop test. The familiar >> extraction operator extracts a string from the *fin* file stream and places it in a local string object called *line*. Within the loop, the string just read is displayed via a *cout* statement. The loop continues to iterate until the EOF marker is detected.

It is important to analyze the window positioning during the file read operations. Given a file containing the strings "Andy", "Janet", and "Ron", the first *fin >> line* statement extracts the characters 'A', 'n', 'd', 'y' from the *fin* file stream and terminates when the CR character is encountered. This results in the file window being positioned at the first CR character, as follows:

The next *fin >> line* statement skips the CR and LF characters and extracts the characters 'J', 'a', 'n', 'e', 't' from the *fin* file stream, leaving the window positioned at the next CR character, as follows:

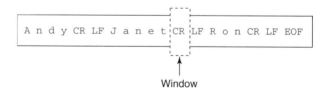

The loop continues to read the remaining characters in the file in this fashion until the end-of-file marker is encountered.

Appending an Existing File. Appending a file means to add information to the end of the file. The operations required to perform this task are as follows:

❏ Define an input/output file stream object and open an existing disk file.

❏ Position the file window at the end of the file.

❏ Get the additional file data items from the user, and write them to the file.

This implementation will be stored in a separate file called *append.cpp*. The code required to append an existing file is almost the same as that for creating a new file. The only difference is that the file must be opened for both input and output. You might be thinking that we are simply appending the file, so it only needs to be open for output, right? However, if you open the file for output exclusively, we will lose the original file contents. So, in order to preserve the original file contents, it must be opened for input/output using the *fstream* class. Also, the file window must be positioned at the end of the file so that a string can be appended to the file. Here's the required implementation code:

```
//append.cpp  IMPLEMENTATION FILE FOR appendFile()

//PREPROCESSOR DIRECTIVE
#include "files.h"       //FOR Files CLASS

void Files :: appendFile()
{
  //LOCAL STRING OBJECT
  string line = " ";    //LINE BUFFER

  //DEFINE APPEND FILE OBJECT AND OPEN FILE
  fstream append(fileName.c_str());

  //FILE OK?
  if (!append)
  {
    cerr << "\nThis file cannot be opened." << endl;
    exit(1);
  }//END IF
  else
  {
      //SEEK END OF FILE POSITION
      append.seekp(0,ios::end);

      //GET FILE FILE DATA ITEMS AND APPEND TO FILE
      cout << "Enter a string or DONE when finished:" << endl;
      cin >> line;
      while (line != "DONE")
      {
          append << line << endl;
          cout << "Enter a string or DONE when finished:" << endl;
          cin >> line;
      }//END WHILE
    }//END ELSE
  }//END appendFile()
```

A file stream object, called *append*, is defined as an object of the *fstream* class. This class is used to open the file for both input and output to preserve the file contents as stated earlier. Next, the statement *append.seekp(0,ios::end)* moves the file window to the end of the file by calling the inherited *seekp()* function. The *seekp()*

function positions the file window a given number of bytes from a specified point in the file. Here we are positioning the window 0 bytes, from the end of the file, *ios::end*. This obviously places the window at the end of the file, right? There are three possible points in the file from which we can position the window: the beginning of the file (*ios::beg*), the current window position (*ios::cur*), or the end of the file (*ios::end*). Once the file window is positioned at the end of the file, a string is read from the user and a **while** loop is entered to continually append strings to the file until the user enters the string "DONE".

Changing an Existing File. The last function we need to discuss is the *changeFile()* function. This function requires the following file operations:

- ❐ Define an input/output file stream object and open an existing file.
- ❐ Get the data item to be changed from the user, and search the file for the data item.
- ❐ Seek the position of the data item to be changed.
- ❐ Erase the old data item from the file.
- ❐ Seek the end-of-file position.
- ❐ Write the new data item to the end of the file.

The idea here is to get the data item to be changed from the user and then search the file for that data item. Once found, we will erase the old data item from the file and ask the user to provide the new data item. The new data item then will be written to the end of the file. Let's get into the code. By the way, this implementation will be stored in a file called *change.cpp*. Here it is:

```
//change.cpp IMPLEMENTATION FILE FOR changeFile()

//PREPROCESSOR DIRECTIVE
#include "files.h"  //FOR Files CLASS

void Files :: changeFile()
{
  //LOCAL STRING OBJECTS AND VARIABLES
  string oldLine = " "; //LINE TO CHANGE
  string newLine = " "; //NEW LINE
  string entry = " ";    //USER ENTRY FOR LINE TO CHANGE
  int windowPos  = -2;   //CURRENT WINDOW POSITION
  bool  flag = false;    //FLAG TO INDICATE FILE STRING FOUND

  //DEFINE INPUT/OUTPUT FILE OBJECT
  fstream change(fileName.c_str());

  //FILE OK?
  if (!change)
  {
    cerr << "\nThis file cannot be opened." << endl;
    exit(1);
  }//END IF
  else
```

```
{
   //GET STRING TO CHANGE FROM USER
   cout << "\nWhich string do you wish to change?" << endl;
   cin >> entry;

   // READ ITEM, TEST FOR EOF, AND SEARCH FILE FOR USER ENTRY
   while ((change >> oldLine) && (flag == false))
   {
       //COMPARE FILE STRING TO USER ENTRY
       if (oldLine == entry)
       {
           //SET FLAG TO TRUE IF FOUND
           flag = true;
           //SEEK BEGINNING OF FOUND STRING
           change.seekg(windowPos + 2,ios::beg);
           //REPLACE STRING WITH *'s
           for (int i = 1; i <= oldLine.length(); ++i)
               change << '*';
           //ADD CRLF
           change << endl;
           //GET NEW STRING FROM USER
           cout << "Line found, what do you wish to change it to?" << endl;
           cin >> newLine;
           //SEEK END OF FILE POSITION
           change.seekg(0,ios::end);
           //ADD NEW STRING TO END OF FILE
           change << newLine << endl;
       }//END IF

       //SAVE CURRENT WINDOW POSITION
       windowPos = change.tellg();
   }//END WHILE
   }//END ELSE

   //WRITE MESSAGE TO USER IF STRING NOT FOUND
   if (!flag)
      cout << "Line not found." << endl;
}//END changeFile()
```

The code begins by including our *files.h* header file that declares our *Files* class. Several local items are defined at the beginning of the *changeFile()* implementation. You will discover their use shortly. A file stream object called *change* is defined for the *fstream* class. The *fstream* class is required here because we will use this object to both read and write the file. The file stream is opened and attached to the disk file name stored in *fileName*.

After the file is opened, the user is prompted to enter the string information to be changed. The user entry is placed in a local string object called *entry*. Next, the first file string is read via a *change >> oldLine* statement. The >> extraction operator extracts this first string from the *change* input file stream and places it in the *oldLine* string object. A **while** loop is then executed to search for the user entry

(*entry*). Notice that the **while** loop will execute until one of two conditions occurs: 1) when the end-of-file (EOF) marker is encountered, or 2) when the string being searched for is found. The loop test reads a file string and automatically checks for the EOF marker. The **if** statement within the loop is used to compare the user entry to the file string just read. If the two strings are equal, the file string is replaced with *'s, and a new string is obtained from the user and written at the end of the file.

If the two strings are unequal, the statements within the **if** are bypassed, and a variable called *windowPos* is set to the current window position. This is accomplished when the *change* object invokes a function of the *istream* class called *tellg()*. [How does this program inherit *tellg()*?] The *tellg()* function returns the current position of the file window. (You should be aware that there is a comparable function, called *tellp()*, defined for the *ostream* class. We are using *tellg()* rather than *tellp()* to be consistent with an input operation.) The value returned by *tellg()* represents the number of bytes the window is located from the beginning of the file. This value is assigned in the program to a variable called *windowPos* that will be used later. After the current window position is saved in *windowPos*, another string is read and tested. Thus, the loop continues to iterate until the end-of-file marker is encountered or the string being searched for is found.

Now, let's take a closer look at what goes on inside the **if** statement. First, a Boolean flag is set to indicate that the string being searched for was found. Next, the file window is repositioned to the beginning of the string just found when the *change* file object invokes an inherited function called *seekg()*. The *seekg()* function positions the file window a given number of bytes from a specified point in the file. Here is the statement that we are using to call *seekg()*:

```
change.seekg(windowPos + 2, ios::beg);
```

This statement places the file window at the beginning of the found string, *old-Line*. The first argument, *windowPos + 2*, contains the number of bytes that the *oldLine* string is located from the beginning of the file. Why are we specifying *windowPos + 2*? Well, let's assume that our file contains the strings "Andy", "Janet", "Ron" and we are searching for the string "Janet". Here is the window status after the first read operation:

This window position is saved in *windowPos* prior to reading the next string. Next, the string we are looking for ("Janet") is read, and the window is now positioned as follows:

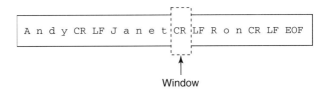

Window

Prior to this read operation, the window was at the previous CR character position, which is saved in *windowPos*. Now, the idea is to erase the string "Janet" by replacing it with *'s. However, in order to write over the string "Janet", the file window must be repositioned at the 'J' character, like this:

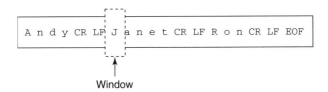

Window

Now, to get to this character, the window must be moved a distance of *window-Pos + 2* bytes from the beginning of the file. Recall that, before the last read operation, the file window was at the CR character just after "Andy". However, after "Janet" is read, the window moves to the CR character just after "Janet". Therefore, if the string being searched for is found, the window must be repositioned to the beginning of this string so that it can be erased from the file. To position the window on the 'J' in "Janet", the window must be moved a distance of *windowPos + 2* from the beginning of the file. This is why we stored the previous window position in *windowPos* just prior to reading the last string. The *+ 2* accounts for the CR and LF characters separating the two strings.

The second argument in the function call, *ios::beg*, tells the compiler to move the window relative to the beginning of the file. So, the first argument in *seekg()* specifies the number of bytes to move the window, and the second argument specifies the starting point. In our case, we must move the window *windowPos + 2* bytes from the beginning of the file. There are three possible starting points for the second argument of *seekg()*: the beginning of the file (*ios::beg*), the current position of the file window (*ios::cur*), and the end of the file (*ios::end*). Thus, we can move the file window so many bytes from the beginning of the file, the current position of the file window, or the end of the file.

Now that the searched-for string has been found, it is effectively erased by replacing it with asterisks. This is accomplished using a **for** loop that iterates a number of times equal to the length of the found string, *oldLine*. Notice the call to the *length()* function in the loop test. Recall that the *string* class *length()* function calculates the length of the calling string object, *oldLine* in this case. The resulting length determines when the loop will terminate. With each loop iteration, an asterisk (*) is written to the file so that the *oldLine* string is overwritten with *'s.

TABLE 12.1 FILE WINDOW FUNCTIONS IN C++

Function	Class	Purpose
tellg()	istream	Returns window position of the input file stream.
tellp()	ostream	Returns window position of the output file stream.
seekg()	istream	Positions window of the input file stream.
seekp()	ostream	Positions window of the output file stream.

The task now is to get the new string information from the user and append it to the end of the file. The user is prompted for the new string, which is obtained by *cin* and stored in a string object called *newLine*. To append the new information to the file, the file window must be moved to the end-of-file position. This is accomplished with a call to the *seekp()* function. The *seekp()*function is analogous to the *seekg()* function used earlier. However, *seekp()* is inherited via *ostream*, and *seekg()* is inherited via *istream*. Thus, the *seekp()* function should be used in conjunction with file write operations and *seekg()* used with file read operations. Actually, either could be used here, because both are inherited by this program. We are using *seekp()* to be consistent with its purpose, because we are about to perform a file write operation. Here is the statement we are using to call *seekp()*:

```
change.seekp(0, ios::end);
```

Notice the two arguments. The first argument, 0, tells the compiler to move the file window 0 bytes from the second argument specification. Thus, the window will be positioned 0 bytes from the *end* of the file. Table 12.1 summarizes the *tell* and *seek* functions available for window manipulation.

After the window is positioned at the end of the file, the *newLine* string is written to the file via the statement

```
change << newLine << endl;
```

After the new string is appended to the file, the **while** loop will break because *flag* has been set to true.

The next segment of code checks *flag* to determine if the string searched for was found during the previous search loop. If the string was not found in the file, an appropriate message is displayed to the user.

The Application Program.   Now all we need is an application program to test our *Files* class. Here is one, called *fileapp.cpp*, that will exercise all of the file operations that we have just developed:

```
//fileapp.cpp  APPLICATION FILE FOR FILE I/O

//PREPROCESSOR DIRECTIVES
#include "files.h"     //FOR Files CLASS

//MAIN FUNCTION
int main()
{
```

```
//DECLARE myFile OBJECT AND LOCAL VARIABLES
Files myFile;
char choice = ' ';

//GET FILE NAME FROM USER
myFile.setName();

//GENERATE FILE-ACCESS MENU
do
{
   cout  << "\n\n\t\tWrite and create a new file (W)"
         << "\n\n\t\tRead and display file (R)"
         << "\n\n\t\tAppend file (A)"
         << "\n\n\t\tChange file (C)"
         << "\n\n\t\tQuit(Q)"
         << "\n\n\n\t\t\tENTER CHOICE --> " << endl;
   cin >> choice;
   choice = toupper(choice);
   switch (choice)
   {
      case 'W':   myFile.writeFile();
                  break;
      case 'R':   myFile.readFile();
                  break;
      case 'A':   myFile.appendFile();
                  break;
      case 'C':   myFile.readFile();
                  myFile.changeFile();
                  break;
      case 'Q':   break;
      default :   cout << "Invalid choice." << endl;
   } //END SWITCH
} //END DO/WHILE
while ((choice != 'q') && (choice != 'Q'));

//RETURN
return 0;
} //END main()
```

Again, you see our *files.h* header file included so that we can define an object for our *Files* class. Function *main()* begins by defining an object called *myFile* of the *Files* class. This object is then used to call our *setName()* function to obtain a disk file name from the user and set the *fileName* member of the class. A menu is then generated on the screen that allows the user to exercise any of the file operations that are part of the *Files* class. Of course, these are the operations that we just developed. Once the user selects a given menu option, the respective class function is called via the *myFile* object. Notice in particular that both the *readFile()* and *changeFile()* functions are called for the "Change file (C)" menu option to allow the user to examine the existing contents of the file via the *readFile()* function prior to entering a string to be changed. That's all there is to it! You now have the knowledge to create and manipulate your own disk files.

DEBUGGING TIP

Testing file handling programs for proper operation can be tricky and time consuming since you can't really see what's going on. So, why not use *cin* and *cout* to test your program via keyboard input and display output for proper operation first, then overload the *cin* and *cout* objects to perform the same operations on disk files once you are certain the program is working properly. Yes, you can overload the standard *cin* and *cout* objects to read and write disk files, rather than the default keyboard and display files. The idea will be to use *cin* and *cout* as intended so we can see what's going on, then overload them to operate on disk files. For example, suppose that we must read a file called *values.txt* from the *A:* drive which contains an unknown number of integer values. As we read the file, we must sum the integer values and write the final sum to a file on the *A:* drive called *sum.txt*. But, before we operate on the files, we will input the values on the keyboard and read them with *cin* then output the sum to the display via *cout*. Once we verify that the program is working correctly, we will use *cin* and *cout* to read and write the disk files. This way we are sure the disk file operations will work correctly. Here's a program that will do the job:

```
/*
THIS PROGRAM WILL OVERLOAD cin AND cout FOR DEBUGGING
FILE I/O
*/
//PREPROCESSOR DIRECTIVES
#include <fstream>   //FOR ifstream AND ofstream
#include <iostream>  //FOR cin AND cout
#include <stdlib.h>  //FOR exit()

using namespace std;   //REQUIRED WHEN INCLUDING iostream


//MAIN FUNCTION
int main()
{
   //DEFINE VARIABLES
   int value = 0;  //INTEGER VALUE TO SUM
   int sum = 0;    //SUM OF VALUES

   //DEFINE FILE OBJECTS AND OPEN FILES
   //ifstream cin("A:values.txt");
   //ofstream cout("A:sum.txt");

   //FILE OK?
   if(!cin)
   {
     cerr << "Cannot open input file" << endl;
     exit(1);
   }
```

```
                if(!cout)
                {
                  cerr << "Cannot open output file" << endl;
                  exit(1);
                }
                else
                {

                  //SUM THE VALUES
                  while (cin >> value)  //READ CHARACTER
                     sum += value;      //ADD TO SUM

                  //WRITE SUM
                  cout << "The sum is " << sum << endl;
                }//END ELSE

                //RETURN
                return 0;
             }//END main()
```

Do you see what we have done in the program? We have commented-out the two lines that define *cin* and *cout* as file objects. This allows us to test the program by entering the values via the keyboard and observing the final sum on the monitor. Once the program is working properly, we simply remove the // comment symbols on the file object definitions. This will overload *cin* and *cout*, forcing them to perform disk file input and output, respectively. Also, notice that we have used *cerr* to display the file error messages. Why?

When testing the program via keyboard input, you must enter a Ctrl-Z character to terminate the loop. The Ctrl-Z character is interpreted as an EOF marker by the compiler.

Have you ever been in a programming contest? If not, you need to get with some of your computer science friends and enter one. They are a blast! Plus you learn a lot! Organizations such as ACM sponsor such contests. You might even want to organize your own contest. Anyway, all input and output for the contest problems is usually in the form of file I/O. The program is judged by reading a judging file, then writing the program results to an output file. The judges then compare the output file your program generates to a master file to determine if the program produced the correct output for the given input. Many of the problems in the contest often require you to determine character and/or word boundaries. To determine these boundaries you must use the *get()* function, because *get()* reads white space as well as non-white space characters. The idea is that white space such as blanks, tabs, and CRLF separate words and we don't count them as characters. Here is a program that will count both the words and non-white space characters in a file:

```
//PREPROCESSOR DIRECTIVES
#include <iostream>      //FOR cin AND cout
```

```
#include <fstream>          //FOR FILE I/O
#include <stdlib.h>         //FOR exit()

using namespace std;   //REQUIRED WHEN INCLUDING iostream OR fstream

//MAIN FUNCTION
int main()
{
  //DEFINE VARIABLES
  char fileChar = ' ';    //FILE INPUT VARIABLE
  int wordCount = 1;      //WORD COUNTER
  int charCount = 0;      //CHARACTER COUNTER

  //DEFINE FILE OBJECT AND OPEN FILE
  ifstream cin("A:wordsIn.txt");    //DEFINE FILE INPUT OBJECT
  ofstream cout("A:wordsOut.txt");  //DEFINE FILE OUTPUT OBJECT

  //FILE OK?
  if(!cin)
  {
   cerr << "Cannot open input file" << endl;
   exit(1);
  }

  if(!cout)
  {
   cerr << "Cannot open output file" << endl;
   exit(1);
  }
  else
  {
     //READ ONE CHARACTER AT A TIME AND LOOP UNTIL EOF
     while(cin.get(fileChar))
     {
         if((fileChar != ' ') && (fileChar != '\n') && (fileChar != '\t'))
           ++charCount;
         else
           ++wordCount;
     }//END WHILE
  }//END ELSE
  cout << "\n\nThere " << wordCount << " words in the file" << endl;
  cout << "There are " << charCount << " non-white space characters in the file"
       << endl;

  //RETURN
  return 0;
} //END main()
```

Here, we have assumed that the program is to read a file called *wordsIn.txt* and write to a file called *wordsOut.txt*, both located on the *A:* drive. First, notice that we have overloaded *cin* and *cout* so that the file can first be tested via keyboard input and display output as discussed in the foregoing debugging tip. Next, you see that the **while** loop uses the *get()* function to read one character at a time. The character is tested for white space and a character counter or word counter are incremented accordingly. Notice that a blank, tab, or CRLF constitute white space. The program assumes that there is no final CRLF, only an EOF, marking the end of the file. Can you see how the logic is working?

Quick Check

1. True of false: File operations in C++ are the same as those in C.
2. List the major operations that are required to create a new file.
3. List the major operations that are required to read an existing file.
4. What is the difference, relative to positioning of the file window between using the *ios::cur* versus the *ios::end* specifications?
5. How does the *change.cpp* program in this section inherit the *tellg()* function?
6. What does the *tellg()* function return to the calling program?
7. True or false: The *tellg()* function should be used with input files, whereas the *tellp()* function should be used with output files.
8. What function must be used to position the file window for an output file?
9. What three predefined starting points are available to the *seekg()* and *seekp()* functions?
10. The distance to move the file window from the specified starting point when using *seekg()* or *seekp()* must be expressed in _____ units.

CHAPTER SUMMARY

A file is a data structure that consists of a sequence of data items. Files provide a means for your program to communicate with the outside world. Any I/O operations performed by your program, even keyboard input and display output, are handled via files. All file I/O in C++ is in the form of file streams that employ predefined classes. The *ifstream* class is used to create input file stream objects, the *ofstream* class is used to create output file stream objects, and the *fstream* class is used to create file stream objects that will be used for both input and output. All three of these file stream classes are declared in the *fstream* header file. File streams that you create are called named file streams. To create a named file stream, you must define a file stream object for one of the *fstream* file classes and attach the stream object to a particular disk file by specifying the file name as the constructor argument when the file stream object is defined. This is referred to a "opening" a file. The file stream class constructor automatically opens the file, while the class destructor automatically closes the file.

Once a file stream is opened, it is ready for processing. The individual data items within a file are accessed via a file stream window. The window must be positioned over the data item to be accessed. When a file is opened, the window is automatically created to access the file data items. Typical tasks that are performed on disk files include writing new files, reading existing files, appending existing files, and changing the information in existing files. The C++ language has various predefined functions to facilitate the coding of these tasks, some of which are given in Table 12.1.

QUESTIONS AND PROBLEMS

QUESTIONS

1. Describe the structure of a file.

2. What is a file stream?

3. What is a file stream window and how is it used during file processing?

4. What three predefined classes provide the basis for C++ files?

5. What header file provides the predefined file class declarations in C++?

6. What two operations must be performed to create a named file stream in C++?

7. Write statements to create the following disk file streams:

   a. A file stream called *fileIn* that will read a disk file called *mydata.txt* from the *A:* drive.

   b. A file stream called *fileIO* that will both read and write a disk file called *mydata.txt* located on the hard drive in a directory called *myDirectory* in a Windows operating system.

   c. A file stream called *addTo* that will append a file whose name is stored in a string object called *name*.

8. True or false: When a file stream is opened for the *ofstream* class the file stream window is placed at the beginning of the file, and all data items in an existing file are overwritten by any subsequent write operations to the file.

9. List the major operations that must be performed in order to change the contents of an existing file.

10. Write a statement that will store the current position of the *myFile* file stream window in a variable called *position*. Assume that *myFile* is defined for the *ofstream* class.

11. Write a statement that will move the file stream window in question 10 to a position that is *position* bytes from the current position of the window.

12. Write a statement that will position the *myFile* file stream window to the beginning of the file. Assume that *myFile* is defined for the *ifstream* class.

13. Write a statement that will position the *myFile* file stream window to the end of the file. Assume that *myFile* is defined for the *ofstream* class.

14. Write a statement that will write a string called *myString* to an output file stream object called *myFile*.

15. Write a statement that will read a string at the current window position of an input file stream called *myFile* and place it in a string object called *myString*.

16. Write a loop structure that will search for a string called *myString* in a file stream called *myFile* and set *flag* to true if the string is found.

Problems

Least Difficult

Perform the following tasks for problems 1–5:

❑ Add the specified function to the *Files* class developed in this chapter.

❑ Write an implementation file for the specified function.

❑ Add the specified function to the application program menu in *fileapp.cpp* in order to test the function.

1. A function called *copy()* that will copy an existing file to a new file.

2. A function called *erase()* that will erase an existing file.

3. A function called *compare()* that will compare the contents of two files and report to the user if they are the same or different.

More Difficult

4. A function called *cleanUp()* that will clean up a file by removing the asterisks inserted by the *change()* function developed in this chapter. The cleaned-up file should have no blank lines or fill characters.

5. A function that will read a file and then rewrite it to a new file with every line preceded by a sequential line number. The line number must be left justified on the screen when the file is displayed.

Most Difficult

6. Using the techniques discussed in this chapter, write and test a program that will handle a parts inventory file of the following information:

❑ Part Name
❑ Part Number
❑ Part Price
❑ Quantity on Hand

Develop functions that will allow a user to create the parts inventory file, read and display the file, append the file, and change information in the file. (*Hint*: Define the parts inventory information as private members of your inventory files class.)

7. Using the techniques discussed in this chapter, develop a class that will process an employee file containing the following information:

❑ Employee name
❑ Employee number
❑ Employee type: salaried, commissioned, or hourly
❑ Employee gender: male or female
❑ Employee wage: annual salary, commission rate, or hourly rate

Develop functions that will allow a user to create the employee file, read and display the file, append the file, and change information in the file. (*Hint*: Define the employee information as private members of your employee file class.) Then, write an application program to completely test your classes.

POINTERS

Chapter Contents

Chapter Objectives

When you are finished with this chapter, you should have a good understanding of the following:

- The concept of a memory pointer.
- The concept of dynamic memory allocation and deallocation.
- How to define static and dynamic pointers in C++.
- How to access pointer data.
- The do's and don'ts of pointer arithmetic.
- Indirection via pointers.
- How to pass pointers to/from functions.
- The concept of indirection using arrays of pointers.
- Object pointers.
- The purpose of a destructor.

INTRODUCTION

Pointers are fundamental to programming in either the C or C++ language. A pointer represents a physical address in memory.

> A **pointer** represents a physical memory address.

Although you may not have realized it, you have been working with pointers already. For instance, recall that an array name actually represents the memory address of the first element of an array. Furthermore, by preceding a parameter with an ampersand, &, you are representing the memory address of the parameter. Therefore, an array name and a parameter preceded with an ampersand are actually pointers. However, these pointers are **constant pointers**, because the address to which they point can never be changed by the program. On the other hand, a **variable pointer** is a pointer whereby the address to which it points can be changed by the program. In this chapter, you will learn how to use variable pointers in preparation for their use in the chapters that follow. Pointers provide a powerful and efficient means of accessing data, especially when the data are part of a data structure, such as an array. This is an important topic, so stay with us.

13.1   THE IDEA OF POINTERS

Let's begin by comparing a pointer to a variable. Assume for a moment that *value1* and *value2* are defined as integer variables and initialized to the values of 10 and 20, respectively. Also, assume that *p1* and *p2* are defined as pointers. The boxes in Figure 13.1 illustrate these assumptions.

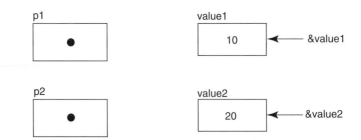

FIGURE 13.1   *P1* AND *P2* ARE POINTERS, AND VALUE1 AND VALUE2 ARE INTEGER VARIABLES.

In Figure 13.1, you see the boxes labeled *value1* and *value2* storing the integers 10 and 20, respectively. Now, you already know that *&value1* and *&value2* represent the memory *addresses* of the variables. Thus, *&value1* locates the box containing the integer 10, and *&value2* locates the box containing the 20. The boxes labeled *p1* and *p2* contain a dot, •, indicating that they do not point to anything at this time.

Because *p1* and *p2* are pointer variables, we can reassign them at any time to point to data in memory. For instance, we can assign the address of *value1* to *p1* and the address of *value2* to *p2*, like this:

```
p1 = &value1;
p2 = &value2;
```

There is no problem with these assignments because *p1, p2, &value1,* and *&value2* all represent memory addresses. What you get is illustrated by Figure 13.2(a).

After these assignments, *p1* and *&value1* both locate the value 10 in memory, and *p2* and *&value2* locate the value 20 in memory. Likewise, both *p1* and *p2* are pointers, so we can assign *p1* to *p2*, like this:

```
p2 = p1;
```

The result of this assignment is illustrated in Figure 13.2(b). Notice now that *p1, p2,* and *&value1* all locate the value 10. In fact, we can alter *p1* and *p2* to point to any address in memory, because they are variable pointers. However, we cannot alter *&value1* or *&value2*, because they are constant pointers, which cannot be altered.

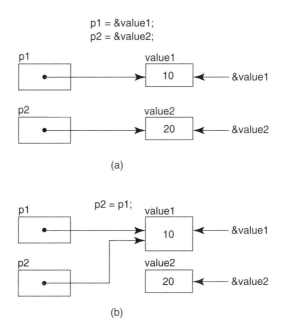

FIGURE 13.2   THE EFFECT OF (A) ASSIGNING THE ADDRESS OF A VARIABLE TO A POINTER, AND (B) ASSIGNING A POINTER TO A POINTER.

It is important to note that in Figure 13.2(b), there is only one *value1*; however, we have three pointers locating this value. Thus, if we change the value of *value1*, there is still only one variable to be changed, not three. For instance, suppose we make the following assignment:

```
value1 = 30;
```

After this assignment, *p1*, *p2*, and *&value1* will all locate the new value, 30, in memory.

Quick Check

1. Suppose that *pchar* is a pointer to a character and *character* is a character variable. Write a statement to make *pchar* point to the character stored in *character*.
2. Write a statement that will make an integer pointer called *p1int* point to the same integer to which an integer pointer called *p2int* is pointing.
3. True or false: If *character* is defined as a character variable, then *&character* can be altered at any time.
4. True or false: If *pchar* is defined as a character pointer, then *pchar* can be altered at any time.

13.2   DEFINING POINTERS AND INITIALIZING POINTER DATA

To define a pointer, you must tell the compiler the type of data to which the pointer is pointing, just as you do when defining a variable. Here's the general format:

POINTER DEFINITION FORMAT

data type being pointed to   ∗ pointer identifier;

Here are some sample pointer definitions:

```
int    *integerPointer;
char   *characterPointer;
double *floatPointer;
```

The first definition says that *integerPointer* will be a pointer to an integer value, the second says that *characterPointer* will point to a character, and finally *float-Pointer* will point to a floating-point value. Note the use of the asterisk, or star, in all the definitions. The star must immediately precede the pointer identifier. This is what tells the compiler that you are defining a pointer variable rather than a common variable. From now on, we will refer to a pointer variable as simply a pointer.

> The **star**, *, in front of a pointer variable denotes "the contents of." In other words, *p1* is read as *the contents of the memory location to which p1 is pointing.* In the preceding pointer definitions, the * indicates the data type to which the pointer is pointing. Thus, the definintion *int *integerPointer* says that the contents of memory to which *integerPointer* is pointing is an integer.

There are two ways to initialize a pointer to point to a value.

1. Allocating memory **statically** by defining a variable and then making a pointer point to the variable value.
2. Allocating memory **dynamically** and initializing a pointer to point to a value.

Static Pointers

Let's define a pointer to an integer and an integer variable as follows:

```
int  *p1;
int value;
```

Using these definitions, we can then make the following *static* assignments:

```
p1 = &value;
*p1 = 25;
```

Figure 13.3 illustrates the results of the preceding operations. Pointer *p1* is defined as a pointer to an integer. Variable *value* is defined as an integer variable. The first assignment makes *p1* point to the variable *value*. The second assignment stores the value 25 in memory where *p1* is pointing. Notice the use of the star symbol, *, again. A star in front of a pointer variable means "the contents of." Therefore, the second assignment reads "Store the value 25 in *the contents of* memory to where *p1* is pointing." Of course, this is the same memory location as *&value*. We can say that **p1* is an **alias** for the variable *value*, because the integer value stored in *value* can also be accessed via **p1*.

There is no ambiguity in the use of the star to define a pointer and to initialize a pointer to point to a value. Both reference "the contents of." When defining a pointer, the * indicates that "the contents of" memory pointed to by the pointer will be a given data type. When initializing a pointer to point to a value, the * indicates "the contents of" memory pointed to by the pointer will be a given value.

We say that this type of initialization is **static** because the allocation of memory used to store the value is fixed and cannot go away. Once the variable is defined, the compiler sets aside enough memory to store a value of the given data type. This

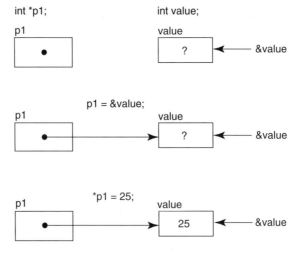

FIGURE 13.3 **INITIALIZING A STATIC POINTER.**

memory remains reserved for this variable and cannot be used for anything else until the function in which the pointer is defined is terminated. In other words, you cannot **deallocate** the memory set aside for a variable. The pointer to that variable can be changed, but the amount of memory set aside for the variable remains.

DEBUGGING TIP

It is very easy to make incorrect assignments when working with pointers. For example, using the foregoing definitions, the following three assignments will create an error:

```
*p1 = &value;
p1 = value;
p1 = 25;
```

In all cases, an attempt is made to "mix apples and oranges." In the first case, an attempt is made to assign an address (&*value*) to a value, because *p1 is a value. In the second case, an attempt is made to assign a value (*value*) to an address, because *p1* is an address. Likewise, in the third case, an attempt is made to assign a value to an address. The correct assignments would be

```
*p1 = value;
p1 = &value;
*p1 = 25;
```

Dynamic Pointers

The second way to initialize a pointer to point to a value is by allocating memory *dy-namically*. By allocating memory dynamically, we mean to set aside memory at run time when it is needed to store a value of a given data type. Then, once the value is no longer needed, we can deallocate the memory and make it available for other use by the system. Again we will define *p1* as an integer pointer, as follows:

```
int *p1;
```

Now, we can initialize *p1* dynamically to point to a value, like this:

```
p1 = new int;
*p1 = 25;
```

Figure 13.4 illustrates the results of these operations. This time, we did not need to first initialize *p1* to the address of a static variable. Rather, the **new** operator creates enough memory to hold an integer value pointed to by *p1*. Then, we stored the value 25 in that memory area. Once memory is allocated dynamically like this, we can deallocate the same memory area by using the **delete** operator, as follows:

```
delete p1;
```

This operation will free up the memory pointed to by *p1* for other use by the program and/or system. It is important to note that the **delete** operator *does not* delete the pointer; it simply releases the memory area to which the pointer points. There-fore, after the preceding statement is executed, *p1* still exists as a pointer that does

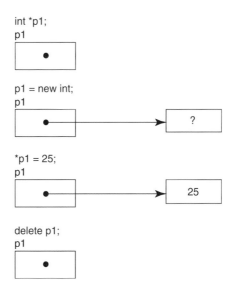

FIGURE 13.4   INITIALIZING A DYNAMIC POINTER.

not point to anything but can be again initialized to point to another integer by using the **new** operator.

> The **new** operator is used to dynamically allocate memory for pointer data, and the **delete** operator is used to deallocate memory pointed to by a pointer.

EXAMPLE 13.1

Determine the output generated by the following program:

```
//PREPROCESSOR DIRECTIVE
#include <iostream.h>        //FOR cout

//MAIN FUNCTION
int main()
{
    //DEFINE TWO POINTERS AND A VARIABLE
    int *p1;
    int *p2;
    int index;

    //INITIALIZE POINTER DATA STATICALLY
    p1 = &index;
    index = 10;

    //INITIALIZE POINTER DATA DYNAMICALLY
    p2 = new int;
    *p2 = 20;

    //DISPLAY POINTER DATA
    cout << "The contents of memory pointed to by p1 is:  " << *p1 << endl;
    cout << "The contents of memory pointed to by p2 is:  " << *p2 << endl;

    //DEALLOCATE MEMORY POINTED TO BY p2
    delete p2;

    //RETURN
    return 0;
} //END main()
```

Solution

The output generated by the program is

```
The contents of memory pointed to by p1 is 10
The contents of memory pointed to by p2 is 20
```

Notice that the program initializes the *p1* pointer data statically and the *p2* pointer data dynamically. Both produce the same results; however, the memory pointed to by *p1* is set aside until the program terminates, whereas the memory pointed to by *p2* is deallocated immediately after the *cout* statement. Notice also how the pointer data are accessed in the *cout* statement. The ∗ is employed to indicate that "the contents of" memory pointed to by the pointer is to be displayed. What do you suppose would happen if the ∗ were omitted? Well, because a pointer is a memory address, you would see the actual memory address, in hex, assigned to the pointer. This leads us to our next topic.

DEBUGGING TIP

Remember to always use the **delete** operator to deallocate the memory for each and every pointer you allocate with the **new** operator. The operating system sets aside memory when you create a dynamic pointer using the **new** operator. Forgetting to use the **delete** operator to deallocate pointer memory results in *memory garbage*—memory that is not being used and cannot be allocated by the operating system for any other purpose. In fact, deallocating pointer memory is often referred to as **garbage collection**. Some languages, like Java, perform automatic garbage collection, but when using C++ the programmer must be the garbage collector.

Quick Check

1. Define a static character pointer called *pchar* and a character variable called *character*.
2. Write a statement to make *pchar* point to the variable *character* defined in question 1.
3. Write a statement to initialize *pchar* defined in question 1 to the character 'A'.
4. True or false: The assignment *pchar* = 'Z' is legal, as long as *pchar* is defined as a character pointer.
5. When a pointer is initialized dynamically, the _____ operator must be used in the pointer definition.
6. Write the statements to initialize a dynamic character pointer called *pchar* to the value 'B'.
7. Write a statement that will deallocate the memory allocated in question 6.
8. True or false: When you deallocate pointer memory using the **delete** operator, the respective pointer is deleted.

13.3   ACCESSING POINTER DATA AND POINTER ARITHMETIC

You have already seen how to access the data pointed to by a pointer through the use of the star, ∗, operator. Remember, ∗*p* means *the contents of memory pointed to by p*. Let's see how we can expand on this knowledge by using a pointer to a string. Consider the following pointer definition:

```
char  *sptr = "HAL";
```

The foregoing definition creates a character pointer called *sptr*. In addition, the pointer data are initialized to the string "HAL". If you were to view the data stored to where *sptr* is pointing via a debugger, you would observe the following:

DEBUGGER RESULTS

> Inspecting *sptr*
>
>   [0]   'H'
>   [1]   'A'
>   [2]   'L'
>   [3]   '\0'

As you can see, *sptr* locates the entire string in memory just as an array name locates an array in memory. In fact, you see that the compiler has placed the string in an array located by the variable pointer *sptr*. Now, what do you suppose you would see on the display after the following *cout* statements were executed?

```
cout << *sptr << endl;
cout << sptr[0] << endl;
```

Even though the pointer data are initialized to a string, *sptr* is still only a character pointer. Therefore, the first *cout* statement will display the single character 'H'. Likewise, the compiler has placed the string into an array pointed to by *sptr*, so the second statement will also produce the single character stored at index [0] in the array, which is the single character 'H'.

Next, what do you suppose will be displayed by the following?

```
cout << sptr << endl;
```

With this definition, *sptr* is simply a pointer to an array of characters. In other words, the compiler will treat it just like an array name when used like this. As a result, the foregoing statement will display the entire string "HAL". Remember, although *sptr* is treated just like an array name in this operation, it is different! When *sptr* is defined as a pointer to a character array, it is a variable pointer and therefore could be altered to point to another location in memory. On the other hand, if *sptr* were an array name, it would be a constant pointer and could not be altered to point to a different location.

Next, consider the following two statements:

```
cout << *(sptr + 1) << endl;
cout << (sptr + 1)[0] << endl;
```

The first statement is read "Display the contents of *sptr* + 1." Because *sptr* locates the first character in the array, (*sptr* + 1) must locate the second array character, right? Therefore, the contents of (*sptr* + 1) must be the character 'A'. This statement doesn't change the pointer location; it simply *offsets* the pointer for the purpose of the *cout* operation. The second statement will produce the same character 'A'. This statement would be read as "Display the character stored at index [0] of location (*sptr* + 1)." This time, the pointer is being treated just like an array name; however it might be a bit confusing, because the character 'A' is located at index [1] in the array. This is true relative to *sptr*, but relative to (*sptr* + 1), index [0] locates the second character in the array, which is the character 'A'. What character do you suppose is stored at (*sptr* + 1)[1] ? You're right if you thought the character 'L'. How about position (*sptr* + 2)[0] ? Again, you would be accessing the character 'L'. Think about it! These concepts are illustrated in Figure 13.5.

Pointer Arithmetic

Unlike an array name, which is a constant pointer and cannot be altered, a pointer is a variable pointer, which can be altered. As a result, you can perform certain arithmetic operations on pointers.

Keep in mind that a pointer is an address. As a result, only those arithmetic operations on addresses that "make sense" are legal. You can add or subtract an integer constant to or from a pointer. Adding or subtracting an integer, say, x, to or from a pointer will produce a new pointer, which is x elements away from the original pointer.

Adding or subtracting a floating-point constant to or from a pointer would not make sense, considering that an address must result from the operation. Likewise, it wouldn't make sense to multiply or divide a pointer by a constant, considering that a pointer is an address.

Here is what you *should not* do:

❐ You should not add two pointers.

❐ You should not multiply two pointers.

❐ You should not divide two pointers.

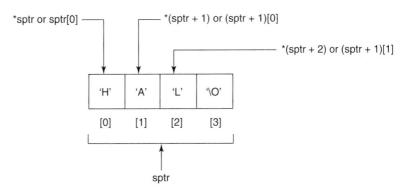

FIGURE 13.5 ACCESSING STRING POINTER DATA.

CAUTION

Performing arithmetic operations on pointers may be hazardous to your system! Pointers can be altered to point anywhere in the system memory, so you could accidentally make a pointer operate in an area of memory being used by the operating system for other system chores. The result of such an accident is usually a system crash, which can only be corrected by rebooting the system.

One thing you *can* do is subtract two pointers when both pointers are pointing to the same array. When you subtract two pointers that point to the same array, you get a constant value, which is the number of array positions, or elements, between the two pointers. So, if *p1* is a pointer that points to index [0] in an array, and *p2* is a pointer that points to index [5] in the same array, then *p2 – p1* will yield the value 5.

Legal arithmetic operations on pointers are *scaled*. This means that when you perform pointer arithmetic, the compiler scales the result relative to the data type being pointed to, rather than bytes of memory. For instance, if a given compiler requires two bytes to store an integer value, then the value will occupy two addresses in memory. So, if *iptr* is a pointer to an integer, then adding 1 to *iptr* yields a pointer that will point 2 bytes, or addresses, away from where *iptr* was originally pointing. Likewise, if *iptr1* points to index [1] in an integer array, and *iptr2* points to index [2] of the same integer array, then *iptr2 – iptr1* will yield the constant value 1, even though the two addresses being pointed to are 2 bytes from each other.

EXAMPLE 13.2

Determine the output generated by the following program:

```
//PREPROCESSOR DIRECTIVES
#include <iostream.h>        //FOR cout

//MAIN FUNCTION
int main()
{
    //DEFINE THREE CHARACTER POINTERS AND
    //INITIALIZE ONE TO A STRING
    char *sptr1;
    char *sptr2;
    char *sptr= "HAL";

    //DISPLAY POINTER DATA
    cout << "*sptr --> " << *sptr << endl;
    cout << "sptr[0] --> "<< sptr[0] << endl;
    cout << "*(sptr + 1) --> " << *(sptr + 1) << endl;
    cout << "(sptr + 1)[0] --> " << (sptr + 1)[0] << endl;
    cout << "*(sptr + 2) --> " << *(sptr + 2) << endl;
```

```
//ADD ONE TO sptr AND OUTPUT STRING
++sptr;
cout << "sptr --> " << sptr << endl;

//SUBTRACT ONE FROM sptr AND OUTPUT STRING
--sptr;
cout << "sptr --> " << sptr << endl;

//WEIRD
for (int i = 0; i < 3; ++i)
  *(sptr + i) = *(sptr + i) + 1;
cout << "sptr --> " << sptr << endl;

//INITIALIZE sptr1, sptr2 AND OUTPUT DIFFERENCE
sptr1 = sptr;
sptr2 = sptr + 2;

//OUTPUT sptr2 - sptr1
cout << "sptr2 - spt1 = " << sptr2 - sptr1 << endl;

//RETURN
return 0;
} //END main()
```

Solution

Here is what you would see on the display:

```
*sptr -->  H
sptr[0] -->  H
*(sptr + 1) -->  A
(sptr + 1)[0] -->  A
*(sptr + 2) -->  L
sptr -->  AL
sptr -->  HAL
sptr -->  IBM
sptr2 - sptr1 = 2
```

The first five single character outputs demonstrate the operations discussed earlier. See if you can verify the output characters knowing that *sptr* is initialized to the string "HAL". The sixth output, "AL", results from adding 1 to *sptr* and then displaying the string located by *sptr*. Adding 1 to *sptr* yields a new pointer that points to the second character in the string. The seventh output, "HAL", is produced by subtracting 1 from *sptr* to make it point to its original location at the beginning of the string. The eighth output, "IBM", results from a **for** loop that adds 1 to each character in the string pointed to by *sptr*. The body of the **for** loop is the single statement $*(sptr + i) = *(sptr + i) + 1$. Think about what this statement does. When *i* is 0, the statement becomes $*(sptr) = *(sptr) + 1$. Doesn't this add one to the value pointed to by *sptr* and assign this sum back to the contents of *sptr*? Well, $*sptr$ is the character 'H'. If you add one to this character value, you get the character 'I'. As a result, the first loop iteration replaces the character 'H' in *stpr* with the character 'I'. Likewise, the second iteration replaces 'A' with 'B' and the third iteration replaces 'L' with 'M'. After the loop terminates, the string pointed to by *sptr* is "IBM", which can be verified by observing the output generated by the respective *cout* statement.

Finally, the last output is produced by initializing *sptr1* to point to the beginning of the string and *sptr2* to point to the end of the string. The output is the value 2, which is the number of elements between *sptr1* and *sptr2*.

Quick Check

1. Define a string pointer called *pstring* and initialize it to the string "C++".
2. Write a statement to display the entire string in question 1.
3. Write a statement to display just the first character of the string in question 1.
4. Write a statement to display just the last character of the string in question 1.
5. Write a statement to display the last two characters of the string in question 1.
6. Suppose that *p1* is a pointer that points to index [5] of an array of double floating-point values, and *p2* is a pointer that points to index [15] of the same array. Then *p2 – p1* will yield the value _____.

13.4 ARRAYS OF POINTERS ⇒ INDIRECTION

We can easily define an array that stores pointers, thus creating an *array of pointers*. Here is how it's done:

```
char *ptrArray[2];
ptrArray[0] = "Dog";
ptrArray[1] = "Cat";
```

The first line of code defines an array of pointers to character data. The star in front of the array name is used to specify an array of pointers. The array size is 2, so this array holds two pointers, or addresses. This definition represents two levels of **indirection**, or **referencing**, because an array name is always a pointer and this pointer points to the pointers contained in the array. Here, one level of addressing is provided by the * pointer specification and the second level provided by the [] array specification.

Indirection has to do with the levels of addressing it takes to access data.

The two lines of code following the array definition are used to initialize the array. The pointer at position [0] of this array is initialized to point to the string "Dog", and the pointer (address) contained at position [1] of the array is initialized to point to the string "Cat". Notice that the "pointer" is initialized to point to a given string.

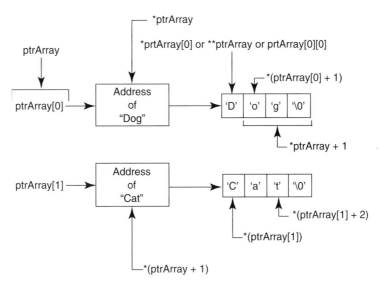

FIGURE 13.6 AN ARRAY OF POINTERS POINTING TO STRINGS.

Although the array is easily defined and initialized, interpreting the indirection gets a bit tricky. Study Figure 13.6 to get an idea of how the array data are accessed using pointers. First, you see that each position in the array is a pointer that locates an entire string. Thus, *ptrArray*[0] locates the string "Dog" and *ptrArray*[1] locates the string "Cat". You also see that *∗ptrArray* and *∗(ptrArray + 1)* locate the same two strings, "Dog" and "Cat", respectively, because the *contents of ptrArray* is the address of the first string and the *contents of (ptrArray + 1)* is the address of the second string. What do you suppose is pointed to by *∗ptrArray + 1*? This statement offsets the contents of the first pointer by 1, resulting in a string pointer that points one character away from the original pointer. Thus, *∗ptrArray + 1* points to the string "og". Next, because *∗ptrArray* locates the entire string "Dog", what do you suppose is located by *∗ptrArray*[0]? You're right if you thought the first character, 'D', of the first string, "Dog". Likewise, *∗(ptrArray*[0] + 1) locates the second character, 'o', of this same string. How would you access the character 'C' in the second string? How about *∗(ptrArray*[1])? Extending this idea, *∗(ptrArray*[1] + 2) will locate the character 't' of the second string.

In all of the above examples, we were ***dereferencing*** the pointers to get at what a given pointer was pointing to. One way to make dereferencing simpler is to re-member that by dereferencing once you get a string, while dereferencing twice gives you a character in the foregoing definition. Remember that dereferencing can occur with a ∗ or a [] specification. So, *∗ptrArray* and *ptrArray*[0] both point to the string "Dog", while *∗(ptrArray[0])*, *∗ptrArray[0]*, *∗∗ptrArray* and *ptrArray[0][0]* will all point to the single character 'D'. Think about it, but don't think too long or you will get a headache!

Let's look at a practical application for an array of pointers.

Example 13.3

Write a program to define an array of pointers, called *names[]*, to strings. Initialize the array pointers to point to the strings "Andy", "Brenda", "Neil", "Lori", and "Doug", and display the strings using the array of pointers.

Solution

First, we must define an array of pointers and initialize the pointers to point to the given strings. This can be accomplished in one line, as follows:

```
char *names[] = {"Andy", "Brenda", "Neil", "Lori", "Doug", NULL};
```

This defines an array of pointers called *names[]*. The pointers point to character strings. There is no array size specified, so the number of pointers in the array depends on the number of initializing string values. The pointers are initialized to point to the five string values given in the problem statement. In addition, the last pointer in the array is initialized to point to **NULL**. The word **NULL** is predefined in the standard C++ library header files, such as *iostream.h* and *stdio.h*. Any pointer can be tested for equality or inequality to **NULL**. As a result, it can be used to terminate a loop that will display the string values. Here's such a loop:

```
int i = 0;
while (*(names + i) != NULL)
{
    cout << *(names + i) << endl;
    ++i;
} //END WHILE
```

The **while** statement displays the strings pointed to by $*(names + i)$. Thus, the first loop iteration will display the string pointed to by $*(names + 0)$, which is the string "Andy". The second iteration will display the string pointed to by $*(names + 1)$, which is the string "Brenda", and so on. The loop terminates when $*(names + i)$ points to **NULL**. In our example, this happens when i equals the value 5, because $*(names + 5)$ was initialized as a pointer to **NULL**. Notice that the loop test is ($*(names + i)$!= *NULL*). Here is the complete program:

```
/*
THIS PROGRAM WILL DEFINE AN ARRAY OF POINTERS TO POINT
TO STRINGS AND THEN DISPLAY THE STRINGS USING POINTERS
*/
//PREPROCESSOR DIRECTIVES
#include <iostream.h>  //FOR cout

//DEFINE AND INITIALIZE ARRAY OF POINTERS TO STRINGS
char *names[] = {"Andy", "Brenda", "Neil", "Lori", "Doug", NULL};

//MAIN FUNCTION
int main()
{
   int i = 0;

//DISPLAY NAMES IN ARRAY UNTIL NULL POINTER IS ENCOUNTERED
   while (*(names + i) != NULL)
   {
```

```
        cout << *(names + i) << endl;
        ++i;
    } //END WHILE

    //RETURN
    return 0;
} //END main()
```

The output produced by the program is

```
Andy
Brenda
Neil
Lori
Doug
```

Quick Check

1. Define an array of pointers called *courses[]* to point to the strings "Calc", "Assembler", and "C++".
2. What is located at *courses* using the array in question 1?
3. What is located at *courses*[2] using the array in question 1?
4. What is located at *courses* + 2 using the array in question 1?
5. What is located at *(*courses*[1] + 3)?
6. The concept of using several levels of addressing to access data is known as _____.

13.5   USING POINTERS AS FUNCTION ARGUMENTS AND PARAMETERS

When you use a pointer as an argument in a function call, you are passing the address that the pointer references to the function. Recall that when you pass an address to a function, you are passing by reference rather than by value. When passing by reference, any operations on the parameter variables within the function will alter the corresponding actual argument variables listed in the function call. Up to this point, you had only two ways to pass variables to a function by reference: 1) by using the ampersand symbol, &, prior to the parameter in the function header, or 2) by passing an array using an array name. Well, think about what you are doing in both cases. You are passing an *address* to the function, right? Because a pointer is an address, we can also pass by reference using a pointer variable. Consider the following program:

```
//PREPROCESSOR DIRECTIVE
#include <iostream.h>   //FOR cout
```

```
//FUNCTION PROTOTYPE
void exchange(int *, int *);

//MAIN FUNCTION
int main()
{
    int value1 = 10;
    int value2 = 20;
    int *pointer2 = &value2;
    cout << "The values before the function call are " << value1
         << "  " << value2 << endl;
    exchange(&value1,pointer2);
    cout << "The values after the function call are " << value1
         << "  " << value2 << endl;

    //RETURN
    return 0;
} //END main()

//FUNCTION WILL EXCHANGE THE TWO PARAMETER VALUES
void exchange(int *p1, int *p2)
{
    int temp;
    temp = *p1;
    *p1 = *p2;
    *p2 = temp;
} //END exchange()
```

At the beginning of this program, a function called *exchange()* is prototyped to accept two integer pointers. Notice the syntax in the prototype. The *int* * specification means that the function expects to receive an integer pointer. Looking at the function definition at the end of the program, you see that the function simply exchanges the two integer values that it receives from the calling program. In function *main()*, you find that two integer variables are defined and initialized to the values of 10 and 20, respectively. Then, a pointer variable called *pointer2* is defined to point to the value of *value2*. In the function call, the address of *value1* is passed using the ampersand symbol, &, as we did earlier in the text. In addition, the address of *value2* is also passed as the second argument via pointer *pointer2*. Therefore, both variables are passed by reference to the function. The function expects to "see" two addresses, because its prototype dictates that it will accept two pointers. The variables are passed by reference, so their values will be swapped by the function. Here is the output generated by the program:

```
The values before the function call are 10  20
The values after the function call are 20 10
```

Look at the actual arguments and the prototype parameters again. You probably don't have any question about the second argument versus the second parameter, because both are pointers. But, what about the first argument versus the first parameter? Is there a problem here, because an & symbol is used for the argument and a * symbol is used for the corresponding parameter? No! Both are addresses of integers; therefore, there is no mismatch between the type of data being passed to the function and the type of data being received by the function.

Next, let's see how strings can be passed to functions using pointers. Look at the following program:

```
//PREPROCESSOR DIRECTIVE
#include <iostream.h>   //FOR cout

//FUNCTION PROTOTYPE
void displayString(char *);

//MAIN FUNCTION
int main()
{
    //DEFINE AND INITIALIZE A POINTER TO A STRING
    char *myString = "Hello World";

    //CALL FUNCTION TO DISPLAY STRING
    displayString(myString);

    //RETURN
    return 0;
} //END main()

//THIS FUNCTION DISPLAYS THE STRING POINTED TO BY *String
void displayString(char *myString)
{
    cout << "The string value is:   " << myString << endl;
} //END displayString()
```

First, you see the function prototype. The prototype shows a void function that will accept a character pointer. Next, you see a pointer defined to point to a string of characters and initialized to the string value "Hello World". Nothing is new here. Looking at the function implementation, you see that the function simply displays the string value whose address is pointed to by *myString*. The function call in *main()* passes the pointer to the function by listing the pointer identifier as the function argument. The pointer already represents an address, so you must never use the ampersand symbol, &, prior to a pointer name in a function call. So, in summary, the address of the string is passed to the function, where it is used to display the string value. That's all there is to it!

The foregoing program represents one level of indirection using a pointer that points to a character string. Next, let's consider two levels of indirection by defining an array of pointers to strings and see how such a structure is passed to and operated upon by a function. We will use the same array of pointers employed in Example 13.3. Here is the definition/initialization again:

```
char *names[] = {"Andy", "Brenda", "Neil", "Lori", "Doug", NULL};
```

Remember, *names* is a pointer to an array of pointers, thereby creating two levels of indirection. Now, we will develop a prototype for a function that will display the string values pointed to by the array pointers. Consider this:

```
void displayNames(char **);
```

Notice that the function parameter is *char ***. The reason that two stars are required is that it requires two levels of indirection to get to the fundamental character elements. Using this prototype, we will write a function to display the string values, as follows:

```
void displayNames(char **names)
{
  cout << "The names in the array are:" << endl;
  while (*names != NULL)
  {
    cout << *names << endl;
    ++names;
} //END displayNames()
```

First, you see that the function header reflects the prototype. Next, you see that a **while** loop is employed to display the string values. The last pointer in the array is initialized to **NULL,** so we can test for the null condition in the **while** statement as we did in Example 13.3. The *cout* statement within the loop displays the strings pointed to by the pointers in the *names[]* array. Observe how the two levels of indirection are working here. To access the individual characters, you must use ***names*; to access the entire string at a given pointer address, you use **names*. Thus, ***names* points to the character 'A', and **names* points to the string "Andy".

The real power of pointers is demonstrated where the loop is incrementing from one string to the next to provide the sequential string display. To do this, you simply increment from one string pointer to the next by incrementing the array pointer *names* using a *++names* statement. That's all there is to it!

Finally, the function call is

```
displayNames(names);
```

Again, you see that you only need to list the pointer array name as the argument in the function call. Putting everything together, you get the following program:

```
/*
THIS PROGRAM WILL DEFINE AN ARRAY OF POINTERS TO
POINT TO STRINGS  AND THEN DISPLAY THE STRINGS BY PASSING
THE POINTER ARRAY TO A FUNCTION
*/

//PREPROCESSOR DIRECTIVE
#include <iostream.h>  //FOR cout

//FUNCTION PROTOTYPE
void displayNames(char **);
```

```
//MAIN FUNCTION
int main()
{
    //DEFINE AND INITIALIZE ARRAY OF POINTERS TO STRINGS
    char *names[] = {"Andy", "Brenda", "Neil", "Lori",
                     "Doug", NULL};

    //CALL FUNCTION TO DISPLAY NAMES
    displayNames(names);

    //RETURN
    return 0;
} //END main()

//THIS FUNCTION DISPLAYS THE STRINGS POINTED TO
//BY THE ARRAY

void displayNames(char **names)
{
    cout << "The names in the array are:" << endl;
    while (*names != NULL)
    {
        cout << *names << endl;
        ++names;
    } //END WHILE
} //END displayNames()
```

 Quick Check

1. True or false: When a pointer is used in a function call, any operations on the pointer data in the function will affect the pointer data in the calling program.
2. True or false: A pointer argument in a function call must have a corresponding pointer parameter in the function prototype.
3. Write a prototype for a function called *foo()* that will receive a pointer to a string.
4. Write a prototype for a function called *foo()* that will receive an array of pointers to strings.
5. Assuming that *myNames[]* is defined as an array of pointers to strings, write a statement that will call the function in question 4.

13.6   OBJECT POINTERS

In earlier chapters, you learned how to define *static* class objects. By static, we mean not dynamic. In other words, static objects do not allocate memory dynamically. You can, however, define object pointers just as you can simple variable pointers. Then, to call an object function, you employ the ***pointer operator***, –>, instead of the dot operator.

Defining Object Pointers

Object pointers are defined very much like variable pointers. Object pointers can be set up as static or dynamic pointers using the following formats:

> ### FORMAT FOR DEFINING STATIC OBJECT POINTERS
>
> *class name object name;*
> *class name *pointer name;*
> *pointer name* **=** **&***object name;*

> ### FORMAT FOR DEFINING DYNAMIC OBJECT POINTERS
>
> *class name *pointer name;*
> *pointer name* = **new** *class name;*

If you are defining a pointer to a static object, you must define the object first and then define a pointer and make it point to the address of the object. When defining dynamic objects, the object name must be a pointer, and the keyword **new** must be employed to create the dynamic object. Notice that the class name must appear again after the keyword **new**. Of course, if you create a dynamic object, you should delete it using the keyword **delete** when you are finished with it.

For example, suppose that we have declared a class called *Rectangle*. Then object pointers can be defined as follows:

```
//DEFINE A STATIC OBJECT POINTER
Rectangle box(1,2);          //DEFINE STATIC OBJECT, box
Rectangle *box1;             //DEFINE OBJECT POINTER, box1
box1 = &box;                 //MAKE box1 POINT TO box

//DEFINE DYNAMIC OBJECT POINTER
Rectangle *box2;             //DEFINE box2 OBJECT POINTER
box2 = new Rectangle(2,3);   //ALLOCATE box2 MEMORY
```

In the first case, a static object called *box* is defined for the *Rectangle* class; then an object pointer called *box1* is defined for the same class. Finally, the address of the *box* object is assigned to the object pointer so that the pointer points to the object. In the second case, an object pointer called *box2* is created for the *Rectangle* class; then an object is allocated dynamically using the **new** operator. Notice that the *box* object has the argument *(1,2)*. This obviously means that a constructor is called when the object is defined. Here, the constructor will initialize the rectangle length to 1 and width to 2. There is nothing new here. The arguments *(1,2)* are passed to the object when it is defined. The object pointer, *box1*, is made to point to this object and, therefore, will reference a rectangle object with a length of 1 and width of 2. Now, look at the dynamic object definition for *box2*. Something *is* new here. The constructor arguments of *(2,3)* are placed *after the class specification*. This is where you must pass constructor arguments to dynamic objects. So, the *box2* object pointer points to a rectangle object whose length and width have been initialized by the constructor to (2,3).

> **PROGRAMMING NOTE**
>
> When initializing data with a dynamic object constructor, the initializing arguments must be placed after the class specification in the **new** statement.

Using the Pointer Operator to Send Messages to Objects

When a pointer is defined for an object, you must use the pointer operator, –>, to send messages to the object. Here's the idea:

> ### SENDING A MESSAGE USING THE POINTER OPERATOR
>
> *object name* –> *function name* **(argument listing)**;

   The pointer operator must be used when the object name is a pointer; otherwise, you use the dot operator.

> **DEBUGGING TIP**
>
> Remember, you must employ dot notation, •, to call functions when using non-pointer objects. On the other hand, you must use the pointer operator, –>, when calling function members using pointer objects. The pointer operator is coded using a dash, –, followed by a right-angle bracket, >, with no spacing.

   Here is a *Rectangle* class similar to the one we declared in Chapter 10:

```
class Rectangle
{
public:
   Rectangle(double l = 0, double w = 0); //CONSTRUCTOR
   double perimeter();                     //RETURN PERIMETER
   double area();                          //RETURN AREA
```

```
    double getLength();                      //ACCESS LENGTH
    double getWidth();                       //ACCESS WIDTH

  private:
    double *length;                          //RECTANGLE LENGTH
    double *width;                           //RECTANGLE WIDTH
}; //END Rectangle
```

Notice that the private members, *length* and *width*, have been defined as pointers. More about this later. Now, let's repeat our earlier definitions for two *Rectangle* objects called *box1* and *box2*. Recall that we defined *box1* to be a pointer to a static object and *box2* to be a dynamic object pointer. Here are the definitions:

```
//DEFINE A STATIC OBJECT POINTER
Rectangle box(1,2);         //DEFINE STATIC OBJECT, box
Rectangle *box1;            //DEFINE OBJECT POINTER, box1
box1 = &box;                //MAKE box1 POINT TO box

//DEFINE DYNAMIC OBJECT POINTER
Rectangle *box2;            //DEFINE box2 OBJECT POINTER
box2 = new Rectangle(2,3);  //ALLOCATE box2 MEMORY
```

Finally, let's send messages to all the functions of the two boxes using *cout* statements. We will use a separate *cout* statement for each message so that you can easily observe the required syntax. Here are the messages:

```
cout << "The length of box1 is:  " << box1 -> getLength() << endl;
cout << "The width of box1 is:  " << box1 -> getWidth() << endl;
cout << "The perimeter of box1 is:  " << box1 -> perimeter() << endl;
cout << "The area of box1 is:  " << box1 -> area() << endl <<endl;

cout << "The length of box2 is:  " << box2 -> getLength() << endl;
cout << "The width of box2 is:  " << box2 -> getWidth() << endl;
cout << "The perimeter of box2 is:  " << box2 -> perimeter() << endl;
cout << "The area of box2 is:  " << box2 -> area() << endl;
```

Observe that each group of four *cout* statements deals with a different box object. Both groups send messages to their respective boxes using the pointer operator. Here is what you would see on the display as a result of the above code:

```
The length of box1 is:  1
The width of box1 is:  2
The perimeter of box1 is:  6
The area of box1 is:  2

The length of box2 is:  2
The width of box2 is:  3
The perimeter of box2 is:  10
The area of box2 is:  6
```

Destructors

The last thing we need to cover, relative to pointers, is the use of a ***destructor*** function within an object. You were acquainted with a destructor as used by the *fstream* classes to automatically close files in Chapter 12. Another use for a destructor is to deallocate memory allocated dynamically by a constructor.

> A ***destructor*** is the counterpart of a constructor and is used to *clean up* an object after it is no longer needed.

Like a constructor, a destructor is called automatically. However, rather than being called when the object is defined, a destructor is called *when program execution leaves the block of code in which the object is defined*. Here are some rules governing the use of destructors:

❒ The name of the destructor is the same as the name of the class.

❒ The destructor cannot have a return type, not even **void**.

❒ The destructor cannot have any parameters.

❒ A class cannot have more than one destructor.

❒ The destructor cannot be overloaded.

Here is another declaration for our *Rectangle* class that includes a destructor:

```
class Rectangle
{
public:
    Rectangle(double l=0, double w=0); //CONSTRUCTOR
    double perimeter();                //RETURN PERIMETER
    double area();                     //RETURN AREA
    double getLength();                //ACCESS LENGTH
    double getWidth();                 //ACCESS WIDTH
    ~Rectangle();                      //DESTRUCTOR
private:
    double *length;                    //RECTANGLE LENGTH
    double *width;                     //RECTANGLE WIDTH
}; //END Rectangle
```

First, look at the private member declarations, and you will see that they are defined as pointer variables. This has been done to facilitate the use of a destructor, because we will use the constructor to allocate memory dynamically for these members. Next, you see that the constructor prototype has not changed from the one you observed earlier. The constructor receives two floating-point values that will be used to initialize the private members of the class. Now look at the destructor prototype. Like the constructor, the destructor has the same name as the class, but its name is preceded with a tilde symbol, **~**. In addition, there is no return type, and there are no parameters. Destructors cannot have a return type, and generally no parameters are needed.

Now, here are implementations for both the constructor and destructor:

```
//IMPLEMENTATION OF CONSTRUCTOR
Rectangle :: Rectangle(double l, double w)
{
  length = new double;
  *length = l;
  width = new double;
  *width = w;
} //END Rectangle()

//IMPLEMENTATION OF DESTRUCTOR
Rectangle :: ~Rectangle()
{
  delete length;
  delete width;
} //END ~Rectangle()
```

In the constructor implementation, you find that the private class members, *length* and *width*, are being allocated dynamically using the **new** operator. Once allocated, each is set with an initializing value received by the constructor. In the destructor implementation, you see that the memory allocated to *length* and *width* is deallocated using the **delete** operator. Notice the destructor header line. The format for the header of this typical destructor is illustrated in Figure 13.7.

So, when an object is defined for the *Rectangle* class, the constructor is called automatically, which allocates memory for the private members of the object and initializes them to the values of *l* and *w* received by the constructor. Then, the destructor is called automatically when program execution leaves the block of code in which the object is defined. The destructor deallocates the memory that was allocated by the constructor.

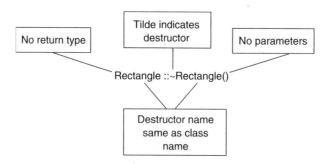

FIGURE 13.7   HEADER FORMAT FOR A DESTRUCTOR.

Let's put everything together in a complete program for our rectangle class. First the header file that declares the class:

```
//Rectangle CLASS DECLARATION  (pRect.h)
class Rectangle
{
public:
    Rectangle(double 1 = 0, double w = 0);    //CONSTRUCTOR
    double perimeter();                       //RETURN PERIMETER
    double area();                            //RETURN AREA
    double getLength();                       //ACCESS LENGTH
    double getWidth();                        //ACCESS WIDTH
    ~Rectangle();                             //DESTRUCTOR

private:
  double *length;                             //RECTANGLE LENGTH
  double *width;                              //RECTANGLE WIDTH
};  //END Rectangle
```

Next, the implementation file:

```
#include "pRect.h"        //FOR Rectangle CLASS

//CONSTRUCTOR IMPLEMENTATION
Rectangle :: Rectangle(double 1, double w)
{
  length = new double;
  *length = 1;
  width = new double;
  *width = w;
} //END Rectangle

//IMPLEMENTATION OF DESTRUCTOR
Rectangle :: ~Rectangle()
{
  delete length;
  delete width;
} //END ~Rectangle()

//IMPLEMENTATION OF perimeter() FUNCTION
double Rectangle :: perimeter()
{
  return 2 * (*length + *width);
} //END perimeter()

//IMPLEMENTATION OF area() FUNCTION
double Rectangle :: area()
{
  return *length *  *width;
} //END area()
```

```
            //IMPLEMENTATION OF getLength() FUNCTION
            double Rectangle :: getLength()
            {
              return *length;
            } //END getLength()

            //IMPLEMENTATION OF getWidth() FUNCTION
            double Rectangle :: getWidth()
            {
              return *width;
            } //END getWidth()
```

And finally the application code:

```
//PREPROCESSOR DIRECTIVES
#include "pRect.h"          //FOR Rectangle CLASS
#include <iostream.h>       //FOR cin AND cout

//MAIN FUNCTION
int main()
{
  //DEFINE OBJECTS
  Rectangle box(1,2);                     //DEFINE  box STATIC OBJECT
  Rectangle *box1;                        //DEFINE box1 OBJECT POINTER
  box1 = &box;                            //MAKE box1 POINT TO box
  Rectangle *box2;                        //DEFINE AN OBJECT POINTER
  box2 = new Rectangle(2,3);              //ALLOCATE box2  MEMORY

  //DISPLAY LENGTH, WIDTH, PERIMETER, AND AREA OF BOX OBJECTS
  cout.setf(ios::fixed);
  cout.precision(2);
  cout << "The length of box1 is:  " << box1  ->  getLength() << endl;
  cout << "The width of box1 is:  " << box1  ->  getWidth() << endl;
  cout << "The perimeter of box1 is:  " << box1  ->  perimeter() << endl;
  cout << "The area of box1 is:  " << box1  ->  area() << endl;

  cout << "\nThe length of box2 is:  " << box2  ->  getLength() << endl;
  cout << "The width of box2 is:  " << box2  ->  getWidth() << endl;
  cout << "The perimeter of box2 is:  " << box2  ->  perimeter() << endl;
  cout << "The area of box2 is:  " << box2  ->  area() << endl;]

  //DEALLOCATE DYNAMIC OBJECT POINTER
  delete box2;

  //RETURN
  return 0;
}//END main()
```

Now we have a multifile C++ program that employs object pointers both statically and dynamically. Take a close look at how pointers are being utilized here. First, the private class members are integer pointers that are being dynamically allocated by the constructor and then deallocated by the destructor. Next, *box1* is being defined as a pointer to a static object, and *box2* is defined as a pointer to a dynamic object. Since *box2* is a dynamic object pointer, it must be deallocated using the **delete** operator when it is no longer needed in the program. The destructor deallocates the pointer data memory within the object, but not the pointer object itself. When this program is compiled, linked, and executed, you will obtain the following results:

```
The length of box1 is:   1.00
The width of box1 is:   2.00
The perimeter of box1 is:   6.00
The area of box1 is:   2.00

The length of box2 is:   2.00
The width of box2 is:   3.00
The perimeter of box2 is:   10.00
The area of box2 is:   6.00
```

 ## Quick Check

1. Write a definition for a dynamic object called *pickUp* for a class called *Truck*. Assume that the *Truck* class has a constructor that initializes the number of wheels for the truck.
2. Write a statement that will send a message to an access function called *getWheels()* that will return the number of wheels on the truck.
3. Write a statement to deallocate the *pickUp* object memory.
4. When should a destructor be used as part of a class declaration?

CHAPTER SUMMARY

A pointer represents a physical memory address. Pointers can be used to point to anything in memory, including other pointers. You can initialize a pointer by allocating memory statically or dynamically. To initialize a pointer statically, you must define a variable first and then make the pointer point to the address of the variable. To initialize a pointer dynamically, you must use the **new** operator. Dynamic memory allocation is most efficient, because memory can be allocated and deallocated as needed in the program.

You can add and subtract integer values to or from a pointer. The result will be a pointer that is displaced from the original pointer value by the number added or subtracted. The displacement is relative to the size of the data pointed to by the pointer. We therefore say that pointer arithmetic is scaled. If you subtract two pointers pointing to the same array, you get the number of elements between the two pointer locations, regardless of the data-type size. You cannot add, multiply, or divide pointers.

Variable pointers can be altered to point to any data of the same type. A constant pointer, like an array name, cannot be changed to point to anywhere other than where it has been originally defined to point.

Pointers can be used as function arguments and parameters. Because a pointer is an address, a pointer parameter is a reference parameter. Therefore, any operations on the pointer parameter within the function affect the pointer data in the calling program.

Pointers can be created to point to static or dynamic objects. When calling function members via a pointer, you must use the –> pointer operator in lieu of the dot operator. An object destructor is the counterpart of an object constructor and is commonly used to deallocate dynamic memory created by a constructor. An object destructor is executed automatically when the program leaves the block of code in which the object is defined.

QUESTIONS AND PROBLEMS

QUESTIONS

1. What is a pointer?

2. Explain the difference between static memory allocation and dynamic memory allocation.

3. Define a static pointer to point to the character 'Z'.

4. Define a dynamic pointer to point to the character 'Z'.

5. Write a statement that will deallocate the memory pointed to by the pointer in question 4.

6. If *p* is defined as a pointer, what is the meaning of *p?

7. Define a pointer to point to the string "This text is great!"

8. What would you see when you view the data pointed to by the pointer in question 7 using your C++ debugger?

9. Given the following pointer definition,

   ```
   char *myMajor = "Computer Science";
   ```

   what output will be generated by the following statements?
   a. cout << myMajor << endl;
   b. cout << *myMajor << endl;
   c. cout << myMajor[0] << endl;
   d. cout << *(myMajor + 1) << endl;
   e. cout << (myMajor + 1)[1] << endl;
   f. cout << *myMajor + 5 << endl;

10. List the arithmetic operations that can and cannot be performed with pointers.

11. Suppose *p1* is pointing to index [2] in a given array and *p2* is pointing to index [7] of the same array. What is the result of subtracting *p1* from *p2*?

12. Define an array of pointers called *myCourses[]* that point to the following strings:
    "Assembler"
    "C++"
    "Data Structures"
    "Data Communications"

13. Write a function that contains a loop that will display each of the strings in question 12 using pointers.

14. Explain why using pointer parameters in a function facilitates passing data by reference.

15. True or false: A destructor may or may not have parameters.

16. Suppose that you have a constructor called *Circle()*. What will be the corresponding destructor name?

17. When are destructors normally used in a C++ object-oriented program?

18. Create a dynamic pointer object called *myCircle* for a class called *Circle*. Assume that the constructor has a single argument to initialize the radius of the circle.

19. Write a statement to call the *getRadius()* function of the *myCircle* object in question 18.

20. Write statement to deallocate the dynamic pointer object you created in question 18.

Problems

Least Difficult

1. Write a program that will fill a character array with a string of up to 25 characters using pointers, and display the string in reverse order using pointers.

2. Write a program that will determine whether a word is a palindrome. Place a word entered by the program user into an array and use pointers to compare the character elements for the palindrome determination. (*Note:* A palindrome is a word that is spelled the same way both forward and backward. Example: "MOM.")

More Difficult

3. Suppose that you have the following strings in an array:

"Bob"
"Andy"
"Janet"
"Brenda"
"Larry"
"Zane"
"Andrew"
"David"
"Ron"

Write a program using pointers to initialize an array with the foregoing names in the order given. Employ a function in the program to sort the names within the array using the following sort algorithm:

For $i = 0$ to Array Size
    For $j = i + 1$ to Array Size
        If *array[i] > array[j]*
            exchange *array[i]* and *array[j]*

Employ another function that uses pointers to display the array names to verify the sorting operation.

Most Difficult

4. A **stack** is a sequential data structure whereby the last element placed into the stack is the first element to be removed from the stack. This idea is referred to as *last-in, first-out* (*LIFO*). The last element placed into the stack is located by a pointer called *top*. Suppose that you use an array to implement a stack and a pointer called *top*. As you add elements to the stack, *top* increments through the array; as you remove elements from the stack, *top* decrements through the array. Adding elements to a stack is called a ***push*** operation, and removing elements from a stack is called a ***pop*** operation.

Write two functions, called *push()* and *pop()*, that employ a pointer called *top* to push and pop character elements to and from a stack contained in an array. Remember, the only legal way to access the stack is through the single pointer *top*. Place your functions in a program that will allow you to test the functions. Here are the function descriptions to help you get started:

Function *push()*:	Places an element onto the stack.
Accepts:	An element to be pushed and a pointer called *top*, which locates the position in the array where the element is to be placed.
Returns:	Nothing.
Function *pop()*:	Removes an element from the stack.
Accepts:	A pointer called *top*, which locates the position in the array from where the element is to be obtained.
Returns:	The popped element.

5. When pushing and popping elements to and from a stack that is being held in an array, you must have a way of determining when the stack is empty or full. You know the stack is empty when the *top* pointer points to array position **NULL**. You know the stack is full when *top* points to the maximum array index. Write two functions called *emptyStack()* and *fullStack()* that will return true if the stack is empty or full, respectively, and false if the stack is not empty or full, respectively.

6. You can use stacks to test a word to see if it's a palindrome. Here's the idea: Enter the word to be tested into two separate stacks. Pop the elements from one of the two stacks and place them in a third stack. Pop the two remaining stacks and compare the popped elements character by character as they are popped. Continue popping until two elements do not match or until the stacks are empty. As soon as you find two elements that are not the same, you don't have a palindrome. On the other hand, if no mismatches have been detected after all the elements are popped, you have a palindrome. Why does this work?

Write a program that uses this idea to test a word to see if it is a palindrome. Employ the functions that you developed in problems 4 and 5.

Use the following class declaration to do problems 7 and 8:

```
class Employee
{
public:
  Employee(string n = "",double r = 0.0, double h = 0.0); //CONSTRUCTOR
  void setData();                 //SETS EMPLOYEE DATA FROM USER
  void calculatePay();            //CALCULATES WEEKLY PAY, WITH OVERTIME
  void displayData();             //DISPLAYS PAYROLL DATA
  ~Employee();                    //DESTRUCTOR

private:
  string name;          //EMPLOYEE NAME
  double *rate;         //HOURLY RATE OF PAY
  double *hours;        //WEEKLY HOURS WORKED
  double *pay;          //GROSS WEEKLY PAY
}; //END Employee
```

7. Code the foregoing class declaration as a header file, and develop an implementation file for the member functions of the *Employee* class.

8. Develop an application file to test the code you developed in problem 7.

9. Create a dynamic invoice object that contains all the information necessary to process one line of an invoice. Assume that the invoice must include the following data and functions:

Data:

      Quantity Ordered
      Quantity Shipped
      Part Number
      Part Description
      Unit Price
      Extended Price
      Sales Tax Rate
      Sales Tax Amount
      Shipping
      Total

Functions:

❏ A function to initialize all the data items to 0, except the Sales Tax Rate, which should be initialized to 5%.

❏ A function to allow the user to initialize all the data items from the keyboard.

❏ A function to calculate the Extended Price of the item.

❏ A function to calculate the Sales Tax Amount of the item.

❏ A function to calculate the Total Amount of the invoice.

❏ A function to display the invoice data with header information in a businesslike format.

Use dynamic pointers to implement the object data.

INTRODUCTION TO DATA STRUCTURES AND ADTs

Chapter Contents

Chapter Objectives

When you are finished with this chapter, you should have a good understanding of the following:

- The importance and characteristics of abstract data types, or ADTs.
- The stack ADT and the concept of last-in, first-out.
- The queue ADT and the concept of first-in, first-out.
- How to code a stack ADT using a C++ class.
- How to code a queue ADT using a C++ class.
- How to code a linked list ADT using a C++ class.
- How to use the STL *stack*, *queue*, and *list* classes.

INTRODUCTION

Abstract data types, or ADTs, provide for data abstraction. You were introduced to data abstraction in Chapter 3. Recall that the idea behind data abstraction is to combine data with a set of operations that are defined for that data in one neat encapsulated package called an ADT. The ADT can then be used by knowing what the operations do, without needing to know the details of how the computer system implements the data or its operations. You have been using data abstraction since Chapter 3 when you first learned about the standard C++ classes, such as the *string* class. In each case, you learned about the structure of the data within the class, the operations that could be performed by a given object of a class, and how to use those operations. You were not concerned about how the computer stores the data or how the operations were implemented. You could concentrate on their use rather than their implementation.

Data abstraction is an important software development and programming tool. When developing software with ADTs, you can concentrate on the ADT data and related operations, without worrying about the inner implementation details of the ADT. Data abstraction provides for generality, modularity, and protection when developing software. The C++ class is the ideal programming construct for implementing ADTs. We will discuss all the facets of an ADT so that you completely understand all of its implications. Then, the remaining sections of the chapter will use object-oriented programming to build three classic ADTs: the stack, the queue, and the linked list. After you learn how to build your own stack, queue, and linked list ADTs, you will be exposed to the STL *stack*, *queue*, and *list* classes.

14.1   THE CONCEPT OF DATA ABSTRACTION REVISITED

Let's begin with a simple definition for an ADT and then look at some important characteristics of an ADT.

An *abstract data type (ADT)* is a collection of data and related operations.

❑ *Abstraction*

The term *abstract* means that the data and related operations are being viewed without considering any of the details of *how* the data or operations are implemented in the computer system. You have been working with abstract data types throughout this book, without knowing it. For instance, consider the floating-point data types used in C++. Have you been concerned about how floating-point values are stored in memory? Have you been concerned about how the C++ compiler implements floating-point operations? Of course not! All that you are concerned about is the general structure of a floating-point value, what operations are available to be used with floating-point values, and how to use these floating-point operations. The implementation details are left to the C++ compiler designer.

This whole idea of abstraction facilitates the design of modular software and the development of algorithms for software design, because abstraction allows us to hide implementation details, thereby facilitating more general thinking.

❐ *An ADT includes both data and related operations.*

Think of an ADT as a black box that contains *private* data and *public* operations. Sound familiar? You know what the box does and how to use it through its *public* operations, or interface. However, you are not concerned about what goes on inside the box. The ADT black box concept facilitates modular software design.

The Data: An ADT defines the data to be operated upon as well as the operations that can be performed on the data. An ADT is not the same thing as a data structure. A data structure provides a way of structuring, or organizing, data within a programming language. You will be concerned about data structures when you implement an ADT, because you will have to decide how to organize and store the ADT data. However, on the surface, you are not concerned with these implementation details in order to access and manipulate the ADT data. The data in an ADT must be private, which means that it is hidden from any operations that are not defined for the ADT.

The Operations: The ADT includes operations, or functions, that manipulate the ADT data. These operations are public, which means that they are used by outside software to access and manipulate the private ADT data. Again, all you are concerned about at the abstract level is what these operations do and how to use them. As a result, the interface to the operations within the ADT must be complete enough to describe totally the effect that they have on the data. However, you are not concerned about how they do what they do.

❐ *An ADT provides a means to encapsulate details whereby the data are completely hidden from their surroundings.*

Recall that *encapsulation* with *information hiding* allows you to combine data with the operations that are dedicated to manipulating the data so tightly that outside operations cannot affect the data. This allows the application program to be oblivious to how the ADT data are stored. In addition, information hiding provides for data protection. Only those operations that are defined for the ADT can operate on the ADT data. As a result, the data cannot be corrupted intentionally or unintentionally by using "unauthorized" operations.

❐ *ADT operations provide loose coupling to the outside world via a function interface.*

The operations defined for an ADT provide the interface between the outside world and the ADT. In other words, the only way to gain access to the ADT is through the ADT operation, or function, interfaces. Again, the ADT is like a black box that is connected to its surroundings via its function interfaces. The function interfaces provide the communications channel between an application program and the ADT. This idea is illustrated in Figure 14.1. This figure should look familiar to you, because it is basically the same figure used to illustrate a class in Chapter 10. As you might now suspect, the class in C++ provides an ideal implementation of an ADT.

By using ADTs during software development, we gain *modularity*, *generality*, and *protection*. We gain modularity, because ADTs can be thought of as black box building blocks during software development. We gain generality, because algorithms can be developed that depend only on the function interface to the ADT without considering the implementation details of the ADT. In addition, once an ADT is developed, it is available for general use in many applications without rewriting the ADT code. We gain protection through information hiding. Private data stored within an ADT cannot be corrupted intentionally or unintentionally.

The preceding definition of an ADT completely describes the C++ class that we developed in an earlier chapter. Recall that a class includes both data (private members) and related operations (public functions) that are encapsulated. In addition, the private member data are completely hidden from anything outside the class. Finally, the class is coupled to its outside world via the class function interfaces (prototypes). That is, to access the class data from the outside, you must invoke the public member functions of the class. This is why C++ is ideal for coding ADTs.

The remainder of this chapter is devoted to building some classic ADTs. As you study these ADTs, keep in mind the general ideas of data abstraction presented in this section.

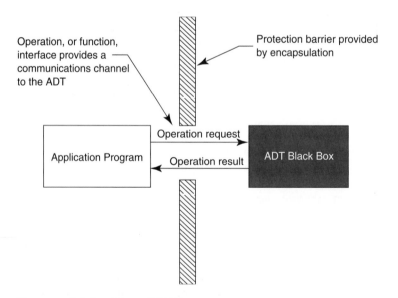

FIGURE 14.1   THE ADT IS LIKE A BLACK BOX THAT IS CONNECTED TO ITS SURROUNDINGS VIA ITS FUNCTION INTERFACES.

Quick Check

1. What term is used to indicate that data and its related operations are being viewed without considering any of the details of how the data or operations are implemented in the computer system?

2. Give an example of an ADT with which you have been working in the C++ language.

3. The ADT black box concept facilitates _____ software design.

4. True or false: A data structure and an abstract data type are the same thing.

5. Data protection in an ADT is provided by _____.

6. The interface to an ADT is through its _____.

7. Why do you gain modularity through the use of ADTs?

8. Why do you gain generality through the use of ADTs?

14.2   THE STACK ADT

You have been introduced to the stack ADT via some of the programming problems in previous chapters. Now it is time to take a closer look at this important ADT. Stacks are common in a wide variety of applications in computer science. For example, you observed the use of a stack when you studied recursion in Chapter 8. With recursion, a stack is employed to save information as the recursive function calls are made. Once the terminating condition is reached, the stack information is retrieved to determine the final recursive function value.

In general, a stack is used to reverse the order of data placed in it. Now, let's see how a stack works, beginning with a formal definition for a stack:

A **stack** is a collection of data elements and related operations whereby all the insertions and deletions of elements to and from the stack are made at one end of the stack called the **top**. A stack operates on the **last-in**, **first-out**, or **LIFO**, principle.

To get the idea of a stack, think of a stack of trays in a spring-loaded bin, such as that which you might find in a cafeteria line. Such a stack is illustrated in Figure 14.2. When you remove a tray from the stack, you remove it from the *top* of the stack. If you were to add a tray onto the stack, you would place it on the *top* of the stack. All insertions and deletions of trays to and from the stack are made at the *top* of the stack. In other words, the last tray placed onto the stack will be the first tray removed from the stack. This characteristic is commonly referred to as *last-in*, *first-out*, or simply **LIFO**. Examples of the LIFO principle are hard to find

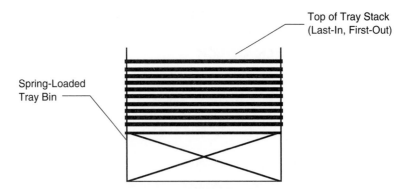

FIGURE 14.2 A STACK OBEYS THE LAST-IN, FIRST-OUT (LIFO) PRINCIPLE, LIKE THIS STACK OF CAFETERIA TRAYS.

in everyday life. For instance, suppose that you enter a grocery store check-out line. If the line is operating on the LIFO principle, the last person in the line would be the first one to be checked out. It might be quite some time until you were able to pay for your groceries, especially if other people keep entering the line. Think about how unfair such a line would be! To be fair, a grocery store line must operate on a ***first-in***, ***first-out***, or ***FIFO***, principle. This principle is associated with *queues* and will be discussed in the next section. Although the LIFO principle is not very common in everyday life, it is very common in many problems that arise in computer science.

Now, let's consider the cafeteria tray stack again. What operations do you suppose could be performed on such a stack? Well, first of all, you can move an empty tray bin into position in preparation for adding trays to the bin. Then, you can begin adding trays to the bin to form a stack of trays. When a single tray is added to the stack, it can only be added at the *top* position and no other position. Adding an element to a stack is referred to as a ***push*** operation. You can remove a tray from the *top* of the stack, and, normally, you can't remove a tray from any position other than the top of the stack. Removing an element from a stack is called a ***pop*** operation. You could also inspect the *top* tray, but no others. You could see if the stack of trays were empty, but if not empty, you would not know how many trays were in the stack. Given the situation, you are forced to access the trays from the *top* of the stack. The stack of trays provides a very good analogy to stacks in computer science, because the operations that can be performed on a stack of trays form the basis for the stack ADT in computer science. Here is a summary of legal stack operations:

- ❐ *createStack()* ⇒ Creates an empty stack.
- ❐ *push()* ⇒ Places an element on the top of a stack.
- ❐ *pop()* ⇒ Returns and removes the top element of a stack.
- ❐ *topElement()* ⇒ Inspects the top element of the stack, leaving the stack unchanged.
- ❐ *emptyStack()* ⇒ Determines if the stack is empty.

Now we are ready to define our stack ADT. Remember, to define an ADT, we must include both a definition for the ADT data as well as any operations that will be needed to manipulate the data. Consider the following ADT definition:

ADT Stack

Operations, or Interface:

createStack()
    Creates an empty stack.

push()
    Adds a new element to the top of a stack.

pop()
    Returns and removes the top element of a stack.

topElement()
    Copies the top element of the stack, leaving the stack unchanged.

emptyStack()
    Determines if the stack is empty.

Data:

A collection of data elements that can be accessed at only one location, called the *top* of the stack.

Implementing the Stack ADT

The foregoing ADT definition provides all the information needed to work with a stack. The operations are clearly defined in order to access and manipulate the stack data. Now it is time to consider the implementation details in order to create stacks in C++. Remember, however, that the following implementation details are not part of the ADT definition. We can always change how we implement the stack ADT, but the stack ADT definition will remain constant.

It is perfectly natural to use a one-dimensional array to hold a stack because of its sequential element ordering nature. Also, we must use a built-in structure to implement our stack, because there is no inherent built-in stack structure available in C++, or most other high-level languages for that matter. However, the ANSI/ISO standard template library does contain as built-in *stack* class that you will study shortly, after you have mastered the building of your own stack class.

Creating a Stack Using an Array.   We will create an array of some arbitrary length and create an integer variable called *top* to keep track of the top element on

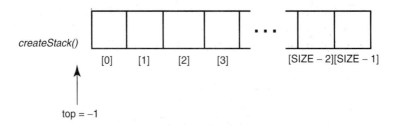

FIGURE 14.3   SETTING *TOP* TO THE VALUE −1 WILL CREATE AN EMPTY STACK.

the stack. Remember, we only need to keep track of the top element of the stack, because, by definition, access to the stack elements must be through the top of the stack. To initialize the stack, we will set *top* to the value −1, as shown in Figure 14.3.

First, look at the array. It is defined with indices ranging from [0] to [*SIZE* − 1] and, therefore, can hold *SIZE* elements. The array will be used to hold a stack so that the first stack element will be placed at position [0] in the array, the second stack element at position [1], and so on. We will create an integer variable called *top* that will "point" to the array index that locates the top element in the stack. In Figure 14.3, the value of *top* is set to −1 to indicate that the stack is empty. The value −1 is used to indicate an empty stack condition, because there is no −1 index in the array. So, using this idea, all we have to do to create a new empty stack is to define an array and set *top* to the value −1. How do you know if the stack ever becomes empty when processing the stack data? Of course, the stack is empty if the value of *top* is −1. The algorithm required to create a stack using our array implementation is straightforward. Here it is:

createStack() **Algorithm**

```
    BEGIN
        Set top = −1.
    END.
```

Now we are ready to start pushing elements onto the stack.

Pushing Elements onto a Stack.   The first element pushed onto an empty stack will be placed in position [0] of the array. However, before the first element can be placed into the array, the value of *top* must be incremented to point to position [0]. Let's suppose that we have created a character array to form a stack of characters. Then we execute the following operation:

push('A')

The push operation causes the value of *top* to be incremented from -1 to 0, and then the character 'A' is placed at position [*top*], or [0], of the array. Next, suppose we execute another push operation, like this:

push('B')

This push operation causes *top* to be incremented from 0 to 1, and then the character 'B' is placed on the top of the stack, which is now array position [1]. Lastly, let's execute a third push operation, like this:

push('C')

Now we are pushing the character 'C' onto the stack. Again, the value of *top* is incremented, and this character is placed into array position [*top*], or [2]. This sequence of three push operations is illustrated in Figure 14.4.

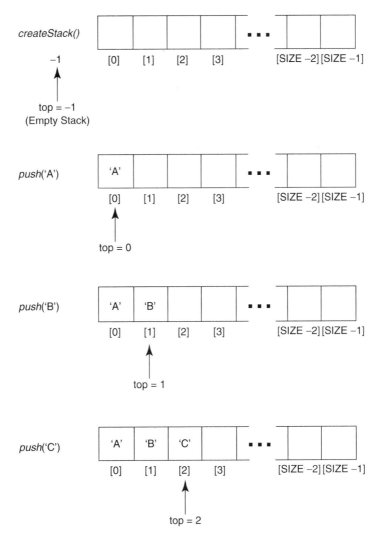

FIGURE 14.4   THE EFFECT OF CREATING A STACK AND PUSHING THREE CHARACTER ELEMENTS ONTO THE STACK.

It is important to note that the value of *top* must be incremented *prior* to placing the element on the stack. Thus, we say that the *push()* operation preincrements the stack pointer, *top*. Here is an algorithm for *push()*:

push() **Algorithm**
BEGIN
    If the stack is not full
        Increment *top*.
        Place element at array position [*top*].
    Else
        Display full stack message.
END.

Notice that a test is made to determine if the stack is full, because you cannot push an element onto a full stack. When would our stack be full? Well, the stack is full when the array is full, right? The maximum array position is *SIZE* − 1, so the stack will be full when *top* has the value *SIZE* − 1.

Popping Elements from a Stack.   Now we are ready to illustrate several popping operations. Given the stack in Figure 14.4, suppose that we execute a single pop operation, like this:

pop()

What happens to the stack? Well, *top* is pointing to the *last* element placed on the stack (the character 'C') so all we need to do is to remove the element at array position [*top*], or [2]. However, once the element is removed, the value of *top* must be decremented to locate the new top of the stack. Thus, in Figure 14.4, the character 'C' at position [2] is removed, and the value of *top* is decremented from 2 to 1 to locate array position [1], which is the new top of the stack.

Next, suppose we execute a second pop operation. This operation removes the character 'B', and *top* is decremented to array position [0]. Finally, if we execute a third pop operation, the character 'A' is removed from the stack, and *top* is decremented to the value −1, indicating an empty stack. This sequence of events is shown in Figure 14.5. Remember that the *pop()* operation decrements *top* after the element is removed from the stack. Thus, we say that the *pop()* operation postdecrements the stack pointer. Here is an algorithm for *pop()*:

pop() **Algorithm**
BEGIN
    If the stack is not empty
        Remove element at array position [*top*].
        Decrement *top*.
    Else
        Display empty stack message.
END.

Notice that a test must be made to determine if the stack is empty, because you cannot pop an element from an empty stack. How do you know when the stack is empty? Of course, when *top* has the value −1.

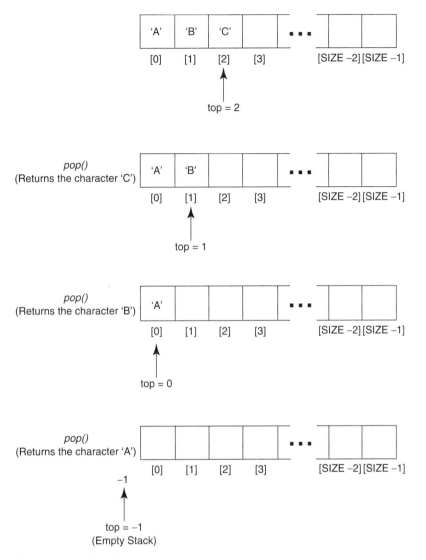

FIGURE 14.5   THE EFFECT OF POPPING THREE CHARACTER ELEMENTS FROM THE STACK IN FIGURE 14.4.

One final point: Although the stack is empty after the three popping operations in Figure 14.5, the array still contains the 'A', 'B', and 'C' character elements. However, these elements are no longer part of the stack. They could be accessed by reading the array. However, remember that, by definition, an ADT restricts the data access to only those operations defined for the ADT. Therefore, the only possible way to access the array is through the stack operations, *push()* and *pop()*, defined for the stack ADT. Any direct array access would violate the idea of an ADT. This is why object-oriented programming is ideal for implementing ADTs. With object-oriented programming, we can make the array a **private** data member of a class, thereby restricting its access to only those operations defined for the ADT. As a result, the ADT data are completely hidden from the outside world.

Inspecting the Top Element of a Stack. The last operation of our stack ADT that we need to illustrate is the *topElement()* operation. Recall that this operation makes a copy of the top element on the stack, leaving the stack unchanged. So, let's assume that we start with the stack in Figure 14.4 and execute a *topElement()* operation, like this:

topElement()

Like the *pop()* operation, the *topElement()* operation reads the element at array position [*top*]. However, unlike the *pop()* operation, *topElement()* does not decrement the stack pointer, *top*. This operation is illustrated in Figure 14.6.

The algorithm for *topElement()* is straightforward. Here it is:

> *topElement()* **Algorithm**
> BEGIN
>   If the stack is not empty
>   Copy element at array position [*top*].
>   Else
>   Display empty message.
> END.

Coding the Stack ADT. We are now ready to code our stack ADT. We will code the ADT as a class to enforce encapsulation and information hiding. Here is the stack ADT class coded as a C++ header file called *stack.h*:

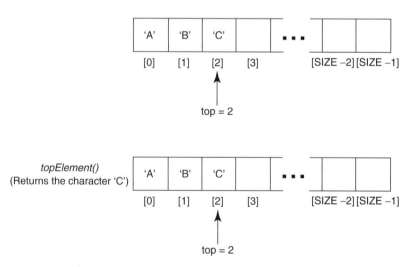

FIGURE 14.6 THE EFFECT OF THE *TOPELEMENT()* OPERATION.

```
//STACK CLASS DECLARATION (stack.h)

#ifndef STACK_H
#define STACK_H

const int SIZE = 5;                    //MAXIMUM STACK SIZE
enum {EMPTY = -1, FULL = SIZE - 1};    //DEFINE EMPTY = -1
                                       //AND FULL = SIZE - 1


class Stack
{
public:
 Stack();                      //CONSTRUCTOR FOR createStack()
 bool emptyStack();            //CHECKS FOR EMPTY STACK
 bool fullStack();             //CHECKS FOR FULL STACK
 void push(char c);            //PLACE ELEMENT ON TOP
 char pop();                   //REMOVE ELEMENT FROM TOP
 char topElement();            //INSPECT TOP ELEMENT

private:
 char s[SIZE];    //CHARACTER ARRAY TO HOLD THE STACK
 int top;         //top LOCATES TOP ELEMENT OF STACK
}; //END Stack
#endif
```

First, you see a constant, called *SIZE,* defined. This constant will dictate the maximum size of the array, or stack. Next, you see enumerated data elements defined. We set *EMPTY* to the value −1 to designate an empty stack. Then, we set *FULL* to the value *SIZE* − 1 to designate a full stack. You know why *EMPTY* is set to −1. But why is *FULL* set to *SIZE* − 1? Well, theoretically, the size of a stack is limited only by the amount of memory available in the system to hold the stack. However, because we are using an array to hold the stack, the maximum stack size is limited by the size of the array. The size of this array implementation is *SIZE*, which means that the last array index is [*SIZE* − 1]. Therefore, when the top of the stack is located at array index [*SIZE* − 1], the stack is full.

The stack ADT is defined as a class called *Stack.* The public members of the class include the operations defined for the stack ADT. First, you see the *Stack()* constructor. This constructor will take the place of the *createStack()* operation. Remember how a constructor works? When an object is defined for a class, the constructor is automatically called to initialize the private members of the class. Here, the constructor function will be coded to set the value of *top* to *EMPTY*, or −1. Isn't this what the *createStack()* operation must do? We could not use the name *createStack()*, because a constructor must have the same name as the class.

Next, you see the *emptyStack()* function listed. This function will return the Boolean value true if the stack is empty, or false if the stack is not empty. The next function defined is *fullStack()*. This function will be used to determine if the stack is full. The function will return the Boolean value true if the stack is full or false if the stack is not full. (What constitutes a full stack?) You have noticed that in our formal ADT definition, we did not have a *fullStack()* operation, and, in theory, no such operation is needed for the stack ADT. However, *fullStack()* is required in this implementation, because we are using a finite array to hold the stack.

The last three functions defined for the class are *push()*, *pop()*, and *topElement()*. You already know the purpose of these functions. However, take a close look at each function prototype. The *push()* function accepts a character, *c*, to be pushed onto the stack. It does not return any value, because it will simply place *c* into the array at the top position. The *pop()* function does not have any formal parameters, because it will read the element at the top position of the stack array. The return type of *pop()* is a character, because it will return the popped element to the calling program. Likewise, the *topElement()* function does not require any formal parameters, because it simply reads the top element of the stack. The return type is character, because it will return a copy of the top element to the calling program.

The private members of the class are the character array, *s[]*, and the integer variable, *top*. The size of the array is *SIZE*, which means that the stack can hold *SIZE* elements. However, remember that the last array index is [*SIZE* − 1]. It goes without saying that array *s[]* will hold a stack of characters whose top element is located by *top*.

PROGRAMMING NOTE

The C++ class fully encapsulates the stack ADT. As a result, only those operations defined in the class can operate on the stack data. Even though the stack is being implemented with an array, the stack array is private and, therefore, cannot be corrupted by any operations outside of the class. When using the stack, you are forced to use only those operations defined by the stack ADT. This is why encapsulation and information hiding are so important when creating ADTs. As you can see, the class in C++ inherently provides the encapsulation and data hiding required by ADTs.

Now we need to look at the implementation file for the *Stack* class functions.

```
//STACK IMPLEMENTATION FILE (stackop.cpp)

//PREPROCESSOR DIRCTIVES
#include "stack.h"    //FOR stack CLASS
#include <iostream.h> //FOR cin AND cout

//IMPLEMENTATION OF Stack() CONSTRUCTOR
Stack :: Stack()
{
 top = EMPTY;        //SET TOP TO -1
} //END Stack()

//IMPLEMENTATION OF emptyStack()
bool Stack :: emptyStack()
{
 if (top == EMPTY)    //IF STACK EMPTY RETURN TRUE
   return true;       //ELSE RETURN FALSE
 else
```

```
    return false;
} //END emptyStack()

//IMPLEMENTATION OF fullStack()
bool Stack :: fullStack()
{
  if (top == FULL)        //IF STACK FULL RETURN TRUE
    return true;          //ELSE RETURN RETURN FALSE
  else
    return false;
} //END fullStack()

//IMPLEMENTATION OF push()
void Stack :: push(char c)
{
  if (!fullStack())       //IF STACK NOT FULL, INCREMENT TOP
  {                       //AND ADD ELEMENT TO STACK
    ++top;
    s[top] = c;
  }
  else
    cout << "The stack is full!" << endl;
} //END push()

//IMPLEMENTATION OF pop()
char Stack :: pop()
{
  char c;                 //TEMP VARIABLE TO HOLD ELEMENT
  if (!emptyStack())      //IF STACK NOT EMPTY, RETURN ELEMENT
  {                       //AND DECREMENT TOP
    c = s[top];
    --top;
    return c;
  } //END IF
  else
  {
    cout << "The stack is empty!" << endl;
    return '#';           //RETURN '#' TO INDICATE STACK EMPTY
  }  //END ELSE
} //END pop()

//IMPLEMENTATION OF topElement()
char Stack :: topElement()
{
  if (!emptyStack())      //IF STACK NOT EMPTY, RETURN ELEMENT
    return s[top];
  else                    //ELSE RETURN '#' FOR EMPTY STACK
  {
    cout << "The stack is empty! " << endl;
    return '#';
  }  //END ELSE
} //END topElement()
```

The file is named *stackop.cpp*. You see that the stack header file, *stack.h*, is included in this file. The first implementation is for the constructor function, *Stack()*. This function simply creates a new stack by setting *top* to *EMPTY*, or –1. Next, the *emptyStack()* function returns true if the stack is empty or false if the stack is not empty. What constitutes an empty stack? Of course, when the value of *top* is –1. This is the test that is made in the **if/else** statement. Remember that *EMPTY* is defined as –1, and *FULL* is defined as *SIZE* – 1.

The structure of the *fullStack()* implementation is similar to *emptyStack()*. However, *fullStack()* checks to see if the value of *top* is equal to *FULL*. Recall that *FULL* is defined in the header file as *SIZE* – 1. This value is the maximum array index value. When *top* reaches *SIZE* – 1, the array is full, thereby making the stack full.

The implementation of the *push()* function employs an **if/else** statement to check for a full stack condition. You cannot push an element onto a full stack. The condition is checked by calling the *fullStack()* function. If the stack is not full, the value of *top* is incremented, and the character, *c*, received by the function is stored in the stack array at position *s[top]*. If the stack is full, an appropriate message is displayed.

The *pop()* function employs an **if/else** statement to check for an empty stack condition. You cannot pop an element from an empty stack. Here, the *empty-Stack()* function is called as part of the **if/else** statement. If the stack is not empty, the element at array position *s[top]* is obtained and assigned to the local variable *c*. (Why is a local variable required here?) The value of *top* is then decremented, and the character, *c*, is returned to the calling program.

Finally, the *topElement()* function is similar to the *pop()* function in that it checks for an empty stack condition and, if the stack is not empty, returns the character at array position *s[top]*. Notice, however, that the value of *top* is not altered, thereby leaving the stack unchanged.

Now all we need is an application program to test our stack ADT. Here is one that will do the job:

```
//PREPROCESSOR DIRECTIVES
#include "stack.h"            //FOR stack CLASS
#include <iostream.h>         //FOR cin AND cout

//MAIN FUNCTION
int main()
{
  char c;                     //CHARACTER TO BE STACKED
  int number = 0;             //NUMBER OF CHARACTERS TO BE STACKED
  int count = 0;              //LOOP COUNTER

  Stack stk;                  //DEFINE STACK OBJECT

  //OBTAIN NUMBER OF ELEMENTS TO STACK
  cout << "You cannot enter more than " << SIZE
       << " elements.  \nHow many elements do you have to enter? " << endl;
  cin >> number;

  //PUSH ELEMENTS ONTO STACK
  while (count < number)
  {
```

```
    ++count;
    cout << "\nEnter a character element:  ";
    cin >> c;
    stk.push(c);
  } //END WHILE

//INSPECT TOP ELEMENT OF THE STACK
cout << "\nThe top element of the stack is:  "
     << stk.topElement() << endl;

  //POP AND WRITE STACK ELEMENTS
  cout << "\nThe contents of the stack were:  " << endl;
  while (!stk.emptyStack())
     cout << stk.pop() << endl;

  //ATTEMPT TO POP AN EMPTY STACK
  stk.pop();

//RETURN
 return 0;
} //END main()
```

The program begins by including the stack ADT header file, *stack.h*. There are several local variables defined at the beginning of *main()*. These variables will be used to process the stack information, as you will see shortly. An object called *stk* is defined for our *Stack* class. The user is first prompted for the number of characters to be entered onto the stack. A **while** loop is used to push the entered characters onto the stack one character at a time. Notice that the **while** loop will execute as long as the number of characters entered is less than the number dictated by the user. The user is prompted within the loop to enter one character at a time. After the character is read from the user, it is pushed onto the stack by calling the *push()* function.

The next segment of code inspects and displays the top character on the stack with a call to the *topElement()* function.

The final segment of code pops the entire stack and displays the stack elements one character at a time. A **while** loop is used to pop and display the stack elements. The loop is controlled by making a call to the *emptyStack()* function. As a result, the loop will execute until the stack is empty.

Finally, notice that a single call to *pop()* is made after the stack is emptied. This call is made to test the *pop()* function relative to an empty stack. Here is a sample run of the program:

```
You cannot enter more than 5 elements.
How many elements do you have to enter?
3↵

Enter a character element:  A↵

Enter a character element:  B↵

Enter a character element:  C↵

The top element of the stack is:  C
```

```
The contents of the stack were:
C
B
A

The stack is empty!
```

Observe what has happened. The user entered three characters in the order 'A', 'B', 'C'. The program shows that the last character entered, 'C', is on the top of the stack. Then, the contents of the stack are popped and displayed. Notice that the output order is reversed from the input order because of the LIFO principle. Also, notice that the message says "The contents of the stack *were:*". We must use past-tense phraseology because we emptied the stack during the loop. Finally, the attempt to pop an empty stack resulted in the appropriate message to the user, thus verifying the integrity of the *pop()* function.

Quick Check

1. Suppose that the user filled a stack using the application test program in this section. What would happen if a call was made to the *push()* function after the stack was full?

2. Because we are using an array implementation for a stack, why can't you randomly access the stack elements using array operations, rather than accessing them through *top*?

3. With our array implementation of a stack, a *push()* operation requires that the stack pointer be _____.

4. True or false: With our array implementation of a stack, the stack is full when the value of *top* becomes equal to *SIZE*, where *SIZE* is the maximum number of elements that the array can hold.

5. With our array implementation of a stack, the stack is empty when the value of *top* is _____.

6. What is the functional difference between the *pop()* function and the *top-Element()* function?

7. There is no *fullStack()* operation defined for the stack ADT. Why did we have to include a *fullStack()* function in our implementation?

14.3 THE QUEUE ADT

A *queue* is another important ADT in computer science. There are more examples of queues in the real world than stacks, because queues have the *first-in, first-out*, or *FIFO*, property. For instance, the grocery store line mentioned in the last section is a queue. Aircraft in a holding pattern waiting to land at a busy airport represent a *queuing* operation. As aircraft approach the airport traffic area, they are placed in a holding pattern so that the first one in the pattern is the first one to land. We say that the aircraft are being *queued* into the pattern. A computer scientist would never say that the aircraft are being *stacked* in the pattern, right? Can you think of other real-world examples of queuing operations?

Recall that the LIFO property of stacks reverses the order of the stack elements from input to the stack to output from the stack. Queues, on the other hand, exhibit the FIFO property which preserves the order of the elements from input to output. Now for a formal definition of a queue.

> A **queue** is a collection of data elements in which all insertions of elements into the queue are made at one end of the queue, called the **rear** of the queue; and all deletions of elements from the queue are made at the other end of the queue, called the **front** of the queue. A queue operates on the **first-in**, **first-out**, or **FIFO** principle.

From this definition, you see that queue access occurs at one of two ends of the queue. If an element is added to the queue, it is added to the rear of the queue just as in a grocery store checkout line. On the other hand, if an element is removed from the queue, it is removed from the front of the queue, as with the grocery store line. Of course, you can't remove an element from the middle of the queue or from an empty queue.

We are now ready to define our queue ADT as follows:

ADT Queue

Operations, or Interface:

createQ
Creates an empty queue.

insert()
Adds an element to the rear of a queue.

remove()
Removes an element from the front of a queue.

frontElement()
Copies the front element of a queue, leaving the queue unchanged.

emptyQ()
Determines if the queue is empty.

Data:

A collection of data elements with the property that elements can only be added at one end, called the **rear** of the queue, and elements can only be removed from the other end, called the *front* of the queue.

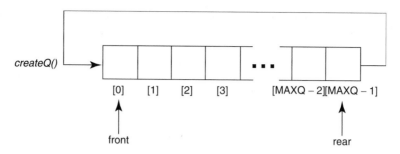

FIGURE 14.7 **SETTING *FRONT* TO 0 AND *REAR* TO *MAXQ* − 1 WILL CREATE A QUEUE USING A CIRCULAR ARRAY IMPLEMENTATION.**

Implementing the Queue ADT

Like a stack, the queue ADT is not predefined in C++ or most other programming languages. Therefore, we must implement it using something that is predefined in the language. Again we will use the versatile array to implement the queue. However, we need to make use a special array called a ***circular***, or ***wraparound***, array. Look at the array in Figure 14.7 to see how we can create a queue using a circular array.

Creating a Queue Using a Circular Array. You see an array whose size is $MAXQ$ and highest index is $MAXQ - 1$. To make the array hold a queue, we need to initialize two integer variables that locate the front and rear of the queue. Here, *front* is initialized to 0 so that it locates position [0] of the array, and *rear* is initialized to $MAXQ - 1$ so that it locates the last array position. Thus, an appropriate algorithm for *createQ()* is

> *createQ()* **Algorithm**
> BEGIN
>> Set *front* = 0.
>> Set *rear* = $MAXQ - 1$.
> END.

Now, here's the idea behind a circular array. When we are using an external integer variable, such as *front* or *rear*, to locate elements in the array, we will advance the variable through the index range of the array, in our case from 0 to $MAXQ - 1$. When the variable needs to be advanced past the last array index, $MAXQ - 1$, we will force it to the first array index, 0. Thus, the variable will be advanced as follows:

$$0, 1, 2, 3, \ldots, (MAXQ - 1), 0, 1, 2, 3, \ldots, (MAXQ - 1), 0, 1, 2, 3, \ldots$$

This way, the advancing process can continue in a circle indefinitely. All we need to accomplish this task is an **if/else** statement, like this:

> If *rear* == $MAXQ - 1$
>> Set *rear* = 0.
> Else
>> Set *rear* = *rear* + 1.

Here you see that the **else** statement increments *rear*, unless the value of *rear* is $MAXQ - 1$. If this is the case, *rear* is set to 0. Of course, we will do the same thing with *front* to make it wrap around.

Now we are ready to begin inserting and removing elements to and from the queue. Remember, we will insert elements at the rear of the queue and remove elements from the front of the queue.

Inserting Elements into a Queue.   To insert an element into the queue, we must first advance *rear* and then place the element at array position [*rear*]. Thus, suppose we start with the array shown in Figure 14.7 and execute the following three insertion operations:

> *insert('A')*
> *insert('B')*
> *insert('C')*

The sequence of events created by these three operations is illustrated in Figure 14.8.

We begin with the queue being initialized using *createQ()*. Remember that *createQ()* initializes *front* with the value 0 and *rear* with the value $MAXQ - 1$. When the first character, 'A', is inserted into the queue, the value of *rear* must be advanced prior to the character being placed in the array. However, because *rear* locates the last array index, $MAXQ - 1$, the value of *rear* is forced to 0 using the wraparound idea. Once *rear* is advanced to 0, the character 'A' is placed at array position [*rear*], or [0]. Notice that both *front* and *rear* locate the character 'A'. This is *always* the case when there is only one element in the queue.

The second character to be inserted is the character 'B'. Again, *rear* is advanced to locate the next array position. This time, however, the value of *rear* is *not* $MAXQ - 1$. Therefore, 1 is added to *rear* so that it locates the next sequential array position, [1]. The character 'B' is then placed at array position [*rear*], or [1].

The third insert operation places that character 'C' at array position [2]. Notice that *front* has not been affected by the insert operations and locates the first character inserted into the queue.

Here is an algorithm that reflects the *insert()* operation at this point:

> **Initial** *insert()* **Algorithm**

> BEGIN
>   If the queue is not full
>   If *rear* == $MAXQ - 1$
>   Set *rear* = 0.
>   Else
>   Set *rear* = *rear* + 1.
>   Place element at array position [*rear*].
>   Else
>   Display full queue message.
> END.

The first thing that must be done is to check for a full queue. How do you know when the queue is full? Or, for that matter, how do you know when the queue is

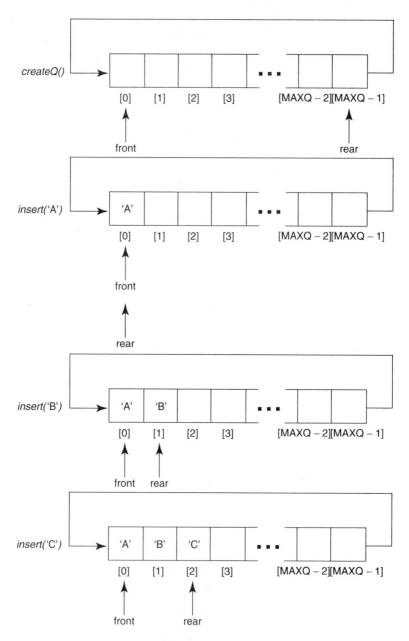

FIGURE 14.8 **THE EFFECT OF CREATING A QUEUE AND INSERTING THREE CHARACTER ELEMENTS INTO THE QUEUE.**

empty? Because we are using an array implementation, the queue is full when the array is full, and the queue is empty when the array is empty, right? But, how can we use *front* and/or *rear* to determine when the array is full or empty? Your first thought might be that the queue is full when an element is placed in the last array position, thereby making *rear* take on the value $MAXQ - 1$. But, from Figure 14.7, you see that this condition also reflects an empty queue condition. In fact, because of the circular nature of the array, there is no way to determine a full or empty queue condition using the values of *front* and *rear* unless we alter the nature of our implementation. Think about it!

The simplest way to determine an empty or full queue condition is to count the number of elements being inserted and removed from the queue. When an element is inserted into the queue, we will increment an element counter. When an element is removed from the queue, we will decrement the element counter. In this way, the queue is empty when the counter value is 0 and full when the counter value reaches the size of the array, *MAXQ*. To do this, we must add an additional processing step to our *insert()* algorithm that will increment the element counter. Here is a modified *insert()* algorithm that will permit us to determine a full queue condition:

Modified *insert()* Algorithm

BEGIN
    If the queue is not full
        Increment element counter.
        If *rear* == $MAXQ - 1$
          Set *rear* = 0.
        Else
          Set *rear* = *rear* + 1.
        Place element at array position [*rear*].
    Else
        Display full queue message.
END.

You should be aware that there is another way to implement a queue using a circular array that doesn't require an element counter to determine the empty/full conditions. However, this implementation requires that you sacrifice one array position by not allowing any queue elements to be placed in this position. This implementation will be left as a programming exercise at the end of the chapter.

Now, back to the algorithm. If the queue is not full, the element counter is incremented, and the **if/else** wraparound statement is executed to advance *rear*. Once *rear* is advanced, the element is placed in array position [*rear*]. Note that *rear* must be advanced prior to placing the element in the array. Of course, if the queue is full, no action is taken on the queue, and an appropriate message is displayed.

Removing Elements from a Queue.   Let's remove the three elements that were inserted in Figure 14.8 by executing the following *remove()* operations:

remove()
remove()
remove()

This sequence of events is illustrated in Figure 14.9. Elements are removed from the front of the queue. As a result, the first element to be removed from the queue is the character 'A' at array position [*front*], or [0]. Once the element is removed, *front* is advanced to the next circular array position. Now the character 'B' is at the front of the queue. The second *remove()* operation removes this character and advances *front* to position [2]. Now the only remaining element in the queue is the character 'C'. Notice that both *front* and *rear* locate this character, because it is the only element in the queue. A third *remove()* operation removes the character 'C', leaving an empty queue. How can it be that the queue is empty, because *front* and *rear* are not in their initialized positions? Moreover, *front* has moved ahead of *rear*. Is this a problem? No! Remember how we have defined an empty and a full queue? It does not matter where *front* and *rear* are located in determining the empty or full queue conditions. All that matters is the value of the element counter. If the element counter is 0, the queue is empty. If the element counter is *MAXQ*, the queue is full.

Here is an algorithm for the *remove()* operation:

> *remove()* **Algorithm**

```
BEGIN
    If the queue is not empty
        Decrement element counter.
        Remove the element at array position [front].
        If front == MAXQ – 1
            Set front = 0.
        Else
            Set front = front + 1.
    Else
        Display empty queue message.
END.
```

The algorithm begins by checking for the empty queue condition. If the queue is not empty, the element counter is decremented, and *front* is advanced via the **if/else** wraparound statement. If the queue is empty, an appropriate message is displayed.

Inspecting the Front Element of a Queue.   The next thing we need to do is to develop the *frontElement()* operation. Suppose we execute the following statement on the queue created back in Figure 14.8:

> *frontElement()*

The results of this operation are shown in Figure 14.10. Here you find that neither *front* nor *rear* is affected by the *frontElement()* operation. The operation simply returns the front character of the queue. The following algorithm will support this operation:

> *frontElement()* **Algorithm**

```
BEGIN
  If the queue is not empty
    Copy the element at array position [front].
```

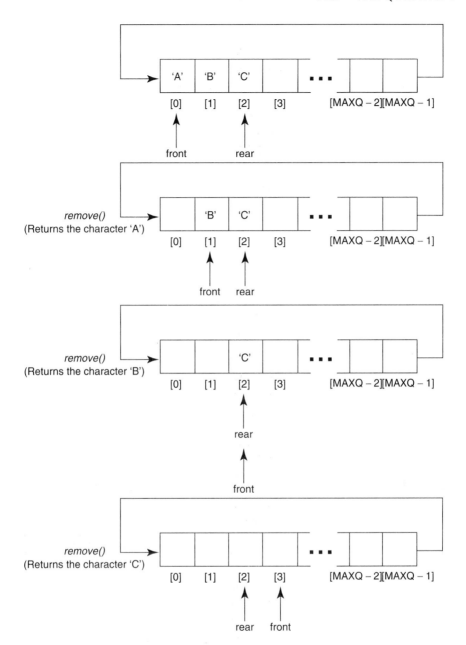

FIGURE 14.9 **THE EFFECT OF REMOVING THREE CHARACTER ELEMENTS FROM THE QUEUE IN FIGURE 14.8.**

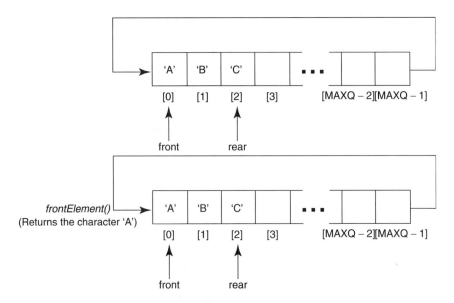

FIGURE 14.10 **THE EFFECT OF INSPECTING THE QUEUE CREATED IN FIGURE 14.8.**

Else
        Display an empty queue message.
END.

If the queue is not empty, the algorithm simply copies the element at the front position of the queue. Comparing this to the *remove()* algorithm, you find that there is no operation on the element counter or the *front* position locator.

Coding the Queue ADT.   We are now ready to code the queue ADT. To assure encapsulation and information hiding, we will code the ADT as a class. Here's the class declaration:

```
//QUEUE CLASS DECLARATION (queue.h)

#ifndef QUEUE_H
#define QUEUE_H
const int MAXQ = 5;             //MAXIMUM QUEUE SIZE
enum {EMPTY = 0, FULL = MAXQ};  //DEFINE EMPTY = 0 AND
                                //FULL = MAXQ

class Queue
{
public:
 Queue();                 //CONSTRUCTOR TO IMPLEMENT createQ()
 bool emptyQ();           //CHECKS TO SEE IF QUEUE IS EMPTY
 bool fullQ();            //CHECKS TO SEE IF QUEUE IS FULL
 void insert(char c);  //ADD ELEMENT TO REAR
```

```
        char remove();              //REMOVE ELEMENT FROM FRONT
        char frontElement();    //INSPECT FRONT ELEMENT

    private:
        char q[MAXQ];           //CHARACTER ARRAY TO HOLD THE QUEUE
        int front;              //front LOCATES FRONT ELEMENT OF QUEUE
        int rear;               //rear LOCATES REAR ELEMENT OF QUEUE
        int elementCount;  //ELEMENT COUNTER
    }; //END Queue
    #endif
```

The foregoing file is coded as an include file called *queue.h*. At the beginning of the file, you find the same type of constant and enumerated data definitions as we coded in the stack ADT. Notice, however, that *EMPTY* is defined with a value of 0, and *FULL* is defined with a value of *MAXQ*. These definitions will be used when testing the element counter for the empty and full conditions, respectively.

The public functions that are listed in the class are those defined for the queue ADT, with the exception of the *fullQ()* operation. Why do we need a *fullQ()* operation for our implementation? The same reason that we needed a *fullStack()* operation for our stack implementation. We are dealing with a finite array data structure. Note also that the *createQ()* operation is implemented by the class constructor.

The private section begins by defining a character array called *q[]* as a private member. As a result, this queue will store character elements. The size of the array is *MAXQ*, where *MAXQ* has been defined as the constant 5 for example purposes. There are three private integer variables: *front*, *rear*, and *elementCount*. You now should be aware of their use in this implementation. Again, it is important to stress the hiding of these private class members. No operations outside of the class can affect the contents of *q[]* or the values of *front*, *rear*, or *elementCount*. As a result, any queue object created for this class cannot be corrupted by intentional or unintentional operations outside of the queue class.

Next we need an implementation file to define the class functions. The file is called *queueop.cpp* and is provided as follows:

```
//QUEUE IMPLEMENTATION FILE (queueop.cpp)
#include "queue.h"       //FOR queue CLASS
#include <iostream.h>    //FOR cin AND cout

//IMPLEMENTATION OF Queue() CONSTRUCTOR
Queue :: Queue()
{
  front = 0;                      //SET FRONT TO FIRST ARRAY POSITION
  rear = MAXQ - 1;                //AND REAR TO LAST ARRAY POSITION
  elementCount = EMPTY;           //SET q ELEMENT COUNTER TO 0
} //END Queue()

//IMPLEMENTATION OF emptyQ()
bool Queue :: emptyQ()
{
```

```
 if (elementCount == EMPTY)     //IF q  EMPTY, RETURN TRUE
   return true;                 //ELSE RETURN FALSE
 else
   return false;
} //END emptyQ()


//IMPLEMENTATION OF fullQ()
bool Queue :: fullQ()
{
 if (elementCount == FULL)      //IF q FULL, RETURN TRUE
   return true;                 //ELSE RETURN FALSE
 else
   return false;
} //END fullQ()


//IMPLEMENTATION OF insert()
void Queue :: insert(char c)
{
 if (!fullQ())                  //IF q NOT FULL
 {                              //ADD ONE TO ELEMENT COUNT
   ++elementCount;
   if (rear == MAXQ - 1)        //INCREMENT REAR USING WRAPAROUND
     rear = 0;
   else
     ++rear;
   q[rear] = c;                 //INSERT CHARACTER INTO q
 } //END IF
 else
   cout << "The queue is full!" << endl;
} //END insert()


//IMPLEMENTATION OF remove()
char Queue :: remove()
{
 char c;                        //TEMP VARIABLE TO HOLD ELEMENT
 if (!emptyQ())                 //IF q NOT EMPTY
 {
   --elementCount;              //DECREMENT ELEMENT COUNT
   c = (q[front]);              //SAVE FRONT ELEMENT
   if (front == MAXQ - 1)       //INCREMENT FRONT USING WRAPAROUND
     front = 0;
   else
     ++front;
   return c;                    //RETURN SAVED FRONT ELEMENT
 }
 else
 {
   cout << "The queue is empty" << endl;
   return '#';                  //RETURN '#' TO INDICATE QUEUE EMPTY
 }  //END ELSE
}  //END remove()
```

```
//IMPLEMENTATION OF frontElement()
char Queue :: frontElement()
{
 if (!emptyQ())                    //IF q NOT EMPTY
   return q[front];                //RETURN FRONT ELEMENT
 else                             //ELSE RETURN '#' FOR EMPTY q
 {
   cout << "The queue is empty!" << endl;
   return '#';
 }  //END ELSE
}  //END frontElement()
```

In this file, all of the queue algorithms discussed earlier have been coded. Compare each coded function to its algorithm so that you understand what's going on. There were no algorithms developed for the *emptyQ()* and *fullQ()* operations, because they are so straightforward. Observe that the code for the *emptyQ()* and *fullQ()* functions simply tests the element counter for an *EMPTY* or *FULL* condition. Recall that *EMPTY* is defined as 0 and *FULL* is defined as *MAXQ*.

The following application file, called *queueapp.cpp*, has been created to test our queue ADT:

```
//APPLICATION FILE TO TEST THE QUEUE ADT (queueapp.cpp)

//PREPROCESSOR DIRECTIVES
#include " queue.h "  //FOR queue CLASS
#include <iostream.h> //FOR cin AND cout

//MAIN FUNCTION
int main()
{
  char c;                          //CHARACTER TO BE QUEUED
  int number = 0;                  //NUMBER OF CHARACTERS TO BE QUEUED
  int count = 0;                   //LOOP COUNTER
  Queue q;                         //DEFINE QUEUE OBJECT

  //GET NUMBER OF ELEMENTS TO QUEUE
  cout << "You cannot enter more than " << MAXQ
       << " elements. \nHow many elements do you have to enter? " << endl;
  cin >> number;

  //INSERT ELEMENTS INTO QUEUE
  while (count < number)
  {
    ++count;
    cout << "\nEnter a character element: ";
    cin >> c;
    q.insert(c);
  } //END WHILE
```

```
//INSPECT FRONT ELEMENT WITHOUT CHANGING QUEUE
cout << "\nThe front element of the queue is: "
     << q.frontElement();

//REMOVE AND WRITE QUEUE ELEMENTS
cout << "\n\nThe contents of the queue were: " << endl;
while (!q.emptyQ())
     cout << q.remove() << endl;

//ATTEMPT TO REMOVE FROM EMPTY QUEUE
q.remove();

//RETURN
return 0;
} //END main()
```

The test program defines *q* as an object of class *Queue*. Elements are then inserted into *q* one at a time from user entries via a **while** loop. Notice that the loop executes as long as the number of elements entered does not exceed the number of elements the user specified for entry. Once the user elements are inserted into the queue, the front element is inspected by a call to the *frontElement()* function. The next segment of code removes and displays the queue elements. If the queue is not empty, a **while** loop is entered to remove and display all of the queue elements one at a time. The termination of the loop is controlled by a call to *emptyQ()*. As a result, the loop statements will execute, removing and displaying one element with each iteration, until the queue is empty. Finally, a single call is made to *remove()* in an attempt to remove an element from an empty queue. This call was made to test the *remove()* function. Here are the results of executing the test program:

```
You cannot enter more than 5 elements.
How many elements do you have to enter?
3↵

Enter a character element: A↵

Enter a character element: B↵

Enter a character element: C↵

The front element of the queue is: A

The contents of the queue were:
A
B
C

The queue is empty!
```

In this test run, the user has entered the characters 'A', 'B', and 'C'. The front character, 'A', is copied and displayed to verify the *frontElement()* function. Then all of the characters of the queue are removed and displayed. Notice that the characters are displayed in the same order in which they were entered, thereby verifying the FIFO principle. The last line on the display verifies that the *remove()* function checks for the empty queue condition.

Quick Check

1. Suppose that the user filled a queue using the application test program in this section. What would happen if a call were made to the *insert()* function after the queue was full?

2. True or false: With our array implementation of a queue, an *insert()* operation requires that *front* be advanced prior to placing the element in the array.

3. Write the pseudocode required to advance *front* for the circular array implementation of a queue.

4. True or false: With the circular array implementation of a queue, *front* can never have a higher value than *rear*.

5. Using the circular array implementation of a queue, how can you tell when there is only one element in the queue?

6. Theoretically, the size of a queue is unlimited. Why did we have to include a *fullQ()* function in our implementation?

7. Explain how to determine when the queue is empty and when the queue is full using our array implementation.

14.4   THE LIST ADT

You have already been dealing with lists, even though we have not made a formal definition of a list, but now is the time to do so.

A *list* is a *sequence* of data elements whose basic operations are insertion and deletion of elements to and from the list.

The arrays, stacks, and queues that you have studied so far are lists. Each of these lists represents a *sequence* of data elements. The term *sequence* implies ordering. This means that the list has a first element, a second element, and so on. In an array, the elements are ordered from the first array position to the last array position. In a stack, the elements are ordered from the top of the stack (last element in) to the bottom of the stack (first element in). In a queue, the elements are ordered from the front of the queue to the rear of the queue. Stacks and queues, however, are special kinds of lists, because the insert and delete operations are defined to be at the end(s) of the list. An array has no such restriction, because you can access the list randomly, inserting and deleting elements from any position in the list. Thus, stacks and queues must be sequentially accessed, whereas arrays can be randomly accessed.

In each of the lists you have studied so far, the sequencing of the elements is ***implicit***. This means that the element sequence is inherent to the structure definition. The sequencing of elements in an array is given implicitly, because the first element is stored in position [0], the second element in position [1], and so on. Thus, given any element in the array, you can always locate its successor element. Given the element at array position [5], you know that its successor is at array position [6]. In a stack, the sequencing of elements is given implicitly from top to bottom. Given the element located at *top*, you know that the next element is located just beneath the top element. In a queue, the sequencing is from front to rear. Given an element located at *front*, you know that its successor is located just behind the front element. In all of these lists, once you locate the first element, you can locate the second, and so on, via the natural ordering of the structure. However, there is one kind of list where the sequencing of elements must be provided ***explicitly***. This means that given any element in the list, the location of its successor must be clearly specified, because its location is not inherent within the natural sequencing of the list elements. Such a list is called a ***linked list.***

Linked Lists

First, consider the following formal definition of a linked list:

> A ***linked list*** is a sequential collection of data elements such that, given any element in the list, the location of its successor element is specified by an *explicit* link, rather than by its natural position in the collection.

Now, here's the idea: A linked list consists of a sequence of ***nodes***. A node contains two things: an ***element*** and a ***locator***, or ***link***. The element is the information that is stored in the node, and the locator is the link that locates the *next* node in the list. This idea is illustrated in Figure 14.11.

The element part of the node may contain a simple integer, character, or string as well as an entire structure that contains many other data elements. For instance, the element part of a node could be a record that contains your name, address, and telephone number. We will call this the *info* part of the node. The locator part of the node is the explicit locator, or link, to the next sequential node in the list. We will call this the *next* part of the node. We say that *next* locates, or points to, the next node in the list. Now, look at the sample linked list in Figure 14.12.

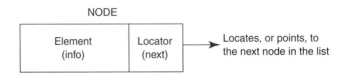

FIGURE 14.11   A SINGLE NODE IN A LINKED LIST.

FIGURE 14.12   **A LINKED LIST CONTAINING THREE NODES.**

The linked list in Figure 14.12 contains three nodes storing character information. The first node is located by a locator called *first*. We must always have a means of locating the first node in the list and will usually designate this as *first*. Notice that *first* locates, or points to, the first node in the list. The first node locates, or points to, the second node, and so on. The last node points to *NULL*, because there are no more nodes in the list. We will use the term *NULL* to designate the end of the list. It is easy to see that the list is sequentially ordered from the first to the last node and the ordering is given explicitly via the *next* part of each node.

Now we need to develop some notation that will be used to discuss linked lists. We will implement our linked list using pointers and, therefore, refer to a node locator as a pointer. Here is some notation and terminology that will be employed when discussing linked lists:

> *node(p)* refers to the entire node pointed to by *p*.
> *info(p)* refers to the information part of the node pointed to by *p*.
> *next(p)* refers to the next, or pointer, part of the node pointed to by *p*.
> The *predecessor node* to *node(p)* is the node just before *node(p)*.
> The *successor node* to *node(p)* is the node just after *node(p)*.

This linked list notation and terminology is illustrated in Figure 14.13. Of special interest is *next(p)*. *next(p)* is always a pointer and points to *node(p)*'s successor node, unless *node(p)* is the last node in the list. If this is the case, *next(p)* has the value *NULL*.

To familiarize yourself with this notation, consider the following algorithm:

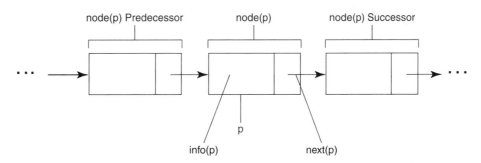

FIGURE 14.13   **NOTATION AND TERMINOLOGY USED WITH LINKED LISTS.**

BEGIN
    Set *p = first.*
    While *p ≠ NULL*
        Write *info(p).*
        Set *p = next(p).*
END.

Can you determine what the algorithm does? Well, notice that *p* is made to point to the first node in the list by setting *p* to *first.* Then, the **while** loop will execute as long as *p* is not equal to *NULL.* Each time the loop is executed, the information in the node pointed to by *p* (*info(p)*) is written and *p* is advanced to point to the next sequential node in the list. In other words, the list is *traversed* from the first node to the last. At each node, the information stored in the node is written. Now that you have a general feel for a linked list, it is time to define our linked list ADT, as follows:

ADT Linked List

Operations, or Interface:

createList()
    Creates an empty list.

insertNode()
    Adds a data element to the beginning of the list.

deleteNode()
    Removes a specified data element from the list.

traverseList()
    Traverses the list, processing the list information as required.

emptyList()
    Determines if the list is empty.

Data:

A sequential collection of data elements.

Implementing the Linked List ADT

The natural way to implement a linked list is by using pointers. As you can see from the ADT definition, we have defined five linked list operations. We now need to show how pointers can be used to implement these operations. For each of the operations, we will develop an algorithm using the linked list notation given earlier. Then, we will code the algorithms in C++.

Creating an Empty Linked List.   The first thing that must be done before building a linked list is to create an empty list. An empty list will be a list with no nodes in it, right? So, to create a list without any nodes, all we need to do is set *first* to *NULL*, as in Figure 14.14.

Remember that 1) we will be using pointers to implement our linked list, 2) *first* will be the pointer that locates the first node in the list, and 3) *NULL* will define the end of the list. So, if we make *first* point to *NULL*, we have an empty list. Here's the simple algorithm:

createList() **Algorithm**

> BEGIN
>   Set *first* = *NULL*.
> END.

Inserting a Node into a Linked List.   Next, we need to develop an algorithm to insert a data element into the linked list. Because the linked list data elements are contained in nodes, this operation requires that a node be added to the list. Looking at the ADT definition, you see that we will always add a node at the beginning of the list. To accomplish this task, we need to do four things:

1. Create a new node.
2. Fill the node with the data to be stored.
3. Make the new node point to the first node in the list.
4. Make *first* point to the new node.

For example, suppose that we have a linked list of the two characters 'A' and 'B', in that order. Then, we execute the following operation to insert the character 'C' into the list:

insertNode('C')

The sequence of events that must be performed to insert a new node containing the character 'C' at the beginning of the list are shown in Figure 14.15.

To create the new node, we simply make a temporary pointer, *p*, point to an empty node. As you will find out shortly, a node will be coded as a record, called a *struct* in C++, that contains a data, or *info*, member and a pointer, or *next*, member. The new node struct will literally be created from nothing using dynamic memory allocation and the **new** operator. So, to create a new node and make *p* point to this node, we will use the following statement in our algorithm:

Set *p* = new *node.*

first ⟶ NULL

FIGURE 14.14   AN EMPTY LIST IS CREATED BY MAKING *FIRST* POINT TO *NULL*.

Initial List

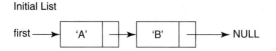

1. Create a new node.

2. Fill the new node with data

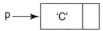

3. Make the new node point to the first node.

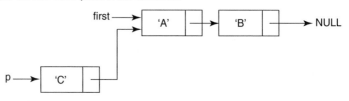

4. Make first point to the new node.

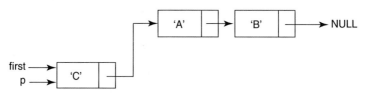

FIGURE 14.15 INSERTING A NODE AT THE BEGINNING OF A LINKED LIST.

Next, the information part of the new node is filled with the data element, in this case the character 'C'. To accomplish this task, we will place the following statement in the algorithm:

Set *info(p)* = 'C'.

This statement says to "place the character 'C' in the information part of the node pointed to by *p*."

Once the data are in the new node, we must add the node to the list. The node is to be added at the beginning of the list, so we make the new node point to the first node in the list. Notice from Figure 14.15 that, prior to this step, *first* is pointing to where the new node needs to point. As a result, all we need to do is to assign *first* to the pointer, or *next*, part of the new node. The following pseudocode statement will accomplish this task:

Set *next(p)* = *first.*

The foregoing statement says to "Assign *first* to the pointer part of the node pointed to by *p*." Performing this assignment places the new node at the beginning of the list. However, *first* is now pointing to the second node in the list and needs to be moved to point to our new node. Our new node is currently being pointed to by *p*. Thus, to make *first* point to the new node, all we have to do is to set *first* to *p*, like this:

Set *first* = *p*.

That's all there is to it. Here's the complete algorithm:

insertNode() **Algorithm**

BEGIN
  Set *p* = new *node*.
  Set *info(p)* = data element.
  Set *next(p)* = *first*.
  Set *first* = *p*.
END.

Make sure that you understand how the four statements in the above algorithm accomplish the four tasks shown in Figure 14.15, especially in light of the notation that is being used. You might have noticed that, because our *insertNode()* algorithm places the new node at the beginning of the list, the character 'C' is placed out of its natural order, relative to the other nodes in the list. An ***ordered linked list*** is a linked list whereby all the data elements are in some natural order from the first node to the last node in the list. To create an ordered linked list, our *insertNode()* algorithm must be changed to search the list for the correct insertion point prior to adding the node to the list. This will be left as an exercise at the end of the chapter.

Deleting Data from a Linked List.   Deleting data from a linked list requires that we delete the node containing the data from the linked list. Deleting a node from a linked list is the most difficult operation to be performed. As a result, we will develop several algorithm levels, working up to one that can be coded in C++.

Looking at the ADT definition for *deleteNode()*, you see that we must delete a specified data element from the list. This means that, given an element to delete, we must search for the element in the list. Then, once the element is found, adjust the list pointers to eliminate the node that contains the element to be deleted. So, our first-level algorithm becomes

deleteNode() **Algorithm (First Level)**

BEGIN
  Search the list for the element to be deleted.
  Adjust the list pointers to eliminate the node that
  contains the element to be deleted.
END.

Searching a Linked List. We will employ a simple sequential search to find the node to be deleted. This means that, beginning with the first node, we must test the element stored in the information part of the node against the specified element to delete and advance to the next node, repeat the testing procedure, and so on, until we get to the end of the list. Here is an algorithm that will do the job:

Linked List Search Algorithm

```
BEGIN
  If the list is empty
     Write an appropriate message.
  Else
     Set p = first.
     Set predP = NULL.
     Set found = false.
     While (NOT found) AND (p ≠ NULL)
          If info(p) == element
             Set found = true.
          Else
             Set predP = p.
             Set p = next(p).
END.
```

The first thing that must be done is to test for an empty list, because you cannot delete a node from a list that is empty. If the list is empty, an appropriate message is written to the user; otherwise, the search process is started.

There are two key pointer variables employed for the search. We will use the pointer *p* as a pointer to traverse the list, beginning at *first* and ending when *p* becomes *NULL*. In addition to *p*, we will employ another pointer called *predP* that follows *p* through the list as the search progresses. As a result, the pointer *predP* will always point to the node just prior to the node to which *p* is pointing. Recall that this is the predecessor node to *node(p)*. This idea is illustrated in Figure 14.16.

A **while** loop is employed to control the search. Notice that the loop tests for two conditions: (NOT *found*) and (*p* ≠ *NULL*). The **AND** operator requires that both tests be true for the search to proceed. As a result, the search will stop when either the element is found or when *p* becomes *NULL*. Within the loop, we use an **if/else** statement to test the information contained in *node(p)*. If *info(p)* is equal to the element being searched for, the Boolean variable is set to true, and the loop

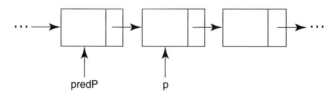

```
predP              p
```

FIGURE 14.16   DURING THE LIST SEARCH PROCEDURE, *P* WILL POINT TO THE NODE BEING TESTED, AND *PREDP* WILL POINT TO THE PREDECESSOR NODE TO *NODE(P)*.

will break. Otherwise, both pointers are advanced to the next respective node in the list. Do you see how the statement *Set predP = p* makes *predP* point to *node(p)* and the statement *Set p = next(p)* makes *p* point to *node(p)*'s successor node?

So, when the search loop is broken, *p* is pointing to the node to be deleted, and *predP* is pointing to this node's predecessor. But, what if the element being searched for was not in the list? In this case, *p* will move all the way through the list and stop when it becomes *NULL*. Also, what if the node to be deleted is the first node in the list? Well, in this case, *p* and *predP* will not be advanced at all and will have their original values of *first* and *NULL*, respectively.

Deleting a Node in a Linked List.   Next, let's develop the pseudocode required to actually delete a node from the list. This task follows the foregoing search algorithm, so we will use the values of *found*, *p*, and *predP* to delete the required node. Here's the delete algorithm:

Delete Algorithm

```
BEGIN
    If (found)
     If (predP == NULL)
        Set first = next(p).
     Else
        Set next(predP) = next(p).
     Else
          Write a message that the element was not
          found in the list.
   END.
```

Here, the first thing to do is to check to see if the element being searched for was found during the search. If *found* is true coming out of the search algorithm, the element was found, and the node must be deleted. Otherwise, the element was not found and an appropriate message must be written to the user. If the element was found, a nested **if/else** statement is employed to delete the respective node. If the node to be deleted is the first node in the list, we simply make *first* point to the second node in the list by setting *first* to *next(p)*. This deletes the first node in the list. How do you know if the node to be deleted is the first node in the list? Of course, *predP* has the value *NULL* after exiting the search algorithm. If *predP* does not have the value *NULL,* the node to be deleted is not the first node in the list. In this case, the nested **else** makes the pointer from *node(p)*'s predecessor jump around *node(p)* and point to *node(p)*'s successor. This is accomplished by setting *next(predP)* to *next(p)*. The diagram in Figure 14.17 illustrates this operation:

Now putting the search algorithm together with the delete node algorithm, we get an algorithm for our ADT *deleteNode()* operation that can be coded in C++. Here is the final algorithm:

deleteNode() **Algorithm**

```
BEGIN
  If the list is empty
```

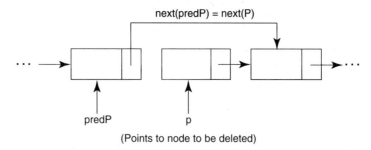

next(predP) = next(P)

predP

p

(Points to node to be deleted)

FIGURE 14.17 SETTING *NEXT(PREDP)* TO *NEXT(P)* DELETES *NODE(P)* FROM THE LIST.

           Write an appropriate message.
    Else
        Set *p = first.*
        Set *predP = NULL.*
        Set *found* = false.
        While (NOT *found*) AND (*p ≠ NULL*)
            If *info(p) == element*
                Set *found* = true.
            Else
                Set *predP = p.*
                Set *p = next(p).*
        If (*found*)
            If (*predP == NULL*)
                Set *first = next(p).*
            Else
                Set *next(predP) = next(p).*
        Else
            Write a message that the element was not found
            in the list.
    END.

Traversing a Linked List. You have already observed a traversal algorithm. Here is one that is customized to fit our ADT definition for *traverseList()*:

        traverseList() **Algorithm**

BEGIN
    If the list is not empty
        Set *p = first.*
        While *p ≠ NULL*
          Write *info(p).*
          Set *p = next(p).*
    Else
        Write a message to indicate an empty list.
    END.

The algorithm begins by checking for an empty list. If the list is not empty, a temporary list pointer, *p*, is initialized to the beginning of the list. A **while** loop is then executed to process the information stored in the nodes. In this case, we are simply writing the node information, *info(p)*. Once the node information is written, *p* is advanced to point to the next node in the list. The loop continues writing the node information and advancing *p* through the list until the value of *p* becomes *NULL*. Of course, an appropriate message is written to the user if the list is empty.

Checking for an Empty List.   To complete our ADT implementation, we must develop an algorithm for the *emptyList()* operation. Recall that this operation simply checks to see if the list is empty. How do you know when the list is empty? Right, when *first* has the value *NULL*. As a result, the algorithm is

emptyList() **Algorithm**

```
BEGIN
   If first == NULL
      Return true.
   Else
      Return false.
END.
```

As you can see, *emptyList()* returns the Boolean value true if the value of *first* is *NULL*; otherwise, it returns the value false. We can now call upon this operation in the other operations when we need to test for an empty list.

Coding the Linked List ADT.   We are now ready to code the linked list ADT. How do you suppose that we will code it in C++? You guessed it, using a class to assure complete encapsulation with information hiding. First, the class declaration:

```
//LINKED LIST CLASS DECLARATION FILE (list.h)
#ifndef LIST_H
#define LIST_H

#include <iostream.h>   //FOR cin, cout, AND NULL

//NODE STRUCTURE DECLARATION
struct node
{
   char info;      //INFORMATION PART OF NODE
   node *next;     //POINTER TO NEXT NODE
}; //END node

//LIST CLASS DECLARATION
class List
{
public:
   List();      //CONSTRUCTOR TO
                //IMPLEMENT  createList()
   ~List();     //DESTRUCTOR TO DEALLOCATE LIST MEMORY
   void insertNode(char c);      //FUNCTION TO INSERT A NODE
```

```
              void deleteNode(char c);      //FUNCTION TO DELETE A
                                            //SPECIFIED NODE
              void traverseList();          //FUNCTION TO TRAVERSE LIST
              bool  emptyList();            //FUNCTION TO TEST FOR
                                            //EMPTY  LIST
        private:
          node *first;   //DEFINE first AS A POINTER TO NODE STRUCT
        }; //END List
        #endif
```

The class declaration is placed in a header file called *list.h.* Before the *List* class is declared, a **struct** called *node* is declared. A **struct** is how C++ implements a record. Think of a struct as class that contains *only public* data members. The data members can be different data types, but are all public by default. No function members are allowed in a struct.

> Think of a **struct** as a class that contains only public data members. The data members can be different data types, but are all public by default.

Now, back to our linked list. Remember that a linked list node has two parts: an information part and a pointer part. As a result, the *node* struct has two parts. The information part is defined as a character member called *info.* This means that our linked list will hold character data. The pointer part of the node is defined as a pointer member called *next.* Notice that the data pointed to by *next* is the struct itself, called *node.* This means that the *next* pointer will point to a struct that has the same definition as the *node* struct in which *next* is defined. Isn't this what we want to do? The *next* pointer in a node needs to point to another node of the same structure, right?

Following the *node* struct declaration, we declare a class called *List.* The class must consist of the linked list node structure and the functions required to operate on that structure. All we have to do to define the entire linked list is define a pointer to the first node in the list. From here, each node locates its successor node via its *next* pointer. So the single private member of the class is a pointer, called *first,* which will locate the first node in the list. Notice that *first* is a pointer to our *node* struct.

The first function declared in the class is the class constructor, called *List().* This constructor function implements the *createList()* operation and will be coded to set *first* to *NULL.*

The second function declared is the class destructor, called *~List().* This is an ideal application for a destructor! We will be generating new nodes by dynamically allocating memory. When we delete a node, we will deallocate the memory required for that node. So, why not deallocate the memory allocated to the entire list by using a destructor when we are done processing the list? In other words, our *~List()* destructor will delete the entire list by deallocating all memory allocated to the list when we are done processing the list. This function is not part of our ADT definition and is only included because of the use of dynamic memory allocation.

Next you see the remaining four operations required for the *Linked List* ADT. You are now aware of the purpose of these four operations. The task at hand is to code the respective algorithms developed for these operations as part of an implementation file. The function implementation file is called *listop.cpp*. Here it is:

```
//LINKED LIST IMPLEMENTATION FILE (listop.cpp)

//PREPROCESSOR DIRECTIVES
#include "list.h"        //FOR list CLASS
#include <iostream.h>   //FOR cin AND cout

//IMPLEMENTATION OF CONSTRUCTOR List()
List :: List()
{
 first = NULL;
}   //END List()

//IMPLEMENTATION OF DESTRUCTOR, ~List()
List :: ~List()
{
  node *p;              //DEFINE p AS A POINTER TO
                        //THE NODE STRUCT
  node *temp;           //DEFINE temp AS POINTER TO
                        //THE NODE STRUCT
  p = first;            //SET p = first
 while (p!= NULL)       //TRAVERSE LIST UNTIL p = NULL
 {
   temp = p -> next;    //MAKE temp POINT TO NEXT NODE IN LIST
   delete p;            //DEALLOCATE node(p)
   p = temp;            //MAKE p POINT TO NEXT NODE
 }   //END WHILE
}   //END ~List()

//IMPLEMENTATION OF insertNode()
void List :: insertNode(char c)
{
 node *p;               //DEFINE p AS A POINTER TO
                        //THE NODE STRUCT
 p = new node;          //ALLOCATE MEMORY FOR node(p)
 p -> info = c;         //PLACE CHAR IN info(p)
 p -> next = first;     //INSERT node(p) AT BEGINNING
 first = p;             //MOVE first TO node(p)
}   //END insertNode()

//IMPLEMENTATION OF deleteNode()
void List :: deleteNode(char c)
{
 bool found = false;    //INITIALIZE found TO FALSE
 node *p;               //DEFINE p AS A POINTER TO NODE STRUCT
 node *predP;           //DEFINE predP AS A POINTER TO NODE STRUCT
 p = first;             //START p AT first NODE
 predP = NULL;          //START predP AT NULL
```

```
//IF LIST EMPTY, WRITE EMPTY MESSAGE. ELSE
//SEARCH FOR ELEMENT TO BE DELETED
if (emptyList())
  cout << "\nYou cannot delete a node from an empty list!" << endl;
else
{
  while (!found && p != NULL)          //TRAVERSE LIST UNTIL FOUND
                                       //OR p == NULL
  {
      if (p -> info == c)              //TEST info(p)
        found = true;
      else                             //ADVANCE POINTERS
      {
        predP = p;                     //CATCH predP UP TO p
        p = p-> next;                  //ADVANCE p
      }  //END ADVANCE ELSE
}  //END SEARCH LOOP


//DELETE NODE IF FOUND, ELSE WRITE NOT FOUND MESSAGE
if (found)
{
      //DOES node(p) HAVE A PREDECESSOR?
      //IF NOT, DELETE first NODE, ELSE DELETE node(p)
      if (predP == NULL)
      {
        first = p -> next;             //MOVE first TO SECOND NODE
        delete p;                      //DEALLOCATE node(p)
      }  //END DELETE first NODE

      else
      {
       predP -> next = p -> next;      //MAKE NEXT(predP) JUMP
                                       //AROUND node(p)
        delete p;                      //DEALLOCATE node(p)
      } //END DELETE node(p)
} //END IF FOUND
else                                   //WRITE NOT FOUND MESSAGE
      cout << "\nThe character '" << c << "' is not in the list!" << endl;
  }  //END SEARCH ELSE
}  //END deleteNode()


//IMPLEMENTATION OF traverseList()
void List :: traverseList()
{
 node *p;                              //DEFINE p AS A POINTER TO  NODE STRUCT
 p = first;                            //START p AT first NODE


//IF LIST IS NOT EMPTY, TRAVERSE LIST
//AND WRITE info(p). ELSE WRITE LIST EMPTY MESSAGE
if (!emptyList())
```

```
{
  while (p != NULL)                        //TRAVERSE LIST UNTIL p = NULL
  {
    cout << p -> info << " -> ";           //WRITE info(p)
    p = p -> next;                         //ADVANCE p
  }  //END WHILE
  cout << "NULL " << endl;                 //WRITE "NULL"
}  //END IF NOT EMPTY
else                                       //WRITE EMPTY LIST MESSAGE
    cout << "\nThe list is empty!" << endl;
}  //END traverseList()

//IMPLEMENTATION OF emptyList()
bool List :: emptyList()
{
  if (first == NULL)
    return true;
  else
    return false;
}  //END emptyList()
```

Now remember, we are implementing our linked list ADT using dynamic pointers. The first implementation that you see in the foregoing code is for the constructor, *List()*. This function simply initializes a new list by setting *first* to *NULL*. Next, the destructor function, *~List()* begins by defining temporary pointers, *p* and *temp*, to the *node* struct. The pointer *p* is initialized to point to the first node in the list by setting it to *first*. A **while** loop is then executed until the value of *p* becomes *NULL*. Within the loop, *temp* is set to the next node in the list, and the **delete** operator is executed to deallocate the memory being used by *node(p)*. Once the node memory is deallocated, *p* is advanced to the next node in the list by setting *p* to *temp*. (Why do we need *temp*?)

The remaining function implementations simply reflect their respective algorithms. However, take special note of how dynamic pointers are employed to code the algorithm. For example, notice how the *insertNode()* function allocates memory for a new node by executing the **new** operator. The statement *p = new node* allocates memory dynamically for a *node* struct and then makes *p* point to that struct. In the *deleteNode()* function, the statement *delete p* deallocates the memory occupied by the *node* struct to which *p* is pointing. The pseudocode operations used in our algorithms are implemented in C++ using pointers, as summarized in Table 14.1.

Make a sincere effort to understand how each of the algorithms developed in this section is coded using dynamic pointers in the foregoing implementation file. You now possess all the knowledge required to understand this code.

TABLE 14.1   LINKED LIST PSEUDOCODE VERSUS C++ POINTER CODE

Pseudocode	C++ Pointer Code
info(p)	*p -> info*
node(p)	**p*
next(p)	*p -> next*

Last but not least, we need an application file to test our linked list ADT. Here is the one that we used:

```cpp
//APPLICATION FILE TO TEST LIST ADT (listapp.cpp)

//PREPROCESSOR DIRECTIVES
#include "list.h"       //FOR list CLASS
#include <iostream.h>   //FOR cin AND cout

//MAIN FUNCTION
int main()
{
   char c;                 //CHARACTER TO BE INSERTED INTO LIST
   int number = 0;         //NUMBER OF CHARACTERS TO BE INSERTED
   int count = 0;          //LOOP COUNTER
   List l;                 //DEFINE LIST OBJECT

   //INSERT SPECIFIED NUMBER OF ELEMENTS INTO LIST
   cout << "How many nodes do you want to insert? " << endl;
   cin >> number;
   while (count < number)
   {
      ++count;
      cout << "\nEnter a character element:  ";
      cin >> c;
      l.insertNode(c);
   } //END WHILE

   //TRAVERSE AND WRITE LIST ELEMENTS
   cout << "\n\nThe contents of the list are:  ";
   l.traverseList();

   //DELETE A SPECIFIED CHARACTER  FROM THE LIST
   cout << "\nWhich character element do you want to delete? ";
   cin >> c;
   l.deleteNode(c);

   //TRAVERSE AND WRITE LIST ELEMENTS
   cout << "\nThe contents of the list are:  ";
   l.traverseList();

   //RETURN
   return 0;
}  //END main()
```

The application file name is *listapp.cpp*. The code begins by including the *list.h* header file as well as other standard header files that are required. An object, *l*, is defined for the *List* class. The user is then prompted to enter any number of list elements. Is the user restricted to some maximum number of elements as with our stack and queue implementations? No! This is the advantage of using a dynamic pointer implementation. As long as memory is available, we can add as many elements to the list as we want. (Why were we limited with our stack and queue implementations?)

Once a list is constructed, the list is traversed by calling *traverseList()* to display the list elements. Then the user is prompted to delete a specified character from the list. The character is deleted, and the list is traversed and displayed again. Here's a sample run:

```
How many nodes do you want to insert?
3↵

Enter a character element: A↵

Enter a character element: B↵

Enter a character element: C↵

The contents of the list are: C -> B -> A -> NULL

Which character element do you want to delete? B↵

The contents of the list are: C -> A -> NULL
```

Quick Check

1. True or false: In a linked list, the sequencing of the nodes is implicit.
2. The two parts of a linked list node are the _____ and _____.
3. If *node(p)* is the last node in the list, the value of *next(p)* is _____.
4. True or false: In a pointer implementation of a linked list, we know that the list is empty when the value of *first* is zero.
5. What happens if you reverse the order of steps 3 and 4 in the insertion process illustrated in Figure 14.15?
6. Will the list search algorithm given in this section detect multiple occurrences of the same element in a linked list?
7. What happens if the statements *Set predP = p* and *Set p = next(p)* are reversed in the linked list search algorithm?
8. Write an algorithm using the pseudocode notation developed in this section for the list destructor function, *~List()*.

14.5   THE STANDARD TEMPLATE LIBRARY, OR STL

Now that you are thoroughly familiar with stacks, queues, and linked-lists, it is time to tell you that all are available in the ANSI/ISO Standard Template Library, or STL. The STL provides several data structure container classes shown in Table 14.2. These classes are called *container classes* because the objects of these classes "contain" other objects. You have already worked with the *vector* class, now it is time to discuss the *stack*, *queue*, and *list* classes. A course in data structures will most likely cover other data structures in general and STL container classes shown in Table 14.2 not covered here.

TABLE 14.2   CONTAINER CLASSES AVAILABLE IN THE STL

Class	Description
Deque	Random access indexed queue structure.
List	Unbounded non-indexed sequential access structure with head and tail.
Map	Collection of key-valued pairs.
Priority Queue	Queue with front element always largest element.
Queue	FIFO structure.
Set	Ordered list.
Stack	LIFO structure.
Vector	Indexed random access array structure.

The STL *stack* Class

The *stack* class is defined in the *stack* header file. Thus to use it, you must include the *stack* header file at the beginning of your program. The primary functions available in the *stack* class are listed in Table 14.3.

You are familiar with most of these from our earlier discussion of stacks. As you might suspect, the *empty()* function returns a Boolean value of true or false, depending on whether or not the stack is empty. The *push()* function places its *element* argument on the top of the stack. Notice from the table that, unlike the non-void *pop()* function that we developed, the *stack* class *pop()* function is a void function that removes, but *does not return* the top element of the stack. You must use the *top()* function to return the top stack element. However, *top()* does not remove the element. So, how do you both return and remove the top element? You must call *top()* followed by a call to *pop()*. The *size()* function is convenient because it returns the size of the current stack. Here's a program that exercises the *stack* class functions:

```
//PREPROCESSOR DIRECTIVES
#include <stack>        //FOR stack CLASS
#include <iostream>     //FOR cin AND cout

using namespace std;   //REQUIRED WHEN INCLUDING iostream
```

TABLE 14.3   FUNCTIONS AVAILABLE IN THE STL *STACK* CLASS

Function Prototype	Purpose
bool empty()	Returns true if stack is empty.
void pop()	Removes, but does not return, the top element of the stack.
void push(element)	Places *element* on the top of the stack.
int size()	Returns the number of elements in the stack.
stack_type top()	Returns, but does not remove the top element of the stack.

```
//MAIN FUNCTION
int main()
{
  int number = 0;        //NUMBER OF CHARACTERS TO BE STACKED
  int count = 0;         //LOOP COUNTER
  char c = ' ';          //CHARACTER TO STACK

  //DEFINE CHARACTER STACK OBJECT
  stack<char> stk;

  //OBTAIN NUMBER OF ELEMENTS TO STACK
  cout << "\nHow many elements do you have to enter? ";
  cin >> number;

  //PUSH ELEMENTS ONTO STACK
  while (count < number)
  {
   ++count;
   cout << "Enter an element:   ";
   cin >> c;
   stk.push(c);
  } //END WHILE

 //DISPLAY STACK SIZE
 cout << "\nThe stack has " << stk.size() << " elements.";

 //INSPECT TOP ELEMENT OF THE STACK
 cout << "\n\nThe top element of the stack is:   "
      << stk.top() << endl;

 //POP AND WRITE STACK ELEMENTS
 cout << "\nThe contents of the stack were:   " << endl;
 while (!stk.empty())
 {
    cout << stk.top() << endl;
    stk.pop();
 }//END WHILE

 if(stk.empty())
    cout << "The stack is empty" << endl;

 //RETURN
 return 0;
} //END main()
```

We have highlighted the stack-related code in bold so that you can quickly see what's going on. First, notice that a preprocessor directive is provided to include the *stack* class. Next, an object called *stk* is defined for the class. However, notice the syntax of *stack<char> stk*. This tells C++ that our stack will be a stack of characters, *<char>*. One of the problems with the stack class that we created earlier was that the class and function implementation code would have to be totally rewritten each time we wanted to create stacks for different types of data elements. Since the *stack* class is a container class which uses a template, we can tell C++ the type of elements to stack when we create an object for the class. This is one of the purposes of a template. Templates allow you develop generic classes and functions for arbitrary data types. For example, we can create a stack of strings in the same application program by changing the definition to *stack<string> stk*. That's all there is to it!

Now, looking back at the program, you see that the user is prompted to enter the number elements to stack, then the *stk* object calls the *push()* function to stack each user entry. After the loop exits, the *stk* object calls the *size()* function within a *cout* statement to display the number of elements that were pushed onto the stack. Next, the *top()* function is called within a *cout* statement to display the top element of the stack. The second **while** loop empties the stack by calling *top()* and *pop()* in tandem to display and remove the top stack element with each loop iteration. Notice that the loop test employs a call to *empty()*. Finally an **if** statement calls the *empty()* function to assure that the stack is indeed empty. Here is a sample run:

```
How many elements do you have to enter? 3↵
Enter an element: A↵
Enter an element: B↵
Enter an element: C↵

The stack has 3 elements.

The top element of the stack is: C

The contents of the stack were:
C
B
A

The stack is empty
```

Now, let's see how easy it is to revise our program to create a stack of strings. Here's the same basic program, with the modified code highlighted in bold.

```
//PREPROCESSOR DIRECTIVES
#include <stack>        //FOR stack CLASS
#include <iostream>     //FOR cin AND cout
#include <string>       //FOR string CLASS

using namespace std;    //REQUIRED WHEN INCLUDING iostream

//MAIN FUNCTION
int main()
{
    int number = 0;     //NUMBER OF CHARACTERS TO BE STACKED
    int count = 0;      //LOOP COUNTER
    string s = " ";     //STRING TO STACK

    //DEFINE CHARACTER STACK OBJECT
    stack<string> stk;
```

```
//OBTAIN NUMBER OF ELEMENTS TO STACK
cout << "\nHow many string elements do you have to enter? ";
cin >> number;

//PUSH ELEMENTS ONTO STACK
 while (count < number)
 {
    ++count;
    cout << "\nEnter a string:   ";
    cin >> ws;
    getline(cin,s);
    stk.push(s);
 } //END WHILE

//DISPLAY STACK SIZE
cout << "\nThe stack has " << stk.size() << " elements.";

//INSPECT TOP ELEMENT OF THE STACK
cout  << "\n\nThe top element of the stack is:   "
      << stk.top() << endl;

//POP AND WRITE STACK ELEMENTS
cout << "\nThe contents of the stack were:   " << endl;
while (!stk.empty())
{
    cout << stk.top() << endl;
    stk.pop();
}//END WHILE

if(stk.empty())
    cout << "The stack is empty" << endl;
 //RETURN
 return 0;
} //END main()
```

See how easy that was! We simply included the *string* header file and defined our stack object using the syntax *stack<string> stk*. This is the beauty of using a template class—you can easily change the type of data the class will operate on. Of course, we also had to use *getline()* to read the strings from the keyboard.

Also, you should be aware that the STL *stack* class allows you to assign one stack to another. So, if *stack1* and *stack2* are two stack objects of the same type, then you can copy the contents of *stack2* to *stack1* with the statement *stack1 = stack2*. Finally, you can also compare stack objects directly using the relational operators of ==, !=, <, >, <=, and >=. The stacks will be compared relative to the number and value of the stack elements. That makes for a very versatile class.

The STL *queue* Class

The *queue* class is defined in the *queue* header file. Thus to use it, you must include the *queue* header file at the beginning of your program. The primary functions available in the *queue* class are listed in Table 14.4.

TABLE 14.4 FUNCTIONS AVAILABLE IN THE STL *QUEUE* CLASS

Function Prototype	Purpose
bool empty()	Returns true if queue is empty.
queue_type back()	Returns, but does not remove, the rear element of the queue.
queue_type front()	Returns, but does not remove, the front element of the queue.
void pop()	Removes, but does not return, the front element of the queue.
void push(element)	Places *element* at the rear of the queue.
int size()	Returns the number of elements in the queue.

Notice that the *front()* and *back()* functions return the front and rear elements of the queue, respectively, but *do not* remove the elements. You must use the *pop()* function to remove an element from the front of the queue. To insert elements to the rear of the queue you must use the *push()* function. Here is a program that exercises some of these functions.

```
//PREPROCESSOR DIRECTIVES
#include <queue>      //FOR queue CLASS
#include <iostream>   //FOR cin AND cout

using namespace std; //REQUIRED WHEN INCLUDING iostream

//MAIN FUNCTION
int main()
{
   int number = 0;   //NUMBER OF CHARACTERS TO BE QUEUED
   int count = 0;    //LOOP COUNTER
   char c = ' ';     //CHARACTER TO QUEUE
   char front = ' '; //FRONT QUEUE ELEMENT
   char rear = ' ';  //REAR QUEUE ELEMENT

   //DEFINE CHARACTER QUEUE OBJECT
   queue<char> q;

   //OBTAIN NUMBER OF ELEMENTS TO QUEUE
   cout << "\nHow many elements do you have to enter? ";
   cin >> number;

   //PUSH ELEMENTS ONTO QUEUE
   while (count < number)
   {
    ++count;
    cout << "Enter an element:  ";
    cin >> c;
    q.push(c);
   } //END WHILE

   //DISPLAY QUEUE SIZE
   cout << "\nThe queue has " << q.size() << " elements.";
```

```
//INSPECT FRONT QUEUE ELEMENT
cout << "\n\nThe front element of the queue is:   "
     << q.front() << endl;

//INSPECT REAR QUEUE ELEMENT
cout  << "\n\nThe rear element of the queue is:   "
     << q.back() << endl;

//REMOVE AND WRITE QUEUE ELEMENTS
cout << "\nThe contents of the queue were:   " << endl;
while (!q.empty())
{
    cout << q.front() << endl;
    q.pop();
}//END WHILE

if(q.empty())
    cout << "The queue is empty" << endl;

//RETURN
return 0;
} //END main()
```

Again, we have highlighted the queue-related statements in bold. Notice the *queue* class must be included in the preprocessor section, then an object defined for the class. Like the *stack* class, the *queue* class is a template that requires the data type of the object elements in the object definition. Once an object is defined, it can be used to call any of the class functions as shown in the program. Here is a sample run of the program:

```
How many elements do you have to enter? 3↵
Enter an element: A↵
Enter an element: B↵
Enter an element: C↵

The queue has 3 elements.

The front element of the queue is: A

The rear element of the queue is: C

The contents of the queue were:
A
B
C

The queue is empty
```

Make sure you see how the program generated this output. Also, like the *stack* class, the *queue* class allows you to assign queue objects of the same type as well as compare queues using the Boolean relational operators.

The STL *list* Class

The *list* class is defined in the *list* header file. Thus to use it, you must include the *list* header file at the beginning of your program. The primary functions available in the *list* class are listed in Table 14.5.

TABLE 14.5 FUNCTIONS AVAILABLE IN THE STL *LIST* CLASS

Function Prototype	Purpose
bool empty()	Returns true if list is empty.
list_type back()	Returns, but does not remove, the last element of the list.
list_type front()	Returns, but does not remove, the first element of the list.
void merge(aList)	Merge with *aList*.
void pop_front()	Removes, but does not return, the first element of the list.
void pop_back()	Removes, but does not return, the last element of the list.
void push_front(element)	Places *element* at the front of the list.
void push_rear(element)	Places *element* at the rear of the list.
void remove(element)	Remove all occurrences of *element*.
void reverse()	Reverse element order.
int size()	Returns the number of elements in the list.
void sort()	Sort elements in ascending order.
void swap(aList)	Exchange values with *aList*.

Look at all the things you can do with the *list* class. Here is a program that exercises some of these funtions:

```
//PREPROCESSOR DIRECTIVES
#include <list>        //FOR list CLASS
#include <iostream>    //FOR cin AND cout

using namespace std;   //REQUIRED WHEN INCLUDING iostream

//MAIN FUNCTINOS
int main()
{
   char c;              //CHARACTER TO BE INSERTED INTO LIST
   int number = 0;      //NUMBER OF CHARACTERS TO BE INSERTED
   int count = 0;       //LOOP COUNTER

   list<char> list1;    //DEFINE LIST OBJECT
   list<char> list2;    //DEFINE LIST OBJECT

   //INSERT SPECIFIED NUMBER OF ELEMENTS INTO LIST
   cout << "How many nodes do you want to insert?
   cin >> number;

   while (count < number)
   {
     ++count;
     cout << "\nEnter a character element:   ";
```

```cpp
       cin >> c;
       list1.push_front(c);
   } //END WHILE

//INSPECT FIRST ELEMENT OF LIST
cout << "\nThe first element in the list is "
     << list1.front();

//INSPECT THE LAST ELEMENT OF THE LIST
cout << "\nThe last element in the list is  "
     << list1.back();

//DELETE A SPECIFIED CHARACTER  FROM THE LIST
cout << "\nWhich character element do you want to delete? ";
cin >> c;
list1.remove(c);

//SORT THE LIST
list1.sort();

//COPY list1 TO list2
list2 = list1;

//REVERSE list2
list2.reverse();

//REMOVE AND WRITE ELEMENTS IN list1
cout << "\nThe contents of the list1 were:  " << endl;
while (!list1.empty())
{
  cout << list1.front() << endl;
  list1.pop_front();
}//END WHILE

//list1 NOW EMPTY?
if(list1.empty())
     cout << "list1 is empty" << endl;

//REMOVE AND WRITE ELEMENTS IN list2
cout << "\nThe contents of the list2 were:  " << endl;
while (!list2.empty())
{
  cout << list2.front() << endl;
  list2.pop_front();
}//END WHILE

//list2 NOW EMPTY?
if(list2.empty())
     cout << "list2 is empty" << endl;
//RETURN
return 0;
}  //END main()
```

Here is a sample program run:

```
How many nodes do you want to insert? 5↵
Enter a character element: H↵
Enter a character element: E↵
Enter a character element: L↵
Enter a character element: L↵
Enter a character element: O↵

The first element in the list is O
The last element in the list is H

Which character element do you want to delete? L↵

The contents of list1 were:
E
H
O
list 1 is empty

The contents of list2 were:
O
H
E
list2 is empty
```

Look at the program output and compare it to the highlighted code in the program. Notice how easy it is to copy as well as sort a list. You should now have all the knowledge needed to understand the program. See how easy it is to use the STL classes?

CHAPTER SUMMARY

The definition of an ADT includes the following key concepts:

❐ *An ADT provides for data abstraction.*

❐ *An ADT includes both data and related operations.*

❐ *An ADT provides a means to encapsulate and hide information details whereby the ADT data is completely hidden from its surroundings.*

❐ *ADT operations provide coupling to the outside world via a function interface.*

Data abstraction is an important software development and programming tool. When developing software with ADTs, you can concentrate on the ADT data and related operations, without worrying about the inner implementation details of the ADT. Data abstraction provides for generality, modularity, and protection when developing software.

Three classic ADTs are the stack, queue, and linked list. The stack ADT provides for a collection of data elements whereby elements are always added and removed from one end of the stack, called the *top* of the stack. As a result, stacks operate on the last-in, first-out (LIFO) principle, which reverses the ordering of data elements from input to the stack to output from the stack. The queue ADT provides for a collection of data elements whereby elements are always added to the rear of the queue and removed from the front of the queue. Thus, queues operate on the first-in, first-out (FIFO) principle, which preserves the ordering of data elements from input to the queue to output from the queue. The linked list ADT provides for a list of data elements whereby elements are always added to the beginning of the list (with the exception of an ordered linked list) and removed from a specified position in the list. Linked lists consist of nodes that contain an information part and a pointer part. The pointer part of any node locates the next sequential node in the list. Arrays, stacks, and queues provide for implicit sequencing of data, whereas linked lists provide for explicit sequencing of data.

Object-oriented programming is ideal for implementing ADTs because of its data hiding ability. When an ADT is coded as a class, only those operations that are defined for the ADT can be used to access and manipulate the ADT data.

The C++ Standard Template Library, or STL, provides a rich and robust set of standard ADTs at your disposal so that you do not need to "reinvent the wheel" when coding many of these common data structures and related algorithms.

QUESTIONS AND PROBLEMS

QUESTIONS

1. Why is data abstraction an important software development tool?

2. What three things are gained by using ADTs during software development?

3. Suppose that we implement a queue using a noncircular array. The queue is initialized so that *front* = *rear* = 0. Then, as we add elements to the queue, we increment *rear* and insert the element into the array at position [*rear*]. When we remove elements from the queue, we remove the element at position [*front*] and increment *front*. What problem is encountered with this implementation? Can the problem be corrected? If so, how? What do you suppose the disadvantage is to this implementation versus the one given in this chapter?

4. How do you know that there is only a single element in a queue using the implementation discussed in this chapter?

5. Suggest a way of implementing a queue using a noncircular array. (*Hint:* Always keep *front* at position [0] in the array.) What is the disadvantage of this implementation compared to the circular array implementation?

6. Would a compiler use a stack or a queue to keep track of return addresses for nested function calls?

7. Use the stack ADT to write the pseudocode required to remove the element just below the top element of a stack.

8. How must the class header files for the stack, queue, and linked list ADTs given in this chapter be changed to store integers?

9. How must the class header files for the stack, queue, and linked list ADTs given in this chapter be changed to store floating-point numbers?

10. How must the class header files for the stack, queue, and linked list ADTs given in this chapter be changed to store structures (structs)?

11. Use the queue ADT to write the pseudocode required to move the element at the rear of the queue to the front of the queue.

12. Suppose that p is pointing to some given node in a linked list. What is pointed to by the expression *next(next(p))*?

13. Suppose that p is pointing to some given node in a linked list. What information is accessed by the expression *info(next(p))*?

14. Verify, through desk-checking, that the linked list *deleteNode()* algorithm developed in this chapter works for the last node in the list.

PROBLEMS

Least Difficult

1. Change the stack ADT implementation given in this text to store integers. Write an application program to test your integer stack.

2. Change the queue ADT implementation given in this text to store floating-point numbers. Write an application program to test your floating-point queue.

3. Code the linked list ADT given in this chapter, and write an application program to test the following features:
   ❐ Deleting the first node in the list.
   ❐ Deleting the last node in the list.
   ❐ Deleting a node from an empty list.

4. A palindrome is a word that has the same spelling both forward and backward. Three examples are the words MOM, DAD, and ANNA. Write a program that uses a stack and a queue to determine if a word entered by the user is a palindrome.

5. Write a program that uses only stacks to determine if a word entered by the user is a palindrome. (*Hint:* You will need three stacks. Why?)

More Difficult

6. A problem with the array implementation of a stack is that the array is finite, thus requiring a *fullStack()* operation. A dynamic pointer implementation of a linked list does not have this limitation. Implement the stack ADT using a dynamic linked list. (*Hint:* Make the top of the stack point to the first node in the list. In fact, replace *first* with *top*. Then always insert and delete at this first node when you push and pop data, respectively.)

7. You can implement a queue in a circular array without using an element counter to determine the empty/full conditions. To do this, you must sacrifice an array position so that no element is ever stored in this position. In this implementation, *front* will locate the empty array position, and the empty position will always precede the actual front element in the queue. This idea is shown in Figure 14.18. With this implementation, the queue is empty when *front = rear,* and the queue is full when *rear* + 1 = *front.* To insert an element into the rear of the queue, you must preincrement *rear.* To remove an element from the front of the queue, you must preincrement *front.* The queue can be initialized to an empty condition by setting *front = rear = MAXQ* − 1. Write a program using object-oriented code for this implementation. Be sure to write a test program to

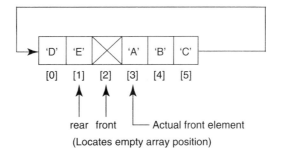

**FIGURE 14.18   AN ALTERNATIVE WAY TO IMPLEMENT
A QUEUE USING A CIRCULAR ARRAY.**

see if the implementation works. Does it really matter relative to data abstraction which implementation is used for the queue: this one or the one given in the chapter? Both implementations do the same thing relative to the ADT definition, right?

8. A problem with the array implementation of a queue is that the array is finite, thus requiring a *fullQ()* operation. A dynamic linked list does not have this limitation. Implement the queue ADT using a dynamic linked list. (*Hint:* Make *front* point to the first node in the list and *rear* point to the last node in the list.)

9. Change the linked list ADT given in this text to store structs consisting of a name, address, and telephone number. Write an application program to test your linked list.

Most Difficult

10. An ordered linked list is one in which the information in the list is ascending or descending from the first node to the last node in the list. To develop an ordered linked list ADT, the *insertNode()* operation needs to search for the proper insertion point of the information being added to the list prior to inserting the node into the list.

    Develop an ordered linked list ADT to store character data in ascending order, from the beginning to the end of the list. (*Hint:* You will need to employ two pointers as we did in the *deleteNode()* operation.) Write an application program to test your ordered linked list.

11. Modify the ADT developed in problem 10 to store a list of address structs, where each struct contains a name (last, first), address, and telephone number. The list should be in ascending order according to the last name. Write an application program to test your address list.

12. Write a program using the STL to create and test a queue of strings.

13. Write a program using the STL to create and test an ordered linked list of strings.

MULTIDIMENSIONAL ARRAYS

Chapter Objectives

When you are finished with this chapter, you should have a good understanding of the following:

- How to define multidimensional arrays in C++.

- How to access multidimensional arrays using direct assignment, reading/writing, and loops.

- How to pass multidimensional arrays to/from functions.

- Cramer's rule for solving simultaneous equations.

- How to construct a program that uses multidimensional arrays to solve simultaneous equations using Cramer's rule.

INTRODUCTION

A multidimensional array is simply an extension of a one-dimensional array. Rather than storing a single list of elements, you can think of a multidimensional array as storing multiple lists of elements. For instance, a two-dimensional array stores lists in a two-dimensional table format of rows and columns, where each row is a list. The rows provide the vertical dimension of the array, and the columns provide the horizontal array dimension. A three-dimensional array stores lists in a three-dimensional format of rows, columns, and planes, where each plane is a two-dimensional array. The rows provide the vertical dimension, the columns provide the horizontal dimension, and the planes provide the depth dimension of the array.

In this chapter, you will learn about two- and three-dimensional arrays: Arrays larger than this are seldom needed in programming. The chapter will conclude with a comprehensive problem-solving exercise employing two-dimensional arrays to solve sets of simultaneous equations using Cramer's rule.

15.1   TWO-DIMENSIONAL ARRAYS

The most common multidimensional array is the ***two-dimensional*** array shown in Figure 15.1. Here, you see that a two-dimensional array contains multiple rows. It's as if several one-dimensional arrays are combined to form a single rectangular structure of data. As a result, you can think of this rectangular data structure as a ***table*** of elements.

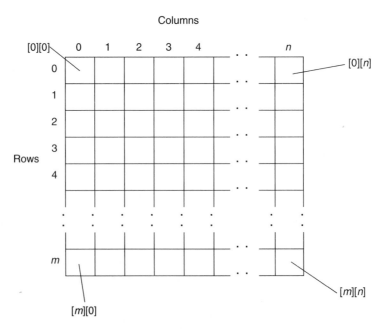

FIGURE 15.1   THE STRUCTURE OF A TWO-DIMENSIONAL ARRAY.

Observe that the two-dimensional array in Figure 15.1 is composed of elements that are located by rows and columns. The rows are labeled on the vertical axis and range from 0 to m. The columns are labeled on the horizontal axis and range from 0 to n. How many rows and columns are there? Each dimension starts with index [0], so there must be $m + 1$ rows and $n + 1$ columns, right? As a result, we say that this two-dimensional array has a dimension, or size, of $m + 1$ rows by $n + 1$ columns, written as $(m + 1) \times (n + 1)$.

How many elements are in the array? You're right: $(m + 1)$ times $(n + 1)$ elements! How do you suppose a given element is located? You're right again: by specifying its row and column index values. For instance, the element in the upper left-hand corner is located at the intersection of row 0 and column 0, or index [0][0]. Likewise, the element in the lower right-hand corner is located where row m meets column n, or index $[m][n]$. We say that two-dimensional arrays in C/C++ are ***row major ordered***. This means that the row index is listed first, followed by the column index.

Defining Two-Dimensional Arrays in C++

You define a two-dimensional array in C++ almost the same as you define a one-dimensional array. Here's the general format:

> ### *TWO-DIMENSIONAL ARRAY FORMAT*
>
> *element data type   array name* **[***number of rows***][***number of columns***];**

The only difference between this definition and that required for a one-dimensional array is found within the size specification. You must specify both the row and column sizes, as shown.

EXAMPLE 15.1

Given the following two-dimensional array definitions, sketch a diagram of the array structures showing the respective row/column indices.

a. `float table[5][7];`

b. `const int ROWS = 5;`
`const int COLS = 7;`
`float table[ROWS][COLS];`

c. `const int CURRENT = 26;`
`const int RESISTANCE = 1001;`
`int voltage[CURRENT][RESISTANCE];`

d. `const int WEEKS = 6;`
`const int DAYS = 7;`
`int may[WEEKS][DAYS];`

e. `const int ROW = 57;`
`const int SEAT = 10;`
`bool seatOccupied[ROW][SEAT];`

Solution

a. See Figure 15.2(a). This is a rectangular array, or table, whose rows range from 0 to 4 and columns range from 0 to 6. Remember that, because array indices start with [0], the last index in a given array dimension is one less than its size. The array name is table, and it will store floating-point values.

b. See Figure 15.2(a) again. This array is identical to the first array. The only difference here is in the way the array is defined. Notice that the row and column indices are defined as [*ROWS*][*COLS*], where *ROWS* and *COLS* are defined as constants.

c. See Figure 15.2(b). Here, the rows are called *CURRENT* and range from 0 to 25. The array columns are labeled *RESISTANCE* and range from 0 to 1000. The array name is

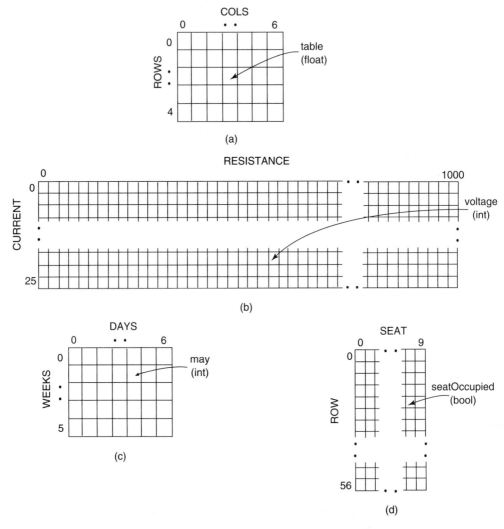

FIGURE 15.2   FOUR TWO-DIMENSIONAL ARRAYS FOR EXAMPLE 15.1.

voltage, and it will store integer elements. Obviously, the array will store the *voltage* values corresponding to *CURRENT* values from 0 to 25 and *RESISTANCE* values from 0 to 1000, using Ohm's law.

d. See Figure 15.2(c). This array is constructed to store the dates for the month of May, just like a calendar. Look at a common calendar if you have one handy. Isn't a given month simply a table of integers whose values are located by a given week and a given day within that week? As you can see from Figure 15.2(c), the array structure duplicates a monthly calendar. The rows are labeled 0 through 5, representing the six possible weeks in any given month. The columns of the array are labeled 0 through 6, representing the seven days of the week.

e. See Figure 15.2(d). This last array also has a practical application. Can you determine what it is from the definition? Notice that it is an array of Boolean elements. The rows range from 0 to 56, and the columns range from 0 to 9, as shown. The array name is *seatOccupied.* Suppose that you use this array to store Boolean values of true and false. Then, this array could be used in a reservation program for a theater or airline flight to indicate whether or not a given seat is occupied or not occupied.

EXAMPLE 15.2

How many elements will each of the arrays in Example 15.1 store, and what type of elements will they store?

Solution

a. The array in Figure 15.2(a) will store 5 × 7, or 35 elements. The elements will be floating-point values.

b. The array in Figure 15.2(b) has 26 rows, from 0 to 25, and 1001 columns, from 0 to 1000. Thus, the array will store 26 × 1001 = 26,026 integer elements.

c. The array in Figure 15.2(c) has 6 rows and 7 columns and, therefore, will store 6 × 7 = 42 integer elements.

d. The array in Figure 15.2(d) has 57 rows and 10 columns and will store 57 × 10 = 570 Boolean elements.

The foregoing figures can be verified by using the *sizeof()* function. The *sizeof()* function returns the *number of bytes* required to store an expression or a data type. So, coding the following statements will display the number of elements in each array:

```
cout << sizeof(table)/sizeof(float) << endl
     << sizeof(voltage)/sizeof(int) << endl
     << sizeof(may)/sizeof(int) << endl
     << sizeof(seatOccupied)/sizeof(bool) << endl;
```

Here, the *sizeof()* function is called twice to calculate the number of elements in each array. Notice that the size of the array in bytes is divided by the size of the data type of the array in bytes. The quotient, therefore, should be the number of elements that the array can store, right? You should be aware that the preceding code is totally portable between systems that might represent data types using a different number of bytes. This calculation will always determine the *number of elements* in the respective array, regardless of how many bytes are employed to store a given data type.

Accessing Two-Dimensional Array Elements

You access two-dimensional array elements in very much the same way as one-dimensional array elements. The difference is that to locate the elements in a two-dimensional array, you must specify a row index and a column index.

You can access the array elements using direct assignment, reading/writing, or looping.

Direct Assignment of Two-Dimensional Array Elements.   The general format for direct assignment of element values is as follows:

TWO-DIMENSIONAL ARRAY DIRECT ASSIGNMENT FORMAT
(inserting elements)

array name [row index][column index] = element value;

TWO-DIMENSIONAL ARRAY DIRECT ASSIGNMENT FORMAT
(copying elements)

variable identifier = array name [row index][column index];

First, you see the format for inserting elements into a two-dimensional array, followed by the format for obtaining elements from the array. Notice that in both instances you must specify a row and column index to access the desired element position. The row index is specified first, followed by the column index. By using the arrays defined in Example 15.1, possible direct assignments for insertion might be

```
table[2][3] = 0.5;
voltage[2][10] = 20;
may[1][3] = 8;
seatOccupied[5][0] = true;
```

In the first case, the floating-point value 0.5 is placed in row [2], column [3] of the *table* array. In the second case, a value of 20 is inserted into row [2], column [10] of the *voltage* array. Notice that this voltage value corresponds to a current value of 2 and a resistance value of 10 when using Ohm's law. In the third case, a value of 8 is placed in row [1], column [3] of the *may* array. Finally, the last case assigns the Boolean value true to row [5], column [0] of the *seatOccupied* array.

By using the same arrays, direct assignment statements to copy elements might be

```
sales = table[0][0];
volts = voltage[5][100];
today = may[2][4];
tomorrow = may[2][5];
seatTaken = seatOccupied[3][3];
```

In each of these statements, the element value stored at the row/column position within the respective array is assigned to a variable identifier. Of course, the variable identifier should be defined as the same data type as the array element being assigned to it.

Remember that copy operations have no effect on the array elements. In other words, the elements are not actually removed from the array; their values are simply "copied" to the assignment variable.

Reading and Writing Two-Dimensional Array Elements.   *cin* statements can be used to insert two-dimensional array elements, and *cout* statements can be used to copy array elements, like this:

```
cin >> table[1][1];
cout << table[1][1];
cin >> voltage[5][20];
cout << voltage[5][20];
cin >> may[1][3];
cout << may[1][3];
if (seatOccupied[3][1])
   cout << "true" << endl;
else
   cout << "false" << endl;
```

Again, you can see that both a row and a column index must be specified. The *cin* statements will insert elements obtained from a keyboard entry. The *cout* statements will then copy the array element just inserted and simply "echo" the user entry back to the display. Notice that the last *cout* statement is contained within an **if/else** statement to determine if the element is a Boolean true or false value. This statement will produce a true or false on the display, depending on the contents of location [3][1] of the *seatOccupied* array.

Using Loops to Access Two-Dimensional Arrays.   As you know, loops provide a more efficient way to access arrays, especially when working with large multidimensional arrays. The thing to remember with multidimensional arrays is that *a separate loop is required for each dimension of the array.* In addition, the loops must be nested. Thus, a two-dimensional array requires two nested loops.

Look at the calendar pictured in Figure 15.3. As you have seen, this calendar can be stored in memory using a two-dimensional array. How do you suppose you

May

	Sun [0]	Sat [1]	Mon [2]	Tue [3]	Wed [4]	Thu [5]	Fri [6]
week [0]							1
week [1]	2	3	4	5	6	7	8
week [2]	9	10	11	12	13	14	15
week [3]	16	17	18	19	20	21	22
week [4]	23	24	25	26	27	28	29
week [5]	30	31					

FIGURE 15.3   MAY CALENDAR.

might go about filling the calendar with the dates required for a given month? A logical approach would be to fill in all of the dates of week 0, from *Sun* to *Sat,* then go to week 1 and fill in its dates, then fill in the week 2 dates, and so on.

Think about what the array indices must do to perform this filling operation. The week index would start at [0], and then the days index would begin at [0] and increment through the days of the week to [6]. This will fill the first week. To fill the second week, the week index must be incremented to 1, with the days index starting at [0] and incrementing to [6] all over again. To fill the third week, the week index is incremented to 2, and the days index incremented from [0] to [6] again. In other words, you are filling in the dates week by week, one week at a time. Each time the week index is incremented, the days index starts at [0] and increments to [6], before the week index is incremented to the next week.

Does this suggest two loops, one to increment the week index and a second to increment the days index? Moreover, doesn't this process suggest that the days loop must be nested within the week loop, because the days must run through its entire range for each week?

Here's the general loop structure for accessing elements in a two-dimensional array.

> ### *LOOPING FORMAT FOR ACCESSING TWO-DIMENSIONAL ARRAY ELEMENTS*
>
> **for (int** *row index = 0; row index < row size; ++row index*)
>   **for (int** *col index = 0; col index < col size; ++col index*)
>   *Process array*[*row index*][*col index*]

You see that the column index loop is nested within the row index loop. Thus, the column loop runs through all of its iterations for each iteration of the row loop. The actual insertion takes place within the column loop. Let's look at an example to get the idea.

EXAMPLE 15.3

Write a function using loops to fill a calendar array for the month of May. Write another function to display the May calendar.

Solution

We will begin by defining the month array as before.

```
const int WEEKS = 6;
const int DAYS = 7;
int may[WEEKS][DAYS];
enum dayOfWeek {Sun,Mon,Tue,Wed,Thur,Fri,Sat};
```

In addition, you see that an enumerated data type called *dayOfWeek* has been defined. This enumerated data type will be used to access the days of the week within the array, as you will see shortly.

Next, we must write a function to fill the array with the dates for May. But first, we must consider the function interface. The function must receive the array, get the dates from the user, and return the filled array to the calling program. Thus, the function-interface description becomes as follows:

Function *fillMonth():*   Obtains dates of the month from the user and fills a two-dimensional integer array.

Accepts: A two-dimensional integer array of size $WEEKS \times DAYS$.

Returns: A two-dimensional integer array of size $WEEKS \times DAYS$.

Now, here's a function that will do the job:

```
//THIS FUNCTION WILL FILL A 2-DIM ARRAY FOR A
//CALENDAR MONTH
void fillMonth(int month[WEEKS][DAYS])
{
 cout << "Enter the dates of the month, beginning Sunday of the first\n"
      << "week in the month.  If there is no date for a given day\n"
      << "enter a 0.  Press the ENTER key after each entry." << endl;
 for (int week = 0; week < WEEKS; ++week)
   for (int day = Sun; day < Sat + 1; ++day)
   {
    cout << "\nEnter the date for week " << week
         << " day " << day << ":  ";
    cin >> month[week][day];
    }  //END DAY LOOP
 }  //END fillMonth()
```

The first few lines of the function provide a few simple directions to the user. The array-filling operation takes place within the two **for** loops. Notice that the *week* loop is the outer loop, and the *day* loop is the inner loop. Here's how it works: The *week* counter begins with 0, and the *day* counter begins with *Sun*. As a result, the first date is inserted into *month[0][Sun]*, corresponding to Sunday of week 0 in the month. Notice that the array name is *month*. How can this be, because we defined *may* as the array name? Actually, the *may* array will be the argument used in the function call. However, *month* is the formal parameter listed in the function header. Thus, the function will receive the *may* array from the calling program, fill it, and return it to the calling program. The reason we used a different array name (*month*) in the function is to make it more general. For example, additional arrays, such as *june, july, august,* and the like, could be defined to create arrays for these months. Again, these would act as arguments when calling the function. The respective month arrays (*june, july, august,* etc.) could then be filled separately using separate calls to this same function. In each case, the function parameter *month* would take on the array argument used in the function call. Now, back to the loops. After an element is read into *month[0][Sun]*, the inner **for** loop increments the *day* counter to *Mon*, and an element is read into *month[0][Mon]*. Notice that the *week* counter remains the same. What is the next array position to be filled? You're right: *month[0][Tue]*. In summary, the inner *day* loop will increment from *Sun* to *Sat* for each iteration of the outer *week* loop. Thus, the first iteration of the outer *week* loop will fill:

```
month[0][Sun]
month[0][Mon]
month[0][Tue]
month[0][Wed]
month[0][Thur]
month[0][Fri]
month[0][Sat]
```

The second iteration of the outer *week* loop will fill the second week, like this:

```
month[1][Sun]
month[1][Mon]
month[1][Tue]
month[1][Wed]
month[1][Thur]
month[1][Fri]
month[1][Sat]
```

This filling process will continue for weeks 2, 3, 4, and 5. The looping is terminated when a value is read into the last array position, *month*[5][*Sat*].

Now, let's look at a similar function to display our May calendar once it has been filled. Again, consider the following function interface description:

Function *displayMonth()*:   Displays the two-dimensional-calendar month array.

Accepts: A two-dimensional array of size *WEEKS* × *DAYS*.

Returns: Nothing.

Here is the completed function:

```
//THIS FUNCTION WILL DISPLAY THE CALENDAR MONTH ARRAY
void displayMonth(int month[WEEKS][DAYS])
{
 cout << "\n\n\t\tCALENDAR OF THE MONTH"
      << "\n\n\tSun\tMon\tTue\tWed\tThur\tFri\tSat" << endl << endl;
 for (int week = 0; week < WEEKS; ++week)
 {
   cout << endl;
   for (int day = Sun; day < Sat + 1; ++day)
    cout << '\t' << month[week][day];
 } //END WEEK LOOP
} //END displayMonth()
```

Again, *month* is the formal parameter defined in the function header. The first part of the function statement section simply writes the header information required for the calendar. Then, the nested **for** loops are executed to display the array contents. The basic loop structures are the same as those we discussed for the filling operation: The *day* counter is incremented from *Sun* through *Sat* for every iteration of the *week* loop. Thus, the array contents are displayed in a row-by-row, or week-by-week, fashion. Notice that a *cout* statement is used to display the element values. The *cout* statement is the only statement within the inner **for** loop.

Now, putting everything together, here is the entire program:

```
/*
THIS PROGRAM WILL FILL AND DISPLAY
A 2-DIM ARRAY FOR A CALENDAR MONTH
*/
```

```
//PREPROCESSOR DIRECTIVE
#include <iostream.h> //FOR cin AND cout

//GLOBAL CONSTANTS AND ENUMERATED DATA
const int WEEKS = 6;
const int DAYS = 7;
enum dayOfWeek {Sun,Mon,Tue,Wed,Thur,Fri,Sat};

//FUNCTION PROTOTYPES
void fillMonth(int month[WEEKS][DAYS]);
void displayMonth(int month[WEEKS][DAYS]);

//MAIN FUNCTION
int main()
{
  //ARRAY DEFINITION
  int may[WEEKS][DAYS];
  //FUNCTION CALLS
  fillMonth(may);
  displayMonth(may);

  //RETURN
  return 0;
} //END main()

//THIS FUNCTION WILL FILL A 2-DIM ARRAY FOR A
//CALENDAR MONTH
void fillMonth(int month[WEEKS][DAYS])
{
  cout << "Enter the dates of the month, beginning Sunday of the first\n"
       << "week in the month.  If there is no date for a given day\n"
       << "enter a 0.  Press the ENTER key after each entry." << endl;
  for (int week = 0; week < WEEKS; ++week)
   for (int day = Sun; day < Sat + 1; ++day)
    {
     cout << "*\nEnter the date for week " << week
          << " day " << day << ":  ";
     cin >> month[week][day];
    }  //END DAY LOOP
}  //END fillMonth()

//THIS FUNCTION WILL DISPLAY THE CALENDAR MONTH ARRAY
void displayMonth(int month[WEEKS][DAYS])
{
  cout << "\n\n\t\tCALENDAR OF THE MONTH"
       << "\n\n\tSun\tMon\tTue\tWed\tThur\tFri\tSat" << endl << endl;
  for (int week = 0; week < WEEKS; ++week)
  {
    cout << endl;
    for (int day = Sun; day < Sat + 1; ++day)
      cout << '\t' << month[week][day];
  } //END WEEK LOOP
}  //END displayMonth()
```

First, you see that *WEEKS, DAYS,* and *dayOfWeek* have been declared globally so that all functions have access to them. Notice that the statement section of *main()* is short. Function *main()* simply defines the array and calls the two other functions. In each function call, the actual array argument, *may,* is employed. As stated earlier, other monthly arrays could also be defined to create additional monthly calendars. In fact, all 12 months could be defined to create a yearly calendar. To fill or display a given month, you simply use that array name in the respective function call.

Assuming that the user executes this program and keys in the proper dates for may, the program will generate the following calendar display:

CALENDAR OF THE MONTH

Sun	Mon	Tue	Wed	Thur	Fri	Sat
0	0	0	0	0	0	1
2	3	4	5	6	7	8
9	10	11	12	13	14	15
16	17	18	19	20	21	22
23	24	25	26	27	28	29
30	31	0	0	0	0	0

We have used a structured approach in the foregoing example to show you how two-dimensional arrays must be passed to/from functions. However, an OOP approach would have created a class which contains the *may* array as a private member and the *fillMonth()* and *displayMonth()* functions as public members. As a result of the tight binding within the class, the *may* array would *not* need to be passed to/from the functions, right?

EXAMPLE 15.4

Write a program that uses an array to store the names of all the students in your C++ course. Use one function to insert the student names into the array and a second function to display the contents of the array once it is filled. Assume that there are no more than 25 characters in any student name and the maximum course size is 20 students.

Solution

First, an array must be defined to hold the student names in your C++ course. The student names will be C-strings, so we must define a two-dimensional array of characters so that each name string will occupy a row in the array. Consider the following:

```
const int MAX_STUDENTS = 20;
const int MAX_CHARACTERS = 26;
char cpp[MAX_STUDENTS][MAX_CHARACTERS];
```

Here, the array name is *cpp,* and it is defined as a character array with 20 rows and 26 columns. This will allow for 20 name strings with a maximum of 25 characters per C-string. (An extra column must be provided for the null terminator character.)

Next, we will work on the function that obtains the student names from the user. We will call this function *setStudents()*. Here is the function interface description:

Function *setStudents()*:	Obtains student names from the user and fills a two-dimensional character array.
Accepts:	A placeholder for the number of students and a two-dimensional character array of size *MAX_STUDENTS × MAX_CHARACTERS*.
Returns:	The number of students and a two-dimensional character array of size *MAX_STUDENTS × MAX_CHARACTERS*.

This interface requires that the two-dimensional *cpp* array be passed to the function and then returned filled with the student names. Of course, passing an array to a function is easy, regardless of its size, because you simply use the array name as the function argument. Here is the complete function:

```
/*
THIS FUNCTION GETS THE STUDENT NAMES FROM THE
USER AND ENTERS THEM INTO THE ARRAY
*/
void setStudents(int &n, char students[MAX_STUDENTS][MAX_CHARACTERS])
{
 cout << "Enter number of students:   ";
 cin >> n;
 for (int row = 0; row < n; ++row)
 {
    cout << "\nEnter student number " << row + 1 << ":   ";
    cin >> ws;
    cin.getline(&students[row][0],MAX_STUDENTS);
 } //END FOR
} //END setStudents()
```

Again, you see a different name employed for the array in the function header. This makes the function more generic, because you might want to use this same function to fill other arrays from other classes. The function begins by prompting the user to enter the number of students in the class and then reading this number and assigning it to a reference parameter called *n*. The value entered will provide a maximum value for the row counter in the **for** loop. Next, you see a single **for** loop. Is there a problem here, because we are filling a two-dimensional array? No, this single loop is all that is required, because we are filling the array with strings, not individual characters. Notice that the loop counter increments only the row index. The column index is fixed at [0]. This will place the first string in the array beginning at [0][0], the second string at [1][0], the third string at [2][0], and so on. The standard *getline()* function is used to read the C-strings. Recall that, *cin* >> will terminate when a white space character is encountered, thereby interpreting first and last names as two separate strings. Look at the argument used in the *getline()* function call. An ampersand symbol is used to tell *getline()* to place the string beginning at the *address* associated with *students[row][0]*. When reading strings into a two-dimensional array, we must tell the compiler to insert the string beginning at a specified address. So, the first string is inserted into the array beginning at the memory address associated with index

[0][0], the second string begins at the memory address associated with index [1][0], and so on.

Next, we will write a function called *displayStudents()* to display the array of student names. Here is the interface description for this function:

Function *displayStudents():*	Displays the strings of a two-dimensional array.
Accepts:	The number of students and a two-dimensional character array of size
	MAX_STUDENTS × *MAX_CHARACTERS.*
Returns:	Nothing.

The parameter listing for this function will be identical to the previous function, because it accepts the same array structure. Here is the entire function:

```
//THIS FUNCTION DISPLAYS THE CONTENTS OF THE ARRAY
void displayStudents(int n, char students[MAX_STUDENTS][MAX_CHARACTERS])
{
 cout << "The students entered in the array are:" << endl;
 for (int row = 0; row < n; ++row)
  cout << "\nArray position [" << row << "] [0]   " << &students[row][0];
} //END displayStudents()
```

Again, you see a single **for** loop employed, because we need to reference only the beginning address of each string. The ampersand symbol is required in front of the array name in the *cout* statement to specify the string address. Without the ampersand, you would only see the first character of each string. (Why?)

PROGRAMMING TIP

Multiple C-strings are stored in two-dimensional arrays row by row. When accessing C-strings that are stored in a two-dimensional array, you must specify the beginning address of the string. This is done by using the ampersand symbol, &, prior to the array name and specifying the respective string row and fixing the column at zero, like this: *&stringArray[row][0].*

In addition to displaying the student names, the *cout* statement is formatted to display the array position of each name string. Here is a sample of what you would see on the monitor:

```
Array position [0][0]   Brenda Snider
Array position [1][0]   Anna Simon
Array position [2][0]   Doug Hahn
Array position [3][0]   Steve Weston
```

Finally, the entire program follows:

```
/*
THIS PROGRAM WILL FILL A 2-DIM CHARACTER ARRAY WITH
STRINGS ENTERED BY THE USER  AND THEN DISPLAY THE
FILLED ARRAY
*/
```

```cpp
//PREPROCESSOR DIRECTIVE
#include <iostream>    //FOR cin AND cout

using namespace std;    //FOR iostream

//GLOBAL CONSTANTS
const int MAX_STUDENTS = 20;
const int MAX_CHARACTERS = 26;

//FUNCTION PROTOTYPES
void setStudents(int &n, char students[MAX_STUDENTS][MAX_CHARACTERS]);
void displayStudents(int n, char students[MAX_STUDENTS][MAX_CHARACTERS]);

//MAIN FUNCTION
int main()
{
 int number = 0;            //ACTUAL NUMBER OF STUDENTS
 char cpp[MAX_STUDENTS][MAX_CHARACTERS];  //DEFINE ARRAY
 setStudents(number,cpp);      //CALL FUNCTION TO FILL ARRAY
 displayStudents(number,cpp);  //CALL FUNCTION TO DISPLAY ARRAY

 //RETURN
 return 0;
} //END main()

/*
THIS FUNCTION GETS THE STUDENT NAMES FROM THE
USER AND ENTERS THEM INTO THE ARRAY
*/
void setStudents(int &n, char students[MAX_STUDENTS][MAX_CHARACTERS])
{
 cout << "Enter number of students:  ";
 cin >> n;
 for (int row = 0; row < n; ++row)
 {
   cout << "\nEnter student number " << row + 1 << ":  ";
   cin >> ws;
   cin.getline(&students[row][0],MAX_STUDENTS);
 } //END FOR
}  //END setStudents()

//THIS FUNCTION DISPLAYS THE CONTENTS OF THE ARRAY
void displayStudents(int n, char students[MAX_STUDENTS][MAX_CHARACTERS])
{
 cout << "The students entered in the array are:" << endl;
 for (int row = 0; row < n; ++row)
   cout << "\nArray position [" << row << "] [0]   " << &students[row][0];
} //END displayStudents()
```

Again, notice that we have used a structured approach in this example. An OOP approach would have defined the number of students and array as private class members and, therefore, not require them to be passed to/from the functions.

Quick Check

1. Given the following two-dimensional array definition:

    ```
    double sample[10][15];
    ```

    What is the maximum row index? What is the maximum column index?

2. What will the following statement display when applied to the array defined in question 1?

    ```
    cout << sizeof(sample)/sizeof(double) << endl;
    ```

3. Write a statement that will read a value from the keyboard and place it in the first row and last column of the array defined in question 1.

4. Write a statement that will display the value stored in the second row and third column of the array defined in question 1.

5. Write the code, using **for** loops, that will display the elements of the array defined in question 1 in row/column format.

6. Write a prototype for a function called *display()* that will display the contents of the array defined in question 1.

7. Write a statement to call the function in question 6.

8. A two-dimensional array in C++ is _____ major order.

15.2 ARRAYS OF MORE THAN TWO DIMENSIONS

Arrays of more than two dimensions are required for some applications. In this text, we will only consider three-dimensional arrays, because few common applications require larger arrays. The easiest way to picture a three-dimensional array is to imagine a cube such as that shown in Figure 15.4. Think of a three-dimensional array as several two-dimensional arrays combined to form a third dimension, depth. The cube is made up of rows (vertical dimension), columns (horizontal dimension), and planes (depth dimension). A given element within the cube array is located by specifying its plane, row, and column. The plane indice is specified first, followed by the row indice, followed by the column indice. See if you can verify for yourself the element positions indicated in Figure 15.4.

Now, let's look at a practical example of a three-dimensional array so you can see how one is defined and accessed in C++. Think of this excellent textbook as a three-dimensional array where each page of the book is a two-dimensional array made up of rows and columns. The combined pages then form the planes within a three-dimensional array that make up the book. Let's suppose there are 45 lines on each page that form the rows for the array and 80 characters per line that form the columns of the array. If there are 1000 pages in the book, there are 1000 planes in the array. Thus, this book array is a 45 × 80 × 1000 array. What are the array elements, and how many are there? Well, the array elements must be characters, because characters form the words within a page. In addition, there must be 45 × 80 ×

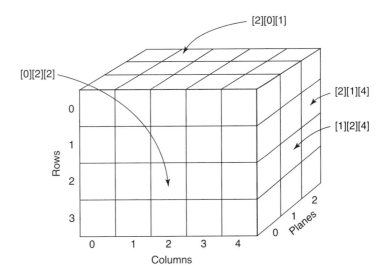

FIGURE 15.4 A 3 × 4 × 5 THREE-DIMENSIONAL ARRAY.

1000 = 3,600,000 of them, including blanks, because this is the size of the book in terms of rows, columns, and pages.

How might our book array be defined in C++? How about this:

```
const int PAGES = 1000;
const int LINES = 45;
const int COLUMNS = 80;
char textBook[PAGES][LINES][COLUMNS];
```

You should be able to understand this definition from your work with one- and two-dimensional arrays. There are three dimensions [*PAGES*], [*LINES*], and [*COLUMNS*] that define the size of the *textBook* array. A three-dimensional array in C/C++ is **plane major ordered.** This is why the plane size is specified first, followed by the row size, followed by the column size. The array data type is *char,* because the elements are characters. Of course, additional arrays could be used to create arrays for other books of the same general dimensions, right? Well, theoretically yes, but just one of these book arrays would be too large for most PC systems. In most systems, the definition would result in a *array size too big* error when the program is compiled.

Next, how do you suppose you might access the book information? The easiest way is to use nested loops. How should the loops be nested? Because the array is plane major ordered, the page loop must be the outermost loop, and the column loop the innermost loop. This leaves the row loop to be inserted between the page and column loops. Translating this to our book array, you get

```
for (int page = 0; page < PAGES; ++page)
        for (int line = 0; line < LINES; ++line)
                for (int column = 0; column < COLUMNS; ++column)
                        Process textBook[page][line][column]
```

By using this nesting approach, the column loop is executed 80 times for each iteration of the line loop, which is executed 45 times for each iteration of the page loop. Of course, the page loop is executed 1000 times. This **for** structure would process elements one line at a time for a given page. Notice the use of the variables *page, line,* and *column* as the loop counters. These variables must be different from the constants (*PAGES, LINES, COLUMNS*) used to define the array, because they are local to the **for** loops.

CAUTION

When you define an array, C++ actually sets aside enough primary memory to store the array. This memory is reserved exclusively for the defined array and cannot be used for other programming or system chores. In other words, a large array "eats up" a lot of memory. For instance, the foregoing book array contains 3,600,000 character elements. Each character requires 1 byte of memory to store, so C++ will allocate about 3515K bytes of user memory for the book array. If the array is defined too big, it would create an *array size too big* error during compilation. So be careful that your arrays don't get too big for your system to store. There are other, more memory-efficient, ways to store large amounts of data—a dynamic linked list.

EXAMPLE 15.5

Given the foregoing *textBook* array definition:

   a. Write a program segment that could be used to fill the book.

   b. Write a program segment that could be used to print the entire book.

   c. Write a program segment that could be used to print page 2 of the book.

Solution:

   a. Using the three foregoing nested loops, you could fill the book, like this:

```
for (int page = 0; page < PAGES; ++page)
        for (int line = 0; line < LINES; ++line)
                for (int column = 0; column < COLUMNS; ++column)
                        cin.get(textBook[page][line][column]);
```

The innermost loop employs a *get()* function to read one character at a time and place it in the indexed position. The *cin* extraction operator (>>) will not work here, because >> ignores white space, which would obviously be part of the text material.

   b. A *print* object is employed in the innermost loop to print the book. Of course, a class would have to be created for this object that directed output to the system platform printer.

```
for (int page = 0; page < PAGES; ++page)
  for (int line = 0; line < LINES; ++line)
  {
     print << endl;
```

```
          for (int column = 0; column < COLUMNS; ++column)
              print << textBook[page][line][column];
      } //END MIDDLE FOR
```

Notice the single *print* statement used in the middle loop to provide a CRLF after a given line has been printed.

   c. You need only two loops to print a given page number, as follows:

```
      for (int line = 0; line < LINES; ++line)
      {
        print << endl;
        for (int column = 0; column < COLUMNS; ++column)
              print << textBook[1][line][column];
      } //END FOR
```

Observe that the *page* index is fixed at [1] within the *print* statement in order to print page 2 of the book. (Remember that the first page of the book is actually at page index [0].) How could this segment be modified to print any page desired by the user? Think about it! This will be left as an exercise at the end of the chapter.

Quick Check

1. What problem might be encountered when defining large multidimensional arrays?
2. A three-dimensional array in C++ is _____ major ordered.
3. Define a three-dimensional array of integers that has 10 planes, 15 rows, and 3 columns.
4. How many bytes of storage are occupied by the array that you defined in question 3 if each integer requires 2 bytes of storage?
5. Write the code necessary to display the contents of the array that you defined in question 3, one plane at a time.

PROBLEM SOLVING IN ACTION: SIMULTANEOUS EQUATION SOLUTION

PROBLEM

Recall from your algebra class that a set of simultaneous equations exists when you have two or more equations with two or more common unknowns. For instance, consider the following:

$$7x - 5y = 20$$

$$-5x + 8y = -10$$

Here you have two equations and two unknowns. To solve the equations, you must find both x and y. This is impossible using just one of the equations alone, but does not present a problem when both equations are solved "simultaneously," or together. One thing you might remember from algebra class is that in order to solve simultaneous equations, there must be at least as many equations as there are unknowns. This is why you cannot solve for two unknowns using a single equation. However, two unknowns can be solved using two or more equations.

DETERMINANTS

A common way to solve simultaneous equations is by using determinants. You might recall from algebra that a **determinant** is simply a *square array*. By a square array, we mean an array that has the same number of rows and columns. Here is a simple 2×2, called an **order** 2, determinant:

$$\begin{vmatrix} A_1 & B_1 \\ A_2 & B_2 \end{vmatrix}$$

The elements are A_1, B_1, A_2, and B_2. (*Note:* These elements will be numeric values when we actually use determinants to solve simultaneous equations.) Notice the vertical "bars" on the left and right sides of the array. These bars are used to indicate that the array is a determinant. This determinant is called an order 2 determinant, because it has two rows and two columns. There are also order 3, order 4, order 5, and so on, determinants. In each case, the determinant is a square array. Here is an order 3 determinant:

$$\begin{vmatrix} A_1 & B_1 & C_1 \\ A_2 & B_2 & C_2 \\ A_3 & B_3 & C_3 \end{vmatrix}$$

Expansion of a Determinant

A determinant is said to be expanded when you replace the array with a single value. An order 2 determinant expansion is the simplest. To get the idea, look at the following:

$$\begin{vmatrix} A_1 & B_1 \\ A_2 & B_2 \end{vmatrix} = A_1B_2 - A_2B_1$$

Imagine the two diagonals in the determinant. There is one diagonal running from top-left to bottom-right. We will call this the *down diagonal,* which forms the product A_1B_2. The second diagonal runs from bottom-left to top-right. We will call this the *up diagonal,* which forms the product A_2B_1. In the expansion on the right side of the equals sign, you see that the up-diagonal product is subtracted from the down-diagonal product.

EXAMPLE 15.6

Expand the following determinants:

a. $\begin{vmatrix} 20 & -5 \\ -10 & 8 \end{vmatrix}$

b. $\begin{vmatrix} 7 & 20 \\ -5 & -10 \end{vmatrix}$

c. $\begin{vmatrix} 7 & 5 \\ -5 & 8 \end{vmatrix}$

Solution

a. $\begin{vmatrix} 20 & -5 \\ -10 & 8 \end{vmatrix} = (20)(8) - (-10)(-5) = 160 - 50 = 110$

b. $\begin{vmatrix} 7 & 20 \\ -5 & -10 \end{vmatrix} = (7)(-10) - (-5)(20) = -70 - (-100) = -70 + 100 = 30$

c. $\begin{vmatrix} 7 & 5 \\ -5 & 8 \end{vmatrix} = (7)(8) - (-5)(5) = 56 - (-25) = 56 + 25 = 81$

Expansion of an order 3 determinant is a bit more challenging. Here is a general order 3 determinant again:

$$\begin{vmatrix} A_1 & B_1 & C_1 \\ A_2 & B_2 & C_2 \\ A_3 & B_3 & C_3 \end{vmatrix}$$

To manually expand this determinant, you must rewrite the first two columns to the right of the determinant, and then use the diagonal method, as follows:

$\begin{matrix} A_1 & B_1 & C_1 & A_1 & B_1 \\ A_2 & B_2 & C_2 & A_2 & B_2 \\ A_3 & B_3 & C_3 & A_3 & B_3 \end{matrix} = A_1 B_2 C_3 + B_1 C_2 A_3 + C_1 A_2 B_3 - A_3 B_2 C_1 - B_3 C_2 A_1 - C_3 A_2 B_1$

Here, you create three down diagonals that form the products $A_1B_2C_3$, $B_1C_2A_3$, and $C_1A_2B_3$, and three up diagonals that form the products $A_3B_2C_1$, $B_3C_2A_1$, and $C_3A_2B_1$. The three up-diagonal products are subtracted from the sum of the three down-diagonal products. This is called the "method of diagonals" for expanding order 3 determinants. We should caution you, however, that the method of diagonals does not work for determinants larger than order 3. To expand determinants larger than order 3, you must use the method of *cofactors*. The cofactor method is a recursive process.

EXAMPLE 15.7

Expand the following order 3 determinant:

$$\begin{vmatrix} 6 & -2 & -4 \\ 15 & -2 & -5 \\ -4 & -5 & 12 \end{vmatrix}$$

Solution

Rewriting the first two columns to the right of the determinant, you get

6	−2	−4	6	−2
15	−2	−5	15	−2
−4	−5	12	−4	−5

Now, multiplying the diagonal elements and adding/subtracting the diagonal products, you get

$$+ (6)(-2)(12) + (-2)(-5)(-4) + (-4)(15)(-5)$$
$$- (-4)(-2)(-4) - (-5)(-5)(6) - (12)(15)(-2)$$

Finally, performing the required arithmetic gives you

$$+ (-144) + (-40) + (300)$$
$$- (-32) - (150) - (-360)$$
$$= -144 - 40 + 300 + 32 - 150 + 360$$
$$= 358$$

As you can see from the preceding example, expanding an order 3 determinant can get a bit tricky! You have to pay particular attention to the signs. One simple sign error during your arithmetic will result in an incorrect expansion. Wouldn't it be nice if a computer program could be written to perform the expansion? This is an ideal application for a C++ function, because the expansion operation returns a single value.

An Order 2 Determinant Expansion Function.   Let's write a C++ function to expand an order 2 determinant. We will assume that the elements in the determinant are stored in a 2 × 2 array. This array must be passed to the function, and then the function must evaluate the array and return a single expansion value. Here is the function interface description:

Function *expand()*: Expands an order 2 determinant.

Accepts: A 2 × 2 array.

Returns: The expansion value.

By using this interface description, the function prototype becomes

```
double  expand(double determinant[2][2]);
```

The function name is *expand()*. The formal parameter is *determinant*[2][2], because this is the size of the array that will be expanded. The data type of the returned expansion value is *double*. Now, the *determinant* array has row indices, which range from [0] to [1], and column indices, which range from [0] to [1]. Here is the array showing the row/column index layout:

$$
\begin{array}{cc}
[0][0] & [0][1] \\
[1][0] & [1][1]
\end{array}
$$

Remember that these are only the array indices and not the elements stored in the array. Recall that to expand the determinant, the up diagonal must be subtracted from the down diagonal. Thus, the product of indices [1][0] and [0][1] must be subtracted from the product of [0] [0] and [1] [1]. Using this idea in our function, we get a single **return** statement, as follows:

```
return  determinant[0][0] * determinant[1][1]
          - determinant[1][0] * determinant[0][1];
```

That's all there is to it! Here is the complete function:

```
//THIS FUNCTION WILL EXPAND A 2 x 2 DETERMINANT
double expand(double determinant[2][2])
{
  return  determinant[0][0] * determinant[1][1]
            - determinant[1][0] * determinant[0][1];
} //END expand()
```

Writing a function to expand an order 3 determinant will be left as an exercise at the end of the chapter.

Cramer's Rule

Cramer's rule allows you to solve simultaneous equations using determinants. Let's begin with two equations and two unknowns.

An equation is said to be in ***standard form*** when all the variables are on the left-hand side of the equals sign and the constant term is on the right-hand side of the equals sign. Here is a general equation containing two variables in standard form:

$$Ax + By = C$$

This equation has two variables, x and y. The x-coefficient is A and the y-coefficient is B. The constant term is C.

Here is a set of two general simultaneous equations in standard form:

$$A_1x + B_1y = C_1$$

$$A_2x + B_2y = C_2$$

The common variables between the two equations are x and y. Subscripts 1 and 2 denote the coefficients and constants of equations 1 and 2, respectively. Cramer's rule allows you to solve for x and y using determinants, like this:

$$x = \frac{\begin{vmatrix} C_1 & B_1 \\ C_2 & B_2 \end{vmatrix}}{\begin{vmatrix} A_1 & B_1 \\ A_2 & B_2 \end{vmatrix}} \qquad\qquad y = \frac{\begin{vmatrix} A_1 & C_1 \\ A_2 & C_2 \end{vmatrix}}{\begin{vmatrix} A_1 & B_1 \\ A_2 & B_2 \end{vmatrix}}$$

As you can see, the determinants are formed using the coefficients and constants from the two equations. Do you see a pattern? First, look at the denominator determinants. They are identical and are formed using the x- and y-coefficients directly from the two equations. However, the numerator determinants are different. When solving for x, the numerator determinant is formed by replacing the x-coefficients with the constant terms. When solving for y, the numerator determinant is formed by replacing the y-coefficients with the constant terms. Here's an example:

EXAMPLE 15.8

Solve the following set of simultaneous equations using Cramer's rule:

$$x + 2y = 3$$

$$3x + 4y = 5$$

Solution

Forming the required determinants, you get

$$x = \frac{\begin{vmatrix} 3 & 2 \\ 5 & 4 \end{vmatrix}}{\begin{vmatrix} 1 & 2 \\ 3 & 4 \end{vmatrix}} \qquad\qquad x = \frac{\begin{vmatrix} 1 & 3 \\ 3 & 5 \end{vmatrix}}{\begin{vmatrix} 1 & 2 \\ 3 & 4 \end{vmatrix}}$$

Expanding the determinants and dividing gives you x and y:

$$x = \frac{(3)(4) - (5)(2)}{(1)(4) - (3)(2)} = \frac{2}{-2} = -1 \qquad y = \frac{(1)(5) - (3)(3)}{(1)(4) - (3)(2)} = \frac{-4}{-2} = 2$$

Implementing Cramer's Rule in C++. Think about the "functions" you just went through using Cramer's rule to solve the previous set of simultaneous equations. There are three major tasks to be performed:

- ❐ Task 1: Obtain the equation coefficients and constants.
- ❐ Task 2: Form the determinants, both numerator and denominator.
- ❐ Task 3: Expand the determinants.

We have already developed a function to perform the third task. We must now develop C++ functions to accomplish the first two tasks.

To perform Task 1, we must write a function that will obtain the coefficients and constants of the equations to be solved. There are two equations and three items (two coefficients and a constant) that must be obtained from each equation. Does this suggest any particular data structure? Of course, a 2 × 3 array! So, let's write a function to fill a 2 × 3 array from coefficient and constant terms of the two equations that will be entered by the user. Here it is:

```
//THIS FUNCTION WILL FILL AN ARRAY WITH THE
//EQUATION COEFFICIENTS
void fill(double equations[2][3])
{
 for(int row = 0; row < 2; ++row)
 {
   cout << "Enter the variable coefficients and constant for equation "
        << row + 1 << "\nNote the equation must be in standard form."
        << endl << endl;
   for(int col = 0; col < 3; ++col)
   {
        if (col == 2)
```

```
                cout << "Enter the constant term:   ";
            else
                cout << "Enter the coefficient for variable " << col + 1 << ":   ";
            cin >> equations[row][col];
        }   //END COLUMN LOOP
    }   //END ROW LOOP
}   //END fill()
```

Such a function should be nothing new to you, because it simply employs nested **for** loops to fill an array. The function name is *fill()*. It fills an array called *equations* that must be defined as a 2 × 3 array in the calling program. The array will be passed to the function by reference using the array name in the function call. Once the function fills the array, it is passed back to the calling program.

Given the following two general equations in standard form,

$$A_1x + B_1y = C_1$$

$$A_2x + B_2y = C_2$$

The *fill()* function will fill the 2 × 3 array, like this:

$$A_1\ B_1\ C_1$$

$$A_2\ B_2\ C_2$$

As you can see, the first equation coefficients and constant term are inserted into the first row of the array. The second row of the array stores the coefficients and constant term of the second equation. Of course, the function assumes that the user will enter the coefficients and constants in their proper order.

To accomplish Task 2, we will develop a function to form the determinants from the equation coefficients and constants. How can we obtain the coefficients and constants? You're right: from the 2 × 3 array that was just filled! Now, how many unique determinants does Cramer's rule require to solve two equations and two unknowns? Three: a numerator determinant for the *x* unknown, a numerator determinant for the *y* unknown, and a denominator determinant that is the same for both the *x* and *y* unknowns. All of the determinants must be order 2, right?

So, our function must obtain the single 2 × 3 array that was filled with coefficients and constants in the *fill()* function and generate three 2 × 2 arrays that will form the two numerator and one denominator determinant required by Cramer's rule. Here's the function:

```
//THIS FUNCTION WILL FORM THE DETERMINANTS
void formDet(double equations[2][3],double x[2][2],double y[2][2], double D[2][2])
{
  for(int row = 0; row < 2; ++row)
    for(int col = 0; col < 2; ++col)
    {
            x[row][col] = equations[row][col];
            y[row][col] = equations[row][col];
            D[row][col] = equations[row][col];
    } //END COLUMN LOOP
```

```
 x[0][0] = equations[0][2];
 x[1][0] = equations[1][2];
 y[0][1] = equations[0][2];
 y[1][1] = equations[1][2];
} //END formDet()
```

First, look at the function header. The name of the function is *formDet()*. This function requires four parameters: *equations*[2][3], *x*[2][2], *y*[2][2], and *D*[2][2]. *equations*[2][3] is the 2 × 3 array containing the coefficients and constants from the *fill()* function. The *x*[2][2] parameter represents the numerator determinant for the *x* unknown. The *y*[2][2] parameter represents the numerator determinant for the *y* unknown. The *D*[2][2] parameter represents the denominator determinant for both the *x* and *y* unknowns.

Next, look at the statement section of the function. The first two columns of the equation array are copied into each of the determinant arrays using **for** loops. Then, the constant terms are inserted into the *x* and *y* determinant arrays at the required positions using direct assignment. The formation pattern results from Cramer's rule. Notice that in all instances, the determinants are formed using the elements from the 2 × 3 *equations* array of coefficients and constants generated by the *fill()* function.

Now we have all the ingredients for a C++ program that will solve two equations and two unknowns using Cramer's rule. Combining our *fill()* function, our *formDet()* function, and our *expand()* function into a single program, we get the following:

```
/*
ACTION 15-1(ACT15_01.CPP)
THIS PROGRAM WILL SOLVE TWO EQUATIONS AND TWO
UNKNOWNS USING CRAMER'S RULE
*/

//PREPROCESSOR DIRECTIVE
#include <iostream.h>        //FOR cin AND cout

//FUNCTION PROTOTYPES
void fill(double equations[2][3]);
void formDet(double equations[2][3],double x[2][2],double y[2][2],
             double D[2][2]);
double expand(double determinant[2][2]);

//MAIN FUNCTION
int main()
{
  //ARRAY DEFINITIONS
  double equations[2][3];
  double x[2][2];
  double y[2][2];
  double D[2][2];

  //CALL FUNCTIONS TO FILL EQUATION ARRAY
  //AND FORM DETERMINANTS
```

```
  fill(equations);
  formDet(equations, x, y, D);


  //IF DENOMINATOR = 0, WRITE ERROR MESSAGE.
  //ELSE CALCULATE x AND y
  if(expand(D) == 0)
    cout << "\nDenominator = 0.  Equations are unsolvable." << endl;
  else
     cout << "\nThe value of the first variable is: "
          << expand(x)/expand(D)
          << "\n\nThe value of the second variable is: "
          << expand(y)/expand(D) << endl;


  //RETURN
  return 0;
}  //END main()


/*
THIS FUNCTION WILL FILL AN ARRAY WITH THE EQUATION
COEFFICIENTS
*/
void fill(double equations[2][3])
{
 for(int row = 0; row < 2; ++row)
 {
   cout << "\nEnter the variable coefficients and constant for equation "
        << (row + 1) << "\nNote the equation must be in standard form."
        << endl << endl;
   for(int col = 0; col < 3; ++col)
   {
        if (col == 2)
           cout << "Enter the constant term:   ";
        else
           cout << "Enter the coefficient for variable " << (col + 1) << ":   ";
        cin >> equations[row][col];
   }  //END COLUMN LOOP
 } //END ROW LOOP
} //END fill()


//THIS FUNCTION WILL FORM THE DETERMINANTS
void formDet(double equations[2][3],double x[2][2],double y[2][2],
            double D[2][2])
{
 for(int row = 0; row < 2; ++row)
   for(int col = 0; col < 2; ++col)
   {
        x[row][col] = equations[row][col];
        y[row][col] = equations[row][col];
        D[row][col] = equations[row][col];
   } //END COLUMN LOOP
 x[0][0] = equations[0][2];
```

```
  x[1][0] = equations[1][2];
  y[0][1] = equations[0][2];
  y[1][1] = equations[1][2];
} //END formDet()


//THIS FUNCTION WILL EXPAND A 2 x 2 DETERMINANT
double expand(double determinant[2][2])
{
  return  determinant[0][0] * determinant[1][1]
          - determinant[1][0] * determinant[0][1];
} //END expand()
```

Observe that all the arrays are defined local to *main()*. The *equations* array is a 2×3 array that will store the coefficients and constants of the two equations. This is followed by definitions for the three 2×2 determinant arrays. The prototypes for our three functions are given prior to *main()*, and the functions themselves are listed after *main()*.

Now, look at the statement section of the *main()*. The *fill()* function is called first to obtain the coefficient and constant terms of the two equations. The actual argument used for the function call is the name of the equations array, *equations*. Next, the *formDet()* function is called to form the required determinants. The actual arguments used in this function call are *equations, x, y,* and *D.* The *equations* argument is required to pass the 2×3 array to the function. The *x, y,* and *D* arguments are required to pass the three determinant arrays to the function and back.

Finally, look at how the *expand()* function is invoked. It is first invoked as part of an **if/else** statement to see if the denominator determinant value is zero. If it is, the equations cannot be solved using Cramer's rule because division by zero is undefined. If the denominator determinant is not zero, the *expand()* function is invoked twice to calculate the first unknown (*x*) within a *cout* statement like this: *expand(x)/expand(D)*. This expands the *x* determinant, expands the common denominator determinant, and divides the two to obtain the value of the first unknown (*x*). The function is called twice again to find the second unknown (*y*).

Given the following two equations

$$x + 2y = 3$$

$$3x + 4y = 5$$

here is what you would see when the program is executed:

```
          Enter the variable coefficients and constant for equation 1
          Note the equation must be in standard form.

          Enter the coefficient for variable 1:   1↵
          Enter the coefficient for variable 2:   2↵
          Enter the constant term:   3↵

          Enter the variable coefficients and constant for equation 2
          Note the equation must be in standard form.
```

```
Enter the coefficient for variable 1:   3↵
Enter the coefficient for variable 2:   4↵
Enter the constant term:   5↵

The value for the first variable is:   −1

The value for the second variable is:   2
```

Do you think that you could develop a similar program to solve a set of three simultaneous equations? You now have all the required knowledge! Guess what you will be doing in the programming exercises at the end of the chapter.

CHAPTER SUMMARY

A two-dimensional array, or table, is a combination of two or more element rows, or lists. It has dimension $m \times n$, where m is the number of rows in the array, and n is the number of array columns. A three-dimensional array is the combination of two or more two-dimensional arrays. It is comprised of rows, columns, and planes. Thus, a three-dimensional array has dimension $p \times m \times n$, where p is the number of planes in the array, m is the number of array rows, and n is the number of columns. In C++, two-dimensional arrays are row major ordered, and three-dimensional arrays are plane major ordered.

A separate **for** loop is required to access each array dimension. In addition, the loops must be nested when accessing multidimensional arrays. Thus, to access a three-dimensional array, the column loop is nested in the row loop, which is nested in the plane loop.

There are many technical applications for arrays. A common use of an array is to store determinants that are used to solve systems of simultaneous equations using Cramer's rule.

QUESTIONS AND PROBLEMS

QUESTIONS

Use the following array definitions to answer questions 1–11:

```
double semesterScores[10];

const int MULTIPLIER = 12;
const int MULTIPLICAND = 20;
int product[MULTIPLIER][MULTIPLICAND];

bool cube[3][7][4];

enum Colors {Brown, Black, Red, Orange, Yellow, Green, Blue,
            Violet, Gray, White};

double colorCode[10][10][10];
```

1. Sketch a diagram showing each array structure and its indices.

2. List the identifiers that must be used to access each array.

3. What are the dimensions of each array?

4. How many elements will each array store?

5. List all of the possible element values for the *cube* array.

6. Write a C++ statement that will display the element in the fourth row and second column of the *product* array.

7. Write a C++ statement that will assign any legal element to the second row and last column of the *product* array.

8. Write a C++ statement that will display the element values in the third row, second column, and third plane of the *cube* and *colorCode* arrays. Assume that the enumerated data type elements will be used as indices to access the *colorCode* array.

9. Write C++ statements that will insert values into the *colorCode* array using the following color code combinations and associated values:
   a. Brown, Black, Red = 1000
   b. Brown, Black, Green = 1000000
   c. Yellow, Violet, Red = 4700
   d. Red, Red, Red = 2200

10. Write the C++ code required to fill each array from keyboard entries.

11. Write the C++ code required to display each array, and include appropriate table headings.

PROBLEMS

Least Difficult

1. Write a program to read 15 integer elements from the keyboard and store them in a 3×5 array. Once the elements have been read, display them as a 5×3 array. (*Hint:* Reverse the rows and columns.)

2. Write a function that will display any given page of the book array used in Example 15.5. Assume that the user will enter the page number to be displayed.

3. Write a program that will store the state table for a 4-bit decade counter (BCD). Write functions to fill and display the state table. Here is what its state table looks like:

State	Count
0	0000
1	0001
2	0010
3	0011
4	0100
5	0101
6	0110
7	0111
8	1000
9	1001

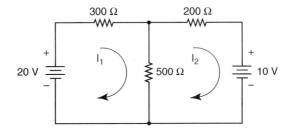

FIGURE 15.5   A TWO-LOOP CIRCUIT
FOR PROBLEM 5.

4. Write a program that employs two functions to fill and print a calendar for the current month.

More Difficult

Employ the program developed in the chapter case study to solve problems 5–7. Modify the program to meet the given application.

5. The circuit diagram in Figure 15.5 shows two unknown currents,

An engineer writes two equations that describe the circuit, as follows:

$$300\,I_1 + 500\,(I_1 - I_2) - 20 = 0$$
$$200\,I_2 + 500\,(I_2 - I_1) + 10 = 0$$

Put these equations in standard form, and solve for the two currents using the software developed in the chapter case study.

6. Look at the lever in Figure 15.6. If you know one of the weights and all the distances of the weights from the fulcrum, you can calculate the other two weights using two simultaneous equations. The two equations have the following general form,

$$w_1 d_1 + w_2 d_2 = w_3 d_3$$

where

w_1, w_2, and w_3 are the three weights.

d_1, d_2, and d_3 are the distances the three weights are located from the fulcrum, respectively.

Using this general equation format, you get two equations by knowing two balance points. Suppose weight w_3 is 5 pounds, and you obtain a balance condition for the following distance values:

FIGURE 15.6   A LEVER/FULCRUM ARRANGEMENT
FOR PROBLEM 6.

Balance point 1:

$$d_1 = 3 \text{ in.}$$
$$d_2 = 6 \text{ in.}$$
$$d_3 = 36 \text{ in.}$$

Balance point 2:

$$d_1 = 5 \text{ in.}$$
$$d_2 = 4 \text{ in.}$$
$$d_3 = 30 \text{ in.}$$

Find the two unknown weights, w_1 and w_2.

7. The following equations describe the tension, in pounds, of two cables supporting an object. Find the amount of tension on each cable (T_1 and T_2).

$$0.5T_2 + 0.93T_1 - 120 = 0$$

$$0.42T_1 - 0.54T_2 = 0$$

Most Difficult

8. Write a function to fill a 3×4 array with the coefficients and constant terms from three simultaneous equations expressed in standard form. Assume that the user will enter the array elements in the required order.

9. Write a function to display the equation array in problem 8.

10. Using Cramer's rule, write a function to form 3×3 determinants from the 3×4 equation array you filled in problem 8.

11. Write a function to expand an order 3 determinant.

12. Employ the functions you developed in problems 8 through 11 to write a program that will solve a set of three simultaneous equations.

13. Use the program in problem 12 to solve the three currents (I_1, I_2, I_3) in the Wheatstone bridge circuit shown in Figure 15.7. Here are the equations that an engineer writes to describe the circuit:

$$2000(I_1 - I_2) + 4000(I_1 - I_3) - 10 = 0$$

$$2000(I_2 - I_1) + 8000I_2 + 5000(I_2 - I_3) = 0$$

$$5000(I_3 - I_2) + 3000I_3 + 4000(I_3 - I_1) = 0$$

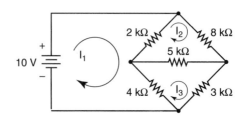

FIGURE 15.7 THE THREE-LOOP WHEATSTONE BRIDGE CIRCUIT FOR PROBLEM 13.

14. Suppose the perimeter of a triangle is 14 inches. The shortest side is half as long as the longest side and 2 inches more than the difference of the two longer sides. Find the length of each side using the program you developed in problem 12.

15. Assume the following table represents the monthly rental price of six resort cabins over a 5-year period.

		YEAR				
		FIRST	SECOND	THIRD	FOURTH	FIFTH
	1	200	210	225	300	235
	2	250	275	300	350	400
CABIN	3	300	325	375	400	450
	4	215	225	250	250	275
	5	355	380	400	404	415
	6	375	400	425	440	500

Write a program that employs functions to perform the following tasks:
❒ Fill a two-dimensional array with the table.
❒ Compute the total rental income for each cabin by year, and store the yearly totals in a second array.
❒ Compute the percentage increase/decrease in price between adjacent years for each cabin, and store the percentages in a third array.
❒ Generate a report showing all three arrays in table form with appropriate row/column headings.

16. Write a program that employs pointers to find the maximum and minimum elements in a two-dimensional integer array. Initialize the array from the keyboard using user entries.

APPENDIX A

QUICK-CHECK SOLUTIONS

| A.I | CHAPTER 1 |

Section 1-1

1. The three major areas of a PCs architecture are the *CPU*, *memory*, and *I/O* areas.
2. A CPU contained within a single integrated circuit is called a *microprocessor*.
3. Arithmetic: addition, subtraction, multiplication, division

   Logic: equal to, not equal to, less than, greater than, less than or equal to, greater than or equal to
4. Three things that are found in a CPU are *arithmetic logic unit (ALU)*, *control unit*, and *internal registers*.
5. A 128-MB RAM has 134,217,728 bytes of memory.
6. Programs stored in ROM are often called *firmware*.
7. Instructions are fetched from memory, decoded, executed, and results are stored back into the internal registers or memory.
8. Instructions waiting to be processed are fetched from primary memory and placed *cache* memory so that they are ready for execution when the CPU needs them.

Section 1-2

1. The major difference between the C language and the C++ language is that C++ allows for object-oriented programming whereas C does not.
2. The steps that must be performed to translate a C++ source code program to an executable program are as follows:
   - Write the source *code, or edit*.
   - Compile the source code into object code.
   - Link the object code to other required routines to form the executable program.
3. Portability is that feature of a language that allows programs written for one type of computer to be used on another type of computer with few or no changes to the program source code.

4. A compiler translates the entire program into machine code all at one time, before execution by the CPU. An interpreter translates then executes one high-level program statement at a time.

5. Machine language, assembly language, high-level language.

6. Your C++ program code is referred to in general as *source* code and has a file extension of *cpp*.

7. The code generated by a C++ compiler is referred to as *object* code and has a file extension of *obj*.

8. The code generated by a C++ linker is referred to as *executable* code and has a file extension of *exe*.

9. To manage the resources of the system.

Section 1-3

1. Any C++ program consists of two sections called the *preprocessor* and *main function* sections.

2. The following is an *#include* directive to include a standard header file called *math.h* into a program:

```
#include  <math.h>
```

3. A subprogram that returns a single value, a set of values, or performs some specific task in C++ is called a *function*.

4. Line comments are inserted into a C++ program using: *d. double forward slashes like this //COMMENT*.

5. Block comments are inserted into a C++ program using: *c. stars and slashes like this /*COMMENT*/*.

6. At a minimum, the program should include the following comments:

- The beginning of the program should be commented with the programmer's name, date the program was written, date the program was last revised, and the name of the person doing the revision. In other words, a brief ongoing maintenance log should be commented at the beginning of the program.

- The beginning of the program should be commented to explain the purpose of the program, which includes the problem definition and program algorithms. This provides an overall perspective by which anyone, including you, the programmer, can begin debugging or maintaining the program.

- Preprocessor directives should be commented as to their purpose.

- Constant and variable definitions should be commented as to their purpose.

- Major sections of the program should be commented to explain the overall purpose of the respective section.

- Individual program lines should be commented when the purpose of the code is not obvious relative to the application.

- All major subprograms (functions in C++) should be commented just like the main program function.

- The end of each program block (right curly brace) should be commented to indicate what the brace is ending.

7. All the executable statements reside or are called from function *main()*.

A.2 CHAPTER 2

Section 2-1

1. English-like statements that require less precision than a formal programming language are called *pseudocode* statements.

2. Some questions that must be answered when defining a computer programming problem are as follows:
   - What outputs are needed?
   - What inputs are needed?
   - What processing is needed to produce the output from the input?

3. To test and debug a program you can desk-check, compile, debug it using a debugger, and run it.

4. Commenting is important within a program because it explains what the program does and makes the program easier to read and maintain.

5. A syntax error is any violation of the rules of the programming language.

6. A logic error occurs when the compiler does what you tell it to do but is not doing what you meant it to do. It is an error in thinking on the part of the programmer.

Section 2-2

1. It is important to use an algorithm in the planning of a program to define what steps are needed to produce the desired final result. An algorithm keeps you from "spinning your wheels."

2. The three major categories of algorithmic language operations are *sequence*, *decision*, and *iteration*.

3. Three decision operations are *if*, *if/else*, and *switch/case*.

4. Three iteration operations are *while*, *do/while*, and *for*.

Section 2-3

1. Abstraction allows you to "see the forest for the trees," because it permits you to initially concentrate on the problem at hand, without agonizing over the implementation details of a computer language.

2. Stepwise refinement begins with the initial abstract algorithm and step by step divides it into one or more related algorithms that provide more and more implementation detail.

3. A codeable level of an algorithm is reached when all the statements have been reduced to the pseudocode operations listed in Table 2.1.

A.3 CHAPTER 3

Section 3-1

1. A *class* describes the data attributes and behavior of its objects.

2. Simple data types that are predefined within a programming language are called *primitive* data types.

3. A set of data elements defined by you, the programmer, to meet a given application is called an *enumerated* data type.

4. Another name for a struct is a *record*.

5. An abstract data type, or ADT, describes the data attributes and behavior of its objects.

6. The three major data type categories in the C++ programming language are the *primitive*, *standard*, and *structured* data categories.

7. Behavior, as related to classes and ADTs, describes how the ADT will act and react for a given operation.

8. A C++ class is ideal for implementing ADTs because it can be used to define the data attributes of the ADT as well as the behavior of the ADT.

9. The behavior of the class is provided by *functions* in C++.

Section 3-2

1. The range of values that is provided via the standard *int* data type in a typical C++ compiler is *–32768 to +32767*. Check your compiler specs for the range that it provides.

2. An *overflow error* occurs when, as a result of a calculation, a value exceeds its predefined range.

3. The two ways that floating-point values can be represented in a C++ program are using either *fixed decimal* or *exponential* format.

4. According to the ASCII character code, the character 'z' is larger than the character 'a'.

5. According to the ASCII character code, the character 'a' is larger than the character 'A'.

6. The primitive data type that contains only two elements, **true** and **false**, is the **bool** data type.

7. White space is any non-printable character.

Section 3-3

1. The two reasons for defining constants and variables in a C++ program are as follows:

   • The compiler must know the value of a constant before it is used and must reserve memory locations to store variables.

   • The compiler must know the data type of constants and variables to determine their data attributes and behavior.

2. The following will define a constant called *PERIOD* that will insert a period wherever it is referenced in a program.

   ```
   const  char  PERIOD = '.' ;
   ```

3. The following will define a variable called *middleInit* that will store your middle initial:

   ```
   char  middleInit = 'C' ;
   ```

4. The following will define a variable called *gpa* that will store your grade point average:

   ```
   double  gpa = 3.25;
   ```

5. The following will define a variable called *age* that will store your age:

   ```
   int  age = 19;
   ```

6. The following will define a variable called *salary* that will store the salary of an employee:

```
double  salary = 52500.00;
```

7. The following values will be returned when these functions are executed:

```
toascii('B') = 66
toascii('?') = 63
```

8. The extended character set defined for the IBM PC must use the **unsigned char** data type.

Section 3-4

1. A class called *string* is part of the Standard C++ Library and is used to create string objects.

2. `const string BOOK = "Structured and Object-Oriented Problem Solving";`

3. 28 bytes of storage are required to store the string "The United States of America".

4. `string ssn = " ";`

5. `string course = "Data Structures";`

6. `cout << course << endl;`

7. `string firstName = "Andrew";`
   `string lastName = "Staugaard";`

8. `string myName = " ";`
   `myName = firstName + lastName;`

9. `cout << myName.length() << endl;`

Section 3-5

1. Enumerated data types allow the programmer to define a problem more clearly and make the program more readable than standard data types.

2. The following will define an enumerated data type called *Automobiles*, which consists of 10 popular automobile brands.

```
enum  Automobiles {Ford, BMW, Mercedes, Chrysler, Volvo,
                   Dodge, Mazda, Porsche, Cadillac, Toyota};
```

3. The compiler assigns the numeric value of 0 (zero) to the first element in an enumerated data type.

A.4   CHAPTER 4

Section 4-1

1. The file that must be included to use *cout* is the *iostream.h* or *iostream* header file.

2. The operator that must be employed to insert information into the *cout* stream is the *<< stream insertion* operator.

3. The following is a *cout* statement to display my name as a fixed string of information.

```
cout << "Andy" << endl;
```

4. The following is a *cout* statement to display my name when it is stored in a string object called *name*.

```
cout << name << endl;
```

5. The escape sequence that must be used to generate a CRLF is \n.

6. The file that must be included to use the *setw()* field-width manipulator is the *iomanip.h* or *iomanip* header file.

7. The following *cout* statement that will display the value of a floating-point variable called *number* left-justified within a field width of 10 columns and a precision of 3 decimal places.

```
cout.setf(ios::fixed);
cout.setf(ios::left);
cout.precision(3);
cout << setw(10) << number << endl;
```

8. The difference between using a \n versus an *endl* within a *cout* statement is that the \n escape sequence only generates a CRLF, whereas the *endl* manipulator generates a CRLF and flushes the output stream buffer.

9. The following code will display the variable *grossPay* in proper currency format:

```
cout.setf(ios::fixed);
cout.setf(ios::showpoint);
cout.precision(2);
cout << grossPay << endl;
```

Section 4-2

1. The operator that must be employed to extract data from the *cin* input stream is the >> *extraction* operator.

2. The following statements will prompt the user to enter a value for an integer variable called *value:*

```
cout << "Please enter an integer :" << endl;
cin >> value;
```

3. Blanks, tabs, and carriage-return line-feeds (CRLFs) are all considered white space.

4. The following statement will read a single white space character and store it in a variable called *whiteSpace*.

```
cin.get(whiteSpace);
```

5. The following statement will display the single white space character read in question 4.

```
cout.put(whiteSpace);
```

6. True: When reading character data, *cin* will read only one character at a time.

7. When using the >> operator to read string data, *cin* >> will terminate when white space is encountered.

8. The *getline()* function can be used as *getline(cin,stringName)* to include white space when reading string data.

9. The following employs the *getline()* function to read a string and store it in an object called *myName*.

```
getline(cin,myName);
```

10. The statement *cin* >> *ws* should be used prior to *getline()* so that any leading CRLFs are removed from the input stream.

Section 4-3

1. The *fstream.h* or *fstream* header file must be included to read/write disk files.
2. The class used to define input file objects is the *ifstream* class.
3. The class used to define output file objects is the *ofstream* class.
4. You test to see if there were any problems opening a file by using an *if(!fileObject)* statement after *fileObject* is defined.
5. `ifstream myInput("data.txt");`
6. `ofstream myResults("A:results.txt");`
7.

```
//PREPROCESSOR DIRECTIVES
#include <fstream.h>      //FOR FILE CLASSES
#include <stdlib.h>       //FOR exit()

//MAIN FUNCTION
int main()
{
  //DEFINE VARIABLES
  int integer = 0;
  int timesTen = 0;

  //DEFINE FILE OBJECTS
  ifstream myInput("A:data.txt");
  ofstream myResults("A:results.txt");

  //INPUT FILE OPEN OK? IF NOT, EXIT
  if(!myInput)
  {
     cout << "The input file cannot be opened." << endl;
     exit(1);
  }//END IF

  //OUTPUT FILE OPEN OK? IF NOT, EXIT
  if(!myResults)
  {
     cout << "The output file cannot be opened." << endl;
     exit(1);
  }//END IF

  else  //LOOP TO READ AND WRITE FILES
  {
    //READ AND PROCESS FILE DATA USING A LOOP
    while (myInput >> integer)
    { //BEGIN LOOP
      timesTen = 10 * integer;   //MULTIPLY INTEGER BY 10
      myResults << timesTen << endl; //WRITE PRODUCT TO OUTPUT FILE
    } //END LOOP
  }//END else

  //RETURN
  return 0;
}//END main()
```

A.5	CHAPTER 5

Section 5-1

1. The order in which C++ performs arithmetic operations is as follows:

$$( ) \; * \; / \; \% \; + \; -$$

Any operations inside of parentheses are performed first, then (from left-to-right) multiplication, division, and modulus, and then (from left-to-right) addition and subtraction.

2. If the statement $x \% 2$ returns 0, x must store an even value.

3. If the statement $y \% 17$ returns 0, y must store value that is divisible by 17.

4. The statement 1/2 % 5 returns 0.

5. Assuming x has the value 1, the expression $(2 - {+}{+}x)$ evaluates to 0.

6. Assuming x has the value 1, the expression $(2 - x{+}{+})$ evaluates to 1.

7. The statement $--x$ is equivalent to the statement $x = x - 1$.

8. *False:* Both operands must be integers in order for the division operator to produce an integer result. However, the division operator will produce a floating-point result when either of the operands is a floating-point value.

9. The difference between using the preincrement operator versus the postincrement operator on a variable is that a preincrement operator increments the variable before any expression involving the variable is evaluated and a postincrement operator increments the variable after any expression involving the variable is evaluated. It is important to be careful as to which one you use, especially when the variable is used as part of a compound expression, because undesirable results can be produced if the wrong incrementing operator is used.

10. The result of 10/100 is 0, becasue both operands are integers, and the / operator generates an integer result when both operands are integers.

Section 5-2

1. The expression $x \mathrel{+}= 5$ is equivalent to the expression $x = x + 5$.

2. The expression $x \mathrel{/}= 10$ is equivalent to the statement $x = x/10$.

3. The expression $x = 10/x$ will compile and execute fine, but it is most likely not what the programmer intended. This expression will divide 10 by x then assign the result back to x. Most likely the intent was to divide x by 10 then assign the result back to x. The required expression would then be: $x = x/10$.

4. The expression $x = x + 5$ makes sense in C++ because it says to "add 5 to x, then assign the result back to x", while in math class the = is interpreted as equals, not assignment.

5. Four different expressions that will increment the variable x in C++ are $++x$, $x++$, $x = x + 1$, and $x \mathrel{+}= 1$.

Section 5-3

1. In order to use a standard function in your program, you must include its *header*, or *include*, file.

2. The answer to this question depends on the compiler that you are using. To get an on-line description of a standard function using the Visual C++ compiler while working in the edit mode, type the function name, place the cursor within the function name and press the **F1** key. You can also select the function from the on-line help index.

3. `cout << tan(45 * 3.14159/180);`

4. *math.h*

5. *toupper('a')*

6. *ctype.h*

7. If the value generated by the *rand()* function is scaled by 10, you will generate values from 0 to 9.

A.6   CHAPTER 6

Section 6-1

1. Operators that allow two values to be compared are called *relational* operators.

2. The difference between the = operator and the == operator in C++ is that the = operator assigns the statement on the right to the variable on the left and the == operator compares two quantities to determine if they are equal.

3. The Boolean value **true** is generated as a result of the operation $4 > 5 - 2$, because 4 is greater than $(5 - 2)$, or 3.

4. The Boolean value **false** is generated as a result of the operation $(5 != 5)$ &&

   $(3 == 3)$, because $(5 != 5)$ is false, making the entire && (AND) statement false.

5. You test string objects for equality or inequality using the == and != operators just like you would test variables of a primitive data type.

Section 6-2

1. False: The logical opposite of greater-than is less-than *or equal-to*.

2. True: When a test expression in an **if** statement evaluates to true, the related **if** statements are bypassed.

3. The correct **if** statement reads as follows:

```
if (x == y)
        cout << "There is a problem here" << endl;
```

   The test expression needs to be a comparison, not an assignment.

4. The && (**AND**) operator must be employed to test if all conditions are true.

5. The || (**OR**) operator must be employed to test if one or more of several conditions is true.

6. For all values of *x* that are less-than or equal to 50.

Section 6-3

1. The following pseudocode needs an **else** statement because, without an **else** statement, both statements, "It's payday" and "It's not payday", would be written when the **if** test is true.

If *today* is *Friday*
    Write "It's pay day".
Write "It's not pay day".

3. True: Framing with curly braces can be eliminated when an **if** or **else** statement section only has a single statement.

4. When comparing two strings, C++ actually performs a subtract operation on the strings.

5. True: An **else** must always be associated with a corresponding **if**.

6. True: Objects of the *string* class are compared using the Boolean relational operators just like any other primitive data type variables.

Section 6-4

1. Indentation is important when operations are nested for code readability and to be able to see at a glance which statements belong to which **if** or **else** statements.

2. False: Any given **else** does not always go with the closest **if**.

   Consider the following pseudocode to answer questions 3 – 6:

   If *value* < 50
       If *value* > –50
           Write "Red"
       else
           Write "White"
   else
       Write "Blue"

3. "Red" will be written when *value* is greater than –50 and less than 50.

4. "White" will be written when *value* is less than or equal to –50.

5. "Blue" will be written when *value* is greater than or equal to 50.

6. The equivalent **if-else-if-else** logic is

   If *value* >= 50
       Write "Blue"
   else
       If *value* <= –50
           Write "White"
       else
           Write "Red"

Section 6-5

1. The selection of a particular case in a **switch** statement is controlled by a *matching* process.

2. If you have *n* cases in a **switch** statement and there are no **break** statements in any of the cases, all of the cases will be executed sequentially when a match is made on the first case.

3. False: There may be times when several subsequent cases need to be executed as the result of a match to a given case.

4. A statement that can be inserted at the end of a **switch** statement to protect against invalid entries is the **default** statement.

5. A common application for a **switch** statement is *for menu-driven programs*.

A.7   CHAPTER 7

Section 7-1

1. False A **while** loop repeats until the test expression is false.

2. False: The **while** loop is a pretest loop not a posttest loop.

3. The **while** loop statements need to be framed, because without the framing, the value of x is never changed and you will have an infinite loop.

4. The correct code for question 3 is as follows:

```
x = 10;
while (x > 0)
{
    cout << "This is a while loop" << endl;
    --x;
} //END WHILE
```

5. The loop will never execute, because the loop test is false. Notice that x is initialized to 1 and is never $< = 0$.

6. This is an infinite loop. Notice that x is initialized to 1 and is incremented with each loop iteration. Thus, the **while** test of $x > = 0$ is always true.

Section 7-2

1. False: A **do/while** repeats until the loop test is false.

2. True: A **do/while** loop is a posttest loop.

3. The value of x is never changed within the loop, thereby creating an infinite loop.

4. The correct code for question 3 is as follows:

```
x = 10;
do
{
    cout << "This is a do/while loop" << endl;
    --x;
} //END DO/WHILE
while (x > 0);
```

5. The loop will execute once, because a **do/while** loop is a posttest loop.

6. This is an infinite loop. Notice that x is initialized to 1 and is incremented with each loop iteration. Thus, the **while** test of $x > = 0$ is always true.

Section 7-3

1. The three things that must appear in the first line of a **for** loop structure are as follows:
   - The loop counter initialization.
   - The loop test expression.
   - The increment/decrement of the counter.

2. True: The loop counter in a **for** loop is altered after the loop body is executed in a given iteration.

3. True: A **for** loop can always be replaced by a **while** loop, because they are basically the same looping structure, just coded differently. However, the **while** loop counter must be changed at the end of the loop body.

4. The loop will execute zero times, because the test condition $x > 0$ is false on the first test.

5. The loop will execute eleven times.

6. The **for** loop body must be framed when there is more than one statement to be executed within the loop.

7. If you have two nested loops, with the inner loop executing five times and the outer loop executing ten times, there will be fifty total iterations. The inner loop will execute five times for every outer loop iteration (5×10).

8. In a down-to loop, the loop counter is always *decremented*.

Section 7-4

1. The statement that will cause only the current iteration of a loop to be terminated is the **continue** statement.

2. The **break** and **continue** statements are normally used as part of an **if** statement within a loop structure.

3. The loop will execute twice. When x is incremented to 1 at the end of the first iteration, the **if(x > 0)** statement will be true in the second iteration, causing the **break** statement to execute to terminate the loop structure.

A.8 CHAPTER 8

Section 8-1

1. Functions eliminate the need for duplicate statements in a program.

    Functions make the program easier to design.

    Functions make the program easier to code and test.

    Functions allow for software reusability.

    Functions make the program more clear and readable.

    Functions provide the basis for classes in OOP.

2. The four major components of a non-void function are a *function header* line, any *local variables* required by the function, a *statement section*, and a *return statement*.

3. All logical paths in a non-void function must lead to a *return* statement.

4. What the function *accepts* and what the function *returns* relative to its calling code.

5. The function header represents the function interface which shows what the function accepts and returns.

6. The three parts of a function header are as follows:
    - The data type of the value to be returned by the function, if any.
    - The name of the function.
    - A parameter listing.

7. A function variable waiting to receive a value from the calling program is called a *parameter*.

8. To return both a value and/or control to the calling program.

9. The difference between an argument in a calling program and a parameter in a function header is that the argument is the value passed to the parameter in the function header. In other words, the parameter receives the argument value from the calling program when the function is called.

10. `double calculatePayment(double amount, double interestRate,`
    `                        double term)`

11. `cout << "You're payment is $"`
    `        << calculatePayment(amount, rate, term);`

    or

    `payment = calculatePayment(amount, rate, term);`

    or

    `annualAmount = 12 * calculatePayment(amount, rate, term);`

Section 8-2

1. **void** must be used as the return data type when a function does not return a single value to the calling program.

2. One-way communication of data from the calling program to a function is provided via *value* parameters.

3. Two-way communication of data between the calling program and a function is provided via *reference* parameters.

4. To specify a reference parameter in a function header, you must use the & *(ampersand)* symbol prior to the parameter identifier.

5. The body of a function is normally located after the closing brace of *main()*.

Section 8-3

1. The primary purpose of a function prototype is to allow the compiler to check for any mismatches between the arguments in a function call and the parameter values that the function expects to receive.

2. A function prototype is located after the preprocessor directives and before function *main()* in a C++ program.

3. True: Parameters listed in a function prototype can be listed only by data type, without any corresponding identifiers.

4. True: Default parameters can appear in either the function prototype or function header, but not both.

5. True: Once a default parameter is specified in a function prototype, the remaining parameters in the parameter listing must be default parameters.

6. When overloading a function, the number and data types of the function parameters will determine how the function will behave.

Section 8-4

1. A constant that has global scope must be placed *outside* and *prior to* function *main()* in a C++ program.

2. A local variable has *block* scope.

3. A variable defined in *main()* must be passed to a function in the same program for that function to have access to the variable.

Section 8-5

1. The statement "There is no way that a C++ function can call itself" is false because C++ supports recursion, which allows a function to call itself.

2. We can describe recursion as a "winding" and "unwinding" process, because recursion "winds" values onto a stack, and when the terminating condition is reached, it "unwinds" the values to calculate the final result.

3. When the terminating condition is reached, a recursive function call is terminated.

4. The pseudocode required to find *factorial(n)*, where *n* is any integer is

   If *n* is 1 Then

   > *factorial(1)* = 1.

   Else

   > *factorial (n) = n * factorial (n − 1)*.

5. False: Recursion uses large amounts of memory to keep track of each recursive call within a stack.

6. True: All recursive problems can also be solved using iteration.

7. Recursion employs a memory data structure called a *stack* to save information between recursive calls.

8. Stacks operate on the *last-in, first-out (LIFO)* principle.

A.9   CHAPTER 9

Section 9-1

1. The two major components of an array are the *index* and *element.*

2. False: Because the elements within a given array must all be of the same data type.

Section 9-2

1. `double testScores[15];`

2. The dimension of the array in question 1 is 1 × 15.

3. The index of the first element of the array in question 1 is [0].

4. The index of the last element of the array in question 1 is [14].

5. `enum Courses{CS1, Calc, Physics, English, Speech};`
   `Courses thisSemester[5];`

6. If the index of the last element in an array is [25], the array will store 26 elements, since the first element index is always[0].

7. An array definition initialized with the integer values −3 through +3 is

   `int numbers[7] = {-3,-2,-1,0,1,2,3};`

   or

   `int numbers[] = {-3,-2,-1,0,1,2,3};`

8. The dimension of the array in question seven is 1 × 7.

9. The contents of the array `char language[5] = {'C','+','+'};` are

`['C'] ['+'] ['+'] ['\0'] ['\0']`

Section 9-3

1. ```
for (int index = 0; index < 15; ++ index)
    cin >> characters [index];
```

2. ```
for (int index = 0; index < 15; ++ index)
    cout << characters [index] << '\t';
```

Section 9-4

1. The array size must be 26 to allow room for the null terminator character.

2. `char course[ ] = "Data Structures";`

3. `char month[10] = "\0";`

4. `month = "May";`

5. `cin.getline(month,10);`

6. `cout << month << endl;`

7. To prevent output of random memory data, and a likely program crash, should the string values not be changed within the program and subsequently written to the monitor.

8. ```
if(strcmp(s1,s2))
    cout << "The two strings are unequal" << endl;
```

## Section 9-5

1. False: Because the array name locates index [0] of the array.

2. `void sample(char characters [15]);`

3. `void test(char &element);`

4. `test(characters [5]);`

## Section 9-6

1. False: To use the vector class, you must include the *vector* header file in your program, not the *vector.h* header file.

2. A template allows you to develop generic classes and functions for arbitrary data types.

3. `vector<string> myVector (5,"");`

4. ```
for(int i = 0; i < myVector.size(); ++i)
{
    cout << "Enter a string: ";
    cin >> ws;
    getline(cin,myVector[i]);
}//END FOR
```

5. ```
for(i = 0; i < myVector.size(); ++i)
    cout << myVector[i] << endl;
```

6. `sort(myVector.begin(),myVector.end());`

7. The *vector*, *string*, *algorithm*, and *iostream* header files.
```

A.10   CHAPTER 10

Section 10-1

1. By a class defining the behavior of its objects, we mean that the class defines how its objects act and react when they are accessed.

2. False: Information hiding is not ensured by encapsulation, because encapsulation dictates only that the data and/or functions are packaged together in a well-defined unit.

3. True: Private class members can be accessed only via public member functions.

4. Combining data with the functions that are dedicated to manipulating the data so that outside operations cannot affect the data is known as *information*, or *data*, *hiding*.

5. False: You *never* pass private data to a public function of the same class.

6. Information hiding is provided by the *private* section of a class.

7. The behavioral secrets of a class are revealed at the *implementation* level.

8. `Truck  myTruck;`

9. `Automobile  myCar;`

Section 10-2

1. The operator employed in a function header that designates the function as being a member of a given class is the *scoping*, ::, operator.

2. The complete definition of a member function that includes the function header and body is called the function *implementation*.

3. `int  Truck::wheels();`

4. A member function that is used specifically to initialize class data is called a *constructor*.

5. The constructor will have the same name as the class.

6. False: A constructor cannot have a return type.

7. A class constructor is called automatically when an object is defined for that class.

8. All member functions of a class carry with them a built-in pointer to the object that called the function, which is called *this*.

9. You can call a non-constructor member function of a class by listing the object name, a dot, and the function name with any required function arguments.

10. A member function that returns only a value of a private class member is called a(n) *access*, or *get*, function.

11. The term "message" is used for a call to a member function because when an object function is called, we are sending information to the object, and the object often responds with information.

Section 10-3

1. Three reasons for using the multi-file approach for developing software are as follows:
    - It allows the creation of smaller, more manageable files.
    - Programs are easier to maintain.
    - The programmer can hide important program code from the user.

2. Header files in a C++ software project provide interfaces to the class objects.

3. A software manufacturer might not supply you with the member function implementation source code to keep you from altering and possibly corrupting the function implementations, or to hide the function implementations for proprietary reasons.

4. A file that identifies the files that need to be compiled and linked to create an executable program is the *project* file.

5. When building a C++ project, the *.cpp* files, such as the implementation and application files, must be added to the project. The header files will be included in the appropriate implementation files or application file using #*include* directives. Some compilers, like Visual C++, also require you to add the class header files to the project.

A.11 CHAPTER 11

Section 11-1

1. A parent class is called a *base* class in C++.

2. A child class is called a *derived* class in C++.

3. A collection of classes with common inherited members is called a *family*.

4. Two reasons for using inheritance are
   - Inheritance allows you to reuse code without having to start from scratch.
   - Inheritance allows you to build a hierarchy among classes.

5. False: The proper use of inheritance would not allow a line class to be derived from a point class, because a line IS *NOT* A point.

6. True: The proper use of inheritance would allow a pixel class to be derived from a point class, because a pixel IS-A point.

7. True: The proper use of inheritance would allow a pickup truck class to be derived from a truck class, because a pickup truck IS-A truck.

Section 11-2

1. True: When declaring a derived class, the derived class is listed first followed by a colon and the base class.

2. True: A public base class allows its public members to be used by any of its derived classes.

3. False: All derived classes of a base class have access to the protected members of the base class.

4. When base class header files are included in multiple implementation and application files, you must use the #*ifndef* directive to avoid "multiple declaration" compile errors.

5. The main reason that *Savings* should not be derived from *SuperNow* is that a savings account is *not* a type of checking account. Such an inheritance would not be natural.

6. *Multiple inheritance* occurs when all the inherited members in a family can be traced back to more than one parent class.

Section 11-3

1. True: A virtual function is always a polymorphic function.

2. False: All polymorphic functions are not virtual functions, because an overloaded function is polymorphic, but not virtual.

3. True: The virtual function interface is identical for each version of the function in a given class family.

4. Overloaded functions are *statically* bound.

5. Virtual functions are *dynamically* bound.

6. The implementation code for a dynamically bound function is determined at *run time*.

A.12   CHAPTER 12

Section 12-1

1. False: A file is a sequential-access data structure.

2. A channel where data can flow between your C++ program and the outside world is called a *file stream*.

3. Standard output in C++ is written to the *cout* file stream.

4. The *ifstream* class is used in C++ to perform input, or read, operations from disk files.

5. True: The *iostream* class is derived using multiple inheritance.

6. `ofstream myFile("C:\\temp\\data.txt");`

7. `fstream yourFile("A:ASCII.txt");`

Section 12-2

1. False: File operations in C++ are centered around classes and classes are not available in the C language.

2. The major operations that are required to create a new file if it does not already exist are as follows:
   - Define an output file stream object and attach it to a physical disk file.
   - Get the new file components from the user, and write them to the file.

3. The major operations that are required to read an existing file are as follows:
   - Define an input file stream object and attach it to a physical disk file.
   - Read the file components and display them to the user.

4. *ios::cur* forces the file window to be positioned relative to the current position of the window whereas *ios::end* forces the file window to be positioned relative to the end of the file when used with *seekg()* or *seekp()*.

5. The *change.cpp* program in this section inherits the *tellg()* function from the *ifstream* class.

6. The *tellg()* function returns the current position of the file window.

7. True: The *tellg()* function should be used with input files, whereas the *tellp()* function should be used with output files.

8. The standard function, *seekp()*, must be used to position the file window for an output file.

9. The three predefined starting points available to the *seekg()* and *seekp()* functions are as follows:
   - *ios::beg* (for the beginning of a file)
   - *ios::end* (for the end of a file)
   - *ios::cur* (for the current position of the file window)

10. The distance to move the file window from the specified starting point when using *seekg()* or *seekp()* must be expressed in *byte* units.

A.13   CHAPTER 13

Section 13-1

1. `pchar = &character;`
2. `plint = p2int;`
3. False: *&character* represents a constant pointer and cannot be changed by the program.
4. True: If *pchar* is defined as a character pointer, then *pchar* can be altered at any time.

Section 13-2

1. `char *pchar;`
   `char character;`
2. `pchar = &character;`
3. `*pchar = 'A';`
4. False: *pchar* must be assigned to another pointer, not a character. The correct assignment would be

   `*pchar = 'Z';`
5. When a pointer is initialized dynamically, the **new** operator must be used in the pointer definition.
6. `pchar = new char;`
   `*pchar = 'B';`
7. `delete pchar;`
8. False: The pointer remains, and only the memory space that was used by the pointer is deallocated.

Section 13-3

1. `char *pstring = "C++";`
2. `cout << pstring << endl;`
3. `cout << *pstring << endl;`

   or

   `cout << pstring[0] << endl;`
4. `cout << pstring[2] << endl;`

   or

   `cout << *(pstring + 2) << endl;`
5. `cout << *(pstring + 1) << *(pstring + 2) << endl;`

   or

   `cout << pstring[1] << pstring[2] << endl;`
6. Suppose that *p1* is a pointer that points to index [5] of an array of double floating-point values and *p2* is a pointer that points to index [15] of the same array. Then, *p2 – p1* will yield the value *10*.

Section 13-4

1. `char *courses[] = {"Calc", "Assembler", "C++", NULL};`
2. "Calc" is located at *courses* using the array in question 1.
3. The string "C++" is located at *courses*[2] using the array in question 1.
4. "lc" is located at *courses* + 2 using the array in question 1.
5. The single character 'e' is located at *(*courses*[1] + 3).
6. The concept of using several levels of addressing to access data is known as *indirection*, or *indirect addressing*.

Section 13-5

1. True: When a pointer is used in a function call, any operations on the pointer data within the function will affect the pointer data in the calling program.
2. True: A pointer argument in a function call must have a corresponding pointer parameter in the function prototype.
3. `void foo(char *);`
4. `void foo(char **);`
5. `foo(myNames);`

Section 13-6

1. `Truck *pickUp;`
   `pickUp = new Truck(4);`
2. `pickUp -> getWheels();`
3. `delete pickUp;`
4. A destructor should be used in a class declaration when private members of the class have been defined dynamically. The destructor function is used to deallocate the dynamic member memory.

A.14   CHAPTER 14

Section 14-1

1. The term *abstract* is used to indicate that data and its related operations are being viewed without considering any of the details of how the data or operations are implemented in the computer system.
2. *double*, *int*, *string* or any of the other data types and classes are examples of ADTs.
3. The ADT black box concept facilitates *modular* software design.
4. False: A data structure provides a way of structuring or organizing data and an ADT defines the data to be operated on, the data structure, as well as the operations that can be performed on the data.
5. Data protection in an ADT is provided by *encapsulation with information hiding*.
6. The interface to an ADT is through its *function interface*.
7. You gain modularity through the use of ADTs, because ADTs are building blocks for use in software development.

8. You gain generality through the use of ADTs, because algorithms can be developed that depend only on the ADT function interface without concern for the implementation details of the ADT.

Section 14-2

1. "The stack is full!" would be displayed on the monitor.

2. You can not randomly access the array holding the stack, because the array is a private member of the *Stack* class and can be accessed only via the stack operations defined for the class which do not include random element access within the array.

3. With our array implementation of a stack, a *push()* operation requires that the stack pointer be *preincremented*.

4. False: The array begins at 0. Thus, *top* must equal *SIZE* – 1 when the stack is full.

5. With our array implementation of a stack, the stack is empty when the value of *top* is *−1*.

6. The functional difference between the *pop()* function and the *topElement()* function is that the value of *top* is not changed with the *topElement()* function and it is with the *pop()* function.

7. We had to include a *fullStack()* function in our implementation of a stack because of the finite storage capacity of an array.

Section 14-3

1. "The queue is full!" would be displayed on the monitor.

2. False: *rear* must be advanced, not *front*, during an *insert()* operation.

3. If *front* is *MAXQ*– 1
      Set *front* = 0.
   Else
      Set *front* = *front* + 1.

4. False: For example, after the last element is removed, the value of *front* can be greater than the value of *rear*.

5. *front* and *rear* have the same value if there is only one element in the queue when using the circular array implementation of a queue.

6. We had to include a *fullQ()* function in our implementation of a queue because of the finite storage capacity of the array used to hold the queue.

7. By using our array implementation of a queue, the element counter is equal to 0 when the queue is empty, and the element counter is equal to *MAXQ* when the queue is full.

Section 14-4

1. False: The sequencing of nodes in a linked list is explicit, because the location of the successor of any given node must be clearly specified in the node.

2. The two parts of a linked list node are the *element* (*info*) and *locator* or *pointer* (*next*).

3. If *node(p)* is the last node in the list, the value of *next(p)* is *NULL*.

4. False: The list is empty when the value of *first* is *NULL*, not 0.

5. If you reverse the order of steps 3 and 4 in the insertion process illustrated in Figure 14.15, the linked list will be lost because *first* will be reassigned to the single new node before it is linked into the list.

6. The list search algorithm given in this section will not detect multiple occurrences of the same item in a linked list. It could be made to detect multiple occurrences by placing the search in a **while** loop and searching for the item until the end of the linked list is reached.

7. If the statements *Set predP = p* and *Set p = next(p)* are reversed in the linked list search algorithm, *p* and *predP* would be pointing to the same node.

8. An algorithm for the list destructor function, *~List()*, is

~List() **Algorithm**
BEGIN
    Set *p = first*
    While *p ≠ NULL*
        Set *temp = next(p)*.
        Delete *p*.
        Set *p = temp*.
END.

A.15   CHAPTER 15

Section 15-1

1. The maximum row index is *9*, and the maximum column index is *14*.

2. 150.

3. `cin >> sample [0][14];`

4. `cout << Sample [1][2] << endl;`

5.
```
for (int row = 0; row < 10; ++row)
    {
        for (int col = 0; col < 15; ++col)
            cout << sample [row][col];
        cout << endl;
    }//END OUTER FOR
```

6. `void display(float sample [10][15]);`

7. `display(sample);`

8. A two-dimensional array in C++ is *row* major order.

Section 15-2

1. A problem that might be encountered when defining large multidimensional arrays is the *array size too big error*. This means that you are attempting to set aside more memory for the array than a particular computer system can allocate.

2. A three-dimensional array in C++ is *plane* major order.

3. `int integers [10][15][3];`

4. To determine how many bytes of storage is occupied by the above array, you can use

`sizeof(integers)`

If your compiler stores an integer in 2 bytes, this calculation becomes

$(10 \times 15 \times 3) \times 2 = 900$ bytes.

```
5. for (int plane = 0; plane < 10; ++ plane)
   {
       for (int row = 0; row < 15; ++ row)
       {
           for (int col = 0; col < 3; ++ col)
                cout << integers [plane][row][col];
           cout << endl;
       }   //END ROW FOR
   }   //END PLANE FOR
```

ASCII Character Table

Dec	Char	Dec	Char	Dec	Char	Dec	Char
0	^@ NUL	32	SPC	64	@	96	`
1	^A SOH	33	!	65	A	97	a
2	^B STX	34	"	66	B	98	b
3	^C ETX	35	#	67	C	99	c
4	^D EOT	36	$	68	D	100	d
5	^E ENQ	37	%	69	E	101	e
6	^F ACK	38	&	70	F	102	f
7	^G BEL	39	'	71	G	103	g
8	^H BS	40	(	72	H	104	h
9	^I HT	41	)	73	I	105	i
10	^J LF	42	*	74	J	106	j
11	^K VT	43	+	75	K	107	k
12	^L FF	44	,	76	L	108	l
13	^M CR	45	-	77	M	109	m
14	^N SO	46	.	78	N	110	n
15	^O SI	47	/	79	O	111	o
16	^P DLE	48	0	80	P	112	p
17	^Q DC1	49	1	81	Q	113	q
18	^R DC2	50	2	82	R	114	r
19	^S DC3	51	3	83	S	115	s
20	^T DC4	52	4	84	T	116	t
21	^U NAK	53	5	85	U	117	u
22	^V SYN	54	6	86	V	118	v
23	^W ETB	55	7	87	W	119	w
24	^X CAN	56	8	88	X	120	x
25	^Y EM	57	9	89	Y	121	y
26	^Z SUB	58	:	90	Z	122	z
27	^[ESC	59	;	91	[	123	{
28	^\ FS	60	<	92	\	124		
29	^] GS	61	=	93	]	125	}
30	^^ RS	62	>	94	^	126	~
31	^— US	63	?	95	—	127	DEL

APPENDIX C

VISUAL STUDIO TUTORIAL

Chapter Contents

INTRODUCTION

Who Should Use This Tutorial?

You should, first of all, have a working knowledge of Windows before you attempt to program in a Windows environment. Knowing how to launch programs from the start menu and use standard Windows menus, buttons, etc. is a minimum. Having a general knowledge of the Windows file structure (i.e., how and where files are stored) will also help you out. You can often pick up these basics simply by surfing the Internet or even by playing a few simple games of Windows solitaire. Once you have the basics down, you will be well equipped to begin to learn how to program in C++.

It helps to know C++ before trying to master the Visual Studio environment. Likewise, it is easier to learn C++ if you are already familiar with Visual Studio. This puts the beginner in a distinct Catch-22. This tutorial is written with the beginner in mind. It attempts to give the new user some insight into the Visual Studio environment without addressing C++ concepts. The drawback is that a new user will probably not have the knowledge of C++ to proceed through the entire tutorial.

Instead, future programmers should attempt to read through enough of this tutorial to become familiar enough with Visual Studio to use it for learning C++. As a novice programmer learns new concepts (such as multi-file projects and classes), he or she can refer to the later sections of the tutorial to learn how to apply these concepts in Visual Studio.

If you do not have any knowledge of C++, you should go through section C.1 to get accustomed to the Visual Studio to use it to learn C++. Once you have a little experience with C++, go through the remaining sections. If you are already familiar with the Visual Studio environment (i.e., you have used Visual Basic, Visual J++, or another Visual Studio product) this tutorial will probably not help you much.

What Is This Tutorial?

We will cover how to use the Visual Studio environment. C++ concepts are not presented. You should use this tutorial in conjunction with a book (or a class) that teaches standard C++ programming. It is possible to read through the all the sections and go through all the examples without knowing anything about C++, but you will probably not gain anything from it.

Why Microsoft Visual Studio?

Some might argue that Visual Studio is too advanced for beginning programmers. This is a valid argument. After all, Visual Studio is an advanced **IDE** (**Integrated Development Environment**). It is the IDE that is used by Visual C++, Visual Basic, Visual J++, Visual Foxpro, Visual Interdev, and others. As a result, if you can program in Visual C++, then learning to program with Visual Basic, Visual J++, et. al. is a matter of learning a new language without learning a new environment.

Others might argue that Visual Studio does too much for beginners. They might say that the debugger catches mistakes too easily, so that new programmers will not learn from them, or that the automation of compile options puts new programmers at a disadvantage if they ever have to deal with a command line based compilers. This is another valid point; however, a new programmer would not know the purpose of all the command line options anyway, and entering these options would simply be the student's algorithm for compiling a program. Sure, new programmers do eventually learn what all the command line options mean, but the same new programmer could instead learn C++ in Visual Studio and learn how to compile with a command line compiler if and when that need arises.

Microsoft Visual Studio is an excellent IDE, and Visual C++ is an excellent implementation of the C++ language. Once a new programmer gets a good handle on the Visual Studio Environment, he or she will be able to concentrate on learning C++ with minimal complications.

C.1   JUMP RIGHT IN: A VISUAL STUDIO OVERVIEW

Getting Started

We will assume that you have already installed Microsoft Visual C++. If you do not have Visual C++ installed, please refer to the documentation that comes with the program.

Launch Visual C++ from the Windows *Start Menu*. You will be sitting in front of a screen that looks similar to that in Figure 1. If your screen has a dialog box showing the "Tip of the Day," click on the *Close* button and you will be left with a screen shown in Figure 1.

Your First Visual C++ Program

This section will take you through building a simple console program. You will begin by creating a new C++ file, then you will type in a very simple program. Finally, you will compile and run the program.

In Visual C++, you must have a *project* in order to compile a program. Similarly, you must have an active *workspace* in which to create a project. If no project exists,

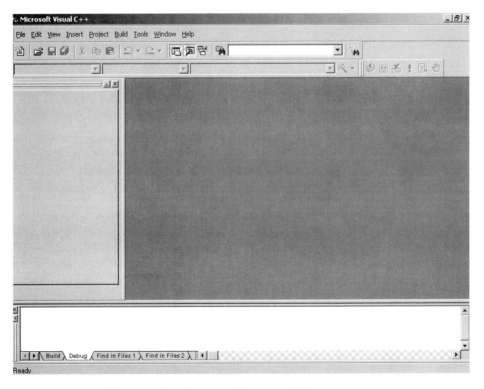

FIGURE 1   EMPTY VISUAL C++ WINDOW.

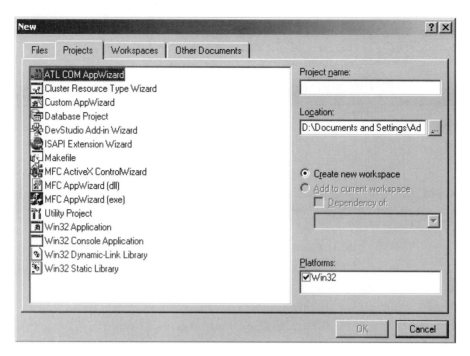

FIGURE 2   A *NEW* WINDOW (*PROJECTS* TAB).

Visual C++ helpfully creates a default project within a default workspace. You will allow Visual C++ to do this when you compile your program.

Creating a New C++ Source File.   The first step is to create a new C++ file. Click on the *File* menu, then click on *New...* in the drop-down menu. A window that is shown in Figure 2 will appear.

Click on the *Files* tab along the top of the screen, and you will be presented with the window shown in Figure 3. Click once on the icon labeled *C++ Source File*. Next type *hello* into the text box labeled *File name:*. (Since *C++ Source File* is highlighted, Visual C++ will automatically add a ".cpp" extension to the end of the file name to identify it as a C++ source file.)

Below the *File name:* text box, there is another box labeled *Location:*. If you know the path of the directory where you would like to create the file, type it in the text box, otherwise click the button to the right of the box to show a dialog window similar to the one shown in Figure 4. Use this dialog window to browse to the folder where you would like to save your new C++ file, then click on the button labeled *OK*. You should see the path of the folder that you chose in the text box labeled *Location*.

The Project Directory.   It is a good idea to save your C++ source file in its own folder. The typical practice is to create a folder with the name of your project (in this example, the project is called *hello*), then create the C++ source file within that folder. If you need to create a folder, then click cancel on the open dialog windows, minimize Visual C++, create the folder, then go back to Visual C++.

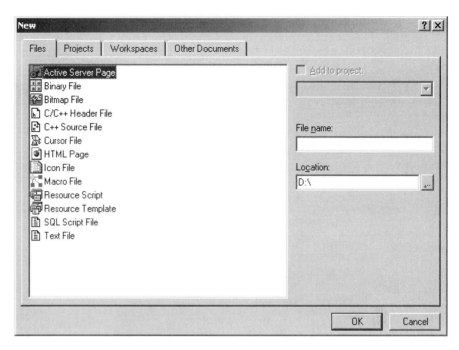

FIGURE 3   A *NEW* **WINDOW (***FILES* **TAB).**

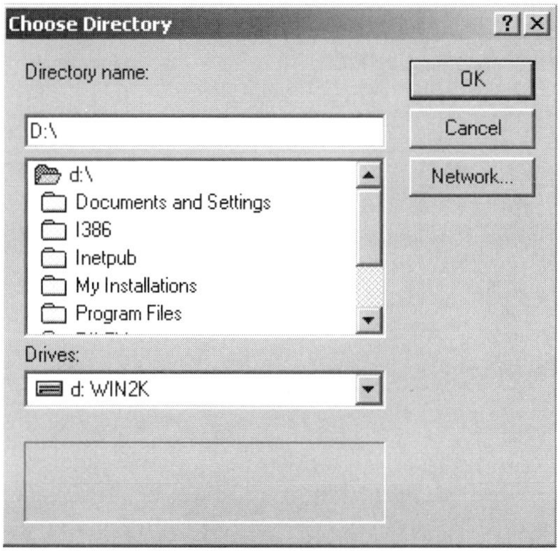

FIGURE 4   *CHOOSE DIRECTORY* DIALOG WINDOW.

Also, keep in mind that since Visual C++ creates several files (including the executable) within the project folder and its subfolders, a 1.44-MB floppy disk is not a good place to create your file. If you need to save your project on a floppy disk, create your file in a temporary folder on the hard drive or on a network drive somewhere. Then, when you are done working, copy *only* the C++ source file to a floppy disk.

Once you have decided where to save your file, click on the *OK* button in the *New* window. You should be presented with a screen similar to Figure 5. Notice that the gray background from Figure 1 now appears as a white edit screen with the cursor blinking in the top left corner of the screen. This is the part of the window that shows the contents of the current file being edited.

Type-in the Code.   Now you are ready to type in your first Visual C++ program. Type the following code exactly as it is shown:

```
#include <iostream.h>

int main()
{
  cout << "Hello World!" << endl;

  return 0;
} //END main()
```

Notice that Visual C++ highlights the C++ keywords *#include*, *int*, and *return*. This is called **syntax highlighting**. Syntax highlighting is one of the many features that Visual C++ provides to make writing programs simpler.

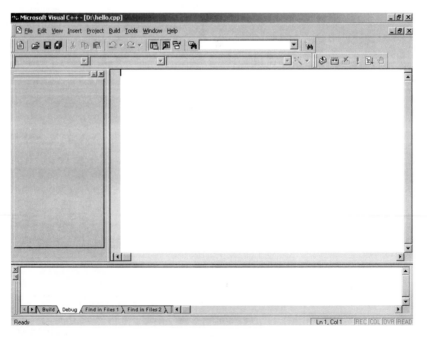

FIGURE 5   **VISUAL C++ WINDOW WITH EMPTY C++ FILE OPENED.**

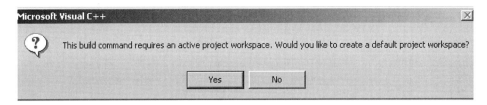

FIGURE 6   **MESSAGE BOX TO CREATE A DEFAULT PROJECT AND WORKSPACE.**

Build the Program.   Now we need to compile, link, and run the program. First, save your file. Either click on the *File* menu then select *Save* from the drop-down menu, or simply type `Ctrl+s` (hold down the `Ctrl` key and type *s*). Now Click on the *Build* menu, then select *Build* from the dropdown menu (or type the `F7` key, which is the "hot key" for the *Build* command). A message box like the one in Figure 6 should appear. Click the *Yes* button to allow Visual C++ to create a default project and workspace.

Your screen should now look similar to Figure 7. If any error messages appear in the bottom portion of the window, make sure that your code is typed in correctly then try to build the program again. If you are sure your code is correct, you might want to ask someone to double-check it for you. It is very easy to miss something when copying code, particularly if you are not familiar with C++.

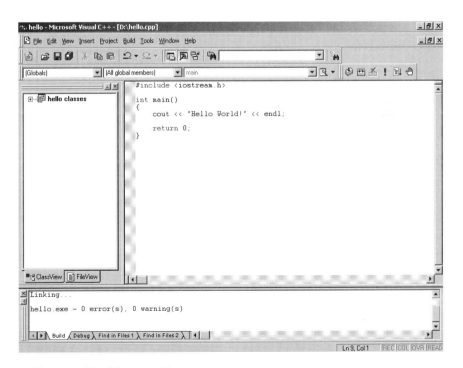

FIGURE 7   **VISUAL C++ WINDOW WITH ACTIVE WORKSPACE AND PROJECT.**

In the event that your code is right and you are still getting an error, you should look for other problems. Your first step should be to quit Visual C++, then reopen it and try to build your program again. If that doesn't help, try rebooting your computer. If you still have trouble, it is possible that Visual C++ is not installed properly. It is also possible that you do not have the file permissions within the operating system to write in the directory where your project is located. If you have built your project on a floppy disk, you may not have enough disk space to build the project. You may need to consult your computer and software manuals and/or technical support.

Exploring the Environment.   In general, your program will compile without any problems and you will be ready to execute it. Before running the program, take a moment to explore the Visual C++ environment now that you have an active workspace and project.

At the left side of the screen is a window containing "hello classes." This is the *Workspace* window. Click on the plus sign (+) next to "hello classes." A folder with the word "Globals" will appear with another plus sign next to it. Click on this plus sign and "main()" will appear underneath it. If you double-click on "main()" or the icon next to it, the editor window will become active, and the cursor will appear at the beginning of the line "int main()" within your code.

At the bottom of the *Workspace* window are two tabs labeled *Class View* and *File View*. By default, *Class View* is the active tab. Click on the tab labeled *File View*. Now the *Workspace* window should show "Workspace 'hello': 1 project(s)" on the first line and "hello files" on the next line. Click the plus sign next to "hello files" and "hello.cpp" will appear. You should recognize this as the name of the file that you typed into the *New* window in the *File Name* text box.

If you look at the very top right corner of the screen, you should see two rows of the standard window buttons (from left to right: *Minimize, Restore/Maximize,* and *Close*). Click the close button on the *lower* row. The editor where you typed the code will disappear leaving nothing but a gray background. (If you are prompted to save at this time, double-check that you haven't accidentally made any unwanted changes to the code, then click *Yes*.) Now double-click on "hello.cpp" in the *Workspace* window. The editor window will reappear, code and all.

Now look at the window at the bottom of the screen. The window that says "hello.exe – 0 Error(s), 0 Warning(s)" is called the *Output* window. Notice that there are several tabs at the bottom of the *Output* window labeled *Build, Debug,* etc. The active tab is the *Build* tab, and, interestingly enough, it contains output created when you built your program.

Notice that on the right side of the *Output* window there is a vertical scroll bar. Right now it is at the bottom of the window. Try scrolling up. You should see that there was more output from the build that had just automatically scrolled past. There is also a horizontal scrollbar along the right part of the bottom of the window. You can scroll right if you want, but there is nothing over there now. Sometimes the output lines are too wide to fit on the screen. Rather than wrap around to the next line, the output will extend off the screen.

Run the Program.   Click on the *Build* menu, then select *Execute hello.exe* (or type ctrl+F5). A console screen will appear showing the output of your program

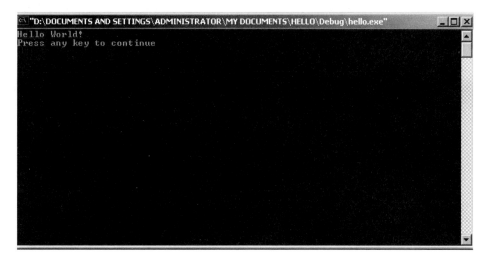

FIGURE 8   CONSOLE OUTPUT FROM *HELLO.EXE*.

and prompting you to press any key as in Figure 8. When you press a key, the window will disappear.

Congratulations! You have just created your first program with Visual C++. Here is a summary of the steps you just performed:

1. Created a new C++ file (*File→New...*, *Files*, *C++ Source File*, enter file name and location)
2. Typed in the code
3. Built the program by compiling and linking it. (*Build→Build)*
4. Ran the program (*Build→Execute*)

C.2   DEALING WITH ERRORS IN VISUAL C++

Syntax Errors

Syntax errors occur when you do not correctly follow the rules of a programming language. For instance, if you forget a semicolon at the end of a line or if you mistype a keyword or a variable name the compiler will generate a syntax error. A program will not compile if it has syntax errors. As a result, these are the first errors you will have to fix. However, most of the time they are easy to find and fix. Visual C++ does an excellent job of finding and helping you fix syntax errors. With most errors, it stops just short of fixing them for you.

Let's create a syntax error in your *hello* program to see how C++ handles it. Delete the semicolon from the end of the line that begins with "cout." Your code should now look like this:

```
#include <iostream.h>

int main()
{
  cout << "Hello World!" << endl

  return 0;
} //END main()
```

Now push `Ctrl+s` to save the file, then push `F7` to build the program. The last line of the *Output* window should now show "hello.exe – 1 error(s), 0 warning(s)." If you scroll up, you will see a description of the error. The line will begin with the full path and filename of the *hello.cpp* file followed by the line number where the error was found in parentheses, then a colon and the description of the error. The error message should read: "error C2143: syntax error : missing ';' before 'return'."

Now that we know where the error is, it's time to fix it. Double-click anywhere on the line that shows the error message. You will be pleasantly surprised to see what happens. Your screen should look similar to Figure 9. The error line in the *Output* window will be highlighted and the error message will appear at the very bottom of the main Visual C++ window. Also, the cursor jumps to the beginning of the line indicated in the error message, and a small marker appears just to the left of the line indicated in the error message. (A missing semicolon always shows up as a syntax error on the line after the line missing the semicolon.)

In a large program this error finding ability will speed up program development tremendously. From here, you can fix the error and rebuild your program. Take

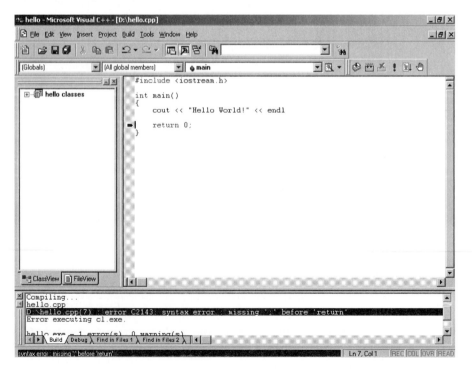

FIGURE 9   VISUAL C++ WINDOW WITH BUILD ERROR.

some time to play around. Delete things, add things—play around with the program and get a feel for the syntax error reporting capability in Visual C++.

Using the Debugger

Syntax errors in code are the least of your worries. *Logic* errors are much harder to find. A logic error occurs when your code does not do what you want or expect it to do. These errors do not keep your program from compiling or running (although sometimes they cause your program to crash), and the compiler will not find them for you. A debugger, however, is a great tool for finding these errors.

To get a feel for the Visual C++ debugger, retype the *hello* program. Here is the original code again:

```
#include <iostream.h>

int main()
{
  cout << "Hello World!" << endl;

  return 0;
} //END main()
```

After typing in the code, hit `Ctrl+s` to save then `F7` to build the program. Now you are ready to *step through* the program. Stepping through the program will run it by executing one line of code at a time using the debugger. To begin, simply press the `F10` key. You will see a console window briefly appear, then disappear, and your Visual C++ window will change to look similar to Figure 10.

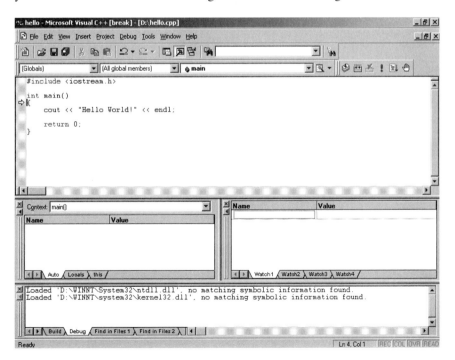

FIGURE 10   VISUAL C++ DEBUGGER WINDOW.

Notice that the *Workspace* window has disappeared from the left side of the screen, and, although the *Output* window is still at the bottom of the screen, it is now set to the *Debug* tab. There are also two new windows just above the *Output* window. The one on the left is called the *Variables* window, and the one on the right is called the *Watch* window. If these windows did not appear, then select the *View* menu, followed by the *Debug Windows* submenu, followed by *Variables*. Repeat this procedure for the *Watch* window if it did not appear.

Look at the menu bar. The *Build* menu has been replaced with a *Debug* menu. If you click on this menu heading, you will see the dropdown menu shown in Figure 11. The only two commands we will use right now are *Step Over* and *Go*. As you can see in Figure 11, the hot key for *Step Over* is F10. This is the key you used to start the debugger and the key you will use to step through the program. The hot key for *Go* is F5. You will use this command to run the rest of the way through the program when you are finished stepping through it.

If you look back at the main Visual C++ screen, you may notice a small yellow arrow next to the opening brace of *main()* (the '{' on the line following "int main()"). This arrow marks the current line of code. The line that is marked with the yellow arrow is the line that will be executed when you hit F10.

Select *Step Over* from the *Debug* menu and you should see the yellow arrow drop down one line. Since that line didn't contain any code, nothing happened, but the arrow should now be pointing at the line with the *cout* statement.

Now hit F10 and your program will write "Hello World!" to the console screen, which is running as a separate program in Windows. Use either the task bar or Alt+Tab to look at the console screen. After verifying that the output is displayed correctly, click anywhere on the Visual C++ window to make it the active window once again. Hitting F10 again will execute the *return* statement, bringing the arrow to the closing brace (}). From here you can keep pushing F10, but Visual C++ will pop

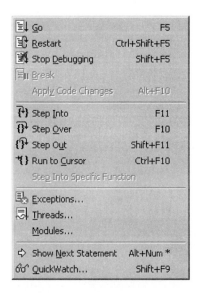

FIGURE 11   THE *DEBUG* MENU.

open unfamiliar files where the code to end the program is located. It's easier to simply push F5 and allow the debugger to run through the rest of the code on its own.

Go ahead and push F5 to allow the program to finish. You may see the console window appear briefly again. If you recall, when you used Ctrl+F5 to execute the program without the debugger, the console window stayed open until you pressed a key to close it. The debugger does not do this; it simply runs through the program and closes the console window.

Finding Logic Errors with the Debugger.   Delete everything in your *hello.cpp* file then type in the following code which contains logic errors. This program is supposed to prompt the user for the number of people to greet, then prompt for each person's name. As you type in the program, see if you can catch some of the logic errors. (*Hint:* There are three logic errors in the code.) Even if you find the errors, type the code exactly as it is shown so that the errors will be there when you use the debugger.

```cpp
#include <iostream.h>

int main()
{
    //DEFINE LOCAL VARIABLES
    int count=0;              //A LOOP COUNTER
    int numberOfPeople=0;     //HOLDS THE NUMBER OF PEOPLE TO GREET
    char name[25]=" ";        //HOLDS THE NAME OF A PERSON TO GREET

    //PROMPT USER FOR THE NUMBER OF PEOPLE TO GREET
    cout << "How many people do you want to say hello to?  " << flush;
    cin >> numberOfPeople;
    cout << endl;

    //PROMT FOR EACH PERSON TO GREET THEN GREET THAT PERSON
    for ( count = 1 ; count < numberOfPeople ; count++);
    {
        //GET THE NAME OF THE FIRST PERSON
        cout << "Please type the name of person #" << count << ":  " << flush;
        cin.getline(name,25);

        //SAY HELLO TO THE PERSON
        cout << "Hello, " << name << '.' << endl << endl;
    } //END FOR

    return 0;
} // END main()
```

After you type in the code, hit Ctrl+s to save, then hit F7 to build the program. (If you end up with any syntax errors, fix them, then try to build the program again.) Now, hit Ctrl+F5 to run the program. What happens? Figure 12 shows a sample output of the program.

When the program runs, it first prompts you for the number of people to greet. In the sample run, we entered 4. After that, the program doesn't act right. Rather

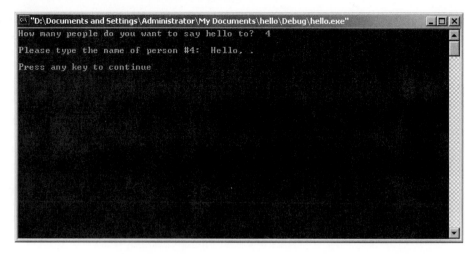

FIGURE 12 SAMPLE OUTPUT OF THE *HELLO* PROGRAM WITH LOGIC ERRORS.

than prompting for four names, it writes the name prompt once, then immediately outputs "Hello, ."

Before using the debugger, you should look at the output and decide where to look for the error. Right away, you should suspect the *for* loop, since the program only runs through the code within the loop one time. This is good enough to get a start, so press a key to make the run window disappear, then press F10 to start debugging.

Press F10 one more time to get to the first line of actual code. Now take a moment to look at the *Variables* window. Right now, the *Auto* tab is active, and the window is showing the variable *count* with a random value, since the line where *count* is initialized to 0 has not yet been executed.

Click on the *Locals* tab. You will see all three local variables that exist in the program (*numberOfPeople*, *name*, and *count*) along with their values, which are currently random memory garbage. Press F10 once and watch what happens. The values of *name* and *count* have turned red. Click back on the *Auto* tab. Notice that *numberOfPeople* has appeared on the list of variables. Press F10 again and watch what happens. This time, *count* disappears from the list, and the value of *numberOfPeople* has turned red.

The *Auto* tab shows only the variables that are in the current line of code (which will be executed on the next *Step Over*) and the previous line of code. When the value of a variable has just been changed, it turns red. The *Local* tab shows a list of all variables that are local to the current function, in this case *main()*. When a variable's value is changed, that variable turns red.

Since there are only three variables in this program, the *Local* tab will make it easy to see everything that is going on, so click on the *Local* tab. Then turn your attention to the variable *name*. You may have noticed that *name* has a small plus sign next to it. Click on the plus sign, and the variable (which is a C-string variable) will expand so that each of the 25 characters set aside to represent the variable appears on a separate line. Since the value is still random memory garbage, it isn't easy to see. So, press F10 again to execute the line that initializes *name* to blanks.

Now the line after the *name* line (labeled with "[0]") shows a value of "32 ' '." This is the ASCII value of the first character in the string (32 is the ASCII code for the blank character). The character itself is shown after its ASCII code, enclosed in single quotes. The rest of the characters (lines labeled "[1]" through "[24]") all show an ASCII value of 0, which is called the **null terminator** character. A null terminator indicates the end of a C-string. If you don't understand all of this, don't worry—just make a mental note that it is possible to look at individual characters in a string should you ever need to.

Click on the minus sign next to *name* (where the plus sign was) to hide the individual characters. It's time to continue searching for the logic errors. Press F10 to execute the *cout* statement, then press it again to execute the *cin* statement. You'll notice that the arrow doesn't move to the next line after you execute the *cin* statement because the program is expecting input here.

You need to enter a number into the console screen where the program is running. Use the task bar or Alt+Tab to switch to the console window, then type in the number 4 and press Enter. Look at the Visual C++ window. The arrow will now have moved on to the next line. In the *Variables* window you should find that the value of *numberOfPeople* is now 4. Press F10 again, and the program will enter the *for* loop.

Before executing the next line, look at the value of *count* in the *Variables* window. Its value should be 0. Now press F10 and watch what happens to the value. The arrow goes to the next line, and the value of *count* changes to 4. This isn't supposed to happen! The value should become 1 because that is what the *for* statement sets it to the first time in the loop. There is something wrong with this statement.

If you look at the *for* statement, you'll see that it ends with a semicolon; however, *for* statements should not normally end with a semicolon (even though C++ syntax allows it). This is the first error. The semicolon causes the program to execute the single *for* line four times rather than executing the loop four times.

Now that you've found the first error, press F5 to allow the program to finish executing, then delete the semicolon from the end of the *for* statement. Press Ctrl+s to save the change, then press F7 to build the program again. Now, run the program again by pressing Ctrl+F5. What happens this time? As you can see from Figure 13, there are still errors within the program. First, the program never read in the name of person #1. It just skipped by without waiting for input. Also, the program should have prompted for a person #4, but it stopped after #3.

You'll have to step through the program again to find these errors. You might guess from the output that there is a problem with the *cin.getline()* statement the first time it runs in the *for* loop. You should also see that the loop is running one time less than it should be. Armed with that knowledge, it's time to debug again.

Press F10 twice to begin debugging. Click on the *Locals* tab in the *Variables* window to show all the local variables. Step through the program using F10. Enter the value 4 when you are prompted for the number of people, and stop when you get to the *for* statement. Press F10 one more time and look at the variables. The value of *count* is now 1, which is what it should be. Execute the next line of code and the

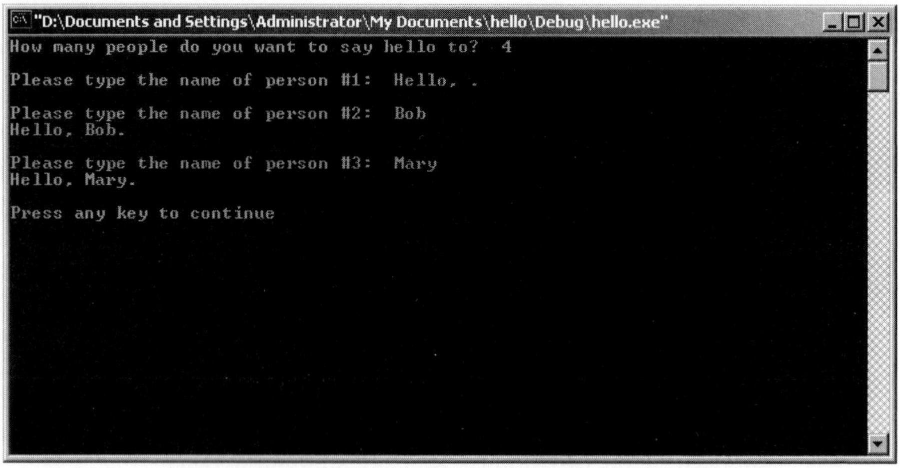

FIGURE 13   SAMPLE OUTPUT OF *HELLO* **PROGRAM WITH ONE LOGIC ERROR FIXED.**

arrow will be at the *cin.getline()* statement. Since this is the first time through the loop, this is one of the problem areas that you need to look at.

Now press F10. You know from executing *cin* statements in the debugger that the program should stop here until you enter a value into the console window; however, the arrow continues to the next line without waiting for input. Now you know what happened. But, why did it happen? This will be revealed shortly.

Let's find the next error. Continue stepping through the program. You will see the arrow jump back up to the *for* statement after the last line of code within the loop. Keep stepping through the program. Notice that *count* increments each time through the *for* loop. Also notice that each time you execute the *cin.getline()* statement you have to switch to the console window where the program is running and enter a name.

After the third time through the loop, the arrow jumps back up to the *for* statement, but then jumps to the *return* line next. Stop right there and check your variables. You'll see that the value of *count* is 4. You know that the program should be going through the loop four times; therefore, the loop should be executed when *count* is equal to four. If you look at the *for* loop though, you'll see that in order for the loop to execute, *count* must be less than *numberOfPeople*. If you look at the value of *numberOfPeople*, you'll see that it is also 4. Since 4 is not less than 4, the loop does not execute the last time. This is the error.

Press F5 to finish debugging. The last error is an easy one to fix. Simply change the test in the *for* loop from *count < numberOfPeople* to *count <= numberOfPeople*. The other problem is a little tougher to figure out. It turns out to be a quirk of the C++ language having to do with input buffers and carriage-return-line-feeds. It suffices to say that you should always place the following line before a *cin.getline()* statement:

```
cin >> ws;
```

Whenever a *cin* statement is used to read in data, it does not clear out the input buffer, and *cin.getline()* does not take that into account. It follows that whenever a *cin.getline()* statement appears after a *cin* statement, it reads what is left in the buffer rather than prompting for more input. If you didn't catch that, don't worry about it. Just remember that a *cin* before a *cin.getline()* requires a *cin >> ws*. Here is the complete, corrected code, with the required corrections highlighted in bold type:

```
#include <iostream.h>

int main()
{
    //DEFINE LOCAL VARIABLES
    int count=0;              //A LOOP COUNTER
    int numberOfPeople=0;  //HOLDS THE NUMBER OF PEOPLE TO GREET
    char name[25]=" ";     //HOLDS THE NAME OF A PERSON TO GREET

    //PROMPT USER FOR THE NUMBER OF PEOPLE TO SAY HELLO TO
    cout << "How many people do you want to say hello to?  " << flush;
    cin >> numberOfPeople;
    cout << endl;

    //PROMT FOR EACH PERSON TO GREET THEN GREET THAT PERSON
    for ( count = 1 ; count <= numberOfPeople ; count++)
    {
        //GET THE NAME OF THE FIRST PERSON
        cout << "Please type the name of person #" << count << ":  " << flush;
        cin >> ws;
        cin.getline(name,25);

        //SAY HELLO TO THE PERSON
        cout << "Hello, " << name << '.' << endl << endl;
    } //END FOR

    return 0;
} //END main()
```

Make the required changes. Then build and run the program to assure that it is working correctly.

Using the Watch Window

The *Variables* window can get very crowded in a program with more than three of four variables. There are also times that you may want to keep an eye on an expression rather than on just variables.

To learn how to use the *Watch* window, use the corrected program from the last section. With the program open, hit F10 to begin debugging. Once the debugger is started, you can use the *Watch* window. The premise behind the *Watch* window is simple: you simply type the variable name or expression whose value you want to watch. If you look down at the *Watch* window, you will see a dotted rectangle in the *Name* column and another in the *Value* column. Click on the rectangle in the *Name*

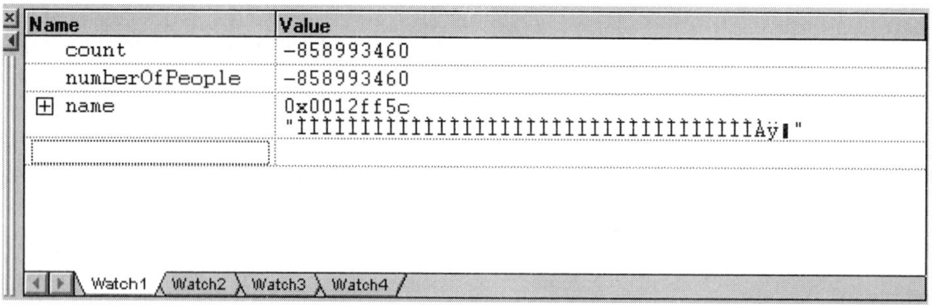

FIGURE 14 WATCH WINDOW SHOWING UNINITIALIZED VARIABLES.

column. The cursor will appear in the rectangle. Now type "count" in the box and hit Enter. The *Value* column will show an error because the program execution is not yet running your code. Hit F10 again and the uninitialized value of *count* will appear.

Find the variable name *numberOfPeople* within the code and double-click it with your mouse to highlight it. Once it is highlighted, use your mouse to drag it to the dotted rectangle on the second row of the *Watch* window in the *Name* column. The row should now contain *numberOfPeople* in the *Name* column and its uninitialized value in the *Value* column. This is an alternative way to add a variable to the *Watch* window.

Now add a watch for *name* using whichever method you prefer. Notice that *name* has a plus sign next to it, just like it did in the *Variables* window. This can be used to look at individual characters that make up the string exactly the same way as it worked in the *Variables* window. Your watch window should now appear as shown in Figure 14.

In this program, it may also be useful to know when the *for* loop will break. You can enter the conditional statement *count <= numberOfPeople* contained in the *for* statement into the *Watch* window by either typing it in the next row or by highlighting the expression and dragging it to the next row. You can now step through the program.

Notice that the value of *count <= numberOfPeople* is represented by a "1" when it is true and a "0" when it is false. In general, this is how Boolean values are represented in both the *Watch* and *Variables* windows.

Take some time to play around with the *Watch* window to get a feel for how it works. Try entering different expressions such as *1+2* and *count − numberOfPeople*. When you feel comfortable with the use of the *Watch* window, click on the *File* menu and select *Close Workspace* from the dropdown menu.

C.3 VISUAL C++ PROJECTS

Until now, you have probably pictured the C++ source file as the basis for C++ programming. You started with an empty file, filled it with code, and allowed the compiler to create a default project around it. It is now time to look at it from a different perspective. Visual C++ provides several different types of projects—each type can be thought of as a template, or framework, for which you, the programmer, provide functionality. The default project which Visual C++ built around the *hello.cpp* file was a *Win32 Console Application*. You didn't write the code that caused a console window to appear, and you didn't write the code that prompted the user to "Press any key to continue" when the program was finished running. The *Win32 Console Application* project (in conjunction with Windows) took care of that. What you did was fill in the gap between the opening of the console window and the "Press any key to continue" prompt.

To create a program in Visual C++, you begin with a project, and you plug in your own C++ source code to provide functionality. When you think about it that way, you should not have any trouble imagining how one project can contain several files.

Creating a New Project

If you have a project open, click the *File* menu and select *Close Workspace* from the dropdown menu. Click on the *File* menu then select *New...*from the dropdown list, or simply type *Ctrl+n*. You will be presented with the *New* window with the *Projects* tab active. Click on the *Projects* tab if it is not active. You will see a list of the projects available in Visual C++. *Win32 Console Application* is listed third from the bottom. Click it once to highlight it.

Now you need to choose a location and a project name. Keep in mind that you are creating a project rather than a file. Visual C++ will create a folder in the location that you choose and it will call the folder by the project name. Type "rps" in the *Project Name* text box, then choose a location for your project and click *OK*. In case you're wondering, "rps" stands for *Rock-Paper-Scissors*. Another window similar to Figure 15 will appear to prompt you for more information on your project. Make sure "An empty project" is selected, then click *Finish*. One more window will appear asking you to finalize your choices. Click *OK* and your project will be created.

Adding Multiple Files to a Project

Now you need to add a file to the project. Press *Ctrl+n* to bring up the *New* window as shown in Figure 16. Since you have a project open, the window defaults to the *Files* tab. Click once on *C++ Source File* to select it, then enter "rps" in the *File Name* box. The *Location* box defaults to the project folder, so there is no need to change it.

Notice the checkbox labeled *Add to project*. Since this is checked, this file will be added to the project. It is possible for a file to exist within the project folder, yet not be part of the project, so you want to make sure this box is checked. If the file is not added to the project, it will not be compiled with the project, and it might as well not exist.

Click *OK* and you will be presented with an empty source file. Type in the following code. (*Note:* This code is contained on the CD that came with your text. The file is called *rps.cpp* and is located in the *VisualTutorial* directory. To insert the file into your edit window, click on the *Insert* menu item, then click on *FileAsText....*

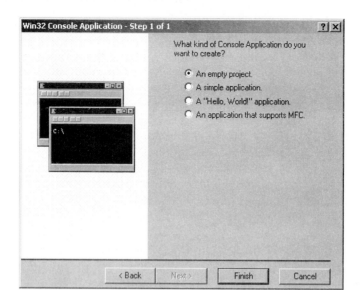

FIGURE 15 WIN32 CONSOLE APPLICATION WIZARD.

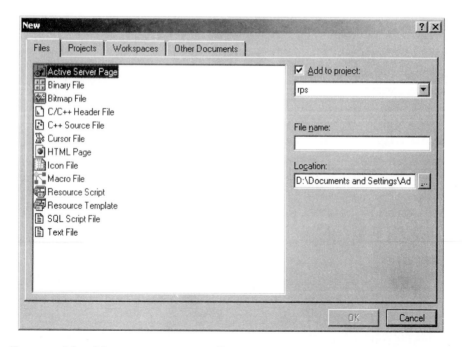

FIGURE 16 NEW WINDOW ON FILES TAB WITH RPS PROJECT OPEN.

Place your CD in the CD drive and select the *VisualTutorial* directory on the CD so that it appears in the *Look in:* directory box. You should now see all the files within this directory. Double-click on the *rps.cpp* file. This should place the *rps.cpp* code within the project edit window. You can also download the file from the *VisualTutorial* directory at the text Web site and insert the downloaded file using the *Insert* menu option just described.)

```cpp
//ROCK-PAPER-SCISSORS PROGRAM FILE (rps.cpp)

//PREPROCESSOR DIRECTIVES
#include <iostream>
#include <string>
using namespace std;

#include <stdlib.h>      //FOR srand() AND rand()
#include <time.h>        //FOR time() (USED FOR RANDOM SEED)
#include "rpsGlobals.h"  //FOR RPS PROTOTYPES AND CONSTANTS

//MAIN FUNCTION
int main()
{
    //DEFINE LOCAL VARIABLES
    int wins=0;       //NUMBER OF ROUNDS THE PLAYER HAS WON
    int losses=0;     //NUMBER OF ROUNDS THE PLAYER HAS LOST
    int pAttack=0;    //PLAYER'S CURRENT ATTACK
    int cAttack=0;    //COMPUTER'S CURRENT ATTACK
    char again=' ';   //TO PROMPT WHETHER TO PLAY AGAIN

    //INITIALIZE RANDOMIZATION
    srand(time( NULL ));

    //DISPLAY PROGRAM DESCRIPTION
    writeProgramDescription();

    //BEGIN do / while LOOP FOR PROMPTING TO PLAY AGAIN
    do
    {
      //CLEAR VARIABLES
      wins=0;
      losses=0;

      //PLAY GAME
      //THE for LOOP WILL BREAK AFTER THE LAST ROUND
      //OR WHEN wins OR losses IS OVER HALF OF ROUNDS
      for( int i=0 ;
          i<ROUNDS && wins<(ROUNDS / 2)+1 && losses<(ROUNDS /2)+1 ;
          i++)
      {
          //SHOW CURRENT ROUND AND SCORE
          cout << "Round " << i+1 << ':' << endl;
          writeScore(i,wins,losses);
```

```
        //GET PLAYER'S ATTACK
        pAttack=getPlayerAttack();

        //ECHO ATTACK
        cout << "You attack with " << writeAttack(pAttack) << '.' << endl;

        //GENERATE COMPUTER'S ATTACK
        cAttack = rand() % 3;

        //WRITE COMPUTERS ATTACK
        cout << "Computer attacks with " << writeAttack(cAttack) << endl;

        //DECIDE WHO WINS
        writeRoundResult(wins, losses, pAttack, cAttack);
    } //END FOR

  //SHOW FINAL SCORE
    cout << "FINAL SCORE:" << endl;
    writeScore(i,wins,losses);

    //DECLARE WHO THE WINNER IS
    writeFinalResults(wins, losses);

    //PROMPT USER TO PLAY AGAIN
    cout << "\n\nPress 'Y' then <ENTER> to play again."
         << "\nPress any other character then <ENTER> to quit."
         << endl;
    cin >> again;
    } //END WHILE
    while (again=='Y' || again=='y');

    return 0;
}// END main()
```

Several constants and function calls are not defined within this code. In the interest of simplifying things, they have been separated out into different files. The constants and the function prototypes exist in a file called *rpsGlobals.h*, which is included in this file with a *#include* statement.

To create this file, press *Ctrl+n* to open the *New* window. Click on *C/C++ Header File* to select it, then type "rpsGlobals" in the *File Name* box. The location will automatically be set to the project folder, so make sure *Add to project* is checked and click *OK*.

You will be presented with another blank file. Type in the following code or use the *Insert* procedure described earlier to insert the *rpsGlobals.h* file from the text CD or Web site.

```
        //GLOBAL VALUES FOR ROCK-PAPER-SCISSORS (rpsGlobals.h)

        //DECLARE CONSTANTS
        const int ROCK = 0;
```

```
                    const int PAPER = 1;
                    const int SCISSORS = 2;
                    const int ROUNDS = 5;

                    //FUNCTION PROTOTYPES
                    void writeProgramDescription();
                    void writeScore(int round, int wins, int losses);
                    int getPlayerAttack();
                    string writeAttack(int attack);
                    void writeRoundResult(int &wins, int &losses, int pAttack,
                    int cAttack);
                    void writeFinalResults(int wins, int losses);
```

Now, all that is left is the actual code for the functions. Press *Ctrl+n* again to bring up the *New* window. Select *C++ Source File*, and type "rpsFunctions" in the *File Name* box. Once again, the location should be correct, so make sure *Add to project* is checked and click *OK*. Type this code into the edit window or use the *Insert* procedure described earlier to insert the *rpsFunctions.cpp* file from the text CD or Web site.

```
//FUNCTIONS FOR ROCK-PAPER-SCISSORS (rpsFunctions.cpp)

//PREPROCESSOR DIRECTIVES
#include <iostream>
#include <iomanip>
#include <string>
using namespace std;

#include "rpsGlobals.h"    //FOR RPS PROTOTYPES AND CONSTANTS

//THIS FUNCTION WRITES A PROGRAM DESCRIPTION MESSAGE
void writeProgramDescription()
{
   //HEAR IS THE PROGRAM DESCRIPTION
   cout << "         ROCK - PAPER - SCISSORS" << endl << endl;
   cout << "It's time to play Rock-Paper-Scissors against the computer.  Decide"
        << endl;
   cout << "what your attack is, then see what the computer chose.  Play best"
        << endl;
   cout << "of " << ROUNDS << ", then decide whether to play again.  "
        << "Remember that" << endl;
   cout << "Rock smashes Scissors, Scissors cuts Paper, and Paper covers Rock."
        << endl << endl;
}//END writeProgramDescription()

//THIS FUNCTION DISPLAYS THE SCORE
void writeScore(int round=0, int wins=0, int losses=0)
{
   cout << "   Player: " << setw(4) << wins << flush;
   cout << "   Computer: " << setw(4) << losses << flush;
   cout << "   Draw: " << setw(4) << round-(wins+losses) << endl;
}// END writeScore()
```

```cpp
//THIS FUNCTION PROMPTS FOR THE PLAYER TO ENTER ATTACK
//THEN READS IT IN AND RETURNS IT
int getPlayerAttack()
{
    //DEFINE LOCAL VARIABLE
    int attack=0;

    //DISPLAY PROMPT
    cout << "0  ROCK" << endl;
    cout << "1  PAPER" << endl;
    cout << "2  SCISSORS" << endl;

    //READ IN ATTACK UNTIL A VALID VALUE IS ENTERED
    do
    {
       cout << "What is your attack?  " << flush;
       cin >> attack;
    } while (attack!=0 && attack!=1 && attack!=2);

    return attack;
} //END getPlayerAttack()

//THIS FUNCTION WILL RETURN A STRING TO REPRESENT AN ATTACK
//GIVEN THE ATTACK NUMBER
string writeAttack(int attack=0)
{
    //DECIDE WHICH STRING TO SEND BACK
    switch (attack)
    {
    case ROCK:
      return "ROCK";
      break;

    case PAPER:
      return "PAPER";
      break;

    case SCISSORS:
      return "PAPER";
      break;

    default:
       return "ROCK";
       break;
   } // END SWITCH
} //END writeAttack()

//THIS FUNCTION DISPLAYS THE RESULTS OF A ROUND GIVEN PLAYER
//AND COMPUTER ATTACKS. IT ALSO ACCEPTS wins AND losses BY
//REFERENCE AND INCREMENTS WHEN NEEDED
void writeRoundResult(int &wins, int &losses, int pAttack=0, int cAttack=0)
```

```
{
   //WRITE THE RESULTS
   switch ((pAttack - cAttack + 3) % 3)
   {
   case 0:
      //IT WAS A TIE
      cout << "Its a tie." << endl << endl;
      break;

   case 1:
      //PLAYER WON
      cout << "You Win!" << endl << endl;
      ++wins;
      break;

   case 2:
      //PLAYER LOST
      cout << "Computer Wins." << endl << endl;
      ++losses;
      break;
   } //END SWITCH
} //END writeRoundResult()

//THIS FUNCTION DISPLAYS THE FINAL RESULTS OF THE PROGRAM
void writeFinalResults(int wins=0, int losses=0)
{
   if (wins>losses)
   {
      cout << "YOU WIN THE GAME!!!" << endl;
   } //END IF
   else
   {
      if (wins<losses)
      {
         cout << "The computer won." << endl;
      } //END IF
      else
      {
         cout << "It's a draw...but you didn't lose." << endl;
      } // END ELSE
   } //END ELSE
}//END writeFinalResults()
```

You should now make sure that all three files are saved. If you click on the *FileView* tab of the workspace window (at the left side of the screen), then click on the plus next to "rps files," you will see three folders listed. If you double-click on the *Source Files* folder, you will see the *.cpp* files listed, and if you double-click on the *Header Files* folder, you will see the *.h* file listed. Double-clicking on any of these file names will open the file (if it is not open) and move it to the front of the code editing portion of the screen. You can then push Ctrl+s to save that file.

When all the files are saved, push F7 to build the program. If you have mistyped anything, the compiler will let you know it now. Use the error messages in the *Output* window to fix any syntax errors if the program doesn't compile. After it compiles correctly, run it.

It is sometimes helpful to split a large program into several files. For instance, if a program has several functions that do calculations and several others that display messages on the screen, it may be helpful to separate those categories of functions so they are easier to find later. When you do this, it is a good idea to create a header file to contain all global information (such as constants and function prototypes) and include it in each C++ file. In general, programs that you will write while learning to program will not be large enough to warrant this kind of separation, but you should know how to do it.

Adding Classes to a Project

To create a class, you can add source files and header files one at a time as described in the previous section, but Visual C++ offers an easier way. In this section, you'll create a simple class using the *New Class...* command.

If you have a project open, click the *File* menu and select *Close Workspace* from the drop-down menu. Create a new project by pressing Ctrl+n and selecting *Win32 Console Application*. Name the project "geometry," and click *OK*. In the next window, make sure *An Empty Project* is selected then click *Finish*. Click *OK* in the window that follows and you'll be ready to start.

Let's create the class right away. If the *ClassView* tab is not active in the *Workspace* window, click on it. The window should have a line that says "geometry classes" with a plus sign to the left of it. Right click on the text, then select *New Class...* from the dropdown menu. A window similar to Figure 17 will appear. Type "Rectangle" into the *Name* text box then click *OK*.

Visual C++ will now create files called *Rectangle.cpp* and *Rectangle.h*. You can open these files by clicking on the *FileView* tab of the *Workspace* window, clicking the plus sign next to *geometry files*, clicking the plus sign next to either *Source Files* (for *Rectangle.cpp*) or *Header Files* (for *Rectangle.h*), then double-clicking on the file name. However, Visual C++ provides an easier way to create member functions and variables.

In the *Workspace* window with the *ClassView* tab active, click the plus sign next to *geometry classes*, then click the plus sign next to *Rectangle* when it appears. Under *Rectangle* is a list of the class's member functions. Visual C++ has already added a constructor function called *Rectangle()* and a destructor function called *~Rectangle()*.

You will need to add variables to contain the length and width of the rectangle as integers, and functions to calculate the perimeter and area of the rectangle. Begin by adding the variables. Right-click on *Rectangle* in the *Workspace* window and select *Add Member Variable* from the drop-down menu. You will be presented with a window similar to Figure 18.

Type "double" in the *Variable Type* box, and type "length" in the *Variable Name* box. Click on the radio button next to *Private* to make the variable private, then click *OK*. Repeat the process to create a private double named "width."

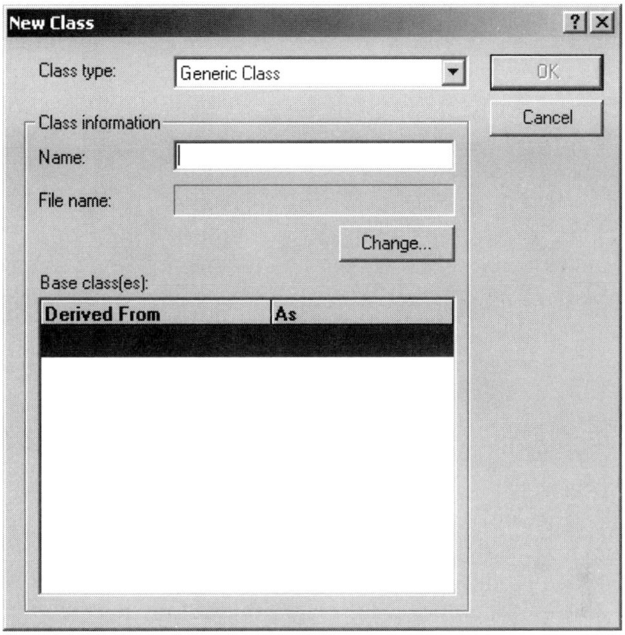

FIGURE 17   NEW CLASS WINDOW.

To add member functions to our *Rectangle* class, right-click on *Rectangle* within the *Workspace* window, and select *Add Member Function....* A window similar to Figure 19 will appear. Type "double" into the *Function Type* box and "perimeter" into the *Function Declaration* box. Click *OK.* (The *Rectangle.cpp* file will open, but ignore that for now.) Repeat the process to create a public member function of type double called "area."

Now add a new member function of type void. This will be the *setLength()* function, so it will have to accept a parameter. Type "void" in the *Function Type* box and then type "setLength(double l=0.0)" in the *Function Declaration* box. Notice that if you want a default parameter, this is where you set it. Repeat this to create a function of type void called *setWidth()* that accepts a double called *w* with a default value of 0.0.

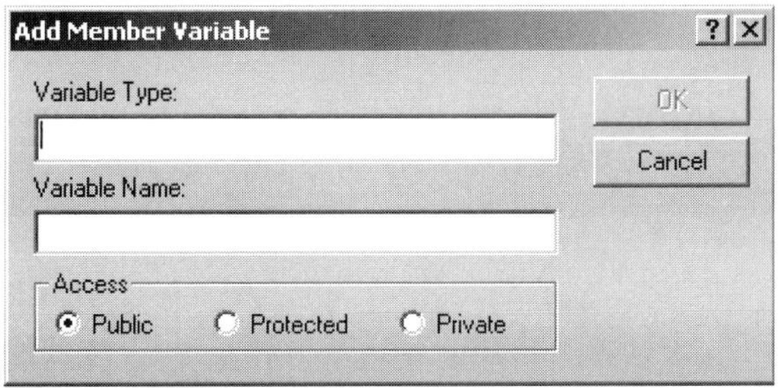

FIGURE 18   ADD MEMBER VARIABLE WINDOW.

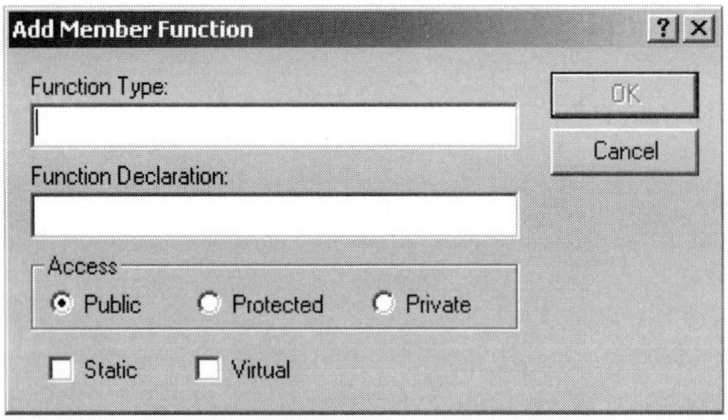

FIGURE 19 *ADD MEMBER VARIABLE* WINDOW.

You should now have a screen similar to Figure 20. Type the following code into the constructor (*Rectangle::Rectangle()*):

```
length=0;
width=0;
```

Now put this code into the perimeter function (*Rectangle::perimeter()*):

```
return (2 * length) + (2 * width);
```

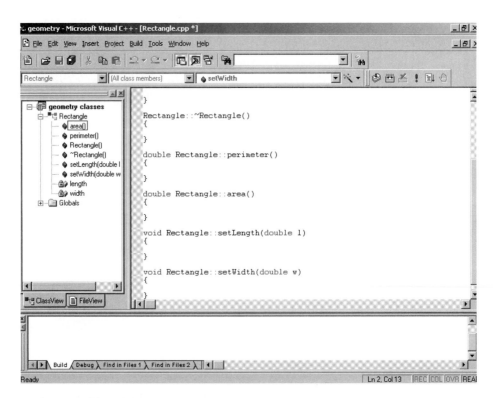

FIGURE 20 *RECTANGLE* CLASS WITH EMPTY MEMBER FUNCTIONS.

Place this code into the area function (*Rectangle::area()*):

```
return length * width;
```

Place this code into the *setLength()* function (*Rectangle::setLength()*):

```
length=1;
```

Place this code into the *setWidth()* function (*Rectangle::setWidth()*):

```
width=w;
```

When you have entered the code, press Ctrl+s to save the file. The rectangle class is now complete. It may help you to see exactly what the compiler has done, so right click *Rectangle* in the *Workspace* window and select *Go to Definition* from the dropdown list. The file *Rectangle.h* will open in the editor. Aside from a very small amount of Visual C++ specific information, this file should look exactly as if you created it yourself (except for commenting).

You may now create a new C++ source file to test the class functions. Press *Ctrl+n* again to bring up the *New* window. Select *C++ Source File*, and type "geometry" in the *File Name* box. Once again, the location should be correct, so make sure *Add to project* is checked and click *OK*. Type the following code into the edit window or use the *Insert* procedure described earlier to insert the *geometry.cpp* file from the text CD or Web site.

```
//GEOMETRY PROJECT MAIN FILE (geometry.cpp)

//PREPROCESSOR DIRECTIVES
#include <iostream.h>   //FOR cin AND cout
#include "Rectangle.h" //FOR Rectangle CLASS

//MAIN FUNCTION
void main()
{

    //DEFINE LOCAL VARIABLES
    Rectangle rect; //RECTANGLE OBJECT
    double l=0.0;   //LENGTH OF RECT
    double w=0.0;   //WIDTH OF RECT

    //SET LENGTH AND WIDTH
    cout << "Enter the length of the rectangle:  " << flush;
    cin >> l;
    rect.setLength(l);

    cout << "Enter the width of the rectangle:  " << flush;
    cin >> w;
    rect.setWidth(w);

    //DISPLAY THE PERIMETER AND AREA
    cout << "The perimeter is " << rect.perimeter() << endl;
    cout << "The area is " << rect.area() << endl;
} //END main()
```

Now press F7 to build the project and correct any syntax errors that you might have made typing-in the code. Run the project to test the *Rectangle* class functions.

Using the Debugger with Functions and Classes

Two crucial areas of the debugger have not been covered yet in this tutorial: the differences between stepping over, stepping in, and stepping out of statements, and setting breakpoints.

If you consult Figure 11, you will see that in addition to the *Step Over* command that you used to step through the program, there are also *Step Into* and *Step Out* commands. To see the differences between these commands, make sure you have the *geometry* project from the previous section open, then press F10 to begin debugging.

Use F10 (the *Step Over* command) to step through the program until you reach the statement *rect.setLength(l)*. (When you are prompted for a length, type any number you want.) Now press F10 one more time to run this line. You might expect the debugger to go to the code within the *setLength()* function, but this does not happen. The debugger executes the function as if it was just another program statement. The debugger "steps over" the function.

Keep pressing F10 until you are at the statement *rect.setWidth(w)*. This time, instead of pressing F10 to step over the function, press F11 to step into the function. The debugger will now open the *Rectangle.cpp* file, and it will be ready to step through the *setWidth()* function.

Use F10 to step through the function. When you reach the end of the function, keep stepping through, and the debugger will jump back to the *geometry.cpp* file. You should be ready to execute the first *cout* statement.

Press F11 to step into the *cout* statement. The debugger will jump into the *perimeter()* function in *Rectangle.cpp*. Instead of stepping through this function, press Shift+F11 to step out of the function. The debugger will jump back to *geometry.cpp*. The debugger executed the rest of the function, then handed control back to you within *main()*.

You should notice that the program flow did not move to the next line. There are actually two functions in this line: the *perimeter()* function which you entered and an output function used by *cout*.

If you always step into code, you might accidentally step into a built-in function. In fact, Visual C++ will actually allow you to change the built-in code. This could be hazardous to your system and require you to reinstall the compiler. In general you should not step into any of the Visual C++ built in functions. If you aren't careful, the debugger allows you to step all the way down to assembly level code, and then you'll really lost. If you find yourself hopelessly buried within unknown source files within the debugger, it's a good idea to simply press F5 to allow the program to finish running or Shift+F5 to stop the debugger.

Breakpoints are another feature of the debugger with which you should be familiar. If you are still in the debugger, press F5 to let the program finish. Open the *geometry.cpp* file if it is not already open. (To do this, click on the *FileView* tab in the *Workspace* window, click on the plus next to *geometry* files, click on the plus next to *Source Files*, then double-click *geometry.cpp*.)

Right-click anywhere on the line that contains *rect.setLength(l)*. Select *Insert/Remove Breakpoint* from the drop-down list. A red dot will appear to the left of the line. Now open the *Rectangle.cpp* file. Within the *setWidth()* function, create a breakpoint on the line that contains *width=w* by right clicking on the line and selecting *Insert/Remove Breakpoint* from the drop-down list.

Now you should begin debugging. Instead of pressing F10 to step through the program, press F5 to run the program in the debugger. (This is called the *Go* command.) The program will begin to run. The console window will appear and prompt you for a length. Enter any number, then press Enter. After this, the program appears to freeze. If you click on the Visual C++ window, you will see that the program execution has halted at the line where you set the breakpoint.

At this time, it is important to point out that if you run the program with Ctrl+F5, it will ignore all breakpoints. However, since the *Go* command runs the program within the debugger, it will halt when it reaches a breakpoint in the code.

Now use F10 to step through the code until you come to the line containing *rect.setWidth(w)*. Remember, you set a breakpoint within this function. When you reach the breakpoint line, press F10 one more time to step over it. What happens?

Since the program encountered a breakpoint within the function, it halted the program flow when it reached the breakpoint, even though you stepped over the function. The debugger opened the *Rectangle.cpp* file and it is ready to execute the line where you inserted the breakpoint. Right-click on this line and select *Remove Breakpoint* to get rid of the breakpoint on this statement.

Take some time to play around with stepping into/over/out of statements and with inserting and removing breakpoints. These are very important features of the debugger and you should be familiar with using them. When you are done, click on the *File* menu and select *Close Workspace* from the drop-down menu.

C.4   VISUAL C++ 6 SPECIFIC COMMENTS

Visual C++ 6 is a very good compiler and is generally compliant with the ANSI/ISO standard with one notable exception: *string*. This is forgivable as the standard did not contain the *string* type until after Visual C++ 6 was released, and Microsoft has created a fix so that you can use the string type.

To use the *string* type, you normally have to include *string.h* along with *iostream.h* to use *cin* and *cout* with strings and *iomanip.h* to use *cout* formatting. In Visual C++ 6, you should include *iostream*, *iomanip*, and *string* (notice that the ".h" is dropped). You should also type *using namespace std;* on a line with your preprocessor directives. Thus, a program that uses the *string* class with *cin* or *cout* would contain the following:

```
#include <iostream>
#include <string>
using namespace std;
```

If you need to use formatting functions such as *setw()*, your program must contain:

```
#include <iostream>
#include <iomanip>
#include <string>
using namespace std;
```

You cannot also include *iostream.h* or *iomanip.h* as your program will not compile.

Visual C++ 6 is a very good and easy to use program, but, like any large program, it's not perfect. You are bound to run into some strange behaviors if you use it long enough. If it does not seem to be working properly, simply closing the program then reopening it will usually fix it. If that doesn't work, try rebooting your computer.

CONCLUSION

It is beyond the scope of this tutorial to cover every aspect of Visual C++ 6, but after going through it, you should have a good working knowledge of the environment. Several features of the program have not even been mentioned here; however, everything you need to get started using Visual C++ 6 to create programs is here. Good luck.

C++ QUICK REFERENCE

KEYWORDS

asm	delete	int	sizeof	unsigned
auto	do	long	static	virtual
bool	double	new	struct	void
break	else	operator	switch	volatile
case	enum	private	template	while
catch	extern	protected	this	
char	false	public	throw	
class	float	register	true	
const	for	return	try	
continue	friend	short	typedef	
default	if	signed	union	

CONVERSION FUNCTIONS

Function Name	Header File	Operation
toascii()	ctype.h	Converts a character to ASCII value.
tolower()	ctype.h	Converts a character to lowercase.
toupper()	ctype.h	Converts a character to uppercase.

MATH FUNCTIONS (MATH.H)

Function Name	Header File	Operation
abs()	math.h	Returns the absolute value of the argument.
acos()	math.h	Returns the arc cosine of the argument (radians).
asin()	math.h	Returns the arc sine of the argument (radians).
atan()	math.h	Returns the arc tangent of the argument (radians).
cos()	math.h	Returns the cosine of the argument (radians).
hypot(a,b)	math.h	Returns the hypotenuse of a right triangle whose sides are a and b.
log()	math.h	Returns the natural log of the argument.
log10()	math.h	Returns the base 10 log of the argument.
pow(x,y)	math.h	Returns x raised to the power of y.
pow10(y)	math.h	Returns 10 raised to the power of y.
rand()	stdlib.h	Generates a random number between 0 and $2^{15} - 1$.
srand()	stdlib.h	Initializes the random-number generator and should be used prior to rand().
sin()	math.h	Returns the sine of the argument (radians).
sqrt()	math.h	Returns the square root of the argument.
tan()	math.h	Returns the tangent of the argument (radians).

STL LIST CLASS FUNCTIONS

Function Prototype	Purpose
bool empty()	Returns true if list is empty.
list_type back()	Returns, but does not remove, the last element of the list.
list_type front()	Returns, but does not remove, the first element of the list.
void merge(aList)	Merge with aList.
void pop_front()	Removes, but does not return, the first element of the list
void pop_back()	Removes, but does not return, the last element of the list
void push_front(element)	Places element at the front of the list.
void push_rear(element)	Places element at the rear of the list.
void remove(element)	Remove all occurrences of element.
void reverse()	Reverse element order.
int size()	Returns the number of elements in the list.
void sort()	Sort elements in ascending order.
void swap(aList)	Exchange values with aList.

STL STACK CLASS FUNCTIONS

Function Prototype	Purpose
bool empty()	Returns true if stack is empty.
void pop()	Removes, but does not return, the top element of the stack.
void push(element)	Places *element* on the top of the stack.
int size()	Returns the number of elements in the stack.
stack_type top()	Returns, but does not remove the top element of the stack.

STRING CLASS OPERATIONS

Function	Description	Use of

s.empty()	Returns true if the string *s* has no characters.	`string s;`
		`s.empty()`
		`returns true`

s.length()	Returns the length of *s*.	`string s = "Hello World";`
		`s.length()`
		`returns 11`

s1 == s2	Returns true if *s1* equals *s2*, else returns false.	`string s1 = "Hello World";`
		`string s2 = "hello world";`
		`s1 == s2`
		`returns false`

s1 != s2	Returns true if *s1* does not equal *s2*, else returns false.	`string s1 = "Hello World";`
		`string s2 = "hello world";`
		`s1 != s2`
		`returns true`

s1 < s2	Returns true if *s1* is less than *s2*, else returns false.	`string s1 = "Hello World";`
		`string s2 = "hello world";`
		`s1 < s2`
		`returns true`

s1 > s2	Returns true if *s1* is greater than *s2*, else returns false.	`string s1 = "Hello World";`
		`string s2 = "hello world";`
		`s1 > s2`
		`returns false`

s1 = s2	Copies, or assigns, *s2* to *s1*.	`string s1 = "Hello World";`
		`string s2 = "hello world";`
		`s1 = s2;`
		s1 now contains "hello world"

s = s1 + s2	Concatenates *s2* to *s1* to form *s*.	`string s;`
		`string s1 = "Hello";`
		`string s2 = "World";`
		`s = s1 + s2;`
		s now contains "HelloWorld"

s1 += s2	Appends *s2* to *s1*.	`string s1 = "Hello";`
		`string s2 = "World";`
		`s1 + = s2;`
		s1 now contains "HelloWorld"

STL QUEUE Class Functions

Function Prototype	Purpose
bool empty()	Returns true if queue is empty.
queue_type back()	Returns, but does not remove, the rear element of the queue.
queue_type front()	Returns, but does not remove, the front element of the queue.
void pop()	Removes, but does not return, the front element of the queue.
void push(element)	Places *element* at the rear of the queue.
int size()	Returns the number of elements in the queue.

STL VECTOR Class Functions

Function Prototype	Purpose
void begin()	Places iterator at beginning of the vector.
vector data type back()	Returns, but does not remove, the last element of the vector.
bool empty()	Returns true if vector is empty.
void end()	Places iterator at end of the vector.
vector data type front()	Returns, but does not remove, the first element of the vector.
void pop_back()	Removes, but does not return, the last element of the vector.
void push_back(element)	Places *element* at the end of the vector.
int size()	Returns the number of elements in the vector.

GLOSSARY

Abstract class A base class for which objects will never be created.

Abstract data type (ADT) A collection of data and related operations.

Abstraction Looking at things in general terms, ignoring detail.

Access function A get function used to return the value(s) of a private class member(s).

Actor In object-oriented analysis, an actor represents anything that must interact with the system. An actor can be a person, an organization, or another system.

Address A value that designates the memory location of a data element.

Algorithm A series of step-by-step instructions that produce a solution to a problem.

Argument A value used within a function call.

Arithmetic and logic unit (ALU) That part of the CPU that performs all arithmetic and logic operations.

Array An indexed data structure that is used to store data elements of the same data type or class.

Assembler A program that translates assembly language into machine language for a given CPU.

Assembly language A language that employs alphabetic abbreviations called mnemonics that are easily remembered by you, the programmer.

Association A relationship in an object-interaction diagram that represents a pathway of communication between two objects.

Attribute of a class The data members that make up a class provide the class attributes, or characteristics.

Base class A class from which one or more other classes are derived. Also called a superclass.

Behavior Used to describe how an ADT, or class object, will act and react for a given operation.

Block scope The accessibility, or visibility, of a local variable defined in a given block of code, such as a function.

Bus A signal path within a computer system.

Button A GUI component that, when clicked, generates an event.

Cache High-speed RAM that is usually contained within the same chip as the CPU. Instructions waiting to be processed are fetched from primary memory and placed in the cache so that they are ready for execution when the CPU needs them.

Calling program The code that calls, or invokes, a function.

CASE (Computer-Aided Systems Engineering) tool Software products that automate the phases of the software development life-cycle and are used to generate the required graphics with either the structured or object-oriented paradigms.

Casting Temporarily converting one type of data to another, as in type casting.

Checkbox A GUI component that allows the user to select one of two possible states: checked or unchecked.

Choice box A GUI component that allows the user to chose one of several items in a pop-up menu listing.

Circular array An array that wraps around such that the first element of the array follows the last element of the array.

Class (abstract level) An interface that defines the behavior of its objects.

Class (implementation level) A syntactical unit that describes a set of data and related operations that are common to its objects.

Class diagram Used in object-oriented design to show both the private data members which provide the attributes of the class and the function members which provide the class behavior.

Compiler A program that translates an entire program into machine code all at one time, before it is executed by the CPU.

Compiling The process of translating source code to machine, or object, code using a compiler.

Compound statement Several statements framed by curly braces.

Concrete class A derived class for which objects will always be created.

Constructor A special class function that is used to initialize the data members of an object automatically when the object is defined.

Context diagram A graphic that shows the entire system as one process and the external entities with which the system must interact. A context diagram defines the system boundaries.

Control structure A pattern for controlling the flow of a program module.

Control unit That part of the CPU that directs and coordinates the activities of the entire system.

Dangling else   An **else** that is not associated with a corresponding **if**. A dangling, or misplaced, **else** problem often occurs when improper framing is used within nested **if/else** logic.

Data abstraction   That property of an ADT that allows you to work with the data elements without concern for how the data elements are stored inside the computer or how the data operations are performed inside the computer.

Database   A collection of related files.

Data hiding   That property of a programming entity, such as a class object, that shields private data from operations that are not predefined to operate on the data.

Data type   A particular category of data elements.

Declaration   Specifies the name and attributes of a value but does not reserve storage as in a class declaration.

Default parameter   A function parameter that is assigned a default value in the function prototype or the function header, but not both.

Definition   Specifies the name and attributes of a variable or object and also reserves storage as in a variable or object definition.

delete operator   Deallocates memory created dynamically by the **new** operator.

Derived class   An inherited class, or subclass, that will include its own members as well as members inherited from its base class.

Destructor   The counterpart of a constructor that is used to "clean up" an object after it is no longer needed. Normally used to deallocate memory which was dynamically allocated to an object by the object constructor.

Dimension   The size of an array, such as $m \times n$, where m is the number of rows and n is the number of columns in the array.

Dynamic binding   Dynamic binding occurs when a polymorphic function is defined for several classes in a family, but the actual code for the function is not attached, or bound, until execution time.

Editor   A program that allows you to enter, save, and edit a source code program.

Element   A data value. In particular, a data value stored within an array.

Encapsulation   To package data and/or operations into a single well-defined programming unit.

Entity relationship diagram (ERD)   A graphic used to formalize data relationships in order to build system databases.

Enumerated data type   An ordered set of data elements that the programmer defines for a particular application.

Escape sequence   A special formatting character for text output.

Event   An action generated by a program user activating a GUI component, such as clicking button.

Event handler   A function used to process a GUI event.

Family   A group of classes related through inheritance.

Fetch/execute cycle The basic cycle that takes place when a program is executed by a CPU. The four basic operations of the cycle are *fetch*, *decode*, *execute*, and *store*.

Fibonacci sequence A sequence of numbers such that the first two numbers in the sequence are 0 and 1. Then, each additional number is the sum of the two previous numbers in the sequence.

Field An area used to store a meaningful collection of characters, such as your name.

FIFO First-in, first-out; FIFO is associated with queues.

File A data structure that consists of a sequence of data items usually associated with program I/O. A means by which the program communicates with the "outside world"; a sequence of data items stored in secondary memory; a collection of related records.

File scope The scope of a global constant or variable created prior to *main()* that is accessible to any block of code in the same file.

File stream A channel for data to flow between the program and the outside world.

File window The means for a program to communicate with a file. The file window locates data within the file for processing.

Firmware Software stored in ROM.

Fixed repetition loop A loop that will be executed a predetermined number of times.

Function A subprogram designed to perform specific tasks, such as those performed by an algorithm.

Function body The statement section, or implementation, of a function.

Function header The first line of a function that defines a common boundary, or interface, between the function and its calling program.

Function prototype A model of the interface to the function that is used by the compiler to check calls to the function for the proper number of arguments and the correct data types of the arguments.

Get function An access function used to return the value(s) of a private class member(s).

Global identifier A constant, variable, object, or data structure that is visible to the entire program.

Graphical component A graphical object within a graphical user interface, such as a button, text field, choice box, and so on. Also, a graphical image such as a rectangle, ellipse, point, line, polygon, etc.

Graphical user interface, GUI A window-based program whereby input and output are handled via graphical components and program control is event driven via the components.

High-level language A language consisting of instructions, or statements, that are similar to English and common mathematical notation

Icon   A small graphic in a GUI.

Identifier   A symbolic name associated with a constant, variable, function, data structure, class, object, and so on.

Implementation   The body of a function.

Index   An integer that locates an element within an array.

Indirection   Related to the levels of addressing it takes to access data.

Information hiding   Accomplished when there exists a binding relationship between the information, or data, and its related operations within an encapsulated unit so that operations outside the unit cannot affect the information inside the unit.

Inheritance   That property of object-oriented programming that allows one class, called a derived class, or subclass, to share the structure and behavior of another class, called a base class, or superclass.

Instance   In object-oriented programming, an example, or specimen, of a class. We say that an object is an *instance* of a class.

Instruction set   The set of machine instructions designed for a given CPU.

Interface   Something that forms a common boundary, or barrier, between two systems.

Interface of a class   The set of all **public** function prototypes that forms a boundary to a class.

Interface of a function   The function header that forms a common boundary between the function and its calling program.

Internal registers   That part of the CPU that provides temporary storage areas for program instructions and data

Interpreter   A program that translates and executes one high-level statement at a time. Once a given statement has been executed, the interpreter then translates and executes the next statement, and so on, until the entire program has been executed.

IS-A   The link between a derived class and its base class.

Iteration   A control structure, also called looping, that causes the program flow to repeat a finite number of times.

Keyword   A word that is predefined and recognized by a programming language.

Layout chart   A graphical aid in laying out text output for a display screen or the components within a GUI window.

LIFO   Last-in, first-out; LIFO is associated with stacks.

Linking   The process of combining object files needed for a program execution to form an executable file.

Linked list   A sequential data structure where, given any element in the list, the location of its successor element is specified by an *explicit* link, rather than by its natural position in the structure.

List   Another name for a one-dimensional array.

List box   A GUI component that allows the user to chose one or more items within a scrolled item listing.

Local identifier   A constant, variable, object, or data structure that is defined within a given block of code, such as a function. Local variables have block scope.

Logical data flow diagram (LDFD)   Used to model the flow of data within the current system during structured analysis. A LDFD is a graphic that shows the logical movement of data within the system and the processes being performed on that data without regard to the physical software or hardware devices that are operating on the data.

Logic error   An error created when the computer does what you tell it to do but is not doing what you meant it to do. Such an error is usually an error in thinking on the programmers part.

Loop control variable   A variable that is tested with each loop iteration to determine whether or not the loop will continue.

Machine language   The binary code, called machine code, that forms the instruction set for a given CPU.

Main memory   *See* primary memory.

Manipulator   A function or special command that produces input or output formatting within a file stream.

Member   Any item declared in a class.

Menu   A set of user-selectable options.

Menu bar   A container on the top of a window for holding menus.

Menu item   A selectable item within a menu.

Menu separator   A line between two menu items.

Message   A call to an object function.

Message box   A GUI component, sometimes called a text box, that displays a message of some kind.

Method   In object-oriented programming, another name for a class function.

Microprocessor   A single integrated-circuit (IC) chip that contains the entire central processing unit (CPU).

Misplaced else   An **else** that is not associated with a corresponding **if**. The misplaced, or dangling, **else** problem often occurs when improper framing is used within nested **if/else** logic.

Mnemonic   An assembly language instruction abbreviation.

Multidimensional array   An array with more than one dimension.

Multiple inheritance   Multiple inheritance occurs when the inherited class members can be traced back to more than one base class.

Multiplicity   Used in an object interaction diagram to show how many objects on each side of an association participate in the relationship.

Nested looping   Looping structures that are located within other looping structures.

new operator   Used to dynamically allocate memory in C++.

Nonvoid function   A function that returns a single value to the calling program.

Object   An instance, or specimen, of a given class. An object of a given class has the attributes and behavior described by the class that is common to all objects of the same class.

Object interaction diagram   In object-oriented design, they are used to show the relationships between the system objects.

Object program   The binary machine-language program generated by a compiler; usually has a file extension of *.obj*.

Object-oriented analysis (OOA)   Employs use-case and class modeling to describe the current as well as future system in terms of existing objects and new or modified objects.

Object-oriented design (OOD)   The process of determining how the new system is to satisfy the client's needs through the construction of object interaction and class diagrams, as well as other UML tools such as sequence and collaboration diagrams.

Object-oriented paradigm   A software engineering methodology that employs objects and object interaction to attack complex problems in a natural way, like we humans tend to think about things.

Object-oriented programming (OOP)   A form of programming whereby data and related operations are specified as classes whose instances are objects. The data and related operations are so tightly bound so that only those operations defined for a class can affect the class data. This idea of encapsulation and information hiding allows the easy formation of ADTs.

One-dimensional array   An array with one row and n columns that has a dimension of $1 \times n$.

Operating system, OS   A collection of software programs dedicated to managing the resources of the system.

Overflow error   An error that occurs when a numeric data type value exceeds its predefined range.

Overloaded function   A function that has different behavior depending on the number and/or type of arguments that it receives. An overloaded function is statically bound at compile time.

Paradigm   A model that provides a way of thinking about things.

Parameter   A variable or object appearing in a function prototype that receives an argument value when the function is called.

Parameterless constructor   A constructor that does not contain any parameters.

Physical data flow diagram (PDFD)   Depicts actual physical entities of the proposed system such as a "C++ *xyz* function" during structured design, not just logical entities like a process as in the LDFD of the structured analysis phase.

Pixel   A picture element which is a point of illumination on a display screen.

Pointer   A direct program reference to an actual physical address in memory.

Polymorphism   Occurs when a function has the same name but different behavior within a program. Both overloaded and virtual functions exhibit polymorphism in C++.

Portability   That feature of a language that allows programs written for one type of computer to be used on another type of computer with few or no changes to the program source code.

Posttest loop   A loop that tests a condition *after* each loop iteration as in the **do/while** loop structure.

Preprocessor   The first part of a C++ program that acts as a smart text editor before any translation is performed.

Pretest loop   A loop that tests a condition each time *before* a loop is executed, as in the **while** and **for** loop structures.

Primary memory   Used to store programs and data while they are being "worked," or executed, by the CPU.

Private member   A member of a class that is accessible only to the public functions of the same class. Private members of a base class are *not* inherited by a derived class.

Problem abstraction   Provides for generalization in problem solving by allowing you to view a problem in general terms, without worrying about the details of the problem solution.

Program   A set of software instructions that tells the computer what to do.

Project file   A file that identifies the files that need to be compiled and linked to create a workable C++ program.

Project manager   A program development tool which links several parts of a program together to build a complete workable program.

Programmer-defined function   A block of statements, or a subprogram, that is written to perform a specific task required by you, the programmer.

Protected member   A member that is accessible to both a base class and any subclasses of the base class in which it is defined. Thus, a protected member of a base class is accessible to any descendent derived class within the family, but not accessible to things outside the class family.

Prototype   A copy of the function header used by the compiler to check for correct calls to the function.

Pseudocode   An informal set of Englishlike statements that is generally accepted within the computer industry to denote common computer programming operations. Pseudocode statements are used to describe the steps in a computer algorithm.

Public base class   A base class that allows all of its public members to be public in its derived classes.

Public member   A member of a class that is accessible outside the class within the scope of the class. A public member of a base class is inherited by any derived classes of the base class.

Queue   A primary memory storage structure that consists of a list, or sequence, of data elements. All insertions of elements into the queue are made at one end of the queue, called the *rear* of the queue, and all deletions of elements from the queue are made at the other end of the queue, called the *front* of the queue. A queue operates on the *first-in, first-out,* or *FIFO,* principle.

Radio button   A state (on/off) button within a group of buttons that can be selected or deselected. Only one button within the group can be selected at any given time.

Random-access memory (RAM)   Volatile, read/write memory.

Rapid prototype   A quickly-built software package that models the target system during analysis or design.

Reading   The process of obtaining data from something such as an input device or a data structure; a copy operation. A read operation is usually a nondestructive operation.

Read-only memory (ROM)   Nonvolatile system memory that contains firmware.

Record   A collection of related fields. Implemented as a **struct** in C++.

Recursion   A process whereby an operation calls, or clones, itself until a terminating condition is reached.

Recursive function   A function that calls itself.

Reference parameter   A function parameter, preceded by an ampersand (&), that provides two-way communication between the calling program and the function via the address of its related argument.

Return value   A value returned by a nonvoid function. The value replaces the function name in the calling program.

RGB value   Actually three values, from 0 to 255, representing the intensity of the colors red, green, and blue, respectively, in a graphical component.

Run-time error   An error that occurs during the execution of a program.

Scenario   In object-oriented analysis, a sequence of tasks that are performed for a given use-case.

Scope   The largest block in which a given constant, variable, object, data structure, or function is accessible, or visible within a program.

Search   The process of finding a given data element. In particular, searching for a given element within an array.

Secondary memory   Nonvolatile memory, such as disk memory, used to store programs and data between program runs.

Selection   A control structure where the program selects, or decides, between one of several routes depending on the conditions that are tested.

Sentinel controlled loop   A loop that terminates when a given sentinel value is entered by the user.

Sentinel value   A value that terminates a sentinel controlled loop.

Sequence   A control structure where statements are executed sequentially, one after another, in a straight-line fashion.

Set function   A function used to set the value(s) of a private class member(s).

Side effect   The process of altering the value of a global variable.

Single inheritance   Single inheritance occurs when all inherited class members can be traced back to a single base class.

Software engineering   A discipline whose goal is to produce error-free software that considers all the what-if scenarios, is cost-effective, and meets all the client's needs.

Software life cycle   A set of phases which describe a logical process used by software engineers to develop fault-free, cost-effective software that meets all the client's needs.

Source program   The program that you write in the C++ language that normally has a file extension of *.cpp*.

Sort   The process of placing data elements in order. In particular, sorting the elements within an array.

Stack   A primary memory storage structure that consists of a list, or sequence, of data elements where all the insertions and deletions of elements to and from the stack are made at one end of the stack called the *top*. A stack operates on the *last-in, first-out*, or *LIFO* principle.

Standard function   A predefined operation that the C++ compiler will recognize and evaluate to return a result or perform a given task.

Star, *   In front of a pointer variable, the star denotes the contents of the memory location where the pointer is pointing.

Static binding   Occurs when a function is defined with the same name, but with different prototypes and implementations. The actual code for the function is attached, or bound, at compile time. Overloaded functions are statically bound.

Stepwise refinement   The process of gradually adding detail to a general problem solution until it easily can be coded in a computer language.

Stream   A channel for data to flow between your program and the outside world.

String   A collection of characters.

Structure   A collection of data members, or data fields. Also called a **struct** in C++ or a record in general.

Structured analysis   Employs logical data flow diagrams (LDFDs) to model the flow of data within the current system using a top/down methodology.

Structured design   A methodology that requires software to be designed using a top/down modular approach. A structured design requires formalization of the new process models in the form of physical data flow diagrams (PDFDs) and functional decomposition.

Structured paradigm   A software engineering methodology that employs top/down functional decomposition that breaks the original complex problem down into smaller, more manageable subproblems.

Structured programming   Structured programming allows programs to be written using well-defined control structures and independent program modules called functions in C++.

Submenu   A menu within a menu.

Syntax   The grammar of a programming language.

Syntax error   An error created by violating the required syntax, or grammar, of a programming language.

System memory   ROM firmware that stores system-related programs and data.

Terminating condition   A known condition that terminates a recursive function call.

Text area   Several lines of editable or non-editable text on a GUI.

Text field   A single line of editable text on a GUI.

Truth table   A table that shows the results of a logic operation on Boolean values.

Type cast   Converts data of one type to a different type, temporarily.

Unified Modeling Language (UML)   A language, or notation, for modeling systems that provides techniques to specify, visualize, construct, and document systems. The UML can be used for non-software business system modeling as well as software system modeling.

Use-case   Used in object-oriented analysis. A use-case represents a pattern of behavior exhibited by the system as the result of a dialogue between the system and an actor. The collection of all the system use-cases specifies all the ways in which to use the system.

Use-case scenario   A sequence of tasks that are performed for a given use-case.

Utility function   A private function.

Value parameter   A parameter that allows for one-way communication of data from the calling program to the function via a copy of its related argument.

Venn diagram   A class family diagram that illustrates the common members within the family.

Void function   A function that performs some procedural task or returns multiple values, rather than returning a single value to the calling program as in a nonvoid function.

Virtual function   Functions that have the same name but different implementations for various classes within a class family. A virtual function is a polymorphic function that is dynamically bound.

Virtual memory   Hard-disk memory that is being used by the CPU as RAM when no more actual RAM is available.

Visibility   That part of the program code in which a constant, variable, object, data structure, or function is accessible.

White space Blanks, tabs, new lines, form feeds, and so on, are all forms of white-space.

Writing The process of generating data to a display monitor, printer, or file. In addition, data can be written to variables and data structures. A write operation is usually a destructive operation.

INDEX

LICENSE AGREEMENT AND LIMITED WARRANTY

READ THE FOLLOWING TERMS AND CONDITIONS CAREFULLY BEFORE OPENING THIS DISK PACKAGE. THIS LEGAL DOCUMENT IS AN AGREEMENT BETWEEN YOU AND PRENTICE-HALL, INC. (THE "COMPANY"). BY OPENING THIS SEALED DISK PACKAGE, YOU ARE AGREEING TO BE BOUND BY THESE TERMS AND CONDITIONS. IF YOU DO NOT AGREE WITH THESE TERMS AND CONDITIONS, DO NOT OPEN THE DISK PACKAGE. PROMPTLY RETURN THE UNOPENED DISK PACKAGE AND ALL ACCOMPANYING ITEMS TO THE PLACE YOU OBTAINED THEM FOR A FULL REFUND OF ANY SUMS YOU HAVE PAID.

1. **GRANT OF LICENSE:** In consideration of your payment of the license fee, which is part of the price you paid for this product, and your agreement to abide by the terms and conditions of this Agreement, the Company grants to you a nonexclusive right to use and display the copy of the enclosed software program (hereinafter the "SOFTWARE") on a single computer (i.e., with a single CPU) at a single location so long as you comply with the terms of this Agreement. The Company reserves all rights not expressly granted to you under this Agreement.

2. **OWNERSHIP OF SOFTWARE:** You own only the magnetic or physical media (the enclosed disks) on which the SOFTWARE is recorded or fixed, but the Company retains all the rights, title, and ownership to the SOFTWARE recorded on the original disk copy(ies) and all subsequent copies of the SOFTWARE, regardless of the form or media on which the original or other copies may exist. This license is not a sale of the original SOFTWARE or any copy to you.

3. **COPY RESTRICTIONS:** This SOFTWARE and the accompanying printed materials and user manual (the "Documentation") are the subject of copyright. You may not copy the Documentation or the SOFTWARE, except that you may make a single copy of the SOFTWARE for backup or archival purposes only. You may be held legally responsible for any copying or copyright infringement which is caused or encouraged by your failure to abide by the terms of this restriction.

4. **USE RESTRICTIONS:** You may not network the SOFTWARE or otherwise use it on more than one computer or computer terminal at the same time. You may physically transfer the SOFTWARE from one computer to another provided that the SOFTWARE is used on only one computer at a time. You may not distribute copies of the SOFTWARE or Documentation to others. You may not reverse engineer, disassemble, decompile, modify, adapt, translate, or create derivative works based on the SOFTWARE or the Documentation without the prior written consent of the Company.

5. **TRANSFER RESTRICTIONS:** The enclosed SOFTWARE is licensed only to you and may not be transferred to any one else without the prior written consent of the Company. Any unauthorized transfer of the SOFTWARE shall result in the immediate termination of this Agreement.

6. **TERMINATION:** This license is effective until terminated. This license will terminate automatically without notice from the Company and become null and void if you fail to comply with any provisions or limitations of this license. Upon termination, you shall destroy the Documentation and all copies of the SOFTWARE. All provisions of this Agreement as to warranties, limitation of liability, remedies or damages, and our ownership rights shall survive termination.

7. **MISCELLANEOUS:** This Agreement shall be construed in accordance with the laws of the United States of America and the State of New York and shall benefit the Company, its affiliates, and assignees.

8. **LIMITED WARRANTY AND DISCLAIMER OF WARRANTY:** The Company warrants that the SOFTWARE, when properly used in accordance with the Documentation, will operate in substantial conformity with the description of the SOFTWARE set forth in the Documentation. The Company does not warrant that the SOFTWARE will meet your requirements or that the operation of the SOFTWARE will be uninterrupted or error-free. The Company warrants that the media on which the SOFTWARE is delivered

shall be free from defects in materials and workmanship under normal use for a period of thirty (30) days from the date of your purchase. Your only remedy and the Company's only obligation under these limited warranties is, at the Company's option, return of the warranted item for a refund of any amounts paid by you or replacement of the item. Any replacement of SOFTWARE or media under the warranties shall not extend the original warranty period. The limited warranty set forth above shall not apply to any SOFTWARE which the Company determines in good faith has been subject to misuse, neglect, improper installation, repair, alteration, or damage by you. EXCEPT FOR THE EXPRESSED WARRANTIES SET FORTH ABOVE, THE COMPANY DISCLAIMS ALL WARRANTIES, EXPRESS OR IMPLIED, INCLUDING WITHOUT LIMITATION, THE IMPLIED WARRANTIES OF MERCHANTABILITY AND FITNESS FOR A PARTICULAR PURPOSE. EXCEPT FOR THE EXPRESS WARRANTY SET FORTH ABOVE, THE COMPANY DOES NOT WARRANT, GUARANTEE, OR MAKE ANY REPRESENTATION REGARDING THE USE OR THE RESULTS OF THE USE OF THE SOFTWARE IN TERMS OF ITS CORRECTNESS, ACCURACY, RELIABILITY, CURRENTNESS, OR OTHERWISE.

IN NO EVENT, SHALL THE COMPANY OR ITS EMPLOYEES, AGENTS, SUPPLIERS, OR CONTRACTORS BE LIABLE FOR ANY INCIDENTAL, INDIRECT, SPECIAL, OR CONSEQUENTIAL DAMAGES ARISING OUT OF OR IN CONNECTION WITH THE LICENSE GRANTED UNDER THIS AGREEMENT, OR FOR LOSS OF USE, LOSS OF DATA, LOSS OF INCOME OR PROFIT, OR OTHER LOSSES, SUSTAINED AS A RESULT OF INJURY TO ANY PERSON, OR LOSS OF OR DAMAGE TO PROPERTY, OR CLAIMS OF THIRD PARTIES, EVEN IF THE COMPANY OR AN AUTHORIZED REPRESENTATIVE OF THE COMPANY HAS BEEN ADVISED OF THE POSSIBILITY OF SUCH DAMAGES. IN NO EVENT SHALL LIABILITY OF THE COMPANY FOR DAMAGES WITH RESPECT TO THE SOFTWARE EXCEED THE AMOUNTS ACTUALLY PAID BY YOU, IF ANY, FOR THE SOFTWARE.
SOME JURISDICTIONS DO NOT ALLOW THE LIMITATION OF IMPLIED WARRANTIES OR LIABILITY FOR INCIDENTAL, INDIRECT, SPECIAL, OR CONSEQUENTIAL DAMAGES, SO THE ABOVE LIMITATIONS MAY NOT ALWAYS APPLY. THE WARRANTIES IN THIS AGREEMENT GIVE YOU SPECIFIC LEGAL RIGHTS AND YOU MAY ALSO HAVE OTHER RIGHTS WHICH VARY IN ACCORDANCE WITH LOCAL LAW.

ACKNOWLEDGMENT

YOU ACKNOWLEDGE THAT YOU HAVE READ THIS AGREEMENT, UNDERSTAND IT, AND AGREE TO BE BOUND BY ITS TERMS AND CONDITIONS. YOU ALSO AGREE THAT THIS AGREEMENT IS THE COMPLETE AND EXCLUSIVE STATEMENT OF THE AGREEMENT BETWEEN YOU AND THE COMPANY AND SUPERSEDES ALL PROPOSALS OR PRIOR AGREEMENTS, ORAL, OR WRITTEN, AND ANY OTHER COMMUNICATIONS BETWEEN YOU AND THE COMPANY OR ANY REPRESENTATIVE OF THE COMPANY RELATING TO THE SUBJECT MATTER OF THIS AGREEMENT.

Should you have any questions concerning this Agreement or if you wish to contact the Company for any reason, please contact in writing at the address below or call the at the telephone number provided.

PTR Customer Service
Prentice Hall PTR
One Lake Street
Upper Saddle River, New Jersey 07458

Telephone: 201-236-7105